MACRO PRA

SOCIAL WORK

for the

21st CENTURY

SECOND
EDITION

*Dedicated to Desmond Barchetto and
Sara Kaye Siegel: May they willingly join
their voices in the fight for social justice that
awaits their generation later in the 21st century.*

MACRO PRACTICE IN SOCIAL WORK

for the

21st CENTURY

Bridging the Macro-Micro Divide

SECOND EDITION

Steve Burghardt

*Silberman School of Social Work at
Hunter College—City University of New York*

Los Angeles | London | New Delhi
Singapore | Washington DC

Los Angeles | London | New Delhi
Singapore | Washington DC

FOR INFORMATION:

SAGE Publications, Inc.
2455 Teller Road
Thousand Oaks, California 91320
E-mail: order@sagepub.com

SAGE Publications Ltd.
1 Oliver's Yard
55 City Road
London EC1Y 1SP
United Kingdom

SAGE Publications India Pvt. Ltd.
B 1/I 1 Mohan Cooperative Industrial Area
Mathura Road, New Delhi 110 044
India

SAGE Publications Asia-Pacific Pte. Ltd.
3 Church Street
#10-04 Samsung Hub
Singapore 049483

Acquisitions Editor: Kassie Graves
Editorial Assistant: Elizabeth Luizzi
Production Editor: Amy Schroller
Copy Editor: Megan Granger
Typesetter: C&M Digitals (P) Ltd.
Proofreader: Susan Schon
Indexer: Sheila Bodell
Cover Designer: Anupama Krishnan
Marketing Manager: Shari Countryman

Copyright © 2014 by SAGE Publications, Inc.

Printed in the United States of America

A catalog record of this book is available from the Library of Congress.

ISBN 978-1-4522-5745-7

This book is printed on acid-free paper.

SFI Certified Sourcing
www.sfiprogram.org
SFI-00453

13 14 15 16 17 10 9 8 7 6 5 4 3 2 1

Brief Contents

Detailed Contents

Acknowledgments

Many of those whom I thanked in the first edition remain central to this edition and will be mentioned below. Others have since entered my life and have only added to the value of this work. In particular, this edition is much stronger in integrating more clinical skills so that the text is much more inclusive of both macro and micro skill sets. Over the past 4 years, I have been fortunate to work with a set of people in a year-long foundation practice course. They have expanded my appreciation for and awareness of how clinical work, both with individuals and groups, informs macro practice—and how organizing impacts their clinical, individual, and group work. Robyn Brown-Manning, Carolyn Gelman, Chanda Griffin, Delores Hunter, Kyle McGee, Carmen Morano, Moyosore Paupau-Mickens, Beth Reiman, Judith Trachtenberg, and Norma Uriquen have provided me insights and practice wisdom of enormous value. A special shout-out goes to my long-time friend and collaborator Willie Tolliver, who walks the talk of anti-oppression work as few others do. I also extend thanks to Mary Cavanaugh for her clinical and humane insights outside of the classroom, as well as to my wise friend Evelyn Pederson. Finally, I especially would like to thank Samuel Aymer, whose clinical brilliance and personal openness to the social dynamics embedded in practice have contributed so much to our rich and rewarding conversations on the "macro–micro mix" over the past 3 years. The results of those conversations can be found throughout this edition.

As stated before, it is a fortunate person who loves what he or she does more after 35 years than at the start of that career. I am blessed to be such a person because of the extraordinary group of people who have entered my organizing classes and gone on to work in the rough-and-tumble world where the struggle for social justice is ongoing. Cantankerous, smart as can be, and willing to take on the world, as well as the increasingly older white guy in the front of the room, filled with courage and moments of self-doubt—these community organizers have given a richness to my life that I never would have had without them.

Another group of people with whom I have worked and who have added so much are the men and women who toil in the human service organizations that make up those other parts of macro practice—those agency workers, frontline supervisors, managers, and executives who head out each day to work in the trenches with groups others would prefer to forget: the neglected kids in child welfare, the homeless families thrown out of substandard housing, the mentally ill folks others might try to avoid. Their resilience and capacity to carry on each and every day, even as funds fall short—again and again—so others might be able to live with a touch of dignity leaves me humbled at all they do far better than I ever could.

My hope is that this book honors them all.

Others have provided encouragement and support along the way as I completed this new work. Friends who provided the occasional kick in the pants to keep me writing are Mike Fabricant, Kami Franklin, Liz Laboy, Ed Laboy, and Eric Zachary. Silberman School of Social Work colleagues Kristin Ferguson-Colvin, Nancy Giunta, Terry Mizrahi, Associate Dean Andrea Savage, and Dean Jackie Mondros continue to provide encouragement as well. Dr. Mohan Krishna Vinjamuri again used his special mix of analytic brilliance and extraordinary thoroughness to take on the writing of Chapter 9, addressing the Internet and social networking as organizing tools.

One of the two new chapters was written by remarkable young practitioners who have lived their strategic vision, from the classroom we shared and into their life's work. Kristin LeBourveau and Meredith Ledlie-Johnson began discussing how social work had to stretch its definition of the "social environment" to include the work of environmental activists at a time when most of their classmates and professional colleagues thought little about issues such as community gardens, local food markets, hydrofracking, and climate change. As their own stories attest in Chapter 11, the field is slowly awakening to their vision as Earth grows in peril—along with us who inhabit it.

Finally, the remarkable people who continue to write, compile, and maintain the Community Toolbox deserve special mention. Like macro practitioners everywhere, Stephen Fawcett, Jerry Schultz, and Christina Holt of the University of Kansas have toiled without much notice to create a vibrant and rich Internet resource for organizers that has helped countless practitioners across the United States and beyond. I hope readers of this book will take full advantage of it.

That my best editor of thematic coherency and word choice—as well as pants-kicker par excellence—happens to be my wife, Pat Beresford, is another fortuitous part of my life, for which I give thanks every day. Being backed up by our brood of various Bs (and a few other letters)—Lila and Matty and their future 21st century organizer, Desmond; Josh; Lisa and Eric; and Jen and her sweet honeybee, Sara Kaye—rounds out the fullness of my life.

The family at SAGE Publications is a pretty special group, too. Kassie Graves, editor extraordinaire, continues to be a class act in everything she does, whether signaling encouragement, quietly offering improvements, or kindly yet persistently making sure I complete all that needs to be done. I am blessed to be able now to call her my friend.

Elizabeth Luizzi, Amy Schroller, and Megan Granger have provided able assistance in moving the work through its various stages, for which I am most appreciative. I am also again aware of the steady, wise hand of Armand Lauffer on this book. Giving him thanks continues to be a thimble's worth of the debt at play here.

My final thanks still go to a man I met but once: Paulo Freire. The influence of his seminal ideas, first written in *Pedagogy of the Oppressed,* on my life and work cannot be overstated. Understanding how well-meaning educators (including professors of community organizing) can replicate domination through the banking system of education, the importance of genuine respect and belief in others' capacities to find within themselves the resolution to their internalized and external oppression, recognizing the dehumanization of those who oppress and how a transformed relationship with the oppressed leads to a new sense of humanity for us all, the value of posing problems as a vehicle for mutual exploration and eventual dialogue . . . the list of what his writings have given me is a long one that has become fundamental to how I try to live my life. My other hope for this book is that it uses his words in ways that further expand his contribution to a lifetime fight for social justice, a fight that will continue throughout the 21st century.

The author and SAGE gratefully acknowledge the contributions of the following reviewers:

Lynn Agre, *Rutgers State University*

Steven Applewhite, *University of Houston*

Sheli Bernstein-Goff, *West Liberty University*

Cassandra Bowers, *Wayne State University*

Fredi Giesler, MSW, PhD, *University of Wisconsin Oshkosh*

Dorlisa J. Minnick, *Shippensburg University*

Anne Powell, *University of Kansas*

Kathleen (Kat) Walsh, *Millersville University of Pennsylvania*

Introduction

THE FOCUS OF THIS SECOND EDITION

As with the first edition, the focus of this book is in one sense very personal: It is about the lives of individual macro practitioners and, to a lesser but still significant extent, about the micro practitioner as well. Rather than being a sociological examination of organizations, communities, and the profession, its emphasis is on the dynamic interaction between one's own personal and professional development, the political and organizational contexts in which a dedicated practitioner works, and the strategic choices undertaken throughout one's career.

Specific attention is paid to how one can utilize these dynamics in ways that can heighten the political and personal meaning of one's daily work, whether as a grassroots organizer, clinical worker, community-based supervisor, or executive. As such, the text will also weave in the personal stories and political dilemmas of committed people who have decided that their life's work is primarily through macro practice, not individually focused change. At the same time, the "personal" focus of this text consciously breaks down the divisions between community organizers and clinical social workers—neither practice approach can be as engaging, diagnostically insightful, or empowering (with clients/community members *and* oneself) without using the skill sets and frameworks of the other. This text seeks to demonstrate some of the ways this can be done.

One of the central ways this new edition will make this connection is through utilization of the Council on Social Work Education's (CSWE) core competencies for practice. By demonstrating how each chapter's particular focus on skills, frameworks, and values is tied directly to social work's professional practice competencies, faculty, field instructors, and students together can note how their own assignments connect to professionally identified skills and values that unite the field. Each chapter will identify the specific competencies so professional learning is deepened. Furthermore, my friend and Silberman School of Social Work colleague Glynn Rudich—former director of field education at the school and now assistant dean of Student Services—and I have written a "Field Instructor's Guide" that for the first time joins textbook skills, professional competencies, and field practicum assignments. In this way, both new and experienced field instructors have a "learning bridge" from classroom to field so that textbook activities and fieldwork experiences complement each other rather than remaining remote and disconnected.

Macro Practice in Social Work for the 21st Century: Bridging the Macro-Micro Divide takes the first half of Netting, Kettner, McMurtry, and Thomas's (2012) definition of macro practice—"professionally guided intervention(s) designed to bring about planned change in organizations and communities" (p. 28)—as the focus for how to improve the lives and communities with whom we work. The "circumstances leading to the need for planned change" (p. 28) that they identify as the other primary focus of their work is here filtered through the personal and political dilemmas of macro practitioners as they struggle within the unique demands of their work at different stages of their professional careers: the grass-roots organizer with intense commitments to social justice and few resources and, at times, little personal insight into his or her impact on the work; the new supervisor with those same commitments now forced to supervise staff and use his or her authority in uncomfortable ways; the executive whose daily life is inside a bureaucracy or boardroom, yet who seeks to remain committed to the work of the grassroots organizer that he or she once was.

To unify this case approach, the book will follow the career paths of two fictional macro practitioners, Ellis and Kay. In the first edition, they met up after years apart on the heady night of November 5, 2008, in Grant Park, Chicago, where they reviewed what they had done professionally and what they were planning to do. For the second edition, they have met up again in 2012 after the less heady but still exhilarating reelection of Barack Obama. The changes they have undergone over the past 4 years are reflective of new chapters in this book—one on political advocacy, the other on environmental activism. All of Ellis's and Kay's stories, of course, continue to be based on the experiences of many real people who have worked as community practitioners (both organizers and managers), as well as clinical and organizing students whom I have met and learned from over the years.

Once again, these two practitioners, Ellis and Kay, having met in school as grassroots community practitioners, will begin building their relationship together by discussing one of the animating yet rarely stated career issues that exist among macro practitioners in social work: *One of them is an organizer who has decided to do his progressive work in social work, while the other sees herself as a social worker who is committed to organizing.* Carried out over 20 years and unfolding chapter by chapter as career choices are made, their composite stories are drawn from real organizers and managers to deepen each chapter's meaning for both new and experienced macro practitioners. In short, their stories bring to life their beliefs, the strategic decisions they made as organizers, the dilemmas such choices created, the specific roles they played in their communities and organizations, and the ensuing career choices each made. It is hoped that through such stories, macro practice—and, in part, a dynamic micro practice as well—will come alive for the reader.

THE OUTLINE OF THE BOOK

While this second edition includes important substantive additions, the actual outline of the book remains straightforward. Based on my 4 years of experience with others in developing a foundation practice course, the textbook is now broken into five sections that correspond to the five primary phases of practice development: pre-engagement, assessment and engagement, relationship building, intervention, and evaluation. Within the sections, each chapter centers on the particular skill sets and competencies every committed activist undertakes as new roles and responsibilities emerge across a macro practitioner's career. Once again, the book starts with stories from when Ellis and Kay were students new to community organizing and then moves, chapter by chapter, through roles they undertake as leaders of grassroots campaigns, directors of organizing programs, and, over time, managers and directors of larger and larger agencies. Through this approach, I seek to break down the false dichotomy between the highly committed (albeit naïve) young activist and the highly experienced (albeit compromised) older manager, replacing it with a more vital (and mutually respectful) relationship consistently in service of bettering both. Likewise, one tends to be deeply "macro" and political, the other more "micro" and interpersonal. As we will also see, both organizer and social worker, as they learn from each other, can have meaningful careers of lasting impact.

Learning Objectives

Furthermore, Chapters 2 through 13 will be structured with the following learning objectives:

- At the beginning of each chapter, *the text will identify the core CSWE competencies as a way to inform faculty, field instructors, and students of how the specific skills, activities, and values of the chapter are connected to the social work profession.* The chapter will conclude with an activity or exercise specifically designed to further strengthen these competencies.
- There is now a *"Field Instructor's Guide" available for all students and field instructors using this book so that foundational assignments combine real-life application from the field to the text—and from the text to the field.* By also integrating them with core competency Education Policy and Accreditation Standards, this edition significantly advances professional accreditation standards for every school and every agency that uses this text.
- *Another goal is to provide the reader with the primary strategic tasks and activities associated with each level of macro practice.* For example, every new macro practice intervention begins with a community assessment. It is also a way for new

community practitioners to learn about their community and to begin working with a handy strategic tool that helps them learn what strategy and tactics are all about. The next chapters explore different kinds of campaign demands or program expectations that require other strategic skills for more experienced organizers. In this way, the reader gets to reflect on the more advanced strategic thinking associated with his or her own career development. The same occurs in later chapters as more experienced organizers begin to decide whether to be lifetime organizing directors or agency managers and executives—a pivotal career decision for every macro and many micro practitioners.

- After reviewing the primary tasks related to each chapter's principal strategic activity, *there will be an analysis of the ways those tasks are approached by different people.* Through the illustrative material of the ongoing case study of our two practitioners and their colleagues, each chapter will also address *the weave of differing values, perceptions, and social dynamics that are at play within any organizing campaign or agency project. This will include examples of how the "micro and macro divide" can be diminished.* How we do our work often matters as much as what we do. To that end, we will explore how good people with slightly different frameworks of intervention can end up working in ways that reflect powerful distinctions in values (who should lead and why); their assessments of racial, gender, and other social dynamics at play in the work; and the degree of conflict or consensus they seek through their campaigns.

- As discussed earlier in this introduction, the explosion of worldwide activism between 2010 and the present has in part occurred because of the influence of the Internet, smartphones, tablets, YouTube, and myriad software programs, which have made all forms of practice more immediate, accessible, and connected than ever before. To see just how profound these changes are, when the first edition of this book was being written and Barack Obama was campaigning for the White House, Twitter was a geek's pastime. Facebook was used by fewer than 40 million Americans, compared with 160 million today [2012]. Smartphones were still largely a professional luxury. But in this cycle, virtually every American voter not only has a [smart] phone but also increasingly uses it to go online. . . . "Everything you want to do online you can do on mobile." (Scherer, 2012)

These shifts to user-friendly, immediate, cyber-based technologies are having a profound impact on all forms of social work practice—from flash-mob tactics for activism to apps for cognitive-behavioral therapy. In the first edition, Mohan Krishna Vinjamuri in one chapter examined how the Internet had affected organizing campaigns as seen through the response to California's Proposition 8 defeat of gay rights, but this edition will consistently explore how one can use various Internet and cyber-based technologies in one's practice.

- The end of each chapter provides a more complete listing of other tasks, tactics, and strategic issues that may be associated with that chapter's primary focus. To that end, each chapter will provide the subject outline of the invaluable Community Toolbox and links to the appropriate webpages at the Community Toolbox website (http://ctb.ku.edu/en). Located at the University of Kansas, this remarkably rich web-based resource, created by Stephen Fawcett, Jerry Schultz, Christina Holt, and the Community Toolbox team, will provide readers with excellent to-do lists for specific tactics (how to run a meeting, develop a flyer, etc.).

- My experience as student, teacher, and organizer is that too many texts incorporate so many lists and typologies that it becomes difficult to distinguish task from process and targeted outcomes from targeted populations. This text seeks to emphasize the key strategic choices and tactical activities a practitioner makes as he or she moves through a career, not every choice and all activities. The Community Toolbox provides the exact tool, technique, and approach one might need so that practitioners' need to "do" does not interfere with what Fisher and Karger (1996) assert is community practitioners' responsibility to undertake "a profound re-examination of the values on which their society and their way of life are based" (p. 19). The hope here is that a committed community practitioner sees that getting the job done doesn't mean we don't have time to grapple with how we go about doing it. Societal transformation and personal transformation require a little bit of both.

- The next learning objective flows from the above: *helping practitioners develop both their strategic choices and capacity to live with the dilemmas those choices create.* A great practitioner not only works with others to make sound strategic choices about what to do and how to do it but also fosters the capacity for people to live with what those choices *will not do.* For example, a consensus-based strategy more easily increases your number of participants, but it may dull their clarity on the actual causes of a problem. Likewise, a charged political analysis of a school reform effort by local educational leaders may clarify their limitations, but it may also frighten off potential allies. *Developing a practitioner's internal capacity to live with the external opportunities and limits to a group's strategic approach* is at the heart of this book.

- The final objective is perhaps the most demanding. By examining the strategic options and dilemmas of the macro practitioner as he or she develops a professional career, I will seek to incorporate Paulo Freire's transformational methodology into the discussion as well. As he made clear in *Pedagogy of the Oppressed* and other works (Freire, 1996, 2000a, 2000b), many of those who seek to help the oppressed and disenfranchised all too often unknowingly replicate the same forms of oppression and domination they seek to undermine. Though I first undertook this examination in the Reagan Era through *The Other Side of Organizing,* it remains all the more germane in "the interesting times" known as the early 21st century.

As the first and second chapters make clear, the dynamics of our political economic discourse are shifting as rapidly as at any time since the late 1950s. To replicate the same discourse of the past 30 years inside macro practice without attempting our own transformational work would seem a lost opportunity we can ill afford. Each chapter addresses how that transformational activity is embedded in the daily weave of personal choice and strategic emphasis that every macro practitioner makes.

This attention to how one practices does not imply a substitution of process over content; those other circumstances that Netting and her colleagues (2012) address remain paramount for any macro practitioner's work. As I make clear in Chapter 2, economic and political relationships are primary factors that affect us in our work, determining the type of practice and programmatic choices we make daily. However, the primacy of objective conditions does not make subjective, interpersonal concerns irrelevant. We can and must unite our personal interactions with our attention to societal concerns. Indeed, neglecting these issues is often detrimental to both inspired organizing and effective management. Who can be truly committed to the long-term fight for social justice if the campaign is won at the expense of one's physical and spiritual health? Who honestly believes that the client's voice will be heard through that grant when the work group meetings one attends to win it leave team members frustrated and in tears?

Macro Practice in Social Work for the 21st Century: Bridging the Macro-Micro Divide has been written not to guarantee the right answers but to make sure some of these questions are asked in the first place. Through such questions, if they are asked honestly and often enough, a macro practitioner can perhaps develop the humility Freire (2000a) demands of anyone who seeks to work with the oppressed. In our struggle to remain open to the answers others may bring us lies our freedom to grow with them, perhaps the most fundamental prerequisite for long-term community work that is transformative and not incremental.

THE CONTENT OF THE BOOK

As for the content of the book, the fundamental content of the first edition has been retained. It makes me happy that a lot of the original content still holds up. As with the first edition, the original framework and focus on organizers' personal dilemmas as they carry out their professional practice is still being used pretty much *in toto*—albeit with even more current references and, where applicable, updates on other methods' choices. That the original content continues to enrich people's lives a little is as much as I ever could have hoped in terms of influence. (Actually, being a well-read footnote in countless organizing schools based on the works of Paulo Freire, Miles Horton, and Septima Clark would have been even better, but I'm not complaining!) Furthermore, many students and practitioners in the field were appreciative of the chapters that analyzed supervisors', managers', and executives' lessons on how they have maintained an active vision of social justice while running large agencies and programs. Seeing a way forward in their career without "selling out" inspired younger social workers, and it was equally satisfying for experienced professionals to receive affirmation for living their values and commitments regardless of their position inside social work agencies and programs.

While the text develops along a career path for macro practitioners, it does so by focusing the stories of the two former Obama supporters on the most important skills they need to continue being effective in their roles—first as organizers, later as directors and managers. Skills therefore range from knowing how to do a community needs assessment (an entry-level skill) to developing a coalition-based campaign (a more advanced organizing skill). New supervisors learn to set boundaries with their staff while remaining true to their vision of self-determination, while managers run meetings and create projects that handle dynamics of race and racism in the workplace. An organizer comes to see the value of interpersonal, "clinical" effectiveness, while a more individually focused practitioner sees her effectiveness grow through a better strategic sense of the larger social and political order. As stated earlier, each chapter ends with a review and description of vital practice tools found on the Internet and through social media. The chapter review is followed by a Community Toolbox outline of other concrete skill sets one can apply within the framework of that chapter's issues, lessons, and career choices.

As stated earlier, the work integrates both CSWE core competencies and field instructor material to provide a better fit with social work program's accreditation requirements and to connect actual field experience to the text. The book also has two new chapters that are reflective of the ongoing changes in practice. One details the kind of political advocacy that more and more social workers and their local professional chapters undertake as they seek improved legislation and more influence in electoral politics. The other is on the exciting, emerging (or, as the chapter authors attest, *reemerging*) environmental activism that social workers are now practicing—a true meeting of "micro" and "macro." The environmental activism chapter was written by Kristin LeBourveau and Meredith Ledlie-Johnson, who embody the career path reflective of our fictional activists, Ellis and Kay. As will be seen in their writing, working from a passionate commitment to their own internal strategic visions, LeBourveau and Ledlie-Johnson are building careers of strategic innovation and meaningful impact that will inspire others to follow the model of genuine engagement they are carving out for themselves.

Chapter Outline

Broken into the five foundational practice segments, the book begins with Section I on *pre-engagement*, explaining the long-term historical and personal assumptions that led to the development of this practice model of "macro and micro" (Chapter 1) and then moving on to place today's organizing, management, and social work practice in the context of the rapidly changing 21st century's political economy (Chapter 2).

In Section II, the *engagement and assessment* section, the book explores a practitioner's personal and professional development as he or she begins assessing communities and programs. Chapter 3 examines "professional use of self" through tactical self-awareness as applied to community needs assessments. Chapter 4 deepens the engagement process by examining the impact of "the unconscious in organizing" as seen through outreach. Chapter 5, perhaps the most difficult chapter in the book, synthesizes the issues of pre-engagement and engagement in a practice framework as "the social construction of practice." This chapter also examines some of the ways macro and micro skill sets can be applied in complementary fashion so that the field begins to break away from the "either/or-ness" of macro *versus* micro practice.

Moving on to Section III, on *relationship building,* Chapter 6 focuses on the dynamics of power while addressing leadership development inside a human services framework, a topic that has been much written about over the past 20 years, albeit primarily for the corporate sector. Chapter 7 develops campaign strategy while clarifying the not-so-hidden realities of race, class, and gender that can impact such campaigns even among progressive activists, as relationships are either strengthened or harmed through attention or inattention to the micro aggressions of oppression so often woven into everyday life.

There are four chapters within Section IV, the *intervention* section. Chapter 8 focuses on strategic development. It is a core chapter in the book, as it delineates the various levels of organizing for a community practitioner and applies detailed activities and experiences to practice so that the practitioner learns as much as possible about how to do organizing from the chosen model of practice. Chapter 9, written by Dr. Mohan Krishna Vinjamuri, explores the growing impact of social network organizing and other profound shifts occurring in macro practice from the Internet, both in electoral politics (exemplified by Obama's campaign) and other, more grassroots efforts related to mobilizing for social justice (as seen around the battle for gay/lesbian marriage and the defeat of Proposition 8 in California, culminating in the historic Supreme Court rulings in June 2013). This chapter goes on to explore the even wider impact of the Internet and social media on world transformational change, to which all social work must attend. In keeping with the rapid changes underway in both society and social work itself, Chapter 10 addresses the vital role played by social work practitioners in the policy advocacy and political arenas. As seen through case examples of former social work students who now are skilled and adroit practitioners within the political arena, this chapter demonstrates how social workers can have a growing legislative and electoral impact to bolster the profession's mission. Chapter 11, written by Kristin LeBourveau and Meredith Ledlie-Johnson, focuses on how social work must expand its definition of the "social environment" to include the natural environment itself. Framing their presentation within path-breaking work they themselves have done, such as community gardens, local food markets, opposition to hydrofracking, and response to climate change, their chapter shows how the field is awakening to their vision that as Earth grows in peril, so do we all—if we do not act.

Section V, on *transitions and evaluation,* focuses primarily on two processes of evaluation: the external data practitioners must utilize in their decision making and their own internal evaluation of their values as they apply them in the lifelong, dilemma-filled arc between career choice and principled commitment. Looking at the social worker who decided to do organizing, Kay, Chapter 12 analyzes the dilemmas of the organizer-turned-supervisor. The chapter shows how both one's "internal strategic vision as a tool" and the self-reflective (i.e., "clinical") evaluation work of the grassroots organizer can positively impact the effectiveness of the new supervisor, without compromising his or her commitments to social justice. Chapter 13 examines the choices made by the organizer who works in social work and moves on to a wider, more politically demanding role with broader strategic responsibilities beyond the grassroots. It details the evidence-based forms of strategic support that managers and executives committed to social justice and client/staff voice can undertake without losing executive responsibility to bottom-line fiscal constraints.

Chapter 14, in the book's conclusion, returns to a set of social and political issues that confront the engaged 21st century practitioner, whether organizer or clinician or executive, if he or she is to be situated within a larger social movement capable of supporting transformative social change as this century unfolds.

This work is meant to be developmental, weaving back and forth between strategic/organizational demands and personal concerns as they occur in each practice situation (first as an organizer, later as a program director and manager). Thus, there are consistent references to practice in the early 21st century (a contextual issue related to the political economy) and the practitioner's personal abilities and professional interests in concrete situations as they occur in the job (a process issue related to implementation). When joined together, these sets of political and personal conditions create a dynamic engagement between these issues that is the reality of how actual macro practice—indeed, all practice—is performed.

A CLOSING DILEMMA OR TWO

Developing a methodology that experientially centers on concrete examples of practice presents two concrete problems. First, as Fisher and Karger (1996) suggested earlier, most books on practice present discussions of theory in sections separate from those on practice, an unfortunate dichotomizing of professional practice that leads many practitioners to dismiss theory as too general or too abstract to be of much use. At the same time, I agree with what Corrigan and Leonard (1978) stated:

> Social workers demand two contradictory things from theory: they want a theoretical insight into their work that will promise them some form of a breakthrough in their practice, emanating from their present situation; at the same time they expect the theory that this theory springs from to be encompassed by their practice. Such theory cannot exist, for theory . . . comes at least in part from outside practice. . . . For social workers who simply want to discover new practice, without struggling with a set of ideas that come from outside that practice, we can offer nothing much. (p. 6)

I again try to resolve this dilemma by posing certain theoretical problems (like the nature of the welfare state, the organization and delivery of social welfare services, etc.) that must be addressed by the practitioner in his or her work, *but not necessarily directly within it on a day-to-day basis.* Corrigan and Leonard's (1978) book, as well as Fabricant and Fisher's (2002) more recent and organizationally focused *Settlement Houses Under Siege,* complement this work because the former uses theory to explore welfare state relations and the latter to explore organizational dynamics within the welfare state. Their respective analyses help explain how certain theoretical ideas (on the welfare state, on the shifting workplace demands of cost containment, etc.), once understood, can affect practice for the better by rooting one's strategic vision within this larger social context. At the same time, this book focuses on the personal–political dynamics of organizing/management of the individual organizer or manager and the creation of democratic leadership/collective voice in ways the works mentioned do not. This has the benefit of involving practitioners (including clinicians) in a series of concrete, daily issues that affect their lives, which touch on theoretical ideas that readers then may wish to pursue through an examination of these other important works (Ganz, 2010).

There also will be reflective exercises woven through each chapter and concrete activities at the conclusion of each, at least one of which will connect to CSWE EPA standards. The reflective exercises serve two purposes. First, they are designed to increase reflective learning, whether as a student in a classroom or as a practitioner in an agency. Developing one's critically reflective capacity is a fundamental requirement for ongoing transformational work, as such capacity helps one consistently sift personal judgments, values, experiences, and the present tactical choices one must make (Scharmer, 2009; Senge, 2006).

The second purpose is based on how most practitioners learn. Some of the theoretical discussions undertaken here are difficult and, as Corrigan and Leonard (1978) point out, can frustrate the reader because they are not initially applicable to the work he or she is doing at the moment. These reflective activities are placed, literally, at some of those difficult moments so readers can both reflect on and see eventual applicability later in their careers or in helping frame the strategic direction to their stance as progressive macro practitioners throughout their careers, not just while doing grassroots work. The concrete activities, on the other hand, are designed to show ways the chapters' material may be of immediate use. In also connecting readers to core CSWE competencies, the work is further strengthened for sustained and meaningful application.

The final issue relates to what we call the people who want and need social services and either organize to get their needs met or arrive at the agency door to see what's possible. Back in the '80s, I wrestled with a variety of options before sticking with *clients,* arguing that our work, if done well, could lead to other options. It's nice to report that, years later, the number of community-based interventions and the focus on strengths among those with whom we work makes the term *community members* more suitable today. Whether this term resonates with ideas of leadership and engaged citizenship in the 21st century depends on how the practice develops among these community members and the practitioners with whom they work.

Such shifts in language and meaning are key tests of whether today's macro practice is political in ways that benefit those who have been marginalized—and those who sit in the White House. For in such personal decisions are born the transformative activities leading to lasting social change that has the potential to alter far more than our practice relationships. On that hopeful irony, this book strives to become a small part of that transformation.

REFERENCES

Corrigan, P., & Leonard, P. (1978). *Social work practice under capitalism.* London: MacMillan.

Fabricant, M., & Fisher, R. (2002). *Settlement houses under siege: The struggle to sustain community organizations in New York City.* New York: Columbia University Press.

Fisher, R., & Karger, H. (1996). *Social work and community in a private world: Getting out in public.* New York: Addison-Wesley.

Freire, P. (1996). *Letters to Cristina.* New York: Taylor & Francis.

Freire, P. (2000a). *Pedagogy of freedom.* New York: Rowman & Littlefield.

Freire, P. (2000b). *Pedagogy of the oppressed* (30th ed.). New York: Bloomsbury Academic.

Ganz, M. (2010). *Sometimes David wins.* New York: Oxford University Press.

Netting, F. E., Kettner, P., McMurtry, S., & Thomas, M. L. (2012). *Macro social work practice* (5th ed.). New York: Pearson.

Scharmer, O. (2009). *Theory U: Learning from the future as it emerges.* New York: Berrett-Koehler.

Scherer, M. (2012, August 27). Elections will never be the same. *TIME Magazine.* Retrieved from http://www.time.com/time/magazine/article/0,9171,2122255,00.html

Senge, P. (2006). *The fifth discipline: The art and practice of the learning organization.* New York: Crown.

The second edition of *Macro Practice in Social Work for the 21st Century* has been redesigned so that its overall structure outlines a practice framework consistent with foundation-level courses used across the country. Along with the alignment of Council of Social Work Education Educational Policy and Accreditation Standards (EPAs) core competencies in each chapter, the 14 chapters have been organized so that they are consistent with all social work practice frameworks: *pre-engagement, engagement, relationship building, interventions, and transitions and evaluation.*

Likewise, the chapter-by-chapter activities and reflection exercises have been designed to meet both the EPA standards and competencies of the field, as well as to engage the student in the type of practice skill, knowledge, and behavior consistent with that phase of practice development. Thus, activities in the "pre-engagement" phase, which are designed for new practitioners to test their assumptions and beliefs about their role, how their agency operates, and opportunities and constraints within the profession, are necessarily quite different from those in the "interventions" phase, which includes many more hands-on tactical and strategic activities.

One final note: Real practice, of course, does not move neatly from one phase to the next. A new social work intern can be trying to reflect on pre-engagement issues while attending a citywide coalition meeting on possible food stamp reductions caused by the "federal sequester"—a potential crisis for her agency and the people with whom they work that will be requiring intense activity. Later on, in the midst of, say, a lobbying effort involving professionals and community members, that same intern and her field instructor may pause during supervision to reflect on limits and new possibilities of activism caused by the political climate—factors that are at the heart of pre-engagement work.

In short, only books, not real life, can be crisp and clean! The sections that follow are designed simply to aid in learning about each phase, not as a primer for how the activities and reflections of the phases appear in the real world. With that caveat, may what follows be a partial guide to the development of each reader's transformational practice.

Section I
Pre-Engagement

In many ways, the pre-engagement phase of practice can be one of the most difficult for the new social work intern. People enter the social work profession to do things—help people, empower groups, build community, save the world!—not to sit around and think about how best and why to do the work or how their agencies operate in today's world as opposed to 30 years ago. And yet professional development requires the new professional to do just that. What distinguishes a professional's skills from others' is the capacity for reflection in the midst of action—what Paulo Freire (2000) called "praxis." It distinguishes reaction—even justifiable reaction to social injustice or personal hurt—from critically reflective activity by the willingness to think deeply about the assumptions one is operating from. (Is this a potential ally I am upset with? Am I upset by the behavior or the intent of the actors involved? Are we developing responses based on what we can do in 2014 or the way people worked in 1984 or 1994?) "Pre-engagement" is technically the earliest phase of a professional's career, where someone new to the profession or agency is given materials about the agency, asked to study the agency organizational chart, and required to attend meetings and events to "study" what the agency is all about. In reality, it is also the training ground that begins to socialize a professional to the importance of maintaining ongoing reflection and assessment of the activities he or she undertakes. Otherwise, action without reflection over time becomes mindless activity, just as reflection without action becomes intellectual passivity.

The two chapters that make up "Pre-Engagement" are designed to serve two primary phases. The first, "Starting Before the Beginning," lays out the origins of this textbook. As such, it is a model for how "work"—even the work of a textbook—comes about—what preceded its writing, what led to its particular emphases on skill sets and strategic focus. The ensuing questions and reflective activities are therefore designed to help you reflect on your own assumptions for why you do this work and what you like to do. It can help you see the limits or boundaries of what can be undertaken, as well as principles that guide you no matter what you decide to do.

The second chapter seeks to contextualize what practice looks like in the 21st century. It was purposely created to break through the often-debilitating assumption that pervades some sectors of the profession: If only we social workers all worked harder, poverty would be erased and injustice overcome. Often, this stems from one fundamental strategic error that all too often has occurred in macro work. This error is to imagine that what worked in 1964 or 1974, when social movements were far more robust in the United States, will work in 2014 and beyond. Modeled after the political economic and social dynamics employed by Robert Fisher (1994) in *Let the People Decide*, the chapter lays out the interplay between the changes in the political economy and the ensuing roles of social workers that emerged and transformed as homelessness and homelessness advocacy evolved. The chapter will also allow students, faculty, and field instructors to reflect on the distinctive contours of practice in today's climate so that future work can be as strategically effective and personally meaningful as possible.

REFERENCES

Fisher, R. (1994). *Let the people decide.* Boston: Twayne.
Freire, P. (2000). *Pedagogy of the oppressed.* New York: Seabury Press.

CHAPTER 1

Starting Before the Beginning

Historical Origins, Strategic Assumptions, and Professional Development: The Creation of a Textbook

As with any other body of work, a textbook does not emerge whole cloth—or virtual text—from spontaneous combustion. To be read correctly, somewhere in its "pre-engagement phase," the book's author must spell out the underlying influences that animate the choices made, whether they be case studies from students, selected quotations from various authors, or the author's own predispositions based on lived experience—in this case as a grassroots organizer, an academic, a community-based consultant, and a human being. Doing so early on, before beginning the heavy slog of reading a textbook (or working on a political campaign or accepting a job inside an agency), expands the reader's choices. By the end of this chapter, you'll know whether you want to begin. If past history is a guide, a few will wish to read no more. Some—it is hoped more than a few—will be inspired. May sufficient numbers learn enough throughout that the following pages make a difference in your work.

UPDATE TO THE SECOND EDITION: THE WORST OF TIMES, THE BEST OF TIMES—OR "INTERESTING TIMES"?

The origins of this book's first edition were threefold. For the second edition, as the reader will see toward the end of this introduction, there is now, 4 years later, a resilient albeit humbling fourth origin. The first edition was written at a time when the rarified air of "hope and change" was being inhaled by progressives everywhere. Four years later, the air seems less rarified and far more pungent: the continuing sway of the Tea Party in political discourse; the Republican Congressional sweep in 2010; the bailout of Wall Street that seems to have left Main Street far behind; and a frighteningly high unemployment rate that refuses to fall. But wait—there is more: in 2010 and 2011, the Arab Spring, dictators toppling like dominoes; universal health care, no matter its flaws, added to the welfare state after 50 years of effort; Occupy Wall Street popping up in 800 American cities, embraced by the suddenly class-conscious 99%; gay marriage the law of the land in 11 states and an American president in support of it; and then, in November of 2012, the reelection of Barack Obama, upending Republican certainties and becoming the only president besides Franklin Delano Roosevelt (FDR) to be reelected with unemployment rates above 8%. There is so much to be scared of and disappointed about . . . so much to be excited by and worthy of fighting for. This second edition begins during a time when core beliefs, starkly contrasted in bright reds and blues, are being challenged across America.

The hope here is that this edition makes a small contribution to meeting some of those challenges for those of us who toil in the forgotten margins of the 2012 campaigns—where poverty is multigenerational and schools are without heat before hurricanes and floods, where children live at risk and without safety and elders weep silently in their isolated rooms. We in human services must be rigorous and steely eyed in our strategic assessments as we chart the direction of our profession over the coming years: The people with whom we work and the issues to which we dedicate our lives were absent from the 2012 electoral discourse. Such absence—and with it, a corresponding decrease in influence—can be corrected only through diligent, strategic leveraging of our ideas and issues in coalitions and campaigns that make these concerns impossible to ignore.

As part of that strategic leveraging, this work also more openly seeks to bridge some of the divides that exist in social work—beginning by showing ways to lessen the divisions between "micro" and "macro" practice that haunt our field. There is no way to increase funding for, say, domestic violence or homeless shelters or mental health budgets if, within the profession, organizers and managers remain distant from clinicians and group-work practitioners. Likewise, clinical social workers who use their numerical supremacy as justification for marginalizing organizers and administrators from professional discourse and teaching do so at their own peril, as such division gives added political strength to those who would cut social services beyond the bone and into its heart. Trivializing and diminishing natural allies who can gain from each other while more powerful economic and political forces look to end entitlements is a fools' game none of us can win. This edition attempts to show ways to connect our different approaches to social work practice as complementary, not conflicting, so that our unity is strengthened in ways that provide resilience to our work at a time when we can expect to be tested again and again by more conservative forces.

In keeping with every social work program's understandable accreditation responsibilities, each chapter also integrates with the chapter's skill set the Council on Social Work Education's core competencies based on Educational Policy and Accreditation Standards, thus easing the difficulties in demonstrating how core curriculum with a macro focus meets the profession's standards. This has been done without diminishing the emphasis on either Paulo Freire's attention to "dialogue" or the importance of Elaine Pinderhughes's analysis of power and privilege as it appears in frontline practice. In a world steeped in conflict, where some perceive compromise as a defeat, finding common ground within the profession in the pursuit of social justice is perhaps itself a political act—and a personally fulfilling one, too.

CONTINUING ORIGINS I: THE AGE OF REAGAN

A new set of influences unique to this edition will be presented as the fourth origin later in this introduction, but I begin with the original three, as they still influence the content of this text. The first origin to this work began a while back, in 1982, a time when the ascent of Ronald Reagan was complete and the unfolding of the conservative paradigm was beginning to be felt throughout America. I wrote a book titled *The Other Side of Organizing* in part because of the devastating impact Reagan's election had on progressive organizing at that time. In the late 1970s, progressive community activists, whether rank-and-file trade unionists, feminists, or neighborhood organizers fighting the latest round of "city crisis" budget cuts, were united by the common assumption that our nation was about to swing back to a far more progressive phase. After all, the conditions commonly assumed to augur a progressive upswing were present everywhere: an economy that placed working people in peril, with both double-digit inflation and skyrocketing unemployment rates; a weakened system of authority caused by Watergate; and unending rounds of "city crisis" cuts that devastated services and increased felt needs throughout the poorest communities. So many of us were so sure that this mix of diminished political authority, increasing economic need, and objectively difficult living conditions could lead in only one direction: to a progressive realignment of workers, people of color, women, and other disenfranchised folk who, in combination, would have the power to change our nation's course as had occurred in the 1930s and 1960s.

It didn't exactly work out that way. Culminating in the personal and political devastation that so many progressive people experienced with the 2004 reelection of George W. Bush to a second term as president of the United States, early 21st century community practitioners reeled with the jarring awareness that more than 25 years had elapsed since liberal thought and liberal action had been off the defensive. Not that there were no pivotal worldwide achievements during that time: The Berlin Wall fell, along with the Soviet bureaucracy; Nelson Mandela was released from prison, and apartheid was vanquished; the Chiapas of Mexico gave a heroic face (or at least a mask) to the struggles of indigenous Americans; through microeconomic loans, Third World women courageously joined economic and social development within their communities; AIDS was seen as simply a virulent disease of marginal people until gay activists forced the world to think and act otherwise; and wired young activists showed the rest of us how to use the Internet to organize international movements, first against Nike's sweatshops, later against the World Trade Organization.

Likewise, while some of the motivation for *The Other Side* also emanated from what I described as "the sad, quiet truth" that too many organizers took too little joy from what we did and the way we did it, that is happily no longer true. Today, young activists aren't afraid to have fun. Community practitioners have learned from Abbie Hoffman that a hearty laugh and a little color in the middle of your protest march can be a good thing. Likewise, gay activists and third-wave feminists have led the way in helping the rest of us openly embrace sexuality, freedom of expression, and a touch of pink as we go about the otherwise mundane tasks of daily political struggle. As seen in the early phases of Occupy Wall Street in 2011, it's nice to see that people who like to boogie can want to change the world, too. (Emma Goldman, you'd be proud!) Finally, Native American, African American, Asian American, and Latino activists have not shied away from embracing the spiritual traditions of their ancestors as integral to our work, helping the rest of us learn that progressive reform devoid of spiritual meaning can be very hollow indeed.

Nevertheless, such successes could not disguise that there was another, often more successful kind of organizing going on as well, from the Reagan Era forward: the rise of Islamist fundamentalism and its fanatical opposition to modernism, signified most powerfully through its subjugation of women; the movement of conservative American Christianity from the religious to the political sphere, felt in treatment of textbooks on evolution, repeal of sex education in schools, the attack on women's reproductive rights, and a proposed constitutional amendment banning gay marriage; the use of terrorism as a powerful tool against modern military and economic might, culminating (but hardly ending) on a beautiful September day over America's East Coast; and the ragged separation of the United States into the warring colors of red and blue. And through it all, an entrenched belief was seeping throughout our nation's communities and neighborhoods: that personal and communal happiness could occur only through the accumulation of economic wealth and individual acquisition (whether of status, power, or *things*), all of it preferably privatized. Entwined within that belief was another assumption that further marginalized progressives from mainstream America: To think otherwise was at best a waste of time and more likely a sign of one's lesser capacity to compete in the global market. Updating Social Darwinism with a late-20th-century gloss of celebrity, the smartest folks, knowing all this already, worked only to free up the market further to grow, not regulate its excesses (Krugman, 2009). The rest of us, as Tea Party activists continue to preach, were simply to get out of the way.

ORIGINS II: STUDENTS OF COMMUNITY PRACTICE KEEP ON KEEPIN' ON

During those long years, I was fortunate enough to have classroom after classroom of community organizing students and social administration majors—macro practitioners—who never gave up their beliefs opposing both the inevitable triumph of conservative thought and the assumed incapacity of marginalized and oppressed people to rise above their conditions to make a better world. Whether educating me in the early '90s on the indigenous struggles emerging in South America or 15 years later offering stories of heartbreak and inspiration about the homeless LGBTQ kids of color fighting for services in Greenwich Village, these students showed me that social change and social justice still mattered and that there were ways one could go about achieving nothing less, even in conservative times.

I was honored to find that the core material of *The Other Side of Organizing* also mattered to them. They continued to find value in the still-all-too-overlooked role of the community practitioner and the ways one goes about doing his or her actual work as fundamental strategic imperatives in working effectively with the disenfranchised and the oppressed. Instead of deep opposition, they could see that the "micro" attention to the personal and the "macro" awareness of the sociopolitical in combination made them better practitioners.

Having now read and reread the works of Freire over the past three decades and borne witness to countless organizing efforts as well, I am more convinced than ever that the ways we work with the oppressed and disenfranchised either socially reproduce the same marginality they have all too often experienced or liberate *us all* to live more fully in the world than we had before. This book will seek to foster this latter kind of transformation in the macro practice that community organizers and administrators undertake—and in the micro practice of clinical social workers, too.

Creating such transformative change won't be easy. As the untiring efforts of students and activists also made clear year after year, the simple truth is that community practitioners have long toiled in soil found mostly on the side of steep mountains. The grinding effort to get people to come to meetings, take on the landlord, fight back against the developer, or work together for school reform has often been backbreaking. After a while, one can believe in the capacity of people to do great things and still grow exasperated when almost nobody shows up. It could come to seem like pretty lonely work . . . and at times it has been. That those who hung in there during those hard times kept returning to chapters from *The Other Side* as part of the way to see them through those difficulties motivated me to update the work for the continuing challenges of the conservative period still evident in the early 21st century.

ORIGINS III: THE TIME OF "HOPE AND CHANGE" WITH OBAMA

Thus, a key thread woven throughout this book emanates from the toil of that long, steep climb since 1982 and the lessons gained, while painful, that allow us to learn from our history. However, when I began writing the first edition, this focus on using the lessons within a conservative period was not just a key thread; it was pretty much the entire bolt of cloth. That, needless to say, changed with the ascent of Obama to the presidency of the United States in 2008. For, as the noted historian of community organizing Robert Fisher (2008) remarked as that campaign went on, "history moves." Fisher had a smile on his face as he spoke that.

As Fisher (2008) pointed out, history often seems to move slowly, seemingly glacially at times, incrementally at best. People then go about the business of living in regular ways, with modest assumptions, based on the belief that "this is the way the world is." Civic involvement wanes, and organizers grow more exasperated; the domination of the con-servative economic and political elite seems complete. For example, Daniel Bell (2002), one of the nation's most esteemed sociologists in mid-20th-century America, wrote as much in his best-selling *The End of Ideology*. Except for "the Negro problem," which he saw confined primarily to the South, and the apathy of college students, he proclaimed that the United States could look forward to a period of healthy, consensus-based, and harmonious pluralism. The book sold best in the early '60s. There were fewer copies sold by the middle of the decade. History moved.

In late 2007 and 2008, history moved again, suddenly and rapidly, in ways that no sane community practitioner could or would have predicted at the beginning of 2007. I am not going to recount what is already well-known to any reader of this text about the stunning ascent of Obama, former community organizer, to the presidency of the United States.[1] What mattered at the time for a community practitioner was the seismic shift that could and did occur within a broad swath of the American populace as the electoral cam-paign went on. Its deeper meanings will not be known for years to come, but there are three aspects that still suggest exciting possibilities for community practice while Obama is president of the United States (and seemingly afterward as well):

1. In running a campaign based in part on community organizing principles that emphasized a new relationship between the leader and the led, the Obama campaign in

2008 heightened expectations of what was expected of both him and those who worked with and voted for him. While much of this focused on his political formulation of finding "common ground between red and blue," such a participatory model laid the groundwork for far more mobilization of the grassroots than did previous electoral strategies. His campaign's efforts to mobilize, train, and expand the numbers of electoral activists through the Internet and the ensuing state- and district-level campaign efforts created larger numbers of street-level activists than had ever been seen in a 20th century election. In turn, this mobilization carried with it the kind of expectation for something transcending "the little victories" common to organizing of the late 20th century. President Obama and all who support him have since been challenged as to how they have gone about securing victories to justify further, expansive mobilization. While the past 4 years have made clear that the United States is deeply divided on his presidency, this text will continue to work from the assumption that extraordinary mobilization by progressives seen during Obama's first presidential election will have to continue throughout his second term if the welfare state as we know it is to remain intact.

2. Obama's 2008 electoral campaign showed evidence that he began to address power dynamics between leaders and followers as something other than a zero-sum game. One of the most important—and, as of this writing, least discussed—aspects of that Obama campaign is his demand that members of his team get along, that factional (and highly personal) struggles for turf and power would not be acceptable, and that the demeaning and enraged ego-based fights between staff members so common in other campaigns (and among White House staff, including those of Democrats) would not be tolerated. Espousing external democracy while practicing antidemocratic turf wars has been a long-time contradiction in political life that Obama and his closest staff seemed intent on diminishing. While 4 years in the Oval Office have led to a serious critique of how much this internal democratic process continued under Obama (Barofsky, 2012), as is made clear in Chapter 5, there is still much to learn from this early model of participation and power that can be applied in other arenas of organizing.

As will be discussed throughout this book, macro practitioners likewise have long recognized that some human service organizations' leaders set high standards in their mission statements regarding respect for clients and community members, only to treat their staff in demeaning ways that over time further marginalize those with the least power (Fabricant & Fisher, 2002). There are also distinct models of organizing that separate the organizer from the organized in ways that replicate forms of "difference" that unconsciously re-create the very power dynamics of marginality that Obama himself has opposed in his own story (Obama, 1995/2004). Obama's attempts in 2008 and after to reconstruct a new model of power sharing within his own team created the active possibility that macro practitioners, whether activist or administrator, can engage in similar kinds of power sharing, especially as they climb off the steep mountains of the past and enter new, more level terrain that can seem more easily traversed than perhaps it is. This text will examine how to do this in its emphasis on democratic leadership development as an organizer and in team building as a manager or supervisor.

3. That in 2008 a significant majority of Americans, including 43% of Whites, chose a Black man to lead them out of the economic, political, and environmental morass occurred for reasons beyond the Bush Administration's Iraq debacle, the collapse of the financial system, and the failure of the federal government to respond to Hurricane Katrina (McClellan, 2008). Weakening alongside these systemic failures has been the stranglehold on discourse related to state intervention, the inevitable "goodness" of the free market, and the inherent wisdom and all-around greater intelligence of those aligned with individualism and acquisitiveness as opposed to forms of community and mutually beneficial reciprocity.

Obama became extraordinarily popular with those who voted for him in part because he represented to them a new way of thinking about themselves and what can be done to better American society. While some commentators continue to refer to Obama as a blank slate even after his reelection, few have noted that the slate is not so much empty as open to challenging the political orthodoxy of the past 30 years. As seen in the contentiousness over his overhaul of the health care system (Barofsky, 2012), his challenge to traditional free-market thinking caused widespread antagonism because the dominant neoliberal agenda received its first systemic threat since the 1970s. While his economic policies related to the financial crisis and ongoing economic stagnation have been met with widespread skepticism from many progressives (Stiglitz, 2012), there is little question that Obama's presence in the White House has been a flashpoint of opposition for conservatives not seen since the first term of FDR.[2] Community practitioners (and social workers in general), once derided for seeking this kind of progressive discourse that is still under way in 2013, continue to have an opportunity to engage in this debate in ways not possible for more than a generation. This text is written in ways meant to help further that discourse.

NEW ORIGIN IV: HISTORY MOVES AGAIN . . . INTO "INTERESTING TIMES"

So in 2008, history moved—toward Obama and toward new ideas and possibilities for what we as a country and a people can be. Unlike the Reagan Era, the early "Time of Obama" was thus an exciting one for community practitioners. That said, the past 4 years have taught us that this is not a time for rest and relaxation. For as Fisher (2008) mentioned in his talk about the time in which we now find ourselves, this time can also be brief. "Historical times such as the one we are entering make possible new alignments, but only if we work hard at it, before another shift occurs," he stated. "We need to use the time that we have well" (Fisher, 2008; see also Fisher, 1994).

Perhaps the primary lesson of 2009 to 2013 is that we all could have used our time better. Yes, President Obama relied more on Wall Street than Main Street in his financial decision making (Barofsky, 2012; Krugman, 2009; Stiglitz, 2012). So did FDR in his first term (Schlesinger, 2003). What FDR had to protect him from the conservative tendencies in his own party and among Republicans was an organized, progressive movement comprising militant trade unions, socialists, communists, social democrats, a social work rank and file, and tenant activists—almost all of them demanding financial and social reform that went far beyond the FDR agenda (Jansson, 2011; Reisch, 2013). Such a movement gave added authority and heft to progressive voices inside FDR's Cabinet, such as Frances Perkins and social worker Harry Hopkins (as well as FDR's wife, Eleanor). In 2009 to 2013, such a movement was replaced with a fragmented set of progressive interests, including a diminished trade union movement (often on opposing sides from environmentalists); highly institutionalized, Beltway advocates such as the American Association of Retired People (AARP); civil rights organizations lacking the leadership, direction, and purpose of their predecessors; and human service activists dedicated more to their own short-term programmatic interests (health care, mental health, domestic violence, education, etc.) than to a unifying set of commitments on which a genuine social movement could be built (Weil, Reisch, & Ohmer, 2009). With the riveting exception of the recent Supreme Court rulings that were fueled by the seismic shifts in Americans' support for gay marriage, how can Obama during his second administration tilt further left in a time of crisis when, unlike FDR, he lacks the leverage of a powerful progressive current helping him combat more conservative trends?

A potential shift in social movements did occur in September 2011 with the birth of the Occupy Wall Street (OWS) movement in New York City and, soon after, across the United States in more than 800 cities. It drew its inspiration from two sources. Its first was its rallying cry of "We are the 99%!" and fierce opposition to the wealth and privilege of the 1%. This simple slogan captured much of the progressive American imagination because it clarified and made whole a set of economic grievances pent up for years: student debt and housing debt; the steep rise of economic inequality; the loss of secure, well-paying jobs. Such unity had been missing from much of progressive-movement work for a generation.

The second inspiring source was the notion of OWS itself. While "the 99%–1%" clarified what was wrong with America, OWS inspired activists to embrace what was right. The movement was less about the seizure of property (although some anarchists might claim otherwise) and more about the *reclaiming of the commons*—an ancient right of citizens to lay claim to places for equal discourse, equality before the law, a sharing of alms (in OWS's case, two well-cooked meals a day), shelter, and even an occasional hug. Anyone who visited the Zuccotti Park site in New York City or dozens of other encampments across the country was struck by the sense of care and commitment people showed one another. Furthermore, OWS was perhaps the first economically driven social justice movement where clinicians of all stripes staffed "empathy tables" and remained available to provide counseling to burned-out activists. While later strains would emerge inside the movement once the encampment was forcibly removed by the police, 2011 to 2012 was marked by an inspiring moment of what alternatives to market exchange (and its increasingly expensive costs) could look like for the 99% increasingly falling behind the economic wealth and social privilege of the 1%.

OWS activists regained both attention and some credibility with their response to the devastation wrought by Hurricane Sandy along the East Coast in the autumn of 2012 and into the winter of that year. Unlike most of their ideological ancestors, who viewed direct service as a bane to social justice work, Occupy Sandy activists soon sprang into action in relief and recovery efforts in Brooklyn, Staten Island, Long Island, and New Jersey. Because of their hard-won and recent experience in mobilizing hundreds for direct action over the previous year, complete with well-honed social media sites such as OWS Text, OWS Newsletter, and Occupy.net, OWS-ers in large numbers immediately sprang into action, setting up coordinated, on-the-ground relief efforts before either the Red Cross or the Federal Emergency Management Agency arrived. By demonstrating a commitment to direct relief as well as direct action, OWS activists have remained a vital part of a still modest but nevertheless significant alternative current to present-day discourse. As such, these forces, in combination with an increasingly restive (and obviously damaged) labor movement, environmentalists, feminists, LGBTQ activists, and social service progressives, may serve as President Obama's much-needed left flank as he continues to do battle with those seeking to undermine the welfare state.

Therefore, the second thread to be woven through this book is about using our time well to create lasting progressive change. While written as a textbook, it is a textbook with a decided point of view: The early 21st century is an extraordinary historical moment for community practice that we must take advantage of to correct some of the mistakes of free-market excess, financial usury, environmental degradation, and indifference to communal and individual suffering of those most marginalized and ignored over the past 25 years. (The inspiring example of LGBTQ activism and the Supreme Court rulings can be found in Chapter 9.) As 2008 to 2010 made clear, community practitioners need to get busy articulating and acting on our progressive agenda, or someone else—perhaps someone from the Tea Party—will.

ADDRESSING PROGRESSIVE STRATEGIC MISTAKES FROM THE PAST . . . AND PRESENT

New possibilities and old lessons can be woven together only if we address a few strategic mistakes right away so that they don't reappear later.

Two strategic issues of the past still stand out that require serious reassessment. The past 4 years have also made clear that there is a third, present strategic perspective we need to fine-tune or court expanded marginalization within the halls of economic and political power. First, the politics of victimization, while in part rooted in the conditions of social oppression for many communities with whom we work, has too often fostered a sense of entitlement devoid of reciprocity that both has alienated us from hard-working allies and is strategically bankrupt. After all, who built a sustained organizing campaign for economic and social change (as well as needed traffic lights or a better school lunch) on the basis of the "obligated few" organizing on behalf of the "dependent many"?

Furthermore, such a perspective carries with it the underlying assumption that oppressed people's voices cannot be sustained in the ongoing historical challenges they confront to live fully in the world. Obama ran his 2008 and 2012 campaigns on the assumption that regular people had as much to offer as anyone else in the building of a successful electoral strategy. Rather than relying only on elites to mastermind his success, he and his staff worked with others with the expectation that they could deliver. Having such high expectations is the opposite of victimhood. In short, organizing in the 21st century from a stance of either victimization or dependence is clearly untenable for long-term progressive transformation.

Second, for the past 25 years, progressive activists have in the main focused on campaigns that are defensive in character and lacking in a coherent, overarching vision that unites people in a longer-term perspective on how their particular campaign connects meaningfully to others. While there have been notable and inspiring international struggles such as the Chiapas and the growth of women's economic and social independence in the Third World, most U.S. domestic strategies have all too often fought against the right wing's assaults on the welfare state or the prerogatives of the free market (company closings, outsourcing, etc.). While the work has been of great value, *the loss of a coherent vision regarding what we want and not simply what we are against* that could unite and inspire people in the manner akin to the conservative movements of today is a challenge that progressives must meet. While OWS activists have been motivated by the reemergence of the commons as an inspiring example of what people want, progressives everywhere need to continue refining what we seek and not only what we fear.

A progressive American presidency (or, at the state and local levels, governorship and city councils/mayoralty) cannot be sustained if those who build social movements are reflexively defensive and lacking in a larger, positive vision that connects us all and that can then be articulated and brought to life by political leaders. As the conservative movement did over the years, progressives need to focus on their own inspiring stories, models for change, and exemplars of both leadership and program that can bring that vision to life, thus sustaining activity that translates to policy and policy to programs that substantially improve the lives of others.

A third strategic error within social work and progressive movements in general has been the no-longer-viable assumption that the welfare state can be maintained and expanded without serious, systemic reckoning as to how and by whom both entitlements and services can be paid. Leading political actors in both political parties at all levels of government see deficit reduction as the primary long-term task of their fiscal stewardship. Such retrenchment is to be done through reduction in labor costs, pension benefits, and a scaling back of entitlements, including Social Security, Medicare, and Medicaid (Bartels, 2008). *Were all these policies enacted, it would be the death of the welfare state as we know it.* Ignoring the seriousness of the shifts under way in the welfare state would be devastating.

There are policy alternatives that could stimulate growth and improve tax revenues needed to diminish unemployment, stimulate the economy, and—yes—fund the welfare state itself. As Nobel Prize-winning economist Joseph Stiglitz (2012) has written,

> Reverse the Bush era tax cuts for millionaires, end the wars and scale back defense spending, allow the government to negotiate drug prices, and, most importantly, put the country back to work. [This] would do more than anything else to improve the country's fiscal position . . . the distribution of income . . . and make money available for investments that could improve future growth. (p. 211)

Were these policies enacted, economic growth through robust government intervention would positively impact the welfare state as well—and, in today's competitive global economy, such policies are being fiercely opposed by economic and political actors that remain hostile to such an agenda.

Obviously, these early years of the 21st century are, as the Chinese saying warns, "interesting times." The full saying is, "Beware of living in interesting times, for such times are filled with tumult." *Tumult* is usually defined as a mix of "noisy commotion and emotional upheaval," which is accurate enough but woefully incomplete. Far more than emotional upheaval is at play here. It is social upheaval as well—the re-creation or the end of the American Dream; the restoration or the eradication of the middle class; the hardening of the 1% against the 99% or the emergence of social unity and common purpose. In the main, social work has been able to stand slightly apart from these kinds of stark national policy choices for most of its professional existence. No more. Whether a clinician working with children at risk, agency executive struggling with budget losses and increasing demand, or grassroots organizer seeking social justice, we all must be prepared to enter the fierceness of this debate as never before.

This edition will continue to address positive ways to handle these strategic errors and missteps.

THREE UNDERLYING ASSUMPTIONS ON WHICH TO BUILD A SOCIAL WORK PRACTICE IN THE 21ST CENTURY

Using the above strategic observations to begin shaping our own positive vision for change, *Macro Practice in Social Work for the 21st Century: Bridging the Macro-Micro Divide* is built around three assumptions related to progressive practice, two of which informed *The Other Side of Organizing* and a third that recent political history and long-time personal experience have proved to be invaluable in maintaining a meaningful stance of personal and political engagement—whether one is a grassroots organizer, clinical practitioner, frontline supervisor, or agency executive.

The first assumption is that the dominant contours of the historical period in which social work practice is carried out are a reflection not only of the status quo but also of the level of struggle between the contending forces in society. Until very recently, we practiced within an American epoch that was further to the right than under Reagan. As harsh as that time was, the Bush presidency's inability to easily undo Social Security and the existence of tepid but nevertheless real funding (as opposed to cuts) for AIDS-related research were reflections of past victories won by progressives that could not be overturned even at the height of conservative power. Likewise, with the authority of the financial system and the Bush presidency replaced by the ascendancy of the Obama Administration—followed by 4 years of increased division and rancor across the political spectrum, leading to policy impasse and widespread public antipathy to almost all political and economic actors—it is an extraordinary time when new progressive thought regarding income redistribution, state regulation, environmental safeguards, and, yes, a more progressive welfare state may be possible to argue for as one of the fundamental alternatives now present in our national discourse.

That said, embedded within these new opportunities are resilient challenges to progressivism that community practitioners cannot ignore: The Tea Party's antigovernment, free-market ideology and antipathy to bipartisanship have widespread support throughout Congress; attacks on lesbians and gays, some of them within communities of color, keep occurring, often backed by state legislative mandates; the ability of capital to move abroad remains unchecked, thus diminishing opportunities for domestic growth; and entitlements remain under attack at their foundation (Bernstein, 2008).

As the past 4 years have made clear, the president of the United States, no matter how progressive his intentions, does not determine progressive outcomes simply because he occupies the White House. It is thus imperative that all social workers, from community-based organizers and managers to frontline clinicians, view the larger context in which they work not as fixed by whoever sits in the executive office. To be strategically effective, *all social work practitioners* instead must situate their work within a dynamic context that is constantly subject to changes among *all* the social forces of the early 21st century. *To understand this is to recognize that whether times are bleak—as they were so recently and can at times seem to be now—or exciting—as they were in 2008—the necessity of engaged, strategically astute activism (in both its organizing and managerial forms) remains vital as a corrective to other forces at play that otherwise would further mitigate progressive change.* The second chapter of this text therefore addresses the unique strategic focus of social work practitioners within the dynamics of present-day economic and political conditions, using this focus as a way for macro *and* micro practitioners to practice their own dynamic interpretation—their own diagnosis—of community conditions and their ensuing practice choices for action.

While developed primarily through the prism of macro practice, it is important to underscore that from the introduction through the final chapter, this text seeks to end the binary separation between "micro" and "macro." While there are of course differences in clinical work and community organizing, overly rigid distinctions in the field have undermined organizers' appreciation for and utilization of individual skills needed for better community engagement, the running of meetings, and work with groups, as well as interpersonal insights into dynamics of power and privilege. Likewise, practice method rigidity has also limited clinical social workers' capacity for understanding the mix of social and political dynamics' impact on human behavior, a proactive and flexible understanding of how agency constraints can impact clinical treatment, and holistic diagnoses that empower clients to examine not only their own actions but those emanating from the larger social order. This text examines how to bridge the macro–micro divide in ways that empower all social workers to be more proactive and empowered in the work we do and in the debates we, too, must enter on the local, state, and national stages.

Second, every method of social work practice (macro or micro, individual, group, community, or administration) therefore carries within it certain ideologies that serve to reproduce either dominant–subordinate or self-determining relationships among its participants. As Corrigan and Leonard (1978) long ago noted in their still trenchant analysis of welfare state functions, ideology is embedded in the practice of social workers and the organizational delivery of those services. The use of red tape, the expectation of distance between organizer and community member, the use of distinct language patterns based on professional norms and standards that separate workers and community members into elites and non-elites, and the definition of practice as solely a helping process combine to communicate powerful social messages to people who enter our doors.

In short, such forms of practice inform community members—regardless of many professionals' stated sentiments—that their position in society, as again reflected in their relationship to an agency or organizing group, is marginal; that their rights are limited to requesting assistance, not that they can be genuine partners in the overall delivery and maintenance of services; and that their voice, when raised, is appreciated only as long as it is in agreement. *Social work practice—whether organizing or clinical, group or administration—that consciously undercuts the dominant attempts within*

social welfare to re-create deferential social relationships is therefc
politics—the politics of self-determination.

For just as Obama's initial attempts to minimize in-fighting within hi
his organizing experience that was grounded in valuing the voices of the peopic
he worked, this text consciously develops a methodology of intervention based on Freii
work and its emphasis on reconfiguring the helping relationship into a transformative one—
for community member and practitioner alike. As such, this text seeks to transform macro
and micro practice in ways that both improve the lives of the people with whom we work
and liberate us all to live more fully and joyfully in the world of which we are a part.

Finally, to remain genuinely progressive in any historical period in ways that foster a
politics of voice and self-determination with those with whom we work, organizers, clini-
cians, and managers must maintain an active, **internal strategic vision** *of their work that*
transcends both historical moment and immediate circumstance. Since the writing of *The*
Other Side of Organizing, a lot of organizers have moved on to become program directors
and then executives in first small and then large community-based agencies; some folks have
gone into foundations and high-level public service; some have gone into private practice.
Remarkably, many have done so without losing their commitment to either social change
and social justice or their belief in people's and communities' efficacy in changing lives.

As this book will address in its later chapters, what does change is the nature of the
dilemmas community-based supervisors, managers, or executives face and the ongoing
evaluation they must make between career advancement and continuous commitments of
a lifetime. With their new positions, they must respond to accountability from above in
ways that organizers do not (or at least perceive they do not). *However, it is not the dilem-*
mas they confront but the **internal strategic vision** *they hold that determines whether their*
career path is one of increasing distance and disengagement from their roots. Such a vision
is not dependent on the position one holds—whether grassroots organizer from Chicago
or president of the United States. Rather, it is determined by the internal vision we carry
within ourselves as we go about our external work.

By internal strategic vision, I mean something quite clear: *Such a vision is framed in*
values that are consecrated in action *so that your decisions about*

what you do,

whom you do it with,

how you do it,

and the roles you and others play

are seen in your core values consecrated in action that are always filtered through that
vision.

As such, this internal vision is a *strategic tool* accessible and usable for what one does and how one does it: for example, what grants can and cannot be applied for, the degree of community member voice in decision making, how meetings are run, and who speaks before a group. Not all community organizers carry an internal strategic vision, and some executives of multimillion-dollar agencies do (see Chapter 13). As will be argued midway through this book, in the transition from organizer to supervisor, what greatly determines one's long-term commitment to social justice is not the role one plays but the clarity of the internal strategic vision one carries, day in and day out, and acts on.

For just as a politically conservative period such as the late 20th and very early 21st century was limited in what it could do partly by the progressive victories of the past, the process of our work carries with it the politics of the future. Today we are living within a starkly challenging moment where most political actors seek little middle ground and instead hold out conflicting images of the role of government, the free market, and how the American public should pay for future generations in need. The eventual ability to move from progressive to transformative societal change therefore will be dependent on the degree to which these different visions unfold, in action and in discourse, and in so doing come to excite the American prospect once again. Holding the dynamic tension between these debates and our own willingness to struggle so that progressive opportunity comes to sustained life is a core task in 21st century social work that this book hopes to strengthen.

Having framed the beginning of this book with these strategic assumptions and beliefs—a core task of any pre-engagement process—let us turn to an examination of the broader historical context in which these assumptions—and this book and the readers' own social work practice—rest while yet being unendingly influenced by larger economic and political forces that shape us as well.

REFERENCES

Barofsky, N. (2012). *Bailout: An inside account of how Washington abandoned main street while rescuing wall street.* New York: Free Press.

Bartels, L. M. (2008). *Unequal democracy: The political economy of the new gilded age.* New York: Russell Sage Foundation.

Bell, D. (2002). *The end of ideology.* New York: Free Press.

Bernstein, J. (2008). *Crunch: Why do I feel so squeezed (and other unsolved economic mysteries).* New York: Berrett-Koehler.

Corrigan, P., & Leonard, P. (1978). *Social work practice under capitalism.* London: MacMillan.

Derber, M., & Young, E. (Eds.). (1972). *Labor and the New Deal.* New York: Da Capo Press.

Fabricant, M., & Fisher, R. (2002). *Settlement houses under siege: The struggle to sustain community organizations in New York City.* New York: Columbia University Press.

Fisher, R. (1994). *Let the people decide: Neighborhood organizing in America.* New York: Twayne.

Fisher, R. (2008, May). *20th century lessons for 21st century solutions.* Talk presented at the Hunter College School of Social Work 50th Anniversary Celebration, New York.

Gerstle, G. (2001). *American crucible: Race and nation in the 20th century.* Princeton, NJ: Princeton University Press.

Jansson, B. (2011). *The reluctant welfare state* (7th ed.). New York: Cengage Learning.

Krugman, P. (2009). *The return of depression economics and the crisis of 2008.* New York: W. W. Norton.

McClellan, S. (2008). *What happened: Inside the Bush White House and Washington's culture of deception.* New York: Public Affairs.

Obama, B. (2004). *Dreams from my father: A story of race and inheritance.* New York: Three Rivers Press. (Original work published 1995)

Reisch, M. (2013). *Social policy and social justice.* Thousand Oaks, CA: Sage.

Schlesinger, A. (2003). *The politics of upheaval: 1935–1936, the age of Roosevelt* (Vol. III). New York: Houghton-Mifflin.

Stiglitz, J. E. (2012). *The price of inequality.* New York: W. W. Norton.

Weil, M., Reisch, M., & Ohmer, M. (2009). *The community organizing handbook.* Thousand Oaks, CA: Sage.

NOTES

1. I have a personal story that in its light way suggests how different the discourse may now be. For years, people at weddings and other social functions have asked me what I do. In going over the list, whenever I mentioned "community organizing," people would nod indifferently, sometimes remarking "how nice it is that some people still did that." At a wedding in late 2008, my brief mention of occupation elicited active interest, even excitement: "Oh, really! Wow! . . . How exciting! Tell me about what an organizer actually does . . . ." Stumbling a bit, I climbed down off that mountain and began to do just that.

2. The greatest periods of programmatic success for FDR occurred during the height of the industrial labor movement. Likewise, Lyndon B. Johnson's landmark domestic legislation was passed with the civil rights movement near its apogee. See *Labor and the New Deal,* edited by Derber and Young (1972), and *American Crucible: Race and Nation in the 20th Century,* by Gerstle (2001).

CHAPTER 2

Developing Pre-Engagement Skills Through an Understanding of Context

"History Moves"

"OH, WHAT A LONG NIGHT!" TWO SOCIAL WORK PRACTITIONERS' 2012 POST-ELECTION CONNECTION ON SKYPE

Ellis Frazier clicked the Skype icon and was soon connected to his smiling, tired-looking friend, Kay Frances, in New York. Whereas 4 years ago they had met up in Chicago's Grant Park for what they both knew was the most exciting political moment of their lives—the election of Barack Obama, the first African American president—tonight they were connecting virtually.

"Hey, girlfriend, feelin' good? I guess we can relax now. Man, I can't say it's been easy these last few months. I was worried right up until CNN announced Ohio."

"Worried? I've been worried for 2 years! Ever since the Tea Party and the conservative victories in 2010, I've had my heart in my throat. Things haven't exactly been going social work's way these days." She paused and took a sip of green tea. "Truth is, I'm still worried about that. The closest anyone mentioned poverty was Romney's '47%' crack about dependent Americans. I sure hope these next 4 years get better on that score than the last 4."

Her African American friend looked serious for a moment. "Well, when Obamacare kicks in, lots of poor people will benefit, especially young ones. And expanded policies on food stamps

---

are helping more low-income people than in our history. Our man just did that one on the side, when nobody was paying much attention. Coulda been a lot worse." Ellis chuckled. "Look at that! Now I'm the conservative one! Things do change, don't they?"

"Hey, you and I have changed so much over the years . . . that's been great! But seriously, there are more desperate poor people in our programs than ever before. Poverty's worse, inequality's worse than it's been in 70 years, and yet Congress acts like the only problem is government. Ellis, you're better on these economic things. What the hell is going on anyway? So many people are suffering! Why does Obama's push for change seem so hard, still?"

Ellis paused and rubbed his eyes. "Back when we were in school a million years ago, you were always better about reading how people felt. I was the data guy, the macro man. I think part of what's going on is that different people are in a lot of pain but read that data in different ways. Three quarters of those red-state voters are worse off than they were 10 years ago, but their solution is less government, not more. They think an unregulated free market is the magic pill. We think government aid's the major answer."

He paused again, trying to smile. "The truth is, nobody truly knows what the hell comes next. Nobody. It's a whole new world."

"It sure is." Now it was Kay's turn to pause as she struggled to find the right words. "You know, it still goes back to how good we are at assessing the community we're a part of. Yeah, pretty amazing. I never understood as well as I do now how important it is that community organizers and social work managers spend time on *our* diagnosis—like clinicians do, only different. You know, assessing the political and economic conditions, again and again, so we can gauge what's actually possible." She smiled at last. "I guess Obama just did a better community needs assessment than Romney, only the community was the whole country!"

They both laughed loudly this time, for Kay's mention of "community needs assessment" reminded them of the first project they'd done together back in their first macro class. They knew they'd gone about it a little less effectively than Obama had. Ellis looked at the smiling White woman with the recent gray streaks in her ashy brown hair. "Oh, wow, you're bringing back memories! And like you finally taught me back then, even if I was kicking and screaming—those clinical skills of reading people matter in that assessment, too."

"True enough. And you made me see that I could trust my gut as long as I checked it with a few more data points for evidence." She laughed again. "Years ago, we were kinda red and blue in our own way. Back then, in that first macro course, we wanted to kill each other. I hated you and all your politically correct organizer jargon about fighting for social justice and ending oppression." She pointed her finger through the Skype picture, her hand momentarily

(Continued)

(Continued)

looming large. "And you couldn't stand all my talk about helping people and the long, honorable tradition of service of the social work profession."

"Hey, some of that talk still drives me crazy." He paused for only a second. "And you helped me see that some P.C. organizers couldn't care less about how they treated people. And, yeah, social justice and social work can go hand in hand."

"Well, we're sure aligned now. It's because of you that I see issues of oppression aren't just add-ons to our work. They're in the middle of everything we do, including every agency I've worked for. And all across the U.S. of A."

"Gee," Ellis replied with just a wisp of irony. "Over the years, a 'red' organizer who grew to care about helping people and a 'blue' social worker who fights oppression through her agency. Who woulda thunk?" Across the miles, he tipped his mug of tea in Kay's direction. "I guess if we can change, maybe the country can, too!

Kay gave a rueful smile. "Well, that's true, but it took a lot of effort to convince each other. I guess we've got to stay in the trenches. If all Obama hears from is the Tea Party on the right, what kind of assessment can he make? We progressive folks have to keep that assessment moving toward us!"

Educational Policy 2.1.9—Respond to contexts that shape practice. This chapter develops core competencies regarding how "social workers are informed, resourceful, and proactive in responding to evolving organizational, community, and societal contexts at all levels of practice. Social workers recognize that the context of practice is dynamic, and use knowledge and skill to respond proactively. Social workers continuously discover, appraise, and attend to changing locales, populations, . . . and emerging societal trends to provide relevant services; and provide leadership in promoting sustainable changes in service delivery and practice to improve the quality of social services."

DEFINING MACRO PRACTICE: HOW COMMUNITY PRACTITIONERS FRAME THEIR "DIAGNOSIS"

Community practitioners deepen their abilities for later relationship building and effective intervention through the time spent in pre-engagement reflecting on and learning about the historical influences impacting the profession, social work agencies, and practice itself. While not dwelled on every day, these influences help explain the key issues community practitioners deal with as they go about their work. *Key pre-engagement practice issues include: (a) the focus of the intervention, (b) the roles one may play, and (c) the types of assessments undertaken.*

The focus of the intervention: As the opening case study vignette implies, one of the core distinctions of macro practice, whether one is a grassroots organizer or social work administrator, is the *focus of the intervention*. The assessments macro practitioners make are different from those of professionals who work with small groups or individuals. Individual and small-group interventions are defined as either clinical/case management or clinical/mutual aid group interventions. Netting, Kettner, and McMurtry (2008) focus on organizations, communities, and policy, while Rothman, Tropman, and Erlich (2000) substitute "small groups" for "policy" as the arenas in which macro practitioners work. Others prefer the policy arena as the primary focus, arguing that communities and organizations fit within the larger domain of policy analysis and legislative action (Gilbert & Terrell, 2002; Jansson, 2004; Karger & Stoesz, 2001). As such, all these definitions in some way equate macro practice with collective, large-scale intervention.

The practitioner roles in the intervention: These interventions are as distinctive as *the roles assigned to those who undertake them* and, as such, are as old as social work itself. Social welfare history books and policy texts are replete with 19th century descriptions of friendly visitors working with downtrodden individuals (the predecessors of caseworkers and clinical social workers who work with individual clients); settlement-house workers providing language and hygiene classes for the European immigrants crowding into northern cities (the forebears of group workers engaged in today's mutual aid/support groups); and labor/suffrage activists fighting for labor rights and the rights of freed slaves and women to vote (the forerunners to community organizers working to end environmental racism, for parents' rights in schools, for child welfare, etc.; Fisher, 1994; Jansson, 2004; Trattner, 1998).

Over time, as populations in need grew in size and interventions expanded their scope, those who ran these more expanded programs began to define themselves as another kind of macro practitioner, the social work administrator (Bonner, 2002). These social welfare administrators were the predecessors to today's social work agency managers and leaders (Blau & Abramovitz, 2007; Jansson, 2004).

Macro practice assessments of interventions: As important as these distinctions are in defining the focus of intervention and the ensuing roles that either macro or micro practitioners play, they still do not provide a conceptual understanding beyond the obvious: Working with lots of people requires a different kind of activity than working with only one or a few. The more pertinent analytical distinction between macro- and micro-practice interventions is through the *type of assessments* that different practitioners undertake. For the micro practitioner, it is the biopsychosocial assessment of the individual (Mattaini & Lowery, 2007; Saleebey, 2008). But what would a biopsychosocial assessment for a community look like? What variables fit in that broader kind of assessment?

In the case study vignette above, Kay and Ellis made reference to two assessments: the one they undertook together in graduate school as part of their macro practice class and Obama's assessments of the whole country in 2008 and 2012. Are these the same kinds of assessments, differing only in the size and breadth of what a potential presidential candidate was diagnosing versus what two young graduate students were? Of course not.

A Case Example of Macro Practice Level-One Assessments: The Rediscovery of Homelessness

That two social work students and a presidential candidate were engaged in different kinds of assessments is obvious: Running for president of the United States requires answering different questions than does helping a community agency decide whether to expand services either for the homebound elderly or at-risk youth. But I would argue that skilled macro practitioners need to understand both what Obama sought to answer and what Kay and Ellis investigated 15 years ago, for each adds critical information that the other needs to be fully effective.

Based on the assessments undertaken, we can understand this more easily by examining *how and why the focus of intervention regarding the homeless has changed over the years.*

• In the early 1970s, when I was a young organizer starting out in New York City, there seemed to be neither homeless people nor homeless advocates. There were, of course, "Bowery bums," those chronic alcoholics living on the seedy streets south of Houston Street, but they had nothing to do with macro practice or organizing. Most of them were attended to by religious folks, not social workers and especially not community practitioners, who were busy fighting against poverty, for an end to the Vietnam War, and to expand open admissions in public universities (Fisher, 1994).

• A few years later, a new group began to show up on streets *north* of Houston Street. While the alcoholics had been mostly men, these people seemed to be mostly women, and they carried large bags of apparel and other items with them. Often talking to themselves and sometimes not very clean, they began to be seen by a few social workers from nearby settlement houses or mental health clinics, especially on the West Side of Manhattan. Macro practitioners would be fighting the cuts caused by the "city crisis" (Fabricant & Burghardt, 1992; Tabb, 1992), as well as for expanded welfare rights, an end to poverty, and for youth employment. Those "bag ladies," while deserving of care, were somebody else's issue.

• By the late '70s into the early '80s, larger and larger numbers of people, including families, were now living on streets all over the city. As South of Houston was increasingly gentrified, more and more of the former Bowery residents joined the numbers of old women found in northern sections of the city. Advocates for the homeless, as they were now called, organized large demonstrations and began class-action lawsuits demanding that the homeless have a right to shelter. Macro practice through community organizing and advocacy was the primary homeless intervention of the day (Baxter & Hopper, 1981; Fabricant, 1985).

- Twenty-five years later, New York City settled a class-action suit with legal advocates while continuing to support an array of homeless shelter providers in their joint efforts to diminish the size of the homeless population. Homeless advocates, now organized in long-standing coalitions at the city, state, and national levels with their own funding streams, continue to mobilize for better services, more affordable housing, homelessness prevention, and an expansion of shelter clients' rights. Macro and micro practitioners can be found throughout the homeless services system.

REFLECTIVE QUESTION

What is the level-one assessment of the issue your organizing campaign or agency is working under in this period in history? What is it for a clinical practitioner? How has it changed from 20 years ago?

THE POLITICAL AND ECONOMIC FRAMEWORK FOR COMMUNITY OR ORGANIZATIONAL INTERVENTIONS

This brief history of how people assessed and intervened around homelessness in New York City underscores two critical issues that macro practitioners must weigh as they make other judgments in their practice about what to do.

First, while social work macro practitioners rarely intervene directly in large-scale economic matters, the people with whom they work and the choices of service intervention or direct action undertaken are greatly affected by such factors. The chronic alcoholics of the 1950s through the early 1970s were contained and (made invisible) within one of the least attractive neighborhoods of Manhattan: South of Houston, or as we call it today, SoHo. By 2010, SoHo was one of the wealthiest neighborhoods in all of New York, with one-bedroom apartments selling for more than a million dollars. In 1970, a single cot in a flophouse cost one of these men a quarter for the night. Kept invisible through an undesirable location not well-known to the larger public, their problems were easily perceived as of their own making. Only as the economic engine of gentrification and expensive cooperative housing development began to displace the flophouses and make their presence less desirable uptown did others begin to notice them as part of a growing social problem that came to be known as homelessness.

Understanding the Political–Economic Calculus

The bag ladies had been similarly displaced as gentrification overtook the West Side of New York City as well, forcing these poor, older women (many of whom had been deinstitutionalized from mental hospitals a few years earlier) out of their single-room-occupancy hotels (SROs) and into the streets (Baxter & Hopper, 1981). Their increasing visibility on the streets of Manhattan signaled not only an increase in social need but also *shifts in economic relationships* as once-cheap housing was redeveloped into luxury apartments.

Equally important, that developers were able to raze large apartment buildings filled with poor people also required a *new political calculus between these economic actors and political leaders*. After all, there had been zoning laws and regulations on the books that precluded wholesale evictions of destitute people. That calculus found expression in an amendment to old housing laws from the 1950s, popularly known as J-51 legislation. The J-51 amendment allowed developers and landlords to empty their buildings if they were completely renovating them for condominium and cooperative conversion (McKee, 2008). Partial renovation on individual apartments or in small buildings continued to provide modest tax abatements as in the past. The impact of this amendment was to speed up the process of full-scale rehab, leading to larger and larger numbers of poor people evicted into the streets (Baxter & Hopper, 1981).

How could housing developers be given such a legislative gift by politicians in what was perceived to be one of the most politically progressive cities in the United States? The simple answer might be greed: Politicians got bought off by developers' contributions. This is accurate as far as it goes; housing developers in New York City have always been huge contributors to major politicians' coffers (Conason, 2008; Tabb, 1992). However, for macro practitioners to be effective over the long term, especially given the massive change under way that is reconfiguring today's political and economic equations, we need to dig more deeply to understand the underlying reasons for both this "developers' amendment" *and* the eventual creation of the largest homeless shelter system in the nation.

In the early-to-mid-1970s, the politics of New York City remained highly progressive. At the same time, the city's fiscal situation was growing weaker and weaker as the national economy entered its most serious recession since the 1940s (Sale, 1975; Tabb, 1992). Forced to pay more and more funds to outstanding debt obligations, the city's revenues were in trouble. Given this financial squeeze, housing developers' promises to convert low-tax SROs and flophouses to high-tax cooperatives shifted the political equation to make the amendment feasible. In short, the economic value of the increased tax revenues for the financially strapped city *reconstructed and expanded the authority of economic actors to act,* even if it meant the eviction of thousands of people into the ranks of those who became known, seemingly overnight, as the homeless.

The long-term pull toward progressive reform of New York City was being pushed powerfully aside by economic need and political support for the open ascension of housing developers and their financial backers as far more central to the city's revitalization than the progressive reformers, trade unionists, New Dealers, and community activists of the past (Conason, 2008; Fisher, 1994; Reisch & Andrews, 2001; Tabb, 1992).

Not that homeless advocates lacked the strategic capacity to fight back. By using the city's historic reputation for progressive reform and the powerful, visible evidence of countless numbers of poor people suffering in its streets, homeless advocates successfully countered some of the developers' prerogatives for economic growth with the right of the city's most vulnerable citizens to shelter. Throughout the late 1970s and early 1980s, homeless advocates were untiring as they campaigned for guaranteed shelter, an expansion in low-income housing, and increased services (Fabricant, 1985). As mentioned in the last item in the case example above, by the mid-1980s, besides winning the right to shelter, many advocates moved from organizing against homelessness to managing the largest homeless shelter system in America.

REFLECTIVE QUESTION

In what ways have the macro and micro practice roles surrounding your issues changed over the past 20 years? How dynamic is this context in your community?

HOW THE ECONOMIC AND POLITICAL BALANCE OF POWER FRAMES A MACRO PRACTITIONER'S LEVEL-TWO COMMUNITY ASSESSMENTS

While successful in limiting rampant development's impact on the most vulnerable, by the early 1980s, homeless activists, as well as other macro practitioners, were confronted with the daunting reality that their voice in the political and economic discourse of the city had been greatly changed. As the Reagan years went on, it had become clear in New York and every other American city that those who financed and owned luxury housing developments would in ways be more central to the discourse on what is acceptable in the mix of economic development and social welfare expenditure for the next 25 years than progressive actors had been in the 1960s. Thus, for example, it is no accident that between 1960 and 1980, the level of social welfare expenditure grew 110%, the federal tax system (critical to state revenue expansion) had a corporate tax rate of 53%, the poverty rate in the nation decreased to 10.1%, and the ratio of wealth between the top 10% and the bottom 10% was 8:1. Between 1980 and 2000, expenditure on social welfare dropped 30%, the corporate tax rate was cut to 18%, the level of poverty rose to 15.1%, and the wealth ratio between the top and bottom tenths grew to 18:1 (Jansson, 2004; Klein, 2007; Krugman, 2003, 2009c; Phillips, 2003, 2008).[1]

This long historic example of New York City's housing development, homelessness, and shelter creation could be applied in any other American community over the past three decades. Its delineation clarifies one of the central distinctions between macro practitioners and others. *This initial, level-one stage of a macro practitioner's assessment includes attention to these kinds of political and economic dynamics that frame the ensuing choices that agencies, community leaders, and others make on their strategic options for change and/or service enhancement.*

Thus, a macro practitioner begins his or her unique set of tasks through an examination of the dominant political and economic balance of power of our larger society that frames the contours to "what is." In turn, this level-one framework of "what is," politically and economically, outlines the overall contours to the day-to-day work of all social workers—whether organizers, clinicians, or managers—that are created out of the level-two community assessments that are the focus of the next chapter.

Undertaking this political–economic assessment is critical to a macro practitioner's strategic effectiveness because it helps him or her choose the correct interventions for the time and place in which he or she is working. This is why judging tactical choices from one period of history to another can be so difficult. That in 2013 macro *and* micro practitioners can be found working with the homeless on supportive housing programs while their 1960s counterparts, fighting the war on poverty, paid little attention to those men on the Bowery neither makes the latter uncaring nor the former less committed to social change. The mix of economic factors and political calculations that shaped the focus of each of their interventions was profoundly different.

HISTORY MOVES: OPENING
MACRO PRACTICE TO A NEW CALCULUS

It was this kind of level-one political and economic appraisal that Kay, at the beginning of the chapter, was referring to regarding Obama's "community needs assessment of the whole country." As he traveled the country in 2006 to 2007, the calls from the heartland of America for his presidential candidacy led him to assess his opportunities differently than he had before. The heartfelt cries from White middle Americans for him to step forward caused him to reflect that the calculus of what is possible in electoral politics in the United States was shifting dramatically throughout the country. Calculus, after all, is concerned with the "*laws of changes attending a slight alteration in the form of the function*" (*Merriam-Webster's Universal Unabridged Dictionary,* 1979).

Obama sensed more than a slight alteration that spoke to changes under way in America's political–economic calculus. As every reader of this text knows, the Iraqi military debacle that was fought on false claims (Clark, 2005; Isikoff & Corn, 2007), the violation of standards regarding torture that diminished this country's standing in the world (Sands, 2008), the failure of the Bush Administration to respond either adequately or humanely to the devastation wrought by Hurricane Katrina (Cooper & Block, 2007), and the unfolding corruption of both Bush appointees and key Republican political leaders (Klein, 2002; McClellan, 2009) all combined to redefine for the first time in generations a different assessment of what was and wasn't acceptable in political discourse and the type of political leadership the nation desired (Connolly, 1993). Obama, perhaps before anyone else, began to see that what was possible had begun to change inside the dominant equation of what made up American political life. By 2008, the authority behind the political part of the discourse on "what is" was beginning to change.

Then, as Obama's unlikely 2008 candidacy grew, an economic earthquake opened up across America. While events continue to unfold with a rapidity that makes up-to-the-moment descriptions of the crisis problematic here, what can be outlined are the underlying systemic issues at play that are dramatically altering the economic part of the calculus in level-one political and economic discourse.

Beneath the home foreclosures, Wall Street firm closings, Big Three auto bailouts and bankruptcies, and credit crises lies an epochal failure of how our economic system operates and the rules that have governed that system's operations. This is a stunning turnaround. After almost 30 years of hegemonic dominance in deciding how the world would operate on financial matters, the totality of conservative leaders' economic and social failures has left a gaping hole in people's assumptions about "what is" that has not been popularly witnessed since the 1930s. As Michael Lewis and David Einhorn wrote in early 2009,

> [Americans have] been viewed by the wider world with mistrust and suspicion on other matters, but on the subject of money even our harshest critics have been inclined to believe that we knew what we were doing. . . . This is one reason the collapse of our financial system has inspired not merely a national but a global crisis of confidence.

The 2008-to-2010 financial crisis was different from other economic downturns of the past 40 years. For example, the city crisis of the 1970s that was the backdrop to the emergence of homelessness cited above came about through the city's overreliance on short-term bonds to pay for social service and public infrastructure expansion that came due without adequate revenues. The ensuing regulations by the state to correct this fiscal problem were overseen by financial managers from the same firms that in 2009 collapsed. While a serious problem in Northeastern and Midwestern cities in the 1970s, the problems were relegated to a few municipalities, especially those with long histories of progressive taxation, expansive social services, and public-sector unionism. Perceived as spendthrifts, these urban actors would be part of the conservative agenda's justification for antistate regulation and antiwelfare state intervention that dominated the Reagan years and beyond (Phillips, 2003, 2008; Sale, 1975).

Unlike the city crisis of the '70s, the financial crisis of 2008 to 2010 is not relegated to what fiscal conservatives would characterize as a few socially progressive bad apples of the Northeast. As nationwide systemic problems, they extend beyond the "blame game" of individuals, as complicit as many of them may be (Krugman, 2009a). As we witnessed in the more recent 2012 electoral campaign, these dynamics will not be resolved for years and perhaps decades to come. As economists have noted, they include the following:

- "Our financial catastrophe . . . required all sorts of important, plugged-in people to sacrifice our collective long-term interests for short-term gain. The pressure to do this in today's financial markets is immense. Obviously the greater the market pressure to excel in the short term, the greater the need for pressure from outside the market to consider the longer term. But that's the problem: there is no longer any serious pressure from outside the market. The tyranny of the short term has extended itself with frightening ease into the entities that were meant to . . . discipline Wall Street" (Lewis & Einhorn, 2009).
- Those regulators created out of the New Deal to watch over investment decisions of banks and other investors in our marketplace no longer provided the balanced oversight required of them under law (Krugman, 2003). Indeed, the true scandal of the Madoff Ponzi scheme, whereby investors worldwide lost more than $65 billion, was that informed whistleblowers had attempted for years to alert the Securities and Exchange Commission to his firm's illegal maneuvering, only to be blocked again and again. As financial writers Lewis and Einhorn (2009) wrote, "Created to protect investors from financial predators, [by 2008] the commission has somehow evolved into a mechanism for protecting financial predators with political clout from investors."
- The conservative state's approach to ending the crisis in 2008 devolved into six different strategies for seven different bailouts (Lewis & Einhorn, 2009). It's quite a list. Among the action items are these: Bear Stearns was allowed to be sold to JP Morgan for rates below bankruptcy filings, while Freddie Mac and Fannie Mae, the government-sponsored housing investors, were nationalized. Venerable Lehman Brothers collapsed; a week later, the giant insurer AIG was given enormous government loans to stay afloat. The inconsistency of these efforts, joined to the minimal oversight demands these loans and bailout funds required (no demand to invest funds in cities or to stop foreclosures on working people's homes, no limit to bonuses), placed the government's economic minions under far-lessened authority to act without discretion.

- The presidents of the Big Three auto companies (GM, Ford, and Chrysler) traveled by individual jets to Washington to beg for bailout money for their failing companies. Arriving with neither a corrective management plan nor an explanation for their stunningly wasteful travel arrangements, these former titans of the American economy were initially scorned and forced to return to the Capitol to make their requests again (Krugman, 2009c). Only the threat of 2 million workers across America losing their jobs (from auto and associated industries) managed to win the bailout package of $4.5 billion. That GM and Chrysler have now gone through bankruptcy has further eroded their overall authority as economic and political actors. Obama's unprecedented election in 2008 and the rise of the populist Tea Party movement both speak to the vacuum created by the diminished authority of late-20th-century economic actors and their political allies.

- These shifts in regulatory and financial power have had a significant impact on Americans not seen for generations. As researchers at Stanford and Brown Universities reported in 2012, "In 2007, the last year captured by the data, 44 percent of families lived in neighborhoods the study defined as middle-income, down from 65 percent of families in 1970. At the same time, a third of American families lived in areas of either affluence or poverty, up from just 15 percent of families in 1970" (Leonhardt, 2012).

- These changes in income can be better grasped through a striking historical comparison: "Since median inflation-adjusted family income peaked in 2000 at $64,232, it has fallen roughly 6 percent (through 2012). You won't find another 12-year period with an income decline since the aftermath of the Depression" (Leonhardt, 2012).

- Furthermore, "the share that has been going to anyone but the richest Americans has been declining. The top-earning 1 percent of households now bring home about 20 percent of total income, up from less than 10 percent 40 years ago. The top-earning 1/10,000th of households—each earning at least $7.8 million a year, many of them working in finance—bring home almost 5 percent of income, up from 1 percent 40 years ago" (Leonhardt, 2012). In other words, unlike what occurred across the 20th century, in the 21st century, economic and social inequality is increasing.

All these precipitous shifts are reflective of the drastically changing global economic position of the American economy, *especially for wage earners.* This in part explains some of the political volatility seen in Congress and that we have witnessed in Wisconsin, Ohio, and California state legislatures over the past few years. Such dynamics will continue to be at play for the foreseeable future. Social workers, whether macro practitioners or micro clinicians, ignore such dynamics at their own peril.

Obama campaigned in 2012 on a platform demanding growth through greater taxes on the rich, as well as still-unknown changes to entitlement programs, including Medicare, Medicaid, and perhaps Social Security, and discretionary funding. Over the objections of conservative members of the House of Representatives, those in the top 2%

will now be taxed more as a way to increase revenues. How these policy changes and shifting political alignments will eventually impact social welfare remains to be seen—and must be watched by anyone involved in social work, education, health, or mental health. Over the coming years, there will be new tax plans, calls for structural reform (from both the right and the left), and other seismic shifts in our economic and political landscape that will transcend what has been discussed above. What matters here for macro *and* micro practitioners is the shift in level-one assessments under way regarding the political and economic calculus of

- what is and isn't acceptable for the state to do,
- who are society's most credible actors in moving our nation to a stable and sustainable system once again, and
- who is deserving of state intervention—both *regulatory* (to protect the community from harm) and *redistributive* (to help lift up those deserving of that lift).

Just as the financial crisis of the '70s and political demands of the day reconfigured the political and economic discourse in ways that ushered in the Age of Reagan for three decades, so now does the ongoing Obama presidency signal that this discourse will continue to be rewritten in new and dramatic ways unseen in the United States for more than 40 years. Such intense drama is created because the primary actors are both extremely different and equally unconvincing to the other. On the one hand, the combination of political miscalculation, malfeasance, and dishonesty of the Bush Administration, coupled with the systemic failures of the early 21st century economic system and its leaders to address the greater and greater declines in middle and lower incomes and heightened inequality, have created an opportunity of enormous magnitude for progressive social interventions unseen since the 1960s. On the other hand, the tremendous fears of the size of the American debt, the rising deficit, and the increasing competition from the low-wage economies of China and India have kept the political discourse dominated by a conservative framework arguing for growth through the diminished role of the state—especially the welfare state (Banjo & Kalita, 2010).

In short, the dynamics at play in American society will require more, not less, activism from anyone committed to a robust nonprofit sector in American society. For those of us who toil, directly or indirectly, through the welfare state, maintaining focus on level-one assessments so that our voices are heard in the larger political discourse seems a fundamental responsibility–and opportunity. I nevertheless need to warn macro and micro practitioners alike about the work ahead. The first assumption under which this book and its predecessor have been written needs to be reiterated here: *The dominant contours of a historical period in which practice is carried out are a reflection not only of the status quo but also of the level of struggle between the contending forces in society.* For just as conservative presidents of the past 30 years were unable to undo some central progressive legislation of the 1930s and 1960s, the first 4 years of Obama's presidency made clear that there is no guarantee the conservative gains since Reagan will disappear easily. If anything, *volatility* seems to be the operative word for years to come. Poverty was not discussed in either the 2008 or 2012 elections. At the same time, immigrants voted for Obama in record percentages because his administration suggested ways to end the enormous legal, social, and economic barriers immigrants confront. Some states have codified greater restrictions on unions; other states saw their voters legalizing same-sex marriages. Obviously, such see-saw shifts dotted across the nation suggest that the social and economic dynamics of what it means to be fully integrated into a global world are all issues still at hand that macro practitioners will need to confront in the years ahead. What was written 30 years ago remains apt today:

> The impact of the international economic crisis on social workers' lives is not about to go away by merely leaving it out of our analysis or by making a list of priorities for a just society tacked on to the end of our work. Some of these concrete problems are: high competition for entry-level jobs with non–social workers; dilution of skill areas; the substitution of accountability measures (paper work) for clinical services. All of these are problems addressed by social workers every day, some opting for increased professional rivalries, others searching for joint coalition and collaborative work. With all that's going on in the field, it seems all the more mandatory that practice frameworks, if they are to begin meeting social workers' real needs, must move away from the safety of generalization to the more tumultuous, risky world of concrete experience. After all, that's where social workers are and what they deal with. The task is a great one, and this work certainly won't attempt all of it. But the era of social welfare we are entering, as the above economic analysis suggests, is going to be dramatically demanding: *everything*, including the nature of practice and the structure of social services, is open to challenge and to change. At the same time, its outcome is not predetermined by either present statistics or current power relationships. If this were true, in the 1930s working people—including social workers—would have accepted bread lines and poverty, and in the 1960s Rosa Parks and her children would still be riding at the back of the bus. The shape of events is determined by people, all of us, and by our willingness to understand and to seek to change the world for the better. (Burghardt, 1982, p. 21)

Where the above analysis proved wanting was in its assumed expectation that "everything . . . is open to challenge and to change," at least as far as progressive change is concerned. The challenge and change of the next 30 years were met by conservative forces more than equal to the demands they set for remaking our society. They, not social welfare activists, read the temper of the times in a way that we did not (Whalen & Flacks, 2002).

As we move fully into the 21st century, we need not make that mistake again—as long as we stay attuned to the dynamics at play within level-one assessments. As we all know too well, once again cuts are being demanded of social welfare and educational programs—end the debt, and lower the deficit by slashing entitlements, not reforming them (Krugman, 2009c; Stiglitz, 2012). But must the times become again like 1982? Legislation mandating redistributive taxes from the wealthy to the poor has been passed for the first time in two generations. Some of the debate in Washington on how to tackle long-term growth focuses on investments in infrastructure and spending on education and social welfare as the better stimulus for economic growth, compared with wide-scale entitlement reduction (Krugman, 2009b). Such arguments—while still not as powerful as other, more conservative demands—speak to the shifts in authority, and in organizing possibilities, that have not been present in this nation for a long, long time. Responding to the cuts in the short run will inevitably be painful; interpreting and acting on how later budgetary decisions of political and economic leaders unfold is an opportunity any social work practitioner must seize.

REFLECTIVE QUESTION FOR EDUCATIONAL POLICY 2.1.9

Consider present-day political debates about the economy and the role of government (especially as it relates to the welfare state, such as Social Security, Medicare, and Medicaid). Looking at both sides of the debate, how will their positions dynamically impact your role? Community members' concerns and issues? The functioning of your agency?

How can you develop an argument that extends your agency issues to larger ones useful to the ongoing political debates inside state and federal legislatures?

Living and working within this remarkable period of American history that the early 21st century has become, we need to unite our consistent hope for what can be with a constant vigilance for what actually is and is not happening in our neighborhoods and communities. Only through such reflective efforts—key tasks of the pre-engagement phase of practice—can the calculus of change under way come to benefit those most in need. For that to occur, in Chapter 3 we turn to what macro practitioners often do best: level-two community assessments.

THE COMMUNITY TOOLBOX

The Community Toolbox has a number of sections that break down models of how organizing can build community capacity. A good place to start is with its first major section on the model for change, as well as how to look for other tools, many of which will be referred to in later chapters. See http://ctb.ku.edu/en/tablecontents/chapter_1001.htm.

The Community Toolbox's Model for Change

Section 1. A Community Toolbox Overview and Gateway to the Tools

Section 2. Some Ways of Doing the Work of Community Change and Improvement: An Overview

Section 3. Our Model of Practice: Building Capacity for Community and System Change

Section 4. Troubleshooting Guide: Common Problems in Community Work and How to Address Them

Section 5. Our Evaluation Model: Evaluating Comprehensive Community Initiatives

Section 6. Some Core Principles, Assumptions, and Values to Guide the Work

Section 7. Working Together for Healthier Communities: A Framework for Collaboration Among Community Partnerships, Support Organizations, and Funders

Section 8. Some Lessons Learned on Community Organization and Change

Section 9. Community Action Guide: A Framework for Addressing Community Goals and Problems

Section 10. Using Internet-Based Tools to Promote Community Health and Development

Section 11. Participatory Evaluation

They also provide access to other organizing models that you may wish to review. Such model review can help you with both immediate assessment needs and making level-one assessments. Go to http://ctb.ku.edu/en/tablecontents/chapter_1002.htm.

Some Other Models for Promoting Community Health and Development

Section 1. Developing a Logic Model or Theory of Change

Section 2. PRECEDE/PROCEED

Section 3. Healthy Cities/Healthy Communities

Section 4. Asset Development

Section 5. PATCH (Planned Approach to Community Health)

Section 6. Institute of Medicine's Community Health Development Process (CHIP)

Section 7. Ten Essential Public Health Services

Section 8. Communities That Care

Section 9. Community Readiness

Section 10. The Strategic Prevention Framework

Section 11. Health Impact Assessment

Section 12. PAHO Guide for Documenting Health Promotion Initiatives

Section 13. MAPP: Mobilizing for Action Through Planning and Partnerships

REFERENCES

Banjo, S., & Kalita, M. (2010, February 2). Once robust charity sector hit with mergers, closings. *Wall Street Journal*, p. 1.

Baxter, E., & Hopper, K. (1981). *Private lives/public spaces: Homeless adults on the streets of New York City*. New York: Community Service Society.

Blau, J., & Abramovitz, M. (2007). *The dynamics of social welfare policy*. New York: Oxford University Press.

Bonner, T. (2002). *Iconoclast: Abraham Flexner and a life of learning*. Baltimore, MD: Johns Hopkins University Press.

Burghardt, S. (1982). *The other side of organizing: Resolving the personal dilemmas and political demands of daily practice*. Rochester, VT: Schenkman Books.

Clark, W. (2005). *Petrodollar warfare: Oil, Iraq, and the future of the dollar*. Baltimore, MD: New Society.

Conason, J. (2008). *It can happen here: Authoritarian peril in the age of Bush*. New York: St. Martin's Griffin.

Connolly, M. (1993). *The terms of political discourse*. Boston: Wiley-Blackwell.

Cooper, C., & Block, P. (2007). *Disaster: Hurricane Katrina and the failure of homeland security*. New York: Holt.

Fabricant, M. (1985). Creating survival services. *Administration in Social Work, 10*(3), 71–85.

Fabricant, M., & Burghardt, S. (1992). *The welfare state crisis and the transformation of social service work*. Armonk, NY: M. E. Sharpe.

Fisher, R. (1994). *Let the people decide: Neighborhood organizing in America*. New York: Twayne.

Gilbert, N., & Terrell, P. (2002). *Dimensions of social welfare policy*. Boston: Allyn & Bacon.

Isikoff, M., & Corn, D. (2007). *Hubris: The inside story of spin, scandal, and the selling of the Iraq War*. New York: Random House.

Jansson, B. (2004). *The reluctant welfare state: American social welfare policies—Past, present, and future*. Pacific Grove, CA: Brooks/Cole.

Karger, H., & Stoesz, D. (2001). *American social welfare policy: A pluralist approach*. Englewood Cliffs, NJ: Prentice Hall.

Klein, N. (2002). *Fences and windows: Dispatches from the front lines of the globalization debate*. New York: Picador.

Klein, N. (2007). *The shock doctrine: The rise of disaster capitalism.* New York: Metropolitan Books.

Krugman, P. (2003). *The great unraveling: Losing our way in the new century.* New York: W. W. Norton.

Krugman, P. (2009a). *A country is not a company.* Cambridge, MA: Harvard Business School Press.

Krugman, P. (2009b, February 5). On the edge. *New York Times,* p. A27.

Krugman, P. (2009c). *The return of depression economics and the crisis of 2008.* New York: W. W. Norton.

Lewis, M., & Einhorn, D. (2009, January 4). The end of the financial world as we know it. *New York Times.* Retrieved from http://www.nytimes.com/2009/01/04/opinion/04lewiseinhorn.html?pagewanted=all

Leonhardt, D. (2012, July 23). A closer look at middle-class decline. *New York Times.* Retrieved from http://economix.blogs.nytimes.com/2012/07/23/

Mattaini, M., & Lowery, C. (Eds.). (2007). *Foundations of social work practice: A graduate text.* Washington, DC: National Association of Social Workers Press.

McClellan, S. (2009). *What happened: Inside the Bush White House and Washington's culture of deception.* Washington, DC: Public Affairs.

McKee, M. (2008). *How the landlords weakened our rent laws, how tenants lost—and how we can win back what we have lost.* Retrieved from http://www.tenantspac.org

Merriam-Webster's universal unabridged dictionary. (1979). Springfield, MA: Merriam-Webster.

Netting, F., Kettner, P., & McMurtry, S. (2008). *Social work macro practice.* Boston: Allyn & Bacon.

Phillips, K. (2003). *Wealth and democracy: A political history of the American rich.* New York: Broadway.

Phillips, K. (2008). *Bad money: Reckless finance, failed politics and the global crisis of American capitalism.* New York: Viking Adult.

Reisch, M., & Andrews, J. (2001). *The road not taken: A history of radical social work in the United States.* New York: Brunner-Routledge.

Rothman, J., Tropman, J., & Erlich, J. (2000). *Tactics and techniques of community intervention.* Florence, KY: Wadsworth.

Sale, K. (1975). *Power shift: The rise of the southern rim and its challenge to the eastern establishment.* New York: Viking Press.

Saleebey, D. (2008). *Human behavior and social environments: A biopsychosocial approach.* New York: Columbia University Press.

Sands, P. (2008). *Torture team: Rumsfeld's memo and the betrayal of American values.* New York: Palgrave MacMillan.

Stiglitz, J. E. (2012). *The price of inequality: How today's divided society endangers our future.* New York: W. W. Norton.

Tabb, W. (1992). The New York fiscal crisis. *Review of Business, 14*(1).

Trattner, W. (1998). *From poor law to welfare state: A history of social welfare in America.* New York: Free Press.

Whalen, J., & Flacks, R. (2002). *Beyond the barricades: The sixties generation grows up.* Philadelphia: Temple University Press.

NOTES

1. As Princeton economist Paul Krugman noted in 2003,

income inequality has now returned to the levels of the 1920s. . . . The thirteen thousand richest families had almost as much income as earned by the twenty million poorest households. . . . (Furthermore) the number of Americans with million dollar incomes doubled from 1995–1999, while the percentage of their income that went to federal taxes dropped by 11 per cent. (p. 20)

As he also noted,

this increase in economic wealth for the very rich and increased misery for the poorest of the poor has been matched by the political assault on social welfare programs that goes to the heart of the modern welfare state. To briefly highlight those programs, the New Deal of the 1930s inaugurated old-age insurance (now called Social Security), unemployment insurance, workers' compensation, and a variety of public initiatives to alleviate poverty, its hallmark being aid to families with dependent children (AFDC). Based on a convergence of militant industrial trade unions and reform-minded capitalism in the 1930s, these programs were joined in the 1960s by important civil rights-led initiatives. Responding to generations of racist and sexist policies, that legislation included Medicaid, Medicare, community-based antipoverty initiatives, and affirmative action programs. These are the programs that have been under attack since the Reagan Administration. (p. 89)

This attack reached its fulcrum under a Democratic presidency—that of Bill Clinton—and the passage of the 1996 Personal Opportunity and Work Responsibility Act, which replaced AFDC. A mix of fiscal and social policies, this sweeping legislation limited aid to 60 months in a person's lifetime; required work activities; prohibited legal immigrants from receiving food stamps and Social Security Insurance; required teen parents to live at home or under adult supervision; and limited food stamps for able-bodied, single, unemployed adults to 3 months every 3 years. Furthermore, this shift in federal policy had been matched by the states' reversal on welfare expenditures. Between 1970 and 1996, for example, New York City had decreased its welfare benefits by 48%, Tennessee by 58%, and Texas by 68%. These radical shifts in social policy did not come about because of the United States' relative expansiveness in welfare expenditures. By 1995—when the push for this federal rollback began to build up steam from the Gingrich-led assault inside Congress—U.S. public social expenditures represented about 17.1% of the gross national product, the lowest among 10 comparable industrial nations and a little more than half the other nations' average level.

Section II

Engagement

"Engagement" is the early phase of professional activity where the practitioner begins (a) the process of assessing the strengths and needs of the community, group, or individual with whom he or she is working, and (b) engaging with others in ways that deepen the clarity and accuracy of the assessment under way.

Of course, there is a reciprocal process under way in this phase: *The people with whom you are working also are engaging with and assessing you.* Recognizing this dynamic, Chapters 3 and 4 integrate two skill sets: concrete assessment skills as one undertakes learning about both the people with whom one is working and the conditions under which they live, and one's own capacity and personal comfort with undertaking those assessment skills as varied as data mining (an obvious "hard" quantitative skill) and engaging with new and varied people (an equally obvious "soft" qualitative skill).

Chapter 3 delineates the specific assessment skills you will need to learn about a community or group with whom you are working. Knowing how to assess hard data and actual trends in economic, political, and social life within one community as opposed to another is critical to strategically effective work. One will also need to speak with informed actors—from professional leaders to community folks—to buttress such hard data with people's perceptions of and interest in such trends. (One can't initiate a campaign around trends that people have no interest in!) Of course, someone good with data may be less comfortable with the person sipping coffee across from him or her at the local coffee shop—and vice versa. Chapter 3 goes on to delineate a core professional skill set—*professional use of self*—as applied to the macro practitioner. Through what I have named *tactical self-awareness,* the practitioner can learn a different, internal form of assessment—assessing your own strengths and limits in the shifting contexts of your work and, from that ongoing assessment, how to become tactically more effective over time in all that you are called on to do.

Chapter 4 deepens this mix of engagement and assessment by exploring the *unconscious in organizing.* By exploring areas of unanticipated struggle that inevitably occur for the practitioner over time, the chapter seeks to unravel the dilemma of all transformational practice: *How can a person have the courage—the chutzpah—to seek to change the world and yet remain humble and open to others as he or she engages with people whose own points of view might be markedly different?*

As explored in Chapters 3 and 4, assessment and engagement require both relational and analytical skills to be successful. In practice, these skill sets have often been divided between "micro" and "macro" tracks for clinicians and organizers/administrators, leading to false and damaging dichotomies between practice methods. Chapter 5 lays out a *social construction of practice* that demonstrates ways for all social work practitioners to use both sets of skills as fundamental to a vitally engaged and transformative practice.

CHAPTER 3

Using Engagement Skills to Improve Community Assessments

Joining "Micro" and "Macro" Through Tactical Self-Awareness

THE PREPLANNING BEGINS

The two macro practitioners were about to sign off when Ellis sat back and whistled for a moment. He could see Kay's bemused expression.

"Kay, remember when we hugged back in Grant Park in '08? We were so hopeful and happy. And I had some disappointment, too. Thought for sure that anti-gay Proposition 8 in California was going to be defeated, but it wasn't. Thought marriage for me and Rob was off the table for a long, long time. But now the Supreme Court's hearing the case—and the fight's being led by a Republican lawyer!"

"And look at Maine and Washington State! People voted it in!"

"And Obama was the first sitting president to support us!" Ellis shook his head in silent wonder. "It's crazy times, but maybe that man in the Oval Office assesses some things better than we give him credit for."

"Like they say, it's a lot harder to govern for change than to campaign for it. He and his people know how to crunch numbers way better than we did."

(Continued)

(Continued)

"He sure keeps doing that 'ongoing assessment' work better than we started out, don't you think?"

They both laughed, remembering their first difficult work together. As they signed off from Skype, each was reflecting on how they met in 1990 in their first macro-organizing class, and their dreaded group assignment—a community assessment of their own choosing. Sitting together in a small classroom, there were four of them in the group: Ellis; Kay; Esperanza, an older Puerto Rican woman who'd gone back to college after her children were grown and had completed her undergraduate degree in 3 years; and Jill, a quiet White woman whose luminescent brown eyes grew tight only when Kay and Ellis argued, which was often.

"So we chose Harlem to look at. There's so many oppressive conditions there, I say we just take poverty and racism and that's enough. I mean, look at how poverty's grown over the last 10 years!" Ellis was as emphatic as he was certain as the group members met for the first time.

"Well, yeah, sure, but couldn't we slow down a bit and find out why we chose Harlem? It's not the only community in New York. It's not even the only Black neighborhood. We must have our own reasons. Couldn't we start there, at least a little?" While less certain, her voice trembling slightly, all the group members noted that Kay was no less emphatic in her request.

"*You're* telling me about Black neighborhoods?" Ellis gave Kay a withering look.

"I wasn't telling anybody anything. I was just trying to slow down and learn about each other and why this assignment might matter in some special way to each of us." She looked at the others for support. "Maybe we all can agree on a focus together after that."

"Whatever." Ellis continued to stare at Kay. "I just hope we move on to the work sooner rather than later. Racial oppression isn't solved with talk-talk-talk."

Esperanza spoke up. "So let's take a minute or two, okay? I chose to look at Harlem because it's pretty close to my community, East Harlem, and my daughter's first middle school was there. We could even walk to school from our apartment, but the school was so bad I had her transferred out in a month. That was 10 years ago. Now I see that the cuts in education keep coming, but they keep talking about school reform, too. I want to see if that school has gotten any better." Without speaking, Jill got up and wrote "Schools" on the blackboard.

Kay spoke next. "I worked for 4 years in a homeless shelter, and some of the staff I got to be friends with come from Harlem. They told me about what a great place it was, with the Apollo Theatre, restaurants like Sylvia's, the architecture, the famous churches with Adam Clayton Powell, Jr. It also has one of the largest numbers of homeless shelters in the city. So I thought I could learn more about how people handle homelessness, even with all the poverty and drugs the papers are writing about. People up here may have answers about how to get people into permanent housing that we could learn from, I'm sure." Jill paused, and then wrote "The homeless" and "Local resources."

It was Ellis's turn. "I already know Harlem. I don't need a tourist's trip to visit there. Walk away from 125th Street and you'll see problems galore: poor housing, men and women out of work, kids with nothing to do except hang out and end up in jail. Poverty goes up, prison levels go up, too. Like they say, when America gets a cold, the Black community gets pneumonia. Hey, the issues in Harlem come from the conditions of oppression created over the last 350 years. If we're going to help young people, whatever we do up here better deal with that reality." Jill wrote "Poverty," "Oppression," and "Prisons" on the board. Wordlessly, Ellis got up and added "Youth."

Jill was the last to speak. "My best friend in high school lived in Harlem until she was 13. Then something happened to her brother, and her family moved to Long Island. She told me she was happy to be with so much green all around her, but she missed the friends and family members she saw on the street every day. Her family came back to church there every Sunday, a 2-hour commute each way. It always amazed me that she never complained about the trip." She paused, and looked keenly at her group members. "I thought it would be great to find out why." Kay wrote "Connections" and "People" next to "Local resources."

"So now what do we do? The whole community is too big to work on." Ellis looked at the blackboard. "Youth, schools, oppression, poverty, homelessness, and the people and resources to fight back. How do we narrow this down to make it mean something?"

"And make it manageable so we get it done?" added Esperanza.

Their first meeting broke up soon after—the three women pleased with their progress, the lone man frustrated that they were still talking and not doing something. Much to Ellis's dismay, it would take them a month of meetings, twice a week, to make their project both meaningful and manageable. Looking back, he would later say it was one of the most painful group experiences of his time at school. It was also, he readily admitted, one of the best learning experiences.

Educational Policy 2.1.1—Identify as a professional social worker and conduct oneself accordingly. This chapter emphasizes core competencies related to how social workers "practice personal reflection and self-correction to assure continual professional development; attend to professional roles and boundaries; and demonstrate professional demeanor in behavior, appearance, and communication."

THE PREPLANNING PHASE TO COMMUNITY ASSESSMENT: CLARIFYING ASSUMPTIONS OF *COMMUNITY*

Strategic Step 1: The Preplanning Begins to Clarify Assumptions on Why the Work Matters for the Group

While often given short shrift, one of the most important phases of a community practitioner's work occurs during what others have called the preplanning phase of a group (Glasser, Sarri, Sundel, & Vinter, 1986; Rothman, 2008). Preplanning is when people discuss and clarify the basic assumptions of what community (or problem) they are examining. During preplanning, a community group frames the basic ways it will approach the actual planning and assessment undertaken. While preplanning can appear to be less labor intensive than sifting data, interviewing people, and analyzing trends, its work is the foundation on which the assessment will be measured for its effectiveness.

For example, our four students of macro practice in the case study each carried distinct assumptions about the community they were about to assess.

- Esperanza spoke in terms of a *geographic community,* one made distinct from others by certain assumed physical borders that made Harlem different from East Harlem (Fellin, 2000; Warren, 1987). Such geography has set limits to its borders even though the actual borders may be defined not only by space but also by shifts in population (East Harlem is more Hispanic; Harlem is more African American) or activities (the commercial strip of 116th Street is seen as the dividing line between the south—East Harlem— and north—Harlem).
- Kay's interest in the homeless given shelter in Harlem and those who worked with them related to a *functional community.* Her emphasis was on the shared activities and functions of a group of people responding to a particular problem. Added to her definition was interest in the particular resources of the community applied within this functional community, a dimension of *bridging social capital* among organizational members. Bridging social capital is created among those networks of affiliations that join professionals and community members in shared activity so that a defined problem across that community—in this case, the functional community concerned with homelessness—is dealt with more effectively than otherwise might occur (DeFilippis & Saegert, 2007; Putnam, 1994).
- Jill's story of her best friend highlighted a *community of shared interest and affiliation.* While similar to a functional community in its shared interests found at church, its emphasis is on the *bonded social capital* that does not necessarily extend beyond the particular church itself. While less integrative, functionally, across a larger community's population (it was, after all, just one church), it adds deeper emotional ties of long-term affiliation that a functional community will not (Anton, Fisk, & Holmstrom, 2000; DeFilippis & Saegert, 2007; Putnam, 1994).
- Finally, Ellis's mix of historic conditions and common problems of an entire group of people refers to the classic *solidarity community* based on race, religion, ethnic heritage, or ideology. As such, it can be located inside both geographic and functional communities as long as groups recognize and find common solidarity in that reference. For example, such a community of shared interests based on historic background remains of prime

concern to people of color, has a more varied response among some White ethnic/religious groups (Reform Jews and Lubavitcher Jews in the United States), and is less easily defined for White Protestants (Winters & DeBose, 2002).

REFLECTIVE QUESTIONS

What is the definition of *community* that your campaign or agency works from? What is the strength in that definition? Is there a potential limitation?

Why Preplanning Matters

It is through the airing of what people mean by *community* that a group begins to sort through what it is interested in assessing and why. This sifting matters, because otherwise a group's members could be looking at the same issues through different lenses. Data collected, interviews undertaken, and implications drawn would all appear with different emphases: Ellis would locate connections to the past, while Kay would be trying to interpret the same data for the future. Jill would be drawn to what happened inside a bonded community, while Esperanza would seek data to spot trends across a geographic community and perhaps beyond. As community groups have limited resources, especially related to time and money, the necessary sifting of assumptions so that a group agrees on what it will and will not be addressing is the bedrock on which the group's eventual results will be evaluated.

Finally, with the exception of Jill, whose focus was drawn to affiliated church activities in the area, all the others mention the defensive and reactive posture common to poorer neighborhoods and their professional allies in the early 1990s. Esperanza thought about assessing what happened at one school, not in the whole school system. Kay was concerned about how to work with the homeless on housing relocation. Even Ellis, while concerned about systemic issues, had begun to narrow his focus to one group of people—youth—rather than considering all the residents of Harlem.

As such, their implicit level-one assessments took as a given that a poor community in the 1990s was worse off than it had been and that its actors would be fighting an uphill battle for community needs to be met. Fitting this level-one assessment into their overall practice framework was a necessary adaptation to the political and economic dynamics of the day. Had they been looking for and proposing wide-scale social movement activity or a more far-reaching set of demands on what they thought was achievable, they would have been strategically ineffective before they began their actual work. Today's macro practitioners will be called on to make their own level-one assessments under conditions that may be quite distinct from those of Ellis, Kay, and their classmates.

FROM PREPLANNING ASSUMPTIONS TO PLANNED ACTION: CHOOSING MEANINGFUL TARGETS AND TIMELINES

THE HARLEM GROUP GETS BUSY

"I don't care about what social workers want! It's what young people of Harlem want and need that matters!"

"Ellis, will you stop speaking about 'the people'? Aren't social workers people? Aren't we?" Kay and Ellis were disagreeing for the third time that afternoon.

Finally Esperanza interrupted them both. "Listen up, you two! Ellis, Kay wants to look at youth programs to see what they need so they can be improved. Kay, Ellis wants to make sure young kids of color have their voices heard. You know, it is possible to do both. Something could benefit the program professionals and the kids. It's not one or the other, right?"

"I just don't trust the focus on what professionals in programs have to say. Professionals have been living off the lives of poor people forever." Ellis folded his arms across his chest and turned away from his combatant.

"And I don't trust something so vague that it just ends up making some political point but doesn't do anything to actually help anybody. What good does it do to remind people they're oppressed if you don't do anything to help?" Kay bit into her pencil, chewing the final piece of eraser off.

"Esperanza's right." Jill spoke for the first time that afternoon. "Let's just start by focusing on prospects for youth in Harlem and go from there. We don't even know what we're concretely talking about yet. Maybe if we look at some actual data we can narrow down what we're looking at. Is it job prospects? School prospects? After-school prospects? Let's do the work and find out." Jill looked at Kay. "That means we can look at programs as well as people." Kay nodded in quiet assent. "And of course we have to talk with young people, Ellis. They're central to our work, right?"

Ellis was quiet for a moment, then pulled a neatly sorted folder from his briefcase. "Actually, I did some data sorting already. I went over to the Community Planning Board and got data on all the issues we've been discussing: poverty, test scores, numbers of homeless." He ruffled through the material, selecting two pages that were both heavily marked with yellow highlighter. "These data sets stood out. The first one shows school dropout rates in Central Harlem." He pointed across a bar graph, showing the upward trajectory. "All the data show increasing dropout rates." He went on to explain three other highlighted graphs on the next page that connected these rates to where the dropouts lived, the percentage who came from single-parent homes, and levels of poverty.

The group was silent with their admiration for Ellis's work. "Where'd you learn to do that?" Esperanza asked.

Ellis blushed, then quickly looked away. "You know, when I was in school. I was always into math, liked to see what underlay things." He pointed at the pile of papers on the table. "This kind of work is fun for me."

For once, Kay laughed warmly. "Hey, no wonder we always fight! I hate math, and math hates me." Kay shyly reached into her large and obviously messy book bag and pulled out a single piece of paper. "I did speak with my field instructor, and she gave me a list of all the youth agencies in Harlem. Turns out there's a task force of social workers who meet once a month to discuss common problems and advocate on their agencies' behalf. My field instructor gave me the name and numbers of the chairperson to contact." She smiled again at Ellis. "Between your data sets and my contacts, maybe we could get something done!" A small grin momentarily appeared on his face as well.

While they were talking, Jill had been quietly writing on the blackboard. At the top were lists of specific tasks: collection of data, interviews with program professionals, interviews with youth in programs/not in programs, and interviews with community leaders. "Here's some things for us to do. How about we divide up? Ellis, you're good at data, so you handle that. Kay, you've got your task force, so you do those professionals. Esperanza, you probably know community leaders already, so maybe you could take them. I like to write lists, so I'll be the recorder/keeper of everyone's records." Her fellow group members looked at her, then began clapping. The quietest group member had gotten them to move!

She hesitated for a second, embarrassed by all the attention. "So let's set timelines for all the things in each section." They quickly did so, making specific suggestions within each other's lists of contacts, other data sources, and possible leads for more information.

Then Esperanza spoke again. "Hey, let's not forget one thing: Our macro teacher says we have to walk the streets, too, in pairs, and get to know the neighborhood as well as the people in it. So maybe we can get to know some of the kids that way. Okay?"

The group nodded in agreement. Then they drew straws to pair up. Naturally, Ellis and Kay wound up together.

Strategic Step 2: The End of the Preplanning Phase—"Problems" Are Tactically Clarified and Assessment Choices Are Made . . . at Last!

The minor skirmish between Ellis and Kay in the above scenario is symptomatic of the classic confrontation that occurs in almost every initial macro-organizing class: an argument between community organizers like Ellis who are motivated by ideological beliefs and who enter social work to find a well-paying, progressive job, and social workers like Kay who decide to do organizing as the best example of what the profession has to offer. Such differences crop up in the preplanning phase of a community group's work because each type of practitioner is having his or her core assumptions tested by the other. The battle over targets that so often occurs in groups is not only about the difficult choices one must make to effectively manage the assessment work; it is also about the struggle to guarantee that core beliefs about who matters will not be discarded. (The issue of who matters will be discussed in greater detail in Chapter 7.) Esperanza and Jill helped bridge the divide between Ellis and Kay by helping them see that their extremes could be encompassed within the same framework. By including both the voices of young people and a review of existing program needs, the group guaranteed that the target focus would have *meaning* in what it eventually accomplished. Working to bridge different group members' core interests is a primary task an organizer undertakes in this often tumultuous and important phase of a group's development.

Joining Targets to Meaningful Goal Achievement

Jill broke through the group impasse and began to move toward problem clarity by sorting the target as "youth in Harlem" and the goal as "to better their prospects." While still vague, *prospects* was understood to mean both issues that concerned young people *and* programs that could meet them because of the clarifying, albeit intense, arguing of Ellis and Kay that had ensued in the preplanning phase.

In this way, the goal itself becomes a filtering lens as group members go about their tasks of data collection, interviewing, and analysis. As implied above, if a strategic goal is too vague ("helping youth"), the tasks at hand remain equally broad, forcing a group to later reassess as the questions asked and the answers given remain too broad for actual use. Likewise, a goal that is too specific (to help one particular program run better), while more manageable, may lack the meaning to one's work that a community group seeks for its young people. "Helping the prospects of young people" has enough specificity to clarify the direction of a group's efforts while remaining open enough to guarantee that key actors (both youth and professionals) are part of the group's eventual recommendations for change.

FROM ANALYZING A SOCIAL PROBLEM TO DISTINGUISHING "FELT NEEDS" LEADING TO ACTION

Both Ellis and Kay were wrapped up in compelling and heartfelt arguments about problems important to them. What they were not doing was using the assessment process to move through problem definitions so that the eventual focus of their group's efforts was actionable and thus tactically meaningful. One of the hardest issues new practitioners have to confront is the difference between the genuine injustice of a social problem and a community's desire to act on that problem through a well-worked-out campaign. The importance of engaging with community members is that they serve as a powerful barometer in directing a group from a *heartfelt issue to a felt need*. Deploring the level of unemployment among young people (a genuine and heartfelt problem) and waging a campaign that all box stores in a community fill at least 75% of their entry-level positions with neighborhood youth between the ages of 16 and 23 (a potential felt need) is a difference in focus and strategic effectiveness.

Practitioners thus use preplanning and engagement phases of their assessment process to accomplish the following:

- *Analyze social problems* in the community, using survey and other forms of aggregate data to distinguish what seem to be key issues or problems of the community or neighborhood.
- *Understand the nature of the problem* so that issues eventually worked on will target solutions that resolve at least some of that problem's cause (or lay a foundation for doing so). Decrying a lack of housing is insufficient; focusing on a city's plans for low-income housing or housing lenders' loan programs for low- and moderate-income housing has located a source of an issue that, were it successfully challenged, could actually alter the housing market of a neighborhood. Such clarity moves a group from abstract, albeit heartfelt, concern to potential activity. While such a campaign may be long and require many levels of engagement, planning, and action, it is nevertheless a powerful antidote to the despair of widespread analysis of issues without focus ("the problem is too big").
- *Clarify the problem* in ways that can lead to focus and action. Knowing a source of the problem—the city has not supplied financial assistance for low-income housing development—shines a bright light on where things are wrong (lack of financial assistance) and how to make them right (use city revenues from the capital budget for this neighborhood). *Combining an analysis with what's wrong and a way forward to make it right* can create powerful energy in what would obviously be a long-term campaign.
- *Finally, this sifting process of problem definition helps community members and groups arrive at issues that they experience as **felt needs**.* The difference between a "need" and a "felt need" is the difference between a group of people bothered by conditions in the world and a group acting on the world to make it a better place for themselves and others. Practitioners engaged in community assessments need to go through the seemingly long process of moving from problem analysis to felt need so that together with community members they can *find issues that people care enough about and experience in ways that will motivate them to act*. The next section explores the strategic issues at play that go into how this process occurs.

Connecting Meaningful Goals to Manageable Targets as You Move From Problem Definition to Action

Staying open to problem definition throughout, the assessment thus begins to move forward with planned tasks and strategic direction. Using the goal as a filter, a community group then separates out tasks that are manageable based on the group's resources related to *time, technology, and financial costs*. All three resources serve as balancing weights to the meaningful power embedded in the strategic goal. One may hold "change the world" as an overarching goal, but having a day or two a week to accomplish something that profound may require rethinking either your resource commitment (can you really give up all your sleep?) or making the goal itself more concrete and realizable. For our four practitioners above, manageability required a careful assessment of all three resources.

- *Time:* Work on this group assignment had to take place when members were not doing fieldwork (3 days a week), not in class (part of 2 other days a week), and did not work (three had part-time jobs of 20 hours a week, and Esperanza was in a work-related school program that let her go to school 1 day a week while she worked 10-hour days the other 4 weekdays). Such time constraints are typical for both social work students and people running community programs with volunteer members. This means that weekends, weeknights, and other free hours are the "time resource" this group has to work with.
- *Technology:* In 1990, Google was neither a powerful web search engine nor a verb used by people seeking information. While information could be found on the web, Ellis's legwork regarding the local Community Board was far more common for hard data searches than it will be in the 21st century. Today, web-based information can far more easily facilitate a group's need for hard data on the conditions of a particular program, population, or problem within a community. The Internet has greatly enriched community groups' capacities to mine data to develop powerful arguments related to needs and resources for a community group. For example, geographic information systems are used within many large urban as well as rural areas and are capable of tracking issues such as the impact of hurricanes on streets and neighborhoods so that zoning regulations can be strengthened. It is possible for citizens to report potholes, street crime, and transit problems using smartphones with city-based apps (see Esri, n.d.). Whether neighborhood blight (Shlay & Whitman, 2006) or community food assessments (Cohen, 2002), the use of hard data found on the Internet has so greatly strengthened a group's capacity and the ease with which it can make its arguments for change widely known that *not* using the Internet today would diminish a community group's credibility.

That said, the risks of technology have shifted from professionals' struggles to utilize it to the dangers of overreliance on Internet-based information as a substitute for on-the-ground assessments of real people affected by the issue under review. Ellis's visit to the Community Board for data also created the opportunity to meet and interact with people from the community being assessed. The value of adding texture to the search engine's hard data on a community by gleaning informal information from such interactions as a practitioner goes about his or her work cannot be underestimated.

Furthermore, there are class and racial biases associated with both web utilization and the information collected via the web (National Urban League, 2009). Poor community groups, especially groups working with those most often perceived as being on the margins of public discourse (like the homeless in the 1970s), have sparse webpages and use their resources on program development, not Management Information Systems development. Their webpages likely will not reveal the work being done with a teen fathers' program, housing efforts with undocumented workers, or antiviolence activities on behalf of homeless LGBTQ youth.

Finally, not all of a community's members are comfortable with or have access to personal computers. While the web has great potential to create a broader and more democratic experience (see Chapter 9), it can do so only if its users make the effort to extend its use throughout their communities to those least able to afford it.

With these caveats, today's Internet technology still creates enormous opportunities to collect relatively accurate hard data that can help a group pinpoint what it is seeking to assess. Because of its accessibility, the Internet can also allow group members to spend that much more time in the community interviewing people, including community leaders; professionals concerned with the program, population, or problem; and those most directly affected by the issue at hand (in this case, youth). In short, while people's work, school, and familial demands have diminished the amount of time they have to make thorough assessments, technology has provided them more time than was possible when Kay, Ellis, Jill, and Esperanza were beginning their assessments in the 1990s.

- *Financial costs:* While the costs of a community assessment may seem minimal for a group such as the one discussed above, there are hidden costs that a socially aware practitioner must identify as assignments are divided among a group's members. Hours spent interviewing could be hours spent at a part-time job. Travel costs related to either public transportation or car mileage (gas, oil, tolls) may be a factor. An entire day spent walking the streets of a neighborhood means food costs, even if only the cost of a slice or two of pizza. Some people, especially women, will have child-care costs, either directly financial or in cooperative arrangements that cost them extra hours later in the week. Taking time to reflect on and showing respect for the varied financial demands on different group members is one of the ways practitioners establish their legitimacy with others. It also allows every group member to honestly assess what he or she is capable of doing for the group so that the tasks at hand are reliably and responsively handled.

Taken together, the resources of time, technology, and financial costs help a group sift through the *meaningful–manageable matrix* between desired goals and available resources. Group members then can focus more clearly on the targets under assessment, the breadth of needs they will attempt to delineate, and the boundaries (whether geographic, functional, solitary, or bonded) of the community itself. After listening to the debate between Ellis and Kay that helped her sort out the matrix that could satisfy them both, Jill successfully moved the group from a discussion about youth and professionals to prospects for youth, giving the matrix a manageable, programmatic focus that pleased Kay without delineating which programs those would be. That, after all, was the meaningful part of the assessment that required input from the youth themselves, central to Ellis's concerns.

Thus, the meaningful–manageable matrix is the sifting tool a group uses to handle its first practice dilemma: Too broad a focus, and they can't get anything done; too narrow, and it may not matter what happens. The prod for *concrete specificity* also helps a group get to work. Given limited time, how big a community are we looking at? What can we learn from data sources on the Internet, and what must be learned from direct contact with others? And who is a reliable informant? That professional who runs an after-school program has credibility, but will she admit to gaps in service? That young person can speak openly about his own needs, but does he know what others his age care about? How much time and expense can a group afford to invest in making certain its members are meeting people who are truly reflective of the community they are assessing?

GROUP EXERCISE: MOVING FROM PROBLEM ANALYSIS TO FELT NEED

In groups of at least three people, list a series of problems in a community you all live in or are a part of (it could be your school community as well):

_____

_____

Now, as much as possible, identify the sources of these problems. Put a check mark by any source that seems a target capable of change:

_____

_____

Clarify which issues seem to be more visible and realistic targets for change:

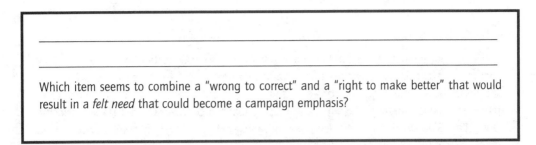

Which item seems to combine a "wrong to correct" and a "right to make better" that would result in a *felt need* that could become a campaign emphasis?

THE STORM BEFORE THE LULL: ASSESSING NEEDS VERSUS STRENGTHS, OPPRESSION VERSUS OPPORTUNITY, AND THE EXPERTISE OF PROFESSIONALS VERSUS THE VOICE OF THE PEOPLE

As any experienced group worker or community organizer knows, groups often erupt along harsh battle lines as members must decide not only what they want to do but also how they want to do it (Middleman & Wood, 1989; Salmon & Kurland, 1995). Ellis and Kay's group was no different.

A GROUP STRUGGLES TO GROW

"So listen, you two, could we argue a little less here?" Esperanza was looking directly at Ellis and Kay. "We have some hard decisions to make and I'd like to get home and make dinner before 7 p.m. So . . . which part of Harlem? There are a million people in the whole community. So what makes sense? And prospects for youth about what? Employment? Education? Health? And which youth? Youth 13 to 17? Youth 17 to 21? And how are we going to find them and the people who work with them?" Esperanza's voice took on a slight edge of frustration as more and more questions emerged. She looked at her watch and sighed heavily.

"Ellis already gave us an option with his data. Why not just look at Central Harlem? That seems big enough to matter, but it's not the whole huge community," Kay spoke quickly in response. "My task force list has about eight agencies right there."

"Um . . . I like the idea of Central Harlem, Esperanza. We could handle that, and it still is, well, you know," Ellis smiled, "central to the community. What goes on here affects the rest of the community." Everyone smiled. Ellis and Kay had finally agreed on something!

Kay went on quickly. "I heard from my supervisor that these groups are doing some excellent work with those new after-school programs. I know we could talk to them about what they're doing. I'd love to see what's working so we could pass it on to others."

(Continued)

(Continued)

Ellis quickly jumped in, the irritation back in his voice. "Excuse me, but before we go to how cool things are, could we examine the actual conditions on these data sheets and compare them elsewhere? I mean, yeah, people can do nice work, but what if that work has been compromised by underfunding? Let's make a little comparison between Central Harlem and the Upper East Side District on the same programs. I will bet you 2 to 1 that we're underfunded up here, even though the need is greater!"

"Come on Ellis, don't we have enough to do on this project? I'm sure the after-school people can tell us their resource issues. After all, they know . . ."

Ellis quickly interrupted. "There you go again, trusting what a few professionals say, making it easier on us by avoiding reality. I am *certain* that a little historical trend data will show us the kind of discrimination and oppression for these Black and Latino kids that some people don't want to admit to. Maybe making it easy on us is just a cop-out . . ."

"Hey, Ellis, I didn't say anything like that!" It was Kay's turn to interrupt, her cheeks turning red with anger. "I just said let's see what's working! Besides which, what exactly is wrong with speaking with professionals? If they work here and care about the kids, aren't they part of the community in some way, too? Or is the only good community assessment one that focuses on the victims of oppression? Couldn't people be doing something right as well? Even those professionals you think are jerks?"

The two argued for another 5 minutes, neither giving ground to the other. Finally, Jill got up and started to pack her book bag. "I'm already late to my waitressing job downtown." She looked at Kay and Ellis, her voice wavering as she spoke. "I say make a comparison. A good assessment needs trends to make sense of what's going on. So what's the big deal, Kay? And, Ellis, we're *in* social work! Do you honestly think everyone working those 12-hour days for less pay than teachers' is a sell-out? Why don't you guys just calm down and meet in the middle? My God, we're doing a community assessment here, not planning World War III! Stop making yourselves each other's enemy, okay?"

Esperanza was packing up her bags as well. "So, since you guys monopolized all the time, you get to stay here and finish this up. We've got Central Harlem. We've got these new after-school programs as our focus. So let's compare the past and talk to professionals about the present. And kids, too. Just take a breath and spend time on a work plan . . . we've only got 4 weeks to get this project done." She looked at Kay and Ellis like the mother she was as she made her last comment. "And if each of you could see the other's point of view, just a little, we'd all get the results we want. Kay, talking about the past doesn't mean we ignore good stuff in the present. Ellis, talking to professionals on what's working doesn't mean we forget about injustice." She slung her large book bag over her shoulder as she walked to the door. "Lighten up, okay? And put together sensible timelines for what we've got to do before you leave!"

Ellis and Kay looked down at their notes, embarrassed. Jill had made them see how strident they'd been. And from Esperanza, they'd seen how childish they were acting. Their arguing behind them at least for the moment, they quickly got to work.

The storming that occurred here encapsulates what inevitably occurs at some stage of a group's development as group members must make decisions on how they are going to move ahead. *In that discussion of "how" is embedded the way the core values within the assessment will be expressed.* While there are always minor variations, those arguments most often entail three distinct yet overlapping themes.

Needs/Strengths, Oppression/Opportunity, and the Expertise of Professionals/the Voice of the People

As we saw with Kay and Ellis, the debate will be argued as one *versus* the other, as if the topics were dichotomized and one's choice canceled the other out. That's why the storming occurs; group members, caught in the ambiguity of a group's project formation, overemphasize what matters most to them, hoping to guarantee its place in the project. That the eventual emphasis might be an amalgam of *both* rather than *either/or* may seem obvious, but it is rare in a group's formative stage that this kind of battle does not take place (Middleman & Wood, 1989). In community assessments, such struggles are common to group life and become reflective of core strains that have existed inside the social work field for generations (Abramovitz, 1999; Blau & Abramovitz, 2007; Fisher & Karger, 1996; Jansson, 2008).

Needs Versus Strengths

Twenty-five years ago, community assessments were called community needs assessments, and the focus was overwhelmingly on the problems, disparities, and deficits that could be found in some part of

1. a community's functions—economic production, distribution, consumption; socialization and social control; and participation and support (Fellin, 2000; Warren, 1987);

2. populations—youth, the elderly, LGBTQ, infants, children in foster care, and so on; or

3. structures—education, social services, transportation services, and linkages to other communities.

As Saleebey (2008) cogently argued, such a deficit focus undercuts the strengths, resiliency, and capacity of communities, especially those whose objective conditions are in part limited by conditions of economic and social oppression and social stigma.

Saleebey (2008) argued that for macro practitioners and others to focus only on needs was to further marginalize already oppressed communities and groups. By instead locating the variety of forms of resiliency, organizational capacity, and assets present in communities, this strength-oriented perspective reconfigured how one went about analyzing the what and how of communities and their members in a resonant and powerful way that corrected the balance between actual needs and the capacity of a community to meet them.

This, of course, was the underlying point to Kay's argument. Ellis's was to guarantee that the historical and present-day realities of oppressive and discriminatory resource allocation in comparison with other communities and groups not be ignored as well. New practitioners (as Ellis and Kay were at the time) fought as hard as they did so that these core dimensions to their community assessment would be neither ignored nor trivialized. Finding a balance between awareness of discrimination and marginalization and not focusing exclusively on deficits and victimization is part of the filtering that group members do as they develop their community assessment project.

Oppression Versus Opportunity

One of the longest debates among American organizers, social workers, and policy-makers concerned with poverty and social welfare relates to one's interpretations of the social conditions impacting people's lives (Blau & Abramovitz, 2007; Jansson, 2008; Reisch & Andrews, 2002). As we can see from the above case study, Ellis is acutely aware of the historic markers of oppression and discrimination that are woven into the conditions of the Harlem community's life. As such, he frames his interpretation of present-day problems within long-term and systematic issues of purposeful discrimination, economic inequality, and conscious marginalization that have long afflicted the community he is assessing (National Urban League, 2009). The identified problem—whether prospects for youth or concerns of the elderly—will always have a comparative, trend-influenced perspective so that any possible inequalities will be highlighted and appear central to eventual problem definition and proposed solutions. Actions would incorporate this principled attention to the past as work was undertaken.

Kay, on the other hand, sought out the opportunities presently at play so that their group could recommend meaningful activities that actually impacted the youth. Her focus, while not denying past injustices, centered on what could be done in the immediate present based on resources and interests of programs and the people who ran them. The problem at hand would have an immediacy and *pragmatic* attention to action based on what could benefit youth, regardless of the past.

The discussion on oppression and opportunity that macro practitioners undertake eventually gets filtered through the mix of *principles and pragmatism* common to all policy debates (Jansson, 2008), especially as they impact programmatic recommendations for a targeted group whose needs may be both large in the present and historic in the making. Kay and Ellis were arguing in ways familiar to almost all groups as practitioners refine their assessments to be both principled and pragmatic in their analysis of social problems and what they propose to do about them (Alinsky, 1989a, 1989b).

Professional Expertise Versus the Voice of the People

Ellis and Kay also argued over the *key community informants*—that is, who was most credible in evaluating the needs and assets of the community under review. Any assessment must have *reliable* informants, people whose answers to your questions accurately portray the program, population, or issue for an entire group of people and not just from their own points of view. Likewise, community respondents' answers on trends, problems, and assets must also have a high degree of validity; what they say must carry the authority of soundness and thoroughness regarding the issue at hand. Ellis's desire to hear from young people reflected his belief in the validity of their experience, regardless of whether it could be generalized beyond themselves. In turn, Kay wanted the reliability offered by professionals' wider scope, even though such scope may extend beyond their programmatic interests.

This kind of tension between professional experience and community member voice extends back more than 50 years in social work, as seen in the profession's Code of Ethics (National Association of Social Workers, 2009). As such, this issue is resolved not with an either/or answer but through the mix of both sets of representatives in one's assessment. Esperanza and Jill forced Kay and Ellis to compromise on an age-old problem of the field so they could complete the course assignment. Selecting the mix of community members and professionals to interview in your own community assessment—all fit within the mix of principles and pragmatism that drive any good community project—will be part of the sifting process that you and your group undertake as well.

At the conclusion of this chapter, there is a topical outline from the Community Toolbox on the specific steps and tools you can use for your own community assessment. While we continue to frame the broader strategic issues at hand that impact your practice choices—and your career options—you are invited to use the outline and assess the rich material from the webpage for the step-by-step tools you will need as your projects unfold.

EXERCISE: CREATING A MEANINGFUL–MANAGEABLE MIX

Choose a campaign you or your agency is involved in: _____

Outline what and who the campaign is attempting to influence and change in terms of

Needs/strengths:

_____

_____

(Continued)

(Continued)

Oppression/opportunities:

_____

_____

Professional expertise/member voice:

_____

_____

How could the campaign be made more manageable?

_____

_____

More meaningful?

_____

_____

THE FIRST STEPS IN YOUR *PERSONAL* DEVELOPMENT OF YOUR *PROFESSIONAL* BEST PRACTICES: MAKING TACTICAL CHOICES . . . AND STRATEGICALLY LIVING WITH THEM

The arguments under way between Ellis and Kay at surface level are about the kinds of tactical choices their group needs to make to get the assignment done: Who do we talk with? Who matters? What are the boundaries of the community we are assessing? Too small and modest? Too big and vague? How much of the past do we compare to the present? How much do we focus on the programs as they are today? As such, these choices are powerfully reflective of the general strategic direction a group will take as its project unfolds. Those are the *professional judgments* of you and the people with whom you work about what you seek to accomplish.

That said, how you respond to different tactical choices in your work is part of your *personal and professional development* into a great practitioner as well. Underlying Kay and Ellis's arguments is something beyond professional strategic judgment. *There is also the personal fear that what matters to one will be ignored, left out, or trivialized by the other, especially after the group has made its tactical choices on how to mix the amount of focus on oppression/opportunity, needs/strengths, and expertise/voice.* Kay and Ellis are not only arguing; they are also in the beginning stages of their own professional development in living with the choices a group makes that may not totally reflect their own values, beliefs, and personal comfort.

Best practice in macro work is not only about the choices you make in the meaningful–manageable matrix of your project; it is your personal capacity to live within that mix once choices are made. Kay needs to toughen up and pay attention to larger social conditions and dynamics of oppression. Ellis needs to lighten up and allow that not every social work program is a source of control and marginalization of the people he cares about. One's ability to work on the choices a group makes *and* the dilemmas created by the inevitable limits that such choices create is a personal challenge that anyone committed to a life of meaningful social change and social justice must undertake throughout his or her career. It is, in many ways, the kind of "micro" intrapersonal issue that clinical social workers easily embrace and many macro practitioners find more difficult.

Happily, there is also a paradox embedded in this personal and professional challenge that any practitioner can embrace: The more you are able to handle your tactical choices and their limits, the more likely you will begin to embody the qualities of openness, flexibility, and humility that are at the core of Paulo Freire's (2000) charge to practitioners who seek to work with the oppressed:

> Dialogue [the ongoing, reciprocal work done among macro practitioners and community members] cannot exist without humility. The naming of the world, through which people constantly re-create that world, cannot be an act of arrogance. Dialogue, as the encounter of those addressed to the common task of learning and acting, is broken if the parties (or one of them) lack humility. How can I dialogue if I always project ignorance onto others and never perceive my own? How can I dialogue if I regard myself as a case apart from others? . . . How can I dialogue if I consider myself a member of the in-group of "pure" men, the owners of truth and knowledge for whom all non-members are "these people"? . . . Someone who cannot acknowledge himself to be as mortal as everyone else still has a long way to go to be at the point of encounter [with those with whom he works]. (p. 90)

Through one's personal capacity to admit to limits, one's professional capacity to transform the way one works with others becomes more, not less, powerful. Of course, seeing limits as opportunities for growth is an enormous paradox as well: *How can one have the courage to try to change the world and be humble at the same time?*

LEARNING TO GROW PROFESSIONALLY THROUGH "LESS IS MORE": THE DEVELOPMENT OF TACTICAL SELF-AWARENESS

This is where the development of tactical self-awareness can make a difference. As we can see from the early struggles between Ellis and Kay, some of their disagreements stemmed from the different ways they approached problem solving early in their group's development. Ellis wanted to get down to work and move things along; Kay desired a chance to talk things through and to check in with each other before getting down to the rest of the work. Their differences in pace (one fast, one more measured) and focus of interest (one on task, one on process) are reflective of key dimensions to one of the profession's key domains: *the conscious use of self.*

However, "use of self" has been written about primarily for caseworkers, where transference and countertransference issues are endemic to practice (Maguire, 2001). The social caseworker uses available tools to minimize long-term problems created by such intrapsychic phenomena: Regular clinical supervision, knowledge of cultural and social psychological differences, the spatial limits of an office, and the temporal limits of 45-minute (or less) sessions are all used to maintain practice effectiveness. Such aids help the caseworker and the client overcome what are otherwise emotionally charged problems within the therapeutic process.

Few of these aids exist for the community practitioner. He or she works with varying numbers of people in rarely neutral settings, often at irregular hours. Supervision, when it exists, is structured around the political and strategic concerns of the group. Furthermore, many community practitioners (like Ellis) are predisposed to mistrust the presumably "gloppy" process interests of case and group workers: The task is everything, and the process, if it matters, is a concern for leadership development, not for personal issues related to oneself. Anything else is just talk.

The reality, of course, is that community practitioners, whether organizers or managers, are as much engaged in process as any clinical worker is. As we can see through Ellis and Kay's arguments, the emotional strains are certainly as intense. This is why, in part, so many organizers leave community organizing after a few years—not because the work is finished but because they are too exhausted, personally, to continue. Instead of the experience being a mellowing process, as Perlman (1989) called long-term professional work, it becomes a justification for exhaustion. The result is that many social work agencies and communities lose some of their most skilled professionals just when they could be of most service (Maguire, 2001).

One of the ways organizers can avoid burning out is through a different appreciation of the use of self, using an approach that looks at personal issues in terms of the community organizing experience, drawing on both casework and community organizing literature to create a viable methodology—one that actively incorporates the self into the socially and politically tumultuous world of organizing. What follows is an attempt to do just that.

A CASE EXAMPLE OF THE PERSON IN THE ORGANIZING PROCESS

An example of how an individual's personal makeup affects the organizing process occurred during a legislative session where social workers were intently lobbying for their issues. A young organizer was speaking with me about her lobbying efforts on food stamp legislation. It was a complex and exciting task, one she relished. If passed, the new procedural guidelines would have tremendous impact on thousands of people. The vote was expected to be close, but she looked forward to the effort, complete with arm twisting, late-night negotiations, and constant haggling as the vote drew close. Later in the conversation, we happened to speak about casework, and she visibly cringed when I suggested she also might like being a caseworker. "Never! I haven't the right to do that kind of work—there's too much power over the individual. I'd never do it." When I mentioned that she seemed to relish the power at the legislative level, which could affect thousands of people, her consternation grew. "But there's a difference—one's individual, the other's collective. I want to help communities, not just one person." She and Ellis have a lot in common.

As she later admitted, however, her initial response to my query had been personally, not politically, based. While she still felt politically correct in choosing organizing over casework, part of her justification had centered on her discomfort with intense personal interaction. Unfortunately, the blanket political justification also had diminished her effectiveness as an organizer. Personality is not destiny, but since *people* implement strategy, one's own personal understanding becomes tactically necessary. This otherwise effective organizer later found herself limited in her arm-twisting techniques. She was highly effective when working in groups, but lobbying's one-on-one interaction left her awkwardly inarticulate. If she had been more aware of this personal limitation, her ensuing difficulties, repeated throughout the legislative session, might have diminished.

THE INTROSPECTIVE CUTTING EDGE OF ORGANIZING

As the above example suggests, the introspective cutting edge of organizing is neither a political nor a personal issue but one of *tactical self-awareness*: How aware are you of your personal skills in the array of organizing settings that you are part of daily? Can you distinguish between objective and personal limits? Did that important contact at the fundraiser turn you down because her funds were already committed or because your own discomfort in social situations dampened her interest in your organization? Did the plans for the large rally fall apart because people truly weren't interested or because, like Kay, you don't have the necessary attentiveness for the minor details beforehand?

There are no easy answers, but the rest of this chapter will focus on how heightened tactical self-awareness can increase one's organizing effectiveness.[1] As we will see, the community assessment group's struggles to create an effective plan of action would have been diminished had Ellis and Kay been developing their own tactical self-awareness of the organizing situation at hand.

The term *tactical self-awareness* has been chosen carefully, for the phrase emphasizes both personal temperament regarding one's preferred approaches to problem solving and the specific organizing techniques required at that strategic phase of the group's development.[2] Tactical self-awareness, with attention to both one's personal and political skills, is an extension of the relationship Saul Alinsky (1989b) discussed in his classic *Rules for Radicals*. In analyzing the failure of some organizers to grow beyond a certain elementary level of skill, he stated:

> [Those who failed] memorized the words and related experience and concepts. Listening to them was like listening to a tape playing back my presentation word-for-word. . . . The problem . . . was their failure to understand that a specific situation is significant only in its relationship to and its illumination of a general concept. Instead they see the specific action as a terminal point. They fail to grasp the fact that no situation ever repeats itself, that no tactic can be precisely the same. (p. 23)

However, Alinsky (1989b) was stating only that tactics are different in each new situation. An individual is different, too, with distinct emotional and personal responses to the event, its participants, and the host of tactical considerations evoked by each strategic context. If each new strategic situation demands a fresh look at tactics, it also needs a quick reappraisal of the people involved in implementing them . . . including oneself.

The basic assumption of tactical self-awareness, by emphasizing simultaneous personal and tactical changes in varying contexts, opposes the Great Organizer Theory of Organizing. This theory (and one that almost every organizer has succumbed to at times) goes like this: *Every organizer should be able to perform well within all important strategic situations, from running the office (the autonomous, neat, punctual organizer, like Jill) to running the demonstration (the collective, spontaneous, charismatic organizer, similar to Kay).* Furthermore, anyone who can't perform all these tasks should seriously consider a different profession.

A number of organizers have taken up this alternative job consideration after reading Alinsky's (1989b) list items:

> While idealized, the best organizers should have all of them to a strong extent, and any organizer needs at least a degree of each: (1) curiosity; (2) irreverence; (3) imagination; (4) a sense of humor; (5) a bit of a blurred vision of a better world; (6) an organized, rational personality; (7) a well-integrated political schizoid; (8) a strong ego; (9) a free and open mind. (p. 46)[3]

Alinsky (1989a, 1989b), always the provocative tactician, undoubtedly wrote this list with an eye toward some of the smug younger organizers of the late '60s. However, anyone who reads this list, whether grayish '60s activist or 21st century third-wave feminist, will feel understandably defeated. For example, after my own reading, I proceeded to eliminate everyone I knew from the "best" category, and only a few squeaked into Alinsky's "any organizer" slot. Yet, as I mused on the list while continuing my organizing, I realized something was missing in his analysis. At times, such as during large demonstrations, I was a terrific organizer: I functioned well, spoke clearly, got along with everybody, and even digested my food with ease. At other times, doing routine office work, I was a klutz— about as effective as an Adam Sandler character on a blind date, without the humor. Did this mean I was only half an organizer, half effective?

All organizers will ask the same thing, particularly after certain organizing problems recur. If the problem is strictly tactical, they can find suitable political alternatives. For example, you don't wage a petition campaign when people can't decide what the problem is, nor do you attack the landlord when the rest of the group still likes him. That's simple enough and fits the general guidelines Alinsky (1989a) was writing about. Ellis calmed down and got to work on the assessment when Esperanza pointed out to him the group's need for a clear purpose before getting started. Most organizers learn this within 6 months.

But *real* organizing, the day-to-day, garden variety of three-person meetings, bungled conference calls because someone forgot the number, gulped lunches, overlooked details, and late-night, laughter-filled drinks at the bar, isn't easily fit into abstract strategic formulas. *In reality, an organizer is engaged in the implementation of tactics every day and thus is an embodiment, personally, of the tactics themselves.* If some of those situations are personally discomforting, the tactic won't be as effective as it might otherwise be. Kay was bothered by Ellis's pushiness. Ellis grew irritated with Kay's desire for check-ins. The objective for a community practitioner is to learn how to work with whatever form of discomfort you feel in ways that minimize potential organizing problems in the future.

The young woman working on food stamp legislation, discussed above, had just this type of problem. In her discomfort with direct, individualized interaction that had potential conflict, she presented the bill so poorly in her one-on-one meetings that a few moderately sympathetic legislators began to suspect both her and her program. Yet later that night at a group strategy session, the organizer could skillfully synthesize different bits of political information on how votes were lining up, and her final presentation was instrumental in charting the next day's lobbying efforts.

In fact, she was no different from any other practitioner. Equally important, her choice of *tactics* in the lobbying situation had been correct. The failings were her personal inhibitions in highly specified organizing activities, inhibitions she could have predicted beforehand. She had functioned not as a heroine but as a human—good in some areas, a little shakier in others.

REFLECTIVE QUESTION

What is the key distinction between *professional use of self* and *tactical self-awareness* for the community-based practitioner?

A PRACTITIONER'S SEARCH FOR INTERNAL BALANCE IN THE MIDST OF AN ORGANIZER'S AMBIGUOUS WORK

Organizers can begin to become more tactically self-aware by recognizing, rumors to the contrary, that they are just like other people in their varying effectiveness at work. In doing so, community practitioners can become much more open to the subjective concerns of psychologists and clinical social workers. One helpful role model is Carl Rogers (1980), who years ago developed a series of still-popular propositions related to personality development that explain some of the subjective reasons for one's constantly shifting tactical effectiveness. While written for a different audience, the propositions (based on years of research) are still illuminating:

1. A [person] reacts to the field [environment] as it is experienced. This perceptual field is, for the individual, reality.

2. The [person] has one basic tendency and striving—to actualize, maintain, and enhance [himself or herself].

3. Behavior is basically the goal-directed attempts of the [person] to satisfy its needs as experienced in the field as it is perceived.

4. Emotion accompanies and facilitates such goal-directed behavior.

5. Any experience that is inconsistent with the organization or structure of self may be perceived as a threat, and the more of these perceptions there are, the *more rigidly the self-structure is organized to maintain itself* (italics added).

6. Under certain conditions, involving complete absence of any threat to self-structure, experiences that are inconsistent with it may be perceived and examined and the structure of the self revised to assimilate and include such experiences. (pp. 115–116)

Later, we will return to the last point with its element of active, personal change. Rogers's (1980) first four propositions underscore the point that a person's behavior is always a response to his or her existing need to experience reality in a way that allows him or her to be comfortable with both the environment and his or her sense of fit in that reality. Second, Proposition 5 makes clear that when one's environment is in some way personally threatening, it is natural to become defensive (consciously or otherwise) and thus *rigidly responsive* (tactically less effective) to the surrounding world. In other words, the self (emotions and all) is personally mobilized to maintain its perception of a safe environment, even if political/organizational concerns and tactical flexibility suffer as a consequence (Shriever, 2003).

To use a concrete example, it was neither accident nor political inconsistency that the food stamp organizer was tongue-tied in individual confrontation and yet skillful in group interaction. Her personal makeup, complete with its own history, emotions, and behaviors, made her better able to actualize her entire range of skills in one situation (the group) and less able in another (one-to-one). Without attempting psychoanalysis, we can see from Rogers's (1980) formulation that, in the particular context of individual conflict, what was going on beneath the organizer's awkwardness had served not a political but a personal purpose—engaged, individual conflict had been avoided effectively.

Strategically, if organizers can view their personalities as being as potentially variable as any other tactic, they are freer to adapt their personal attributes to particular situations, letting others perform in those more difficult contexts or, if that's not possible, building recognizable supports so that tactical problems are minimized.[4] Rather than berating yourself for being a lousy organizer because you can't do well in, for instance, social situations where important contacts can be improved, a little tactical self-awareness frees you to more easily use other abilities in a more dynamic and personally liberating manner. You're not so hot on social contacts? How about your colleague, who is as gregarious as he is disorganized on follow-up? Let him have the main tasks at the social function, and you can handle the later phone calls. By affirming your strengths and admitting to limits, you humbly begin to open yourself up to the tactical flexibility great practice requires.

TACTICAL SELF-AWARENESS WITH THE TASK-ORIENTED PRACTITIONER

The awareness of how personal effectiveness varies from situation to situation is important for all practitioners to consider, but perhaps even more so for organizers, for most tend to identify themselves as task-oriented rather than process-oriented personalities. Indeed, in brief surveys with about 100 student organizers and 30 practicing organizers, it was found that more than 70% considered themselves task oriented—the type of people who focus on the actual work, are disinterested in the procedures of how the work is done, worry mostly about outcomes, and devalue social interaction over goal achievement.[5] This orientation thus tends to ignore an organizing project's demands for a longer-term, more open-ended practice when it comes to group engagement, leadership development, and reflection on what's working and not working. Being task oriented is helpful, of course, especially as a group gropes toward understanding what it can accomplish, needs to take risks on new ways of working, and has to meet deadlines.

To look at the implications from Rogers's (1980) work again, one can see that the more a person views reality as time limited and sharply focused in its demands, the more he or she will emphasize task-oriented, impersonal, concrete roles and actions. Furthermore, one can thus correctly screen out more personally intense, emotional concerns. ("Cut out all that talk-talk-talk!" Ellis cried. "We have work to do!") To have a longer-term or more relational focus, with its heightened interpersonal complexity and variability in the process itself, would greatly increase the emphasis on intuitive, personalized situations. It is equally likely, of course, that the personal discomfort of the task-oriented practitioner would increase in such situations as well.

Task orientation, then, is not "the right way to organize"; it is simply the adaptive style of most organizers. As stated before, it is often helpful. However, *organizers need to learn that one's personal strength in some aspects of practice is not the same as an immutable law of how things must get done.* The daily life of an organizer touches on innumerable events that demand a more subtle mix in one's perspective. Indeed, most organizers go through enough tactical variation in a week to touch on almost every type of strategic situation—individual discussions, group meetings, social events, and so forth. The following case example, analyzed in detail, helps explain what can happen to a task-oriented practitioner when he or she does not account for personal dynamics in certain organizing situations.

An organizer, working in a poor neighborhood of a large city, was having his first large meeting of concerned community members. They had gathered to discuss local problems, and the organizer, a solidly task-oriented person, was actively trying to find out the main problems people wanted action on. People had been discussing both personal and community issues, and the meeting was about an hour old. The following narrative took place:

Organizer:	We've been talking about a number of things tonight, and we ought to start listing ones that people feel are the most important. Who'd like to start?
Mr. O (immediately):	Where the smell's from . . . the sewers.
Organizer:	Any other problems that ought to be discussed?
Mr. F:	Well, what we need are some stop signs around here. We should have a stoplight on the corner so the kids don't get hurt.

Organizer (looking around somewhat blindly):   What would you call that? (*There was silence, and finally someone said, "Safety."*)

(*People in general were looking at the organizer somewhat strangely. After a brief pause, Mr. M. brought up the topic of the streetlights again. A wider, informal discussion then ensued in the group.*)

Organizer (interrupting the informal discussion):   Okay, we've got recreation because somebody mentioned parks for the kids. Are there any other problems in the area worth looking into?

Mr. P: Garbage collection.

Organizer: Let's see now, we've got the garbage collection, and the sewers. Now what would you call that? (*Again, people looked at him oddly.*)

Organizer (continuing):   Could we call it sanitation? (*There was no reply for a time and then some brief nodding.*)

(*The meeting broke up soon afterward with a small committee formed. It never functioned.*)

The first and most obvious criticism one could make about the organizer's performance was that his needless use of abstract categorization around concrete issues only confused people—his educated class bias was showing. *There is only one problem with this criticism: The organizer almost never spoke like that anywhere else.* Given his desire to be effective, his previously demonstrated talents, and his generally concrete approach to work, what happened?

The answer is simple. Working in a new group of predominantly poor people had not only excited him but also made him nervous with anticipation. That nervousness manifested itself not in hemming and hawing but in heightening the specific, categorical, and abstract clarity of each and every topic. *Such obsessive categorization may have been dysfunctional tactically, but not personally.* Its abstract unity was the evening's closest approximation to satisfying the practitioner's own personal need for some concrete, *organized* success.

His behavior had helped resolve the underlying nervousness he felt in the new and exciting situation; it may have been unnecessary, but his own *personal* fit with the amorphous context was better for the effort. As Rogers (1980) would say (in Proposition 5): "Any experience which is inconsistent with the organization or structure of self may be perceived as a threat, and the more of these perceptions there are, the more rigidly the self-structure is organized to maintain itself" (p. 218). Or, as the organizer later put it, "I grabbed at something to calm me down."

ORGANIZING SITUATIONS AND THEIR DOMINANT PERSONALITY DEMANDS

It might be helpful here to look at the variety of situations in which organizers eventually find themselves. While the variations on each category are endless (the social, informal party may be used for fundraising when a valued financial contact unexpectedly appears, day-to-day routines may be upset by anything from a fire to a firing), the typology in Table 3.1 is based on interviews with experienced organizers regarding their most common situations, the kind that you inevitably will be called on to respond to, whether you like it or not. In general, they range from the informal and social (with an emphasis on interpersonal, process skills) to planning activities, with their greater demands for intellectual, task-oriented abilities. Each naturally carries certain types of personal difficulty to match its strengths.

The dominant positive and negative characteristics in these organizing situations were selected by organizers in an informal survey over a 2-year period. (Done yearly since then, the results have not varied in more than 30 years.) They are meant not to be exclusive but to serve as aids in helping organizers better examine their own personal effectiveness throughout the organizing situations in which they will find themselves.

In general, people identify themselves in either the more personal, intuitively demanding situations (informal parties, new meetings, interpersonal routines), as Kay does, or the more intellectually precise situations (office routines, formal meetings, ongoing group activity), as Ellis does.[6] This is consistent with industrial psychologists' findings on other people's problem-solving abilities, either task or process oriented. These situations are as follows:

- *Informal gathering:* Parties, social events, late-night bar conversations after a meeting; these events are common to community development, social action, and labor organizing strategies. People want to know with whom they are working, at least a little, and task-oriented, intellectually intense organizers like Ellis most frequently have difficulty here as they feel there's nothing worth talking about, it wastes valuable time, and so forth. Others use this time quite profitably—and can have fun in the bargain!
- *New meeting of an open-ended group:* Most common in community development strategies, but always part of any unfolding strategy or campaign, new meetings are a time when people explore common problems, present themselves to the group, check out who is in attendance, and generally talk a lot. They want to leave with some sense of purpose and not be either too overwhelmed by the tasks ahead or distrustful of the group's approach. An intense, outcome-focused organizer can often push the group too fast or overwhelm them with detail; others, who are more process oriented, may forget to show any results from the meeting. But if you establish a modest goal beforehand and use helpful structural reminders to allow the group to cohere (have a coffee break, include notes

Table 3.1   Organizing Situations and Their Dominant Personality Demands

High Process Oriented (Personal)		More Intuitive	More Intellectual	High Task Oriented (Impersonal)	
Informal party	*New meeting (informal group)*	*Individual day-to-day work*	*Formal gathering (competing reference groups)*	*Ongoing planning group*	*Militant demonstration*
Most Common Personal Strength in Above Settings					
Sociable, cooperative, talkative, good-natured, efficient	A. *Office routine:* Tidy, persevering	Ideological clarity, formal poise		Technical, analytical expertise	Adventurous, headstrong
	B. *Interpersonal routine:* Responsible, personal, verbally clear				
Most Common Personal Difficulties in Above Settings					
Avoidance of personal engagement	Pushes group too fast, overloads content	A. Sloppy, forgetful, inefficient	Role conflicts, role strain	Overfocused, overidentification within group	Fear of conflict, overreaction to conflict (heightened anger)
Awkwardness, discomfort in nonintellectual tasks	Overstates future outcomes	B. Forgetful, inefficient in conversation, too much formality/ informality			

to yourself on your copy of the agenda about relaxing), new meetings end up being less anxiety provoking than often expected.

- *Day-to-day office routine:* No organized group does anything if it doesn't maintain its operations. Everyone knows that. However, knowing that and becoming efficient are two very different things for organizers who prefer a little more personal contact or excitement every day. Others, like Jill, perform extremely well here and are valuable in their ability to pay the bills on time, keep prompt schedules, and so on. One common technique for those seeking to become more efficient is to ask their tidier friends for helpful hints. (This has been an area of great difficulty for me all my life. By taking some concrete hints from colleagues on how to use lists, how to build up an easy filing system, and so on, I've made some progress over the years. Some.)

- *Interpersonal routines:* These are all the phone calls, brief chats, short lunches, and street raps that an organizer engages in every day of the week to follow up with individuals. They call for some efficient skills in one's office work but are intuitively demanding as well. Some organizers hate the phone or prefer political discussions to personal matters; they may end up being too brusque. Others, in their anxiety to please, may have a delightful conversation, only later realizing they forgot the reason they called in the first place. Either case demands you follow two simple rules: (a) Remember why you contacted the person by writing it down somewhere (the act of writing increases retentiveness). (b) Remember that people are human, and allow for personal issues to be raised without viewing it as diversionary (if you have to, write that down, too!). The use of tactical self-awareness is important here, where the lack of formalized meetings or events minimizes the use of other, more structural supports.

- *Formal gathering (competing or conflicting reference groups):* These are formal, occasional events in one's work—cocktail parties before important conventions or conferences, obligatory organizational functions (forums, conferences), and coalitions. They most often involve social action and social planning strategies and create role strain because their surface functions and their underlying purposes may be either unclear or problematic. (Two competing groups may be equally attractive in meetings. How do you decide?) Those who are uncomfortable with such political ambiguity and/or uncertain how they and their organizations fit in with such situations have difficulty here. Only by being thoroughly prepared, especially about one's own positions, can an organizer expect to be comfortable.

- *Ongoing planning group:* Once an organization has established itself (especially in social planning and community development strategies), ongoing group meetings are necessary to coordinate work, share information, and analyze progress. Real intellectual analysis may matter here, where someone like Ellis can shine. What can develop, however, are common forms of goal displacement; one must stay attuned to other, less visible concerns or face the possibility of overspecialization and ignorance about newly developing organizational or community issues. Making certain that someone is responsible for maintaining and extending the group's outreach work is an obvious structural solution, but individuals over time can also train themselves to be more intuitively responsive to new issues as they develop.

- *Militant demonstration:* Used in community development, social action, and labor organizing strategies, militant actions can be exciting and effective galvanizers to even greater commitment and success. For those who shy away from conflict, they also can be frightening experiences. I have also seen people become too excited, using the emotionally charged event to ventilate an unrelated, deep anger. As such events are so public, it is important that organizers and their coworkers select their roles carefully, allowing more verbally confident and gregarious types to perform the publicly expressive roles while others handle the demonstration's order and safety. This minimizes both personal difficulties and potentially embarrassing public miscues.

THE STEPS TOWARD DEVELOPING TACTICAL SELF-AWARENESS

By identifying one's personal comfort in the above organizing situations, the organizer can begin to structure ways to improve performance in areas of lesser effectiveness while maintaining strengths. The structure you develop should emphasize two operational principles:

1. **Be modest in your personal goals.** Everyone knows you're supposed to work with groups in a way that does not build false expectations, the type that either can never be met or are so grandiose that solid achievements appear worthless. And so it is with oneself. You haven't efficiently organized the office's routines over the past month? Instead of berating yourself over the failure, start organizing your appointment book for the next week. By being modest, you have a chance at success that can spur you on to even larger tasks. (If you like, think of this process as community development for one!)

2. **Actively use your personal strengths to work on areas of difficulty.** No person is exclusively process or task oriented, and few situations are, either. You're uncomfortable at parties? Why not tend bar or help serve food? This more focused task will fit your own personal makeup better and creates enough work to help you relax a bit. One can reverse the content if the difficult situation relates to task-oriented groups. By being both modest and aware of how to use your strengths in every situation, you can and will effect personal change.

An organizer can then begin using the organizing process in ways that help him or her lessen particular errors of the past. Increased effectiveness, rather than being viewed as art or just experience, is respected as a deepened ability to combine one's intuitive and intellectual skills in ways that help differentiate the political and personal elements of the organizing process.

A brief example of this process would probably look like the following:

- As a good organizer, you make some tactical mistakes (and good organizers are *always* making mistakes) at some organizing event. (Choose your most challenging type of event from Table 3.1.)
- Recognizing your mistakes, you go home and for the rest of the evening berate yourself for being such a colossal failure.

- After a while, fatigue sets in and some of the self-hatred instilled by "great organizer" theories begins to wear off. The tactically self-aware practitioner can now use this slight distance from the situation to analyze what happened. Ask yourself the following questions:

  - Where and when was I effective?
  - When did people respond well, and when did I get results?
  - What was I doing, specifically, that seemed to excite or irritate people?
  - Was the problem in my implementation, or were there hidden agendas floating around?

- As you explore these answers through both introspection and later talks with others, a sifting process occurs, one that allows you to recognize strategic mistakes, others' hang-ups, and your own personal inflexibility.
- Away from the context of the actual work, you, a tactically self-aware organizer, begin to integrate new elements into your behavior, allowing yourself to have a few structural supports in future situations so that overall tactical effectiveness is maintained.

Or, as Rogers (1980) put it in more theoretical language (Proposition 6):

Under certain conditions, involving primarily complete absence of any threat to the self-structure, experiences which are inconsistent with it may be perceived and examined and the structure of the self revised to assimilate and include such experiences. (pp. 67–68)

**REFLECTIVE ACTIVITY FOR EDUCATIONAL
"POLICY 2.1.1: BUILDING TACTICAL
"SELF-AWARENESS**

Choose an event that had success and struggles for you, too:

_____

_____

What worked well for you?

_____

_____

What did not go as well?

_____

_____

On reflection, which part of the problem related to your tactical inflexibility?

_____

_____

Is there a way you can use your tactical strengths as a support within this situation?

_____

_____

What other preplanning supports can you use with others in the future?

_____

_____

Although Rogers (1980) was discussing therapeutic issues, the process related to tactical self-awareness isn't really much different. Such introspection and reflective work may not be easy, but one's willingness both to engage in personal introspection and to use tactical supports in personally challenging organizing situations can help move one, over time, from a mechanistic application of tactics to a more fluid use of self in any variety of strategic contexts. Thus, the next time a similar situation occurs, you free yourself from personally discomforting tasks by taking different assignments—or, if that's not possible, giving yourself structural cues to ease the situation (notes on your agenda, etc.).

There always will be moments of greater and lesser success, of course, but the application of tactical self-awareness over time uses experience as a tool for ongoing learning and not as a static "artistic" place where old organizers someday arrive by accident. This is why task-oriented organizers can grow to work well with individuals and highly process-oriented caseworkers can learn to handle large political groups. Neither type of individual has been born with certain irrevocable work styles. Each practitioner is made, again and again, by both contextual and environmental demands and his or her willingness to engage personally in further understanding those demands as they change.

With experience, you can extend your use of this introspective tool beyond your own personal growth and increased tactical effectiveness. Looking at yourself means increasing your willingness to look at others, too, and helping judge their personal fit in different situations. Nancy Wehle's recollection in *The Other Side of Organizing* (Burghardt, 1982) is still apt today. An organizer doing liaison work in the Bronx, she recalled the following example:

> I dislike confrontation. I link it to my own background that emphasized the virtues of stoicism, since confrontation involves a show of emotion, anger. I end up being very uncomfortable, even though I know confrontation is needed, and end up putting off any display until it's almost too late.
>
> However, looking at the issue of confrontation from another perspective (otherwise known as turning a sow's ear into a silk purse), I know there are people who feel the same way I do. I've been able to connect up to their hesitancy in challenging authority. An example occurred at a senior citizen center that was in jeopardy. Their funding was about to be terminated and they had gone the route of appeals and appointments and meetings. While talking to the director of the center, I suggested picketing and a demo at downtown City Hall, if all else failed. The director became hesitant and uptight. I knew what she was talking about when she said that wasn't her style. I was able to be supportive, understanding my own discomfort in those situations. Instead, we talked about someone else taking main responsibility and she staying in the background. She agreed, and the protest march was organized successfully. (pp. 118–119)

A less experienced organizer in the same situation would probably have ended up straining relations with the director and potentially jeopardizing the strategic demands of the center. After all, the ABCs of organizing are clear regarding militancy: If all other means have been tried and have failed, of course you have a legitimate right to use it! As few politicians want to be seen openly disagreeing with a group of seniors, this joint use of militancy and rightful need might go far in saving the center.

In this case, Wehle saw through the prism of her own personal struggles with militancy to the director's real issue—*she didn't oppose staging a protest as long as she didn't have to be in it.* This personal recognition of a politically necessary tactic had not always been immediately obvious. However, by being able to identify the director's statements with her own discomfort with militancy, Wehle supportively helped the director distinguish tactically between her own personal needs and those of the center. No arguments on the legitimacy of protest, the just needs of the seniors, or anything else would have worked as well. Indeed, as the director generally agreed with those arguments, any discussion of them would have distracted her from her personal difficulties.

Wehle's use of tactical self-awareness avoided such barriers. *A sweet strategic irony had occurred—the one that underlies the effective use of tactical self-awareness in all situations: She had admitted to personal limits and allowed for political growth at the same time.*

CONCLUSION

Community assessments serve multiple purposes for any social work agency or grassroots campaign. As such, they are a systematic undertaking with great strategic value in helping one learn the way a community perceives a problem, what the contours of the problem are, and how to begin addressing the issue. This is also the initial level of engagement by which a practitioner begins to build trust, demonstrate respect, and frame the role he or she will be playing in the long work ahead.

As a fundamental task of engagement, such assessments also reveal a macro practitioner's degree of comfort in approaching this work: sifting data as opposed to talking with community members, analyzing a report or facilitating a focus group. Developing your tactical self-awareness on the work's mix of "process" and "task" functions can only strengthen how well that trust is built as well as how thorough and accurate your information gathered is.

It's important to reiterate that tactical self-awareness is not a panacea that can correct for the political limits of a diminished resource base or lack of wide-scale progressive social movements. Its application, however, is designed for any period of history, not just ones of seeming passivity or intense activism. With this recognized, tactical self-awareness can have one final underlying benefit. Starting with community assessment, by understanding and engaging with the entire organizing process, you not only deepen the practice experience but also lessen the likelihood of unnecessary exhaustion. As we will see in Chapters 8, 12, and 13, this self-reflective work helps prepare you to more effectively adapt to new roles, situational demands, and expectations as your career advances. Experience no longer burns you out over the years but, instead, makes you better able to deal with the shifting tides of all macro practice work. After all, in seeking to change the world, what can be wrong with changing ourselves along the way?

THE COMMUNITY TOOLBOX

The Community Toolbox website has a number of rich tools related to community assessments that a practitioner can take advantage of. See http://ctb.ku.edu/en/tablecontents/chapter_1003.htm.

Assessing Community Needs and Resources

REFERENCES

Abramovitz, M. (1999). *Regulating the lives of women: Social welfare policy from colonial times to the present*. Cambridge, MA: South End Press.

Alinsky, S. (1989a). *Reveille for radicals*. New York: Knopf Doubleday.

Alinsky, S. (1989b). *Rules for radicals*. New York: Vintage.

Anton, A., Fisk, M., & Holmstrom, N. (2000). *Not for sale: In defense of public goods*. New York: Westview.

Blau, J., & Abramovitz, M. (2007). *The dynamics of social welfare policy*. New York: Oxford University Press.

Burghardt, S. (1982). *The other side of organizing*. Cambridge, MA: Schenkman.

Cohen, B. (2002). *Community food security assessment toolkit* (Report prepared by IQ Solutions for the Economic Research Service Food Assistance and Nutrition Program). New Brunswick, NJ: Rutgers University.

DeFilippis, J., & Saegert, S. (Eds.). (2007). *The community development reader.* New York: Routledge.

Dombroski, T. (2000). *Creative problem solving: The door to individual success and change.* Bloomington, IN: iUniverse.

Esri. (n.d.). *What is GIS?* Retrieved from http://www.esri.com/what-is-gis/index.html

Fellin, P. (2000). *The community and the social worker.* Pacific Grove, CA: Brooks/Cole.

Fisher, R., & Karger, H. (1996). *Social work and community in a private world: Getting out in public.* New York: Addison-Wesley.

Freire, P. (2000). *Pedagogy of the oppressed.* New York: Continuum.

Glasser, P., Sarri, R., Sundel, M., & Vinter, R. (1986). *Individual change in small groups* (2nd ed.). New York: Free Press.

Jansson, B. (2008). *The reluctant welfare state: Engaging history to advance social work practice in contemporary society* (6th ed.). Pacific Grove, CA: Brooks/Cole.

Maguire, L. (2001). *Clinical social work: Beyond generalist practice with individuals, groups, and families.* New York: Wadsworth.

Middleman, R., & Wood, G. (1989). *The structural approach to direct practice in social work: A textbook for students and front-line practitioners.* New York: Columbia University Press.

National Association of Social Workers. (2009). *President's initiative: Institutional racism and the social work profession: A call to action.* Washington, DC: Author.

National Urban League. (2009). *The state of Black America 2009: Message to the president.* New York: Author.

Perlman, H. H. (1989). *Looking back to look ahead.* Chicago: University of Chicago Press.

Putnam, R. (1994). *Bowling alone: The collapse and revival of American community.* New York: Simon & Schuster.

Reisch, M., & Andrews, J. (2002). *The road not taken: A history of radical social work in the United States.* New York: Brunner-Routledge.

Rogers, C. (1980). *A way of being.* Boston: Mariner Books.

Rothman, J. (2008). *Strategies of community intervention.* Peosta, IA: Eddie Bowers.

Saleebey, D. (2008). *Human behavior and social environments: A biopsychosocial approach.* New York: Columbia University Press.

Salmon, R., & Kurland, R. (1995). *Group work practice in a troubled society.* Binghamton, NY: Haworth.

Shlay, A. B., & Whitman, G. (2006). *Research for democracy: Linking community organizing and research to leverage blight policy.* Paper presented at the annual meeting of the American Sociological Association, San Francisco. Available from http://www.allacademic.com/

Shriever, J. (2003). *Human behavior and the social environment: Shifting paradigms in essential knowledge for social work practice* (3rd ed.). London: Allyn & Bacon.

Warren, R. (1987). *The community in America.* New York: University Press of America.

Winters, L., & DeBose, H. (2002). *New faces in changing America: Multiracial identity in the 21st century.* Thousand Oaks, CA: Sage.

NOTES

1. Since writing this in the early 1980s, I have learned that similar management tools have been developed and are used inside many corporate and nonprofit offices to help teams better problem-solve and communicate together. They include the DISC problem-solving series and Myers-Briggs personality assessments (Dombroski, 2000).

2. With this noted, there is no suggestion that one's personality is unchangeable—in fact, the opposite is true. As one lives through certain situations, one's personality can and will change, as will the situations themselves. It is thus necessary to be that much more aware of these changes as they occur in oneself and in others so that one can maximize *ongoing* strategic effectiveness.

3. With the exception of number 7, these points relate to personal characteristics. Point number 7, however, is a political prescription ideologically bound to a form of liberalism other organizers reject, and it should be viewed as being as politically motivated toward a particular ideology as any other political statement.

4. I am convinced that a lack of personal awareness about one's effectiveness in varying situations is a major reason why so many organizers burn out in their late 20s. Having denied or felt they had to deny personal discomfort with any number of tasks, they come to realize that the immediate payoffs in such work don't seem worth all the personal strain and opt for an entirely different line of work.

5. This is consistent with the previously mentioned DISC Profiles, especially "Drivers" and "Calculators."

6. Interestingly enough, people who fell into either primary category frequently felt comfortable in demonstrations. However, on closer examination, their particular comfort depended on the function they selected to perform at the big event. Process-oriented people enjoyed engaging others in protest, speaking, and so forth, while others enjoyed maintaining the demonstration's safety and order (serving as marshals, being in charge of organizing speakers, etc.). The varied task and process functions of large-scale demonstrations seem to allow room for just about everybody . . . as long as they approve of the use of protest in the first place!

CHAPTER 4

The Unconscious in Organizing

The Struggle to Build Authentic Relationships in Community Interventions

---

DIGGING DEEP

Ellis stood behind Kay in the bodega directly across from the school as she ordered for them both. The older Latino man behind the counter smiled as he handed her a plastic bag bulging with two full plates of *arroz con pollo,* complete with red beans and a few sweet *platanos.* Kay had ordered the meal with a perfect Spanish accent obtained during her 2 years of Peace Corps work in Honduras.

"Gracias, señor!" Kay smiled, continuing in Spanish. "Looks great!" She paused, then asked him directly, "Do you get many kids in here after school? They must be hungry!"

"Kids always hungry. Good thing for me they are!"

"What's the busiest time for you with them?"

He paused, looking carefully at her. Kay simply smiled, her face open. Suddenly uncomfortable, Ellis headed for the door. "I'm asking 'cause we're trying to learn about how young people are doing around here. We're social workers." Ellis stood in the doorway, trying not to glare at her.

"They're mostly good kids, the ones in school. It's the ones that aren't who cause the problems. Drugs an' all. But they sell their stuff two blocks over. Cops keep 'em away from the school."

"So the kids from school do come in. Even later in the day?" Kay was interested in who came in from the after-school program.

(Continued)

(Continued)

"Sure. Half-hour before school starts, kids buyin' cakes and coffee. Lunchtime, chips and soda. Some of the kids buyin' beef jerky late in the day before they head home." He paused as he gave her change for their meals, switching to English for the first time. "All them's good kids."

Kay thanked him and walked out to join Ellis, who was sitting on a nearby bench. "You think he cares that we're social workers, Kay?" He dug into a piece of chicken, his tone less defensive. "You sure do have the gift of gab."

"So I like people. Can't hurt, can it? I mean, the more people we know and know us, the more we might learn." She bit into a fried *platano*.

"Good information isn't just from data. It's from people, too. Speaking with everyday folks shows respect. Working in Honduras, I came to believe in *con la gente,* not *por la gente . . . with* the people, not *for* them."

Ellis looked at her, quietly impressed. They ate in silence the rest of the meal, sharing the pile of thick napkins at the bottom of the bag.

A half-hour later, after a quick check of IDs and a mention of why they were there, a school security guard was escorting them to the basement where the after-school program was held. Ellis and Kay knew they had a full afternoon ahead of them, with two focus groups of teachers and young people, as well as one-on-one interviews with the director and assistant director. Kay's supervisor had called the director, an old friend, who graciously made the arrangements. She whispered in Ellis's ear how excited she was to be doing this, unable to contain the wide grin on her face. While less openly enthusiastic, he nodded in agreement.

The guard looked back at them as she walked down the stairs. "You two are in luck today. The after-school corporation's CEO dropped in, so you'll have a chance to talk with her, too. She oversees the entire city!"

Kay's eyes widened for a second, and she quickly looked at her companion as they walked into the small office. Kay went in first; the two had agreed beforehand that she would be the primary questioner with the director while Ellis transcribed, and they would reverse roles for the focus group. Two women—a younger African American woman with dreadlocks tightly wound in a brightly colored scarf that matched the print of her dress and an older White woman wearing an impeccably tailored Donna Karan business suit—were standing to greet them.

After brief introductions, they promptly settled around a small blue-and-white Formica table. "So, fire away!" The young director, Dawn Ashley, looked at Kay. "Luckily, Mrs. Anderson has about 20 minutes, so she agreed to answer any questions about the origins of the program. She's the actual founder."

Kay looked blankly at the director, then Ellis, then Mrs. Anderson. "Mrs. Anderson? Um, thank you for taking the time for us. I mean, I know you must be busy, and our course assignment can't be that important with all you have to do. I mean, we really appreciate it. Um, it's a surprise that you have the time, so we won't take long . . . um."

Without missing a beat, Ellis took up the questioning. "Mrs. Anderson, could you tell us the specifics of when and why you started this program?" Unlike most of his questions directed at Kay, his tone here was calm, his manner composed. "You have programs here in Central Harlem and, among others, one on the Upper East Side. Of course, local community board data show dropout rates are 45% in Central Harlem, yet only 26% downtown. Does this lead to you running each program differently?"

Mrs. Anderson looked momentarily thrown off guard as she took in the depth of his question, but then she relaxed. Her posture grew more erect as she began to respond, using other data as well. Soon, she and Ellis were deep in conversation. Kay picked up Ellis's pen and notepad and began to write. Except for goodbyes, she didn't say another word throughout the interview.

At the end, Ms. Ashley shook Kay's hand, then warmed as she looked at Ellis. "Ellis, Mrs. Anderson was so impressed with how you handled yourself! You came prepared with data that made us both think, but you didn't throw bombshells. Having a calm tone with those rough statistics made a big difference in getting us to hear you, believe me. Maybe there *are* some disparities between our program and those downtown. Thank you!" Ellis mumbled a brief thank you in return, suddenly shy at her affirmation.

Because their interview ran over, the two graduate students had no time to debrief about what had happened to Kay. Working together in the next focus group with the young adults who made up the after-school mentors and assistants, Kay and Ellis's questions were answered with ease and honesty by the motivated young men and women in the room. They clearly loved the program and its potential.

One of their notebooks was full as they headed into the room for the last group interview. Seven students, all between the ages of 13 and 17, were sitting there, laughing, as one of them—a tall, dark-skinned African American boy with a hoodie covering his head—regaled them with some story of a hallway incident earlier in the day. Seeing Ellis and Kay walk in, he yelled, "Hey look, y'all, we got us a salt-and-pepper team to talk to!" The group laughed in unison as the two sat down in front of them.

A young Latina with large gold hoop earrings and tiger-skin boots spoke up. "More like salt and oregano!" Ellis quickly blushed at the mention of his light mocha skin tone. He looked down at his notebook, suddenly tongue-tied.

Kay, looking around at the group, started to laugh as well. Her eyes took in the entire multiracial, multihued group sitting in the first two rows of the classroom. "Hey, if you ask me, we got a whole set of herbs here: pepper, oregano, garlic, cinnamon, and me, the salt." She laughed

(Continued)

(Continued)

again. "Not much green, though. No basil at all." The group energy immediately shifted toward Kay and her light touch.

"So before we begin, could we make a circle? I worked in Honduras for 2 years, and people in the villages, when they met, sat together where everyone could see each other, young and old." She smiled again. "I guess Ellis and I are the old folks, right? But that circle means we're sharing a little bit better, okay?" Without a moment's hesitation, the young people broke the rigid classroom setting into a large circle.

Kay turned to Ellis, who quickly whispered in her ear, "That was great, Kay, for real. I'll be right back. Need a bathroom break. Don't wait for me." Ellis quickly exited the room. He returned 45 minutes later. His one contribution was to profusely thank the group for their time.

The two walked quietly to the subway, both more tired than they'd realized they would be. A small diner next to the subway station flashed its "Hot Coffee" sign in neon red and blue as they approached. Ellis looked at Kay and quickly asked if she'd like a cup so they could debrief.

They both waited for the coffee to arrive, agreeing to share a plate of french fries as well. Stirring his coffee slowly so none slopped over into the saucer, Ellis looked at Kay as if for the first time. "Well, I think we got a lot of good material from the interviews, but the truth is, I gotta say, you were great. So open with the guy who owned the bodega, and, man, you really can relate to kids." He took a long gulp of coffee. "And you didn't back off at all when those kids started in!" He shook his head, a wistful look on his face. "I mean, you are *with* those kids, they could tell." He paused only for a second. "So what happened with that CEO lady? She was the person I figured you'd be best with!"

Kay looked embarrassed. "Oh, man, that was so bad!" She drank her entire cup before speaking. "I love kids, and I can totally relate to people who run bodegas and work in shops. You know, the little people. But as soon as I get near someone in an expensive suit, I freeze. Clam up. Put me in a classroom with kids, and I can do anything. Put me in a boardroom, and I can barely remember my name." She started in on her second cup of coffee.

Ellis looked at her, that wistful smile back on his face. "It's so weird, Kay. I could have gone and worked in a boardroom, given my fancy Ivy League credentials. But I saw how rigged this system is for most kids of color, and I knew what I wanted to do was work with them. I want to do that more than anything in the world!" He looked glumly at the black-and-white tile floor of the diner as if he'd lost something that couldn't be found. "And as soon as I get near them, I freeze. What the hell is that about? How come the very people I care about the most make me so uneasy, while Mrs. Anderson's a breeze?"

"Life sure is complicated." They both laughed, signaling for another plate of fries. They stayed in the diner, talking, until it closed 3 hours later.

Educational Policy 2.1.7—Apply knowledge of human behavior and the social environment. *This chapter demonstrates the core competency for how macro practitioners "are knowledgeable about human behavior across the life course ... and the ways social systems promote or deter people in maintaining or achieving health and well-being." By looking at practitioner dynamics, the chapter further demonstrates how social workers can "utilize conceptual frameworks to guide the processes of assessment, intervention, and evaluation ... [as they] apply knowledge to understand person and environment."*

COMMUNITY ENGAGEMENT BEGINS WITH YOU: AN ORGANIZER BUILDS RELATIONSHIPS THROUGH THE "LITTLE THINGS" TO MAKE "BIG THINGS" POSSIBLE

Initiating a community assessment, as Kay and Ellis are, is a clear way to start developing a program or project. This assessment is the opening tactic of an organizer's engagement with a community. It is, however, only the scaffolding on which engagement is constructed. In reality, it truly commences through the ways a community practitioner conducts the assessment itself: how he or she relates with others, to whom he or she chooses to listen, the way others are made to feel more or less a part of the tactic at hand, whether in the early stages of assessment or at a campaign's targeted conclusion (a rally, conference, or program opening). In short, for community practitioners committed to transformation, how we work matters as much as what we work on.

The awareness that macro practice's inter- and intrapersonal process is indeed political grew out of one of the greatest insights of the Brazilian educator Paulo Freire (2000). Working with Brazilian peasants on literacy, he came to understand that he and his fellow teachers of literacy were dispensing far more than the alphabet as they went about their work.

> A careful analysis of the teacher-student relationship ... reveals its fundamentally *narrative* character ... [which] involves a narrating subject (the teacher) and patient, listening objects (the students). ...
>
> The outstanding characteristic of this narrative education, then, is the sonority [sound] of words, not their transforming power. ...
>
> Narration ... leads the students to memorize mechanically the narrated content. Worse yet, it turns them into "containers," into "receptacles" to be "filled" by the teacher. ...
>
> This is the "banking" concept of education. (p. 71)

As an alternative, Freire (2000) goes on to write:

But the humanist, revolutionary educator cannot wait [for transformative struggle to start from this didactic, top-down narrative]. . . . From the outset, her efforts must coincide with those of the students to engage in critical thinking and the quest for mutual humanization. His efforts must be imbued with a profound trust in people and their creative power. (p. 75)

Through the investigation of his own literacy work, Freire had learned that simply teaching people to read and write did little to transform their lives if the way literacy was taught replicated the same dynamics of coercion, oppression, and marginality under which poor people already lived. Instead, he wrote that a different level of *interpersonal engagement* between teacher and student based on mutual trust in their capacity to learn and work together was the only way to foster an alternative to the marginalization that other teaching interventions replicated. This profound insight applies no less to community organizing, where people are working together to improve the conditions of a particular community and its members.

To apply Freire's insight to community practice means that every tactic we choose has transformative possibilities among the people with whom we work. It also means that every tactic has the potential to have the sound of social justice, equality, and anti-oppression without fostering it. As we can see with Kay and Ellis, this work begins as soon as one enters a community to begin a preliminary assessment: Talks with a bodega owner, a program director and her boss, mentors, and students are all part of some narrative as well. Is it a narrative of openness and opportunity, of genuine engagement with others—*con la gente*—or a series of tasks designed to get the job done—*por la gente*—that has the sound of engagement without the deeper meaning? How well one comes to assess one's own and others' personal development to answer such a question positively is a profound and lasting dimension to every form of professional practice.

Most discussions of community engagement begin with the work of framing the issue at hand. As we saw in the previous chapter, Ellis, Kay, Esperanza, and Jill were doing just that as they sought to narrow the scope of their inquiry to something meaningful and manageable. All groups do this. What's also at play here, however, is not only the choice of issues in which to engage but how the organizers of that engagement go about building relationships with others: whom they seek out, the level of respect shown in the conversations, the comfort they exhibit in their presence. *In short, the way organizers conduct themselves with others builds the transformative narrative of the future engagement they are seeking . . . or does not.*

REFLECTIVE QUESTIONS

Explore a recent assessment and/or other activity by your campaign or agency. In what ways were the ideas and issues from the community sought out? Did their ideas influence for the better in some concrete ways the conclusions of that assessment? Or was the assessment designed simply to confirm what the leadership was already doing?

THE STRATEGIC NARRATIVE OF "LITTLE THINGS"

As we see from the above case example, at different times both Kay and Ellis exhibited a series of seemingly little things that helped them begin to establish positive and powerful relationships with key actors important to their assessment. (We will return to their other, obviously less effective dynamics in the latter sections of this chapter.) These little things are part of any community practitioner's growing effectiveness in community work.

Kay demonstrated respect for information gathered from community people who were without visible status, power, or influence. Her openness with the small bodega owner, starting with her ability to speak his first language, demonstrated a stance of sincerity toward those who lived and worked in the community. If consistently practiced over time, these small street engagements (whether at a bodega, beauty salon, barber shop, security guards' front desk, or playground) signify to residents that an outside community practitioner genuinely has their interests at heart. It is in this way that a new organizer or macro practitioner achieves Erlich and Rivera's (1998) dictum that outside organizers must seek out and learn from the members of the community first and foremost.

Ellis interviewed professionals with directness and clarity, using his relaxed manner and data to demonstrate reasons for otherwise too-busy professionals to take their project seriously. Just as Kay demonstrated respect for the bodega owner, Ellis did the same for the professionals they would need to work with. He did so with thorough preparation so that the limited time he had with executives would not be spent on generalities requiring later follow-up that might not be given. The bedrock of trust in professional relationships is reliable, accurate, and usable information that community practitioners have gathered to show others there is a reason to develop the relationship further. As we will see in Chapter 10, two of the greatest constraints an agency executive has are too little time and too many disparate sources of information and influence vying for his or her attention (Bennis, 2009; Senge, 1994). By laying down a foundation of substance at the early stages of his relationship with the after-school leaders, Ellis established reasons for them to stay connected with him, should the need arise. Built over time, this kind of reliability and directness becomes invaluable in achieving larger goals of community engagement in any campaign a practitioner might undertake.

Kay met the young people where they were, on their terms, and in ways that made them comfortable without surrendering her own interests. Teenagers are at a developmental stage where their testing of adults is both an aggravation and a necessity. Trying on adult behaviors and ideas isn't easy; the back and forth between childishness and mature reasoning is as aggravating for those trying out the behaviors as for those on the receiving end of these pogo-stick–like actions. It could not be otherwise, for they need to learn which roles and responsibilities fit them best. How adults respond to them helps provide some of the answers to these developmental tasks. As with other marginalized groups (Hefner, 1998), learning who responds well and who runs for cover goes a long way in helping them determine where they belong in the world the organizer is seeking to change.

Kay's ability to laugh at the teens' street humor and banter with them signaled her comfort with their presence that transcended, at least momentarily, any doubts about her willingness to see them on their terms. As we saw from the previous chapter, Kay is a process person, one comfortable in social situations and undefined professional roles. This comfort allows her to adapt to their approach to her in ways that signify her trust, which Freire (2000) identified as critical to this kind of work: "A real humanist can be identified more by his [or her] trust in the people, which engages him [or her] in their struggle, than by a thousand actions in their favor without that trust" (p. 60).

Bantering about skin color at the beginning of a focus group may seem trivial and is hardly a mark of the kinds of external struggle found in organizing campaigns.[1] It is, nevertheless, a significant little thing. As such, it is a passing moment fraught with potential meaning because it signifies young people's attempt to define themselves in relationship to one another and to those adults who have just entered their lives. While minor, it carries an implicit challenge to the new organizers in the room to accept or not accept such social bantering as *part of who they are, not as something to be changed.* Whether you're reacting to a young person's call-out or an older community person's disagreement on tactical choices ("You say we need to focus on the landlord, but I say it's sanitation not picking up garbage that's the problem."), how you genuinely respond to that challenge will go a long way in building sustainable and transformative change in the community work you and community members are undertaking.

By neither backing off from the teens' racial humor nor being thrown by it, Kay signaled that she accepted them on their terms. Because she did not immediately assert her defined role as focus group leader sent by the director to meet with them, she demonstrated the respect and trust Freire (2000) spoke of above as fundamental to beginning to develop a new relationship between those helping and those being helped. That said, by beginning with respect, she did not cede her responsibilities of running the group but instead challenged the young people to immediately reconvene in a new seating arrangement she had learned from a Honduran village council.

To combine showing immediate respect for the people you work with and weathering a challenge to rethink what you will all do together is a powerful task that confronts every macro practitioner. To hear and respect disagreement without simply capitulating to where the people are takes significant practice in community work. Kay, with the young people, and Ellis, with the directors, showed the right mix of openness and chutzpah not only to get the answers they needed but also to give them the confidence to respect others across from them *and* push their agenda. To be only where the people are gives them nothing; after all, what good is an organizer if it's all the same conversation? *An effective organizer, I would argue, is where the people are, plus one. Meeting them where they are signifies respect for them and what they are doing and thinking; "plus one" includes the challenge to consider ways to go beyond that.* And why not? Community organizers want to change the world, and if that doesn't take chutzpah in the 21st century, what does (Senge, 1994; Senge, Scharmer, Jaworski, & Flowers, 2005)?

Why Little Things Mean a Lot

This attention to seemingly minor moments in the early engagement of an organizer with a community group may seem overdone, but it is not. History shows us that a community organizer and the group he or she is working with, when they lack power, may be perceived as not very important as they try to change the world. That initial moxie or chutzpah—seen by some as obnoxious and by others as courageous, even perhaps heroic—therefore also takes psychological tenacity and unyielding effort when there is little success on the horizon. Courageously staying the course when one's power over others is limited is admirable. But what happens when you achieve a taste of power, and suddenly jobs, resources, and access are part of your domain? How do you keep from turning that chutzpah into arrogance, that respect for others into fear of outsiders? How can one remain more like the true revolutionary hero Nelson Mandela and not become like the former Zimbabwean freedom fighter turned dictator Robert Mugabe?

This dilemma, originally analyzed by Robert Michels's (2009) critique of the German Social Democratic Party through his famous phrase "the iron law of oligarchy," has long been discussed in social work classrooms and is part of the critical analysis leveled at human services in radical writings such as INCITE!'s (2007) *The Revolution Will Not Be Funded*. Both works argue that there will be *an inevitable corrupting of progressive people once they attain power*: Open, flexible, and democratic decision making will be lost because the accountability demands of the job and the psychological makeup of the now-power-laden leaders mandate such erosion.

In short, the drive to change the world turns into a drive to control it once organizers have power. But is this kind of psychological and sociological determinism really accurate? Is it inevitable that with power a person loses both his or her commitment to social justice and openness to those with less power (Palmer, 2004)? To understand why this erosion of commitment need not be, let's return to where Ellis and Kay were each less successful in how they conducted their needs assessment. Paradoxically, it is in the examination of their obvious limitations that we will find (in Chapter 11) how a macro practitioner can develop the capacity to remain open and democratic throughout his or her career, no matter the role or level of power. For by exploring the unconscious in organizing, chutzpah meets humility.

Ellis grew so uncomfortable in both the bodega and the classroom that he removed himself. Likewise, Kay grew tongue-tied as soon as she met the founder of the after-school program. Such lapses are all the more ironic when you consider what Kay and Ellis had argued about earlier. Based on their arguments about the community and the social work profession, one would expect Kay to be most comfortable with a professional such as Mrs. Anderson, while Ellis would be most at home with the young folks and community members of Harlem. But a deeper understanding of their own development and the environments that shaped them led to different outcomes—and to the beginning of mutual respect for each other. As Kay and Ellis began to know each other's stories—how their actual behavior was shaped by their environments—the beginning of trust was possible. This insight is crucial for all practitioners, micro and macro, to strive for in their engagement with others.

As suggested in the previous chapter, tactical self-awareness works from the dynamic that often what you do best in other tactical situations may create a limitation (the successful task organizer can't pause for reflection; the process-oriented macro practitioner gets the group mobilized and then can no longer get group members to reach a decision). As we see with Kay's and Ellis's stumbles, often what we care about the most—what we are most passionate about, aspire to, and believe in—can also cause us the greatest discomfort. Mrs. Anderson was the epitome of the successful professional Kay aspired to be, yet in her presence, Kay lost herself. The power of seeing a representation of her own professional aspirations threw her for a loop. Likewise, Ellis's deeply held beliefs on both the oppressive social conditions and inherent potential of young people of color undermined his initial reactions to their offhand banter. His passionate desire to be with them was greater than his ability to relate to them. Just as Kay couldn't speak in front of her perfect role model, Ellis was overwhelmed by the opportunity to work directly with the people who mattered most to him.

These two experiences, written about in similar variations for years in logs of community practitioners starting out in their careers, are both built on the axis of *external power and internalized oppression* that every practitioner confronts throughout his or her career. Thus, macro practitioners, perhaps more than most, are finely attuned to power dynamics— who has power, how it is used or abused, what positions of authority have more power than others. Mrs. Anderson had a formal position of authority and had used her power to create after-school programs. She likewise dressed the part that executives of most large agencies do. Whether she used or abused it was not known to Kay; her powerful presence and the construction of meaning that Kay unconsciously gave Mrs. Anderson caused her own uneasiness. The executive didn't do anything to Kay to cause her discomfort. Something within Kay did that.

Ellis, in a similar manner, grew rigid and uptight in the social banter of the young people he cared about so much. These seven kids of color—obviously successful enough to be in this program and clearly from the exact neighborhood he had advocated for his community assessment group examination—were the embodiment of the people Ellis had hoped to work with in his career. That they represented his ideal did not mean that in the real world they would show up in an idealized state. Walking into the room, they engaged in a little confrontation, a little adolescent humor (they were, after all, teenagers!), a little edgy give and take. That it was extremely unlikely their humor would escalate to rowdiness didn't matter. What caused Ellis to grow uptight in their presence came from within him, not from them.

That these young practitioners had shortcomings is both obvious and commonplace to any kind of professional practice. What's at play here is not just people's inevitable errors in judgment or struggles to work more effectively in all areas; how we set about correcting our limitations matters far more. Are we to use solely our willpower and the same tenacity of effort that gives macro practitioners their chutzpah? Do we try to eliminate our emotional shortcomings on the road to a more perfect practice? Or is there perhaps a different approach that, while more difficult in the short run, can avoid the "inevitable" grasping of power once we become successful?

Freire (2000) again provides us with a different way to approach learning as a lifelong experience: "[Instead of the banking model of teaching], if we see that people, in order to be, are always in the act of becoming, as unfinished, incomplete beings in and with a likewise unfinished reality . . . the unfinished character of [people] and the transformational character of reality recognizes that education be an ongoing activity."

That in order for every person "to be" is through "becoming" is an enormously liberating way for practitioners trying to change the world to see themselves as they go about their work. To affirm our incompletion is to develop a deeper dimension of tactical self-awareness where its practice is in part to keep us open to *embracing what we do not do well* as part of our work in remaining strategically flexible, open to others, and, over time, humble with or without external power. For if we can embrace the unconscious in organizing, we can admit that we are always becoming, too—not only at the start of our careers but throughout. To do that, we can look more closely at the unconscious in organizing.

CLARIFYING MURKY MATERIAL

First, I am using a small fragment of Freud's original conceptual paradigm, obviously as outdated a therapeutic intervention as many now find Marxism to be for working-class political action. That said, while Freud's method of treatment finds few followers in the 21st century, his original analytical insights into the workings of human behavior and personality continue to find widespread support (Danto, 2005). I am discussing the unconscious as one of three inseparably linked elements of one's mental and emotional makeup, the others being the conscious and the preconscious (Freud, 2005). What distinguishes the unconscious, as Freud noted, is its nonverbal and unseen character—that is, "where the relationship between a symbol (work object, person, etc.) and what it represents has been buried and distorted, so that the symbol becomes a disguised and disguising representative of unconscious levels of psychological process" (p. 418).

In concrete terms, this all means that the unconscious is not easy to understand in some reasonable, straightforward way, especially for people who want to get on with the work. Willpower and tenacity of effort are not going to overcome its presence as if it were some gap in our formal knowledge. This kind of undertaking cannot be resolved by studying it, reading a book, or finding a few articles on the Internet. There are few handy reference libraries, blogs, or chat rooms for one's unconscious. Instead, it seems that we each develop, in unendingly creative ways, a set of defenses, which range from projection (used at first by Ellis toward Kay with the bodega owner) to mental lapses (Kay's sudden inarticulateness with Mrs. Anderson) to far more intricate patterns of behavior (such as Ellis's leaving the classroom and returning at the end of the session). Such actions—*often the opposite of one's intentions*—are a key to understanding and becoming comfortable with one's own unconscious in the act of *becoming* . . . and in the genuine acceptance of personal limits to perfection that is a mark of a great practitioner.

When we embrace it, the unconscious becomes an inseparable yet distinct part of the process of our human development. As humans, we seek equilibrium within our environments (Shreiver, 2003). Naturally, then, this process of adaptation will be in constant change, reacting in relation to a person's situational requirements. This means that the unconscious, as an inseparable yet distinct element in this process, will have *varying* degrees of influence on the actual behavior of an individual. In the previous examples, such as Kay's loss of fluency, its influence can be great. At other times, as with Ellis's discomfort in the bodega, other factors (such as the preconscious) will be more dominant; one may not be comfortable in open, social situations due to one's temperament (Rothbart, 2013). The point here is that all these factors play important roles in our daily lives, changing our behavior and, over time, our behavior shaping future unconscious activity as well.

The Politics of the Unconscious

There are also political reasons for being aware of the impact of the unconscious. To do otherwise is to ignore what Baxandall captured in Wilhelm Reich's early writings: brilliant analysis of the social forces affecting personality development. Writing in the early, less controversial part of his career, he stated:

In short, life in capitalism is not only responsible for our beliefs, the ideas of which we are conscious, but also related, unconscious attitudes—for all those spontaneous reactions that proceed from our character structure . . . therefore emotions as well as ideas are socially determined. . . . Every social order creates those character forms which it needs for its preservation. In class society, the ruling class secures its position with the aid of education and the institution of the family, by making its ideology the ruling ideology of all members of all society. *It is not merely a matter of imposing ideologies, attitudes, and concepts. . . . Rather it is a matter of deep-reaching process in each new generation; of the formation of a psychic structure which corresponds to the existing social order in all strata of the population.* (Reich & Baxandall, 1972, p. xviii; italics added)

Why would this process related to character structure be otherwise? For example, many macro and micro practitioners would agree with the notion of the conservative socializing role of schools, where capitalist values of order, time, and obedience are reinforced daily, or in a more personal realm, that the nature of the traditional nuclear family is patriarchal. Such patterns are not accidental but are constructed for the perceived *positive* societal functions they serve: Schools help create a suitably trained and obedient workforce; nuclear family structure reinforces a system of organization that enhances values of hierarchy and patriarchy (Anyon, 1997; Bowles & Gintis, 1976; Corrick, 1998). Such forms of organizations, as repressive as many of us feel they are, are nevertheless helping create a stabilized, acquiescent, and adaptable workforce needed for large capital formation and expansion common to industrialized societies. That such forces were at play in the early 20th century when Reich wrote about them hardly means they are less powerful in the early 21st century.

Thus, it is equally no accident that any work-related process around the struggle for socialization and resocialization at the office or in the factory will parallel the intrapsychic conflict within the individual. In political terms, the class struggle, as Braverman (1971) brilliantly demonstrated, is always carried out both militantly (strikes, sit-downs, etc.) and on a day-to-day, often apparently random level (slowing down productivity levels, trying to "work to rule," never speaking first to supervisors, etc.). And, as Freud (2005) wrote, on the intrapsychic level, a person from childhood onward experiences and reexperiences a daily struggle between sublimated, instinctual impulses and more consciously experienced needs and demands from the larger society. *As in the office, struggle need not be militantly expressed to be actively present.*

Looked at broadly, if the social needs of the society are such that the dominant forms of socially reproduced behaviors will demand more and more sublimation, the ensuing struggle will create more exaggerated forms of defenses, or neurotic symptoms (Horney, 1988). It is thus no accident that the Industrial Revolution, the period of greatest industrial expansion in our history, and the Victorian age, with its exaggerated forms of proper manners (and, not surprisingly, heightened sexual aberrations), occurred simultaneously. The economic need for rapid expansion coincided with the personal need for intense behavioral emotional repression (Lasch, 1989). Today's global world and its economic need for a flexible, transient workforce, and the corresponding lack of organizational loyalty personally expressed by Generation Xers and Millennials, is today's expression of this dynamic (Sujansky & Ferri-Reed, 2009).

Thus, the development of character structure within the individual and the collective patterns of society naturally seem to interweave in inextricably linked ways—not in some dichotomized fashion ("I'm into politics and don't have time for this interpersonal mush!" or "I'm a caseworker, and all this political stuff is just too big and vague for me to deal with!"). Instead, there is always an ongoing, changing *unified complementarity* between these processes. Indeed, I would argue that one of the most powerful ways to socially "divide and conquer" is not only by class, sex, and race but also by personality. There is increasing specialization in our personalities—there are places to be intellectual, places to be emotional, and never the two shall meet, be it on the job (where depersonalization increases as skill requirements decrease), or in one's personal life (where relationships are more fractured by external demands and thus less permanent). These problems are greatly influenced by economic forces, but the intrapsychic forces, when placed in the context of this preeminent relationship, demand specific attention. The worlds of "macro" and "micro" meet again—within one's self!

Furthermore, to do otherwise would be to ignore the inherently radical nature of Freud's early writings on the unconscious: Here he developed the dynamic relationship between societal demands and individual urgings. In this relationship, what can be resolved without conflict is resolved in the conscious; what cannot (and, in quite revolutionary fashion, Freud argued that many of one's urgings cannot be satisfied through contemporary social situations) will find itself in the unconscious. Thus, by creating an inherently *antagonistic* relationship between individual wishes and urgings (sexual or otherwise) and societal demands, Freud's unconscious takes on a subversive quality worthy of exploration by organizer and caseworker alike (Danto, 2005).

Recognizing this, it follows that since the unconscious is timeless (and thus develops throughout our social existence as we *become,* again and again), we can expect that a person's capacity to acknowledge and work with unconscious and conscious material can serve to liberate a community practitioner to even greater individual potential—potential that in turn can place greater demands on society to meet the expectations developed from such potential. Put simply, a less divided person is less easily conquered.

REFLECTIVE QUESTIONS

Reflect on your own behavior and situations where you became uncharacteristically tongue-tied or perhaps the reverse by overdoing what the situation required. Likewise, reflect on your own response to people when you were less than your best self. Why do you think these things happened? Talk with a trusted friend or colleague so you can mutually explore, reflect, and learn together the power of the unconscious on your own work as a part of your "becoming."

DEEPENING THE USE OF TACTICAL SELF-AWARENESS: ACCEPTING LIMITS TO TRANSCEND THEM

And yet, as any experienced practitioner knows, healing divisions isn't easy anywhere. In dealing with the unconscious, precisely because its function is to hide and distort, the potential for internal splitting is always present, always lurking in our work, as unconscious material is expressed in disguised and hidden ways again and again.

However, embedded in this difficult process lie elements of its potential solution. It begins with the humbling recognition that self-knowledge can never be so mastered as to be completed in some nicely rounded form. Instead, by accepting whatever limits to awareness we may possess, rather than denying them, we come to actively work with and respect them in a way that frees us to be even more flexible in our work. *In experientially making this humble recognition, we free ourselves to replace the entrenched battle to control all our own actions (conscious and unconscious) with the more muted struggle to accept and understand those actions.* Experienced and reflected on over time, such knowledge helps us integrate both strengths and weaknesses in all our daily activities. As Freire (2000) wrote, the midwifery of liberation is always painful.

As so many women friends have informed me regarding that other midwifery experience, the birth of a child dispels the pain of labor that came before, too. That so much earlier pain could be transformed so easily into love seems to make its embrace all the more worthy in other parts of our lives. When one embraces the unconscious, tactical self-awareness is deepened along the way, making one a more able person, a more flexible strategist, and a better—and, ironically, more humble—practitioner.

REFLECTIVE QUESTIONS

How can a community-based practitioner recognize the impact of unconscious material on his or her work? Is there a way to correct for it in some situations? What could Ellis do beforehand in working with the kids? What could Kay do with the executive?

This process of courageously working for social change while accepting the inevitability of our personal limits naturally has parallels in other macro practice work. For example, we would never demand that a community group take on the entire fiscal crisis of the public sector in confronting its own housing problems. *While striving to understand the crisis,* the group would do much better to spend its energy on their landlords, specific redlining issues, housing subsidies for the mentally ill, and so forth. By freeing themselves from trying to attack all the related issues surrounding their consciously felt problems, they focus their activity modestly enough to both achieve concrete success and, through that organizing experience, actively understand other, less directly related problems.

This organizing approach is part of our ABCs. We can do the same with our own conscious and unconscious material. Here our more modest, personal approach helps us focus on positively integrating such material into our understanding. As this necessarily admits to both strengths and limits on any one person's ability, we easily extend *all* our available resources. By thus *respecting* limits instead of ignoring or denying them, we are able to stay attuned to the emotional and nonrational aspects of our daily practice, integrating such knowledge into other strategic considerations. In doing so, we deepen our uses of tactical self-awareness in the process.

A personal example of this process was written by a young organizer, Paula Kindos (Burghardt, 1982) as she described her difficulty in working at a neighborhood center in the Bronx. Some of the problems were in the objective situation; others, as she admitted, were less clearly defined. In particular, she found herself unwilling to admit to frustrations and anger she felt about some of her work assignments.

> I really was growing to hate the place and myself. My unprofessional, critical opinion of myself [she blamed herself at this time for disliking the assignments] was proven four times in four months. I was under some very stressful situations at the agency and personally never felt comfortable in the neighborhood, either. . . . I didn't feel like I could talk to anybody . . . [and] I eventually came down with a very bad respiratory infection . . . with the main advantage being able to miss 4 days at the office. How's that for evading something you really didn't want to face?
>
> I can see now that it was easier at the time of this job for me not to face up to the problems around frustrating, anxiety-provoking incidents. I must admit that today, however, I can cope one hundred percent better with these emotions on the job. I cannot explain why or how, but I find things at the office easier to tolerate. I think it all started when I began being a little more verbal and expressive of my feelings, which helped me understand more of where I was coming from.
>
> For example, one day recently, after holding back several long weeks, I told my director what I felt about my work project—that it could be tossed into the garbage can for all I cared. . . . I felt there was no support from her, that the committee I was setting up was a joke, and so on. Afterwards, we could talk, and some of my complaints became less extreme. But also it felt like a huge burden had been removed from my back and new horizons were created. . . . The dramatics weren't from myself, it was my imagination, too. . . . When I just started to get that stuff out, both myself and my work got better! (pp. 114–115)

As Kindos related later, she had spent so much energy on suppressing her frustrations (feeling she didn't have a right to them, that they weren't justified since the work was to help people, etc.) that she actually damaged her effectiveness—damaged it to the point that she repeatedly got sick to avoid the emotionally charged and confusing work at the office. Once she admitted to their reality and expressed them openly to her supervisor, the highly intense (and denied) personal struggle over maintaining a totally consistent set of emotions and behaviors related to her work began to lessen. By acknowledging her different moods and attitudes within the context of her assignments (some great, some boring), she was freed to more fully engage in the work itself. The outcomes for Kindos were in fact two-fold: Not only did she improve as an organizer, but she never got sick at work again!

REFLECTIVE QUESTIONS

What is the secret to becoming more effective as a community-based practitioner with your unconscious material? Is there a paradox in how you can become more flexible and effective?

The value in heightened awareness of conscious and unconscious material in one's work extends beyond oneself. As a deepened element of tactical self-awareness, it can help one understand certain dynamics within larger group situations. A perceptive organizer, attuned to the rational and nonrational in organizing, can often spot and help dissipate hidden agendas that are created by deeper, more complicated emotional factors. An extremely thoughtful case study on just these dynamics was written by Noreen Murray (Burghardt, 1982), an organizer involved in recreation programs in a borough of New York City. The dynamics are interesting enough to warrant its entire presentation.

My assignment in the agency for the year was to implement a decentralization plan for the agency, working with 22 established groups throughout the borough. Each of these groups belonged to an overall planning and steering committee [which] was unique to my borough and added a twist to the assignment. Not only were they the most active section (I had 200 basketball teams between the boys' and girls' leagues) but they were also the most militantly opposed to the changes.

Of course, there was little in the "plan." The agency had apparently discovered little money in the till around budget time last spring. They also found that athletics cost them a lot to run. As social service staffs were already skeletal, our recreation program became a likely target for economizing. The plan our administration developed was that in each of five geographic sections of the borough I would be responsible for coordinating the basketball and baseball seasons. There had previously been a staff of two supervisors, three secretaries, and five or six part-time referee maintainers for the area alone. The groups would still have to pay the same entry fees, and "pitch in and get the job done" on a volunteer basis. Furthermore, the agency implemented this plan without ever consulting anyone directly involved in the leagues.

Needless to say, when the plan was announced, the parents were not too happy. They were clearly getting less for more, as well as having to live with "an inexperienced young girl" (a direct quote about me) running their sports program. They were also being given more control than ever before over rules and policy but they generally perceived the changes as constituting an agency cop-out. The steering committee became tighter than ever before and devised a plan to run their own program. They wanted to join with the other leagues in the agency at play-off time. The plan was tentatively accepted by the larger agency, and then rejected. As the group needed the other agency teams for any kind of meaningful play-off, they had no choice but to give in to the overall agency plan.

This situation required me not only to exploit all my assets but also face and deal with my liabilities (emotional and professional). Here I was, old conflict-avoiding, anger-suppressing Noreen faced with 22 furious men whom I had to work with on a job I did not want. (Incidentally, the agency had informed me of this new assignment one week before it was to go into effect. The steering committee wasn't the only angry one around.)

My first direct encounter with the parents was in July. It was a meeting to inform them of the agency decisions to reject their plan to operate independently, and to introduce me. . . . Both the parents and myself were each boiling about the whole process, they openly, in the meeting, and afterwards over a few beers. . . . In fact, I kept trying to be a good agency person, but I felt so betrayed that I had an instant bond with the steering committee. . . . I went home feeling as though we'd made an alliance and could work together. *In a way I was right, but naïve about the intervening process that would have to occur before they could let go of their anger and sense of betrayal. I was unprepared for what would take place in the fall.*

. . . Over the summer, instead of reading up on sports programs, exploring the agency structures and trying to prepare for the job ahead of me, I simply ignored its coming. I attended training sessions on scheduling in a fog and concentrated my energies in running another, unrelated community program in the borough.

When fall arrived, so did the basketball season. It was hell. Sixty-hour weeks, constant phone calls—60 and 70 a day—no secretary; and true to their word, no committee volunteers despite the fact that they know how to schedule. Withholding their expertise resulted in their having to play a very reduced schedule, but they were determined to show the agency up for its false promise of delivering the same service of the past.

I was prepared for their not helping; but not for their fever pitch anger toward me at the monthly fall meetings. With no one else present from the downstairs office, I was the target for their genuine fury. Alas, it was taking them months to work out their anger as a group, and I was the one they were working it out on. The combination of working so hard, being still resentful toward the agency, and putting up with a lot of harassment with no help caused me to go through what I now call an "interesting conversation." I got mad at the steering committee and I hated my job. (How dare they behave in such a disgusting manner to me, sports are dumb, etc., etc.) I forgot all about the agency role and transferred my impotent anger at it onto the job, my tasks, and the group.

By this time, it was quite clear to just about everyone that I wasn't effective in the program. Luckily, my supervisor and I have an open relationship, and she was able to explore some of the deeper reasons for my anger and what it was doing to the work. Over a stretch of about four weeks she was able to help me put things back into perspective and get both me and my priorities in working shape again. The thread of this whole situation was anger—both mine and the group's without any outlet for my own feelings. I knew that one can't go running around the office screaming at one's bosses (although I did a little of that); one must maintain more composure than that. What I did not know was how to cope with my anger on a systematic basis.

In the meantime, the parents were also unable to reach the downtown office with their continued rage and so exploded at me—and passively let a program they loved be damaged in the process, which only kept stoking the fires. As I had insufficient emotional clarity on what was going on, we ended up being at each other's throats for a lot longer than necessary. . . . After my discussions with the supervisor and repeated individual contacts with leaders that provided a little "neutral time" away from the group, we began to make some real headway, but the entire episode was much more painful than it had to be. (pp. 152–153)

As Murray herself astutely realized, some of her own and the group's ineffectiveness—indeed, their furious fighting with each other—was related to displaced emotions. (More "clinical" insight applied within an organizing environment!) They felt unable to directly focus their anger at the agency, so they used each other as handy (and wrong) targets. Equally important, Murray and the steering committee *avoided* the necessary preplanning to the recreational work as an unconscious response to actions they disapproved of. "Being in a fog" is unconsciously a nice way to avoid yelling at your boss (or fearing you'll yell too loud once you start), but it also keeps you from doing your job. As Murray, who was trained in both casework and community organization, put it:

At base, in this situation, was the transfer of anger I made from the agency to the steering committee. What I should have done was engage in some serious dealing with the anger toward the agency and then negotiated to relieve the most troublesome aspects of the situation. Instead, I ignored the whole thing until it was in my lap.

Baptism by fire has taught me that a few quiet hours spent in thought and reflection on what's in the gut and how it's affecting the mind-set are not only well spent but crucial, especially at those times that I least feel like doing it. Having been through all this, I know that I am functioning at it competently. I would not have been able to do that if I hadn't acknowledged, owned, and accepted my disappointment and anger at being the target. It very nearly caused me to forget everything I know about professional behavior and "social work process." With all that confused emotion, I began with the project as if I'd never worked before.

Part of me still wants to say, "Dammit, I have every right to be resentful and disgusted with the agency." This may be true, but that does not mean that I have every right to be angry and unprofessional toward my clients, even if they do behave in a hostile way toward me. Getting clear on my own attitudes and emotions is the only way that I'm now able to look on my tasks separately from the agency and its problems. (Burghardt, 1982, p. 153)

The recognition of how emotions impact one's practice, especially when they are unconsciously misdirected, can be a humbling experience. Accepting the power of the unconscious always means that one will never be entirely certain of totally mastering each and every situation, no matter how sharp the practice skills. But these two examples make clear how much easier work can become once a person identifies the powerful unconscious emotionally linked up within one's trying situations. Both Kindos and Murray were tremendously relieved and increasingly flexible, *both personally and strategically,* once they had broadened the use of tactical self-awareness to include obscurely related emotional issues in the work itself.

REFLECTIVE QUESTIONS

In your own work experience, what has happened when you have not confronted issues that upset you? What later happened? What impact did this have on your group's unfolding strategic plan of action?

Over time, if a practitioner actively recognizes this continuous interplay between conscious and unconscious material, invaluable skills are enhanced, for there is a meaningful irony in admitting to personal limitations in changing the world. As stated before, we come to do our work in a more coherent and flexible manner and, in the process, learn to respect our limits rather than antagonistically avoid them.

The freedom of recognizing personal limits allows us to work much harder on more political limits—for being less fearful of *our* actions, we more fully engage in the actions of society. Our increased flexibility gained in a consistent use of tactical self-awareness makes our practice more dynamic and alive to all that changes in the world—be it in politics, in people, or in ourselves.

Finally, there is a deeper, more political dimension to embracing our limits as well. One of the great dilemmas in political history is the replication of oppression by political, revolutionary groups who fought for social justice, only to repeat similar forms of domination and dictatorship once they seized power (Michels, 2009). The most common reason cited for returning to such repressive ways is that there was some inherent failure in the group's political line—that is, the seeds of the new leadership's arrogance and oppression were present in their political ideas. While this of course may be part of the reason for such failings, Freire (2000) makes clear that these failings are also internalized within us. As he insightfully wrote in relationship to the struggle for oppressed people to develop their own forms of learning, the slow process of discovery of one's internal oppression is a mutual journey for us all:

> The fundamental problem [in the early stage of one's work with the oppressed] is this: how can the oppressed as divided, unauthentic beings, participate in developing the pedagogy of their own liberation? Only as they discover themselves to be "hosts" of the oppressor can they contribute to the midwifery of their own liberation. As long as they live in the duality in which *to be* is *to be like* and *to be like* is *to be like the oppressor,* this contribution is impossible. The pedagogy of the oppressed is an instrument for their critical discovery that both they and their oppressor are manifestations of their dehumanization. (p. 48)

Tactical self-awareness is designed to further our own liberating pedagogy of discovery by helping us all struggle to be all of who we are, strengths and limitations included. As we do this work—and it is a lot of work—over time we come to see that what we have perceived as normal dichotomies in life are in fact constructions of our own internal psychological and cognitive divisions—good versus evil, zero-sum games of power (*if you win, I lose*), task versus process, touchy-feely versus objective reality. Such divisions, instead of structuring our world for easy wins and neat categories of understanding, come to be experienced as false dichotomies within our own makeup that we must struggle to diminish if we are to more fully and flexibly handle the responsibilities in our work . . . first without power and then with. (Chapters 11 and 12 explore this with supervisors and then with executives.)

Tactical self-awareness, in its embrace of strengths *and* limitations (both conscious and otherwise), is meant to be one's own midwifery tool for personal growth. By affirming our strengths and allowing for limitations, over time we replace the inauthenticity of a divided, static identity with an always-emerging self that weaves together our courage to change the world with our humble awareness that we need to keep changing, too.

STEPS TO STRENGTHENING YOUR TACTICAL SELF-AWARENESS

Of course growth, personal or otherwise, always means upsetting established relations. An individual may want to change, may wish to become the most tactically self-aware person alive, and still be stymied in how to begin. I have found this especially true when people are analyzing their own motivations and actions rather than those of others. But a real understanding of others, in the course of an active relationship, can rarely take place without genuine understanding of oneself.

So what to do? Once you have established that you want to be involved in deepening your tactical self-awareness (which can be as difficult a decision as any poor tenant finally choosing to confront a landlord), there are a few applied practice processes that you can use.

1. The first involves role-playing on particular events related to specific political or community issues that are highly charged within the group. For example, you actually may be involved in a tenant group that is actively pushing rent control legislation, and certain key landlords and legislators may be hurting your organization's efforts. Undoubtedly, they will not be well liked by the group members. This antagonism creates an ideal role-playing situation where you have a number of key group members, *especially* those most hostile to the group's enemies, positively and sincerely enact a scene that supports a landlord's interests. Other group members will be called on to play appropriate tenant roles.

   If done sincerely (otherwise it is all worthless), the outcome invariably will be the same: The "landlords" will not play their roles well, while the "tenants" will experience little role difficulty. However, *the crucial factor in the post-role-playing analysis is not the discomfort found in the role conflict; it is the manner in which that discomfort expresses itself in each individual.* For some individuals, the discomfort will lead them to totally deny the role, reverting to a tenant's position; others, usually assertive types, will become sullen and withdrawn; still others will appear awkward. Whatever the behavioral response, it is often a key ingredient in a person's array of defenses used in personally difficult situations and should be looked at accordingly.

2. Once a person identifies his or her particular pattern, that person can begin identifying where such behaviors (awkwardness, withdrawal, etc.) have occurred and, through an ongoing exploration, begin positively dealing with such problems. Thus, the withdrawn role-player realizes he does the same thing in social situations; another role-player, who laughed uproariously throughout the acting,

remembers she does the same thing whenever confronted with high-level, task-oriented situations. Such perceptions then help both see and act on the personal stress of problematic situations.

3. More emotionally laden material cannot always be exposed within the direct work of a community group, however. Sometimes, as the examples at the beginning of the chapter suggest, the motivations behind one's behavior are either too difficult or too personal to examine in public view. Here, more individualized role-playing activities suggested by Mary C. Schwartz (1978; Cooper & Lesser, 2007) can be helpful. Taking place in front of only one person skilled enough to help an individual, this type of role-playing can still be used in nontherapeutic situations. Schwartz (1978, p. 229) lists five steps to be used:

   a. The concerned individual first identifies the intractable or consistently unsettling problem facing the practitioner and the way he or she is interacting with the person or group. The practitioner is then asked to select a scene and person in his or her past life that was similar to the present interaction in some respects.
   b. The individual then plays out the selected scene. One first plays oneself, then changes chairs (placed in the room for this purpose) and, continuing the dialogue, assumes the role of the other person. This procedure is continued until the dialogue is completed.
   c. The individual plays the scene again. However, he or she describes as fully as possible the underlying feelings of each person taking part in the dialogue.
   d. The scene is played again, this time with the resolution the practitioner would have preferred had he or she been given a chance to relive the situation.
   e. Finally, the problematic practice interaction is reenacted, using the procedures in the previous three steps to complete the entire sequence.

   As Schwartz (1978) was quick to point out, this much more emotionally laden role-playing often leads to discomfort and resistance by the practitioners. One should go only as far with such material as possible. If you are the guide behind the role-playing, it is important to be both tactful and understanding, for sometimes the resistance relates to unresolved conflict within an individual. With this recognized, Schwartz was nevertheless able to help her fellow practitioners decrease their own discomfort and better understand the deeper emotional issues that were underlying their distress.

4. Schwartz presented many examples. One concerned a young practitioner who wanted to shake an angry mother who would not allow her son to become what he wanted. Furious at the mother, she felt the woman was unable to respect her son's wishes and dramatically sided with the child. However, in the role-play it became clear that the practitioner, as a young adult, had talked angrily with *her*

mother when her mother would not accept her career goals. Obviously, after the role-playing, the practitioner could see that the emotional stress and overreaction on her part in dealing with the boy's mother was caused in part by her own history. Once clearer on her emotions, she could function more effectively in her work with this mother's entire set of problems, not just the one related to her son.

This form of engaged introspection on emotional content is worthwhile only for people who are genuinely interested in such exploration and who have fellow workers to support them in this activity. It is mentioned here as a practice available to people regardless of their practice context, but it is more demanding than the less introspective form of "role conflict"-playing first suggested.

5. Finally, there is another method of personal problem solving for individuals that goes beyond the reach of any community-based practice situation: therapy. It is not necessarily a corrective for social ills, but when a person finds himself or herself in personally disquieting (and organizationally dysfunctional) behaviors that may be *intellectually understood and yet unresolved,* therapy can be an excellent aid in lessening these problems (Cooper & Lesser, 2007). I have certainly learned this personally and am a better practitioner—and happier person—for the effort.

However, you may not feel you want or need such intense emotional introspection, and I have not been writing about the unconscious in organizing to force community practitioners into clinical treatment. The point of analyzing the impact of the unconscious on the organizing process and on developing a deeper level of tactical self-awareness is not to *force* individuals to use this or that tactic but merely to encourage them to be open to *all* tactics. Indeed, the more we explore the constantly varying forms of practice, the more likely *every* practitioner—from caseworkers to organizers to managers—will use tactics developed by others.

REFLECTIVE ACTIVITY FOR EDUCATIONAL POLICY 2.1.7

With a partner, reflect on a strength of yours shaped by your environment from the past:

_____

Now share a limitation as it impacts your work in community engagement:

_____

For the partner, reflect on what you have learned from your partner's story. How would it impact your engagement and work with him or her?
Now reverse roles!

_____

_____

THE COMMUNITY TOOLBOX

The Community Toolbox has some vital activities to help a practitioner better understand communication and ways of working with people that require deeper awareness of one's own relationship skills and personal impact as an organizer or community member. It also provides some great, concrete tools for promoting group outreach. Go to http://ctb.ku.edu/en/tablecontents/chapter_1005.htm.

Promoting Interest in Community Issues

Section 1. Developing a Plan for Communication

Section 2. Using Principles of Persuasion

Section 3. Preparing Press Releases

Section 4. Arranging News and Features Stories

Section 5. Approaching Editorial Boards

Section 6. Preparing Guest Columns and Editorials

Section 7. Preparing Public Service Announcements

Section 8. Arranging a Press Conference

Section 9. Using Paid Advertising

Section 10. Creating Newsletters

Section 11. Creating Posters and Flyers

Section 12. Developing Creative Promotions

Section 13. Creating Brochures

REFERENCES

Anyon, J. (1997). *Ghetto schooling: A political economy of urban educational reform.* New York: Teachers College Press.

Bennis, W. (2009). *On becoming a leader* (4th ed.). New York: Basic Books.

Bowles, S., & Gintis, H. (1976). *Schooling in capitalist America: Educational reform and the contradictions of economic life.* New York: Basic Books.

Braverman, H. (1971). *Labor and monopoly capital.* New York: Monthly Review Press.

Burghardt, S. (1982). *The other side of organizing.* Cambridge, MA: Schenkman.

Cooper, M., & Lesser, J. (2007). *Clinical social work practice: An integrated approach* (3rd ed.). Boston: Allyn & Bacon.

Corrick, J. A. (1998). *The industrial revolution.* New York: Gale Group.

Danto, E. (2005). *Freud's free clinics: Psychoanalysis and social justice, 1918–1938.* New York: Columbia University Press.

Erlich, J., & Rivera, F. (1998). *Community organizing in a diverse society* (3rd ed.). Boston: Allyn & Bacon.

Freire, P. (2000). *Pedagogy of the oppressed.* New York: Continuum.

Freud, S. (2005). *Collected works* (Vol. 5). New York: Basic Books.

Hefner, K. (1998). The movement for youth rights: 1945–2000. *Social Policy, 21*(2), 26–38.

Horney, K. (1988). *The neurotic in our time.* New York: Houghton-Mifflin.

INCITE! Women of Color Against Violence (Ed.). (2007). *The revolution will not be funded: Beyond the non-profit industrial complex.* Cambridge, MA: South End Press.

Lasch, C. (1989). *The culture of narcissism.* New York: Norton Books.

Michels, R. (2009). *Political parties: A sociological study of the oligarchical tendencies of modern democracy.* Ithaca, NY: Cornell University Library.

Palmer, P. (2004). *The undivided self.* New York: Basic Books.

Reich, W., & Baxandall, L. (Eds.). (1972). *SexPol.* New York: Vintage Books.

Rothbart, M. (2013). Temperament. *Encyclopedia on Early Childhood Development.* Retrieved from http://www.child-encyclopedia.com/en-ca/child-temperament/according-to-experts.html

Schwartz, M. C. (1978). Helping the worker with countertransference. *Social Work, 23*(2), 218–236.

Senge, P. (1994). *The fifth discipline: The art and practice of the learning organization.* Cambridge: MIT Press.

Senge, P., Scharmer, O., Jaworski, J., & Flowers, B. (2005). *Presence: Exploring profound change in people, organizations and society.* London: Nicholas Brealey.

Shreiver, J. (2003). *Human behavior and the social environment: Shifting paradigms in the search for essential knowledge for social work practice.* London: Allyn & Bacon.

Sujansky, J., & Ferri-Reed, J. (2009). *Keeping the Millennials: Why companies are losing billions in turnover to this generation—and what to do about it.* New York: Wiley.

NOTE

1. As we will see in Chapter 7, social tensions are often a powerful internal dynamic to many organizing campaigns and human service agencies as well.

CHAPTER 5

The Social Construction of Practice

Where "Macro" and "Micro" Meet on the Road Toward Personal and Community Transformation

---

MICRO MEETS MACRO . . . AND LIKES IT!

"Hey, who woulda believed it?" Ellis grinned across the cubicle at his new office mate. "From fighting in class to working together on the same project in the field!" Due to job transfers at his first-year social work field placement, he had had to change to a new agency. Surprising everyone but Kay, he'd asked to work with her. Their community assessment had gone so well that there now was follow-up work to shape their strategic recommendations into an actual campaign issue for Kay's agency. Since it promised to be work that spread beyond Central Harlem, Kay's supervisor was happy to have an extra pair of hands, especially from someone whose talent with research was so obvious.

Kay reached over and handed him two keys. "In honor of your arrival, I got keys for this office and the bathroom made for you." She smiled. "So you owe me big!" Ellis took the keys and gingerly shook them in his hand.

"Why a bathroom key? Agency afraid of outsiders using the facilities?"

"Yeah, right." Kay's voice held a touch of sarcasm. "When the agency took over the building space a few years ago, this was how it was. They weren't going to waste money on new locks for every floor when keys are a lot cheaper. Are you always gonna be paranoid?"

Ellis blushed and laughed at himself. "Old habits die hard, Kay. Sorry."

During their 5-hour talk in the diner, they had both shared a lot of their histories as a way to unlock the mysteries as to why each had been thrown off guard during the interviews. Kay grew up with a single mom in a one-bedroom Brooklyn apartment, seeing her austere and aloof father only on the occasional holiday when she was young and almost never after her teen years. Ellis had come from an intact family of strivers, his mom a pediatrician, his father a corporate lawyer who had moved their family to an exclusive Connecticut suburb when Ellis was 4 and his sister 3. A day student at a well-regarded prep school, he'd had a warm and supportive family, along with every material advantage except social acceptance. A popular kid at school, at home Kay longed for a complete family around her Christmas tree and at family gatherings. Ellis, on the other hand, grew up yearning for someone with whom he could just hang out.

"No biggie. Look, we agreed back in the diner that I'd lighten you up and you'd keep me focused." She flicked a rubber band in his direction. "So lighten up!" Ellis ducked his head and started to laugh just as their supervisor walked in.

An hour later, Ellis and Kay were on a bus headed toward a meeting of a service coalition across town. After that, they'd be meeting with kids who might be part of a youth council for the after-school program. Their assessment had been a big hit with the director and her boss. "Kay, this stuff looks good, I think—most of it anyway. This will be the first youth council I've worked with since I was on one in high school!" He paused for a second. "What issue do you think they'll want to work on?"

"We'll soon find out! I'm hoping they will go for jobs like we suggested in the assessment, but you never know." She looked over at Ellis and smiled. "And don't forget about these professionals, my friend. This coalition needs your expertise on data mining. I already told the coordinator about you. When she saw your demographic comparisons between school districts, she really got excited. They are trying to come up with a longer-range plan for better funding, and she's sure you can help." Kay also had shown the coalition leader their community assessment as a way of demonstrating what Ellis was capable of.

"Hey, did you show her the cool information you got from those kids? You really got them to open up in no time. Not everybody can get kids to talk about their pressures at home. That information made it possible for us to advocate for the job-creation program and youth council. Those kids can take on a real issue that affects their lives for the short and long term."

"Yeah, well, if that's the issue that gets 'em going. You never know, though. They're great kids. But get ready, Ellis, it won't be that simple. A lot of the kids will need some one-on-one work to get ready for job interviews. Do you know some of these kids have never even been out of Harlem? They'll need clinical casework as much as jobs."

(Continued)

(Continued)

"Clinical casework? Uh-oh." Ellis looked at his new friend warily. "I'm not into that. One-on-one is not for me and what I want to do."

"Yeah, well, our supervisor, Ms. Fortes, gave us both a day a week on individual work. You knew that when you signed up."

"I know, I know. Because of you, I'm gonna try. But I'll need your help. Damn, I thought macro practice was just that—macro, major, the big kahuna. I signed up to work on the conditions that affect people's lives, not their daily hassles. Youth councils fighting for jobs, that I like. How each kid feels about it…" he shrugged and looked downcast.

"Look, I'm not comfortable with data, but I know it's important. You help me, and I'll help you, okay?"

"Yeah, sure, I'm with you." Ellis sighed as they got off the bus, then grinned wryly. "Truth is, I got issues with some issues, Kay." They both laughed. "I just thought social work would be a lot easier than this!"

Educational Policy 2.1.10(a–d)—Engage, assess, intervene, and evaluate with individuals, families, groups, organizations, and communities. This chapter provides a framework that "involves the dynamic and interactive processes of engagement, assessment, intervention, and evaluation at multiple levels." Those engaged in both macro and micro forms of practice will have examples as to how they can gain the "skills to practice with individuals, families, groups, organizations, and communities."

FROM ENGAGEMENT TO RELATIONSHIP BUILDING: FRAMING THE ISSUE

While on the bus, Kay and Ellis began discussing a central focus for macro practice: framing issues in ways that both capture people's attention and get them engaged enough that they commit to action. Beginning with their own community assessment, they were hoping the kinds of issues related to jobs for kids would draw the youth council's energy and activism. Unlike a social problem, which can be real but does not in itself lead to *concreteness, specificity, or action* (Alinsky, 1989; Homan, 2004; Rubin & Rubin, 2007), an "issue" for an organizer is like yeast for a baker. Once agreed to, an issue rises to the top of a group's agenda because

- ✓ it contains enough self-interest to create self-motivation,
- ✓ has concreteness so that it can be acted on, and, with work,
- ✓ becomes specific enough that it can be achieved and built on by the group over the long haul (Homan, 2004; Rubin & Rubin, 2004; Staples, 2004).

Because of their community assessment, Ellis and Kay moved from discussing data on poverty in Central Harlem—a real problem without any focus or specificity—to an issue such as jobs for the after-school program kids. Whether these inexperienced practitioners could engage the young people so that this jobs issue became their own was much of the work that lay ahead for Ellis and Kay. We will return to their work on issue development with the young people later in the chapter.

EXERCISE

Define a social problem that has come from your community assessment:

_____

Break the problem down into a manageable issue:

- Concreteness:
- Specificity:
- Actions:

    o 1.
    o 2.
    o 3.

This chapter has started here with an exercise so that you can keep referring to it—your own specific actions as a way to ground you, the reader, in details that matter to your work. You should refer to it as the chapter issues develop. This is important because the chapter moves quickly to a wider and more difficult set of issues: *how to develop a practice model that breaks away from the dichotomies between individual and community work so that an intuitive practitioner such as Kay and an intellectual practitioner such as Ellis each develop the necessary set of complementary skills that can make their practice transformational—for themselves and for the people with whom they work.* To that end, this chapter will work toward achieving the following objectives:

- To show how to unite the "community" and the "individual" regardless of method
- To examine how there is value rather than a cause for pessimism in working with both the strengths and limitations of one's organizing efforts, even as the cause of social justice remains paramount
- To demonstrate how to utilize both intuitive and intellectual skills to expand one's ability to grapple with social and interpersonal dynamics at play in one's practice that help move from tentative engagement to relationship building

- To discuss how to use one's own tactical self-awareness and appreciation for one's own strengths and limitations to develop tactical flexibility and diminished adherence to outmoded or romanticized, ineffective strategies
- To embrace a model of "macro" and "micro" skills as fundamental to all forms of excellent social work practice

ISSUES ABOUT ISSUES: THE HISTORIC "MICRO–MACRO" DEBATE IN SOCIAL WORK

While Kay and Ellis's discussion began with issue formation, it soon evolved to one as old as the profession of social work itself: Is the issue at hand to be thought of as individual or community in focus? After all, how one answers the question often determines the way one analyzes an issue in the first place (Lowery, Mattaini, & Meyer, 2007; Saleebey, 2008). Kay and Ellis's brief discussion on macro or micro work reflects one of the longest-running debates within social work. Whether the warring followers of Jane Addams and Mary Richmond, Flexner's (Bonner, 2002) near-hundred-year-old dictum of "from case to cause," or the 1970s split into macro and micro practice, this profession has sought to resolve how best to work with those in need. For community-based practitioners, the struggle can seem unique: *Do we do anything clinical? Is it all about the "social" in social work? How do I bring these two issues together . . . should I even bother?* Ellis's discomfort with one-on-one interaction and Kay's unease in front of data sets could lead each to opt out of what a community group or individual actually seeks to work on. Likewise, Kay's concerns are not unlike a clinical practitioner's: *Am I ignoring genuine personal needs by focusing on "social" problems? Is there a way to do clinical work and be an organizer? Should I even bother?*

Finally, there is one additional question for them both: *Is there a way to avoid making what would be the wrong method choice for an important issue because of the professional's personal discomfort with that choice?*

These questions reflect one of the underlying crises of social work practice: the inability to describe a developed practice framework that adequately reflects the daily concerns of the social work practitioner and the community member(s) he or she is working with without sacrificing the historical claims of the field. An established macro text captures this dilemma powerfully:

Given the complexity of macro interventions, practitioners may begin to feel overwhelmed. Is it not enough to do good direct practice or clinical work? . . . Our answer is that professional practice focusing only on an individual's intra-psychic concerns does not fit the definition of social work. Being a social worker requires seeing the client as part of multiple, over-lapping systems that comprise the person's social and physical environment. . . . Social workers unwilling to engage in some macro-practice types of activities when the need arises are not practicing social work. Similarly, social workers who carry out episodes of macro practice must understand what is involved in the provision of direct services to clients at the individual, domestic unit, or group level. (Netting, Kettner, & McMurtry, 2007, p. 18)

The importance of developing *and then utilizing* a practice framework capable of holding both micro and macro perspectives without succumbing to abstract notions of what one should do has never been greater. This is no small matter, for 21st century political debates have made it clear that practitioners and community members alike are facing a set of economic and political demands for contraction of services and shrinkage of the social welfare state as never before. With the economy in free fall and both political parties focused on a significant trimming of the deficit, practitioners no longer have any guarantee that our society will meet, however slowly, the demands of the disenfranchised and poor. None of us can expect our practice, regardless of method choice, to easily connect client/community need with an accessible, responsive social welfare system. Indeed, if the worker cutbacks and the withdrawal of entitlements of the past 25 years are measures of a system's responsiveness, we can expect that heightened community needs will be met with a mix of organizational resistance (more cost containment) joined to ideological indifference (more political support for privatization and individual effort). Social service cutbacks continue to be a major threat in the 21st century across the United States, Canada, and all of Europe (Bernstein, 2008).

The early 21st century crisis of our political and economic marginality is reflected in our ongoing crisis in practice framework development. Some models do make clear that there are practice constraints created by fiscal issues. As Netting et al. (2007) put it: "Decision makers often consider cost even before the urgency or necessity of a change. This means the change agent must understand how such decisions are made . . . and address cost issues in advocating for change" (p. 341).

Working with a generalist practitioner framework, the authors carefully delineate the necessary skills of a social work macro practitioner operating within those constraints. Their analysis goes on to develop a practice picture of a social worker's *highly successful* entry and engagement inside the various systems of social welfare that may unintentionally underplay the degree of struggle workers must face to do meaningful work. Likewise, their work has been helpful in delineating macro practice work into "episodes" so that the new practitioner can see the variety of arenas in which he or she will work. A real advance over the past two decades, their work allows practitioners to try on skill sets necessary for effective community-based work. What remains is to see what actually may be going on inside each stage of community-based work—the weave of clinical case for individuals and organizing for the community—that informs daily practice.

The day-to-day reality of social workers inside agencies struggling with cost containment and increased client need is that there is another side to daily practice: frequent, angry resentment from overworked workers; frustration with bureaucratic red tape and other nonsensical regulations; the pain of seeing clients and communities suffer while needed services are cut back . . . all the while living with the awareness that these micro issues often get in the way of long-term organizing efforts. As one worker said, "How do I get back to fighting the cause of the disease when I can't even get enough Band-Aids to treat the wound?"

The frustration wrought by the dilemma of too few resources and too many needs continues to be what it was 30 years ago: Over time, too many practitioners, while wanting to maintain their macro systems/resource skills, begin to sharply divide up their practice lives. Some see interpersonal change as too secondary for their concern and opt for organizing work that emphasizes only political strategies, seeing themselves fighting antiglobalization struggles and engaging in Occupy efforts through their volunteer work alone. Others (in greater numbers) decide that meaningful work can be found only through treatment and become private practitioners or, more likely with today's HMO (Health Maintenance Organization) restrictions, part-time private practitioners who make extra money in the evening while tiredly holding on to a direct-service job during the day.

Both groups feel that the other's choice is a waste of time. The attempt to find new ways for meaningful practice is sacrificed on the divided altar of either organizing or clinical paths of work. As I will address in the latter half of this book, this same false division can happen to some organizers who move on to administrative positions, feeling their organizing days belong to the distant time of their politicized youth. None of this need be true.

Some of the best organizing literature has encountered this problem. Ross's (1967) classic work mentions the importance of understanding process in community work, even mentioning a community practitioner's clinical role. However, the term is meant metaphorically, with "diagnosis" extended to community problems at large—a nice way of redefining one's political assessment skills but hardly the type of skill that looks at the specifics of the practice process itself.

Happily, present-day texts recognize the importance of relationships, going on to stress that building them is of enormous value. For example, Eichler's (2007) work on consensus organizing has a number of delightful stories about how relationships improve organizing strategy. He goes on to explore the basis for how friendship and organizing relationships are built, with an emphasis on reciprocity, or mutual sharing of tasks and responsibilities. For him, recognizing the value of relationships as a key to organizing strategy is essential.

However, even here the focus on relationships in organizing remains at the level of art, of something intuitively learned. New practitioners are still left to ponder how one systematically develops the listening, engagement, and relationship skills needed to build long-term and effective community-based interventions. Left at a descriptive level of what to do, new practitioners adopt either an organizing or a clinical stance, because most frameworks still stress, at least implicitly, *that such dichotomies exist*—that since case-workers deal with individuals, theirs is primarily interpersonal work, and that for organizers, who work with communities, the emphasis must be sociopolitical and task based. (As Ellis might say, even relationships become a task!)[1]

Other recent works go on to focus on relationship building in terms of leadership development. For example, Sen and Klein (2003) write of how organizers must distinguish development from identification of leaders:

> Identification requires matching a person's skills to tasks, but not much more. Development is more time consuming and riskier. It requires reflection and planning as well as systematic teaching . . . it requires helping people think through who they want to be, as well as who they are in this moment; having some knowledge of a leader's learning style and history; and designing a cycle of learning that makes room for diverse styles. (p. 18)

Their work goes on to stress a set of task-based assignments that allow leaders to develop a powerful voice, weaving in attention to cultural dynamics as well so that the type of leadership that emerges in a group is reflective of the larger population one has targeted to reach.

REFLECTIVE QUESTIONS

?

Working with the issue you identified at the beginning of the chapter . . .
What are its concrete tasks?

a. _____

b. _____

c. _____

In thinking about process, how well are people working together?

_____

In what ways would the process of the work be improved through improved relationship building?

_____

Senge, Scharmer, Jaworski, and Flowers (2004) wrote about this organizing/development dilemma:

> Our normal way of thinking cheats us. It leads us to think of wholes as made up of many parts, the way a car is made up of wheels, a chassis, and a drive train. In this way of thinking, the whole is assembled from the parts and depends on them to think effectively. . . . [However,] unlike machines, living systems, such as your body or a tree [or a community], create themselves. They are . . . continually growing and changing along with their elements. . . . What seems tangible is continually changing. (p. 22)

As the immensity and rapidity of global change confront us daily in a multiplicity of images, types of information, and varied platforms, macro practitioners, too, need forms of learning that end the outmoded dichotomies of the past and replace them with, as Senge et al. (2004) suggest, "deeper levels of learning [that] create increasing awareness of the larger whole—both as it is and as it is evolving—and actions that increasingly become part of creating alternative futures" (p. 23).

To do this, we have to change traditional practice frameworks that, while beginning with a firm declaration of placing the individual within a social context, nevertheless descriptively ignore the *concrete* realities of how systems really affect practice or what impact people and their personal needs have on organizing itself.

The real world of 21st century social work practice is much less tidy on the ground. *As its messiness cannot be avoided, it therefore has been all too often neatly divided between types of practitioners: Caseworkers and clinical social workers feel and engage interpersonally with emotions; organizers and macro practitioners think and engage in political strategy with thoughtful tactics. Such dichotomies can occur within macro practice as well: Administrators deal with accountability systems from above, with funders and their quantifiable outcomes; organizers respond to accountability flowing from below, with people and their social conditions and needs.*

Through this *overemphasis on difference in methods, there is a resultant loss of developing complementary skills across methods as a richer form of intervention.* Instead, the sharp separation between individual and community work is then perceived as a necessary adaptation to the hard realities of the real world rather than as an unfortunate limiting of how people must learn, reflect, and act on the world. If, as Senge and his colleagues (2004) suggest, we must learn to see the world as whole, don't we need a practice framework that assumes we will observe and then act on the whole as well?

FROM CONFLICT TO INNOVATIONS IN PRACTICE: OBSERVING AND ACTING ON THE WHOLE

This impasse between methods (or tracks) can be diminished by experimenting with highly innovative frameworks for practice. What follows, flowing out of my own experience as an organizer, in work with human service managers and executives, and with students of community and clinical practice, was first called "the other side of organizing" and can be extended to "the other side of management" as well. As I have learned, this other side—the interpersonal, emotional realities of practice life—is directly, simultaneously connected to the external, strategic community work being carried out as an organizer in the streets, community coalitions, and agency meetings in which one works.

To incorporate both sides remains a primary goal of my work. Doing so has demanded the use of a framework different from *the standard models of practice that perhaps too easily separated micro from macro. A framework open to the demands of the dynamic flow of the 21st century calls for any practitioner's active understanding and use of both community and casework principles and techniques.* Moving away from a dichotomy between methods and tracks to an appreciation of their interdependence within client-and-community engagements then led me to a deeper awareness of the similarities in approach. This in turn challenged me to explore *how every practitioner can incorporate these similarities into his or her work* in a far more holistic and dynamic interplay between the individual and the community or agency in which he or she works.

Finally, in trying to join the theoretical works of such divergent writers as Freire, Rothman, Saleebey, and Wheatley, there was a reexamination of how one *experientially* combines theory and practice into a *transformational framework* capable of blending the personal/individual and social/community dimensions of practice into an active, engaging system that discards method/track dichotomies in one's professional life.

What follows is thus first a description of what this kind of practice actually looks like and how it is done. We'll look at how one joins presumably personal and strategic issues consistently in one's work, *regardless* of method. Finally, I attempt to move beyond a description of the practice to present the *outlines of a consistently engaged, transformational framework that lies underneath all forms of practice, whether one is working with an individual or a community group.* It is hoped that this paradigm contains within it a partial outline of the kind of dynamic practice that can prepare social work practitioners for the real work we face in the early 21st century.

THE TRANSFORMATIONAL PRACTITIONER'S ROLE: THE SOCIAL CONSTRUCTION OF "WHERE THE PEOPLE ARE . . . PLUS ONE"

Every organizing situation is focused through the prism of societal conditions. Some of them are historical and relate to the epoch in which one is living (Bush conservatism and neoliberal market ideology; Obama's 2008 transformative, interventionist governmental model leaning toward economic redistribution and social equality; the expectation after 2012 that the economy is still moribund and requires a reining in of deficits). Others relate to the immediate resources and activity of a neighborhood or organization (what the schools' reading and math scores are like; how many children of the neighborhood are in the child welfare system). Their combined objective nature—a globalized economy that deepens income inequality within the community, or the level of dollars spent on children within that school district—interacts with people's dominant ideas, attitudes, and beliefs *and* their ensuing strategic responses to create a general sense among people of "what is" and "what we can do."

Each period's objective reality exists in part because people come to perceive those conditions as fixed. The natural responses of people to adapt themselves to those perceived realities reinforce each other in mutually supportive ways: "What is" remains that way because people choose to act, for better or worse, in accordance with those perceptions, making daily life that much easier to understand and act on. As Berger and Luckmann (1967) wrote in their classic *The Social Construction of Reality*:

> Habitualized actions retain their meaningful character for the individual although the meanings involved become embedded as routines in his general stock of knowledge, taken for granted by him and at hand for his projects in the future. . . . And by providing a stable background in which human activity may proceed with a minimum of decision-making most of the time, it frees energy for such decisions as may be necessary on certain occasions. (p. 41)

Thus, in the 1960s and early 1970s, people wanting to change things acted in terms of powerful social movements able to deliver substantial reform. Later, in the mid-'80s, AIDS activists did the same, albeit without as much other social movement support, to lead the fight against corporate profiteering related to HIV-AIDS treatments and medicines. Today, in the early 21st century, activists in the United States are in flux as the habitualized actions of the previous 30 years—*the way folks got used to looking at things*—gave way in 2011 to Occupy Wall Street movements in more than 800 communities. Standing in sharp activist contrast to their Tea Party counterparts on the right, this exciting yet still ambiguous movement speaks to the profound social and political changes under way in our 21st century discourse on the political economy and who does and does not have the right and responsibility to affect U.S. social policy. Is it the 1%? The 99%? Will it be through tax redistribution beginning with the wealthy paying more? Or will it be through deficit reduction via the ending of most of the welfare state? Such a polarized debate reflects the underlying sharp social, political, and economic tensions at play across the United States, Canada, and Europe.

Such a debate and its eventual resolution will be determined by the combined impact of available economic resources, popular ideas, perceptions of who has the authority to make decisions, and the level of organizing activity throughout our communities (see Chapter 1). In combination, these variables reinforce each other in ways that structure how activists will seek change. Thus, while knowing that this period's dominant conditions are exploding with rapid change, good practitioners still ground their strategic stance in the objective conditions before them. To do otherwise would be to stand outside of the experiences and expectations of the people with whom one is working—hardly an effective way to work.

That the strategic outcomes sought at the local level can seem modest in comparison to what is occurring at the national level does not mean they are less compelling or less important. They are designed to fit within what is—based on the actual resources, time, and involvement of the people with whom one is working. Therefore, while cast in the objective mold of the community strategist assessing more limited resources and fiscal options compared with his or her '60s counterpart or at the national level, a community practitioner is actually confronting the same subjective problem in his or her work: *where people are*. By definition, today's organizers in the United States are setting out to change the habitualized perceptions of 21st century groups so that their organizing efforts will be as tactically effective as possible today rather than being based on some time in either the distant past or the faraway future.

Regardless of where one is active, *our organizing role* is thus a statement of opposition to the ways things are perceived and structured. This implicit stance with the community group he or she is working with immediately creates a primary contradiction in an organizer's life: *You must be where the people are . . . plus one.* If all you are is where the people are, they don't really need you, do they? At the same time, if you're where the people are plus three, the people will inevitably frustrate you or lead you to manipulate them for your own ends. *"Where the people are plus one" creates the active tension between **respect** (for where they are) and **challenge** (in the "plus one" of new possibilities that make organizing meaningful).*

Thus, an organizer is almost always a little out of sync, strategically and personally, with those with whom he or she works. In periods of quiet, when the organized expression of our community members' concerns is diffuse and even passive, we are actively working to give energetic form to the ongoing work. Here we are heavily directive and purposefully dynamic; our activism complements their less certain, more passive response. Eventually, however, events begin to shift; people are excitingly engaged in all sorts of activity. Now our roles seem transformed; we perceive the need to emphasize constraint, perhaps caution, at various large-scale tactical suggestions emanating from the group. Then the process begins to repeat itself. This was clearly at play after the election of Barack Obama and the fall of the American financial and manufacturing systems, where in 2011 community people moved from passive acceptance of the status quo to a populist anger and condemnation of these economic leaders; "The 1% versus the 99%" has been a rallying cry of progressive action since it was first used, even outside of the Occupy movement.

Whether people are overly passive or wildly optimistic, your role as an organizer creates a certain *organizational and personal tension* within the mix of resources, perceptions, and strategic alternatives within your group. This tension creates enough dynamism to keep the group moving forward as effectively as possible—always seeking a perfect fit within that mixture that never subsides into either resigned passivity ("There's nothing we can do") or agitated frustration ("Why the hell aren't more people joining this important fight?").

The need for this organizational tension means that we often will go through an organizing experience being just a touch outside of most others' organizational perceptions and experiences. *If an organizer is not aware of the implicit personal tension such a role demands, the result is often either unnecessary personal estrangement leading to elitism or harmful organizational ineffectiveness based on romanticism and naiveté.* As we shall see, neither need occur.

An example of these organizing dynamics occurred when I was doing tenant organizing on the West Side of New York a number of years ago. At first, everything and everyone was uninspired: People rarely came to meetings, apathy hung in the air like a thermal inversion, and there were more diverse issues on our agenda than there were tenants in the building. Because of the passive energy in the room, I knew I had to somehow activate their concerns, however modestly framed, into tangible issues. Regardless of the group's initial amorphousness, as organizer it was my job to make our group *real,* bring it to life in some way; otherwise, the whole effort would be lost. Initially, I spent most of my energy just convincing people to show up to weekly meetings. "Plus one" was convincing people it was worth their while to attend a 2-hour meeting on a Tuesday night to discuss housing code violations with a local government official rather than staying home and watching TV.

REFLECTIVE QUESTIONS

Whatever your formal position (clinical worker, organizer, group workers administrator), examine your role in relationship to a group or individual with whom you are working, preferably on the issue identified at the beginning of the chapter. In what way are you "where the people are plus one"? How do you demonstrate *respect* for where they are? How do you demonstrate *challenge* through "plus one"?

It was not an easy time, those long, long months of October and November. This period is what others have called the preorganizing phase, when one's time is spent convincing individuals to attend meetings, staying positive about future gains, leading by modest example—being what has been described as the "enabler" (Rothman, 2008). However, for a new practitioner, it's also a period of nail biting, bouts of depression, and long nights with a friend mulling over why you ever got into organizing in the first place. In my case, for all my knowledge of pre-engagement phases, I was a wreck.

Then, suddenly, things began to happen. One night, the group transformed itself from an apathetic gathering into a concise, tightly knit organization that definitely wanted to go on rent strike—indeed, wanted to spend its rent money on needed repairs—that night! They had rushed by me, strategically, leaving my tidy, efficient plans for collating all recent rent code violations in disarray. I was soon running to catch up with them, trying to figure out ways to keep the energized group going but struggling to add a drop of caution to their efforts. *Getting to where the people are plus one means respecting and joining the intense activism with a challenge to do it in ways that will keep the momentum going over the long haul and not just for a brief, exciting moment or two.* (In this case, if they hadn't filed the code violations first, all their rent money would have still been owed to the landlord, even if they'd spent the funds to fix terrible violations.)

But that rush from disinterested apathy to intensive activism does not just happen. It is created by the push of objective conditions (in the above case, the elevator broke down for the fourth time in 2 months) that had become harsh enough to necessitate a dramatic alteration of the group's collective consciousness. Given both the previous organizing work and the developing changes in objective conditions, previously unconscious feelings and urgings—what Fritz Perls (1973) called *unfinished business* and Reich and Baxandall (1972) called the *unresolved contradictions of capitalism*— were raised to concretely seek new forms of activity that demanded immediate responses. As one tenant put it, "Look, I've been feeling bad about this place for a while but never put it together. I shouldn't have to *feel* bad and walk those damned stairs, too! I feel fine now, and angry, because I see I have a *right* to that elevator! So let's get it fixed tonight!"

It's only natural that an organizer, having been mired in the small routines of everyday organizing, will often trip in the rush to catch up with a group's heightened activism. And why shouldn't we stumble a bit? As implied by Berger and Luckmann (1967) earlier, initially, the repetition of the organizer's daily activity had been created by the group's passivity. Such routines are a lot of what an organizer does—*the work is necessary but a little boring*—and understandably can cut the organizer off from more radical impulses to move the group into dynamic (and, in all honesty, more emotionally satisfying) forms of confrontation with the landlord around the building's problems.

In such times, we're right to be hesitant, for any good organizer will base strategic decisions on (a) available resources and (b) people's engagement in the issues at hand, rather than on whimsy. In truth, it hurts emotionally to throttle the desire to advance a group rapidly in its development because your tactical awareness says you must slow down. *Ugh!* After a few bruises, you don't move so quickly. Underneath that emotional pain is an important point: All the actions that train a community practitioner in repetitive, daily organizational skills (how to follow up with new members, leaflet preparation, etc.) also *socialize* him or her to levels of expectation—both personally, in effectiveness in motivating others, and collectively about what groups are realistically able to accomplish. If the largest event you've ever engaged in involves 50 people, you can't be immediately prepared, personally or organizationally, to deal with 500.

REFLECTIVE QUESTIONS

Reflect on a recent campaign or group activity. Where could your actions have benefited from a reimagining of possibilities rather than the same habits of planning that perhaps needed a little refreshing? Were new people's perceptions as valued as those of old-timers? Should they be?

For these reasons, we can often find ourselves suddenly lagging behind everyone else's expectations for dynamic activity. The West Side tenants' group didn't have any accumulated experiences to suggest they were trying to do too much. And we can catch up only if we have a well-developed set of intellectual and intuitive skills that can note the varying—and often qualitatively different—shifts in either content (what people want to do) or process (how they want to do it) that underlie such rapid change. Never have these challenging dynamics been more at play than they are for the community practitioner in today's tumultuous world of economic uncertainty and political change. Senge et al. (2004) explain it this way:

> [How] a living system continually re-creates itself . . . in social systems such as global institutions depends on both our individual and collective level of awareness. . . . As long as our thinking is governed by habit—notably by industrial, "machine age" concepts such as control, predictability, standardization, and "faster is better"—we will continue to re-create institutions as they have been, despite their disharmony with the larger world. (p. 9)

Only those capable of developing a practice framework that can see and act on the whole, as Senge and his colleagues (2004) suggest, can expect to be a meaningful part of the transformative change under way in American society in the 21st century.

FROM PERSONAL PROBLEM TO ACTIVIST ISSUE . . . AND BACK AGAIN

Kay and Ellis were back in the diner, coffee cups filled to the brim. They looked at each other, disappointment creased beneath their eyes. After an exciting start, their next youth council meetings had been a bust. No one had shown up at the subcommittees they'd excitedly promised to work on.

"Man, this sucks! What happened here? At the first youth council meeting, the kids were so great! I was sure they liked the issue they'd chosen." Ellis picked at the plain bagel he'd ordered.

"Yeah, geez, they even came up with a name for their group that everybody loved." Kay was referring to the Three Bears Youth Council, the name a member had arrived at after the council decided one of the problems identified was too small—getting their music played at school dances—and another too large—working with the cops to get drug dealers away from their school at the height of the crack epidemic.

The group's final choice had moved from a personal problem to a concrete, actionable issue, itself captured in a catchy name: Jobs for a Change. All the youth council members had eagerly signed on to two subcommittees. Ellis's group members would canvas the neighborhood and nearby communities for a list of potential employers, especially larger corporate businesses. Kay's members were focusing on what they and their friends would need for job readiness skills, résumé writing, and interviewing. The first meeting ended with a few hugs and high-fives all around.

That none of the teenagers came to either subcommittee had jolted the young organizers.

"I guess we put too much on them. They're only kids. We needed to talk with them about their fears, help prepare them more. I got so excited I forgot to see how they really felt about all the work ahead."

"Well, yeah, but I don't think it's how the kids felt about themselves here. I started making all those distinctions about 'corporate' and 'big companies.' Making the whole thing more complicated than it had to be. And then we got into job readiness without even explaining it. Too much stuff, too soon."

"I saw Keysha react when we started putting the committees together, but I didn't stop and ask what she was feeling. She looked kinda' wary now that I think about it. I was just so pleased by the names and the excitement that I stopped looking at the people."

"If you ask me, it was the content: corporate jobs downtown and uptown, job readiness, résumés . . . some of them didn't know what a résumé was, but we kept going. There were so many tasks, and we took too much for granted." Ellis drained his coffee cup. "We have to go back to the kids and break the work down into simpler parts. Then let it build from there."

"Maybe we can do that, but I think we need a little debrief on how each of them feels. I want to follow up one-on-one before the next council meeting. Find out what's going on underneath."

"I'll get the agenda ready. Do a little legwork myself on some of the businesses. Make the work clearer, show them actual forms people use to apply for jobs. Back to basics." They left the diner soon after. While there were no high-fives, a brief farewell hug let them know they were on the same path—only the lanes were different.

MICRO MEETS MACRO: COMBINING YOUR INTUITIVE AND INTELLECTUAL SKILLS

Confronted with an unexpected organizing challenge, Kay and Ellis reverted to what each was most comfortable with in assessing the problem at hand: Kay was intuitively drawn to the interpersonal dynamics; Ellis intellectually reviewed the tasks and their interrelated parts. For both of them—and with any practitioner—learning how to be comfortable with one's intuitive and intellectual abilities is a primary challenge if one seeks to develop an engaged, dynamic practice that can observe and act on the problems of one's chosen community. Indeed, one of the central arguments in this book is that the joining of such abilities is fundamental to the mastery of what Paulo Freire (2000) calls *critical reflection*—the ability to live within what I call "The Two Truths of Great Practice": both acting and reflecting, simultaneously, on one's work. *Great practice is not simply one's professional ability to choose the right tactical intervention. It is equally about developing the personal capacity to live with the dilemmas wrought by whatever correct choice you have made: Too much task creates the dilemmas of undermining relationships; too much relationship building, and the work doesn't get done.*

This is why great practice is so difficult, as such classic theorists in social work education as Hilgard (1987), Berengarden and Berengarden (1968), and Gitterman and Germain (2008) have noted. Likewise, organizational development theorists such as Senge (1994) have found the same when analyzing management behavior. All people have tendencies to emphasize one mode or the other in their learning style: Some approach learning through the intuitive, experiential side, others from a more analytical, intellectual point of view. Researchers are now finding that such modes of problem solving reflect the dominance of one of our brain's two hemispheres: the right hemisphere, which tends to emphasize spatial, intuitive, and emotional faculties, or the left hemisphere, with its analytical, temporal, and intellectual abilities. Thus, as Berengarden and Berengarden discovered, some people learn by doing and then generalize from their experience; others begin from an intellectual and abstract understanding and then through experience develop greater intuitive skill.

The challenge for practitioners, however, is that left unchecked, one's predominant personal approach to learning will be reinforced too often as the primary measure of professional excellence—the singular way by which one approaches problems and how to solve them. This tendency toward the creation of habitualized problem-solving approaches to one's environment, as Berger and Luckmann (1967) noted again and again, is the inevitable process of seeking personal equilibrium in an ever-changing world. There is nothing wrong with balance, of course, but too often practitioners opt for the personal comfort in either "only my gut" versus "only my brain" or "individual versus community," rather than the *critically reflective balance* between intuitive and intellectual skills. Kay needed to strengthen her attention to task and what needed to get done so that her group would not be derailed from actual achievement. Ellis had to focus on his own ability to read the intuitive, personal reasons why young people might have been afraid to take on the assignments so that group cohesion and membership unity would increase.

All too often in macro practice, intuitive or experientially based processes are down-graded as secondary skills. Most approaches to macro practice reward *consistently* only those skills that can be measured in content, which robs a practitioner of much of the credit deserved in his or her intuitive, interpersonal work. This then causes him or her to believe that the intellectual, rational, and abstract elements of practice are the most valu-able when in fact both intuitive and intellectual processes are needed.

Equally important, if models of practice infer that intellectual content relates to higher-order thinking, over time most practice situations will come to be defined primar-ily by their outcome-based content alone, thus once again reinforcing the dichotomy between strategic and personal factors of practice. The sooner we concretely analyze the various ways these two styles of thinking/acting are in fact dual strengths in all practice, the sooner a truly dynamic, strategically and interpersonally charged practice will be possible. Like Ellis and Kay, we all may need a lot of time together over long cups of coffee, tea, or other beverages of our choice for that to happen, but the effort seems worth it.

In short, the joining of our intellectual and intuitive capacities is crucial for everyone's effective practice. Intuitive, interpersonal skills deepen the practice experience by helping one understand intellectual content in actual application—*and vice versa*. Freire (2000) understood this as he wrote about the problem-posing requirements of the literacy worker with the illiterate peasant. For him, the transformational nature of his work from a simple illiteracy project of skilled teachers and illiterate peasants to an organizing prospect led by social beings acting on the world against the Brazilian dictatorship was possible only as the worker engaged in genuine relationship with people that was both respectful and demanding. *Using intuitive skills to build authentic relationships with the peasants while posing intellectual issues that related to the larger world of which the peasants were a part was demanding and important work*. It was a process that required the ongoing develop-ment of peasant and worker alike.

ACTIVITY: INTEGRATING 'MICRO' AND "MACRO"

Assess the campaign issue you identified at the beginning of the chapter in terms of what you do and do not like to do.

- Like doing: _____
- Dislike doing: _____
  - Like doing: more task/intellectual _____
  - Like doing: more process/intuitive _____

(Continued)

(Continued)

     o Dislike doing: more task/intellectual _____

     o Dislike doing: more process/intuitive _____

Reflect on what you can do/learn from others to strengthen one disliked area. Whom can you use as a coach or mentor? Can you reciprocate?

    • I commit to making the effort to improve _____.

Remember: This kind of critical reflection takes long-term effort and is not achieved in one or two attempts!

Every macro practitioner confronts the same problem in trying to intuitively sense a community group's receptiveness to new and potentially bold tactics, tactics one's own previous organizing efforts suggest are doomed to failure. This happened with a group of us who had run a tenants' union in Ann Arbor, Michigan. After being part of a huge rent strike for more than a year (with all the attendant moments of success and failure), most of us had some difficulty in accepting new, militant tactics designed by a fellow steering committee member to reawaken interest in the tenants' union throughout the city. She suggested that the union, recently in the doldrums, organize a dramatic run on the largest bank in the city. This bank, disliked by all students for years due to impersonal service, had been voluntarily giving rent strikers' names to landlords, who then placed liens on their accounts. To the woman proposing the event, the run seemed to be a nice blend of political issues and personal antagonisms that could remobilize our efforts. She based its chances for success on others' personal antipathy toward the bank, not just the correctness of the union's position on liens.

To many of us, it was a nice idea—bold but potentially embarrassing. Having been in a lull, all we needed to further lessen our public image and projected clout as a strong tenants' union was a run on the bank that amounted to about $11.86, the sum total in our individual steering committee members' accounts. *Our skepticism was rationally correct.* Students and other community members had been quiet for months, the event was planned in the middle of a Michigan winter, and our energies were already stretched thin. With the organizer's eye for detail, we observed all the organizational limits to success. Our understanding of previous situations had served us well; we had built a strike with more than 1,000 members and an escrow fund of what today would be more than a million dollars and had maintained enough of our initial dramatic success to build a respected tenants' organization. There had been a great deal of initial fervor, but the ongoing success was due to the organizers' attention to the painstaking detail of day-to-day routines.

The routine—*a routine we were comfortable with*, regardless of our radical posture—was antithetical to the boldness of the act. Yet 1,100 people withdrew what today would be more than $250,000 in one afternoon. Soon, the bank was forced to close its doors to other customers, all of which was duly reported on television, radio, and in papers across the state. The success went beyond our wildest expectations and gave the tenants' union new members, greater clout in the community, and needed encouragement to carry on. As one new member put it, "This thing [the bank run] really hit a nerve. My landlord doesn't matter to me one way or the other, but I hate this bank—and that lien stuff stank. When I saw a chance to bother them like they've bothered me, I figured 'why not?' and took my money out. Now I think I'll join the union. Hell, it *feels* good to get one for our side" (italics mine).

It is only by understanding those feelings and giving shape to them, tactically, that an organization's leadership can remain on top of its work. In our case, it had taken one woman, pulling the rest of us reluctantly along, to state again and again that the people would *like* our demonstration. She had based her plan on both her intellectual skills in organizing previous events and on an intuitive hunch gleaned from her discussions with students that they would identify the bank run with their own personal experiences. She was right. By trusting her mix of abilities, she had pushed the union to the forefront of city politics again. It never would have happened if we had relied on what many of us "knew" was best.

On a far larger scale today, the 2008 election of Obama, himself once a community organizer, followed a similar path of intuitive insight beyond the externally defined limits of the early 21st century, as well as intellectual brilliance (his Internet-based fundraising was nothing short of spectacular, and technically brilliant). If he had waited for the right "rational," historically accurate assessment of a Black man's chances for the presidency in 2007, he would still be a senator from Illinois.

THE VALUE IN CRITICAL REFLECTION

As the above examples suggest, the organizer (or any other practitioner) will always be coming up against certain perceived barriers to ongoing effectiveness. Besides objective factors (availability of economic resources and political alliances, etc.), we also face either disinterest from those around us, which forces a highly routinized response, or, in periods of excitement and mass activity, a breakdown of the boundaries of formal organization, which can create chaos and mismanagement. Only if an organizer forces himself or herself to consistently explore how these larger organizing processes are interconnected with the day-to-day work can he or she expect to remain effective for any extended period of time.

Challenging and testing *one's own* set of behaviors and attitudes is hard work. *But if an organizer can accept the dilemma that says organizational success always demands that he or she limit personal adherence to any one tactic, then the strategic tension between ends and means will lessen.* As the run-on-the-bank example suggests, we risk less in not being committed, personally and organizationally, to one tactical maneuver. Our organizations can only gain in their long-term strategic effectiveness. This strategic and personal irony is not as easy to avoid as it seems, for successful tactics, like a comfortable pair of old shoes, aren't easy to part with. The tactical errors that develop, then, are harder to notice because our own sense of fit betrays our ability to identify others' misgivings.

Such mistakes usually fall into two categories. The first, common to newer macro practitioners, is based on a romanticized commitment to highly intense, emotionally satisfying events in the past. (Often these events were those that crystallized their interest in organizing.) Such romanticism creates what Freire (2000) has called *naive consciousness*:

> an oversimplification of problems; by a nostalgia for the past; by over-estimation of the common man; by lack of interest in investigation; by a strong tendency toward gregariousness; by fragility of argument; by a strongly emotional style; by the practice of polemics rather than dialogics; by magical explanations. (p. 18)

These characteristics could be easily applied to many of us active in the student left in the early 1970s and repeated by some (but by no means all) Occupy Wall Street activists today, particularly in the application of militancy. For example, having effectively used protest tactics earlier in the 1960s, we'd begin our later strategy where the others had ended: with nonnegotiable demands and militant demonstrations. This same has been happening recently as well, especially within some of the anarchist sectors of Occupy Wall Street in which activists transpose tactics from Latin America and other parts of the world where long-term movements have for decades been fighting conditions of recognized oppression (Hedges & Sacco, 2012; Sen & Klein, 2003). Rather than retrace the entire set of long and often frustrating processes and failed tactical choices that in fact had legitimated particular protests, *we'd begin where we experienced final success*—success we felt we could relive almost spontaneously. An acquaintance remembered what happened a few weeks after a successful sit-in for a student bookstore on a Midwest campus:

> We were ecstatic. We'd fought for 2 years to get the bookstore, and the sit-in tipped the issue in our favor. To us the administration looked stupid, and we looked strong. Two weeks later, with our sense of power, we decided to get rid of a really reactionary dean. Rather than think the whole thing through, we all immediately decided to take over his office until he quit. We were really certain we'd win—we were so cocky, we actually were looking for a fight to keep the "student struggle going." And we didn't get anywhere—it was a new issue, new people, and we really needed new ideas. Nobody listened to us in the slightest!

This tactical error need not be based on militancy to create this overly emotional commitment to a particular tactic, be it petitioning, bargaining consensually, or whatever. Rather than analyzing what the organizing situation needs tactically, the organizer with naive consciousness will analyze how the tactic can fit into any situation.

REFLECTIVE QUESTIONS

In reviewing your recent campaign, group, or administrative activity, how are some of the tactics or procedures romanticizing where the people are or assuming levels of engagement/opportunity greater than those that actually exist?

How might they be refreshed by a new mix of intuitive and intellectual reflection joined to actions?

The other major organizing mistake that mirrors the above is based on commitments to outdated tactics that once fulfilled particular institutional needs. Personal commitments such as these create what Freire (2000) calls *fanaticized consciousness* (I prefer *static consciousness*). These errors are common to organizers who have worked in situations demanding high levels of accountability inside their agencies. Often found within larger organizations, such practitioners wed themselves to procedures that grow outdated and inappropriate for new groups but are still upheld as the organizations' measure of success. But the fluidity of organizing makes this tactical pattern subtly misleading. If anything, *it verifies the procedures and old content of past programs as the measure of new organizing programs' success.* One organizer, still active in the settlement house campaigns, recalled her consternation when she realized how bored her group of retired unionist seniors were with her overly formalized approach to their work:

> God, I suddenly saw how bothered they were with me! I'd been running meetings as I'd been trained, filing reports based on officers elected and even . . . what specific skills related to organizing [that] people were learning. . . . Real good examples of leadership training but not much about their needs and how they weren't being listened to. They weren't being listened to. They weren't coming around much until one person told me they'd had enough of "that stuff" in their union meetings! They wanted a chance to talk and socialize. . . . My supervisor wasn't pleased with the vague reports, but I had to change.

Here, rather than forcing a tactic into any situation, the organizer undercuts the natural development of the situation by substituting previously used, *formalized* procedures in the organizing process.

REFLECTIVE QUESTIONS

In reviewing your recent campaign, group, or administrative activity, where are some of the tactics or procedures outmoded—that is, based on unexamined assumptions from the past and imposed on the present?

Where might they be refreshed by a new mix of intuitive and intellectual reflection that mixes "micro" and "macro"?

Each organizing error carries with it an unrecognized rigidity: The former is limited because it is based only on one's gut desires; the latter fails because of *too much* rationality. Real strategic effectiveness therefore demands that we develop the necessary blend of intuitive feeling and intellectual thought—what Freire (2000) calls *critical reflection*—that necessarily combines thought and action. Over time, the practitioner grows comfortable with the engaged use of thought; "reflection and action become imperative when one does not erroneously attempt to dichotomize the content of humanity from its historical forms" (p. 52).

At the diner, Ellis and Kay were learning how to be critically reflective by supporting each other in what the other did best. Rather than a fight over intuitive/interpersonal versus intellectual/task approaches to the work, each began to learn from the other what he or she was not comfortable with in his or her own learning style and approach to problem solving.

That it was mechanistic is understandable: How else do you learn to access information and engage in problem solving that does not come naturally to you? At this stage of their careers, the "content of humanity" related both to *what the kids felt* and *what the campaign needed for strategic success*, joined together at the diner by their mutual appreciation for what each person could do more easily. *In this way, collaboration, rather than an obligatory technique to get the job done, becomes a foundation from which to grow and learn together.* What better model for team problem solving could those young people receive than Kay and Ellis sharing their talents?

Like Kay and Ellis, we blend the intuitive and the intellectual elements into our actual work to check the power of the other. Their agenda has room for Kay's interpersonal dynamics and Ellis's focus on job-related tasks. *Thus, the sweet irony behind less adherence to any one organizing tactic or clinical technique is that by admitting to less, we open ourselves to more flexible application to the dynamic interplay between people's reactions and current conditions.*

Obviously, an organizer's ability to develop critical reflection depends on a sharply honed set of intellectual and intuitive skills that keep him or her open to consistent variation in tactics. Many of those *intellectual skills* relate to invaluable political and technical abilities: being adept at interpreting economic and political trends, knowing how to prepare grants, or learning the plethora of rules and regulations surrounding housing code enforcement, for example.

As developed in the previous two chapters on tactical self-awareness, the ongoing organizing dynamics of critically reflective practice clearly suggest that an organizer's kit involves *the organizer*—his or her personality, self-awareness in different situations, and *intuitive ability* to work with varying numbers of people on all sorts of issues (some of them as amorphous as they are deeply personal). The combination of personal and organizational dynamics at play at every stage of a macro practitioner's career is what this book is exploring, whether the social dynamics regarding race and gender in the workplace or the clinical issues of grassroots organizing. For as any experienced organizer or manager comes to learn, we all engage in "therapy" now and then—on the street or in the office. We just don't use a couch!

ORGANIZERS AND CLINICAL SOCIAL WORKERS: METHOD SIMILARITIES

Engaging in such therapy with our community members in no way implies a less interactive, more reflective stance. That would be ridiculous. However, organizers as well as managers must disabuse ourselves of the idea that we deal only with macro or community issues. We tend to forget that, like clinicians, our concern starts with conditions of individual people. The means by which we choose to correct that condition are just different. *That the means are different does not mean they are therefore in conflict with each other.* Ollman (1977) noted this understanding in Karl Marx's most telling writings:

> Marx's materialism is first and foremost a matter of beginning his study of society with the "real individual," who may be viewed strictly as a producer but is just as often seen as both producer and consumer.... He shows that production and consumption are internally related as aspects of the individual's material existence and that information which generally appears under one heading may be shifted to the other with no loss of meaning. *Likewise, the "real individual" has both subjective and objective aspects—he feels as well as does—and again, because of this interrelatedness, his life situation can be brought into focus by emphasizing either feelings or actions.* (p. 114; italics added)

Unlike the organizer, of course, the clinical social worker usually works in as neutral a setting as possible so that he or she may more easily engage intimately with another individual. This allows the practitioner to better understand and respond to emotional issues that develop. Social forces are involved, too—the physical stress of unemployment, the trauma to one's children or oneself of denied economic aspirations, and so forth—and they must be legitimated and incorporated within the therapeutic process (Lundy, 2004). Nevertheless, this deeply engaged clinical process heightens the personal development that an organizer is not able to consider.

While the level of individual responsibility to address emotional content varies, organizers do assume roles that involve us in trying to understand individual people in our communities. Like clinicians, we need to help people overcome resistance to change and to lessen their fears about what such changes might bring to their lives. We evaluate individuals' capabilities for certain tasks, helping the group choose the right people for the right jobs. By developing a bright, energetic, yet inexperienced young woman to lead a community group or helping another capable, highly efficient, and mild-mannered man grow into a role as an organization's treasurer, we are emphasizing both personal/intuitive and intellectual characteristics in our choices as clearly as the therapist who chooses certain personal issues to aid a client in individual, emotional growth.

Indeed, many types of therapists sound a lot like organizers. For example, Jay Haley (1991) describes strategic therapy as follows:

> Therapy can be called strategic if the clinician initiates what happens during therapy and designs a particular approach for each problem. When a therapist and a person with a problem encounter each other, the action that takes place is determined by both of them, yet in strategic therapy the initiative is by the therapist . . . [who] sets goals, designs interventions to achieve those goals, examines the responses he receives to correct his approach and ultimately examines the outcome to see if he has been effective. The therapist must be sensitive and responsive to the patient and his social field, but how he proceeds must be determined by himself. (p. 77)

While an organizer is not in a position to assume that type of responsibility, Haley's (1991) description reads a lot like Rothman's (2008) synthesis of the "enabler" role in community development:

> The enabler role is one facilitating a process of problem solving and includes such actions as helping people express discontents, encouraging organization, nourishing good interpersonal relations, and emphasizing common objectives. . . . [He] is one who has been responsible for initiating a growth of initiative in others. He has been party to a process of participant-guided learning of habits of responsibility, of applied intelligence, and of ethical sensitivity. The indigenous process he has started, or helped to start, is one of growth in democratic competencies. (p. 97)

Thus, we can see that while there are clear differences in emphasis between the clinician and the organizer, they are more a matter of degree than of irresolvable conflict.

Likewise, Saleebey's (2008) strengths-based framework for intervention is equally compatible with the dynamic we seek to establish, as explained here:

[A strengths perspective] assumes [first] that every person has an inherent power that can be characterized as life force, transformational capacity . . . regenerative potential and healing power . . . [second,] . . . that such power is a potent form of knowledge that can guide personal and social transformation . . . [third,] when people's positive capacities are supported, they are more likely to act on those strengths. (p. 18)

A strengths-based perspective sees that the qualities within an individual are capable of both personal and social transformation. It therefore logically follows that a practitioner's ability to move comfortably between strategic interventions for one individual and strategies for the community at large is critical to long-term practice effectiveness—"micro meets macro" in transformative practice all the time.

REFLECTIVE ACTIVITY: (IN GROUPS OF THREE OR FOUR)

For macro practitioners: Look at a recent campaign or program and discuss how using "micro" skills and techniques could help the project, especially through relationship building.

For micro practitioners: Review your work with an individual or clinical group and see where attention to macro issues and skills could strengthen your clinical work.

THE USE OF PARADOX IN ALL SOCIAL WORK METHODS

For the Clinical Social Worker

There is another fundamental methodological similarity between micro and macro practice, a similarity that heightens the importance of integrating both personal and social dynamics in all types of social work: *All strategic practitioners, be they clinicians or organizers, methodologically value the use of contradiction or paradox as a primary change agent in people's behavior.* As we saw with the development of tactical self-awareness by embracing the permanence of our strengths and the humbling openness to change our limitations, paradox and contradiction assume simultaneous limitation and growth. The clinician, seeing individual growth limited by *personal defense,* uses paradox to frustrate the client, forcing the person to find other, deeper sources of strength if he or she is to resolve the paradoxical dilemma before him or her. The organizer, on the other hand, seeing collective growth limited by *societal defense,* uses contradiction to frustrate society (or an organized segment of society), helping motivate people to go beyond previously imposed obstacles to a richer life.

The clinician seeks to frustrate the individual because the limits are perceived by the client as unmovable (or at least comfortably familiar: *I can't change*); the organizer seeks to frustrate a segment of society because its present organization is perceived by people with whom the organizer is working as a barrier more powerful and/or more legitimate than the people themselves: *We can't win/they have all the power.* Each practitioner has recognized the intrinsic yet underutilized strength in the people with whom he or she is working.

In both cases, they then design strategies to expose these defenses for what they are—not real strength but structured weakness that can be overcome. However—and this is the key point—*by definition, the contradiction embedded in each change situation demands that the practitioners be responsive to its opposite. The clinician must legitimate and respect personal defenses, which thus highlights the client's social context; the organizer must respond to the strength of the perceived social limits, which illuminates people's personal reactions and defenses.*

For example, dialectical behavior therapy (DBT) purposely frustrates clients with problematic behavior by both respecting them to make the choices they wish to make and letting them know the negative consequences that may follow as they remake old choices rather than new ones (Linehan & Dimeff, 2001). The DBT therapist has designed an intervention based on contradiction. The client is receiving two simultaneous communications that create inner conflict: "*You are free to choose to do what you want*" and "*Choosing what you want can harm you if that's what you want.*" As time goes by, it is hoped, such conflict forces changes in behavior, for the client is empowered either to stay stuck in the past or to change.

Working one-on-one, the initial responses to this kind of paradox wrought by DBT will be the client's use of resistance, where well-developed defenses and behaviors are triggered by contradictory options. For example, some clients may push the emotional confusion away by abstractly analyzing the nuances involved in opposing directives; others might pose varying degrees of helplessness, beseeching the therapist for aid and comfort on totally unrelated problems; still others will angrily tell the therapist they don't need his or her help at all.

This resistance, whatever its form, is what the clinician has sought to intensify through paradox. The goal is to eventually raise other emotional issues buried beneath the defensive reaction to the contradictory choices. These more buried issues are very powerful, so powerful that the client may have avoided them for years—the very real emotional abandonment of a distant parent; the understandable rage born of being a Black child in a predominantly hostile, White society; and so on. Once consciously recognized, this new and painful material is directly worked on until the client becomes more comfortable with it, integrating this conscious (and no longer traumatic) information into daily life. Making choices that become positive and healthy becomes easier, not harder.

Yet this therapeutic process is hardly as smooth as the above scenario. It is filled with emotional pitfalls of depression, confusion, and anger that can leave both participants stymied. Some of this will be due to the strength and complexity of the resistance itself (intellectualizing, obsessively complaining about other issues, being overly ingratiating, etc.). *It is here, in the midst of the struggle to go beyond established resistance, where the clinical social worker must actively acknowledge both the power of the defenses and the social conditions that helped bring them into being.* For example, a female client does not create out of thin air a sense of helplessness in high-achievement situations; a sexist society that bombards women with the double-bind message that if they succeed they will suffer for it also becomes part of the therapy.

The client's projection of great neediness is understandable under such conditions. Who wouldn't feel needy if the choices were either (1) succeed at work and court personal estrangement or (2) avoid personal condemnation and throttle personal desires for self-actualization. Many caseworkers who have known how to validate a client's social context have later reported spurts of further emotional growth. Whether this occurs or not, the validation of another's social condition naturally deepens the level of mutual trust. As Saleebey's (2008) strengths perspective suggests, it is a concrete signal of respect, or saying, "Yes, you have some good (social) reasons to have built up those walls around you, and those walls must have helped at times. We both must respect that. *And now* maybe with that respect we can help break those walls down, help cushion our fears as we look deeper at other emotional issues." *Respect and challenge is a fundamental, paradoxical dimension to treatment*

This continuous recognition of social context in personal interactions, even in the midst of paradox, is a necessary element for transformative personal change. As the individual legitimates past defenses as *socially* understandable, he or she can more willingly seek to *personally* change them. The practitioner's and client's use of personal and social factors helps a healthier, more self-aware individual emerge.

REFLECTIVE ACTIVITY

Note a community member's personal issues that may be impacting a group.

Examine what might be some of the social factors influencing this behavior.

Plan for a conversation in which these social factors are raised. Practice a way of framing them as part of an individual response that is neither fatalistic ("There's nothing one can do") nor only about the person's individual responsibility.

Remember: Building relationships here takes practice, practice, and more practice!

For the Community Organizer

The organizer and macro-based practitioner necessarily use contradiction in a different fashion when carrying out a campaign with community members. Rather than focusing on conflicted emotions with an individual, he or she emphasizes the contradiction between, say, societal obligation (rights, stated goals, etc.) and societal achievement (limited access of Blacks and women to executive positions, lack of actual community participation, etc.). By using the *social* paradox ("How can an organization profess openness and discriminate at the same time?"), the organizer develops a set of tactics to engage people in both recognizing the paradox and, at the same time, intensifying its elements so that people seek substantial change.

Here, too, the organizer meets resistance. Some people see the problem as too big and choose to focus on minutiae; others personalize the problems and stridently attack individuals rather than the problem itself; still others are demoralized and feel powerless. To weaken the resistance, the organizer uses tactics that are symbols of the social paradox: The collection of code violations is a concrete action directed toward the ongoing differences between obligation (good housing) and achievement (lousy plumbing, broken doors, etc.). By motivating the tenants to recognize that the social obligation is based on an agreement with them, the organizer helps create a number of tactics (petitioning, scheduling an on-site visit of housing inspectors, etc.) that more forcefully demonstrate the contradiction. (The on-site inspector, whether he does his job or not, is a real example of the violated social contract in action.)

Over time, these small tactics, if effectively carried out, also help break down the *group's resistance to attempt substantial change.* (Here, for example, the demoralized tenant who said society won't change sees hope in trying; the one who said the landlord was too powerful decides the group can take him on.) As the resistance changes to activism, a new social organization—in this case, a tenants' group—emerges to help better our lives.[2]

Like a casework intervention based on DBT, this kind of organizing is rarely choreographed with the fluidity and precision of a Balanchine ballet. Often, each tactical suggestion meets a set of defenses frustratingly real in their capacity to immobilize people. *The organizer's intuitive recognition of people's perceptions and personalized reactions to social conditions becomes important here.* It may turn out that the tenant's gloomy perception of change in the building is colored by a difficult marriage; another's tendency to get too angry at wrong targets (for example, blaming the overworked superintendent rather than the landlord) is based on frustration with a boring job. As the actual day-to-day work goes on, the organizer must be able to learn about such problems, trying to help the community group members distinguish between sets of personal as opposed to community circumstances. If this is done correctly, the group's motivation and effectiveness will eventually increase. Quite often, as individuals meet some collective success, they become personally motivated to try to improve individual problems as well.[3]

The continuous recognition of personal responses and needs in the midst of socially conscious strategic action, developed and understood as social contradictions heighten in the community, is key to any organizer's success. With the organizer's help, the community members begin to differentiate a variety of social and personal problems, becoming increasingly able to focus directly on the organization's primary strategic aims. As in the therapeutic relationship, the organizer's use of social and personal factors helps develop a healthier, more *socially* able organization.

USING PARADOX IN YOUR WORK

The necessary use of contradiction or paradox in any form of strategic practice—micro or macro—initially places great mental strain on any new practitioner. The clinical social worker is in an intense personal relationship, yet he or she must develop social awareness to be successful; the organizer works with social problems yet cannot ignore personal issues if those problems are to be alleviated. Kay and Ellis each have a challenge to overcome!

Understandably, then, the predominant focus of each method creates intrinsic allegiance to a form of practice that sidesteps less dominant issues. The caseworker who legitimates social factors may find that the client uses his or her legitimacy as a new defense to avoid deeper emotional issues. The organizer who helps a community member recognize how personal problems cloud his or her strategic perception may become mired in interpersonal relations that the organization cannot handle. In both cases, it obviously takes more than the recognition of both social and personal dynamics to be effective: One's own self-awareness and a capacity to set and keep healthy boundaries, an ability to skillfully read changing practice context, and a solid strategic sense that helps a practitioner recognize when everyone must move on to other issues are all of vital importance.

An example should help here. An organizer related his dawning consternation when he realized his consumer co-op was becoming so personally focused that it might be unable to expand as originally planned:

> One day it hit me that everyone was sitting around and bullshitting about their individual family problems to the point the co-op was falling apart. I'd begun the rap sessions 2 months earlier because a few members were having problems in getting their spouses to help more at home while they were here. Pretty soon, they were using the sessions for every personal gripe imaginable, and our plans for expansion were being ignored. . . . We almost didn't make it out of that mess.

The organizer's problem was not a mere tactical blunder that could be corrected by a simple return to the organization's tasks or some abrupt modification in the group process. *It was his tendency to dichotomize the practice situation:* "We've dealt with the co-op (strategic, content-focused issues) in easily separated categories." As he admitted in long discussions later, he had been unable to recognize that the larger group situation had been laced with personal implications, just as the predominantly personal situation had direct strategic and programmatic consequences. Beyond this recognition, however, was a more important error: his more rational reliance on only the content of the problem before him—that is, an awkward inability to sense intuitively the underlying, less visible dynamics in each situation. *What is important to note here is that one can develop both attributes only if he or she is constantly aware that personal and social, strategic dynamics are always at play in every practice context. What changes is the predominance of one or the other set of issues, not the absence of either personal or social factors.*

As we discussed in Chapters 3 and 4 on tactical self-awareness, the more we develop our internal capacity to embrace both what we do well and how such strengths can humbly reappear as tactical limitations later on, the more likely we will be to maintain an external flexibility in our tactical and strategic choices. As Senge and his colleagues (2004) wrote, "When people start to see from within the emerging whole, they start to act in ways that can cause problems to start to 'dissolve' over time" (p. 51).

Thus, if the organizer had been holistically aware of the potential *social* defenses underlying an open-ended, *personally focused* factor such as the rap group, the setbacks might never have occurred. While he would have been out of sync, personally and organizationally, with the group when it first expressed its desire for only *informal* rap sessions, the co-op's unimpaired effectiveness would have made the initial tension he experienced worthwhile. Being at "plus one" challenges everyone to grow beyond where the people are—practitioners and community members alike.

A more experienced organizer in the Bushwick section of Brooklyn had a very different experience with his youth employment group, which has located some jobs for group members and also been involved in various community development projects for years. While never having read Freire, his work was the essence of critical reflection:

> We work, and we party later, like they want, that's what we do! The kids know where I'm coming from, that I make 'em work their butts off if they're gonna be in this program, but they know that I'm willing to find out where they're at, too, to let them speak their minds as they see things, you know. . . . Every successful or unsuccessful event always has a dance scheduled after it—that was their idea, one show they run. We all have time for personal problems, too, never letting our projects (housing rehabilitation) be the be-all and end-all. That's the only way we've survived, because at times things get very heavy . . . not everyone can get a job, there are a lot of street hassles going on, you name it. But regardless of the

type of stress, I know this group will work, that the kids will stay on the job, even when there's no immediate pay-off for them or for me.... A guy like me has to wear a lot of hats, that's all—and let the kids wear a few, too! I make mistakes sometimes, don't always do everything based on ideas, especially when things aren't working out right, I go with my gut, too. A person like me has to trust himself inside and out.

This organizer has built a small, effective organization, in part by being aware of both the personal and social needs of the group and by using himself "inside and out" to skillfully weave together personal membership needs within the larger concerns of the organization. There is no artificial separation between skill sets, personal development, or group development. For him, it is a given that personal and social problems have to be concretely attended to, using a variety of his skills—and theirs—to make that often seemingly disparate idea a concrete reality. The institutionalization of policies such as the parties (an idea coming from the community members) brings that home to people. Quite simply, *the predominant needs of any one moment can never dominate all the time—and thus you need a set of shifting yet complementary skills to be aware of such needs.* A person who trusts himself or herself completely can wear many hats—and method choices—comfortably, and that is the essence of engaged, dynamic practice.

The personal demands needed to develop this form of practice aren't easy to meet unless they are acknowledged, accepted, and experientially adapted to. Once this happens, the personal tension that leads one to unconsciously adopt less flexible roles will decrease. The unconscious need to envelop any one practice situation with one rigid set of skills or tactics is replaced with a more relaxed openness to actively engage with *predominant yet shifting needs.* Whether a caseworker or an organizer, knowing the potential fluidity of the situation frees one from the constraints of needing total mastery over it.

FUTURE EXPLORATION OF THE MICRO AND MACRO

Future analyses around specific topics need to be developed to more deeply explore these personal, group, and individualized dynamics within social and political contexts. Some being worked on now that will add further understanding to our practice include issues related to the tactical use of self in organizing, cultural competency, the use of "mindfulness" in professional practice, and the weaving together of interviewing and leadership development techniques; others must begin (Ackerman & Maslin-Ostrowski, 2002; Epstein, 1999; Wing Sue, 2010; Wong, 2004). By venturing into uncharted waters, such work may at times reach beyond its grasp. But any experienced organizer knows (and has been part of) too many campaigns and events that could have been strengthened if the practitioner had been willing to more fully understand how the dynamics of social and personal change intermingle in close, interconnected reality. On a broader scale, the dichotomized world between caseworkers and organizers and between organizers and managers must be narrowed if we are to meet the increasing needs and economic constraints forecast for today.

DEVELOPING TRANSFORMATIVE PRACTICE: SOME FIRST STEPS

The interventions described above can be accomplished only through a practice framework capable of incorporating its distinct yet interconnected parts, whether they are analyzed as process and task, intuitive and intellectual, or relational and outcome focused. Furthermore, that practice must be able to critically reflect and act on the tensions wrought by this constantly changing relationship between those parts. I consider such a framework to be transformational in that the changes wrought through this process alter both the organizing process and the people involved in that change together. (This would be true with clinical social work as well.) Freire (2000) noted again and again that such critical reflection in one's work transforms not only those who seek help (or change) but the helper as well, for the change under way is constantly impacting each participant. Used by practitioners and activists elsewhere, especially in the developing world, a transformative methodology grounds itself in certain principles that hold tremendous potential for the social world. The primary principles are spelled out below.

- First, there can be no exclusive elements in any approach to dynamic, transformational practice. The social–personal dynamics of case and community work developed here have explored how one utilizes the *predominant yet shifting emphases* in each practice situation. A more static framework over time creates false dichotomies between various practice methods within the social work process. In practice terms, this either/or methodology unwittingly creates the false belief that clinical social work deals only with the interpersonal dynamics of the individual or that organizing involves only socioeconomic and political concerns of a community group. Likewise, the same impasse between managers working only from above and organizers struggling solely from below creates tensions between community-based practitioners that need not occur. A transformative practice framework, seeing both elements at play all the time, engages in a consistent examination of both social and personal factors simultaneously. This is why, as seen in the earlier co-op example, an organizer must work on political strategy while seeking to understand personal needs and concerns of a group's membership, allowing his or her understanding of dominant needs to determine tactical choices, at times concentrating on personal problems, and at other times responding to political demands.
- Naturally, at any one moment in time, a particular focus will predominate in the practice situation, as any organizer or caseworker would recognize. But this framework

necessarily poses that any social work intervention will have both individual and social issues that interact with each other and will emerge dynamically in that intervention at some point. The organizational tension needed for change is born out of the essence of this process, for it works with the limitation and opportunity of each practice situation's momentary emphasis. For example, at one point in time, an organizer's emphasis is on mobilizing the group. This *active* stance is a response to the group's *passivity*. In a later, frenetic period of group growth, one's role becomes more cautionary to stimulate maximally effective tactics. An equivalent dynamic happens within a transformational clinical process as well.

- The macro practitioner's role seeks to create this tension during the intervention as healthy and necessary work. *Yet this ability to dynamically adapt to such shifts can occur only if the practitioner actively uses "micro" and "macro" skills that can deal with the content of the immediate moment and the process of the future.* As seen in the example of the run on the bank, the intellectual (content-focused) and intuitive (process-focused) skills of great practice develop out of this form of engagement as one seeks to deal with natural elements of each practice situation—action and passivity, stasis and conflict, personal and social, and so on.

- As one works on these contradictory elements together over time, one can understand and act on the social process only *experientially,* combining both theoretical and practice content. As stated above, *the false distinction between intuitive and intellectual skills is replaced here by a consistent use of both qualities.* The practitioner learns to use all of himself or herself (both mind and body) in each practice situation. The politically "hard" organizer's and emotionally "soft" clinical social worker's abilities within us all allow a transformative practitioner to develop a socially charged practice firmly rooted in historical *and* personal circumstance, authentically engaged with the person or people beside the practitioner and the community of which he or she is a part.

- Furthermore, this framework drops the artificial distinction between short-term process goals (which are most often associated with individual, intrapersonal needs) and long-term instrumental goals (most often associated with demands for community change), replacing this distinction with deeper awareness of the dynamics between short-term change and longer-term transformation. This approach sees the emergence of a *permanent process* that shapes instrumental goals, which in turn alters later process developments. Freire (2000) calls this the *constant development of consciousness.*

- *In short, the way we act is as important as the object of that action.* Thus, the example of a clinical social worker willing to validate and use the social context as part of a client's program will be viewed as far more *politically engaged* than the top-down organizer who ignores others' personal development in pursuit of concrete political aims. Likewise, the organizer willing to grapple with his or her coworkers' reactions in the midst of an intense campaign effort is far more *personally engaged* than the caseworker who screens out the social realities of a client's life to highlight particular psychodynamic phenomena more clearly. In both cases, the transformative practitioner is always able to find meaning in his or her work without opting for the falsely dichotomized clinical/political tracks chosen by others who burned out elsewhere.

- Finally, this transformative framework consistently notes that practice is developed and shaped by larger social conditions and not just personal choices. In practice terms, this means that while values, ideas, and skills are necessary tools to practice, they never stand outside of the influence of larger social forces and the political times in which one lives and works. (The year 2013 is very different from 1969, 1989, or 2009!) In turn, of course, such values and skills can and do affect the larger society over time. This is why an effective practitioner always remains cognizant of both personal and social factors within his or her work. This critically reflective skill does two things: It minimizes the effect of any *static* assumption enveloping one's practice, and *it discards the false notion that transformative change can occur only within large-scale social movements.*

Thus, the process of testing limitations and using the strengths of *any* social period allows one to grow and develop within that period—including this one. Once understood, a transformative framework does away with both the false optimism associated with gut-level reactions to past social movements and today's bouts of pessimism that one can implement a change-oriented practice only if there are banners in the streets or elation that a new president can do it all. By actively developing the social–personal dynamics of a practice situation based on keen observation of what today's world is like, a practitioner remains alive to and aware of *as much change as is possible within that context.* The two-sided coin of false idealism and postmodern cynicism is replaced with the less inflated image of *realistic, humane, and engaged activism.*

As stated in the introduction, this long (and difficult) chapter has attempted to delineate concretely what a transformational practice is and how it can be used dynamically by practitioners at both the micro and macro levels. Its objectives were

- uniting the social and the personal regardless of method;
- realizing the value of working with both the strengths and limitations of one's objective situation;
- using both intuitive and intellectual skills in your practice;
- using one's own tactical self-awareness and appreciation for one's own strengths and limitations to help develop both a macro and micro practitioner's tactical flexibility and diminished adherence to outmoded strategies; and
- using this mix of skills to dynamically engage in, assess, and act on the world in a flexible and potentially transformational way for community, client, and practitioner alike.

All these objectives are operational equivalents to some of the principles involved in the transformational practice developed throughout the chapter. It is hoped that this form of practice may have something to offer, especially if we are to remain adept at responding to the heightened needs of the 21st century—even as our immediate resource base may be much more constricted. In this critically reflective manner, we can begin to end some of the imbalance and pessimism in presently dichotomized forms of social work practice.

REFLECTIVE ACTIVITY FOR EDUCATIONAL POLICY 2.1.10(A–D) (IN SMALL GROUPS)

Reflect on the dynamics impacting your practice, and determine *the mix of individual/personal and collective/community factors* that "present" in your work with others. As either a micro or macro practitioner, what is one intuitive skill from "the other side" that could positively impact the dynamics of your practice intervention so that you deepen relationships *and* achieve desired results?

How can a practitioner from a different method help you stretch to look at this other approach with comfort and flexibility?

Who can be your Ellis or Kay?

THE COMMUNITY TOOLBOX

The Community Toolbox provides some excellent tools on how to analyze social problems and achieve clear, strategic goals at http://ctb.ku.edu/en/tablecontents/chapter_1017.htm.

Analyzing Community Problems and Solutions

Section 1. An Introduction to the Problem-Solving Process

Section 2. Thinking Critically

Section 3. Defining and Analyzing the Problem

Section 4. Analyzing Root Causes of Problems: The "But Why?" Technique

Section 5. Addressing Social Determinants of Health and Development

Section 6. Generating and Choosing Solutions

Section 7. Putting Your Solution Into Practice

REFERENCES

Ackerman, R., & Maslin-Ostrowski, P. (2002). *The wounded leader: How real leadership emerges in times of crisis*. New York: Jossey-Bass.

Alinsky, S. (1989). *Rules for radicals*. New York: Vintage.

Berengarden, I., & Berengarden, S. (1968). *Interviewing and personality assessment*. New York: Columbia University Press.

Berger, P., & Luckmann, T. (1967). *The social construction of reality: A treatise in the sociology of knowledge*. New York: Knopf Doubleday.

Bernstein, J. (2008). *Crunch: Why do I feel so squeezed?* New York: Berrett-Koehler.

Bonner, T. N. (2002). *Iconoclast: Abraham Flexner and a life in learning*. Baltimore, MD: Johns Hopkins University Press.

Eichler, M. (2007). *Consensus organizing: Building communities of mutual self-interest*. Thousand Oaks, CA: Sage.

Epstein, R. M. (1999). Mindful practice. *Journal of the American Medical Association, 282*, 833–839.

Freire, P. (2000). *Pedagogy of the oppressed*. New York: Continuum.

Gitterman, A., & Germain, C. (2008). *The life model of social work practice: Advances in theory and practice* (3rd ed.). New York: Columbia University Press.

Haley, J. (1991). *Problem-solving therapy* (2nd ed.). San Francisco: Jossey-Bass.

Hedges, C., & Sacco, J. (2012). *Days of destruction, days of revolt*. New York: Nation Publishers.

Hilgard, E. (1987). *Psychology in America: A historical survey*. Fort Worth, TX: Harcourt Brace College.

Homan, M. (2004). *Promoting community change: Making it happen in the real world*. Florence, KY: Cengage Learning.

Linehan, M. M., & Dimeff, L. (2001). Dialectical behavior therapy in a nutshell. *California Psychologist, 34*, 10–13.

Lowery, C., Mattaini, M., & Meyer, C. (Eds.). (2007). *Foundations of social work practice: A graduate text*. Washington, DC: National Association of Social Workers Press.

Lundy, C. (2004). *Social work and social justice: A structural approach to practice*. Toronto: Higher Education University of Toronto Press.

Minieri, J., & Getsos, P. (2007). *Tools for radical democracy: How to organize for power in your community*. San Francisco: Jossey-Bass.

Netting, F., Kettner, P., & McMurtry, S. (2007). *Social work macro practice*. Boston: Allyn & Bacon.

Ollman, B. (1977). *Alienation: Marx's conception of man in a capitalist society*. Cambridge, UK: Cambridge University Press.

Perls, F. (1973). *The Gestalt approach and eye witness to therapy*. Palo Alto, CA: Science & Behavior Books.

Reich, W., & Baxandall, L. (Eds.). (1972). *Sex-pol: Essays, 1929–1934*. New York: Vintage.

Ross, M. (1967). *Community organization: Theory, principles and practice*. New York: Harper & Row.

Rothman, J. (2008). *Strategies of community intervention*. Peosta, IA: Eddie Bowers.

Rubin, H., & Rubin, I. (2004). *Qualitative interviewing: The art of hearing data*. Thousand Oaks, CA: Sage.

Rubin, H., & Rubin, I. (2007). *Community organizing and development*. Boston: Allyn & Bacon.

Saleebey, D. (2008). *The strengths perspective in social work practice* (5th ed.). Boston: Allyn & Bacon.

Sen, R., & Klein, K. (2003). *Stir it up: Lessons in community organizing and advocacy*. San Francisco: Jossey-Bass.

Senge, P. (1994). *The fifth discipline: The art and practice of the learning organization*. Cambridge: MIT Press.

Senge, P., Scharmer, O., Jaworski, J., & Flowers, B. (2004). *Presence: Exploring profound change in people, organizations and society*. London: Nicholas Brealey.

Staples, L. (2004). *Roots to power: A manual for grassroots organizing*. Santa Barbara, CA: Praeger.

Wing Sue, D. (2010). *Micro-aggressions in everyday life*. New York: Wiley.

Wong, Y. L. (2004). Knowing through discomfort: A mindfulness-based critical social work pedagogy. *Critical Social Work, 5*(1).

NOTES

1. Some recent texts continue to frame relationship building as a task focus that implicitly becomes canned and mechanistic. See, for example, Joan Minieri and Paul Getsos's (2007) *Tools for Radical Democracy*, in which they write about recruitment of new members by "developing a rap," listing eight steps to be covered in a 5-to-7-minute conversation (introduction, self-interest, accomplishments, political education, agitation, call to action, commitment, and data collection). While certainly inclusive, the focus on so many tasks in such a short time leads to abstracting the very relationships we need to build before they have even begun!

2. The same process in obverse occurs when tactical commitments are based on the perceived seriousness and/or legitimacy of the problem itself. Working in the South Bronx, I have personally fallen prey to this tendency. For example, when confronted with the lack of jobs for young people, I and others were extremely demanding with city officials in our request for aid, even though there were few political resources at hand to motivate our cause. Here we were using our emotional commitment to ending the problem to color our choice and use of tactics, fitting the tactics to the situation more by our anger at injustice than by our analysis of the situation itself.

Both of these tendencies have resurfaced in the use of militancy by anti–World Trade Organization activists today. Emboldened by the success of militancy in Seattle in 2001, the same degrees of militancy were applied elsewhere, with far less power and impact, for similar reasons to those discussed above.

3. I have seen this happen frequently, but I am not arguing that work on one successful organizing or therapeutic act can be a corrective for all kinds of social and/or personal problems—only that it may help. It certainly has a lot more potential than doing nothing at all!

Section III
Relationship Building

Perhaps most central to social work practice is relationship building. Without trusting and collaborative relationships, neither effective biopsychosocial diagnoses nor accurate community assessments can lead to sustained change and improvement. The give-and-take of good clinical and community work means that relationships between people are growing in trust, openness, and honesty so that problems can be confronted and solutions can be developed and implemented. Without good relationships, good social work practice can't happen.

Chapters 6 and 7 focus on two often-neglected dimensions of relationship building. Chapter 6 emphasizes how one develops democratic, shared leadership responsibilities over time without denying the differences in power that exist between paid professionals and community members. While integrating both "micro" and "macro" skills, the chapter delineates Paulo Freire's methodology of liberational pedagogy (originally developed for educators) within our North American context of social work practice. In this manner, it challenges traditional social work practice models of "helping" for a transformational alternative of "co-creation" between social workers and those with whom they work.

Chapter 7 emphasizes relationship building as connected to the *highly charged issues of race, gender, sexuality, class, and age,* and how such social dynamics impact—for better or worse—the abilities of people with different social identities to work together. By carefully assessing how often unconscious dynamics of social power and privilege can undermine well-intentioned efforts at relationship building, the chapter goes on to outline the small but necessary steps one can take to embrace social difference as an asset to one's work. Such steps also form a process of *mindful practice* that emphasizes the development of openness, flexibility, and presence in relationship building.

CHAPTER 6

Leadership Development Through Relationship Building

"Embody the Change You Seek"

EYES ON THE FLOOR

The youth council was wrapping up its first meeting. Ellis and Kay had been thrilled to see 15 young people turn out. "They really seem interested in the job fair. This is good," Ellis whispered in Kay's ear as they moved on to the last agenda item. The teens agreed that a job fair inviting possible employers to the school on a Saturday would be exciting and doable. Kay had her concrete activities to help the kids; Ellis could see a way for companies to give back. Given the energy in the room, the two young organizers were on a roll.

"So who can help with the flyer?" Kay asked the assembled group. Suddenly all eyes were on the floor, searching for some invisible speck of dust that only the teens could see. The energy in the room was replaced with an uneasy quiet.

"Come on, guys, a couple can help with the flyer, and I only need two people to come with me and speak to employers. What do you say?" Ellis was trying not to sound desperate.

Finally, Cece, one of the older members, shyly raised her hand. "I'll sit with you, Kay, but I don't know anything about flyers. You gotta show me." The group seemed relieved that one of theirs had spoken at last. "That's great, Cece, great! So who else? You know, you're the leaders of this council. You get to make the decisions and lead this council, not us." Kay was firm as she spoke, Ellis nodding alongside her.

Quiet descended on the room again. Robby spoke up at last. "Aww, Ellis, Kay, you're the leaders, not us. We haven't done this stuff before, you know. You guys are in graduate school! You know that you know more than we do, you know?"

The group laughed timidly at the repetition but did not disagree. "I can't talk to some employer! What would I know what to say?"

Ellis and Kay looked at each other in consternation. Their ideas on leadership development included the young people in central roles from the beginning. While initially excited, the teens were suddenly backing off any real responsibility. What were they to do? They couldn't make them participate; if they tried too hard, they'd lose them all. But if the young people did next to nothing, they'd never feel a sense of their own empowerment. Having a project that left young people as dependent as ever was just as upsetting.

The young organizers headed back to their favorite diner. Their organizing teacher had mentioned dilemmas like these in class, but up close, the lack of leadership in the council felt less like a dilemma and more like a mess. What could they do now?

Educational Policy 2.1.7—Apply knowledge of human behavior and the social environment.

Educational Policy 2.1.9—Respond to contexts that shape practice.

This chapter emphasizes practitioner core competency in both Educational Policy 2.1.7, through its attention to how "social workers are knowledgeable about human behavior across the life course . . . and the ways social systems promote or deter people in maintaining or achieving health and well-being," and Educational Policy 2.1.9 as practitioners become "informed, resourceful, and proactive in responding to evolving organizational, community, and societal contexts at all levels of practice" and can "recognize that the context of practice is dynamic, and use knowledge and skill to respond proactively."

"EMBODY THE CHANGE YOU SEEK": COMMUNITY PRACTITIONERS, LEADERSHIP DEVELOPMENT, AND THE CREATION OF DEMOCRATIC EXPERIENCE

As they are finding out, Ellis and Kay's first brush with recruiting people to lead their own cause can be fraught with both personal anxiety and strategic tension to expand participation and involvement. Most of the organizing literature addresses these issues under topics of community engagement, issue development, and the choice of topics and targets (Homan, 2004; Netting, Kettner, & McMurtry, 2008; Rubin & Rubin, 2007). This emphasis is a necessary part of any organizing campaign and its strategic development; the reader is invited to use the Community Toolbox's terrific tools (cited at the end of this chapter) for concrete steps to take in addressing engagement, member recruitment, and target selection.

As we shall see, such activities are about far more than these tasks, as important as they are. They are also about how leadership is formed and the dynamic interplay between group members and their assumptions about what democracy means *for them*. While the majority of social work literature on leadership still tends to treat the work of leadership development in a descriptive manner, such an emphasis is incomplete.[1] While informative, most leadership literature in social work neither captures the dynamic interplay of relationship building between organizers and developing leaders nor makes clear how the creation of new leaders is fundamental in framing the contours of civic engagement within a democratic society.

Of course, as Ellis and Kay's experience suggests, one's initial foray into leadership development can cause anxiety, difficulty, and concern for any community practitioner. As we saw in the previous chapter, the dynamics between organizer and members begin with the *organizer's strategic push for commitment/the member's pullback from involvement*. Later, it can turn into *the member's push for widespread change/the organizer's tactical pull for long-term effectiveness*. This role strain constructs its own tensions between group members that are partly overcome through the community practitioner's growing awareness that such push–pull dynamics are a necessary part of a campaign's development, as much a part of the job as creating flyers, holding meetings, and setting agendas.

But more is at play than role tension between macro practitioner and group members. As was made clear in Chapters 2 and 3, what kind of leadership we as a nation seek at all levels of community and how such leadership is expressed in terms of decision making, sharing power, and collaboration is now at play in ways not seen for more than 50 years. For the community practitioner, never before have Gandhi's words, rephrased by the leadership writer Peter Senge, been more apt: *"Embody the change you seek"* (Senge, Scharmer, Jaworski, & Flowers, 2004). How an organizer recruits people, works with them on their decision making, handles social tensions affected by power and oppression, and critiques as well as supports their work will construct the type of democratic experience between leader and led that he or she believes is possible.

In short, over time, a community practitioner's actions, *especially in relationship building,* have the potential to *embody the transformative possibility that as the organized gain power, the organizer loses none*. Expressing Steven Covey's (2004) notion of win–win as 100%–100% in concrete form, the way a macro practitioner goes about his or her work is a powerful opportunity by which genuine democratic experience spreads through our society and captures the imagination of a new generation of activists and citizens. Given the collapse of other forms of leadership in our economic and political spheres and the ensuing volatility in today's political discourse, we seem to be at a historic moment where Paulo Freire's (2000) emphasis on the slow, *gradual process of dialogue between helpers and helped that necessarily begins with the frustrated anxiety of the organizer alongside the fear-driven apathy of the organized can be transformed into the shared democratic experience of mutually interdependent leaders, activists, and members.* For as Freire (2000) wrote, "Liberation is thus a childbirth, and a painful one" (p. 49). This chapter explores how the painful, liberating birth of this transformative leadership experience for the organized *and* the organizer can occur.

THINKING ABOUT LEADERSHIP

We need to begin with current ideas on leadership, because leadership is so central to all forms of macro practice. We will address some of these issues in later chapters as organizers move on to positions as directors, supervisors, and executives. Here, we start when the organizer has little or no formal power, and yet he or she is involved with building lasting campaigns and expanding people's organizations. Interestingly enough, in countless discussions with organizers, I have found their lists of accomplishments always related to programmatic development/campaign success that came to be run at least in part by community members. It seems clear that leadership development is to community organization and macro practice what social functioning is to clinical work (Saleebey, 2008).

That so cherished a hallmark of macro practice continues to be so underdeveloped in the organizing and macro practice literature itself is surprising (Austin, Brody, & Packard, 2008; De Pree, 1989, 1993; Heifetz, 1998; Senge, 1994). While there are numerous workshops and training programs on developing grassroots leaders (from the Midwest Academy to the Center for Third World Organizing), their work tends to focus on *the techniques of leadership rather than on the methodology of leadership itself.* With the exception of Eric Zachary's (1998) study of leadership training for South Bronx parent leaders, little work distinguishes grassroots, community-based leadership from other, more traditional forms of managerially based models of leaders and their teams. It is as if leadership development is so universally agreed on as a given objective of practice that it never dawned on anyone to study it as it actually takes place between the organizer and the organized.

Not that there has been little research on leadership itself. A quick Google of the term *leadership* in 2012 led to 527 million hits, while *leadership development* produced an astounding 106 million! A more careful perusal, however, shows that the focus is on the development of individual leaders, who in turn inspire, motivate, and develop their teams. Whether at the esteemed Center for Creative Leadership (www.ccl.org) or the well-known and respected Center for Third World Organizing (www.ctwo.org), the focus has consistently been on locating individuals to lead others from a paradigm that assumes limits on how one can lead and who can do so. While some, such as the Center for Third World Organizing, are greatly committed to recruitment from communities others might ignore, the basic paradigm that determines whether or not power can be shared over time has remained the same.

QUALITIES OF LEADERSHIP FOR THE MACRO PRACTITIONER

The work on leadership itself has had some profound insights over the past 30 years that can be of real benefit to anyone involved in macro practice. Overwhelmingly written by and for the corporate sector, there are four primary themes related to a person's leadership capacity that are deserving of note here:

- Developing the *capacity to distinguish urgency, importance, and one's use of time* to handle the essential demands of one's workday (Blanchard & Johnson, 1981; Covey, 1999, 2003, 2004; Shepard & Hayduk, 2002).
- Developing one's *personal mastery* to better discern what is actually happening as opposed to what one perceives is happening. Through this internal attention to his or her ways of thinking and acting, the leader is also able to engage in *systems thinking*—that is, an ability to examine the underlying problems and issues that impact an organization's development or a campaign's long-term strategy (Argyis, 1991; Schön, 1991; Senge, 1994; Senge et al., 2004).
- Developing *servant leadership* in the way one works with others in a collaborative and "serve first" manner. Inspired by both the classic writings of Lao-Tze and the teachings of Jesus Christ, the work emphasizes that one must serve before leading as a key to one's lasting legacy (Greenleaf & Spears, 2004). Several educational theorists, such as Bolman and Deal (2003), Covey (1999), Sergiovanni (2006), and Heifetz (1998), also reference these characteristics as essential components of effective leadership.
- Emerging recently from the human service field, a *transformative leadership* model has emphasized the notion that "if the work is sacred, then so are you" so that those working in macro practice recognize that their long-term ability to *create a lasting legacy through small, sacred acts each day* includes *self-care* as fundamental to both personal well-being and the model of leadership one hopes to inspire in others (Burghardt & Tolliver, 2009).

The capacities to distinguish urgency from importance and effectively use one's time were most powerfully put forward through the work of the late Steven Covey. Starting with the key insight that a person's ability to slow down his or her reaction time between receiving a stimulus and giving a response was at the heart of effective management, Covey's original work can be of great value for macro practitioners, who are bombarded with the stimuli of campaign and organizational demands each and every day. Covey went on to find that what could help a person become more reflective and less reactive was to distinguish what was an urgent and important demand from an urgent and unimportant demand. The first set of demands, falling into what he called Quadrant I, were real crises and actual deadlines; what "crises" fell into the other (called Quadrant III) were problems and issues that never should have happened in the first place: others' missed deadlines, unreturned phone calls, and missed meetings. The exhaustion and frustration of spending so much time on these Quadrant III activities in turn led people to spend time on passivity-inducing, mindless activities in Quadrant IV, ranging from gossip to mindless net surfing.

One of Covey's key insights was therefore to *work with leaders on what was important but not urgent in Quadrant II:* long-term planning, relationship building, and self-care. His seminal work has helped countless managers, leaders, and others see that how one carefully uses time, including incorporating Quadrant II activities into one's daily life, is fundamental to long-term managerial and leadership effectiveness (Covey, 1999, 2003, 2004).

PERSONAL ACTIVITY

Take a moment to create Covey's four quadrants:

I. Urgent and Important

II. Important and Not Urgent

III. Urgent and Not Important

IV. Not Urgent and Not Important

In reviewing your week, list the activities in the four quadrants. Once completed, identify Quadrant III activities you'd like to lessen, and add in new Quadrant II activities that would help achieve your objective (better planning, relationship building, etc.). See Covey's (2003) *The 7 Habits of Highly Effective People* for more on this topic.

Developing personal mastery and systems thinking allows the underlying causes of problems and concerns to become the primary focus of leaders and their teams. Masterfully synthesizing and building on his MIT colleagues' work on personal reflection and critical thinking, Peter Senge's (1994) *The Fifth Discipline* focused on the mental and emotional faculties necessary both to work collaboratively and to delve into what he called *systems thinking,* the ability to understand and connect the underlying and often interrelated causes of most organizational problems. While his work initially focused on the dynamics of the business cycle, he and his colleagues have gone on to work with both educational institutions and environmental organizations.

To use an example of interest to a young macro practitioner, through systems thinking, one would assess a problem such as poor reading scores in a school and through deep reflection and practice develop a campaign that focused less on an immediate improvement in test taking and more on the interrelated causes of a lack of parental inclusion in a school's life, the transfer of experienced and skilled teachers to other districts, and an imbalance of financial funding across the city or state. With each causal factor requiring different campaign targets and activities, the organizers could use one set of objectives to rally support for the other, deepening the campaign's effectiveness without losing sight of the immediate demand for test score improvement. (See Chapter 8 for a fuller discussion of this process of strategic development.) Such systems thinking is obviously critical to long-term strategic effectiveness and effective leadership.

Senge's (1994) contribution extended beyond systems thinking, for he also brilliantly described the qualities of individual perception (called *personal mastery*) and thought processes (identified as *mental models*) that are needed if systems thinking is to occur. *Personal mastery* refers to how one develops the increasingly effortless ability to perceive "what is" in the world without judgment, projection, or intimidation. Such a quality noted by many commentators about President Obama is his cool demeanor in assessing and responding to grave economic and political problems.

Senge (1994) used the lovely example of the difference between a new, inexperienced potter and a master artisan to explain personal mastery. The new practitioner labors mightily to grab onto and shape the wet, porous clay on her wheel, only to create at best a misshapen, albeit well-intentioned, pot, saucer, or bowl. Ten years later, the inexperienced potter has evolved into the master artisan who seems to throw that same spongy clay while barely moving her hands, only to have a work of art appear soon after. The personal mastery of the artisan is the skillful, open, and flexible way she has applied herself to the same task over which she labored so intensely 10 years earlier. Developing such personal mastery in the effortless interpretation of the economic, political, and social forces that shape a macro practitioner's life and the people with whom you work is, Senge would argue, fundamental in developing the kind of strategic insight one needs as a macro practitioner to have long-term impact on the systems that affect people's lives.

To do this well while working with others also requires attention to what Senge calls *the mental models* one brings to thinking about the tasks at hand. As is made clear in Chapter 3, on tactical self-awareness, one of the ways people express their mental models is through their primary focus on either the tasks or the process of work. Senge clarifies that what one is drawn to, cognitively, may be about a specific type of content and the meanings we attach to certain words or actions. While to the young practitioner this may all sound like too much of a good thing, a brief mention of a few words used in a jobs campaign like Ellis and Kay's can make clear it is not: Employers/bosses, minimum-wage job/entry-level position, and opportunity/access can all mean very different things to different people in the same conversation. Is a boss a threat or an ally? Is a minimum-wage job a first leg up or a symptom of structural racism and sexism? Is access an example of fairness or unfairness?

Senge argues that the awareness of meaning we attach to powerful words used in problem solving, as well as to the task or process focus of how to solve those problems, helps a leader better work with others so that a more collaborative approach to our work together can occur.

REFLECTIVE QUESTIONS

On personal mastery: Reflect on an area of difficulty in your campaign or program. Assess (with others, if possible) assumptions about what is the problem at hand by imagining the benefits that come with the problem remaining unchanged. Who benefits? What is a new way to imagine the difficulty that might free up you and the group?

On mental models: Reflect on your approach to an ongoing campaign or program issue: How much of it is overly task oriented? Process oriented? What needs to be further emphasized to make the campaign even more effective?

Greenleaf and Spears's (2004) contribution of *servant leadership* is valuable because they directly extend the role of leader into the relationship with those with whom one works. Equally important, they document the types of qualities one must have to be successful in their model of relationship building: less directing than serving. The qualities they identify are listening, empathy, healing, awareness, persuasion, conceptualization, foresight, stewardship, commitment to the growth of others, and building community. Many of these qualities are not unlike the best of what a social worker does: Listening, empathy, healing, awareness, and conceptualization have all been written about in most introductory texts (Mattaini, Meyer, & Lowery, 2007; Netting et al., 2008; Saleebey, 2008).

Greenleaf and Spears's (2004) relational emphasis on *foresight* and *commitment to the growth of others* is clearly a powerful example of what macro practitioners do in leadership development as well. Foresight, or the ability to forecast future activities based on events that may not have happened yet but are foretold by the actions of others, is embedded in the push–pull between an organizer and those with whom he or she works. *Such foresight is the basis of a powerfully constructed and dynamic practice where the macro practitioner is where the people are plus one.* Seeing such a skill as something to pass on to others as they develop their own talents is what Greenleaf and Spears identify as a way to diminish the potential elitism that successful forecasting would otherwise create in some. (Who truly needs others if only you can forecast what's next?) Their recognition that a leader's forecasting ability increases rather than diminishes his or her role in developing others for sustained growth in a community is of real value for effective macro practice.

PERSONAL ACTIVITY

Identify someone in your group, preferably someone not already in a formal leadership role, whose actions suggest real leadership ability. What are those actions? Why do they suggest the ability to lead? Reflect on different types of leaders the group may need. After identifying the person, engage in ongoing conversations with him or her that pose questions and issues in ways that elicit personal reflection as the person considers his or her role and responsibilities in the group.

A more human services–based transformative leadership model has built on the work of Senge and colleagues (2004) and the Theory U paradigm developed by Otto Scharmer (2007). Working from a paradigm concerned with long-term environmental devastation of the planet, Scharmer's work traces how teams of people, whether organizations or communities, must move through the fear, judgment, and cynicism that cloud reform efforts before they can arrive within themselves at the possibility of cocreation and communal well-being. Applied within the human services field, a transformative leadership model has emphasized the small, daily actions of meaning between leaders and managers and those with whom they work as the pivotal measure of an organization's capacity to build a sustained, democratic community.

Transformative leadership places primary emphasis on the idea that "if the work is sacred, then so are you." Here the authors pose a challenge of self-care to all social workers, macro or micro practitioners alike (Burghardt & Tolliver, 2009). *The emphasis begins with the practitioner's relationship to himself or herself.* By making a commitment to self-care as fundamental to how one works with others over time, the authors emphasize the small, daily actions with others as the sacred measure of a leader's effectiveness. Their work provides concrete examples of how embodying the change you seek can come to life—or not—within our agencies and communities. Whether you're practicing politeness with everyone who enters your agency, maintaining a neat and well-lit agency lobby, embracing social diversity as an asset and not a threat, or engaging in systems improvements as a form of leadership development, this model offers ways to inspire others without bonuses and to make a legacy through genuine service rather than through the formal position one holds.

PERSONAL ACTIVITY

Reflect on your self-care and its impact on your own leadership style and internal balance inside the campaign or program of which you are a part. Where in the day can you add in more self-care, whether it's walking to and from work, taking 10 minutes to meditate each day, or spending downtime with a good book? Can you make a sacred commitment to yourself to practice the Second Golden Rule: Do unto yourself as you seek to do unto others?

"EMBODYING THE CHANGE YOU SEEK" IN TRANSFORMATIVE LEADERSHIP: MACRO *USES* MICRO

While the above and other works offer meaningful insights as to what individuals may do to inspire and motivate others and to live a life of integrity, the idea that macro practitioners can work with others in ways that allow *all participants to be transformed together* is still underdeveloped. This is not surprising. Leadership models from the corporate sector have little reason to address the conditions from below that emanate from people without power unless they affect the bottom line. Social work values related to self-determination understandably are not part of such a model.

However, when the stated organizing outcomes are progressive, the inattention to the type of leadership being developed can undermine long-term successes in terms of altering power and decision making. For example, the well-known Midwest Academy, a citizen action training center, provides thorough, direct action training for grassroots activists. At the same time, its core essentials of direct action place little to no emphasis on leadership styles and the relationship of the leader to group members that is any different from traditional, hierarchical models.[2]

So we find that a hallmark of our work is well researched for corporate organizations and yet much less understood among those working within communities. This confusing irony increases when we consider one of the standard yet equally understated techniques of daily organizing work in this training process: *the use of ourselves as models of leadership*. If, in the role of enabler, facilitator, advocate, broker, and so on, we are presenting a style of leadership that implicitly constructs what we want others to emulate, it would seem that we need clarity on what *we* are about, too. We therefore better know a bit more about our own daily roles in our presentation of leadership models, including our manner of decision making, how open we are to suggestions, how well we share power, and our own comfort with a genuinely diverse set of leaders and activists.

To do this, of course, means understanding *why* such knowledge is important in an ongoing relationship, a skill that goes beyond any simple self-assignment into a role category such as liaison or advocate. As this chapter will suggest, we have the potential to be even more effective if we can learn to incorporate other social work methods into our work; doing so may make it possible to focus our attention on the full range of human relationships, both personal and political. *We may then find that instead of socially reproducing a set of leaders consistent with standard notions of hierarchy, deference, and so on, we are creating leadership alternatives quite different from traditional models. After all, if we start with the idea that leadership development is not a hallowed goal but a process by which people change themselves and the organizers as they work together on common organizing tasks, then what goes into that process itself will actually determine long-term, sustained transformation among those with whom we work.*

Using Clinical Social Work Skills for Transformative Leadership

Seeking a more transformative model of leadership explains—perhaps ironically—why clinical social work interviewing and assessment techniques can add so much to a macro practitioner's work. Such interviewing skills are important in organizing precisely because the unstructured nature of most community organizing settings heightens the vagueness of the interpersonal process within one's work. As community-based practitioners, we seek people out and conduct interviews on the street, in bars, over lunch, and in crowded rooms. While hardly conforming to the classical contextual specifications mentioned by Garrett, Donner, and Sessions (1995), the shifts from highly content-specific to person-specific experiences that develop in organizing (almost spontaneously at times) occur with remarkable frequency and must be attended to if a person is to be seen in his or her entirety.

Indeed, I will argue that when these events occur, a macro practitioner is confronted with an opportunity of tremendous consequence to his or her work. Not only might trust be deepened between two people as they learn from each other about what at first may be perceived as extraneous (nonstrategic/nonorganizational) issues in each other's lives; if developed correctly, it is also possible for the now personally engaged individuals to begin extending the mechanics of leadership development into the realm of what Freire (2000) calls *critical consciousness*, or what I will more concretely call *critical reflection in action*. As we shall see, this process expands leadership training beyond the immediate work itself (which will be limited and thus highly pragmatic) and instead takes it toward larger social concerns that may necessitate deeper transformations in society—and different types of leadership.[3]

I cannot underscore enough the point that your use of both clinical and community organization skills is not simply to broaden your professional role. If we assume that critical reflection in action demands an ability to intuitively feel and intellectually understand the way the world is organized, this joint mixture of skills becomes the sine qua non of engaged practice. *To begin with, one crucial but often overlooked fact about most organizing situations and leadership is that organizers, unlike executives, initially are expected to undertake leadership development within a context of* **perceived failure.** Often, of course, the failure is not of the group's or individual's making. The responsibility or blame may lie elsewhere, but that does not change the immediate perceptions of the group as to why they are working together.

This is why our purpose in the construction of transformative practice, as discussed in Chapter 5, is to heighten the underlying tensions between what people may perceive about the world and how the world actually is. By definition, those perceptions, no matter how legitimate they may have once been, create an impression that previous community efforts failed to correct problems still needing to be resolved. The experience of having lived with these feelings of at least partial failure imbues people with a touch of resignation, self-blame, doubt, or confusion as to who is right or wrong. People are going to feel uncertain about how much of their problem is due to their own ineffectiveness and how much is beyond their control. This uncertainty will surface in different situations. The practitioner, in recognizing "where people are," will therefore have to focus on altering both the situation *and* people's perception of their past failures regarding that situation. To do otherwise would be disrespectful.

In short, there simply is no way to divide out process (*how people feel*) and content (*what needs to get done*) for the critically reflective organizer concerned with leadership development, even when concrete tasks may be great and systemic change is difficult. The way we work with people will greatly influence what those people do, not only in the short-run campaigns of meaningful direct action but also in addressing the long-term needs for new models of leadership that confront present power relationships in dramatically new forms.

⌐ REFLECTIVE QUESTIONS ──────────

In what ways can you demonstrate respect for "where a group is" by legitimating why they perceive things as too difficult, without creating a sense of defeat? Can you show respect and challenge them at the same time?

Can you note the use of "clinical" and "organizing" skills in this approach?

DEVELOPING LEADERSHIP THROUGH NEW FORMS OF RELATIONSHIP BUILDING

Historically, three dominant strategic alternatives have been used by organizers to get at the complicated process of developing leadership: (1) *changing the situational problem to the exclusion of leadership development*; (2) *developing leaders who are grounded in organizational, not critical, consciousness*; and (3) *developing critical consciousness*, or *critical reflection in action.*

1. *Changing the situational problem to the exclusion of leadership development.* This highly concrete, direct action approach gets the job done (wins the rent strike, maintains the fiscally troubled senior center, etc.) but doesn't take measures to see that the success will be maintained. While undoubtedly stated in terms of self-determination, it actually furthers dependency by shifting the participant's focus of dependence from outside agents of unfairness or oppression to the organizer's more benign but still hierarchically positioned role. Michael Reisch, writing years ago when he was an activist in the antinuclear movement, thoughtfully wrote about this tendency among some of the leaders involved in the Shoreham, Long Island, demonstrations:

> Some of the activists believed that change would be initiated if they worked for the people. What this course of action effectively did was to impose a world view on the people, rather than dialogue with them about their views and those of the [grassroots] organizational leaders. As Freire noted, "This practice is incompatible with a truly liberating course of action, because it replaces the slogans of the oppressors rather than helping the oppressed 'eject' those slogans from themselves." (Burghardt, 1982, pp. 87–88)

Their method of organizing, while grounded in objective reality (the need to get rid of nuclear power), used an imposing process of intervention that short-circuited the development of a people's understanding of their own potential for being agents with the capacity to change that reality.

2. *Developing leaders who are grounded in organizational, not critical, consciousness.* This is easily the most common form of leadership development that takes place within community organizing and other forms of macro practice. It is also understandably popular, for the constraints facing the practitioner—for example, the perceptions of failure, the limited resources and urgent demands for action, and so forth—breed in anyone the desire for immediate results. We therefore latch on to quick ways to establish someone—at times almost anyone!—to serve as a group's leader. The techniques to keep that person in that leadership position, which range from flattery to guilt, are in actuality forms of objectification that socialize him or her to use the same techniques on followers in the future.

This short-cut process has accidentally created two problems: First, it tends to exclude the vast majority of the group from leadership and instead fosters a view of organization that is hierarchically skewed and potentially undemocratic. Second, it perpetuates the use of techniques that cannot ground a person within a changing social context (which would demand constant attention to the process of how one attempts to change those conditions); rather, they foster reliance on the manipulation of others. A well-traveled and almost burnt-out organizer reiterated his experience with some tenant leaders he'd helped train in the past:

> I don't quite understand it—people come and people go, but they just seem to stay the same. I go into a few buildings, get a lay of the land, and find a few people

ready to work. Then things go fine for a while during the initial action . . . but every group but one has lost its group after a year or so . . . a lot of the original people just give up, or don't care. . . . [*How did you work with the leaders in each group? How did you train them? Or didn't they need any?*]

Training? You have time to train somebody in a rent strike? Seriously, though, I'd work with one or two who seemed most interested. Most of those [people] had more enthusiasm, which makes it a lot easier on me. And most had talents, too, but not in this work. What I needed to do was take their talent and direct them toward the group. I'd latch on to them . . . try to make them feel good, help plan their agendas and all the meeting details, and afterwards boost egos and correct a few points. A lot of effort goes into that kind of work, doing hand-holding, reassuring people over the phone, all that "stroking." *The key was to make them feel good enough so you'd get the job done right and people in position to carry on afterwards.* (Italics added)

You can see right away that there's a lot that's right with this organizer's approach. He wants to get the job done correctly, which means he's willing to train others to lead their groups. He's willing to take the time needed to work with their developing leadership needs, without giving up the central rent strike tasks. *But what is the nature of the training?* There were two points specified: immediate facts on how to deal with organizational detail and ego boosting. The former related to a set of techniques divorced from the social context itself (most meeting skills can be learned and are applicable to any situation). Leadership training never generated issues that would, for example, tie in the previous lack of leadership to other social problems or generate discussion about the set of reasons people were encouraged to be passive receptacles of others' efforts toward change.

The latter use of ego boosting, by definition, excluded much of a person's life from the organizational experience. Not that a person doesn't need to be congratulated for work well done; *it's just that respect isn't simply a function of making someone feel good.* The organizer, by objectifying the group's needs into sharply delineated organizational and ego-salving tasks, was himself perpetuating a model of leadership devoid of the critical reflection necessary to creatively act within the world. *For all his good intention (and decent rent strike work), he was creating a model of leadership devoid of attention to the changing social context that would have made the group interventions more meaningful for the members and himself.* By objectifying his work into differentiated categories of either organizational or personal solutions, he never could develop a conscious method of organically joining people's reactions and needs to the larger context of the organizing effort and the social world in which that effort was taking place. Freire (2000) comments as follows:

Critical and liberating dialogue [between the oppressed and the organizers], which presupposes action, must be carried on with the oppressed at whatever the stage of their struggle for liberation. The content of that dialogue can and should vary in accordance with historical conditions and the level at which the oppressed perceive reality. But to substitute monologue, slogans, and communiqués for dialogue is to attempt to liberate the oppressed with the instruments of [their] domestication. Attempting to liberate the oppressed without their reflective participation in the act of liberation is to treat them as objects which must be saved from a burning building; it is . . . to transform them into masses which can be manipulated. (p. 65)

While requiring patience that can at times seem in short supply, taking the time in the midst of the work to pose issues for mutual problem solving would have laid the groundwork for understanding that a campaign is often a long-term *tactic* used to better the changing social and personal conditions of its membership. People may not need ego boosting as much as a chance to learn concretely how to analyze and interpret the problems before them in *their own words*—be it their perceived individual struggles or those flowing from the organizing situation itself.[4]

They then become active people in the situation, not "things for organization." In short, the above organizer's mistake in the midst of much good work was in not validating a person as a human being with *understandable* doubts, misgivings, hopes, and aspirations attached to the group's ongoing efforts—a far more important organizing goal than that found by stroking an individual's ego to create an organizational tool (a group leader).

PERSONAL ACTIVITY

Review a recent campaign or group activity you have been involved in.

How were members encouraged to become leaders, if at all? What concrete activities were used to develop them?

1. _____

2. _____

3. _____

In what ways were they involved in their own development? In what ways did their ideas and suggestions influence the direction of the group?

1. _____

2. _____

3. _____

In what ways did they influence the organizers?

1. _____

2. _____

3. _____

3. A far different model of organizing is found in *developing critical reflection in action*. An example of how this leadership methodology is put into practice was discussed by Debbie Harris, a community activist working with seniors, as she analyzed certain interactions between a group member and herself. As you will see, there is little direct attention at all to developing leaders.

[This man had been monotonously disruptive to her and other group members.] This man had one major area of interest, which was the high cost of beef and the importance of importing larger quantities. I tried to listen [over the year], but two things interfered with truly hearing and responding: (1) the man spoke endlessly, repetitively, and somewhat monotonously; (2) I'm a vegetarian and somewhat turned off to meat issues. . . . Most everyone else seemed fed up with him too. . . .

Finally I met with [him] for another reason—to work out publicity for a congressional representative involved in our Center. We then started a serious discussion on import/exports, price controls, the cattlemen's lobby, etc. I realized he had a good sense of the topic, but was frustrated by lack of direction. Everyone listened, but no one discussed it with him. "I'm just an old man who likes to talk a lot." But for once I really heard him, argued with him, questioned him, and found we were really communicating. . . . We are now actively seeking ways to work on this [meat] problem. . . . I believe my decision to really take him seriously and actively work with him is having an effect on our relationship. He is beginning to give me feed-back on my role as the worker—something I really want. It seems like a two-way dialogue is developing here! (Burghardt, 1982, pp. 93–94)

The organizer in the previous rent strike example worked with group members as tactics to be maneuvered into positions of organizational responsibility. Harris worked directly with people on individualized needs that transcended the organizational context (which saw only an old man to ignore), both to help him *and* to improve her own skills. Instead of ego boosting, she argued; in place of working only to achieve immediate organizational needs (publicity, which would have left her frustrated), she tried to communicate with the man on his terms. In the end, this genuine person-in-situation approach increased the group's resources (a new project with active membership involvement extending beyond the gentleman) and heightened the likelihood that her own organizing skills would improve through ongoing feedback.[5]

Harris's approach to leadership development will be discussed in greater detail later. What is so distinctive here is her willingness to implicitly validate the *elements of failure* in this man's situation by confronting the parts of his immediate concern (the meat) that were overstated or incorrect. It wasn't a matter of stroking his ego at all but, rather, one of confronting him as a person with quite real qualities of strength and weakness. In her willingness to take his arguments seriously—seriously enough to disagree with him—she was beginning to reach toward the deeper social issue embedded in his obsession: his being *politely listened to because he was an old man.* The rent strike organizer would have tried to set up a meat import committee, telling him how this information would eventually help others; those from the "let's do it for them" school would have set up a committee and plunked him down as its token chairman while they did other work.

Other forms of leadership training would have had leaders, but neither would have dealt with the individual in a manner that altered his own consciousness of his situation or how he could change it. Like so many strike leaders trained by the Brooklyn organizer, he probably would have dropped off in activity as soon as the immediate tasks were over (and the ego boosting had stopped). *By immersing herself into his world through engaged conversation* (Wheatley, 2008), Harris necessarily began altering the relationship they shared. She would be a bit less certain; he would be able to respond more fully and could intuitively perceive himself as more than a tactic for manipulation. His effectiveness naturally increased in all areas of work.

PERSONAL ACTIVITY

Reflect on a person in your group who you hope can develop as a leader but who seems to have issues that get in the way of his or her development. Modeling yourself after Harris's approach, what would you include in that conversation about you and your perceptions of this person? About what you saw as necessary to succeed? About what he or she brought to the work and where there were challenges?

Once completed, what can you commit to change and work on? What will you request of this person?

Let's return to Ellis and Kay as they struggle to understand these dynamics with their field instructor so that they can work more effectively with the teens.

GONE FISHIN'?

Ellis and Kay both looked at their field instructor with a mix of fear and longing. Megan Newman was a smart, no-nonsense supervisor who managed to be warm and direct at the same time. While her smile was genuine, for the moment her emphasis was on being direct.

"Look, guys, you can't get a group of young people together, get 'em all fired up about jobs and job fair campaigns and all, and then turn around and immediately expect them to volunteer. People can like the idea of something without believing they can do anything about it. You gotta address that fear while you do the work."

"Address the fear while doing the work? How do we do both? I mean, won't they get distracted if we focus on their emotions? You know, some of them don't do that well in school. Why would we bring up stuff that reminded them of other failures?" Ellis's brow was creased with concern.

"Like Ellis said, we can't stop and just do therapy with them." Kay sounded as anxious as she felt. "Geez, there's so much to do in a campaign like this. It's already on us to make it happen!"

Their field instructor leaned forward. "So let's pause for a second." She looked at them both, her manner calm. "Tell me something, what is your biggest fear with these kids?"

"That we won't get them jobs, or even if we do, they won't have learned anything about themselves. You know, the 'teach a man to fish' thing won't happen," said a worried Ellis.

"That it'll happen in ways where they're no different than they were when they started. That the two of us didn't matter a bit." Kay's normal upbeat manner was gone from the room.

"Those sound like real fears." Newman's voice remained calm yet direct. "Do either of you work with people elsewhere in that way? You know, expecting that so little will happen, unless you both work hard?"

"I had that happen in high school. Worked on a breast cancer awareness drive and ended up doing all the work," Kay replied.

"What'd you learn from that?"

"Never again! I saw just killing myself got the job done, but I was a wreck when it was over."

"I had that happen in high school, too, only the reverse. A group of us were supposed to get involved in Black History Month, inviting speakers and whatnot. The teacher did the whole damn thing. I felt like a cipher."

"So you've been burned by doing too much and you by doing too little. Did you repeat those mistakes?"

"No."

"Never."

"So why do you expect to repeat them with these kids?"

(Continued)

(Continued)

Ellis and Kay both looked perplexed. Kay spoke first. "I just got so anxious about making a difference as an organizer, I forgot all about that. Old habits die hard, sometimes."

"I see these kids and I want so much to happen, but don't want to impose myself on them, that I just left off thinking, period, I guess," Ellis managed a brief laugh at himself.

"So, isn't it possible you might be projecting your own anxiety onto these kids? Turning what's a normal hesitation to get involved into something far bigger than it is?"

Kay and Ellis looked at their field supervisor and silently nodded in agreement. Their organizing supervisor was tying their leadership development work together with clinical skills.

"So in reality, you each can use your own experience to work with these kids, right? By reflecting on our own history, we can often find ways to help people locate their own reasons for why they do what they do." Megan's smile was brighter now. "And then maybe they can more easily get through that impasse."

Kay and Ellis looked at each other again, this time with relief. "Hey, I think we just got a dose of that problem-posing the prof was talking about!" said Ellis. "A little clinical work for the sake of organizing . . . very interesting!"

"Yeah, instead of giving us answers on how to work with the kids, you asked us things to get us to reflect on our own experience to arrive at our own answers." Kay was beaming now.

"And not impose our own anxiety on them," Ellis laughed. "We're the basket cases, not them!" The others joined in the laughter. Ellis turned serious for a second, focused. "We have to trust that the young people can get there in their own way, too. If we let them have their fears without making it a huge deal, then they can get to their strengths a lot quicker." He looked more relaxed than he had in a week.

Their field instructor just leaned back, her hands behind her head. "Hey, guys, one more thing before you meet with the kids again. Don't forget to leave your fishing poles home, okay?"

Ellis and Kay both high-fived their supervisor as they left the room. Megan high-fived them right back.

PERSONAL ACTIVITY

How can you utilize Ellis and Kay's field instructor's approach? What experiences of your own can you use in working with others on leadership? Can you combine a clinical skill in working on leadership issues with others?

JOINING THE "RELATIONAL" TO TRANSFORMATIVE LEADERSHIP: "NAMING THE WORD"

This kind of problem-posing with people as you go about the rigors of community practice sounds nice in this Ellis and Kay case study, you might be saying, but how can you do it in the actual work? A meeting with your field instructor is one thing, but what about when you're in the midst of a real meeting with community members? After all, practice in a community-based setting is often so unfocused that these nuances of communication seem a bit much. How can you really expect to do more than the rent strike organizer? And before we look at how to do this, why should we bother?

Obviously, the joining of personal concerns as part of a longer-term critically reflective process while engaged in organizing is no small matter. To recognize this is to grasp the essence of what Freire (2000) means by "naming the word." *By being able to recognize a person with his or her individual needs, problems, and strengths, especially when the recognition occurs in the midst of activities that usually relegate such "personness" to superficial consideration, you are making a powerful political statement about how you view history and the organizing that takes place within it. It is a history created* **with** *people, not* **for** *people.*

By seeing the person more fully through these actions, you suggest a definition of history as a *history of subjects—of people who choose, in countless ways, to act on the world with others.* As Harris's example made clear, by taking the risk to engage with an individual as fully as possible—including acknowledging *mutual* doubts and fears—*when such engagement is not organizationally necessary in the short run,* you end *any* **implicit objectification of others** *that may have been unconsciously communicated through the rest of your work.* Your problem-posing actions begin to bring to life what Freire (2000) meant by "the word":

> As we attempt to analyze dialogue as a human phenomenon, we discover something which is the essence of dialogue itself: *the word.* But the word is more than just an instrument that makes dialogue possible; accordingly we must seek its constituent elements. Within the word we find two dimensions, reflection and action, in such radical interaction that if one is sacrificed—even in part—the other immediately suffers. There is not one word that is not at the same time *a praxis* (a joining of reflection and action). . . . An inauthentic word, one which is unable to transform reality, results when dichotomy is imposed on its constitutive elements. When a word is deprived of its dimension of action, reflection suffers as well, and the word is changed into idle chatter, into verbalism, into an alienated and alienating "blah." . . . On the other hand, if action is emphasized exclusively, to the

detriment of reflection, the word is converted into activism. The latter—action for action's sake—negates the true praxis and makes dialogue impossible. Either dichotomy, by creating inauthentic forms of existence, creates inauthentic forms of thought, which reinforce the original dichotomy. (p. 87)

Translated a little less abstractly here, leadership development cannot be elevated to transformative dialogue capable of generating critical reflection in action if a practitioner's conception of the task is either all goal directed (action) toward concrete ends, which stifles personal attributes of the people who are integral to that action, or so process oriented (reflection) toward making individuals feel better that one ignores the objective circumstances that brought people together in the first place.

Ellis and Kay wanted to create action, including young people's leadership. When they were met with resistance, their own fears and initial objectifying of the teens led them to personal resignation and a loss of group momentum. Only as their supervisor got them to reflect on their own past high school experiences could they reflect on how valuable such problem-posing might be for the young people. Through this reflection-joined-to-action, they could then commit to genuine responsibility for the jobs campaign. Ellis and Kay would go on to engage the students in their fears about commitment by admitting to their own as well. *The words spoken then would have the authenticity Freire wrote about, because both the organizers and the organized were speaking together from the same mutual regard and understanding that there are good reasons to fear working on a campaign or project together.*

This is why the joining of clinical and community organizing skills within the same practice framework means much more than just multimethod innovation. For example, knowing when a person's reaction to new and untried leadership responsibilities has a personally concealed meaning is the essence of your own *praxis,* which Freire referred to in the previous quotation regarding reflection and action. Your awareness of how these two parts of an individual's organizing and personal lives may be interacting reveals your own willingness to explore reality as fully as the client is in fact perceiving and living it— even when that exploration is not directly or pragmatically beneficial to you or the campaign at hand. In making this clinical linkage of the personal and the concrete, the possibility of dialogue that can transform the world opens up.

Saying the word is not the privilege of some few persons, but the right of every one. Consequently, no one can say a true word alone—nor can he say it for another, in a perspective that robs others of their word. Dialogue is the encounter between [people], mediated by the world, in order to name the world. . . . [Therefore,] human existence cannot be silent, nor can it be nourished by false words, but only by true words, with which [people] transform the world. To *exist, humanly, is to name the world, to change it.* (Freire, 2000, p. 87)

As Debbie Harris's actions suggested, for the practitioner to engage other people as fully as she did is no minor act, even though each interaction may be brief. Her *conversations* with an elderly man were doing precisely what truly engaged practice demands: looking beneath an obscure political statement to see a man personally crying out to be seen. On one level, she used her clinical skills to engage him in a way that heightened the man's motivation, increased his organizational resources, and cut down his obsessive chatter. But in a deeper, more political sense, through her engagement she had exposed herself to the risk of being perceived poorly, of presenting *herself*, with her emotional ideas and arguments, in as open a way as the older man had done earlier. His later involvement was in part a function of having begun to "name the word" with Harris in a way that transformed the world—his world, the one that had previously denied him any engaged place within it, and hers, where she now had an ally and organizing partner and not just an elderly drone.

It was not just that he saw himself differently; *simultaneously, he saw her differently*. Instead of being the great organizer who could assuage his needs or resolve his difficulties, Harris, by arguing with him, by getting *upset,* was exposing herself as a person with emotions, needs, and uncertainties. While Ellis and Kay would be at a different level of conversation with the teens, because they had worked together so briefly, the dynamic interplay would be the same. *Through this conversation in the midst of their campaigns, the elderly man's growing ability to see himself as a subject of history was in part based on removing others like Harris from a position of total authority that left him only to follow—an object to be used by others, one to obsess over silly topics and needless issues.* The ensuing dialogue was so meaningful not only because it was honest but also because it defined the way certain people act together. Instead of a cranky old man being helped by the tolerant organizer, there were two people sharing information—and themselves—so that they might better the organization. *In short, the organized has gained power, while the organizer has lost none.* In such small acts, a transformation of the world is begun.

No one, meaningful organizing experience can transform the entire world, of course—a lot more critical reflection in action involving huge numbers of people will be needed for that! But this book is *explicating a leadership process that can transform the world by the way an individual or group perceive that world, their place in it, and their actions on it.* Freire's (2000) "critical consciousness" is not some magic elixir that unleashes the bottled-up urgings of the masses into society-wide, transformative upheaval. It is simply, yet profoundly, the way people together learn their rights and responsibilities as subjects of history so that they may choose to act on history as fully and as purposefully as conditions of their epoch will allow. It speaks of self-determination in both personal and political terms, never isolating either in ways that allow others the chance to manipulate and distort their place in acting on the conditions of their lives.

If you assume, with Berger and Luckmann (1967), *that reality is both objectively deter-mined and subjectively perceived,* your direct engagement with both these connected aspects of life as you organize will allow people to engage more fully in *their* history, *includ-ing you.* For as they make history, you necessarily become part of it, mutually exploring ways to improve the total reality of your lives together. That you will all be doing so at this momentous time in American history when leadership and authority are being reexamined as they have not been for generations makes this experience all the more important.

GROUP ACTIVITY

At your next small-group meeting, build time into the agenda for members to reflect on an issue where the group seems stuck. Pose questions that seek their genuine input regarding possible answers. Model your own struggle to get things right by speaking to your own difficulties on an issue you dealt with in the past. Make sure your focus is on the internal effort and personal challenge it took to arrive at a solution and not just the eventual success. Invite the group to go through a similar process; use your listening skills to pose follow-up questions so the group probes deeply for answers beneath the surface.

USING INTERVIEWING SKILLS IN ORGANIZING: MACRO *NEEDS* MICRO

The use of clinical social work and community organization skills within the same prac-tice signifies a practitioner's ability to engage in the "subjective" (*how people see things*) and "objective" elements (*the measureable problems the group is concerned about*) of another's reality. In turn, this deeper awareness communicates openness and respect of that reality so that others more fully reveal themselves *with* you. False distinctions between helper and helped are dissolved without sacrificing the genuine contribution each can make to the other's life. For the organizers, then, the use of clinical social work interviewing skills can help him or her transcend the immediate organizational con-straints imposed by a flat interpretation of macro practice to reach a deeper critical consciousness that actively incorporates the personal within the political.[6]

As Garrett et al. (1995) introduced their classic work:

If we zoom in our discussion to be directing our attention primarily to subjective aspects, to feelings, emotions, and attitudes, it is because we recognize that they are as important as the objective facts themselves and are much more likely to be overlooked. . . . We listen to the undertones, because the underlying subjective of "worry" (for example) may be caused by an objective situation that may not be apparent at once. (p. 176)

In other words, at times, paying attention to the emotionality of a response may be the key to a larger or deeper social problem. (This was the work Ellis and Kay's field instructor was inviting them to undertake.) In microcosm, it forces one always to deal actively with what Berger and Luckmann (1967) have identified *as the primary dialectic of society: Society is a human product. Society becomes and is an objective reality. Man is a social product.* Or, put in terms of macro practice and leadership development, society can be described as follows:

- The activities of creating the world (through macro practice)
- make a new world (an organizing campaign's outcomes plus new forms of leadership), which then
- shapes us anew (as subjects of history)
- as we begin to create a new form of macro and micro practice together (dialogue/critical reflection in action),
- transforming the world.

This dynamic, engaged, relational, and transformational process has necessarily linked the interpersonal (subjective) and the macro (objective) parts of life together in an unending series of interactions that demand mutual exploration. Only as this mutual exploration—known as dialogue, at last!—occurs together can the world of our macro practice be understood *and* changed in ways that model genuine self-determination for all. Or, as Freire (2000) might have said, *to name our word with others is to transform our world,* too.

PERSONAL REFLECTION

Reflect on a campaign or program where you began to think differently about yourself and the people with whom you worked in a positive, energized way. What happened that led you to see your potential for acting on the world in a new and more powerful way? How could you create similar conditions within your own group?

Developing Clinical Assessment and Interviewing Skills as a Foundation to Transformative Practice

So what are the specific interpersonal issues in the group or individual that you need to be aware of to create a transformative form of leadership development? And where in a group's organizing are they most apt to be present? In answering the latter question, we can't forget that community-based practice doesn't lend itself to the more easily controlled structure of most clinical social work interviews. Personal issues that an organizer might deal with are hardly scheduled in advance. Likewise, the immediate topic the group is dealing with may have nothing directly to do with the individual. Nothing would be more ludicrous than stopping a highly charged group discussion about taxes and service cuts to explore a particular issue in greater depth because of one or two people's personal intensity about the matter. At the same time, it would be remiss of the organizer not to note such intensity as a reason for later follow-up. The clinical assessment skills found in casework interviewing are designed to help you make follow-up a real possibility and, with it, a chance for genuine engagement together that can get to the heart of transformative leadership.

Besides your own use of tactical self-awareness, which can help you be aware of those situations in which you'll be most effective in picking up others' personal cues, you must begin by knowing what to look for. Garrett et al. (1995) list six items still used today: (1) recurrent reference, (2) opening and closing sentences, (3) concealed meaning, (4) association of ideas, (5) shifts in conversation, and (6) inconsistencies and gaps.

Recurrent References and Opening and Closing Sentences

We'll begin with two processes that overlap in similar ways in both organizing and casework. When people refer again and again to the same issue or begin and end their presentations with the same topic (or one that otherwise hasn't been mentioned), you are getting an indirect message that in some way, this subject matters beyond the topic itself (like the man concerned about beef). Whether the repetition is personally or politically motivated will depend on myriad factors, including the hidden agenda to purposely obscure other items from the practitioner's view. Perhaps noting the intensity with which topics are referred to can help you differentiate between the personal and the political, but one must be careful with intense political convictions that create powerful emotional responses. In general, it is best to be aware of their potential importance as a beginning to a deeper understanding of the group or individual with whom you are working. Given its relatively open presentation, the chances are that follow-up can be easy.

Association of Ideas

The way a person connects different ideas is often a function of that person's particular history, where powerful past emotional experiences will create distinctive reactions in individuals that are unique to them. In my experience, however, the distinctive association of ideas often relates to cultural differences. For example, not everyone thinks in linear, future-oriented, cause-and-effect terms, not because of lesser conceptual ability but because of the particular environmental demands under which they live. I learned this while working in the Morrisania section of the South Bronx, still one of the poorest neighborhoods in New York City. The leader of the storefront action group was an exceptionally talented and perceptive formerly incarcerated man, a 35-year-old African American, who at times made no sense to many of us White, professional organizers in the group. His ideas always seemed to take leaps of logic that were rarely understood. A few people were convinced it was because of a lack of formal education.

However, one day it clicked for a few of us: *His frame of reference* (thus, the association of ideas) was intensely present oriented. The past was over and forgotten, and the future was to be dealt with only when it arrived. Examples were therefore always couched in highly personal terms that rarely included cause and effect. Powerful ideas were developed through the use of metaphors. ("This meeting best be like Slick's head" seemed a little obscure to us until we met Slick and his smooth, bald head.) Once understood, the metaphors were as rich and subtle as any abstract, intellectual statement, but the tendency at first from our own mental models had been to denigrate the pattern of thought itself.

A community practitioner must understand the different contextual/cultural variations that breed varying ways of presenting ideas before analyzing potentially emotional meanings behind those ideas. Instead of forcing others to adopt your frame of reference (which will undoubtedly cause resistance!), you have a chance to broaden your own mental model, learning new ways to express ideas that are equally valid and smart.[7] In turn, we begin to communicate a form of openness with others and a respect for different abilities that then frees people to present themselves as fully as possible.

Concealed Meanings

Organizers and macro practitioners, in their tendency to be task oriented, can grow easily irritated with people who don't stay with a particular topic but seem to wander from the main points of a discussion. We perceive their reaction to certain topics as attempts to disrupt or impede the work of the group, when in fact their reactions may signify far more than obstructionism. (This is especially true if the people don't have a history of obstruction. If they do, then that has to be dealt with in more political terms.) Indeed, when a person tends to overreact consistently on a particular topic or uses such a topic to digress, there may be a much more personal struggle occurring that needs tending to before the person can refocus energy on the group's larger tasks.

A good example of how concealed meanings can be harmful to the flow of your organizing, yet revealing of an individual's need occurred at a New York City–wide labor support group that had formed after another projected round of layoffs. One of the steering committee members, a well-respected activist, became irritable every time anyone used the term *rank and file* or *rank-and-file group*. Normally a quiet and even-tempered speaker, he would angrily demand the floor and go on long harangues about the "philosophy of the rank and file," attacking others for their use of the term, even though their comments were rarely controversial. (The support group had about 100 different trade union activists from across New York City in its membership. For it not to use the term *rank and file* would be like a caseworker avoiding the use of the word *psychosocial* when discussing a client's background.)

A number of people grew angry with him, including me, but requests to tone down his comments made little headway. Remembering Garrett (Garrett et al., 1995), I finally suggested quietly to him (away from the group) that maybe something else was going on to upset him. I suggested we talk together at a later time. While he was initially furious with me, he agreed, and later we were able to get beneath his antagonism.

His angry responses were symptomatic of his gnawing disappointment and frustration with having been unable to build a rank-and-file group within his own union local. While it was not a problem of his own making, he tended to blame himself for the failure of the organizing efforts. Because he had used the term *rank and file* in the leaflets to his fellow workers, the phrase once had been filled with the hope of rekindling solid democratic traditions in his union. With his organizing efforts smashed by leadership maneuvers, hope had turned to bitterness. In turn, the combination of blaming himself for the rank and file's defeat and his own dashed hopes had emotionally redefined the term in ways having little to do with the support group he was now part of. When used at our meetings, the term didn't make him obstructionist; it made him feel his hurt. While our discussion hardly did away with his pain, it did clarify some of the reasons for his overreaction. Not only were his comments more helpful in the future, but the personal recognition of how bad he felt about the organizing failure helped him resume a much more active role in work designed as *support* for rank-and-file groups!

Shifts in Communication and Recurrent References

It is natural that interviewing people in highly fluid, disruptive situations will undercut the smooth flow of conversations. Talking in the street, at a coffee shop, or on a cramped bus may be more common to our work than carrying on structured interviews in office settings, so it is quite possible that shifts in conversation or recurrent references will have as much to do with the noise from the kids next door as with conscious or unconscious needs to avoid certain topics. At the same time, this is not always the case, and a community practitioner needs to learn the difference between objective circumstance and subjective feelings that interfere with straightforward conversation. As Garrett et al. (1995) noted, people may be too uncomfortable with material to carry a discussion further or may unconsciously connect seemingly disparate thoughts.

Nevertheless, this ability to ascertain latent content is perhaps one of the most valuable skills an organizer can have. Such skill can allow one an initial entry, both personally and politically, into the personal hidden agendas of a group or of its members. As in the previous example with the rank-and-file activist, *people miscommunicate to communicate more fully than they consciously dare.* It is your willingness to dare to look beneath the surface on such issues that may begin generating mutual dialogue later on.

INDIVIDUAL ACTIVITY

Reflect on a recent interview/discussion with a community or coalition member whose influence matters in the group. As you review the discussion, were there any of these dynamics perhaps at play that require further follow-up (recognizing the humbling risk in doing so)?

1. Recurrent reference

2. Opening and closing sentences

3. Concealed meaning

4. Association of ideas

5. Shifts in conversation

6. Inconsistencies and gaps

Make sure to speak of your *perception* of what was heard without insisting that it occurred. Ask for clarity, not correctness. And seek support from your micro colleagues, too!

The effective joining of clinical social work and community organization skills, then, goes beyond multimethod work. By being able to interject personal awareness of another's individualized, emotionally based struggle in a macro practice situation that does not objectively demand such attention, you begin to subvert previous assumptions about how people function, what political activity is, and so forth. Slowly, together, you alter perceptions of the world and how to act on it through your own personal mastery: What is—especially what is limited, determined, and oppressive—may not be exactly what was once perceived. As Freire (2000) said, in naming the word together, the organizer and the organized begin to transform the world—as *transformative leaders who share power rather than seek it.*

MACRO MEETS MICRO UP CLOSE AND PERSONAL

"So, Kay and I met with a number of the local employers last week. Some of them seem interested in your group. They said they need good summer help. But they—"

(Continued)

(Continued)

"But?" Eduardo interrupted quickly. "I bet there's a whole buncha 'buts,' aren't there?"

"And why they say *good* summer help? Some of 'em want *bad* summer help, too?" Jacqui got the whole group laughing with her sarcasm.

Ellis looked briefly at Kay, taking a deep breath as he did so. She could see he was making an effort to follow their field instructor's advice, but it wasn't easy. "Hey, I hear you. You're right to be skeptical." Ellis paused, letting his words sink in as he collected his thoughts. A few sets of eyes looked up from the invisible spots on the floor they'd been examining to watch him more closely. "When I was in high school, I got involved in a project where I ended up feeling worse than when I started. I never wanted to work in a group again."

"So why did you? I mean, what got you involved again once you'd been burned?"

Cece's question seemed to animate them all.

"I don't know, really." Ellis was searching for words, a little unsure of himself as the group moved further and further away from the tasks he was more comfortable with. "Actually, a while later a group of us read about a nearby family whose house had burned to the ground. We did a food and clothing drive just to do something. Felt pretty good to be helping out." As uncomfortable as he was, Ellis found himself moving to firmer ground as he spoke. The group members were listening intently.

"So, yeah, I guess I got going again because it felt right. Took a while, though." He paused again, letting his words sink in. "We all have our reasons for not getting involved, right?"

"Eduardo, sounds like you've been burned like Ellis," Kay followed up. "Were you?"

Eduardo looked embarrassed. "Nah, not really. I don't have problems with groups 'n all." He made a sweeping gesture around the group. "These are my buds, ya know what I mean? Hangin' with them is a good thing." He paused for just a second, his voice momentarily quiet. "Just never had no luck lookin' for jobs."

The room stayed quiet but only for a second. "Been there, done that," Jacqui replied.

"Got tired of it all, too."

The group members kept talking for a while about their failed experiences with the job market. Some of them spoke about their parents' difficulties in finding and keeping a well-paying job. Ellis and Kay would check each other out, making sure their time together wasn't turning into a gripe session. Every once in a while they would pose a question that came from a teen's comments. After about 20 minutes, Kay spoke up.

She, too, was nervous. "I'll be honest, I never had these problems. I was this popular White girl in my school, so I got after-school jobs pretty easily. You guys sure have gotten the short end of the stick on that." She paused again, still nervous for having said so much about herself. "The truth is, my problem with groups was different. I would get involved and then do all the work! It was terrible. I'd do a project and be fried when it was over because I'd worked so hard."

"Yeah, I worry about that, too," Cece replied. "I mean, I want to help, but I just can't do too much. I help my mom at home and all . . . ." Others nodded their heads in affirmation.

"So how about we do this together? Ellis and I can approach the employers, and a couple of you can keep track of who says 'yes' and who says 'no' or 'maybe.' Then we'll help with résumés while you recruit some more of your friends to the job fair . . . ." Five young people signed up to do tasks over the next week. Eduardo and Cece agreed to be the cochairs of the group as well.

Later that afternoon, Ellis and Kay adjourned once again to their favorite diner. Along with their usual coffee, they treated themselves to a cheese Danish.

PERSONAL ACTIVITY

Using the above case as a guide, reexamine your approach to posing issues with a group you are working with. What is your example of your own struggle for the group to reflect on? How can it serve as a bridge to breaking down possible resistance? How does it suggest "transformative" leadership and not just weakness?

RECONSTRUCTING THE PRACTITIONER'S ROLE IN LEADERSHIP DEVELOPMENT

It is important to stress here that the above clinical social work techniques, if not joined to the dynamics of the organizing or management process itself, will be as limiting as any other binary, "either/or" approach. Over time, those who engage in strict clinical social work techniques tend to overwhelmingly focus on intrapsychic dynamics, while strictly "macro" practitioners eventually tend to exclude all but political, economic, and programmatic issues from their activity.

This turn toward method rigidity, initially unintentional among practitioners, occurs because most practice methodologies fail to incorporate the dynamics of *self-change* within their frameworks. This, in turn, limits their ability to maintain an active, engaged form of critical reflection with those with whom they work. In fact, too often, a social worker performs his or her role without fully recognizing the powerful institutionalized influences on that role—which, over time, affect one's stance in the world. For a genuinely transformative process to occur, this *leadership process* requires a *much deeper interplay between practice methods that impacts us all.*

Second, one problem-posing group session is hardly sufficient for leadership invested in sharing power in new, critically reflective forms. One needs both patience and persistence in the development of authentic relationships together to give birth to real transformation. The development of a critically reflective practice is impossible if the practitioner and community members do not work together at weaving these two elements back and forth in their work over a significant period of time. Debbie Harris did not take the risks she did, including her own upset, in the first month or two of working together with the seniors.

If community organizers and managers lack the *patience and persistence* to weave multiple method techniques into their work, they will inevitably succumb to the pressured habits wrought by the primary expectations of the job. And why shouldn't they? After all, a social worker, no matter his or her underlying beliefs and commitments, will be hired to do what the agency has advertised for all along: the caseworker for his or her ability to provide concrete services and casework interventions, and the organizer to engage in more collective, organizational/community work.

Operationally, this means that the agency will more quickly reward those who maintain its order and punish—or at least ignore—those who seek a redefinition of how the world—the agency—views those with and without power inside the agency. *Without the conscious interjections of some methodological factor to buffer this push toward routinization and doing things as they have been done, work comes to be performed in ways that unconsciously maintain the larger social order by accepting the world—in terms of agency roles—as far more objective and outside of one's control than it really is.*[8]

Social workers' roles become static and rigid, in the simplest terms, when a caseworker is assumed to engage in and is rewarded *only* for intrapsychic clinical interventions and the organizer/macro practitioner *only* for strategic, organizational interventions. By removing each practitioner's role from a critically reflective engagement with others and himself or herself, one implicitly accepts the institutional order as it is. Each practitioner has abstracted the intervention's human essence into dichotomized terms, easily dividing interpersonal and community–social life into stark method choices of either micro or macro work. As the larger world is only partially apprehended by the caseworker and organizer through this approach, well-intentioned people go on to perform in agency roles that have unnecessarily stripped away the potential for the critical reflection in action discussed throughout this chapter.

REFLECTIVE QUESTIONS

Review your and others' roles inside your agency.

Where are they overly rigid? What could be added/modified that would add more micro to macro? Macro to micro? Identify concrete ways the agency would benefit. What training skills could each offer the other?

Thus, many social workers' interactions with others take on a static and objectified quality as the varied psychological and social phenomena are worked on with respective— and seemingly alternative—diligence. The organizer tries to develop leaders, but like the Brooklyn worker, he or she finds consistent intrapersonal roadblocks to engaged involvement and falls back on ego boosting to get things done. The caseworker works hard with the clients of different backgrounds but finds so many objective problems that he or she eventually prefers to work with people of like social characteristics so that meaningful clinical work can take place. And, of course, hierarchical relationships between client and worker never change. People consciously continue to see themselves as liberal or even radical, but meaningful change through engaged worker–client interactions becomes increasingly difficult. Rewards are then sought exclusively elsewhere, such as in other professions, publishing, or a change in job status.

PERSONAL REFLECTION

Review your own job and what you are doing. Take some important but not urgent time to see where there is room for either macro or micro skills and focus. What have you been letting slip? What can be added or shifted to deepen your own role flexibility?

To perform differently, you must find within your practice paradigm ways to break down tendencies toward static role definition. Freire's (2000) critical reflection in action points in a generally helpful direction, but it needs specificity in terms of macro or micro practice. Therefore, I would argue the following:

- First, the use of critical reflection in action carries with it an element of *risk* that, if accessed consistently over time, keeps you alive to the potential for transformative change (however modest) within the process of your work.
- *Furthermore, the primary risk for each practitioner will be in the consistent use of the less dominant domain of his or her primary method. For the organizer, it is the risk in intuitively trying to understand the personal strengths and needs of community members, which may necessitate deeper interpersonal interventions; for the clinical social worker, it's the risk in intuitively understanding the social and political factors of a community member's life that may demand some form of macro intervention.*
- Risk is, therefore, not about whether you'll do your job. It's the concrete, ongoing exploration of the live tension between the recognized, yet often silent polarities embedded in any engaged practice relationship. *The silence means that they can and often will be ignored at times but not that they are unimportant. For, as anyone who*

has stepped out of formal role expectations knows, such risks create the possibility of transcending the constraints of any one form of practice. Through your willingness to consistently use intuitive skills, you have taken a leap into areas less known and less certain for yourself (and for the agency that your stated role functions represent).

- *In this leap, you are exposing the vulnerability that all of us experience but that many roles are expected or required to hide—except in the role of client or community member.*
- This is why risk helps you transcend a practice situation's limits: Your more open vulnerability resulting from your use of intuition creates an immediate *sharing* between community member and professional. For as the community member begins to experience a relationship with you in both agency- and non-agency-defined inter-actions, there is a far greater likelihood that he or she will begin to see that his or her own roles can be defined by not only failure but also strength.
- Your grappling with the personal (or, for the clinical worker, the social) material in ways that you are not necessarily comfortable with or institutionally rewarded for forces you to approach the client or community member more as an equal than as someone solely to be helped by you. Freire's dialogue has begun.

This is why the consistent use of risk, such as Debbie Harris's, is as potentially radical as Freire (2000) suggests in his discussion of critical consciousness. *In naming the word, one is transforming the world not only in some objective sense but also in the socially conscious way of consistently redefining perceptions of the way the world is between an agency worker and community member.* Instead of rigidly defining what is between worker and community member as an unchangeable relationship in terms of power and sharing, *you are developing your personal mastery with others.* Such personal mastery, developed over time, allows you to more effortlessly present yourself with others in ways that allow for mutual exploration of your world. As Harris found out, her argument with her community member was a catalyst not for permanent disagreement but for mutual feedback and support on the different tasks of the seniors' group. Over time, each participant needed and got feedback, and each had skills to offer in the process of building their organization.

After all, as Harris recognized, her own self-determination depended in part on her ability to stay attuned to the shifts in her practice experience, both personally and politically. Furthermore, her ability to understand a person's individual problems in the midst of organizational demands showed more than multimethod dexterity. The risk in attempting to go beyond the defined limits of her organizing role in her intuitively based confrontation had meant sharing her own personal vulnerability. Instead of concentrating only on the intellectual tasks of the group (action), she used her intuitive sense of a person's struggle (reflection) to begin creating critical consciousness (the joining of action and reflection). *Not only was the client changed, but so was she—to a method of practice that actively understood how to go beyond imposed agency limits and static role definitions.* Naming the word had indeed begun to transform the world for her and for those with whom she worked.

CONCRETE PHASES FOR "NAMING THE WORD"

There are three interconnected phases to this process of transformative leadership development between the organizer and the organized. As a *process of engagement and relationship building,* there are no definite limits to the beginning or ending of one phase or another. Likewise, the consistent use of different skills is not an unending repetition of intuitively expressed techniques. They must flow organically from the situation itself; your own developing personal mastery in what is and isn't possible together will obviously help along the way. After all, there is a job to do, and you aren't expected to search for transformative, trust-inducing experiences at the expense of immediate tasks at hand. Besides, there must be enough joint activity before you can establish any genuine relationship capable of transformation.

Phase 1: Active Work and the Sharing of Self

As stated earlier in the chapter, the initial work between a community group and a practitioner will carry with it the implicit failure of the group to have previously achieved, in some way, its own stated needs and/or interests. Regardless of origin, this sense of failure is fraught with the dangerous potential of maintaining established role patterns accepted by the institutional order: *You enter to help, showing your concern; they accept your help, following your advice.* Even if you create a viable campaign, dominant patterns of leadership–membership remain embedded in the entire practice situation. Self-determination cannot occur.

Therefore, the contradiction here is to present yourself as skillful in the completion of the group's tasks (your reason for being there in the first place) while simultaneously open enough as a person to suggest a more mutually determined definition of the problem and how to end it. *At this stage, this means performing the work but sharing yourself.* Ted Finkelstein, at the time a neighborhood organizer working with tenants in the Bronx, wrote a good example of how this can happen (Burghardt, 1982):

> At first, when organizing in an emergency situation like this one was, there is little time for certain sharing to develop trust together. You have to get the work done, and that's all. But a while after the emergency repairs had been completed, Milton (a new tenant leader) came back to the office. He needed to use the phone to make calls. I attempted to show him how to get the City Emergency Repairs Program involved in his building. We ran into many obstacles. The day became a real learning experience for both of us as we spent literally five hours on the phone with various agencies trying to overcome major snafus in the building. An instant respect and admiration for each other's style grew as we in our own ways tried to

deal with the City. . . . Our anger and tempers soared as we met resistance at every turn. Laughter and talking were the only things that kept us from going insane. By the end of the day we were talking with each other, not at each other. . . . By the time of the next meeting Milton had told most people what we had been through. It appeared a giant burden was off everyone's shoulders at the start of the meeting.

Finkelstein and Milton had emphasized work, but what was going on underneath the activity was a fuller, more complete presentation of self in subtle, yet clear ways. In the midst of work there was admitted frustration, anger, and laughter, along with "instant" respect for each other's styles. The organizer's role expectations demanded activity that centered on the housing bureaucracy. Finkelstein's particular openness and sharing of himself also communicated a message about the method of leadership that, because it was based on his willingness to risk exposure of himself in personal terms, went far beyond formalized definitions of his professional role. One must remember that the work had begun in failure and with a call to Finkelstein for help. His answer could have fit their assumptions, and those most commonly expressed and sanctioned by society, if he had exclusively done the job *for* them.

The radical nature in this stage's process is not just in confronting these assumptions but in Finkelstein's beginning to demand new "modifications" (as Freire, 2000, calls them) by the oppressed to what leadership (and help) really can be: *mutual, shared activity.* The practitioner, it can't be forgotten, is being observed by those who work with him or her, as much as the reverse, for what level and type of skill he or she is bringing to bear on the problem (a directly stated theme) and for less conscious examples of how the world is, such as images of authority, the degree of following demanded in a request for help, and so on (the indirectly stated theme in this phase).

The key problem for the organizer is to present himself or herself in such a way that these indirect themes begin to be externalized *in a manner that allows for the emergence of community members as increasingly equal partners and participants. In this slow incubation and birthing as leaders, they become aware that their heritage has as much resonance within the organizing process as does a macro practitioner in* his or her *more formally institutionalized role.* If the organizer and the organized can begin to do this together, they both begin a process of decoding old themes of internalized oppression that until then have continually limited the definition of the problem situation to its objective characteristics. Freire (2000) writes:

In general a dominated consciousness which has not yet perceived a limit situation in its totality [that it is not solely of their own creation] apprehends only its epi-phenomena [surface level] and transfers to the latter the inhibiting force which is the property of the limit situation [passivity bred by fatalism and a sense that change is impossible]. *This fact is of great importance for the investigation of generative themes.* When [people] lack a critical understanding of their reality, apprehending it in fragments which they do not perceive as interacting with consistent themes of the whole, they cannot truly know that reality. To truly know it, they would need to reverse their starting point: *they would need to have a total vision of the context in order subsequently to separate and isolate its constituent elements and by means of this analysis achieve a clearer perception of the whole.* (p. 104; italics added)

These dynamics, while written obscurely by Freire (2000), underscore why tactical self-awareness can be of such importance to an organizer's effectiveness in redefining what leadership and power sharing can be (see Chapters 2 and 3). By definition, tactical self-awareness is always conscious of context (including, in part, the way others perceive that context). During this initial phase of organizing, you can therefore use the presentation of your self in ways that begin to sweep away Freire's epiphenomena (the small details of everyday life that show people both how the world is *and* their own limits within it) so that a new vision of the context stands before them.

REFLECTIVE QUESTIONS

Reflect on an organizing activity with community members. What skill sets did you bring to the work? In what way were you overly rigid, staying locked in a stance that revealed little about you as a person? Where could you have been more open in ways that could have demonstrated a positive need for support?

By using your skills and simultaneously being tactically self-aware enough to present yourself as a complete person with your own needs and varied skill sets, *you begin suggesting a far more radical image of what **that context** could be like.* Decoding one's sense of the world can't take place by simply talking about a different, more equitable world. *It occurs through some jarring of people's perceptions so that old ideas and assumptions about the world and their place in it can fall away and new ones can begin to be constructed.* Obviously, much of that jarring will come through the ongoing attempt to improve social conditions. This is why organizing campaigns, with their emphasis on reconstituting the social (and personal) order, are so important. They attempt so much that people taking part sense that things—including them—really can change.

Such transformation can take place on a much smaller scale in even the most conservative periods or with modest resources. The need to alter how people perceive themselves and the world of which they are a part is a constant. The question, then, is will there be active attempts at a more radical transformation or not? The active engagement of a practitioner with community members in altering how people work together can prove to be as exciting as Berger and Luckmann (1967) imply in their analysis of how change occurs:

> A "recipe for successful alteration" has to include social and conceptual conditions, the social, of course, serving as the matrix of the conceptual. The most important social condition is the availability of an effective plausibility structure that is a social base serving as the "laboratory of transformation."[9] . . . [And] this plausibility structure will be mediated to the individual by means of significant others, with whom he must establish strongly affective identification. No radical transformation of subjective reality . . . is possible without such identification. . . . *These significant others are the guides into the new reality. They represent the plausibility structure in the roles they play vis-à-vis the individual. . . . And they mediate the new world to the individual. The individual's work now [begins to find] its cognitive and affective focus in the plausibility structure in question.* (p. 55; italics added)

In the larger society, this is in many ways the role that Obama's presence on the national stage in his 2007-to-2008 presidential election campaign played for so many Americans. His ascension to the presidency re-created the "plausibility structure" of so many who see in him a hope for both his leadership and their own place in American society. Whatever disappointments some may have had in his first term, America's shift in what is "plausible" in American politics will forever be different: When a woman or Latino or Asian American runs for the office, there may be excitement but not fundamental surprise at the "implausibility" of that person's candidacy. A macro practitioner plays a similar role on a much more modest but not unimportant stage. This is why an organizer's small personal acts, dealt with consistently, plausibly create so much transformative potential: *The worker makes practice—the community member makes practice—the worker/community member transforms practice.* The context has shifted from one in which formal authorities make history (you, the skilled, yet distant professional) and objects receive that history (the deferential, thankful community members) to one in which people act as subjects of history—together.

Phase 2: The Demand for Sharing the Work

The primary contradiction of the first phase for the practitioner was shaped by the demand for professional skill *and* personal need. While always emphasizing the socially mandated activity of the group, dynamic tension is found within a consistent presentation of vulnerability where none is expected in the practitioner's role as he or she skillfully goes about doing the work. *In this second phase, the dynamic tension is reversed by locating the contradiction between the demand for quality work and an expression of the client's strength.* The process of altering previously constructed, well-internalized roles that have supported the institutional order doesn't rest with just the macro practitioner. Even as the organizer's formal role definition is being broken down in Phase 1, it doesn't follow that others working with him or her will immediately change. As every experienced practitioner knows, cause and effect is much too slippery to be reduced to a singularly powerful variable. (And, in fact, to assume otherwise in this instance would further condescend to a community member's actual reality.) Just because you change doesn't mean others want to!

Nevertheless, eventually the needs in the organizing process subtly reverse themselves. You may be consistently revealing yourself more fully in your "personness" by allowing some vulnerability in how you go about your work, but now it is time to demand that community members assert their full selves by exposing their *strengths consistently, too.* If you don't make this demand, you may succeed in developing your own legitimacy and respect in the group *but solely as its leader.* (For example, how often have you heard community members refer to a presumably excellent and highly popular professional in terms of how the group couldn't survive without him or her?)

Here, then, the ongoing conversation between practitioner and community group members must shift (Wheatley, 2008). If a rigid institutional order is to be undermined by changing ideas about leadership, then signs of deference and internalized oppression must begin to be broken through. The practitioner realizes this for his or her own good; after all, to remain in Phase 1 may create a sense of well-being and, eventually, a type of charismatic charm, but the vulnerability has obviously been false, for *positions* of responsibility remain the same. No world will be transformed by that!

Indeed, on some level this personalized yet traditionally ordered pattern of interaction may seem to suit community members just fine; here you are, working skillfully and responsibly, and you're a nice person to boot! However, the purpose of developing critical reflection in action together is not to find a new leader but to transform the way people act on the world together as transformative leaders. Your skill and vulnerability have combined to suggest that the old themes of authority and excellence need not be rigidly constructed—and, at the same time, that failure and lack of authority aren't necessarily synonymous.

Thus, the crucial moment (*often repeated!*) during this second phase will be the conjuncture of where community members assume responsibility for certain actions that could be performed by you (and perhaps were earlier) and the type of respect given for this work. *If you truly respect them, you will risk demanding success and will be willing to openly, honestly provide constructive feedback for unsatisfactory performance.* You must dare them to be seen as being as fully human as you have attempted to be. That dare can be frightening. You need to be aware of the difference between genuine, personal inabilities to act and internalized forms of oppression that, while beginning to be broken through, continue to exist. But the daring must begin during this phase.

Just as tactical self-awareness was a primary instrument in the earlier phase, here what matters is your willingness to try to intuitively distinguish between personal problems of individuals who *cannot* do some things and those attitudes and behaviors of internalized oppression one can now risk giving up. Finkelstein related such an incident that occurred while doing the tenant work, after two developing leaders did not show up at an important meeting they had promised to attend—one that Finkelstein attended on his day off:

> Later that week I paid a visit to Milton. Che was there also and I had to over-come my nervousness and let them know what I was feeling. I told them I felt they not only let me down personally but they let down the building. They apol-ogized for not showing but they did not feel it was totally their fault. They then volunteered to handle all the arrangements for our next meeting. It had really been tense, but I think they respected me because I had confronted them. . . . We discussed the seriousness of the work if they were to become responsible for a lot of it. *Although I didn't intend to, I gave their commitment level a jolt of reality. They responded with new vigor, and honestly, they pledged to administer the building to the best of their ability.*

There had been, of course, a great deal of activity preceding this shared encounter. Finkelstein never could have given effective constructive feedback if he himself had not been through a previous process where he exposed his own limitations and frustrations that identified his humanity to the group. He had worked with them for months, so his words were within a context of shared activity and mutual commitment. Likewise, his demands were based on no-longer-acceptable behaviors that were maintaining outmoded, oppressive patterns of dominance–submission rather than on personal problems these individuals may still have had. His ability to make such distinctions had developed through previous conversations touching on others' personal issues, such as family strife, alcoholism, and so on. This clinically focused past activity now made it possible to raise demands that signified a respect for their strength, a desire to share work as equals. The consistent attention to matters in the past, flowing out of the intuitive risks taken between practitioner and client, now made possible his demand for social accountability.[10]

REFLECTIVE EXERCISE FOR EDUCATIONAL POLICIES 2.1.7 AND 2.1.9

In a small group, initiate a discussion of the difference between internalized oppression and having personal problems. As the discussion develops, note that the former is connected to dynamics of social power between groups and individuals that foster a continuation of dominant–subordinate arrangements, while personal issues may relate to individual problems and abilities that may hinder a person but are not related to such power relationships. Note as well where dynamics of internalized superiority may be at play here. Be prepared to make this kind of discussion ongoing rather than a one-time activity.

The demands were flowing organically from a leadership problem created through issues members had to confront. Activity was still primarily focused on the tenants' rights campaign but through these new demands from Finkelstein was moving toward mutual effort and sharing of leadership responsibility. These demands cannot and will not be legitimated with respect from the oppressed if they are not viewed as flowing from this common position, one of joint concern among equals. Only through that experienced commitment developed in Phase 1 and continuing in Phase 2 can your demands be heard and respected.

The future commitments and responsibility evident in Milton and Che (as well as in Debbie Harris's meat expert) did not happen because of external pressures. *They responded in a newly engaged manner because through those demands they experienced the dynamic tension found in a new "limit situation" in which they naturally assumed new roles to resolve the problem . . . as transformative leaders.*

This isn't a smooth process, of course. The ebb and flow between old and new behaviors and expectations necessitate an engaged involvement over a long period of time before a real consistency develops between all participants. We shouldn't burden ourselves with the false expectations that this type of work can occur with any more symmetry than anywhere else. To do so is to delve into the romanticism and abstraction born of distant theorizing, the type (both personal and political) that never lives. Lasting change of this kind is based on months and years, not days and weeks. If one has confidence in people—including oneself—that such change can and will occur given a consistent application of these measures, then one can more easily accept the pattern of change in practice.[11] (An example of this approach can be seen in Chapter 8, in the parent leadership work undertaken by Eric Zachary.)

Phase 3: New Relationships, Transformative Leadership, and Shared "Critical Consciousness"—Naming the Word, Transforming the World

As stated at the beginning of the chapter, the primary flaw in leadership development has been its perpetuation of a model of organization that inevitably doomed its community members to an unending cycle of marginality through the same hierarchical relationships found elsewhere. By simply emphasizing the dichotomy between leaders and followers in a context implicitly based on their initial failures, there is little way for a macro practitioner to do more than re-create old patterns of domination with new, benign faces. However, through an awareness of how to join clinical social work and organizing skills in ways that tap the political and personal dimensions of a person's entire life, it is possible to redefine the problem situation in ways that go beyond the ordinary definitions of leadership and reach a collectively shared, mutually supported transformative leadership born, again and again, through critical reflection in action.

Your ability to fluidly move back and forth between intellectually and intuitively focused issues within the practice situation (a critically reflective skill) frees you both to present professional skills and to risk personal vulnerability in ways that begin restructuring the themes of how a problem situation is defined. Tactical self-awareness allows you to be comfortable in exposing your own needs for support and the inevitable fallibility in parts of your performance without falling apart. You have become the artisan organizer effortlessly molding the leadership pot, not breaking it.

The risks you take here suggest an engaged entry into the actual situation others are living through, *not as being the same for all but as being felt and experienced by all, and therefore its change is necessary for the well-being of practitioner and community member alike.* This is what legitimates the later demands of mutual, reciprocal responsibility for the group's actions. A professional's vulnerability has ironically awakened community member strength, which now allows for shared activity between equals. The institutional order, at least in terms of the role definitions of how our problems are defined and acted on, begins to change. And the subjective alteration of reality carries with it the potential for objective change later on: "Man, the social product, makes society, the human product" (Berger & Luckmann, 1967, p. 11).

This is why to name the word is, indeed, to transform the world. While hardly equal to the drumbeat cadence of thousands marching, the quiet sounds of mutual dialogue and genuine conversation between people once perceived as helping and being helped may soon make deeper reverberations than some might expect. You work and converse together so that as many people as possible develop as subjects of history, choosing how you all will act within it. The application of these skills, shared with others and changing as the situation warrants, if successful, then develops the final irony to this model of transformative leadership development: When done effectively, people come to realize they don't need individual leaders and thankful followers at all—they want everyone "naming the word" and "transforming the world" together.

THE COMMUNITY TOOLBOX

The Community Toolbox offers a number of significant skill sets for practitioners seeking to further their leadership development skills. Some of them can be found at http://ctb.ku.edu/en/tablecontents/chapter_1013.htm and http://ctb.ku.edu/en/tablecontents/chapter_1014.htm.

Orienting Ideas in Leadership

Section 1. Developing a Plan for Building Leadership

Section 2. Servant Leadership: Accepting and Maintaining the Call of Service

Section 3. Styles of Leadership

Section 4. Building Teams: Broadening the Base for Leadership

Section 5. Developing a Community Leadership Corps: A Model for Service-Learning

Section 6. Recognizing the Challenges of Leadership

Section 7. Encouraging Leadership Development Across the Life Span

Section 8. Ethical Leadership

Section 9. Choosing a Consultant

Section 10. Promoting Organizational Change and Development

Section 11. Collaborative Leadership

Section 12. Leading Collaboratively: Leadership as a Collaborative Enterprise

Core Functions in Leadership

Section 1. Learning How to Be a Community Leader

Section 2. Developing and Communicating a Vision

Section 3. Discovering and Creating Possibilities

Section 4. Understanding People's Needs

Section 5. Building and Sustaining Commitment

Section 6. Influencing People

Section 7. Building and Sustaining Relationships

Section 8. Learning From and Contributing to Constituents

Section 9. Making Decisions

Section 10. Overcoming Setbacks and Adversity

REFERENCES

Argyis, C. (1991, May–June). Teaching smart people how to learn. *Harvard Business Review, 3*, 99–109.

Austin, M. A., Brody, R., & Packard, T. (2008). *Managing the challenges in human service organizations: A casebook*. Thousand Oaks, CA: Sage.

Berger, P., & Luckmann, T. (1967). *The social construction of reality: A treatise in the sociology of knowledge*. New York: Knopf Doubleday.

Blanchard, K., & Johnson, S. (1981). *The one minute manager*. New York: Blanchard Family.

Bolman, L., & Deal, T. (2003). *Reframing organizations: Artistry, choice, and leadership* (3rd ed.). Hoboken, NJ: Wiley.

Burghardt, S. (1982). *The other side of organizing*. Cambridge, MA: Schenkman.

Burghardt, S., & Tolliver, W. (2009). *Stories of transformative leadership in the human services: Why the glass is always full*. Newbury Park, CA: Sage.

Covey, S. (1999). *Living the 7 habits: Stories of courage and inspiration*. New York: FranklinCovey.

Covey, S. (2003). *The 7 habits of highly effective people*. New York: FranklinCovey.

Covey, S. (2004). *The 8th habit: From effectiveness to greatness*. New York: FranklinCovey.

De Pree, M. (1989). *Leadership is an art*. New York: Doubleday.

De Pree, M. (1993). *Leadership jazz*. New York: Dell.

Freire, P. (2000). *Pedagogy of the oppressed*. New York: Continuum.

Garrett, A., Donner, S., & Sessions, P. (Eds.). (1995). *Garrett's interviewing: Its principles and methods*. Washington, DC: Manticore.

Greenleaf, R., & Spears, L. (Eds.). (2004). *The power of servant leadership*. La Vergne, TN: Ingram.

Heifetz, R. (1998). *Leadership without easy answers*. Cambridge, MA: Harvard University Press.

Homan, M. (2004). *Promoting community change: Making it happen in the real world*. Florence, KY: Cengage Learning.

Mattaini, M., Meyer, C., & Lowery, C. (Eds.). (2007). *Foundations of social work practice: A graduate text*. Washington, DC: National Association of Social Workers Press.

Netting, F., Kettner, P., & McMurtry, S. (2008). *Social work macro practice*. Boston: Allyn & Bacon.

Rubin, H., & Rubin, I. (2007). *Community organizing and development*. Boston: Allyn & Bacon.

Saleebey, D. (2008). *The strengths perspective in social work practice* (5th ed.). Boston: Allyn & Bacon.

Scharmer, O. (2007). *Theory U: Leading from the future as it emerges*. Cambridge, MA: Society for Organizational Learning.

Schön, D. A. (1991). *The reflective turn: Case studies in and on educational practice*. New York: Teachers College Press.

Senge, P. (1994). *The fifth discipline: The art and practice of the learning organization*. Cambridge: MIT Press.

Senge, P., Scharmer, O., Jaworski, O., & Flowers, B. S. (2004). *Presence: An exploration of profound change in people, organizations, and society*. Boston: MIT Press.

Sergiovanni, T. (2006). *Rethinking leadership: A collection of articles*. Thousand Oaks, CA: Corwin.

Shepard, B., & Hayduk, R. (2002). *From ACT UP to the WTO: Urban protest and community building in the era of globalization*. New York: Verso.

Wheatley, M. (2008). *Authentic conversations: Moving from manipulation to truth and commitment.* San Francisco: Berrett-Koehler.

Zachary, E. (1998). *An exploration of grassroots leadership development: A case study of a training program's effort to integrate theory and method.* Unpublished doctoral dissertation, City University of New York Graduate Center, New York.

NOTES

1. For example, one leading macro text devotes three pages to leadership, with a focus on the different schools of organizational management and leadership (Netting et al., 2008, pp. 288–290). Other works have a broader focus on describing the types of members inside an organization or campaign, including its central leaders as well as activists and participants (Homan, 2004; Rubin & Rubin, 2007), without emphasizing how people develop as leaders.

2. Midwest Academy's 5-day direct action workshops list the following topics: (1) identifying the problem; (2) turning the problem into an issue; (3) developing strategy; (4) bringing people to face the decision maker; (5) the decision maker reacting to the group; and (6) winning, regrouping, beginning again. None of the dynamics of power as related to the *internal development of the group* and members' long-term awareness of themselves as consciously distinct leaders are developed. See www.midwestacademy.com.

3. It is no accident, for example, that women's movement rap sessions were called consciousness-raising groups. The intent of these groups was to explore and give support to individual women's problems and, in the process, to consciously connect those parts of their problems that are rooted in social conditions. They then explored personal and social issues and how they intertwine to develop not just leadership (a personal goal) but *leadership in new forms*—that is, without the patriarchal forms of leadership promulgated by men (a social goal).

4. See Chapter 8 for an example of Freire's (2000) problem-posing model that Eric Zachary has developed inside his educational justice organizing efforts.

5. It's interesting to see that Harris gave what she herself had wanted: feedback that included disagreement, not just words of praise (Burghardt, 1982). This obvious but often ignored process is a key element built into critically conscious practice but one of the hardest for a person to develop. It takes both a recognition of its value and tactical self-awareness to do this well. For example, if you are uncomfortable in highly structured situations, don't set up highly individualized meetings with people where this kind of dialogue is going to be attempted for the first time. Your own awkwardness probably will make whatever negative feedback you have to give and receive appear to be more powerful than it is.

6. Let me add here that there is another vehicle that allows personal and social issues to be joined in a manner that actively fosters new and heightened social consciousness: the tremendous social upheaval wrought by widespread social movements such as the civil rights movement in the 1960s, the labor movement of the 1930s, the lesbian/gay movement of the 1980s, and, at least briefly, the Occupy Wall Street movement of 2011 and 2012. What is being written about here is not a substitute for such movements but an adjunct to them when such movements do not exist—and one that can be used during them, too.

7. This does not mean that in broadening your frame of reference you start trying to talk like other people. There is nothing sillier (and more condescending), for example, than Whites trying to talk Black. While it is understandable that many Whites come to love the beauty and smoothness of Black language patterns, it is another thing to start trying to use them (a phenomenon that happens only when they're around Black people, by the way). It sounds artificially stilted, ignores the rather clear reality that one isn't Black, and is the equivalent form of condescension found in statements of understanding another's oppressive conditions that are referred to in Chapter 7. By being yourself and talking naturally, you communicate far more realness than any mawkish attempts to "get down" with others, and it's much more likely you'll win acceptance and respect from them.

This relates to Freire's (2000) important insights regarding "the banking system of education."

8. Berger and Luckmann (1967) go on to discuss this phenomenon in terms of reification:

> To what extent is an institutional order, or any part of it, apprehended as a non-human facticity? . . . [Does it become] reified [seem to exist apart from people's actions and perceptions of it]?
>
> Reification is the apprehension of human phenomena as if they were things, that is, in nonhuman or possibly superhuman terms. . . . Reification implies that man is capable of forgetting his authorship of the human world, and further, that the dialectic between man, the producer, and his product is lost to consciousness.
>
> Narrowing the discussion [on the dialectic of society] to the matter of roles, we can say that, on the other hand, *the institutional order is real only as it is realized in performed roles and that, on the other hand, roles are representative of an institutional order that defines their character . . . and from which they derive their objective sense.* (p. 61; italics added)

9. This is why an organizer needs to be organically grounded to strategies of potential change that need neither naive nor fanaticized consciousness to be successful.

10. Dennis Saleebey (2008) speaks of this when he writes about client strengths and capacities to grow.

11. This is not to say that one can easily accept the *pace of change,* since so much of that is determined by present social conditions. The point here is to recognize the pattern of change within socially quiescent periods and then to mobilize practice efforts with a pattern of consciousness that makes future historical periods much more open to momentous change.

CHAPTER 7

Why Can't We All Just Get Along?

Building Effective Coalitions While Resolving the Not-so-Hidden Realities of Race, Gender, Class, Sexuality, and Age

---

HIDDEN AGENDAS

Ellis anxiously looked around the large conference room where the HIV-AIDS Human Services Coalition was meeting. The only person he knew who was as anxious as he was had to be Kay. Both in the middle of their second-year field placement, he had been assigned the job of technical assistant and liaison to the coalition itself, a group composed of more than 30 social work agencies working on expanding funding for HIV-AIDS education, testing, and funding for their communities. Kay was the representative of a homeless shelter that focused on women and children who were HIV positive. Sitting down the conference table from Ellis, she nervously waved her hand as he distributed materials to members. They each had quickly recognized that they were the only students in the room.

Luckily, Ellis's field instructor had told him that at this first meeting, he could simply listen and learn. Kay had received the same instructions from her supervisor, which had cut the tension in half. Unfortunately, they each had enough stress left over to make them dry mouthed when they haltingly introduced themselves a few minutes later.

(Continued)

(Continued)

Attendance was taken and the previous meeting's minutes read and accepted. The chair, Ms. Irene Winters, was a dynamic White executive from one of the larger multiservice agencies in the city where Ellis was placed. She confidently introduced the first speaker, the chief of staff of a state politician who would be introducing a bill to expand needed services of interest to the group. The coalition had been formed a year previous to influence the powers that be to provide the revenue.

"People, it's my pleasure to introduce one of the lead champions of our coalition. As you know, a year ago, HIV-AIDS services had the least funding of our state's social service revenues. Because of the efforts of State Senator K_____, we are confident that legislation will be secured in the coming legislative session. While she could not be with us today, I'm happy to introduce her chief of staff, William Jefferson, whom I have gotten to know well throughout the last 10 months. William, take it away!"

A wiry, tall African American man sitting next to the chair, wearing a crisp paisley tie that matched his dark blue suit, tugged briefly at his tie as he rose to speak. "It's Willard Jeffries, folks . . . ."

He took the briefest of pauses, looking slightly to the moderator, who nervously laughed, "Oh, of course, I knew that, Willard . . . I always do that! People, Willard has been the best champion we have in this work!"

Pulling on his tie again, Jeffries returned to the business at hand, providing a concise 30-minute talk on where the legislation stood and possible steps the coalition could take to further influence the vote. His summary point was clear. "This coalition made a difference because you had the staying power and the commitment to work together for over a year. We will need that same level of commitment and focused expertise over the next 2 months. I am sure you will do what is needed for us all to be successful."

Ellis and Kay looked briefly at each other, affirming what they took to have been an impressive summation of the legislation at hand. Surprisingly, some of the group seemed to think otherwise.

Complaints over the bill were raised immediately by three members. Two of them were adamant that the word *household* be changed to *family unit,* a word emphasis that would bewilder both students until they met later with their field instructors.

The third member, a Latino executive of a small agency in East Harlem, was upset over a clause in the bill that assumed screening services were one part of a larger medical project at each site. "Providing funding only for those with on-site medical services preempts who qualifies, don't you think? We've been involved for a long time here, and this makes it impossible for a smaller agency to compete. Some agencies have funding streams—"

The lead facilitator cut off the young executive. "We don't have time for all of this right now. If this legislation is going to pass, we have to stay united. This is the best we can do, right,

Willard?" Willard started to speak, only to be interrupted by the chair again. "I mean, it's been a year making this fight, people. I spoke with the deputy mayor last week, and he said we can expect success if we keep our momentum. I think he knows what's what, don't you?"

The room grew silent for only a second, followed by a quick motion to push ahead with the legislation as written. Calling for a vote, the motion passed, 26 to 3, with one abstention... from Kay.

The chief of staff left soon after, brushing past Ellis before Ellis could speak with him. Ellis felt perplexed. Looking at the agenda earlier in the morning, he had expected an upbeat meeting with plenty for everyone to do. What he experienced was far different. Yes, there clearly was success for the group to celebrate. And it was also clear that different members had different agendas. And something else was gnawing at him and leaving him uneasy. Why did something that seemed to be going so well end up feeling so bad?

Educational Policy 2.1.4—Engage diversity and difference in practice. In this chapter, readers will be able to "understand how diversity characterizes and shapes the human experience and is critical to the formation of identity. The dimensions of diversity are understood as the intersectionality of multiple factors including age, class, color, culture, disability, ethnicity, gender, gender identity and expression, immigration status, political ideology, race, religion, sex, and sexual orientation. Social workers appreciate that, as a consequence of difference, a person's life experiences may include oppression, poverty, marginalization, and alienation as well as privilege, power, and acclaim. Social workers

- *recognize the extent to which a culture's structures and values may oppress, marginalize, alienate, or create or enhance privilege and power;*
- *gain sufficient self-awareness to eliminate the influence of personal biases and values in working with diverse groups;*
- *recognize and communicate their understanding of the importance of difference in shaping life experiences; and*
- *view themselves as learners and engage those with whom they work as informants."*

THE STRATEGIC IMPORTANCE OF COALITIONS AND NETWORKS

Ellis and Kay have begun participating in what is one of the most vital and strategic arenas in a macro practitioner's life: the service-based, advocacy-focused coalition. Sometimes identified as collaborations when the goals of the group are short-term and highly specific (Mizrahi & Rosenthal, 2001), *what distinguishes a coalition is the importance of member interdependence to achieve goals and influence targets that on one's own are less likely to be reached.* Using our above example, the 30 members of this HIV-AIDS coalition came together at the height of the AIDS crisis in the early 1990s. They worked as a coalition to influence legislation needed from the state so that each agency would get needed funding for desperately needed services. Such funding would have been impossible to achieve if each of the agencies had worked on its own. As Ellis and Kay witnessed, this multiagency group was influential enough to have legislative officials speaking at its events and supporting its funding efforts—exactly the kind of strategic goals a coalition would be expected to achieve.

Of course, any group of actors this large is going to have dramas of other kinds as well. This is why the care and tending to coalition members' needs for the overall group is such a demanding commitment for its members, as discussions are often longer and more complex than those within other, more unified campaigns (Mizrahi & Rosenthal, 2001; Roberts-DeGennaro & Mizrahi, 2005). As we can see above, for example, some agencies were not pleased with the language the group was using. Coalition members often must struggle to find the right balance in how to frame issues so that different groups who are otherwise in basic agreement on the primary goal can agree sufficiently on other tactics and targets that may impact their agencies' basic belief systems or approaches to work. For example, the emphasis on *household* as opposed to *family unit* would be the kind of compromise language used in a multiagency coalition to keep some religious agencies involved who otherwise might object to the implicit support for gay and lesbian families. In turn, the objections heard by Kay and Ellis would come from other agencies with an activist agenda in support of gay/lesbian rights. Such tensions surface again and again in coalition work. The ensuing work (and rework) toward consensus and compromise among disparate members while moving ahead on primary coalition goals is one of the most demanding maintenance tasks of a coalition's leadership (Roberts-DeGennaro & Mizrahi, 2005).

A second demand unique to coalition work is the degree of influence each member brings to a coalition's activity. As Roberts-DeGennaro and Mizrahi (2005) point out, there are four key conditions to member influence and effectiveness inside a coalition:

- The type and level of resources possessed by member organizations inside the coalition
- Prior working experiences among and between member organizations
- The salience and urgency of the social change goal
- The feasibility of winning

Using the above example, Ellis and Kay's coalition had had enough reason to believe in the issue's winnability at this time of crisis, in part due to its identified urgency and impact on people's lives (its salience) in the early 1990s. *These latter two items are based on one's strategic assessment of the larger political context, the degree of public attention paid to an issue, and whether or not people perceive those affected by an issue as deserving*

(Jansson, 2008; Reisch & Andrews, 2002). For example, 20 years ago, a coalition to help homeowners with distressed mortgages would have been seen as neither winnable nor urgently important and its identified population as less than deserving of public support. By 2009, that would no longer be the case, as evidenced by recent organizing drives and the positive public response to mortgage relief and the stoppage of foreclosures seen throughout the popular press (Said, 2010). (This kind of broader strategic assessment by coalitions can be examined in more detail at the end of this chapter by linking to the Community Toolbox's outline of coalition activities.)

The remaining two items relate to coalition member-to-member factors internal to the group. Prior experiences of working together affect people's perceptions of whom they can rely on, who is committed to the goals of the coalition itself, and who has other, more hidden agendas that can potentially undermine group formation (Burghardt, 1982; Roberts-DeGennaro & Mizrahi, 2005). A hidden agenda may be fairly benign and simply relate to a new member wanting to get to know and be known by other, more established members. However, other hidden agenda items can include a particular purpose of a group member that either has not been embraced by the larger coalition or is in fact potentially damaging to the coalition itself. For example, it is possible for a legislative coalition like the one above to have individual members attempting to use the influence and reputation of the larger group to get to know and influence political targets and funders on other items that could jeopardize the group's effectiveness or alienate targets they have been attempting to influence together. Coalition leadership has the responsibility to prevent such activities from occurring by the way it establishes and oversees the rights and responsibilities of coalition membership. (See the Community Toolbox outline at the end of this chapter to locate these techniques on the website.)

The final condition at play in any coalition is the degree of commitment and level of resources a group member brings to the group. It is no accident that the chair of Ellis and Kay's coalition came from a large, resource-rich agency. Coalition members gain internal influence through the added resources of their personnel's time (agencies with endowments often have staff assigned to policy and advocacy work, while such work is added to the program work of smaller agencies' staff), space (large agencies have more room where meetings can be held), and reputation (older, established organizations often have boards with highly influential members from the political and economic worlds that coalitions seek to influence). Coalitions that also are committed to social justice/social change issues have to seek to balance these powerful resources of more established groups by including in their criteria for leadership the degree of commitment and hard work others are willing to bring as a counterweight that opens up leadership and direction from new, often minority agencies. Utilizing the best of the resources from established members and remaining open to the vitality and innovation that newer members bring to coalitions is a balancing act that takes ongoing patience and persistence from any coalition leadership seeking long-term strategic effectiveness. (The Community Toolbox addresses ways for newer and older members of coalitions to work together effectively.) In this way, the tensions that surfaced between small agencies and the larger ones that we see in the case study can be minimized.

REFLECTIVE QUESTIONS

Has the chair of Ellis and Kay's coalition achieved this kind of balance? How do you know? What might be done to improve the future work of this coalition?

A LOOK INSIDE HUMAN SERVICE COALITIONS: BUILDING OR BREAKING COMMUNITY? HANDLING THE NOT-SO-HIDDEN REALITIES OF RACE, GENDER, CLASS, SEXUALITY, AND AGE

It is clear that coalitions serve a powerful purpose for advancing a social service and social justice agenda. Working in local communities, professional associations, and national formations (Staples, 2004; Weil, 2005), they can be found wherever there is social service work to do and the needs of the marginalized are unaddressed.

However, our short case study above has other forces at play as well. Left unattended, these more subtle social dynamics can either doom a coalition to a one-shot formation or hollow it out so that its potential to incubate and give birth to the interdependent, multiracial, multicultural community we seek never develops. For example, if you examine closely the interplay between the dynamic White chairwoman and the bright African American chief of staff, you'll see lurking beneath that legislative planning the seeds not of community and consensus but of conflict and cleavage.

As the rest of this chapter explores, one of the greatest challenges we confront as progressive people committed to wide-scale social change and social justice is that so many people still experience agency and coalition life as being fraught with social tensions between groups that need not occur . . . and cannot if we are to develop the unified and interdependent voice that the best of coalitions and communities seek. It is indeed striking that Educational Policy 2.1.4 ("Engage diversity and difference in practice"), which frames this chapter, is more than twice as long as almost all the other standards. In this era ripe with the possibilities of transformation, such detailed emphasis underscores why it is fundamental that practitioners "embody the change we seek," both in our agendas' strategic outcomes and in how we conduct ourselves in building relationships, handling disagreement, and sharing power across races, between men and women, and amidst all those other social factors that form the real patchwork of American life.

REFLECTIVE QUESTIONS

In the Kay and Ellis case study above, what tensions emerged between the coalition chair and the chief of staff? Why do you think they happened? Was everyone aware of what transpired? What was the appropriate response by the chief of staff? The chair? Other members of the coalition?

CLARIFYING THE CONVERSATION: SOCIAL OPPRESSION, INSTITUTIONAL RACISM, SEXISM, HOMOPHOBIA, AND THE MICROAGGRESSIONS OF EVERYDAY LIFE

Racism, sexism, homophobia, ageism, ableism, and classism are found in many forms. There are the large, virulent forms of economic and social injustice that objectively discriminate against people of color, women, gays, those with disabilities, and working-class people in general. We see this oppression in the lower incomes, poorer housing, and fewer judicial rights of these groups. Such conditions are often the animating purpose behind much of what all social work practitioners do—whether organizers or clinicians.

As the nationally recognized People's Institute's antiracism workshops make clear (Chisolm & Washington, 1997), there are also institutionalized procedures and standards that discriminate against oppressed people in a slightly less direct but equally powerful manner. This brand of oppression, first identified by Kwami Ture (formerly Stokely Carmichael) and Charles Hamilton (1992) in their work on institutional racism, uses White, middle-class, male standards of performance and behavior as guides against which all others must be measured—and by which many inevitably fail. Affirmative-action programs in schools and businesses across the country have been designed to help eliminate these procedural biases, though the assault on such programs by the Bush Administration and other conservative groups has thrown some programs (especially in public education) into a much more vulnerable status. For example, a powerful report on institutional racism from the National Association of Social Workers (NASW) in 2007 listed no fewer than 10 forms of various procedures and policies that further marginalize oppressed populations inside schools, social work agencies, and programs: "exclusions from unions, organizations, social clubs seniority systems (last hired, first fired), income differentials, predatory lending practices, inferior municipal services, admissions based on test score differentials, education based on mono-cultural school curricula, [and] preconceived potential or ability" (DeSilva & Clark, 2007, p. 6).

Within the profession, these forms of oppression have been attacked for years by social workers, community members, and other practitioners. However, over the past 25 years, people have learned that the realities of race, sex, sexual orientation, age, disability, and class necessarily have a personal dynamic that plays itself out among well-meaning professionals as well. DeSilva and Clark's (2007) report synthesized these dynamics powerfully. While here applied to race, such dynamics can apply to other forms of oppression as well:

> Three subtle types of racism are captured in the concepts of *symbolic racism, aversive racism, and micro-inequities.* **Symbolic racism** is expressed by those who may or may not perceive themselves as racist, but justify their negative judgment of others by asserting that the others do not abide by traditional values of the dominant group. People can perceive themselves as being fair and practicing equality by holding forth certain values, such as "individualism" or "work ethic" or "self-reliance," and take negative action because the focal group does not share those values. So they perceive themselves as operating based on certain "objective" standards or "universal truths" rather than in opposition to the group based on their race (Durrheim & Dixon, 2005). **Aversive racism** is another subtle form of prejudice. People who engage in the practice see themselves as non-racists, but they will do racist things, sometimes unintentionally, or they will avoid people without overt racist intent (Durrheim & Dixon, 2005; Tatum, 2004). Finally, good people can do bad things to others in ways for which there is no formal grievance, but still have negative (sometimes unintentional) effect. This refers to *micro-aggressions* or *micro-inequities.* **Micro-inequities** are "those tiny, damaging characteristics of an environment, as these characteristics affect a person not of that environment. They are the comments, the work assignments, the tone of voice, the failure of acknowledgement in meetings or social gatherings. These are not actionable violations of law or policies, but they are clear, subtle indicators of lack of respect by virtue of membership in a group. . . . These are forms of racism that as members of this society we all commit. People of color may commit these acts or maintain these attitudes against other people of color. The charge is to become able to recognize them and move ourselves and others beyond them to facilitate systemic change. (pp. 15–16)

As we shall see throughout this chapter, we are especially interested in the micro-aggressions among progressive practitioners, for in the main, social work practitioners seem less inclined toward either symbolic or aversive oppression because of the social justice causes they engage in. At play here are the dynamics that occur in coalitions and campaigns that are fraught with both emotional and political havoc of the sort we see between Willard Jeffries and Irene Winters in the above case study. As we can see from the lingering antagonism between the two, the subtle forms of personal oppression and bias that may exist within any coalition member, regardless of our conscious intentions, have perpetuated problems in our practice and with people with whom we work that need not exist given genuine commitment to overcome them.

In talking with and interviewing people on this subject over the years—and now generations—I have discovered that these microaggressions are still all too present throughout social work practice: Many women still find men fearful of "aggressive" women; people of color find too few Whites developing genuine friendships with Blacks, Hispanics, Asians, or people of lesser-status occupations; and gay people, outside of cities such as San Francisco and New York, still see others uncomfortable with their attaining the same rights and respect as their heterosexual colleagues. While the breathtaking election and reelection of America's first Black president and the emerging support for gay marriage in numerous states stand to further alter our nation's response to multiculturalism, it's important to note that on the ground of everyday life, there are still personal struggles of social significance that all social work practitioners must undertake. Social progress, if it is measured in terms of greater personal understanding and mutual respect, is still a daily undertaking for us all.

As the 2007 NASW report on institutional racism makes clear, the cumulative effect of this inability to bridge social differences on a personal level among professionals and community members has direct political implications. First, fewer people from oppressed groups feel comfortable in (or respectful of) the institutions in which they work, thus diminishing the effectiveness of these institutions. Second, the perpetuation of problems between races, classes, and sexes undermines the institutions' legitimacy in the communities they are supposed to serve. When larger-scale activity occurs, as it did in the '30s and '60s and within the gay community throughout most of the '80s, too many social welfare agencies have had too little legitimacy as important actors in the fight against social oppression. Their credibility in providing *islands of decency* (Horton, 1998) that create spaces of transformative possibility among groups is too piecemeal to serve as an arena that can incubate and support wide-scale change. And finally, underneath all these problems, there is a level of protracted, unresolved hostility and hurt that damages each person it touches. Quite simply, life inside too many human services organizations is not as rich and meaningful as it could be.

The pattern of such interpersonal antagonism is a little like many presumably neutralized war zones: uneasy silence masquerading as peace, followed by occasional yet intense flare-ups that remind people of a war-torn past. This occurs because people *want* to do well and yet are either unwilling or uncertain as to how to begin overcoming years of individual and societal misunderstanding, pain, and ignorance. As we shall see, the risk in experiencing this level of vulnerability calls for a lot more than reciting, or even abstractly believing in, the value of equality. For example, a White person must understand that he or she can be deeply involved in fighting racism and still be viewed as a racist by most people of color; indeed, you *will* be (Chisolm & Washington, 1997). We shall examine why and how a White person can accept and understand this as a necessary perception for people of color to have of most Whites (or, in varying degrees, women about men, gays and lesbians about straights, etc.). Coupled with this awareness, of course, is a greater potential for effective practice.

A commitment to the development of a genuinely engaged practice can allow for such contradictions. Rather than posing our social differences as conflict laden (and thus to be avoided), we see that the resolution of social difference will occur over time—that is, in shared activity. For example, on the one hand, a White person initially is viewed as racist by some Blacks; on the other hand, he or she works in certain groups to end racism. Over time, his or her activity reveals that he or she is not as racist as some people have thought. At the same time, the White practitioner relearns elements of racism still within himself or herself that need greater attention. Personal and social differences remain in the midst of growing commonality between people. The limitations created by social differences allow macro practitioners and others to experience greater personal growth that would have otherwise been denied them. This mix of ongoing activity, personal reflection, and mutual growth by all participants is the essence of what Freire (2000) identified as *praxis,* the ongoing reflection-in-action that is the foundation of dialogue between people. Such dialogue, rooted in what Freire paradoxically identifies as the "freeing prospect of our incompletion" (p. 117), allows for a more powerful yet more fully realized give-and-take between people than otherwise could occur. The fight for social justice becomes not only a desired outcome but also a way to better work together.

In short, if a person is willing to accept these limitations and can learn to work *with* them on a combined basis of *legitimate* differences (people of color's experience necessitating careful scrutiny of Whites, women of men, etc.) and simultaneous mutuality (shared needs for good working conditions, more effective methods of practice, etc.), then both personal and political growth are possible for us all.

That said, what makes the microaggressive forms of racism, heterosexism, and sexism discussed here so insidious is their subtle power to undermine otherwise good work between people in campaigns and coalitions. After all, no one walks around a social welfare agency hostilely saying *nigger* or *faggot.* Likewise, most people would rather be caught naked than found being openly condescending to workers of a different occupation. As stated earlier, the postures and conscious beliefs of most social work practitioners are just the opposite, with liberal voting records, commitments to public education, and so on.

However, as I know from having organized with, been friends of, and interviewed numbers of men and women who, because of their particular social characteristics, are often members of oppressed groups, a far different reality seems to exist for them, even today. Their places of work or places from which they have sought help are not always seen as benign institutions. In fact, the words used again and again to describe these agencies were *oppressive, alienating, arrogant, blind to what we're really like,* and even *dangerous.* Few felt that they were wanted or respected for their work; many felt ignored.

Almost all had a level of thinly disguised hostility that, once exposed, ran deep with pain and frustration. The difference between their public postures and private feelings was profound in 1982 and, tellingly, in 2013.

In analyzing the above findings, a number of consistent themes emerged that explain the day-to-day forms of social antagonism and personal ignorance that many other practitioners created in their work. *Almost without exception, the antagonisms were born out of the false contradiction of simultaneously perceiving similarity where there was difference and difference where there was similarity.* As we'll see, working within such *constructed antagonism* creates a type of resolution that only heightens intergroup tensions. Most of the factors in this unfortunate pattern are small microaggressions: an offhand phrase here; a mispronounced name there; an occasional, too-wide smile of welcome or too-firm handshake of farewell. To the person making the mistake, the issue is trivial. As Ms. Winters says in the above case study, "Oh, of course, I knew that, Willard . . . I always do that!" To Willard Jeffries—who, were this story a novel of his life, would remember being called Mr. Jones, Mr. Johnson, Mr. Jefferson, and "you" once or twice a week by people who in fact know his name—there is nothing trivial about any of this. It is not the daily, minor accidents themselves that matter; *it is the cumulative way the reality of that person's life is being constructed by others.* Over time, each mistake traces out a theme of objectification of one's existence that increasingly oppresses and destroys the dignity of that person's life and work. As Freire (2000) outlines with the banking system of education, where educators teach by imposing their ideas on students and listening only for their own answers, to not understand the impact of these errors is to continue to *force* one's own social context onto the lives of others. That is what oppression is all about.

THE NOT-SO-HIDDEN REALITIES OF A PRACTITIONER'S LIFE

What are the not-so-hidden realities found in the day-to-day life of a macro practitioner? There are at least five—with a sixth, more volatile form that is both cause and symptom of the cumulative effect of the others:

1. Objectification

2. Invisible man/woman/spokesperson

3. Individual exception/collective failure

4. Caste scorn

5. Double-bind performance syndrome

6. Fear and loathing

1. *Objectification.* This is an abstraction by which people are unconsciously placed within certain predetermined categories of behavior (including their intentions) by others. Objectification is a form of oppression that most likely asserts itself under stressful circumstances. Such stress need not occur only during moments of highly charged difficulty for an agency. If you aren't genuinely comfortable in the presence of others from a particular social group, your ensuing discomfort can often translate itself into slips of the tongue that appear trivial but are in fact elements of that objectification. The mistaken names referred to above, a common occurrence to almost every person of color and many women and gays, is hardly caused by people's sudden loss of memory. Nor are the slightly longer pauses before introducing "different" people a function of only a sudden need for air. They, too, represent the fear associated with the unconscious, blanket codification of an entire social group as somehow the same and, thus, totally different from oneself. Name confusion and other forms of behavior that suggest discomfort in what should be normal, everyday events are based on the objectifying of individuals by some larger social characteristic; the slight gulps for air are necessary pauses as one's unconscious adjusts to the presumably vast differences created by this abstract coding.[1]

Such small actions are usually symptomatic of many other abstract notions of people. These others will most likely surface at more emotionally charged and difficult times that further identify one's problems with race, sex, sexual orientation, and class. A good, painfully honest example of objectification and its potential for great harm was analyzed by a talented White organizer as she approached her first tenant organizing task in a predominantly Black building:

> The landlord and super had clearly lowered the level of services since the building had become mostly Black. Management also insists that some tenants are destroying any work they do (a lie, though there were some isolated incidents). And yet I, in the back of my mind, too wondered if the tenants *were* at all at fault, and I don't think I would have been predisposed to think this in a White area. . . . This background, unfocused feeling led to my "splitting" everyone. I began to think and view the tenants collectively as *all* good or *all* bad. While ideologically I was on the tenants' side, I was creating visions of what I would be confronted with the first time out—a kind of projection of my growing anxiety. I envisioned a belligerent, angry, hostile, uninterested mob who would stare at me impassively as I blubbered on in a very liberal, very White, girlish, apologetic mess!
>
> This seemed ridiculous, for I had been in the building once before with another organizer and knew this logically wouldn't occur. But the brain lost to the jitters and the background scene and how I was viewing everybody was continuing to plague me. . . . A lot of this I can now see was personal stuff, but I feel the effects of racism were doing their dirty work on me also, in the sense that part of the jitters was to scapegoat the Black tenants by imagining *they* would be prejudiced and nasty and I could then use my stereotypes to blame them for my flubbing.

In another context, one person's mistaken name is another's mistaken sense of an entire group. They each highlight the theme of objectification experienced by all oppressed peoples. *Objectification is so sinister because it creates dissimilarity where none exists.* The human experiences that bind people together—be they the small pleasures of acknowledging consistently one's real name or the larger practice skill that recognizes that every social group's members will have varying degrees of interest in organizing—are the things we must use to begin uniting us. Objectification, of course, does just the reverse.

REFLECTIVE ACTIVITY

For White practitioners: Think back to a large group meeting, classroom setting, or event. Were you aware of the racial composition of the group before a person of color arrived? Or only once that person was present?

For practitioners of color: Do verbal slips and discomfort emanating from a White colleague happen only to you and others of color, or is that person consistently uncomfortable, awkward, etc., with everyone in those situations?

2. *Invisible man/woman/spokesperson.* Feminist women, gays, and people of color frequently mentioned this frustrating dynamic that Ralph Ellison (1992) wrote so brilliantly about in *Invisible Man* and Vaid (1996) analyzed in *Virtual Equality.* The added twist since the 1960s has been the awarding of the spokesperson role to anyone from an oppressed group. "We're either not here and ignored or trotted out and examined for every word," one woman said bitterly. I have seen the dynamics again and again: Introductions are given to everyone but the "different" one, or else he or she is singled out for special mention; questions of a more generalized expertise are directed to everyone except him or her, yet that person is asked *everything* about particular social issues; major public events *always* utilize a variety of races and sexes, while daily policy issues ignore their input.

> It drives me crazy. The agency head always has me right out front when we have site visits, and I've been head of the minority affairs committee for years. But does anyone expect me to have ideas on how to improve our overall delivery system? Do you know that every week I'm asked *something* about what's going on in the Black community, and in four years have never been approached on *anything* about practice that might help White clients, too? . . . Well, if people don't want to know about practice in general, they sure as hell are not going to find out all those interesting tidbits about what's going on uptown, either!

These complaints, echoed by others throughout social work and other professions, again create confusion between the valid social differences between people and the similarities across groups. The subtlety here is twofold. First, no one minds being asked about social issues that directly relate to his or her own experience, as long as it is understood that one is not objectifying a whole range of people by assuming that one person's views can speak for everyone else.[2] It's not as though there are no social differences in our world, and people from oppressed groups see the necessity of analyzing new issues as they impact them and those they are close to. At the same time, how many Whites have been asked for their comments about what the White community is feeling, or "What do men feel about" some issue? I've found that any time a White man is asked that question, he snickers and considers the question absurd. "Life is too complex for such generalities," he says. "And how would I know anyway? I'm not so stupid as to think that I could speak for everyone. It would make the issue trivial." Unfortunately, that trivialization is exactly what's bound up in other spokesperson roles.

Second, to ignore all the skills of an individual not only lessens his or her worth but also makes suspect one's actual interest in the social differences that do exist. If in the full complexity of organizational life, the only thing you talk to a particular person about is sex or race or ableism or sexual orientation (with a little bit on sports scores thrown in for good measure), then the interest in that social topic will be viewed as more a matter of curiosity than of real concern. Naturally, the recipients of this well-intentioned interaction will come to hold back their real responses to the consciously well-intended queries.

Thus, it is quite possible for Whites, straights, and others to see themselves as actively communicating when in fact they are perceived as just blowing hot air. As one assistant director of a major agency in New York put it,

> People always approach me on racial issues to learn something for themselves, not to respect it for what it is and how it already is impacting on their lives. That really gets to be a drag after a while. So with most people, I now just mouth little niceties to keep 'em happy.

Words substitute for dialogue—and too many people can't tell the difference.

The contradiction here is obvious. If one would approach others more often on issues unrelated to social content—areas of commonality—one would eventually learn about the social differences as well. In doing this, one is not being blind to social differences between people; one is placing those differences in a larger context that allows the richness and variability of all people to be seen, legitimated, and respected. In so doing, people speak as visible men and women. They find themselves being treated as subjects of history and can thus see the humanity of the one with whom they are interacting. As Freire (2003) wrote:

Dialogue is the encounter between men [and women] mediated by the world; in order to name the world. Hence, dialogue cannot occur between those who want to name the world and those who do not wish this naming—between those who deny others the right to speak their words and those whose right to speak has been denied them. (p. 88)

Genuine dialogue, then, is concretely visible between equals, both of whom rely on and need each other. Speaking is therefore not between abstract representatives of groups but as men and women seeking to simultaneously understand and act on the world together.

REFLECTIVE QUESTIONS

When is the last time you approached a person of a different social group and sought his or her expertise on an issue unrelated to that person's social makeup? Have you and other staff spoken only to him or her about social matters at meetings when the topic at hand relates to his or her background, or are substantive issues given equal weight?

---

3. *Individual exception/collective failure.* "I always feel under such pressure around here. As a woman, I know I'm viewed well. People are always complimenting me, my work is good, everyone's impressed. And the work is good, you bet it is. I *drive* myself to do well, make certain it's the best I can do, and then and only then do I feel safe. I feel like I *have* to work extra hard, because if I fail, we'll all fail. There's just a sense that as long as I do well, it's great, *but only for me;* if I screw up, well, women can't handle pressure anyway. It's one hell of a burden . . . and half the time I don't even know if it's real!"

This woman, a successful middle-level supervisor in a major social welfare agency in New York, exemplified the stress of the "individual exception" who feared that any minor mistake she made would be held against all women. As it turned out, she had reason for fear. Two weeks after this interview, a proposal for which she had been the coordinator was turned down in Washington. Having found out about and completed the proposal in just 2 weeks, she had experienced tremendous stress in getting the job completed on time. It, along with a rejected grant prepared by a White male in the agency, later were under review at a staff meeting chaired by the director. His analysis of why the two proposals were turned down? "Putting that kind of pressure on a woman had been unfair." As for the other, "It was a shot in the dark anyway. What the hell, nothing gained!" The fact that a male might have had difficulty in handling the work was not mentioned. The supervisor mulled over her response:

That bastard really had me in a bind. If I pointed out his sexism about women not handling pressure well, I was using "women's issues" as a personal defense. If I didn't say anything, all women, including me, were branded as flub-a-dubs who can't cope with "male" pressures. Of course, when I did say something about the "woman can't cope" crap that he was pulling, his response made me sick—he'd said it as a *defense* of women, not a failing!

Thus, in trying to limit the stress on this exceptionally talented woman, the executive director managed to do just the opposite. The imposition of a false social difference had managed to simultaneously heighten personal antagonism and darken the woman's perception of the agency as a supportive place for women to work.

This theme of exceptional success and collective failure has more than one dynamic. Another, perhaps more damaging, variation occurs when people who have commitments to their large membership group perceive themselves in a position to achieve that exceptional success (or where their already-achieved success is seen as the exception). A Black woman described her problem poignantly:

I have always believed that what I did individually would benefit the Black community. It was a real motivator—doing work, creating solid role models, that kind of stuff. But the more I've succeeded, the worse I've started to perform. I don't know what it is, but I can't bring myself to work as hard or get assignments done as quickly as I used to. I feel like it doesn't matter . . . that I'm not helping anybody in the community except myself. It's as if I'm being judged as some unique person unlike anyone else here in Harlem. I know it's neurotic, but I feel so ambivalent working here [in a mostly White institution]. My good work has never been seen as opening up new avenues for Blacks but as another example of why I'm different from others. And messing up? Well, messing up now and then confirms what most people feel about us anyway.

Both women related the dynamics even further. It seems that generalities on race or sex were uniformly negative; good points stressed individual success, often with the implicit sense that such success distanced them from others just like them. When topics about good values, solid family roots, interest in achievement, and so forth were raised in discussions, many straights, males, and Whites either had stereotypically negative assumptions or asked the women to explain their *distinctive* routes to success. The negative categorization had created difference where it didn't exist.

4. *Caste scorn.* When's the last time you talked *with* one of your agency's custodians or office secretaries? Not just mentioning that the weather seemed damp or that the local team won last night, but having a real discussion—one that sought his or her opinions on important subjects, subjects suggesting depth and complexity, where ideas mingled with attitudes? Your answer will tell you something about your real feelings toward people of

different occupational and educational levels. If you're honest, many will recognize that there is a real difference between general commitments to equality and the practicing of equality in everyday life.

Again, this is not to imply that there are no differences between people. Nor am I suggesting that you don't have more in common, experientially, with those doing similar work. But over a year's time, there are always opportunities for enriching one's daily work through the sharing of ideas and experiences with people of different, less influential occupations. Indeed, if one doesn't do this, is the real motivation for attempting to better a community going to come from exclusive professions? Of course not. But one's daily interactions at the office with other workers reveal one's real belief in whether a community's membership can consciously develop itself. And, of course, these often unconscious attitudes are transmitted to community members, regardless of stated positions. For "common folk," like the rest of us, may forgive—but they rarely forget. An administrative secretary at a large human service organization, who asked not to be identified, recounted her experiences at her place of work and back in her community when agency leaders paid her group a visit:

I gotta tell you the truth. I've been working here [a New York settlement house] for 12 years, and only two professionals ever really treated me as an equal. Oh, everybody had everybody calling each other by their first names and we all got cakes on our birthday, which is nice, but so what? They never tried to get to *know* me. I've been working here . . . and got my kids through college because of that paycheck. Here in the neighborhood, I've got respect. I've been active in the church, helping seniors and getting that day care center set up for working mothers like my oldest needs. I know what education is all about and how to get it. . . . The funny thing was, when [the associate director and an educational program director] visited our place because of their grant, I found myself hostile to them. They were so shocked to see me on the Board, and then so *pleased* [she scowled here], that they just got on my nerves. Why didn't they see me before, so there wasn't such a shock? . . . I let 'em stew awhile, too, because I felt so . . . . They got to see what it's like to be ignored. I didn't like myself for the way I felt, but I felt a little bit good, too.

The corresponding reaction by the program coordinator was no less intense:

When we walked in the room and I saw *L* there, I was shocked. Then I was shocked that I felt shocked. Here I was, very progressive politically, and the reality was I had somehow condescended to this woman while at work by never even deigning to know about her life and interests. I've thought a lot about this incident . . . that sense of shock made me realize that regardless of political outlook, a part of me still viewed people in lesser-status jobs as probably stupid or not really able to be involved in the world the way I was. Since then, I've been trying to change, to look at people as people and not just as job categories. Where we can maybe share things. It's been hard, but I think it's been worth it. Boy, I have been learning a lot since then!

Here, learning, like the other experiences referred to in this chapter, cannot be willed into existence by abstractions alone. It can't hurt to have progressive ideas, of course, as long as those ideas don't lull one into thinking ideas and actions are necessarily the same. The above examples reveal otherwise, and for most of us it's therefore important to search out elements of caste scorn that are often too easily dismissed as not relevant to our work. Often our reactions can help reveal our own sense of professional or occupational marginality. An experienced social worker wrote:

One day, I was in my office cleaning the place up when a new social worker walked in and mistakenly took me for the custodian. He wasn't nasty or anything; just asked me to come to his office and help clean up something when I was through. Well, I quickly told him I was no janitor and went back to work. But I was upset! The nerve! Why was he assuming I was a janitor . . . what a lot of crap, etc., etc. Then I couldn't figure out why I was so upset over some simple mistake— hell, I was even dressed in work clothes that day! As I stood there mulling over my confused, diffuse anger, I remembered the last time I'd felt this way—as a student of social work! The role confusion, the loss of status that I felt, was so easily upsetting—because I felt threatened in a way because I wasn't sure of my own self. It's ridiculous, but I felt like my work might be so worthless that one mistake about a custodian and I got the "status shakes." And what the hell did that say about what I felt about custodians?

The "status shakes" are common to people in occupations or professions where the position and influence are open to question. But think for a moment about the differences between one job category and another, including that of custodian and social worker. Caste scorn is created through a set of assumptions that make occupational status distinctions something to be sought rather than minimized. Why? Are the gained distinctions worth the aggravation needed to maintain them? Or is there perhaps a different formulation, one that can respect the distinctive skills of particular occupations while still seeking to approach our commonality—including the common need for legitimating one's worth? As Freire (2000) writes:

[If we seek dialogue together,] dialogue cannot exist without humility. The naming of the world, through which people constantly re-create the world, cannot be an act of arrogance. Dialogue as the encounter of those addressed to the common task of learning and acting, is broken if the parties (or one of them) lack humility. How can I dialogue if I always project ignorance onto others and never perceive my own? . . . How can I dialogue if I consider myself a member of the in-group of "pure" men, the owners of truth and knowledge, for whom all non-members are "these people" or the "great unwashed"? How can I dialogue if I start from the premise that naming the world is the task of an elite and that the presence of the people in history is a sign of deterioration, thus to be avoided? . . .

[Instead,] dialogue further requires an intense faith in humankind, faith in their power to make and remake, to create and re-create, faith in their *vocation to be more fully human* (which is not the privilege of an elite, but the birthright of all). (p. 90; italics added)

As has been developed throughout this book, acting on the world *with* others is not learned through abstract learning alone. Experience, if joining formal training with the use of tactical self-awareness in both social and personal contexts, helps us understand the contradiction embedded in accepting similarities so we can respect and understand genuine difference. "Caste scorn" is born out of static assumptions of difference that codify people into objects less able than oneself to make history.

Genuinely engaged practice is different. Its ongoing interactions use *shared activity and thoughtful reflection* (learning and tactical self-awareness) to generate respect born of similarities (e.g., the secretary's love of learning acknowledged by the education director through dialogue before the site visit) that simultaneously legitimates difference (e.g., the program coordinator's skills needed by the single parents' group, the knowledge of neighborhood strengths and needs best known by the board members). Instead, the more static model that began with assumptions of difference created conflict where none need exist.

EXERCISE

1. Pair up with someone different from yourself. The difference can lie in any significant social dimension, such as race, gender, age, sexuality, disability, or national origin.

2. Discuss a social group different from you that you are comfortable with and another that you have some discomfort with. Each of you should do this before the rest of the activity.

(Continued)

(Continued)

3. Before speaking again, reflect on what allows you to be comfortable with the first group. List at least three reasons. Examples might include the following:

   a. Long-time experience with group members

   b. Learning about them in another setting

   c. Work/school experiences

   d. Family values and interests growing up

4. Now explore the discomfort. Working from your strengths-based reasons, what do you need to learn/do/act on to begin creating more comfort?

   Step 1:

   Step 2:

   Step 3:

- This activity should be undertaken with clear ground rules in place so that no one is attacked for his or her choices or reasons for having made them. People cannot grow to change on such issues if they are shamed or humiliated about where they must engage in the critical reflection to take on such powerful and uncomfortable material.

---

5. *Double-bind performance syndrome.* The double-bind performance syndrome, like all double binds, creates an edge of disorienting unreality to the person living with it. Here, one's performance gets (often at the same time, though from different people) a response of either indifference or intolerance. Either response, as we all know, can be frustrating. However, together, they create enough confusion over how to measure one's own performance that the performance invariably drops. Who can keep doing well when the same quality of work is seen as both very good and very bad at the same time? Over time, of course, such results further validate others' perceptions of why people of color or occupationally lower-status individuals can't perform as well as White males. An experienced Latino organizer described this syndrome well:

It started while I was in college, and it truly drove me nuts. I'd find myself working really hard on papers or projects, and people's comments would be good. Then I'd slough off a bit, and people's comments *would still be just as good*. Then I'd work harder, and someone would rip the work apart. My own sense of what was good and what needed improvement began to get warped. . . . There never was the kind of consistency in feedback that just let me improve while letting me know what was good, too. I had to start guessing, and the tension, the whole unreality of it, really got in the way of me doing my job as well as I wanted to.

As he and others went on to explain, the dynamics were more than frustrating. For example, how do you get angry or upset with someone who has given you a good grade? And, if you ask for feedback, how can you complain about harsh criticism? With all the other compliments, to get ruffled at a strong critique seems like sour grapes!

Finally, like double binds in neurotic families, they eventually damage the person as he or she seeks some way to maintain a form of stability in his or her environment. As another woman put it, "Hell, if I'm damned if I do and damned if I don't, I figure I'll just do what I have to do to get by. If they don't care about my work, I sure as hell am not going to care about theirs!" Unfortunately, this means that over time the person's effectiveness will be lowered, with only the double-bound individual held to blame. Of course, the organization has lost in the process as well, but it may not realize its loss until it's too late.

6. *Fear and loathing.* Each of the above themes complements and often overlaps the others. Individually, analyzed here as separate mistakes and accidental oversights, they often appear minor. Cumulatively, however, they create a knotted pattern of mistrust, antagonism, and tension that unravels sporadically into acts of vitriolic, enmeshed anger. As in the coalition case study at the beginning of this chapter, the masquerade of well-intentioned pretense and studied patterns of good behavior then lie exposed, the rawness underneath revealed at last. The ensuing emotions are as direct and uncomplicated as any bigot's, except perhaps more painful due to the well-intentioned interactions that preceded them. Given the unresolved nature of the hostility, both oppressor and oppressed can and will react venomously to each other. (Imagine what happens when Ms. Winters visits Mr. Jeffries's busy office and repeats her mistake!) The dominant group comes to believe that the minority's interests are now hostile to its own; the minority comes to believe that its interests and beliefs are perceived as alien and irrelevant.

Sometimes the fear and loathing are stated quietly. For example, a medical social worker at a major New York hospital recited what began to happen when she and other Black employees got together at lunch once a month to talk, discuss common problems and concerns, and in general enjoy one another's company:

The first time we got together, somewhat spontaneously, we suddenly found the cafeteria *very* quiet. The second time people just kept looking at us, with fear in their eyes. Then everyone was *super-friendly* in the halls afterward. After the third time, my supervisor called me in to her office and asked, with loads of hemming and hawing, if I was happy here [at work]. When I smiled and said that I certainly planned on staying a long time, she then asked me why, if I was happy, we were all meeting every month! She thought lunch together must mean a Black conspiracy!

The underlying racist assumption was that any time people of color on their own got together in the hospital, they *must* be doing it for reasons hostile to the institution (Tatum, 2004).

The deep-seated fears that color so many responses to issues of race, class, sexual orientation, and gender often have wider repercussions than the brief example above. They can also poison intra-agency and agency–coalition relations for years to come. What makes these flare-ups remarkable is that they are usually triggered by small actions or microaggressions that at other times have gone unnoticed or unremarked on. In this way, they resemble the larger, more socially and collectively conscious reactions seen in the urban riots of the 1960s. Like those riots, they could not occur if there were not a history of unresolved, antagonistic experiences that had accumulated over time. Two examples suggest how painful and complicated that fear and loathing can be:

> The coordinator of an affirmative action program, while sitting at the staff lunch table, overheard a worker mention that their agency, like all others in the United States, suffered from institutional racism and sexism. Out of nowhere, his arm shot across the table, tightly gripping the young worker's arm. Increasing his grip, voice trembling, he angrily demanded examples of "that bullshit on race and sex here." Stunned and infuriated by the attack, the worker foolishly recited small examples [similar to some in this chapter]. The coordinator started yelling, and his best friend at work, the associate director, soon joined in. "We don't have to take that anymore," she exclaimed. "Ten years ago, yes, but not now!" Shocked, the younger worker foolishly asked what "it" was. "We worked hard here! We have this [affirmative-action] program, and we're working on racism and sexism all the time! How dare you say we've got problems here!" Both left the table. In one year, according to the younger social worker, neither has spoken to her since.

A White group worker working in a predominately White senior citizens' center related what happened one day when he and the center's only Black resident advisor were talking about the issue of undocumented workers. The Black worker, with a gruff reputation at the center, was not very sympathetic to their plight. The White worker disagreed, going on to state why he felt that not only did undocumented workers have it hard but that *all* Blacks should also be getting reparations for slavery. The Black worker angrily responded:

> He then directed at me an emotional tirade that welled up out of him from the depths of a soul wounded by racism. "I don't want you to give me *nothing*. I want to work for it. The White man never gave us niggers nothing! They gave everybody else. They gave the Vietnamese a thousand dollars apiece and they aren't even Americans! They don't give us a dime! So don't talk to me about your

"giving" us anything. I expect to work for *my* money! I am *glad* to have my job. The only ones they give money to are the niggers who sit outside and drink and smoke dope. Me, I have to work for *my* money. And if I want to be somebody, I have to do it myself. No one's going to do it for me. And if I don't amount to anything, I've got no one to blame but myself!"

In retrospect, I saw why he was so hostile. First, at the center, the seniors rarely availed themselves of his services. My contributions to the center were lauded, his were ignored. And I never mentioned to him how I perceived this incongruity, how it bothered me or how I wanted to correct it. . . . Secondly, I never once in the past had talked to him about Black issues in a way that showed they were part of *my* life, too, be it Zimbabwe, South Africa, or what have you. And when I finally talked to him, I started to lecture at him [about the rights of undocumented workers] before I had indicated that I had any concerns about the most glaring example of oppression in this country—or the oppression where we worked. Naturally, he became furious when I championed the cause of immigrants without ever having acknowledged these other realities!

This White social worker learned a lot from the experience. Both he and the Black social worker have been groping toward a more trusting work relationship ever since. Frightened by his blindness to his Black colleague's anger, and the latter surprised at its depth, they've seen the joint need to work together. Sadly, the first example's participants have seen no such need, if their continuing nonverbal hostility is any guide. Nevertheless, the affirmative action program remains a showpiece of the agency.

What's important to underscore here is that the people in these examples are writing their history with an element of their own free will, their own choice. While the larger forces of history are constantly determining the nature of social events before us, this element of choice is a contradiction as real as all others discussed here. It speaks to the ability of us all to shape the direction of those events placed before us, helping lay the basis for later events to more powerfully aid our particular causes. For those who see that the not-so-hidden realities of race, sex, and class are always creating themes of major social significance, both collectively and individually, there are always ways we can work to improve that history (hooks, 2003; West, 2001).

Now let's look concretely at a few ways to help ourselves as we fight for social justice and an end to oppression.

BUILDING A TRANSFORMATIVE MACRO PRACTICE: MINDFULNESS AS A TOOL OF ANTI-OPPRESSION WORK

Over the past 20 years, some trenchant work has been undertaken by activists, organizers, and professionals, especially from communities of color and other oppressed groups, on how to combat the dominant "-isms" at work in our society (Chisolm & Washington, 1997; Mallon, 2002; Reisch, 2004; Rivera & Erlich, 1998; Vaid, 1996). In social work, the work undertaken since 1980 by the People's Institute for Survival and Beyond has had a particularly positive impact on how professionals interpret the historical, structural, institutional, and internalized forms of racism that impact the lives of people of color, especially African Americans. Having trained more than 200,000 Americans across the United States, they challenge all practitioners to both understand and act on the dynamics wrought by long-term racial oppression, whether related to the job market, professional advancement, or internalized dynamics that intensify a person of color's marginality and lack of access. Their work has been embraced throughout child welfare in such powerful ways that the state of Texas has passed legislation requiring that the institute's antiracist program be held within all child welfare agencies (see www.pisab.org), and the Casey Family Programs foundation has made it a centerpiece of its effort to reduce the number of children in child welfare by half by the year 2020 (Bell, 2008).

These and other anti-oppression programs by organizations such as Prevention Justice, an AIDS activist group, and Training for Change, which focuses more on student activists, have helped countless macro practitioners learn not only about the deep-rooted structural impediments in American society for people of color, members of the LGBTQ community, and the working class but also about the microaggressions discussed above that can occur within progressive coalitions and groups committed to social change.

At the same time, for all the work inside social work and other macro-based groups and professions, social tensions that undermine or diminish the effectiveness of progressive work persist among well-intentioned and committed people (Mizrahi & Morrison, 1992; Roberts-DeGennaro & Mizrahi, 2005). For example, as Levi and Murphy's (2006) penetrating analysis of the 1999 Anti–World Trade Organization Coalition in Seattle made clear, minority women, racial, and working-class activists felt excluded and marginalized from one of the most celebrated radical coalitions of the late 20th century. Similar concerns have been raised within the Occupy Wall Street movement (Maharawal, 2011).

This profound dilemma in macro practice—*Why can't we, progressive people in coalitions and agencies, get along?*—bewilders so many activists in part because there is an under-appreciation of the power dynamics at play among those who seek change, as well as those targets who resist it. Freire (2000) analyzed the work among those who sought to help the oppressed and the oppressed themselves:

> Another issue of indubitable importance arises: the fact that certain members of the oppressor class join the oppressed in the struggle for liberation. . . . Theirs is a fundamental role, and has been so throughout the history of this struggle. It happens, however, that as they cease to be exploiters or indifferent spectators and move to the side of the exploited, they almost always bring with them the marks

of their origin: their prejudices and their deformations, which include a lack of confidence in the people's capacity to think, to want, and to know. . . . [They] truly desire to transform the unjust order; but because of their background they believe that they must be the executors of that transformation. (p. 60)

All experienced social work practitioners, whether grassroots organizers or clinical social workers or social work administrators, have somewhere in their careers experienced this kind of painful interplay between themselves and others seemingly committed to social justice who nevertheless marginalize others. For Ellis and Kay, it might be as subtle as the microaggressions between a White practitioner and a person of color. For others, it could be the marginalizing of those from minority-based agencies who are denied access to resources or funding. For others, it might be discomfort around LGBTQ folks, the disabled, or professionals perceived to be either too young or too old to be effective.

This kind of interplay occurs as dominant coalition or network members assert, often unconsciously, their power to subjugate others by demanding adherence to their interpretation of the world as they see and act on it. Such oppressive dynamics occur among well-intentioned practitioners because they do not heed one of Freire's (2000) most important insights for professionals working in the helping professions, which he explains here:

Dehumanization, which marks not only those whose humanity has been stolen, but also [though in a different way] those who have stolen it, is a distortion of becoming more fully human. . . . Because [the dynamic between oppressor and oppressed] is a distortion of being more fully human, sooner or later being less human leads the oppressed to struggle against those who made themselves so. . . . This, then, is the great humanistic and historic task of the oppressed: to liberate themselves and their oppressors as well. (p. 44)

Freire's (2000) insight is challenging as well as liberating for practitioners, regardless of their social origins. In his critique of the banking system of education (or any other profession working with the oppressed), he is suggesting that those who seek to help others carry within them the same dehumanizing dynamics of oppression as those whom they are fighting against. In turn, he makes clear that only those who are oppressed can *lead* one toward a new and more fully human way to love and act in the world—to be more fully human as we all are restored to a more fully engaged, humane way to live.

That macro practitioners, because of our socialization, inevitably carry our own internalized constructions of dehumanization and oppression can initially be an enormously humbling challenge. *That said, it can also free us from the unrealistic and inhumane demand that it is our job to liberate others from oppression, as opposed to working with others to free ourselves from our own dehumanization.* The rest of this chapter explores how the individual macro practitioner can do just that to attain the kind of *restorative social work practice*[3] that "integrates an understanding of the importance of culture and personal identity with practice methods and approaches that deal directly with the issues of social justice and inequality" (Gutierrez, Lewis, Nagda, Wernick, & Shore, 2005, p. 44).

FROM PERSONAL DISCOMFORT TO MUTUAL FREEDOM

The Beginning: Embracing Your Discomfort

What all the above stories have in common is how each person's underlying discomfort finally surfaced in ways that led to new insight, personal awareness, and improved relationships as they confronted issues of internalized racism, elitism, and bias that they initially were unaware they harbored. (Similar dynamics are at play in the transformative leadership lessons of practitioners in Chapter 6.) The problem with discomfort, unfortunately, is that most people understandably run from it rather than embracing it. Why would one do so as a mark of improving one's professional practice?

A practice framework that can answer this dilemma is mindfulness. While originally emphasized as part of either spiritual or religious practice, recent years have seen a significant increase of mindfulness in clinical programs such as dialectical behavior therapy (Linehan & Dimeff, 2001) and the professional development of physicians (Epstein, 1999). Its use by professionals has had a clear purpose: using techniques of mindful practice to root out rigid thinking, personal discomfort, and emotional upset so that a more balanced and flexible approach to practice can occur. As Epstein wrote in his seminal article, "This process of critical self-reflection depends on the presence of mindfulness. A mindful practitioner attends, in a nonjudgmental way, to his or her own physical and mental processes during ordinary everyday tasks to act with clarity and insight" (p. 833).

In concrete terms, "critical self-reflection" is right after that "aha!" moment of discomfort when one begins assessing what is and isn't working in a given approach to problem solving or relationship building—for our purposes here, when one of those "not-so-hidden-realities" may surface in upsetting ways (Wong, 2004).

Notice that the objective of mindfulness is neither political correctness nor intellectual brilliance. Instead, Epstein (1999) goes on to pose five levels of professional development that weave together both *explicit knowledge*—what you learn in books and from trainings and teachings—and *tacit knowledge*—what you learn about yourself experientially as you apply knowledge, skills, and behaviors in your actual work over time—in other words, levels of competency! What follows in Table 7.1 are the five levels, applied here to one's ongoing development as a practitioner becoming increasingly comfortable with anti-oppression work and the dynamics of social diversity as they play out in one's work and life.

Table 7.1   Stages of Mindfulness Applied to Anti-Oppression

Levels of Mindfulness (Improving Competency)	Anti-Oppression Capacity
0 Denial and externalization	Refusal to admit to social differences; unwillingness to examine one's own power and privilege
1 Imitation: Behavioral modeling	Mimicking other social group members' behavior; using "politically correct" language in a didactic, nonreflective manner
2 Curiosity: Cognitive understanding	Deepening awareness of differential impact of oppression on other social groups and individuals
3 Curiosity: Emotions and attitudes	Self-awareness of one's own power and privilege as well as one's responses to social difference
4 Insight	Reflection on and increasing flexibility regarding one's behavior and attitudes with social groups and individuals
5 Generalization, incorporation, and presence	Comfort with self and others in all settings; capacity to hold "two truths" of social oppression and individual variability; capable of "beginner's mind" without ignoring conditions of structural oppression

The first two stages are relatively straightforward: At the lowest level (Level 0), one denies and refuses to look at conditions of social oppression and how one may or may not be impacting others through one's own power and privilege. The second level (Level 1) emerges (often after stages of guilt and upset), where one incorporates the messages of oppression without genuine understanding. In some ways the polar opposite of denial, it can lead to "trying on" others' language patterns and styles of behavior in ways that are perhaps well intentioned but nevertheless ineffective in building trusting relationships with others.

The first level of curiosity (Level 2) that Epstein (1999) identifies is the growing understanding of the differential impact of oppression on others—both social groups (the disabled, the elderly, LGBTQ individuals, people of color) and individuals with whom one works and lives. This can be an overwhelming period for inexperienced practitioners, because they begin to "see oppression everywhere"—and as more than one student and young organizer has expressed to me, often with a mix of sadness, anger, guilt, and personal helplessness. These emotions are intensified as the next level of curiosity (Level 3) emerges (this can happen simultaneously with Level 2)—either how one has benefited from one's own social makeup and the attendant power and privilege or not understood how it might be impacting others. This can occur both with White, straight practitioners suddenly aware of the benefits of their social status and among new professionals from oppressed groups (people of color, LGBTQ individuals, etc.) who are stunned to realize that their professional positions carry power and privilege with their clients and groups that they have been denied in other parts of their lives.

Insight is the level (Level 4) where a practitioner has enough explicit knowledge (ongoing study of history, practice, present-day social conditions) and *tacit learning* (experience) to become flexible in and reflective about his or her use of power and privilege as he or she works and lives with others. Instead of being thrown by social differences in a group or between the practitioner and the client, the differences are comfortably acknowledged and worked with so that positive relationships can be established.

Generalization, incorporation, and presence (Level 5) develops over the years among mindful practitioners committed to ongoing self-reflection, openness to learn from others with less power and privilege, and ability to use their own years of knowledge and practice in open, non-elitist, nonjudgmental ways. They can hold the two truths of social oppression for a group of people and the "beginner's mind" that the person in front of them from that social group may have an entirely different story from those structural conditions. Likewise, they are humbly aware of the shifting dynamics of power and privilege and at the same time *use their own to diminish unfairness and increase access and voice.*

What these levels of mindfulness tell us is that a person evolves in his or her development over time—that it is a road filled with struggle, uncomfortable "aha!" moments, and a willingness to keep learning with and from others. As such, it has been detailed here to break away from past, more judgmental ways of examining how to develop as an anti-oppression practitioner. Too much writing—even the better work—discusses how to be a nonracist or nonsexist practitioner in terms of *where one should evolve to, rather than suggesting how one realistically evolves toward that goal.* For example, this (excellent) definition of a nonracist practitioner states the following:

> [Here in this essay,] we have considered criticism of practitioners as "racist" and identified specific practitioner behaviors that are associated with racist attitudes. . . . Four specific skills were suggested as characteristic of non-racist practitioners: (1) the practitioner should possess the ability to perceive in any behavior—other's or one's own—alternative explanations for that behavior, particularly those alternatives which the self might reject as false; (2) the practitioner should possess the ability to sense those verbal and nonverbal cues which would help to identify out of all possible alternatives the one which is most likely or most probable for a given client; (3) the practitioner should have the ability to feel warmth, genuine concern, and empathy for people regardless of their race, color,

or ethnic background; and (4) the practitioner should be able to confront the client when true feelings of warmth, genuine concern, and empathy have been expressed but have been misinterpreted or distorted by the client. (Rivera & Erlich, 1998, p. 118)

This definition's strengths are obvious: a search for different contexts of social and personal reality, an emphasis on skill that can actively integrate different alternatives and approaches for treatment from the client's point of view, and an unromanticized willingness to place some of the responsibility for distortion on the client's shoulders. There is, nevertheless, one fundamental difficulty with this statement: None of it is related to its content. The definition has an implicit static and moralistic quality to it. The reader has the sense of arriving at a more-or-less exalted position that then frees him or her to carry on good work, unencumbered by the problems confronting the rest of us mortals. It is an unintentional error, but to practitioners uncomfortably grappling with their personal responses to social issues, their own personal assessments can leave them feeling either discouragingly inadequate or, over time, unknowingly smug.

The way to avoid either dilemma is by admitting what is now obvious: As adults, none of us can thoroughly eradicate the unconscious emotions and attitudes created by racism, sexism, homophobia, ageism, ableism, and class bias. As the mindfulness chart in Table 7.1 makes clear, by growing comfortable with discomfort, we can consciously lessen it, grow comfortable with others, and, in general, develop mutually trusting relations where we genuinely embrace diversity in all its forms. But completely eradicating one's racism or homophobia is as impossible as thoroughly eradicating one's neuroses.[4] As any good mental health practitioner will tell you, expecting to be neurosis free, especially in periods of stress, is either naive or itself neurotic! Clinicians therefore work to help clients expose the traumas that created these neuroses and actively confront them so clients can recognize how they manifest in daily life. Over time, it is hoped, clients will grow to be happier and more personally integrated individuals. That is quite different from never being neurotic again.

The situation is no different regarding our varied responses to the emotionally charged social issues of this chapter. If in our personal lives we can accept the continuation of our neuroses, while nevertheless actively struggling to minimize their negative effects, then in our macro practice we certainly can learn to deal actively with our own vestiges of racism, sexism, homophobia, and class bias.

To do this carries with it a great risk, however: Developing mindfulness in support of fighting oppression means it hurts, sometimes a lot, to live with occasional reminders of our biases, especially if they reflect expressions of internalized inferiority or superiority (Freire, 2000, 2003). As different situations inevitably create different reactions, we must use tactical self-awareness with a wider and wider number of issues. There is no innocence in tactical self-awareness, especially when we apply it to social justice issues that often matter deeply to us. Many macro practitioners can forgive themselves more easily for personal failings while nagging themselves brutally for racist or sexist reactions we wish we didn't have. This can occur among people of color or lesbians and gays who become overly deferential in ways that upset them given their inherent talent; for Whites and straights, it may be the discomfort of feeling surprised at how talented and capable that person across the table is in areas unrelated to his or her social background. Others reverse this self-criticism process, but the underlying problems are the same. Both forms of this lacerating self-punishment demand ongoing effort through tactical self-awareness, not unrelenting self-blame that usually manifests in liberal doses of initial guilt or shame, overreaction, and eventual remorse. As Freire (2000) wrote so perceptively, "the midwifery of one's own liberation, like childbirth, is always painful" (p. 49).

However, there is a liberating element embedded within the recognition of our unresolved biases: *Everyone shares this problem.* This is not as facile as it first seems. In genuinely *experiencing* the recognition that there are no perfect people out there (including the people we wish we had no biases against), we are presented with everyone's common need to seek ways to resolve such prejudice. Rather than project our insecurity onto others (usually those we hope will forgive us) by making certain groups of people abstractly better, more dignified, and more skillful than they or anyone else could be (which must eventually lead to *their* failure), we can and will find comfort, literally, in the *ongoing realization that this struggle to avoid objectifying others is a universally shared problem.* The masquerades and postures are perhaps different, but few people (other than very young children) sit in the august position of secular priests, untouched by the racism, sexism, homophobia, ableism, ageism, and class bias that permeate society. We can all share that dehumanizing pain, albeit in varying degrees, and thus have reason to share in its resolution.

So we begin this process of transformative practice with a liberating contradiction: the painful realization that one's internalized biases create the potential for greater common understanding. However, here certain conflicts must be confronted early on by everyone involved in fighting for social justice. The social nature of these bias issues imbues them with real conflict, too, for some segments of society gain from these social divisions. *Therefore, if you yourself are not genuinely, fully committed to the resolution of these social problems for the good of your own life, and not just the lives of others, you won't be willing to live with the initial discomfort that the resolution of these problems demands.* There are few immediate rewards for confronting the various forms of oppression in our society, whether on broad issues of national concern or on the daily issues in one's office. Indeed, the more one works on these issues within the immediate circumstances of one's life and work, the less obvious the external rewards for engaged daily commitment may seem. However, recognizing that this commitment is part of what enriches your life makes the pain secondary to the deep satisfaction gained over time from the effort.

PERSONAL EXERCISE

1. Identify places where either internalized superiority or inferiority occurs. How does it manifest (unconscious inattention or over-attention to others' abilities, assumptions of a lack of or too much talent/knowledge, an unwillingness to defer or too much willingness to defer, etc.)?

   When did it occur? _____

   How did it manifest? _____

   Your/others' reactions: _____

2. Reflect on how this internalized construction developed within you. Journal this over the next week or so as you gain insight into how this bias was created even though you had no conscious intention of doing so/feeling that way.

3. Identify steps you can take to begin altering this internalized dynamic without overemphasizing either guilt or anger.

   Step 1:

   Step 2:

   Step 3:

   Step 4:

   (Acknowledge the stage of mindfulness you are at on this issue.)

4. Give yourself permission to work at this over years, not weeks.

5. Join with others who are willing to do this work.

Moving On: Unpacking Your Life Experiences

Once this life commitment is made, the real effort to overcome one's biases in the development of mindfulness begins with oneself. But here I mean a very particular part of oneself: *that set of experiences, responses, and eventual resolution (however incomplete) to eliminate marginalization that one has incurred in the past.* Some people, such as many people of color and lesbians and gays, may experience this every day, perhaps when they walk into a drug store where the clerks suddenly look nervous or while trying to get the server's attention at a prestigious local restaurant noted for its service. But everyone—even upper-middle-class folks who were ostracized at summer camp—has experienced this trauma in one form or another, living through events in which they perceive themselves as vulnerable to others' fear and loathing, the double binds, and the invisibility discussed earlier.

In locating the set of experiences that assaulted and marginalized you, you begin to search out the psychological and social traumas of the self that can *experientially identify the necessary reactions* of others in the community or office. Please note that I wrote "*experientially identify the necessary reactions*," not *identify with* those subjugated to racism, class bias, homophobia, or sexism. Your previous experience identifies the process of resolution of certain forms of oppression that can help you respectfully validate others' forms of resolution, even when your life circumstances are quite different. *The point is to search for similarity in understanding while recognizing differences in conditions, not the reverse.*[5] You thus use your experiences of marginalization and objectification as a tremendous aid in slowly developing bridges between people of quite different backgrounds.

A personal example: An enormous insight for me in my life and work as someone with a lifelong commitment to social justice and racial equality has been the result of the initial deep-seated skepticism and trivialization of these beliefs of mine, often by people with whom I worked. Years ago, my reaction to such responses was anger, which I learned fulfilled others' personal expectations of the father-fighting image of progressive activists. Later, my attempts at withdrawal from discussions on more traditional curricular matters once again proved that I had too much hostility (now mixed in with an obviously growing immaturity, the kiss of death for a middle-aged White man). Neither was a very successful path of accommodation. Eventually, I learned to develop a friendly mask that concealed *very careful* scrutiny of what people were like and how they reacted to events that were of great importance to me as we engaged in give-and-take together. This mix of openness and scrutiny now works with far less difficulty than other modes of past behavior.

However, the hidden value in these earlier experiences (which at times were objectively very difficult for me) can be traced in part to my growing awareness of what it feels like to be ignored, trivialized, left open to attack, and so forth. Such awareness as a White, straight male would be impossible for me to grasp beyond a certain intellectual understanding that oppression damages people. Having had to experientially resolve the tensions embedded in a minor form of marginalization, I have been able to relate to others quite different from me, not by identifying with them but by remembering and legitimating the pain and discomfort that occurs in situations where objectification may be occurring—*even though it is not occurring for me at that time*. The experience in my early academic life of being treated as the exceptional progressive organizer because of certain writing and teaching skills whose professional failures were nonetheless endemic to activist types has helped me not to try to be like a Black person or a gay man but to understand and legitimate why such people must be cautious in many community coalitions and institutional settings . . . *including around me.*

From my much narrower experience of marginalization, I thus have learned why caution and circumspection in dealing with others is a necessary adaptive mechanism that can and will be altered over time—not by protestations of innocence or proclamations of commitment but by *quietly legitimating that caution without verbal response by working together in ways that over time generate mutual respect and trust.* This is what is meant by *respecting differences while sharing commonalities.* Each person of a different race, sexual orientation, class, or sex must necessarily approach this work differently than one whose actions are not subjected to any or few of the above-mentioned oppressive social themes. Knowing that, and working with that understanding, is what allows us to begin reaping the rewards of genuine trust and shared dialogue.

The Middle: Developing Patience for the Testing and Trusting Process

Once you begin attempting to integrate these issues into your life, a new, almost liberating realization begins taking place: Knowing that you will have to deal consistently with your and others' biases means that accomplishments must be measured over years, not weeks.[6] Your responsibility is to confront these issues, not miraculously resolve them (a goal so far achieved by no one). You thus can take comfort in not pressuring yourself to do the impossible. Consistent engagement in issues of oppression and social justice is not a lullaby; however, it is a form of human labor that one can grow comfortable with and, in that increasing comfort, become more strategically effective.

Judy Lipshitz, a committed activist who is now an agency executive, wrote on the changes in her responses to the racism and sexism expressed by some of the community members with whom she worked as a frontline organizer:

> At first, I'd go crazy. I'd almost deny that I heard [racist words] being spoken to me. I felt so stuck that I couldn't respond to him on a gut level. . . . For a while, I grew so upset with these responses that I started to get negative ideas about the project we were all working on [related to security for the elderly].
>
> But some of what was upsetting me was my response. I either wanted to yell at people, to kill them, or else I'd awkwardly blank out and make believe I'd never heard anything while my gut was doing flip-flops. In reality, I couldn't blame them because I didn't know how to really deal with racial issues—I meant well, but I just didn't have it together to comfortably interact with people . . . and I couldn't blame others for that!

Working with people in our security project forced me to deal with race and class all the time, though. I eventually started trying to talk with people who blamed everything on Blacks and Puerto Ricans. The more I did this, the more people responded in ways that no longer frightened me. I started to get comfortable to raise other possible factors, to quietly (and not nervously) point out what I saw as misperceptions, and so on. . . . As we really began to talk, I stopped hating these people—and hating myself. I was very resistant to giving up all that hatred, fearing I'd lose my genuine anger and concern, but that didn't happen. By staying with it, I really felt like I began accomplishing things on race, too, with half the anxiety. (Burghardt, 1982, p. 137)

Her progress, both personal and professional, in confronting racial matters was achieved through her application of tactical self-awareness to emotionally charged situations fraught with social content. By spotting the contexts in which she herself had great difficulty—in this case, situations where racism and sexism were prevalent—she then used her responses to unravel why she reacted so poorly. Instead of maintaining a rigid response of either anger or indifference, she patiently set out to deal with her reactions to such issues over time, allowing needed reflection in action as the issues arose within the work itself to help her improve her responses.

In other words, *utilizing reflective practice over time* allowed her to work on unresolved tensions (her hostility, her blanking out) so that eventually she created a synthesis in her response to bigotry: calmly stated but firm dialogue on alternatives to racist ideas. Each effective response on her part generated effective ways to use the anger. Over time, she was not only a better practitioner but also more relaxed! Problems did not disappear, but she worked with them more effectively. She became a model of the restorative social work practitioner: calmly confronting others with internalized biases as they worked on their social justice campaigns, slowly yet firmly restoring a balance of genuine respect for others, an appreciation for difference, and a commitment to a common cause. This more dynamic approach is the essence of the genuinely engaged practice that is at the heart of this book.

The Power of Patience

The dynamics discovered in confronting inequities within society and among ourselves are not only seemingly timeless; they also are varied, with new people and new situations re-creating old patterns of caution and reticence before trust is established. This is perhaps where some people become either hostile or indifferent to maintaining active commitments to fighting racism, homophobia, and sexism. Each new situation, especially with new people, demands some form of guarded reaction from them toward a macro practitioner who seems to have more power than others. The reaction may be as minimal as it is repetitive: Perhaps it's a new group member's quiet reservation toward you that, on a superficial level, can appear gnawingly unfair. But is it? *After all, your history will not be theirs.* That joint history must patiently be developed *with them,* too, before genuine acceptance can occur.

A gay man active in civil rights struggles, the late Scott Jacobson, recounted his own realization of this dynamic:

> After a couple of years with our employment group, our staff got along really well. Each of us accepted the others openly, and real friendships between Blacks, Puerto Ricans, and Whites had developed. Then a new staff member, Black, came on. I started relating to him just as I did people I'd been with for two years, and this guy stiffened up like I was Dracula. . . . At first I was pissed—I thought I'd really been proving myself on that score. But then I thought about it some more. As a gay person, when I'm first around straights [who don't know I'm gay] I'm *always* cautious, always checking people out 10 times over before opening up. How could it be different for him with me, a White guy? I decided to cool it a bit, let things go more slowly, and eventually things worked out. The good vibes from people helped, too, but going slower actually got things better a lot faster. (Burghardt, 1982, p. 141)

His insight is important: By allowing each new person to define the situation as he or she perceives it, you immediately show a deep respect for that individual that goes beyond words. Instead of imposing a blanket uniformity on events based on the way you have lived your life, your respect for legitimately different interpretations begins the quiet communication Freire (2000) speaks of that can lead to genuine dialogue. If you have enough confidence in your actions and beliefs to patiently allow for those differences to be present, you can see that beginning again with new people becomes less a test than the opening bridge for potentially meaningful relationships.

Patience creates another advantage. We are able to use time to see people as they *really are,* in all their humanness. This means, unfortunately, that some people will be far more difficult than others—indeed, that a few people are too difficult to work with. While the reasons for someone's behavior may be more easily related to some social injustice, they themselves may be so intransigently obnoxious personally (needlessly aggressive, a rip-off artist, unconsciously acquiescent, etc.) that they are intolerable. If this happens—and it does—then don't be around them. After all, everyone else, especially those from the same social group, will certainly be aware of the individual's problems and will view your persevering attempts at friendship and communication as just so much hung-up hogwash. They're right. Time can help distinguish between your own defensiveness, others' understandable reticence or withdrawal, and those few who drive everyone crazy. After a while, if you find yourself reacting this way to a person whom *everyone* dislikes, then the issues to be dealt with are more likely personal, not social, in origin. They should be dealt with accordingly.

Finally, there are certain situations born of objective differences that will take years to resolve. We have to accept that some people who are less financially secure often are unlikely to enjoy your friendship because the material differences, witnessed up close, personally hurt too much. A White social worker involved in neighborhood stabilization, Caren B., wrote about what happened when a staff-wide party was held at her home:

> Everyone had a great time that night. However, I was particularly struck by Barbara and Bob. Barbara [a Black secretary] commented on the size and furnishings in the apartment; and I informed her of the history behind each find. She said she felt it didn't take much money to put it all together, and it didn't have that standardized store look, either. . . . As they were leaving, Barbara kept exclaiming what a wonderful time she had had and how she "loved us." My husband and Barbara and Bob had a nice little chat at the front door before saying good night. It was so warm and nice. . . . I really looked forward to becoming friends.
>
> Soon after, things began to turn with me and Barbara. That week at work, she was coming to Manhattan one day and I mentioned she should stop by our home. Without letting me finish why, Barbara gave me a look that said, "Don't do me any favors. I don't need them." She walked away without a word. I was so stunned I didn't know what to do. . . . Later that week she gave my supervisor a bitchy note saying I was "staying home and setting up office in my apartment!" I couldn't believe it—and four days earlier she'd "loved us!" Well, I decided to be reserved, too, not hostile or turned off, but not faking friendliness either. Things stayed quiet for a while. . . . A few weeks later she came into the office with a new hairstyle and I matter-of-factly remarked that it looked good (it did). A strange, sad look came over her face, and she said, "You're the only one who said anything." She asked to see me at lunch that day, which wasn't possible . . . so the next day we got together to talk over what was going on with us. . . . And our relationship has been growing ever since. (Burghardt, 1982, p. 144)

As Caren related later, during their talk it became clear what had happened. "Barbara had loved her time at the party, but afterwards she found herself feeling strangely hurt and angry. She had allowed herself to be touched. And that sparked feelings of deprivation; 'I'll never have the clothes and furnishings you do.'" To overcome this level of pain together is a remarkable accomplishment for both women. It would have been easier for either of them to let antagonisms born of *material differences* to become the basis for mutual fear and loathing. But they didn't let that happen. The differences are there, still, but their relationship has grown through a combination of three factors: (1) a willingness to let time work to one's benefit; (2) an ability to search for the small, everyday similarities (such as compliments on a new hairstyle) that create links of understanding; and (3) the internal strength to use that small reopening to explore how some differences can and will cause pain between people.

The above case study highlights the patient work that goes into building any meaningful relationship, especially when there are objective social differences that can easily breed antagonism. It's important to emphasize that such work need not culminate in deep friendship to be meaningful, either; such an assumption is too personalistic to be realized with everyone we come into contact with, including all those with whom we work. That's not the point of these efforts. The point is that such work, like all labor born of choice and mutual determination, can be deeply worthwhile. Furthermore, we give birth to a powerful irony in our macro work: By developing patience within ourselves and with those with whom we work, we reserve our energies for the rightful impatience wrought by social injustice found in the larger world.

Culturally competent, mindful practice operates from the fundamental basis that we start with more similarities than differences and that the differences that do exist are overwhelmingly positive, not negative.

From serious similarity/difference issues such as life goals, quality-of-life concerns, and education for our children to more prosaic ones such as our favorite sweets or baseball players, fundamental commonality underlies most of what we do. We can use this growing mindfulness in understanding how to approach others, especially when perceived differences seem to dominate in the early stages of a relationship.

Demonstrating awareness of commonality and difference occurs through small, consistent acts and behaviors, not large statements or political stances. *Taking the time to learn and pronounce another's name correctly is one of those small, yet significant acts that can build bridges between people who assume bridges exist.*

Racism and these other forms of social oppression shadow and undermine America and perhaps always will. Given the United States' long and painful history in dealing with difference, *one of the key skills in cultural competency is to become comfortable with discomfort.* In social service and educational work, there is always a tension between ignored or exaggerated cultural differences. Neither denying racial experience and history nor unnecessarily emphasizing them is helpful. Better to make certain that both commonality of purpose and difference in opinion are acknowledged—not dwelled on.

There Is No Ending: The Key to Long-Term Success by Fighting the Causes and Consequences of Social Oppression

The above is an individual methodology designed to create ways for a practitioner to mindfully embrace differences and commonalities in coalition together as organizers and community members work on combating oppression and social injustice. There is still one other building block that binds this restorative social work methodology together so that the potential for change is ever present: *active commitment to destroying the material forms of oppression that perpetuate racism, homophobia, ageism, ableism, classism, and sexism.* Because the roots of oppression are socially based, one cannot be personally working on better social relations for oneself and one's fellow activists and at the same time be uninvolved in actual struggles to end social injustice. Equally important, there is no better way to develop social understanding than to enter particular fights against social injustice, discrimination, and bias. Every macro practitioner must remember that those who suffer social oppression are never able to disengage from such issues, never able to choose some way to avoid the problems of racism, sexism, homophobia, and class bias.

The easiest way for others to demonstrate this understanding is through their active commitment, in some chosen area, to end social oppression. That's why coalitions are formed—for people and/or organizations with great need and insufficient power to come together and struggle to create social change. The process of engaged theory and practice that this chapter elucidates is the essence of critical reflection that makes it possible for *sharing* to occur in a way that otherwise may never develop. Such shared activity deepens our evaluations of one another so that feelings of trust and partnership can begin to appear. Whether it's working with a clinic's outreach program, helping set up a single parents' project so that teenage mothers can get their high school degrees, or walking a picket line in opposition of mortgage foreclosures, the activity creates a sense of commonality of purpose that is the essence of dialogue. Without this demonstrated commitment to action, all else is pap.

CONCLUSION: DEVELOPING A MINDFUL, ANTI-OPPRESSION SOCIAL WORK PRACTICE

Developing a "mindful" methodology that actively deals with the not-so-hidden realities of racism, class bias, homophobia, sexism, and other forms of oppression means more than adopting a pat formula for behavior. An effective method of restorative social work practice incorporates these elements into one's framework and seeks to resolve them over time in a flexible, open, and tactically self-aware manner. Those elements include the following:

1. A belief that social problems such as racism, sexism, homophobia, and class bias hurt yourself and not just others.

2. A willingness to view your own often unconscious prejudices and internalized constructions of superiority or inferiority as inevitable parts of daily life that (like neuroses) will necessitate a consistent use of tactical self-awareness as a vehicle toward greater mindful practice. You can then use the recognition of this inherent limitation to stay open to ways you can minimize its influence over your behavior.

3. The use of your own experiences of marginalization, whether minor or major, as a vehicle to identify the ways others may be reacting to actual and perceived experiences of social oppression—even when those experiences are not oppressive to you.

4. Recognizing that you patiently develop levels of mindfulness through years, not months, of your work and in your life.

5. Continuing to mindfully practice the two truths of perceiving legitimate social difference and genuine similarities between races, sexual orientations, classes, and sexes so that your strategic interventions in coalitions and campaigns are flexible and multilayered.

6. Appreciating that people must work together for a significant period of time before mutual dialogue is possible and using that awareness to become comfortable with whatever testing develops.

7. A lifetime engagement in fighting structural causes of social oppression. The fight against the structural causes of social problems such as racism and sexism is seen as the primary vehicle by which trust is developed. *For in doing so, one is able to legitimate the social reality that some have suffered greater forms of social oppression without having to deny one's own dehumanization.*

By embracing the social differences within our communities *and* the common experience of pain that almost everyone shares, we free ourselves from the false separation of the social, economic, and personal forms of oppression that exist. Given the present-day economic, political, and social volatility that marks so much of today's discourse, engaging in such work, no matter how seemingly small and how often focused on relationship building, can have a needed ripple effect over time to shift away from such entrenched social hostility. Personal and collective transformation through such mindful acts—with all the accompanying loss of guilt, anger, and frustration—is what frees us to more fully engage with others in the fight for genuine social justice. Because such work together—whether in coalition, community group, agency project, or political campaign—benefits us all.

REFLECTIVE ACTIVITY FOR EDUCATIONAL POLICY 2.1.4

Engaging in Diversity and Difference in Practice: Finding the Commonalities and Engaging With All Those Differences (Small groups)

As Elaine Pinderhughes (1989) wrote in her brilliant classic *Understanding Race, Ethnicity, and Power*, focusing on difference alone can create barriers where they do not exist. That said, because there are real differences and genuine perceptions of difference that impact all school and human services environments, it is equally important also to understand how much commonality we all share. For example, everyone working with people shares deep humanistic concerns for a better society.

To feel one's commonalities with others in one's daily work, however, requires some experiential practice as a reminder of that twofold lesson. If possible, try this with a small group, although you can also do it by yourself.

Respond to the following:

1. Your name and how you like it pronounced

2. Your racial and ethnic identity

3. A family value you had as a child that still matters to you as an adult

4. Any experience of discrimination you have encountered

After you have completed this exercise, reflect on the following:

Note how profoundly similar we are in underlying values to what we and our families have wanted, no matter how socially distinct we seem to be. We have no difficulty in understanding where someone is coming from when we are guided by that awareness!

A key prong to effective cultural competence: Always operate from the assumption of commonalities in values and aspirations with those with whom you work and serve.

THE COMMUNITY TOOLBOX

The Community Toolbox offers a number of sections on cultural competency and anti-oppression work that you will want to check out at http://ctb.ku.edu/en/tablecontents/chapter_1027.htm.

Cultural Competence in a Multicultural World

Section 1. Understanding Culture and Diversity in Building Communities

Section 2. Building Relationships With People From Different Cultures

Section 3. Healing From the Effects of Internalized Oppression

Section 4. Strategies and Activities for Reducing Racial Prejudice and Racism

Section 5. Learning to Be an Ally for People From Diverse Groups and Backgrounds

Section 6. Creating Opportunities for Members of Groups to Identify Their Similarities, Differences, and Assets

Section 7. Building Culturally Competent Organizations

Section 8. Multicultural Collaboration

Section 9. Transforming Conflicts in Diverse Communities

Section 10. Understanding Culture, Social Organization, and Leadership to Enhance Engagement

Section 11. Building Inclusive Communities

REFERENCES

Bell, W. (2008). *An equal voice for America's families.* Retrieved from http://www.casey.org/Newsroom/InterviewsAndSpeeches/2008SEP06_EqualVoice.htm

Burghardt, S. (1982). *The other side of organizing.* Boston: Schenkman.

Chisolm, R., & Washington, M. (1997). *Undoing racism: A philosophy on international change.* New Orleans, LA: People's Institute.

DeSilva, C., & Clark, E. (2007). *Institutional racism and the social work profession: A call to action.* Washington, DC: National Association of Social Workers.

Durrheim, K. & Dixon, J. (2005) *Racial encounter: the social psychology of contact and desegregation.* New York: Taylor & Francis.

Ellison, R. (1992). *Invisible man.* New York: Random House.

Epstein, R. M. (1999). Mindful practice. *Journal of the American Medical Association, 282*(9), 833–839.

Freire, P. (2000). *Pedagogy of the oppressed.* New York: Continuum.

Freire, P. (2003). *Pedagogy of hope.* New York: Continuum.

Gutierrez, L., Lewis, M., Nagda, P., Wernick, S., & Shore, K. (2005). Multicultural community practice strategies and intergroup empowerment. In M. Weil (Ed.), *Handbook of community practice* (pp. 341–359). Thousand Oaks, CA: Sage.

hooks, b. (2003). *Teaching community: A pedagogy of hope.* London: Routledge.

Horton, M. (1998). *The long haul: An autobiography.* New York: Teachers College Press.

Jansson, B. (2008). *The reluctant welfare state: Engaging history to advance social work practice in contemporary society.* Florence, KY: Cengage Learning.

Levi, R., & Murphy, B. (2006). Coalitions of contention: The case of the WTO protests in Seattle. *Political Studies, 54*(4), 651–670.

Linehan, M. M., & Dimeff, L. (2001). Dialectical behavior therapy in a nutshell. *California Psychologist, 34,* 10–13.

Maharawal, M. M. (2011, October 23). So real it hurts: Building a new republic. *Occupied Wall Street Journal.* Retrieved from http://occupiedmedia.us/2011/10/so-real-it-hurts-building-a-new-republic/

Mallon, G. (2002). *Let's get this straight.* New York: Columbia University Press.

Mizrahi, T., & Morrison, J. (Eds.). (1992). *Community organization and social administration.* Binghamton, NY: Haworth Press.

Mizrahi, T., & Rosenthal, B. (2001). Complexities of coalition building: Leaders, successes, strategies, struggles, and solutions. *Social Work, 46*(1), 218–233.

Pinderhughes, E. (1989). *Understanding race, ethnicity, and power.* New York: Free Press.

Reisch, M. (2004). Radical community organizing. In M. Weil (Ed.), *Handbook of community practice* (pp. 272–283). Thousand Oaks, CA: Sage.

Reisch, M., & Andrews, J. (2002). *The road not taken: A history of radical social work in the United States.* Oxford, UK: Taylor & Francis.

Rivera, F., & Erlich, J. (1998). *Community organizing in a diverse society.* London: Allyn & Bacon.

Roberts-DeGennaro, M., & Mizrahi, T. (2005). Coalitions as social change agents. In M. Weil (Ed.), *Handbook of community practice* (pp. 387–399). Thousand Oaks, CA: Sage.

Said, C. (2010, February 20). Mortgage relief funds headed to California. *San Francisco Chronicle,* p. A-1.

Staples, L. (2004). *Roots to power.* New York: Praeger.

Tatum, B. (2004). *Why are all the Black kids sitting together in the cafeteria? And other conversations about race.* New York: Basic Books.

Ture, K., & Hamilton, C. (1992). *Black power: The politics of liberation.* New York: Vintage.

Vaid, U. (1996). *Virtual equality: The mainstreaming of gay and lesbian liberation.* New York: Knopf Doubleday.

Weil, M. (2005). Contexts and challenges for 21st century communities. In M. Weil (Ed.), *Handbook of community practice* (pp. 16–27). Thousand Oaks, CA: Sage.

West, C. (2001). *Race matters.* New York: Beacon Press.

Wong, Y. L. (2004). Knowing through discomfort: A mindfulness-based critical social work pedagogy. *Critical Social Work, 5*(1).

NOTES

1. There are differences, of course, but those are based not on abstract (and often negative) objectification but on genuine appreciation for those social and personal factors of another's life that are legitimately different. More on this later.

2. This problem is perpetuated in many areas, but nowhere more powerfully than through the media, where every minority member and every woman with a moderate position of influence is automatically a "leader." This issue seems especially sharp regarding Blacks and other people of color, where the concern over Black or Latino or Asian leadership is an almost never-ending topic for White policy analysts. Of course, Whites rarely discuss "White leadership" in so narrow a fashion. This form of leadership for people of color is always of the narrowly political/organizational variety, where people are seen representing numbers and not ideas. Such vacuous leadership can, of course, be easily replaced, can't it? The presence of President Obama in the White House may have begun to powerfully reconstruct the answer to that question.

3. My thanks to Willie Tolliver for the cocreation of this term that joins an anti-oppression stance of what we are against with movement toward what *we are for.*

4. As with neuroses, the work here is not to eradicate but to be able to master these issues by lessening their impact on one's attitudes and behavior. Over time, they no longer control you; rather, you control them—a powerful example of personal mastery, not perfection!

5. The most common reversal occurs when people respond to another individual's oppressive conditions with comments that in effect verbally state, "I understand." Perhaps nothing is more infuriating to oppressed people than to hear such nonsense—indeed, they read such comments as ignorantly hostile to their actual experience. Such verbal statements are forms of monologue, as Freire would put it, that justify the speaker's position rather than validating the plight of the oppressed. A better method is to silently validate the condition through acts of solidarity and support (which can range from militant organizing to dropping by the person's office later with a cup of coffee). In doing so, you neither impose similarity ("understanding" equating "sameness of experience") nor deny difference (how you engage in combating that particular form of oppression).

6. I am speaking here of personal, individual, not societal, accomplishments. Naturally, the greater the number of individual achievements, the greater the societal response, and vice versa. That certain tasks shall take a lifetime is no excuse for inaction.

Section IV

Interventions

At the heart of organizing is action—getting results that right social injustice or shift the focus of services to neglected or marginalized groups. For an intervention to make a sustained difference, however, it must also be tactically flexible and strategically adept so that a community group or coalition originally lacking power or influence can gain enough to create change. The intervention phase comprises four chapters that detail how to deepen your strategic effectiveness.

Chapter 8 systematically outlines the various models of organizing strategy at play throughout North American communities. It is designed to help the reader understand that different models of organizing will lead to different tactical emphases and targets for change. It will help the new practitioner *strategically discern* the differences at play in coalitions among actors who seem to have the same desired outcomes, yet seek to go about achieving them in different ways.

In this chapter, the reader also will begin to develop a core part of his or her long-term strategic framework: *internal strategic vision.* Building on tactical self-awareness, this strategic tool has been designed to moor practitioners to their most important values and actions, regardless of the context of their large-scale organizing intervention, thus sustaining their mindful practice in ways that deepen their potential to develop as transformational strategists.

Chapter 9 emphasizes the growing impact of social media on community organizing—indeed, on all social work practice. Through a powerful case study on the LGBTQ community's response to the defeat of same-sex marriage in California in 2008 up until the Supreme Court ruling on the Defense of Marriage Act in 2013, the chapter makes clear how rapid and impactful various social media tools can be in creating and sustaining a campaign.

Chapters 10 and 11 delineate how widespread macro social work interventions are by examining the expanding roles of social workers in political and legislative arenas (Chapter 10) and the environmental movement (Chapter 11). Through case studies of new and experienced practitioners engaged in real-world campaigns while honing and developing their internal strategic visions, *the chapters also underscore how today's interventions require a mix of macro and micro skills.* Moving from "case to cause" on hoarding issues impacting the elderly began at the individual level and evolved over time into legislative action. Likewise, seeing the impact of food deserts on the health of children in poor communities brought together public health workers, clinicians, and organizers in the same community-wide effort. *Reflecting the socially constructed practice model of this text,* all these interventions have been sustained through attention to individual concerns while also addressing the collective needs of the larger community.

CHAPTER 8

From Checkers to Chess

The Strategic Development of a Community Practitioner

USING THE WHOLE CHESSBOARD

"Okay, okay, I admit it. I am excited beyond belief. And I'm terrified. And I can't believe I got the job. And I have no idea what I am doing in it . . . and . . . ."

Kay playfully knocked a tin spoon against Ellis's knuckles. "Slow down, slow down, old man! First, you better only drink decaf today." They were sitting in a booth toward the back of their favorite diner, a special request made by Ellis because of his news. He'd just been offered a statewide position on a sustainable agricultural and local economic development project that involved small-town farmers, nearby poor urban communities, public and private funders, and small businesses. His job was to convince poor communities to create weekend markets for the farmers, who in turn needed to be convinced to provide technical assistance to those same neighborhoods on how to raise a few crops on their own on the small plots available.

As Ellis talked, it became clear that the vision of the director he'd be working for both excited and overwhelmed him. "I mean, this guy and the board that backs him see farming as a tool for gang prevention! And these little farmers' markets as antiracist tools! And then he even connects this small, local farming and the weekend markets I'll be organizing as part of a positive response to globalization!" Ignoring his coffee, Ellis gulped down a glass of water instead. His smiling face managed to crease with consternation as well. "I thought I knew

(Continued)

(Continued)

organizing, but this guy takes it to a whole new level." He finished his water. "Kay, I realized in all my antiracist and youth development work, as good as I hope it's been, I've just been playing checkers. This program operates at a whole other level. This guy's playing chess."

"Checkers? Chess? You lost me," Kay sighed.

"You know what I mean. For the longest time, we both figured a good basic organizing strategy mixed a little bit of process goals in terms of empowering the kids and women we've both worked with, and then a set of tasks and objectives to get something done. We had targets to influence and all, but it was all about tactical choices on who was to speak or who we were trying to reach, not much more than that."

"Oh, come on, sure it was! I've always worked more from the empowerment, community development model that emphasized getting women into leadership as the way to change the world. You've always been into social action and fighting for power given the racism and injustice you see. Those are pretty different strategic models of how to organize, don't you think?"

Ellis looked at her for a long minute before responding. "Yeah, you're right. Different models, same commitments, different tactical choices along the way. But after working with this guy a bit, I still say we've been playing checkers. I mean, I met this guy at an antiracist forum here in the city. I'm fighting racism by confronting indifferent school principals and working with kids on their rights. He's fighting racism by selling apples and growing corn on an abandoned plot?" Ellis paused again, and then went on. "And he manages to connect all of it to how these activities together help counter global markets run by multinationals." He paused again. "I met him a whole bunch of times since, and he's rock hard in his commitments on racism, injustice, and the kind of capitalism that destroys communities rather than rebuilding them. And yet he's going about work with White farmers and Black clergy as if they've always been brothers or something, united in common purpose." This time he drank his coffee. "He told me that transformative change requires deep strategy. Like chess." Ellis looked at his friend, a wry smile on his face. "Kay, there are 64 squares on a chess board and he's playing on every one. I gotta go work with him. No more checkers for me!"

Educational Policy 2.1.5—Advance human rights and social and economic justice. This chapter delineates a framework and practices that will enable students to "recognize the global interconnections of oppression and [be] knowledgeable about theories of justice and strategies to promote human and civil rights" as they incorporate "social justice practices in organizations, institutions, and society to ensure that these basic human rights are distributed equitably and without prejudice."

INTRODUCTION: UNDERSTANDING THE
BASICS OF COMMUNITY ORGANIZING STRATEGY

Ellis's excitement and worry are reflective of the growing pains every community practitioner undergoes as he or she engages in macro practice work on the front lines. An intense commitment to community change and an equally powerful desire to work with others so that such change will occur, once undertaken, quickly merge together into a dawning awareness that community organizing is as demanding and complex as it is fulfilling. To begin with, there are, as Weil, Reisch, and Ohmer (2009) note, at least eight approaches to organizing utilized by human services activists, ranging from confrontational social movements to accommodative social planning. Strategies of organizing have been offered to empower local citizens (Mondros & Wilson, 1994) and transform individual and collective values for social justice and social equity (Hanna & Robinson, 1994), and have been analyzed to explain progressive change as in the '30s and '60s and conservative change as in the '50s and '70s (Fisher, 1994, 2009). Making sense of it all so that one can make effective strategic and tactical choices is important.

As we will explore in this chapter, there are five strategic demands at play if a person seeks to grow strategically into a lifelong, effective community organizer.

1. For the practitioner new to organizing, it is important to understand the historical antecedents to the organizing strategies you are choosing to undertake. By rooting your work inside previous historical events and the choices people made then, you will gain access both to tactics that led to victory and to avoiding mistakes you might otherwise make.

2. An organizer needs to understand the various models of organizing at play within his or her community and across the profession. You need to know the strengths and limitations to these models so that your organizing strategies remain tactically supple and strategically applicable to what you and the people with whom you are working are seeking to accomplish.

3. Likewise, it is necessary to understand what, if anything, unites an organizing strategy compared with, say, a strategy for group work intervention or an individual diagnosis for the micro practitioner. You need clarity on what is going on in a community organizing intervention that distinguishes it from other methods of intervention so that it maintains its authority as a distinctive form of practice in our communities.

4. Next, if you seek a long-term career as a community organizer, over time you must deepen your own strategic sophistication as you are called on to represent your agencies and programs in increasingly larger and often more complex groups, including city-wide coalitions, national issue formations (such as on the fight against HIV-AIDS, homelessness, global configurations on economic development, the environment, immigration, etc.), and

possible political coalitions. You need to understand what distinguishes the checker game of the new activist from the chess game of the seasoned macro practitioner.

5. Finally, the longer you evolve as a community practitioner, the more likely that the dilemmas of maintaining the vision you had as a frontline grassroots practitioner will come into play. It can be a heartfelt struggle, personally and professionally, to resolve the tensions between expanding an organizing campaign's influence while stepping back from the daily person-to-person contact that so often inspired your organizing commitments in the first place. You need to see ways of resolving this dilemma so that the social justice commitments that inspired you at the beginning of your career remain in play later as well.

This chapter will examine each of the above, ending with a case study of one community organizer whose commitment to social justice, racial equity, and fairness is as central to his work today engaging in large-scale education reform efforts as it was 25 years ago when he was a young organizer campaigning for hospital workers' rights through the Healthcare Workers Union Local 1199.

THE HISTORICAL ANTECEDENTS OF COMMUNITY ORGANIZING

Reading various histories of social movements, as Rubin and Rubin (2007) point out, helps an organizer learn both patience and persistence. As they cogently relate, organizers frustrated by the pace of change learn "that while past movements faced lean days in which few joined the fight, there were frequent days of triumph and victory" (p. 218). Needing a reminder of why to stay in the struggle, reading history can help the organizer see that "bad times (of the past) can be turned to good purpose as activists create a shared history of solidarity and pride" (p. 52). When change seems far off, it can be comforting to know that other Black women consciously refused to move to the back of the bus before Rosa Parks, or that the first efforts to change the name of GRID (gay-related immune disorder) to AIDS (acquired immunodeficiency syndrome) were met with active indifference by the medical establishment (Vaid, 1996).

Likewise, history informs organizers of important tactical choices and strategic decisions from other movements—what worked and what didn't, and why. As Rubin and Rubin (2007) stated,

> The now legendary disruptive tactics of organizer Saul Alinsky teach us what can be accomplished by disruptive humor. The nonviolence of Martin Luther King, Jr., makes clear that unarmed people can face billy clubs and win not only symbolic but actual victories. (p. 219)

Such lessons help an organizer determine whether present conditions are reflective of similar circumstances or require other strategic modification (Reisch, 2005).

A historical work of particular value for all organizers inside and outside of social work continues to be Fisher's (1994) *Let the People Decide*. His book thoroughly reviews the history of community organizing, starting with the antislavery movements preceding and following the Civil War; the suffrage movement; and the labor, socialist, and progressive reform movements that began in the first Industrial Revolution and continued through the Depression, finally reconfiguring first as the powerful civil rights movements of the 1960s and then as the identity-based politics of the '70s, '80s, and '90s. (See also Cox & Garvin, 2001; Rubin & Rubin, 2007; Weil, 2005.) Each chapter covers a different social movement and a different historical period, drawing out the kinds of lessons from each movement that Rubin and Rubin discussed, as mentioned above. Recent work extends this analysis as well (Weil et al., 2009).

Fisher's work brilliantly situates social work organizing/reform efforts inside the larger political and economic trends of which they are a part. For example, the community organizing of the Progressive Era at the end of the 19th century and beginning of the 20th century, when settlement houses were a preeminent model for social work reform, took place alongside the crusading socialist efforts of Eugene Debs, the rise in militant industrial unionism throughout the American working class, and the trust-busting efforts of Teddy Roosevelt. Likewise, the conservative and often racist neighborhood club movements of the 1950s are consistent with the anti-Communist McCarthyism, pro–big business ethos that prevailed in that decade. In short, the struggles for influence and strategic dominance of one period inside community organizing and social work are reflective of the same struggles under way with other economic and political actors. A hundred-plus years ago, settlement house reformers struggled for influence over conservative charitable impulses in the field in ways similar to those found among the industrial workers and their more conservative American Federation of Labor craftsmen or Teddy Roosevelt fighting the pro–Standard Oil trust politicians within the Democratic party (Fisher, 1994, 2005). Today's struggles in the profession over the rights of the poor and the voices of youth can find similar interplay with national struggles over health care reform, job creation, and the role of federal government in economic decision making.

Fisher's enormous intellectual contribution helps macro practitioners understand that their efforts are part of the dynamic historic trends of any period; their strategic choices are neither predetermined by other economic and political actors nor operating independently of them. Fisher (2001) later wrote:

> Certainly issues of human agency—leadership, ideology, daily choices regarding strategy and tactics, and so forth—all play a critical role in the life of any effort, but the larger context heavily influences what choices are available, what ideology or goals are salient, and what approaches seem appropriate or likely to succeed. . . . History puts the actions and work of individuals into a larger framework, interweaving the local with the more global, the particular with broader trends, events, and developments in society. (p. 109)

His analysis can help macro practitioners reflect on trends within the 21st century, recognizing that the push–pull within the economic system and other political activities is not unlike the demanding strategic decisions and tactical choices under way within social work.

REFLECTIVE QUESTIONS

- What is the push–pull between current economic issues and how they can be solved by the White House? (More government aid? Less? More free market activity? More regulation?)
- What are the dynamics at your state level? (Are politicians seeking to cut costs? Are there lobbying groups seeking to expand support for the disadvantaged? What does the mix of influence look like?)
- Trends in macro practice? Other types of social work practice? What's happening inside agencies? Human service coalitions? What does the push–pull look like here?

COMMUNITY ORGANIZING MODELS

As Jack Rothman (2008) noted more than 40 years ago as he was developing his seminal material on community practice models in his classroom, there were different kinds of organizers who approached the same community issue in very different ways. There were the fact finders and agency collaborators who used careful documentation and collaboratively based agency coalitions to ameliorate a social problem. Their work focused on *social planning models* of macro practice. Others, stirred by the work of settlement houses and their appeals to democracy and leadership as well as modern-day empowerment efforts first led by feminists, emphasized bringing people together to solve their own problems. Their model is known as the *community or locality development model* of practice. Finally, those inspired by the civil rights and industrial trade union movements of the 1930s and 1960s looked to more ideological and conflict-laden strategies capable of fostering systemic change. These activists used social action models of community organizing.

Rothman's work has inspired generations of organizers, some of whom simply used his work to better clarify their own approaches to macro practice (Weil, 2005) and others who built on his approach from a feminist perspective (Hyde, 2008; Smock, 2003). As such, his rubric helped others differentiate the multiplicity of organizing activities under way in American communities by highlighting the key distinguishing variables at play in model building:

- *What is the belief system or ideology of the group's members in terms of societal problems and their resolution?* The more systemic and historical the stated beliefs, the more likely the group's model will focus on social action targets for change—identifying targets as potentially hostile or adverse to their efforts—and the more open to militant tactics. Likewise, the more present-day focused the group's belief system, the more likely its models will focus on collaboration among actors, including targets, with an emphasis on consensus-building tactics.

- *What is the mix of rights and responsibilities between professionals and community members and the decision-making roles they play in the group?* The more a group emphasizes the importance of systematic data collection and formal knowledge (on zoning, legal rights for tenants, etc.), the greater the emphasis on professional, agency-based decision making. Likewise, the greater the authority given to community members' voices to legitimate a group's efforts, the more tactical choices will be made that focus on member participation and decision making.

- *What is the mix of means and ends in achieving societal improvement?* Rubin and Rubin (2007) nicely capture the dilemma wrought by this classic organizing debate: "Is the transformation of people the goal in itself or is it a means to alter the broader society? . . . Will an improved society make people feel more efficacious or must people first feel empowered before a society will change?" (p. 317). Likewise, they succinctly pose this dilemma for macro practitioners in administrative roles:

> Is the organization a tool to bring about change or is it an end to be achieved? . . . Without a formal organization sustained action is impossible . . . [yet] if the maintenance of the organization becomes too important . . . [it] may displace tackling important issues to its members. (p. 17)

While Rothman (2008) and others detailed a variety of other important variables (such as boundaries of the defined community, conception of beneficiaries, and the basic change strategy), the above three variables remain the pivotal constructs from which distinctive organizing models have emerged (Reisch, 2005; Rothman, 2008; Weil, 2005). In the rush and tumble of organizing for change across the United States since Rothman's typology appeared, it was only natural that a variety of distinct models would begin to sort themselves out, from the conflict-based Industrial Area Foundations (IAF) work that has built on Saul Alinsky's confrontational approach to social change (Chambers & Cowan, 2003) to Mike Eichler's consensus organizing model that maintains the same goals as the IAF while turning conflict on its head, instead consciously working on projects that begin with consensus building as a primary tactical mechanism for community change (Eichler, 2007; Ohmer & DeMasi, 2008).

Perhaps the most thorough distillation of present-day models is presented by Smock (2003), who carefully researched extant organizing activities in 12 cities and located five distinct models of organizing: power based, community building, civic, women centered, and transformative (pp. 33–34; see Table 8.1).

Examining 12 distinct community organizations from across the country, Smock's (2003) work brings into sharp relief the richness and variability of community practice today. Along with Rothman's (2008) work, her work helps macro practitioners involved in the community sift through their answers to questions of means–ends, roles and responsibilities, and systemic beliefs as they construct their own models of intervention. As Table 8.1 suggests, the power-centered model, growing out of the Alinsky tradition, would build disciplined people's organizations to confront political and economic leaders on inequities experienced by the local residents. Likewise, a civic model would look at the same issues as coming from basic instability and thus create citizens' forums to discuss these issues and work within the formal political agencies for resolution to their problems. Her other typologies can help less experienced organizers develop an understanding of how different models impact strategic and tactical choices so that their work maintains a strategic consistency in approach toward desired outcomes.

THE DISTINCTIVENESS OF COMMUNITY ORGANIZING FROM OTHER PRACTICE METHODS: IT'S NOT JUST THE COMMUNITY

Regardless of model emphasis, macro practice is distinctive within social work because of its *focus on social* problems that will in some way require interventions involving communities and organizations (Netting, Kettner, & McMurtry, 2008; Rubin & Rubin, 2007; Weil, 2005). Community organizing is likewise distinctive within macro practice (as well as in other social work methods) because its emphasis on social problems requires *collective activity that necessitates a plan of action involving tactics and targets, some of which the practitioners initially have little or no power to create on their own.*

Whether a social planner from a large agency working in a community-wide human services coalition or a grassroots activist committed to social action strategies needed for social justice, one of the most distinctive qualities of a community organizer is that he or she operates in a role often lacking in direct power and authority to get things done. Because macro practice defines problems as social in character and thus necessitating the collective involvement of other groups, members, and organizations to be solved, a community organizer enters that group with decidedly less formal authority and fewer prescribed role definitions than the caseworker or group worker operating in clinical and micro practice settings. A group worker's membership has usually been predetermined; an organizer often has to recruit members; a caseworker usually works with people who come to him or her for problem solving or service of some kind; the organizer must go to the community, organization, or group to get them to attend. Most clinical practitioners,

Table 8.1 Models of Community Organizing

Model and Case Studies	Theory of Urban Change	Organizing the Community	Impacting the Public Sphere
Power-based model	Build power: Urban neighborhood problems stem from the community's lack of power within the political decision-making process. Solution is to build community's clout so that its interests are better represented within the pluralist public sphere.	People's organization: Build large, formal, highly disciplined "people's" organizations to fight for the community's interests in the public sphere.	Conflict and confrontation: Use conflict and confrontation to demonstrate residents' power and pressure political and economic power holders to concede to community's demands.
Community-building model	Rebuild social fabric: Urban neighborhood problems stem from the deterioration of the community's social and economic infrastructure. Solution is to rebuild the community from within by mobilizing its assets and connecting it to the mainstream economy.	Collaborative partnership: Build broad collaborative partnerships of diverse neighborhood "stakeholder" groups, including nonprofits, business residents' association, and government.	Legitimacy and collaboration: Strive to influence public decision making through consensual partnership with government. Goal is to be recognized as the legitimate representative of the community as a whole.
Civic model	Restore social order: Urban neighborhood problems stem from social disorder and instability within the community. Solution is to restore and maintain the neighborhood's stability by activating both formal and informal mechanisms.	Informal forum: Create informal, unstructured forums for neighbors to meet one another, exchange information, and problem solve.	Accessing existing channels: Use official, bureaucratic channels for citizen interaction with local government to get the city services system to respond to neighborhood problems. Interact with services personnel on an individual-to-individual basis.

(Continued)

257

Table 8.1 (Continued)

Model and Case Studies	Theory of Urban Change	Organizing the Community	Impacting the Public Sphere
Women-centered model	Link public and private spheres: Urban neighborhood problems stem from the fact that the institutions at the core of community life aren't responsive to the vision and needs of women and families. Solution is to reconceptualize private household problems as public issues with collective solutions and to build women's leadership roles within the community.	Support team: Create small teams modeled on a support-group structure. Provide safe, nurturing spaces where residents can gather, provide mutual support, and build shared leadership.	Interpersonal relationships: Seek to build face-to-face relationships with the staff and administrators of public institutions to make programs and services more responsive to the needs of families.
Transformative model	Structural change: Urban neighborhood problems are the symptoms of unjust economic and political institutions. Solution is to challenge the existing institutional arrangements to create a more equitable society.	Social movement: Develop the ideological foundations within the neighborhood for the emergence of a broad-based movement for social change.	Creating alternative frameworks: View the public sphere as dominated by institutions that systematically disempower low-income residents. Seek to alter the dominant ideological frameworks and change the terms of the public debate.

STRATEGIC MODEL-BUILDING ACTIVITY

Your community organizing project: _____

- Primary beliefs: Is the problem at hand primarily defined by you and other stakeholders as

  historical/structural _____, present-day _____,

  technical _____, social (based on race, gender, etc.) _____,

  hostile targets _____, or amenable targets _____?

- Professional practitioner–community member rights and responsibilities have a mix of what?

  Primarily professional and based on formalized knowledge and skill _____

  Primarily member based and based on neighborhood legitimacy _____

  A mix of professionals and some community members _____

  A mix of community members and some professionals _____

- The group resolves means–ends issues with a primary emphasis on

  It is more important for the group to develop leadership capacity than to get immediate results. _____

  It is more important to get results than to develop members at this time. _____

  The program needs to survive even if it means we compromise the way we go about our work. _____

- Better the program be scaled back than we compromise on core values related to what? (Check no more than two.)

  ____ Empowerment

  ____ Civic engagement

  ____ Working with targets as allies who are really enemies

  ____ Ignoring social/historical issues that impact a problem

- Based on your answers, your community project is most like this model:

  Civic _____
  Community building _____

(Continued)

(Continued)

    Women centered _____
    Transformative _____
    Power based_____

- The strengths and limitations of this model for your project are as follows:

Strengths:	Limitations:
1.	1.
2.	2.
3.	3.
4.	4.

whether group or individual, nevertheless have the formal authority to terminate sessions or end a group member's participation, although they use it only as a last resort; most organizers gain authority in a group only over time, as they demonstrate their effectiveness either in accomplishing desired goals or their facilitation of group development. Likewise, a macro practitioner working as a frontline manager in an agency has the authority to call meetings, set agendas, and make changes in the scope and emphasis of a subordinate's work. Were a community practitioner, working in a neighborhood coalition or social justice campaign, to do the same, he or she would most likely quickly lose whatever credibility he or she had.

Such lack of formal authority greatly affects the trajectory and pace of a community practitioner's work. Organizing seems to start slower because so much of what an organizer initially does relates to the outreach and engagement skills discussed in Chapters 3 and 4 (as well as leadership development issues discussed in Chapter 6). This emphasis is a reflection of the limited authority one has in a community intervention.

The early stages of organizing require a community practitioner to develop the skills of influence, not power. The time spent in listening, understanding, problem posing, and give-and-take is both time well spent and, alas, sometimes awfully long. Like a building's foundation, it is this deep digging that ensures later strength and resilience as a group lives through the intensity of problem solving, model emphasis, and goal/target selection. (The Community Toolbox material at the end of this chapter outlines some of the key skills one can further develop for strengthening influence in a community organizing project, campaign, or coalition.)

As a community practitioner, you must therefore grow comfortable with the heightened ambiguity in your role and what you are doing, especially when compared with your group- and casework colleagues, whose caseloads seem ever present and whose workweek is more scheduled. Later on, of course, the tempo in community organizing interventions will grow both more intense and more immediate in its focus as the early work of influence building and engagement is replaced by demanding campaign tactics, timelines, and targets to influence (Staples, 2004). Part of what makes community organizing both so challenging and so exhilarating is that the authority a practitioner has gained at this point will have emerged from the legitimating give-and-take between members as they have worked together. While harder to get, such authority is also more resilient and democratic in ways that can add real meaning to the legacy a macro practitioner begins building from the start of his or her career.

FROM CHECKERS TO CHESS: THE THREE LEVELS OF STRATEGIC DEVELOPMENT

As we can see from the previous section, when starting a career as a macro practitioner, the new community organizer understandably can be overwhelmed by the world he or she has entered. Working in an ambiguous role with little formal authority, a new practitioner would also for good reason latch on to one of the models described above as a way to sort through what it is he or she is actually expected to do to be a strategic community organizer and not just a well-meaning, easily misled activist. While a model is an excellent place to begin, there are, in fact, three levels to model building that are reflective of an organizer's growing strategic capacity to utilize the entire chessboard of macro practice.

Entry-Level Strategy Formation

I call this first stage of a community organizer's strategic development *entry-level strategy formation*. Entry-level strategy is the equivalent of a good checkers game where a skilled player uses a few of the red or black pieces immediately before him or her to make the next move or two on the board. For example, working within the empowerment model outlined by Smock (2003) above, an organizer working on youth development would stress process goals of member capacity building over concrete results, with the target of change being the members themselves and, perhaps, their growing influence inside their school or youth organization. A series of tactics (giving various meeting assignments to selected members, choosing inspiring speakers who also serve as role models, etc.) would adroitly be created over time so that members grow in confidence and skill level. The group's efforts might culminate in a group project or celebration where other community members (parents, school administrators, community leaders) are invited to witness their expanded leadership capacity. If the young people are successful, the other community stakeholders are asked to recruit some of them into newer positions of responsibility, thus leading to a broader and larger effort in the future, with the youthful leaders taking a more significant leadership role than they had in the past.

Worked on over time, this entry-level empowerment strategy would allow the new community practitioner to develop the following basic repertoire:

- Solid skills that connect long-term strategic outcomes (improved leadership capacity of youth, wider acceptance of the group within the larger community) to
- a series of tactical choices whose completion of concrete objectives (selecting effective inspirational/role model speakers, providing assignments that young people new to organizing can successfully take on, etc.) can be linked to those outcomes,
- all of which lead to the long-term strategic goals of wider community acceptance and
- creating future endeavors that could expand youth influence within the community.

Entry-level strategy formation is sufficiently demanding to also challenge the practitioner to consider the belief systems, means–ends debates, and roles, rights, and responsibilities that he or she and the young people develop together: *How much do I assert my direction on the group if they choose a speaker I feel the adult community will disapprove of? How much do I, as a sign of trust, accept a young person's reasons for not completing a job as opposed to challenging him or her not to "get over" on me?* These questions are cause for deep reflection, not pat answers, for they speak to a macro practitioner's long-term commitments toward widespread social change. This is why it is important to underscore that entry-level strategy formation is not a simplistic or easy stage of one's development as a community practitioner. In many ways, it is the most difficult, because one learns whether or not one is suited to both the challenges of community practice and the often indirect types of concrete results that any organizing campaign may deliver.

ACTIVITY FOR ENTRY-LEVEL STRATEGY

Issue: Youth leadership/opportunities for jobs and school-related activities needed for college entrance

Long-term goals:

Process: Youth develop leadership skills of public speaking, group problem solving, and collaboration.

Task: Youth forum (demonstration of skills, talents, leadership)

Targets and timelines: School leadership, local employers, and parents will attend forum in 3 months.

Weekly objectives and related tasks (partial listing):

1. Schedule meetings, secure meeting rooms, times

2. Invite student leaders

3. Discuss ground rules for working together, explore topics of interest, work with group to decide on others to invite

4. Begin discussing possible topics, needed talents/skills for forum

5. Future weeks: At weekly group meetings, invite speakers/trainers, practice skills, review specific tasks for event preparation

Set new tasks and process-related objectives at the end of each weekly meeting with group. The closer to the actual event, the more time spent on concrete tasks and focused student–leader assignments/responsibilities.

Now apply this exercise to your own group or campaign.

_____

Your issue: _____

Long-term goals:

Process: _____

_____

_____

Task: _____

_____

_____

Targets and timelines: _____

_____

_____

(Continued)

(Continued)

Weekly objectives and related tasks (partial listing):

1.

2.

3.

4.

5.

Set new tasks and process-related objectives at the end of each weekly meeting with group. The closer to the actual event, the more time spent on concrete tasks and focused student–leader assignments/responsibilities.

1.

2.

3.

4.

5.

Coalitional Strategy Formation

The second stage is *coalitional strategy formation.* As Mizrahi and Rosenthal's (2001) work documents, coalitional strategies require a practitioner to have mastered entry-level strategies plus the often-hidden agendas of other coalition actors who purportedly are working for the same cause and yet may have other, more organizational objectives at play in the group. (We saw an example of this in the Chapter 5 case study, when three representatives of minority agencies voted against the majority of the group because the leadership was downplaying their concerns related to financing.) Likewise, another agency may have nothing in common with other actors beyond the cause at hand or for momentary legislative purposes of passing or blocking some legislation (Rubin & Rubin, 2007).

Here an organizer must expand his or her use of the chessboard by understanding the underlying issues regarding a coalition's membership. First, why has each member (who represents an agency or group) joined the coalition to solve what seems to be a common problem? What is each member's individual agency or group motivation? Is it the same as each other coalition member's, or are there other reasons for his or her presence? How directly does the coalition's target goal impact each group? If groups have either different reasons or different levels of concern for joining the same coalition, they may be united on the coalition's goal (say, increased state funding for a project or population) but not on how they will work together, what their contributions need to be, and how the group should make decisions.

A practitioner must also learn who has joined the coalition to pursue the coalition's goals and who has joined to influence other members of the coalition. The latter may see the actual goal as secondary to influencing the other members on separate issues or recruiting them to different causes. For example, an environmental coalition may have 30 members in pursuit of changes in laws that affect the building of a nearby cement plant, but within that large membership are three groups attempting to use the group formation as a platform to influence others on topics such as animal rights, nuclear proliferation, or regional climate control.

An organizer utilizing coalition strategies has expanded his or her use of the strategic chessboard by being especially sensitive to the *strategic meaning behind individual coalition members' decisions on tactical choices*. A group member who has tried to link a coalition's concern about an individual cement plant's pollutants to nuclear proliferation may be trying to move a group from a local or state issue to a national issue.[1] Likewise, a coalition member whose funding may be grossly affected by a legislative decision may seek to demand participation from other members who are concerned about but not as affected by the issue (or the reverse could happen, where a powerful coalition member has only minor interest in an issue and ratchets down participation requirements that may weaken the coalition's overall impact).

Understanding different strategic interests related to various tactics, the effective coalition strategist helps the group *cut the issue and the means by which it is dealt with by the coalition* (Burghardt, 1982; Mizrahi & Rosenthal, 2001; Rubin & Rubin, 2007) so that it maintains its focus on the change at hand and preserves as much unity as possible. As Rubin and Rubin (2007) cogently argue, "cutting the issue" means framing it in such a way that each coalition member sees the benefit in working with others and everyone has reason to be supportive, even if the stakes remain greater for some than for others. Having achieved this strategic objective, the skilled practitioner also helps the group define the norms of participation and membership so that individual groups cannot dominate others for their own ends. By cutting the issues so that the coalition goals are broad enough to invite significant participation while at the same time spelling out what is and is not acceptable to pursue, the coalition strategists have gone far in uniting what otherwise would be disparate groups. In so doing, the practitioner has evolved in strategic sophistication by using the "chess pieces" of the coalition for multiple tactical purposes that serve the same strategic outcome: the success of the coalition in achieving its stated goals. His or her use of the chessboard has expanded as well.

ACTIVITY FOR COALITIONAL STRATEGY FORMATION

Coalition and issue: _____

Number of different members: _____

Unifying coalition goal (passing legislation, anti–large development project, national campaign on global warming, antiracism, etc.):

_____

_____

Chosen tactics to achieve goal:

1. _____

2. _____

3. _____

Are all groups aligned on tactical choices? If not, consider strategic reasons for differences:

1. Different agency commitments related to funding issues or alignments with targeted groups

   a. Funding
   b. Alignments
   c. Other reasons

2. Tactics viewed as serving other strategic purposes related to other issues (other political concerns or other campaigns' objectives)

   a. Attempting to influence members on other campaigns
   b. Using coalition to advocate for other causes as first priority
   c. Other

3. Unwillingness to invest resources to participate due to competing demands

   a. Competing demands
   b. Indifferent/token participation
   c. Other

4. What commitments/norms of participation, discussion, and alignment can you and the coalition leadership create that are respectful to the entire membership and still place primary emphasis on the coalition's agenda?

a. Agreement on participant activity and voting rights

b. Norms on discussion items at meetings

c. Alignment on campaign message and other messages of group

d. Other norms and commitments

Transformational Strategy Formation

The most advanced stage of strategy formation is *transformational strategy formation,* where an organizer is using the entire game board for a variety of strategic purposes. What makes this work advanced is not necessarily the complexity of the goals and objectives sought by a group or by someone speaking about issues in a more complicated manner. If anything, practitioners engaged in transformational strategies can often appear to be involved in very simple undertakings (albeit a lot of them). What makes their strategies transformational and thus more advanced is four underlying dynamics:

- *A strategic ability to use different models of organizing at the same time,* even though their approaches may seem quite distinct from each other.
- *A developed set of consecrated values within their internal strategic vision that moors them to bedrock principles of action while allowing for tactical flexibility.* These principles, tested and refined through experience, then allow for short-term tactical and strategic flexibility as well as the wisdom to know when long-term beliefs and practices will be too compromised for transformational work to continue if done in that manner or within that alliance.
- *A strategic flexibility to form alliances and coalitions with groups that may or may not be aligned with them* on other programmatic issues.
- *An organizer's personal mastery of his or her own transformational strategic commitments so that he or she models the change being sought* in the daily activities, group meetings, planning sessions, and campaign work of which he or she is a part (Senge, Scharmer, Jaworski, & Flowers, 2005).

Using Different Organizing Models: The Ella Baker Center of Oakland, California

An organizer draws from a series of planned change interventions from a variety of models, whether empowerment, civic, or power centered. This approach is called *mixing and phasing* by Rothman (2008) and underscored by Smock (2003) as she assesses her transformational model.[2] It was this expansion of the chessboard that so amazed Ellis in the introductory case study example. While fictionalized, Ellis's work in many ways could refer to the work undertaken by Van Jones, Jakadi Imani, and others of the Oakland,

California–based Ella Baker Center, a formerly grassroots-based organization created to campaign against police violence and antiracist work that has grown into a powerful community-based institution focusing not only on police violence but also on "green-collar" jobs that would marry the inner city of Oakland to the far more bucolic and upper-middle-class Marin County (Jones, 2008).

In many ways, the Ella Baker Center's evolution mirrors its transformational strategic development. The center began in the mid-1990s as a deeply committed, social justice–based organization with a skeletal staff fighting racism and injustice as seen through police violence, profiling, and racially disproportionate incarceration. Using a variety of skilled tactics through a power-based model of social justice–based campaigns emphasizing confrontation and clearly defined targets for change, the center's leadership soon realized that fighting for social justice against the police and the courts, no matter how noble, didn't do enough to alter the widespread hopelessness, lack of economic development, and underdeveloped pathways toward a better future that the young people of Oakland desperately sought.

The leadership knew its strategic focus had to deepen to meet young people's needs. What's important to underscore here is that in broadening their strategic emphasis, those leaders did not give up either their analysis of police brutality and unjust imprisonment or their campaigns for social justice inside the criminal justice system. What they instead did was link this power model campaign (in many ways, a traditional antiracist campaign common to the civil rights struggles over the past 40 years) to a civic campaign for green jobs that joined the mostly middle-class environmental movement to causes of inner-city economic development (see www.ellabakercenter.org for more of its history).

Tactical Flexibility Without Loss of Principle

This ability to link different models of organizing inside one overarching vision for change is a core dimension to transformational work. As a group develops this multimodel approach, other parts of the work will reflect a similar mix in its tactical focus. In turn, this flexible focus maintains its underlying bedrock commitments through the little things in the group's work that reflect *its core values consecrated in action*. A further example of this is what the Ella Baker Center, working with the Oakland Apollo Alliance and Laney College, created as a curriculum for its green jobs program. Working with Racquel Pinderhughes, a noted academic scholar on the green economy who was skilled at training and teaching the long-term unemployed, the Ella Baker Center developed a jobs training program that corresponds to other strategic objectives that are the core of the center's vision (www.californiagreensolutions.com).

Briefly outlined, the program does not look particularly distinct from other jobs programs:

- An outreach campaign to possible participants
- Preconstruction and basic skills training

- Laney College Bridge to Solar and Green Construction curriculum
- Social support and case management

Look more closely, however, and you see that the center has remained true to the principles listed below that guided its first antiracist work:

- The outreach was conducted by the Cypress Mandela, a construction trades program originally established to reach long-term underemployed workers, many of them with records of incarceration. As we saw in Chapters 3 and 6, outreach campaigns require an ability to establish trust with the people one is working with and to do so within a framework of multiculturalism and gender inclusiveness. Cypress Mandela's staff had such a skill set to approach and win over people who otherwise might be mistrustful of traditional college outreach programs. By embracing principles of both the civic model and the women-centered model in their outreach, the group was able to reach and sustain participants who otherwise often drop out of such programs.

- The pretraining program set high standards for both attendance and the skill sets one would need for a green job while respecting the lack of opportunity and basic training in job readiness for participants. The program respected the struggles from their backgrounds that left them underprepared for consistent work and provided them with new tools to achieve basic job preparation. At the same time, the program made clear that the technical skill set participants eventually would need for a well-paying job would require other, more demanding skills on which they would receive later training. This mix of respect and challenge addressed in Chapter 5's discussion of leadership development is a critical ingredient to long-term strategic objectives of an empowerment and transformational model of organizing.

- The Laney College Bridge to Solar and Green Construction curriculum, a college credit program, taught technical skills such as how to install solar panels and did so through a learning framework that placed those skills in the context of environmental sustainability and environmental justice. By blending social issues in with technical skills, the program never lost sight of the communities it sought to serve and other, larger social conditions that affected them. Such a weave of the social inside the technical is an exemplar of how social justice values are consecrated in other, seemingly very different kinds of work.

- The program offered paid internships and apprenticeships on the job while continuing to provide case management support. Entering a demanding green construction job doesn't mean that the vestiges of long-term underemployment, economic insecurity, and both internalized and external measures of oppression disappear with the first paycheck. By continuing with social support and case management, the group recognizes that long-term economic and social marginalization requires long-term support to sustain this workforce as well (see www.ellabakercenter.org).

In this more systematic review, it becomes clear that each programmatic activity is screened through the original lens of grassroots social justice and antiracist work while adapting to the immediate demands and opportunities of the present-day context. The center's strategic experience weaves its principled commitments of the past into a multi-model approach to green jobs that transforms a traditional training program into a program of ecology, economic development, individual empowerment, and social justice.

Rather than sacrificing its original commitments, this program makes them an integral part of everything it does. The result is strategic flexibility in the use of different organizing models and a sustained commitment to core values without losing the ability to pragmatically serve the immediate needs of the Oakland community.

ACTIVITY FOR TRANSFORMATIONAL STRATEGY FORMATION

1. Identify a program you are involved in: _____

2. Reflect on and clarify three core values you have had as a grassroots organizer committed to social change and social justice:

    a. _____

    b. _____

    c. _____

3. Identify the core parts of your program, including outreach, group meetings, primary activities (campaign work, leadership training, etc.), and other services.

    a. Outreach _____

    b. Group meetings _____

    c. Primary activities _____

    d. Group maintenance activities _____

    e. Other services _____

4. Identify a way your core values can be consecrated in action and woven into each segment:

    a. Outreach and consecrated value in action (CVIA) _____

    b. Group meetings and CVIA _____

    c. Primary activities and CVIA _____

    d. Group maintenance activities and CVIA _____

    e. Other services and CVIA _____

5. As you reflect on each segment, what organizing models do they encompass (civic, power based, women centered, community building, transformative)?

a. _____

b. _____

c. _____

d. _____

e. _____

DEVELOPING STRATEGIC FLEXIBILITY WITHOUT COMPROMISING CORE VALUES: A CASE STUDY OF A TRANSFORMATIONAL ORGANIZER'S *INTERNAL STRATEGIC VISION*

Developing Parent Leaders While Fighting for Power as the Foundation to Educational Reform

More than two generations ago, the fight over community control of schools that became famous as the Ocean Hill–Brownsville case study (Gittell, 1998) led to a decades-long breach between the powerful New York City Teachers Union, the United Federation of Teachers (UFT), and parent-led alliances for school reform. The racially charged animosity from that time had lived on inside both the UFT and various parent reform groups that sprang up over the ensuing years so that little collaboration occurred, no matter the common cause they might share for improving school performance (Fabricant, 2010).

Over time, shifts did begin to occur as new teacher leadership and different community voices began to be heard. For example, the UFT president Randi Weingarten and Brooklyn-based ACORN activists began forging an alliance on school reform that served as a foundation for other community–union relationships. Thus, in 2006, Weingarten and the Coalition for Educational Justice's (CEJ) leadership, many of whom had begun their school reform efforts by seeking the ouster of an individual school principal, sat down together to work on a powerful educational reform package that extended parent voice inside the schools, expanded use of lead teachers, and focused on middle school improvement as key benchmarks for lasting educational reform in New York City (Fabricant, 2010).

What had happened to lead once-antagonistic actors to work together effectively when 40 years of previous efforts had failed? Was this a strategic alliance of strange bedfellows, inevitably doomed to failure, or a new formation that, in combination with other citywide activist groups, had the staying power and internal capacity to work together for the long haul that all reform efforts require in a large city? Was the alliance between CEJ and the UFT an authentic community–union partnership where the voices of parents were genuinely respected by seasoned union leadership or one that relied on token community involvement, while real decisions occurred only among professionals?

The success of the group in brokering a powerful reform package with the New York City Board of Education and its powerful chancellor, Joel Klein, on middle school improvements, including both more parent voice in school decision making and an expanded use of mentor teachers to guide inexperienced staff in the classroom, suggests that the alliance between parents and union officials was an authentic one, not a shell. That said, the answers to how these parents developed such leadership and sustained authority with these other powerful stakeholders did not lie in some overnight decision to suddenly and serendipitously work together. As with almost all transformational strategic decisions, the answers instead lie in years of organizing among a group of people who carefully built both the internal capacity among the parent membership and the external credibility with other public education stakeholders to make such partnerships possible. As also could be seen at the Ella Baker Center, true transformative activity was possible only with genuine involvement of many people over many years. And like the center and the early organizing role of Van Jones, CEJ cannot be fully understood without examining the experience of its first lead organizer, Eric Zachary.[3]

Zachary began his organizing in the antiwar and antiracist work common to the early 1970s, moving on through his master's in social work with a focus on community organizing and then beginning his professional career as an organizer for the powerful hospital workers' union, 1199. Wanting to invest more of himself at the neighborhood rather than the union contract level, with the kind of people he had grown up with in the working-class, multiracial world of Coney Island, Brooklyn, by 1989 he found himself working in a drug prevention and parent training program at John Jay College designed to improve school performance in some of New York City's school districts. On the face of it, this program, like the Ella Baker Center's, was similar to countless other prevention efforts: substance abuse training, a skills focus on how to run meetings and lead groups. However, Zachary's life and work experience had led him to emphasize two or three core values that, applied in the training itself, made the training transformational. "My mother instilled in me genuine respect for all people so that it's part of my core, it relates to how I believe everybody deserves to be dealt with."

This seemingly simple value of respect was joined to his belief that working-class people of all races often had untapped abilities to lead. In combination, these values and beliefs were translated throughout his John Jay training program as a fundamental orienting principle in its design: "Demonstrate deep respect for adults in everything one did," and "put [those values] toward the service of the learning." With those principles in mind, Zachary internalized a fundamental question that guided how those values would be put to use:

For me, the question is what values guide you and how do you use them to guide your work—how do you manifest them in ways that is the best fit for you . . . to whose service do you put your skills and values to work? For me, it always related to poor and working class people.

Over the years, this powerful strategic vision that emphasized respect for those in the training session, especially because it was conveyed consistently toward people that others in the school system often marginalized, at first found expression through a powerful training design for parent leadership inside New York City schools (Zachary, 1998). Begun at John Jay, its core elements were these:

- As with all good organizing, the training program started with where people are, which translated concretely into these steps:
- Icebreakers that relax people and make them feel comfortable in a learning environment. Many people from oppressed and marginalized communities have not had good experiences in formal educational settings. "Can training use this initial moment to maximize a connection, as occurs in organizing, or not?" Thoughtful icebreakers did just that.
- Agendas for training needed to reflect the participants' concerns, not just the organizers.' The people's voice was therefore a core part of every session, not an add-on.
- Like Paulo Freire's popular education model, Zachary's training "started with people's experiences" as the legitimate focus of the learning, "using it as a bridge to discuss what they need to do that may require new skills."
- Using a group-centered approach that emphasized the collective wisdom throughout the room and not just at the front, the trainer/facilitator worked with the group to arrive at a "collective idea that they have learned from each other." In this way, parents internalized that their learning became more and more horizontal (and thus from one another) rather than vertical, from the trainer/facilitator.
- The training design was all about "setting up a learning environment where it's safe to take risks" in what people can do together. Some of the risks are related to being able to disagree with the trainer, to take a chance that their own ideas are as worthy as a more credentialed member of the group, and the like. Zachary's training design at John Jay fostered an environment in which such risks could be taken. As one parent leader later noted:

People will get embarrassed speaking in English and not want to make a mistake. . . . Sometimes they have a good idea but they don't want to present it. They won't take the risk. . . . People will take the risk at meetings because of the translator but also because they begin to see this is a place where they can take a risk. (Fabricant, 2010, pp. 109–110)

Worked on together over time, the ensuing internalized belief in parents' capacity to give voice to ideas about organizing served as a powerful exemplar of what Freire (2000) meant when he wrote "to name the word is to transform the world" (p. 114). It was the training model's design that used the ongoing give-and-take between parents as a testimony to Zachary's belief that people from all walks of life could indeed act on the world in a powerful, strategic way.

From Training to Organize to Training While Organizing: The Power of the Prep

The dilemma Zachary faced emerged from the very effectiveness of his training program. Parents involved in their schools who came to the John Jay leadership program were personally more effective and engaged in their schools, but Zachary's experience as an organizer inside the powerful hospital union 1199 had made clear to him that without systematic organizing, there could be little lasting change inside the educational system. What good was great training if it didn't foster systemic change? Moving from John Jay to New York University's Institute for Education and Social Policy, in late 1996 he set about with others in the Bronx to create organizing programs that took on more systemic problems inside schools.

With a preeminent focus now on organizing, a new problem almost immediately popped up. Where before he was training people on leadership and strategic skills with little systematic organizing, now there was so much organizing that there was little time for formal training. Here, Zachary refined an important innovation begun by other experienced organizers pressed for time, yet committed to genuine leadership training: *leadership training as a systematic part of the preplanning process of organizing rather than as an adjunct to it.* Leadership development, both for individual parents as they prepared for a speech or for a group of parents working on a press conference, became fundamental to the preplanning work before each and every action in a unique way. Utilizing the same principles within the former training program, Zachary and others from New York University, including Mili Bonilla and Barbara Gross, *began to use preplanning not simply to plan events but to pose issues and dilemmas for people themselves to answer so that they would take gradual ownership of the organizing campaigns.* As Ocynthia Williams, one of the leading parent advocates reflected:

Basically, the training, the preparation gives you confidence, knowledge. I guess the knowledge gives you the confidence, and just knowing that someone else believes that you can, reaffirming what you've learned by telling you that you did a good job at a meeting, or by helping to prepare you for a meeting. In our conversations we discovered certain things by looking at the data. The data says a, b, and c schools have been at this level for a long time and then it makes you think: Why? Why hasn't there been any improvement? And then I guess you have this awareness, not just the academic part. We can now suggest reasons for the data and the school failing. (Fabricant, 2010, p. 176)

- Through the use of prep as an arena for leadership training as the organizing evolved, the parents began to experience leadership, both individually and collectively, as a group-centered activity in which everyone contributes, rather than just the few. In this way, taking on the responsibilities of leadership becomes a shared activity rather than an isolating one (similar to what was discussed in Chapter 5 about leadership development).
- Organizers were selected for this work who demonstrated the same genuine respect for and comfort with the working-class, racially diverse parents involved in their school campaigns. As organizers, they developed their skill sets in ways that helped pull things together through structured interaction and group decision making, trusting that the group would arrive at the right answers in ways the singular organizer/trainer running a campaign primarily alone could not.

Of course, the purpose of the prep work was to develop leaders in organizing campaigns that could affect change inside public schools. Therefore, the results of the organizing activities inside the schools were brought back into future prep work as the group once again reviewed what did and didn't happen. "In this way people get to reflect on what did and didn't work, but not alone. . . . It was through the efforts of the group, not the individual" (E. Zachary, personal communication, June 2009). In this way, the model for leadership that parents internalized was about themselves in relationship to the group, not as solitary leaders.

It is the culmination of this long-term work, starting as a training program at John Jay and evolving first as a parent-led group in the Bronx prepped for coleadership and then into a citywide alliance with other powerful community groups, that made the eventual alliance between parents and union leaders work (Fabricant, 2010). Through the power of the prep and its application to real organizing, its ongoing give-and-take through group-centered leadership, and the safety in which risk taking could occur, Zachary and other parent leaders have created a powerful organizing model for transformational leadership. Today, community folks from across New York can work with other, powerful educational authorities without intimidation or undue deference. Because people's sense of who they are as leaders was framed in part through a powerful, nurturing, *and* challenging environment, when parent leaders finally arrived at the planning table with a powerful figure such as the UFT's Weingarten, they had the internal leadership capacity to work alongside her in ways that demonstrated flexibility without simply agreeing with her. As Herb Katz, UFT vice president, expressed later, "The give and take was real, with real input from all sides, and real respect, too. That doesn't happen overnight" (Fabricant, 2010, p. 219).

Zachary's work demonstrates that an organizer's personal mastery models the change he seeks in terms of coleadership, shared decision making, and the capacity of others to inform a difficult and demanding organizing campaign. As noted earlier, Senge's (1994) example of personal mastery is of the master potter who effortlessly creates a work of art. Such mastery is not about intensely dominating anything, whether a pot or a group of people; it is achieved only through the consistent efforts one makes over time. It is neither a specific skill nor a technique that can be picked up from the printed page or by mimicking another. It is thus perhaps no accident that when speaking about his organizing model, Zachary began by reflecting on his life, not his work:

> I'm not sure I have a model, but whatever it is it flows from the core of my life experiences with all the diverse people I grew up with . . . and the respect I have for who they are. . . . I put that at the service of my learning, and whatever learning goes on in [my] work. (E. Zachary, personal communication, June 2009)

Looking at his work as an organizer, one can see that these deep-seated values of respect, seeing diversity as an asset, and believing learning best happens as a shared experience have been constants in all the work he has done, whether as an organizer for the hospital union 1199, a training developer for parents working out of John Jay College, or the lead organizer in a citywide parents' effort for school reform. Importantly, this has meant that Zachary esteems what others bring to the table without denying his own worth:

> I've always had the belief that the more people from the community are able to own what they're doing, the more involved they'll be. . . . So I never pre-judge what people are capable of answering [about a campaign's choice of tactics], and I don't deny my own experience, either. . . . Having confidence is not the same thing as arrogance. (E. Zachary, personal communication, June 2009)

It is this combination of personal confidence and belief in others that partly explains Zachary's remarkable talent for problem-posing with others during prep time as they work on campaign strategy. Freire (2000) describes problem-posing as follows:

> The problem-posing method does not dichotomize the activity of the teacher-student [organizer/parent leader]: she is not "cognitive" [learning] at one point and "narrative" [teaching] at another. She is always "cognitive," whether preparing a project or engaging in dialogue with students. He does not regard cognizable

objects [strategic ideas] as his private property, but as the object of reflection by himself and the students. . . . The students—no longer docile listeners—are now critical co-investigators in dialogue with the teacher. (pp. 80–81)

For Zachary, problem-posing with those with whom he works has guided him as his own organizing efforts have led him into larger and larger campaigns that necessarily removed him from daily grassroots activities as he worked with major educational stakeholders, sought larger grants, and strategized with other parent leaders from around the city. For at each new level of involvement, strategic issues and complexities grew larger, not smaller. Choosing whether to work in coalition with certain actors or whether to emphasize tactics of confrontation over compromise and conciliation were dilemmas he could not answer on his own:

There have been numerous times since 2006 where we were in negotiations [with the New York City Department of Education] where I had to go back to people to see what to do. . . . We'd have emergency conference calls. My job was to lay out the dilemmas clearly so people knew what our options were. . . . Of course it was more work, but that's what kept us together. (E. Zachary, personal communication, June 2009)

That Zachary consistently would check in with parent leaders as high-level negotiations were under way clarifies the difference between problem-posing as a momentary technique and problem-posing as integral to one's vision and the personal mastery it takes to express it throughout one's life and work. Problem-posing as a technique simply uses questions as another method of inquiry; learning and those who provide it are still objects toward the organizer's already defined strategic ends. Problem-posing as Zachary uses it is tied to his fundamental belief that the meaning of his work, as well as its effectiveness, necessarily must involve parent leaders. His masterful and seemingly effortless series of questions—asked early on as a parent leadership trainer—because it flowed from his deeply held strategic vision, continues to reappear years later in his prep work and in his work as a nationally known organizer for educational reform because it is not a technique but, rather, the only way he knows how to be in relationship with others—whether as trainer, organizer, or human being.

Like watching the master potter, seeing Zachary in action means not really seeing much. He doesn't dominate discussions in a group. If there's a party or celebration related to some work, you'll probably find him serving the drinks or setting up, not giving toasts or working the room. Because he prefers to wear T-shirts and jeans or Dockers (with his keychain conveniently dangling from a belt loop) rather than jackets and ties, you'd never assume he is a significant player in educational reform or that others around the country are seeking to replicate what he and other parent leaders have created. But the parents are aware; they observe the little things he does that reflect his deepest commitments. As Denise Moncrief explains:

> My self-confidence since coming to CC9 [the forerunner to NYC CEJ] has sky-rocketed. I never knew I could speak to people and get them to listen; speak to people and move them; and speak to people and impart knowledge that wasn't trivial. . . . When we did the first rally, and they wanted me to do a speech, and the mission statement, I had thirty seconds of stuff written out. They said you have to make it longer. They encouraged me and Eric walked me through the entire thing. By the second rally, it was "Leave my speech alone! Don't touch it!" No matter what I have wanted to do, I have always felt supported by them. They have shown extreme confidence in me being able to do whatever they need me to do. And that makes me want to produce all the more. (Fabricant, 2010, p. 118)

Because he is a genuine transformational organizer, Zachary's legacy lies in the efforts to reform schools that are led through Denise Moncrief's voice, not his. His entire chess-board is in play.

ERIC ZACHARY'S INTERNAL STRATEGIC VISION FOR THE COMMUNITY-BASED COALITION FOR EDUCATIONAL JUSTICE

Who: Working-class and poor people, often people of color

What issue: Educational justice, parent leadership, creating schools responsive to parents and families as the foundation for reform

How he works: Builds strategies in dialogue with parents; seeks coleadership on all strategic issues; starts where people are and challenges parents for new levels of commitment (plus one); seeks democratic decision making from below; models the change he seeks through small actions grounded in respect for the daily work

Core values consecrated in action: Respect, diversity, fairness, equality, reciprocity, social justice

---

Choose Your Dilemma: A Transformational Strategist Moves on in the Fight for Educational Reform

Any transformational strategist works with tactical and strategic dilemmas through-out his or her career. For example, Zachary handled the dilemma of leadership develop-ment versus accomplishing concrete educational campaign objectives by developing "the power of the prep" to do both. He was well aware of even more fundamental dilemmas related to the reform efforts themselves. On the one hand, "the Coalition for Educational Justice's independence allowed for more creativity and autonomy of action, but operated with far less power inside to influence long-term change." At the same time, over the years of working with the UFT, he saw that "the union had far more power and resources to bring to the table," albeit within a more traditional, institutionalized approach.

In 2009, Zachary was asked by the American Federation of Teachers' (AFT) president Weingarten to help develop a robust community engagement program. Over the next 6 months, he crisscrossed the country, visiting locals in California, Minnesota, Chicago, Philadelphia, and Houston. The positive response led him to present a proposal on community engagement for the union. While to the outside, "community engagement" can sound pretty tame, within almost all unions, such engagement would represent a cultural sea change to successfully implement. Weingarten and Zachary understood that in the 21st century, only through such engagement could unions withstand the attack from the right that has been a major emphasis of the conservative movements of the day. With union membership nationwide down from 32% in the 1950s to 11.3% in 2013, a new paradigm shift in union–community relations had to happen if public educational reform efforts were to include them as they had in the past.

To begin the campaign, the AFT president announced her full support for the effort so that it had the legitimacy and authority to move forward. People used to the more insular, contract-driven focus of the past 40 years would be supported and trained to develop the skills and approaches on how to do this engagement. Weingarten provided resources to hire five experienced, energetic regional organizers and accepted all the personnel selections Zachary and his team made for this new initiative. Together, Zachary and the new organizers are working with about 10 locals in each of the five regions to build this collaborative model. The training curriculum emphasized a number of skill sets that they have labeled "The Five Ms":

1. **Map** the region in terms of resources, important community actors, levels and types of power, and who shared their values and approaches to public educational reform

2. Develop **messages** that are authentic to the union and resonate and connect with the community

3. **Mobilize** to learn how to engage members and citizens in working together in support of shared goals and objectives—both for the community and for the union

4. Learn how to run **meetings** that allow all voices in the room to be heard, and practice shared decision making so that trust is deepened for the long-term work ahead

5. **Move to action** by creating plans that drill down to the schools and what they need as well as work to broaden support through shared agendas on other community efforts

The paradigm shift of inside–outside collaborative work on both union concerns and community interests underscored the need for a long-term strategic perspective on building power solid enough to push back against the forces aligned against them in support of privatization and charter schools as the keys to educational reform (Fabricant & Fine, 2012). Pushing such a paradigm required encouraging local members long used to and still in need of short-term, contract-specific issues to take risks in thinking longer term and to treat community groups as full partners—a risk the AFT president and her new director of the AFT Human Rights and Community Relations Department were willing to take.

Luckily, Zachary was undertaking his efforts alongside a major AFT local based in Chicago, led by the local's president Karen Lewis. Aware of the importance of parental support for any militant action the union might have to take in support of its members, the Chicago UFT had begun its parent engagement work in 2010. They created a community advisory board comprising parents and other community stakeholders 2 years in advance of the strike that occurred in 2012. Equally important, the union demonstrated genuine support for the community's struggles and not just its own, turning out in support of various housing foreclosure campaigns that impacted poor and working-class people across the Windy City in 2011. The result was that when the union struck against Chicago Mayor Rahm Emanuel's efforts to further privatize the school system, widespread support from parents forced him back to the table far sooner than he anticipated, resulting in far more concessions on privatization than expected (Davey & Yaccino, 2012).

Such success has bolstered the union's efforts. For example, one of the new organizers, working with the Philadelphia local president and a range of community groups, helped develop Philadelphia Coalition Advocating for Public Schools—bringing community and student stakeholders into an alliance for the first time. The coalition created its own reform plan for Philadelphia education as a counter to mayoral efforts to privatize 40 public schools. Having now enlisted other unions, such as the Service Employees International Union, the union–community collaboration is recognized as a genuine force not seen in Philadelphia educational reform efforts for years.

Other collaborative efforts are under way in all five regions across the country, developing 12 "town halls" to bring parents, teachers, and advocates together—with an emphasis on mobilizing parents, community members, and union activists around developing bottom-up solutions for our struggling schools. In early spring of 2013, Zachary and his staff brought together 100 people from these regional groups and locals to synthesize a national platform that continues to build the work. While he would be the first to tell you that the work requires as many doses of patience as it does persistence, his commitment to social justice as central to educational reform continues.

ERIC ZACHARY'S INTERNAL STRATEGIC VISION FOR WORKING IN THE UNION MOVEMENT

Who: Union leaders and members as well as working-class and poor parents, often people of color

What issue: Union–parent collaborations, educational justice, parent leadership, creating reform efforts responsive to both unions and parents, and families as the foundation for reform

How he works: Builds strategies in dialogue with union leaders and parents; seeks coleadership on all strategic issues; starts where people are (both union members and community members); challenges stakeholders to new forms of commitment (plus one); seeks democratic decision making from below and across reform groups

Core values consecrated in action: Respect, diversity, fairness, voice, equality, reciprocity, social justice

---

CONCLUSION: FROM ENTRY-LEVEL TO TRANSFORMATIVE STRATEGIST

For the new or less experienced practitioner committed to developing as a transformative strategist, the lessons from this chapter also require one to hone two other qualities alongside the increasing strategic effectiveness that Rubin and Rubin (2007) discussed earlier: *persistence and patience.* Of the two, persistence is perhaps easier for organizers, for they tend to be a stubborn lot in the first place. Persistence in holding on to what you believe and consistently working on your internal strategic vision, your core values, and how they find expression in your daily entry-level strategic work are the continuing tasks that lie ahead for anyone seeking to do transformative work. What distinguishes Van Jones and Eric Zachary from others is their commitment to stubbornly pursuing the same values for the same people, even as their work takes different shapes. Anyone seeking such a transformative path can be expected to maintain that same level of persistence in the consecration of their values throughout their lives.

Patience, of course, is another matter. Macro practitioners are rarely patient folks; the desire to change the world has never emanated from people serenely waiting for it to happen. And to advocate here for organizers to do that kind of waiting would be a huge strategic error! The patience here is a further dimension of the tactical self-awareness discussed in Chapters 3 and 4: One gets to use the whole chessboard in a masterful way only by tolerating the often slow, gradual, and humbling manner in which patience emerges. Like the master potter, transformational strategists must work first with the seemingly unyielding clay of their limited experience, only over time growing to realize the richness that was there all along. For those willing to develop such patience in the persistent search for a better world, such mastery will have been worth the wait.

REFLECTIVE ACTIVITY FOR EDUCATIONAL POLICY 2.1.5

Given this professional standard, with its emphasis on incorporating "social justice in organizations, institutions, and society," examine your group's internal strategic vision and delineate in concrete ways how "social justice" and "human rights" appear inside your organization and the way it operates. As much as possible, distinguish actions and behaviors that bring this competency to life.

Social justice and the commitment to human rights appears in our group/campaign/organization through the following:

Who:

What (issues):

How the work is conducted:

How I conduct my work:

Seen through core values consecrated in action:

A SPECIAL ADDENDUM: HISTORY MOVES? THE EMERGENCE OF OCCUPY WALL STREET

What follows is a personal essay I wrote for Occupy Wall Street (OWS) activists during the intense protests surrounding the movement in 2011 and 2012. It contains strategic reflections related to social movement building that build on strategic issues discussed in this chapter.

CRUSTINESS, POP-UP THREATS, AND THE DILEMMAS OF 21ST CENTURY SOCIAL MOVEMENT BUILDING: STRATEGIC REFLECTIONS ON THE HOT-MESS AUTHORITY OF OCCUPY WALL STREET

Introduction

In the summer of 2012, if one traveled to the various encampments known as "Occupy" (Wall Street, Memphis, Oakland, etc., etc.), a casual visitor would not have been very impressed. For example, in Memphis, encampments contained mostly a group of aging new leftists out of the '60s, a few punk rockers, and some long-term homeless people. Likewise, if one strolled around New York's Union Square Park around 5 p.m. most weekdays, one might be amused but not impressed by much of what seemed to be going on. Right in the center were some crusty folks, complete with sunburned, unwashed faces, sleep-deprived eyes, a tattoo or two dozen, all sitting huddled close together, in part for warmth, in part because they had nowhere else to go. Nearby, there was a table with some snappy black-and-white booklets on anarchism, staffed by an earnest couple dressed in basic black; behind them, in a tight circle, sat eight or nine people from the Think Tank working group, intently discussing the economic and social costs of fracking. They leaned in toward each other, in part because of the three drummers' loud rhythms emanating from a few yards back. A few young people stood taking pictures, excited to be there, anxious to talk to the gray-haired lady with the large peace sign or the old guy dressed as Uncle Sam. A small table held the vestiges of OWS's library, 30-or-so donated books free for the asking; three guys had set up a longer table for the evening meal of rice and beans and veggies. Others milled around, stopping to chat with passers-by.

Not too far away, but as visible as any of the rest, were three police officers standing against a white-and-blue NYPD van. Ten feet farther down were two more, then six more, over by the park's Ghandi statue. An officer, visible because of his white shirt, stood toward the back by the bushes, three more blue shirts next to him. All these police, for not even 200 people? Weeks earlier, back when a few OWS-ers popped back up in Zuccotti Park, the police response had been swift and violent: three male cops dragging down a young woman on the orders of a female white shirt to "get the fuckin' bitch," leaving marks on her neck and bruises on her back still present a week later; another woman soon to become famous because she went into seizure, left to moan and twitch on the ground as officers stood by, doing nothing. Cameras busted, laptops destroyed, wallets and cell phones lost, handcuffs so tight fingers turned numb from the lack of circulation.

To young Occupiers, the increasing harshness of official response to their presence across the country was confusing. How could such a crusty crew evoke such a police presence, and the intimations of more threatening actions? Why had Florida, holder of the Republican Convention that summer, been in such fear of Occupy that they outlawed things such as masks and pieces of string over 6 inches long wherever a public gathering was to be held? People have been marching for the past 40 years at political conventions. Why would New York Police Department teams raid OWS activists' apartments using 3-year-old "open container" warrants as a ruse to search for future demonstration plans, as *The New York Times* reported? Has OWS really been so different from all the other political causes of the previous generation? And if it is different, is it really such a threat to the powers that be?

The short answers to those two questions are (1) yes, at least for a time it was very different, something not seen in the United States for over 30 years, and (2) yes, OWS, in all its hot mess, was seen as a genuine threat to the established order. What follows is an elder organizer's take on why—and the enormous opportunities *and* pitfalls that stand before us.

Part 1: "We Are the 99%!" . . . Occupy!

Everyone knows that the combination of the OWS slogan, "We are the 99%," and OWS-ers' commitment to nonviolent direct action, including occupation of public spaces, crystallized long pent-up frustrations and anger that unleashed hundreds of Occupy movements across the country. In themselves, however, they neither explain what was different about this mix of ideas and action nor why they have been a perceived threat to established political and economic institutions in ways that make OWS distinct from other campaigns of the past 30-plus years.

To begin, the slogan "We are the 99%" is the first to break through the identity- and issue-based movement activism in more than a generation. With its catchy focus on economic and social inequality, *the slogan has provided a unifying consciousness that gives different kinds of people and distinct issues a coherent target—the 1%—and a degree of similarity of purpose—end economic and political inequality and unfairness—that has not been present in progressive movements since the early 1970s.*

Joined to nonviolent direct action and the retaking of the commons, these messages stood in militant opposition to how political and economic business was conducted. *Things were economically grossly unfair, and the political game to make it "better" was fixed as well.* By willingly living under difficult conditions and the threat of immediate removal by the police, *Occupiers with their powerful slogan established a level of authority to counter dominant elites for the first time since the civil rights and antiwar movements of the 1960s.* It was no accident that OWS authority emerged when Congressional approval ratings were at historic lows and banking and finance leaders were perceived by most Americans as greedy and disinterested in the average working person's standard of living.

This OWS counter-authority has been the grave threat to American political and economic leaders. For as we saw throughout 2011 and 2012, when genuine authority rests within non-elites—all that crustiness and hot mess—the dominant discourse on "who is in charge" and "this is how we do things" is fundamentally transformed—not simply the discourse about the route of a march or how long one can stay in a park *but about everything.* A unifying social movement like the civil rights movement of the 1950s and '60s became a systemic threat to Southern White supremacy after Rosa Parks stayed seated on that Montgomery, Alabama, bus—along with the ensuing bus boycott engineered by civil rights leader E. M. Nixon. However, that didn't mean there was one huge transit breakdown engineered by African Americans across the South. Instead, there was something much more powerful: *Black people and their White allies stopped believing that the segregationist world order couldn't be changed.* Everyday people began working against a poll tax in one county, eating at lunch counters for "Whites only" in another city, boycotting a national Woolworth's chain, or not putting their heads down when a White person walked by. Rosa Parks's act shifted the consciousness of a people to look to themselves for answers . . . to see that "the way things were" didn't have to extend to *all corners of their lives.*

The violent response (bombings, murders, beatings, daily intimidation) to this shift in African American consciousness that then arose was not over bus rides. It was because the threat that emerged from Southern Black communities targeted the dominant discourse of *who and what mattered*—and the push was a shift away from racial segregation and the social and economic certainties it brought with it. If the only issue had been sitting wherever one wanted on a bus, Montgomery officials would have jumped at the chance. It wasn't.

OWS, while expressed differently 60 years later, has represented the beginnings of the same threat: Discourse that the American economic and political game is just a little unfair doesn't wash anymore. Almost all identity- and issue-based politics, while often militant and at times effective in getting their demands met, could be radical but not transformational: *Get the (sexist, racist, homophobic) rascal or issue out and/or changed, but the rules stay the same; the game is played at the margins of power, by the rules of the system.*

OWS's presence stated loud and clear that it's time to throw out the game, because the rules are a setup. Its slogans and growing counter-authority came from this intransigent belief-in-action that wider and wider sectors of the 99% intuit is accurate about their own lives, too. The ensuing unwillingness not to listen to official authority—*any authority*—in the same way alters not only whether OWS-ers get to stay in Union Square or Zuccotti Park or in downtown Memphis. Throughout society, managers are not listened to in the same way; school officials aren't believed when they say those test scores or school closings are genuine "educational reform"; stop and frisk is at last understood by more and more New Yorkers of every color as a racist program. Black folks and their White allies from around the country wear their hoodies up. The discourse is changing.

The OWS crusties may be a hot mess, but consciousness has been changed because of what they stood for . . . and where. Your mortgage is underwater and you're about to be evicted? OWS foreclosure groups claim your right to retake your home, and do so. Tired of vertical decision making from elites with no input? Try some of the crisscross mix of horizontalism, where voices are side by side. Can't afford a $200 meal down at your city's trendy dining area? Have a tasty vegetarian meal, served hot and free, each day at 6 p.m. sharp. Want to read a book? Dance a little? Dream? Over there, in the middle of that hot mess, you can.

Unfortunately, with the increasing clarity that OWS had shifted the dominant discourse at least momentarily from elites, the response of those in charge of "public order" had changed as well. After tactically sensing their error in early response to OWS on the Brooklyn Bridge and the infamous YouTube video of a white shirt Macing three young White women, police were noticeably mild-mannered, even friendly, with the Occupiers at Zuccotti Park. Over time, as it became clear that "Occupy" was about far more than a communal love-in downtown, that began to change—and ended abruptly in the late-night winter clearing of Zuccotti Park, complete with violence and intimidation of the media so that the event would not go viral.

As the brutal arrests suggested, this type of police action can be expected to continue. While it is unlikely ever to reach the level of the officially sanctioned murder seen in the South in the 1950s and '60s, the intimidating presence of the security arm of the 21st century state—from police infiltrators taking names in direct-action planning groups to physically violent arrests to longer and longer periods of incarceration—is going to increase. *Such intimidation serves a clear strategic purpose: It is meant to break the will of OWS activists and threaten the movement's public support in ways that allow for the reassertion of how the game is played*—that the rules are really okay, that elites are smarter and know more and act nicer than those crusty, weird kids down at the local park.

Fifty years ago, the long March to Freedom was filled with far more violence but the same strategic and tactical purposes by governing elites. Popular media portrayed Rosa Parks as just an uppity seamstress whose feet were tired, not an NAACP secretary who'd been trained as an organizer for 10 days at the Highlander Center the year before. Freedom Riders Diane Nash and John Lewis were red-influenced and dangerous radicals, not college-educated, church-going leaders of quiet, unwavering conviction. The Long March to Freedom required courage, commitment, and strategic brilliance to withstand the physical and political assault brought against it. Today's March to Equality will require nothing less.

If we are to march as resolutely and effectively as those who came before us, we also have to pay attention to some strategic dilemmas that they had to overcome—and that we must, too. The second part of this essay focuses on what OWS's strategic dilemmas are, with some modest proposals on how to resolve them.

Part 2. Can OWS Sustain the New Discourse? Strategic Considerations to Maintain OWS's Hot-Mess Authority

Occupy was able to alter the national discourse in 2011 and 2012 because the mix of slogans, forms of activism, and creation of the commons across the country in public parks, vacant lots, and esplanades stood in sharp contrast to the hollow political bargains and entrenched and expanding economic inequality that have marked the past 20 years of what passed for political discourse and debate. The world shifted that late summer day, and the potential for a sustained national social movement was born. That said, the present-day quiescence of OWS around the country suggests that the hard work of political organizing requires more than weekly plans and powerful slogans. Whether or not OWS continues to build a powerful movement and sustains that counter-authority depends on resolving the inevitable strategic tensions that this new social movement building has wrought. I will focus on what I consider six primary tensions.

1. *If OWS responds to every social, economic, and political issue in the world, it will come to stand for nothing.* OWS has responded to a wide variety of social, political, environmental, and economic calls for justice that can be found within the needs and interests of the 99%. I would argue that, strategically, OWS's authority stems primarily from its dual focus on economic inequality and reclaiming public space as a right of the people to their commons. Many issues can fall within this focus: from fracking (a clear economic and environmental risk to everyone) to stop and frisk (with its marginalization and incarceration of young men of color, thus removed from the labor market). OWS's strength has lain in the powerful messages related to student debt, foreclosures, under- and unemployment, tax unfairness, privatizing public space, and (on the political front), the auctioning of elections through Citizens United and the lobbying access of corporations. The underlying coherency of these issues allows different work for different campaigns while staying focused on very, very similar targets. Long-haul success requires those touchstones to be made by a larger and larger audience that over time begins to hear the OWS more clearly. Without that clarity, OWS's authority and arguments stand to be lost in the cacophony of issues and arguments that flood mainstream media and its outlets.

2. *This strategic dilemma is intensified if OWS responses are primarily about **what we are against and not what we are for**: Does OWS have solutions, demands, and "asks" for the 99% to support in their own work and lives?* There is no question that OWS's early strength came from its focus on solutions rather than narrow demands and as it created a commons for simple, collective exchange. Over the past 30 years, so much activism has been so narrowly focused that it has been refreshing to step away

from short-term solutions and remind people of the long-term depth of inequality that needs to be corrected. At some point, however, OWS will need to coherently point to a way forward that resonates with the conditions and aspirations of that part of the 99% we expect and need to mobilize. Part of the power of the right rests in its dangerously false yet compelling demands for lessened government, free-market growth, and heterosexual, patriarchal families. As I will mention below, some of OWS does have a powerful positive message in its internal work—taking back the commons, creating places safe to play and to disagree, militantly standing up against the tyranny of the growing police state. That said, if OWS does not create equivalent external messages primarily related to economic inequality and political unfairness, the 99% whom Occupiers seek to reach will grow disinterested and disengaged. Not seeking solutions that build campaigns of lasting power is a form of class and racial privilege that OWS does not want to be labeled with.

3. *Militant direct action leading to arrests can be a **useful tactic** when it **serves the strategic purpose** of building the movement; **when it becomes an end in itself, it undermines the movement's authority.*** The world not only watched but responded to the early arrests across the Brooklyn Bridge, in Oakland, and elsewhere as the velvet glove of state power came off. Over the first 6 months, the state's exposed iron fist helped expand OWS's reach as members of the 99% reacted in anger and disgust. However, over time, as has been seen in Oakland, Seattle, and elsewhere, risking arrest in small numbers and publically unrecognized actions depletes OWS of valuable energy, wastes resources, and serves no tactical or strategic advantage. As occurred in the South 60 years ago, creating actions that court arrest must serve the strategic purpose of exposing state power to a wider and wider audience and/or clarify a form of unfairness, immorality, or inequality that draws more and more actors to our movement.

One possibility is mobilizing direct actions that personalize the 1% (or, even better, the .01%) who are involved in intensifying economic inequality and political unfairness. Targeting the homes, businesses, and country clubs of those who fund SuperPacs through vigils, nonviolent direct-action marches, and street theater would be great entertainment, drive the 1% nuts, and, if protesters are arrested, expose whom the state continues to serve—and build OWS ranks accordingly.

4. *OWS must be a movement open to all; it cannot be a sustained social movement equally supported and created by all.* This is a debate as old as the fight for social justice: Can those who suffer most from injustice actually build and lead the social movements needed to combat it? A close read of the history of progressive social movements reveals that they created organizational forms that invited and sustained those extraordinary few who were exemplars of the oppression and the capacity to fight it—without denying that most of the day-to-day work was carried out by educated activists who used the power

and privilege of their skill sets in the cause of social justice. For every Fanny Lu Hamer there were a hundred college and high school graduates like John Lewis and Diane Nash.

This historical fact carries with it the bitter, bracing insight that many of those who have suffered the most social injustice may not always be in a position to effectively fight against it. The multiple hardships of homelessness, underemployment, family stressors, and environmental threats inside and outside the home understandably minimize the numbers who can consistently and strategically engage in the long-term fight to end oppression. This does not mean that the most oppressed are inherently less able, lack insight, or are indifferent to the conditions of their lives. It means they can't go to a lot of meetings, don't have time to read and study what to do next, and can't go out for coffee and reflect on what happened at the last march. It also means that those who are in a position to engage in long-term strategic struggles need to constantly assess their potential to misuse their power and privilege to marginalize those with fewer resources, preventing them from playing a vital role in ways that contribute to movement building: tactical insights, personal strategies of resilience, and pitching in.

5. *Inequitable dynamics of power and privilege are not only found within the 1%; they exist within the 99%—and, unless examined and worked with, within OWS itself.* Awareness of economic inequality and political unfairness is not a guarantee of personal insight regarding one's own misuse of power and privilege. Issues of racism, sexism, classism, homophobia, ableism, and basic elitism have surfaced enough to cause all of us discomfort. As someone who has been engaged in these issues all my adult life, they cannot be adequately addressed either through heartfelt, once-a-month sessions comprising equal doses of guilt and anger or through genuflections of romanticized piety directed at the oppressed. Instead, this work must be the individual and collective responsibility of each Occupier and in each OWS event or action so that OWS can begin to construct a world where diversity—social, intellectual, and personal—is embraced as a fundamental resource. If we are to stand for what distinguishes OWS from the 1% (and those parts of the 99% who are openly racist, sexist, and homophobic), this work must be seen as just as important as any form of direct action.

6. *While OWS champions the 99% in action, its internal workings are designed for far fewer.* In the 1960s and '70s, we called it "participatory democracy," where everyone attending a meeting got to vote and speak on every issue. It came to be known as "hard-ass democracy," as only those with the hardest asses could stay until the middle of the night and thus win all important votes. General Assemblies and other OWS forums that function in a similar fashion relegate almost every working person with a full-time job to a position of potential marginality. While we need to hold on to the value of horizontalism, it needs to be fit within the context of the working lives of potential Occupiers if OWS is to grow and thrive beyond our present numbers.

Concluding comment: the above strategic issues are dilemmas to be worked on together, not roadblocks to success. OWS demonstrated the potential to be the most important progressive social movement in at least 30 years. To realize potential, however, takes the kind of effort people displayed back in its early formations across the country—minus the thrilling rush that comes with any new, close relationship. The next few years are OWS's testing and trusting time—dilemmas replace certainty, fears intertwine with hopes and expectations. But isn't such struggle worthwhile?

THE COMMUNITY TOOLBOX

The following sections from the Community Toolbox (see http://ctb.ku.edu/en/tablecontents/chapter_1010.htm) can be extremely helpful for macro practitioners seeking concrete skills and techniques to mobilize and maintain interest in strategy development.

Choosing Strategies to Promote Community Health and Development

Section 1. Strategies for Community Change and Improvement: An Overview

Section 2. Community (Locality) Development

Section 3. Social Planning and Policy Change

Section 4. Social Action

Section 5. Coalition Building I: Starting a Coalition

Section 6. Coalition Building II: Maintaining a Coalition

REFERENCES

Burghardt, S. (1982). *Organizing for community action.* Thousand Oaks, CA: Sage.

Chambers, E., & Cowan, M. (2003). *Roots for radicals: Organizing for power, action, and justice.* New York: Continuum.

Cox, F., & Garvin, C. (2001). A history of community organization since the Civil War with special reference to oppressed populations. In J. Rothman (Ed.), *Strategies of community intervention* (pp. 53–77). Peosta, IA: Eddie Bowers.

Davey, M., & Yaccino, S. (2012, September 18). Teachers end Chicago strike on second try. *New York Times.* Retrieved from http://www.nytimes.com/2012/09/19/us/vote-scheduled-on-chicago-teachers-contract.html?pagewanted=all&_r=0

Eichler, M. (2007). *Consensus organizing: Building communities of mutual self interest.* Thousand Oaks, CA: Sage.

Fabricant, M. (2010). *Organizing for educational justice: The campaign for public school reform in the South Bronx.* Minneapolis: University of Minnesota Press.

Fabricant, M., & Fine, M. (2012). *Charter schools and the corporate makeover of public education: What's at stake.* New York: Teacher's College Press.

Fisher, R. (1994). *Let the people decide: Neighborhood organizing in America.* New York: Twayne.

Fisher, R. (2001). Political economy and public life: The context for community organizing. In J. Rothman, J. L. Erlich, & J. E. Tropman (Eds.), *Strategies of community intervention* (6th ed., pp. 100–117). Itasca, IL: F. E. Peacock.

Fisher, R. (2005). History, context, and emerging issues for community practice. In M. Weil, *The handbook of community practice* (pp. 34–58). Thousand Oaks, CA: Sage.

Fisher, R. (2009). *The people shall rule: ACORN, community organizing, and the struggle for economic justice.* Nashville, TN: Vanderbilt University Press.

Freire, P. (2000). *Pedagogy of the oppressed.* New York: Continuum.

Gittell, M. (1998). *Strategies for school equity: Creating productive schools in a just society.* New Haven, CT: Yale University Press.

Hanna, M., & Robinson, B. (1994). *Strategies for community empowerment: Direct-action and transformative approaches to social change practice.* Lewiston, NY: Edwin Mellen.

Hyde, C. (2008). Feminist social work practice. In T. Mizrahi & L. Davis (Eds.), *Encyclopedia of social work* (20th ed.). New York: Oxford University Press.

Jones, V. (2008). *Green collar economy: How one solution can fix America's two biggest problems.* New York: HarperCollins.

Mizrahi, T., & Rosenthal, B. (2001). Complexities of coalition building: Leaders' successes, strategies, struggles, and solutions. *Social Work, 46*(1), 63–78.

Mondros, J., & Wilson, S. (1994). *Organizing for power and empowerment.* New York: Columbia University Press.

Netting, F., Kettner, P., & McMurtry, S. (2008). *Social work macro practice.* Boston: Allyn & Bacon.

Ohmer, M., & DeMasi, K. (2008). *Consensus organizing: A community development workbook; A comprehensive guide to designing, implementing, and evaluating community change initiatives.* Thousand Oaks, CA: Sage.

Reisch, M. (2005). Radical community organizing. In M. Weil (Ed.), *Handbook of community practice* (pp. 287–304). Thousand Oaks, CA: Sage.

Rothman, J. (2008). *Strategies of community intervention.* Peosta, IA: Eddie Bowers.

Rubin, H., & Rubin, I. (2007). *Community organizing and development.* Boston: Allyn & Bacon.

Senge, P. (1994). *The fifth discipline.* New York: Broadway Press.

Senge, P., Scharmer, O., Jaworski, J., & Flowers, B. (2005). *Presence: Exploring profound change in people, organizations and society.* London: Nicholas Brealey.

Smock, K. (2003). *Democracy in action: Community organizing and urban change.* New York: Columbia University Press.

Staples, L. (2004). *Roots to power: A manual for grassroots organizing.* Santa Barbara, CA: Praeger.

Vaid, U. (1996). *Virtual equality: The mainstreaming of gay and lesbian liberation.* Harpswell Center, ME: Anchor.

Weil, M. (2005). *The handbook of community practice.* Thousand Oaks, CA: Sage.

Weil, M., Reisch, M., & Ohmer, L. (2009). *The handbook of community practice* (2nd ed.). Thousand Oaks, CA: Sage.

Zachary, E. (1998). *An exploration of grassroots leadership development: A case study of a training program's effort to integrate theory and method.* Unpublished doctoral dissertation, City University of New York Graduate Center.

NOTES

1. Please note, I am addressing the use of particular issues not on their merits but as examples of how tactics are used for different strategic purposes within coalitions.

2. In Smock's (2003) work, transformation models refer to those strategies seeking to make wide-scale, societal change. While such groups are part of the above definition, it also applies to groups that may be thinking less about societal change than about broad-scale, long-term issues without a structural, historical analysis attached to them.

3. The following quotations are from an interview conducted with Zachary in June 2009. A fuller description of his training design, organizing efforts, and the results of the program can be found in his doctoral dissertation, "An Exploration of Grassroots Leadership Development: A Case Study of a Training Program's Effort to Integrate Theory and Method" (1998).

CHAPTER 9

Think Local, Act Global

A Case Example of 21st Century Macro Practice Using the Power of Social Networking

Mohan Krishna Vinjamuri

STAYING CONNECTED

The two friends were about to sign off from Skype when Kay reminded them both of how much had changed in their professional and personal lives since 2008 in terms of social networking. "Here we are Skyping, and tomorrow I'll be back in my office on a teleconference call with people from four states dealing with the same homeless issues." She pointed her finger toward the Notebook camera and wagged it at her friend 3,000 miles away. "Hey, 4 years ago you were making me take on all this Internet chatter. And look at me now!"

The memory was still fresh for them both. In 2008, the day after the Obama electoral celebration in Chicago had dawned cool and bright. Standing in line at the local café for breakfast, the two sleepy friends shivered as they inched toward the warmth inside the chrome-and-glass doors just yards away.

"Hey, I guess we're not at our favorite diner anymore, are we?" Ellis remarked. "From good ol' coffee served by Florence to lattés near the park. Things change, don't they? Is the diner still there?"

(Continued)

(Continued)

"Nope, they closed years ago. The whole area's different. Got a café like this one, a few clothing stores, and a high-end bike store. People get their free-trade caffeine and then bike over to Central Park, I guess." Kay paused for a second. "Some of it's better; some of it's worse. I miss Florence and that coffee, though." She sighed, only to brighten again as she reached out and tapped Ellis's Obama button on his coat. "Things sure do change, don't they?"

"You got that right." Ellis held the door as they went inside and were directed to a small table, its wooden surface polished to a gleaming dark brown. "One thing that's gotta change is we need to be in touch more. I miss our conversations. We've been through so much together, we can talk shorthand on work stuff. I miss that."

"I was just saying to Esperanza last week how she and I had to connect more often, and she's just across the city!" Esperanza, their former community assessment group member and class den mother, was in charge of a mental health agency that renovated supportive housing. The agency used some of its rental monies to support advocacy for expanding the rights of the mentally ill. "But how do we do that? I mean, none of us is working an 8-hour day, and who can afford the travel?"

"Ahh, Kay, you're so old-school 20th century! How do you think Mr. Obama got all of us so tanked up for his election over the last year? He wasn't visiting us very often, was he?" The waiter, a smiling young man with a bright, multicolored tattoo of the Indian goddess Durga running up his right arm, gently placed two steaming cups of coffee before them. "All we have to do is follow his lead. You know, 'think local, act global.'"

"Huh? I was with you until you turned the old organizing slogan around. Don't you mean, 'think global, act local'?"

"Well, no, not really. Of course we're each involved in our own local work. After all, I'm gonna be in California and you're back in the Big Apple. But when we get stuck on what we're working on and start thinking about our local problems, we need to connect globally to like-minded people like you and me and Esperanza so that we can figure out what to do. Obama's campaign nailed how to turn social networking into political networking. All we have to do is go on Facebook or LinkedIn and create our own group. Then we plan to chat once a week on like-minded issues to help us through. It's called a 'community of practice,' I think."

Kay was beaming. "I get it! So just like we all had our affinity groups for Obama online, we create the same with each other around the country. Open it up to enough people we can learn from and share, but not so many we can't get our local needs met."

"Who knows? Maybe you and Esperanza and I will work on our local stuff with a few other people and somebody'll get a bright idea about doing something national that we each agree to support in our communities. Or maybe not. Maybe we just use it to bounce ideas off of one another and grow our own programs. Nobody knows for sure what's going to happen with the

Internet, but we do know it can connect us in ways that never could have happened when we met back in social work school. My guess is there's some 20-year-old who's already advanced to something else."

"You mean like teleporting?" They both laughed, as Kay had been a *Star Trek* fan since high school. "I can only hope, but your idea sounds great! I'll text Esperanza right now and see what she thinks." Kay whipped out her Blackberry and punched in a brief message before returning to her breakfast.

"Hey, look at you . . . you're 21st century and don't even know it." Ellis paused for a second as he took a bite of his multigrain muffin. "This could be a great way to connect and strategize together, *and* I find myself texting during meals, too. Maybe one of the things we can talk about is how to make these connections work for us without them taking over all our lives."

Kay finished her granola with Greek yogurt and blueberries and burst out laughing. "Gee, that's great, Ellis! So, we get to start our 'community of practice' group with a new practice dilemma! Thanks a lot!"

Educational Policy 2.1.5—Advance human rights and social and economic justice (in new ways). This chapter focuses on the new ways "social workers recognize the global interconnections of oppression and are knowledgeable about theories of justice and strategies to promote human and civil rights." They "understand the forms and mechanisms of oppression and discrimination; advocate for human rights and social and economic justice; and engage in practices that advance social and economic justice."

THE NEW WORLD OF 21ST CENTURY MACRO PRACTICE: SOCIAL NETWORKING AND COMMUNITY ORGANIZING

The extraordinary and highly successful use of the Internet by the Obama presidential campaigns in both 2007–2008 and 2011–2012 was the culmination of a new, globally based form of Internet organizing that had begun back in the 1990s through the efforts of the Zapatistas and their work with the Chiapas Indians in Southern Mexico (Mattiane, 2003). Beginning with a modest effort for fundraising and information sharing regarding the indigenous Indians' efforts against an exploitative oligarchy of landowners and government officials, by the 21st century, it had morphed—and continues to do so—at an exponential rate in ways that macro practitioners are still coming to understand. That said, it is clear that just as print media are forever changed by the Internet, so, too, will be community organizing and other forms of macro practice (Stoecker, 2002). As the Arab Spring of 2011 underscored, any activity that is information based—whether it's a newspaper, a presidential political campaign, or a local crusade for the rights of battered women, displaced elders, or LGBTQ youth—must become comfortable with and utilize the social-networking capabilities offered through the Internet or face being increasingly less effective.

What follows builds on a rich case study from the first edition by examining how Internet organizing has expanded since 2008 in the fight for same-sex marriage. Taken together, the two versions of the study provide a concrete example of how explosive and far ranging the use of social-networking tools can be in developing a grassroots campaign. It begins with the initial response by LGBTQ activists to the passage of Proposition 8, a California referendum that outlawed gay marriage. The original case study was developed by my colleague Mohan Krishna Vinjamuri; he now expands his work by examining the work of the Courage Campaign, an Internet-based organization deeply involved in national efforts directed toward same-sex marriage and other issues of equality. While we did edit the earlier case study slightly, we have left most of it intact, as the organizing lessons, dilemmas, and reflective issues of Internet organizing remain important for all macro practitioners to consider in the years ahead.

BACKGROUND: THE MIX OF OPPORTUNITY AND OPPOSITION THAT BUILDS SOCIAL MOVEMENTS

As so often happens with grassroots organizing campaigns that grow quickly from one community to another, their origins seem to combine a mix of two powerful factors wrought from the juncture of long-time historic, collective experience of oppression and immediate personal awareness that change was not only necessary but long overdue. Such was the case with Rosa Parks, the Birmingham Bus Boycott, and the civil rights movement in the 1950s, when a woman trained as an organizer at the Highlander Center refused to give up her seat to a White man, igniting a crusade mobilizing tens of thousands that went far beyond transportation and transformed American society (Branch, 2006; Fisher, 1994). The mix of long-standing social injustice for African Americans, the personal grievances of World War II veterans (who were now leaders in their segregated Black communities) denied the G.I. benefits on mortgages and education that their White counterparts received, and the emerging prosperity across America in the 1950s that seemingly ushered in a new age of freedom and opportunity created the necessary mix of anger and hope, opportunity and opposition, that organizers seized on to build a movement that transcended the small, incremental efforts of the past and created what seemingly overnight became a sea change (Branch, 2006; Davis, 1999; Williams & Bond, 1988).

An equivalent mixture of harsh conditions and hopeful aspirations was at play for the LGBTQ community in 2008. Since the early 1980s, gay and lesbian activists leading the HIV-AIDS movement had expanded their efforts into civil rights issues of employment, discrimination, and antiviolence so that across the country once-closeted people were now open activists (Shepard & Hayduk, 2002; Vaid, 1995). At the same time, the rise of the fundamentalist and evangelical religious movements that began growing during the Reagan years continued to espouse often virulent, homophobic messages to their communities, resulting in a significant increase in the level of reported antigay violence across America (Chapman, 2008).

The tensions wrought by these social dynamics have resulted in both enormous gains for and antagonistic opposition to gay marriage. Not unlike the Birmingham boycott, seemingly overnight, 13 individual states and the District of Columbia (as well as the entire nation of Canada) have ratified the right of all people to marry as they choose. Other states and their legislatures have done the exact opposite, by passing a constitutional amendment banning marriage and other forms of relationship recognition for same-sex couples. For detailed information about each state's laws regarding marriage and relationship recognition for same-sex couples, go to www.familyequality.org and click on "Equality Maps." When it comes to gay marriage, both opportunity and opposition were at play across the United States—and have continued into 2012 and 2013.

Nowhere did these dynamics develop as fiercely in 2008 as they did in the most populous state in the union—California. Buttressed by a California State Supreme Court ruling that legalized gay marriage, hundreds, if not thousands, of couples quickly married on the steps of city halls across the state, as well as in churches and synagogues in communities large and small. Alarmed at what they perceived as an attack on the sanctity of marriage, powerful religious groups, especially from the Catholic and Mormon churches, used all their legal and legislative power to initiate a statewide referendum known as Proposition 8 opposing the right of gay marriage and overriding the court decision (McKinley, 2009). Because California was home to some of the most progressive unions, civil rights, and environmental groups in the nation—as well as one of the largest and longest-standing openly gay communities in the country, in the San Francisco Bay Area—the battle was joined against Prop 8 with as much ferocity and intensity as any social movement campaign in more than 30 years (Bloch, 2007).

As has been well documented, what happened in California in 2008 while the rest of the nation focused on the ascendancy of America's first African American president was the narrow victory of Prop 8. Given enormous financial and logistical support from the Mormon Church in the latter months of the campaign, the proposition's backers eked out a narrow victory that stunned liberal activists across what was thought to be the most socially progressive state in the nation. Such a defeat, if it had happened during the Reagan and Bush years, probably would have taken months, if not years, to recover from before attempts to mobilize a new response could begin. As this original case study makes clear, however, because of the power of the Internet and the tools of social networking, all it took was two women and 24 hours to reignite the campaign for gay marriage. As will be seen below, 4 years later, this same effort—now national in focus—has been championed in part by Internet organizers at the Courage Campaign. Its efforts are credited in no small part with influencing the Supreme Court's decision to let stand the California Federal Court ruling that had earlier invalidated Prop 8 as unconstitutional.

The stories of Join the Impact (JTI) and the Courage Campaign (CC) raise interesting questions about how the Internet, particularly social-networking platforms, can influence resources, constituencies, coalition building, trust, and identity in community organizing. What unique opportunities do Internet tools offer to people who may not necessarily identify as organizers but want to get involved? How does the Internet make it possible for an organizing community such as JTI or CC to grow so rapidly? How do electronic media influence the formation of new political identities within marginalized groups such as LGBTQ communities? The remarkable story begun by these two women and further developed by four staffers in CC has key organizing lessons for macro practitioners regarding the use of the Internet and social networking as tools for mobilization.

"JOIN THE IMPACT": POST–PROPOSITION 8 AND THE BIRTH OF AN INTERNET-FUELED NATIONAL CAMPAIGN

The day after the passing of Prop 8, Amy Balliett and Willow Witte, two friends and activists—the former living in Washington State, the latter in Ohio—started an e-mail conversation about their next steps to overturn Prop 8. Soon after, on November 5, 2008, Balliett launched JointheImpact.com. As both women had already been organizing folks in opposition to Prop 8 in their respective states, they simply sent out a mass e-mail to friends and other activists to plan their next steps, which included a mass protest.

Balliett and Witte had expected perhaps four cities to become involved in a protest against Prop 8. They assumed that after this protest, they would resume their local activism. By November 10, the national protest they were organizing went international, with more than 10 countries signing on. By November 12, Balliett and Witte were discussing how to become a nonprofit, and by November 14, they were forming a board. What started as an e-mail conversation and a blog eventually mushroomed into an Internet campaign that rallied more than a quarter of a million people, who all took to the streets on November 15, 2008, in more than 320 cities across 11 countries.

Balliett said that it was "incredibly surprising" to her how the JTI online and offline communities snowballed (A. Balliett, personal communication, 2009). By the end of its first day, JointheImpact.com had received 10,000 visitors. Balliett, whose full-time profession is designing websites and developing ways to traffic people to them, said that it typically takes 6 months for a website to receive this many visitors. In the first few days of JTI, she received numerous e-mails from folks suggesting ways to improve the site. She was thrilled that so many people wanted to get involved so quickly. Within 3 days of JTI's launch, Wetpaint, an organization that helps individuals and groups develop their own websites, contacted Balliett to offer its services. Wetpaint is a social-networking tool that, as Balliett describes, "puts the power in the hands of the people" by providing organizers with the resources and tools they need to launch and activate their campaigns (Wetpaint, 2012).

A longtime activist, Balliett created the JTI website for several reasons. She was frustrated with the current model of organizing, where grassroots organizers needed to wait for community organizations and organizing collectives to initiate campaigns. She wanted to put the power and capability to organize directly in the hands of individual organizers. Thus, she started JTI as a call to action. She also wanted to create a website for LGBTQ people to come together and for other communities to obtain information that dispelled myths about LGBTQ folks, provided resources, and stimulated dialogue on LGBTQ rights. In this way, she was developing a classic macro mix of organizing and support so vital to sustainable grassroots campaigns.

REFLECTIVE ACTIVITY

- In what ways could your recent campaign or organizational event have utilized social networking to improve discussion and information sharing with activists and supporters?

_____

_____

_____

- Can you add a discussion board or chat room to your next significant activity? Explore in your team how this can be set up.

_____

_____

_____

JTI's efforts spawned monthly vigils in cities across the nation that have served as vital connecting rods to these and other efforts within the LGBTQ community. Since the launch of JTI, the LGBTQ community has also won significant victories that occurred because of local organizing on the ground in states and communities across the country. Marriage equality gained in three states—Iowa, Vermont, and Maine. These states joined Massachusetts and Connecticut as states that have legalized same-sex marriage. The Matthew Shepard Act, which expands hate crimes legislation to include hate crimes based on sexual orientation and gender identity, has passed in both the U.S. House of Representatives and the U.S. Senate. Initiatives to repeal the "Don't Ask, Don't Tell" policy for LGBTQ people in the military and to strengthen legislation prohibiting employment discrimination based on sexual orientation and gender identity through the Employee Non-Discrimination Act are moving through Congress.

Like all social movements, however, the fight for LGBTQ equality and justice is marked by both victories and defeats. Prop 8, the referendum that sparked the creation of JTI, was upheld by the California Supreme Court in May 2009—only to be later over-turned by a federal judge. At the same time, lesbians and gays continue not to be able either to adopt children or to serve as foster parents in Florida. Boy Scouts of America now allows scouts who are gay to join, but not scout leaders who are gay. Given the ongoing and turbulent social and political dynamics across America connected to gay rights, JTI's efforts initially spawned monthly vigils in cities across the nation that have served as vital connecting rods to these and other efforts within the LGBTQ community. Such connectiv-ity has now been carried on by the Courage Campaign as well.

JTI'S INTERNET TOOLS AND TECHNOLOGIES

As an Internet-based campaign, JTI began using a range of Internet technologies that have provided organizers with a number of strategic tools. These tools offer two key benefits of Internet organizing: *interactivity and interconnectedness* (Stirland, 2008). The JTI website has two main sections. One offers news and information about important events, past and upcoming initiatives, and blogs that provide people with forums for sharing their opinions on a range of issues related to the LGBTQ equality movement. The website also serves as a timeline and archive for significant organizing initiatives sponsored by JTI since November 2008. One can enter the site and learn about the entire history of organizing campaigns related to same-sex marriage following Prop 8.

The other section of the website is interactive. Using Wetpaint, JTI created a social website—a site that anyone can edit and expand with text, photos, and links to online resources. Most of the content on a social website is created by its users, a concept called *end user creation*. One need not have particular technological expertise to edit the site. Social websites are ideal for people who have common interests and need to collaborate around particular problems or issues (Wetpaint, n.d.). Because everyone can contribute to the site, each person can be actively involved in the efforts of the group. Since November 2008, the JTI website has been updated by its users many times each day with new events, status updates on current initiatives, and calls to action. According to Spaeth (2009), citizens are demanding to be part of the story, not just viewers or readers of a story, a phenomenon called "citizen journalism" (p. 441). Through discussion boards and wikis, participants share their opinions about various issues as well as information about protests, rallies, and other organizing events in their localities. One of the most influential media for sharing information and experiences, according to Spaeth, has been videos. The Obama campaign and other Internet organizing campaigns, such as JTI, have shown that videos are among the most powerful communication tools used on social websites because audiences have been found to watch video postings over and over again (Spaeth, 2009).

A social website can be used to centralize the knowledge of a group or a consortium of groups. The JTI online community offers a prime location for states and localities to disseminate information about their current political landscapes and about local initiatives and events. Consequently, anyone who visits the site can find out what is happening across the United States and in countries worldwide at any given time by accessing links to that locality's particular website. Not unlike Ellis's call "to think local, act global," the website allows people to put out a call to action across the Internet for a rally, organize who will be leading the rally, and then spread the word about the details of the rally around the world. *What typically has happened in scheduled face-to-face organizing meetings and strategy sessions over a period of weeks or months is now happening online at any time of day on any day of the week.*

For example, through JTI, nationwide events were organized, such as the rallies at city halls on November 15, 2009, protests of Prop 8, marches to marriage licensing bureaus on Valentine's Day, and Day of Decision campaigns following the ruling of the California Supreme Court on Prop 8. Many types of media and tactics have been used, including street protests, boycotts of companies and products that do not support LGBTQ equality, and letter-writing campaigns to Congress and President Obama. Importantly, discussion boards and blogs provide forums for people to immediately share what they liked and disliked about these campaigns and offer suggestions for improving organizing tactics for the next event.

This mix of community development–like support mechanisms, forums for feedback and exchange that follow a feminist model of reciprocity and relationship, and the classic social-action/power-based focus on immediate change in cities across the nation all combine to suggest the transformative possibilities within the work of JTI and equivalent Internet campaigns of the future. That said, its formation clearly has developed from the extraordinary success of the Obama presidential campaign of 2007–2008. It needs to be looked at carefully for the lessons it provides macro practitioners in the coming years.

INTERNET ORGANIZING GROWS IN SCOPE AND IMPACT: THE COURAGE CAMPAIGN OF 2011–2013

Since writing how opponents of Prop 8 enlisted the Internet and social media to fight for same-sex marriage in California in the dawn of Barack Obama's first term, much has happened in the world of online activism, not just in the area of same-sex marriage and LGBTQ rights and equality in the United States but also on the international stage. We have seen citizens in Egypt, Morocco, and elsewhere in the Arab world seize the power of solidarity to topple regimes that had the grip on power for decades. We have witnessed people mobilize against the oppression of big business on the streets of the financial district in Lower Manhattan and 800 other cities through the Occupy Wall Street movement. And we have experienced an unprecedented movement toward full equality for LGBTQ people in the United States, which includes

- ✓ the defeat of Prop 8 in the California courts,
- ✓ the legalization of same-sex marriage through legislatures or voter referenda in 13 states and the District of Columbia,
- ✓ the repeal of the "Don't Ask, Don't Tell" policy prohibiting LGBTQ armed-services members from disclosing their sexual orientation or gender identity, and
- ✓ the passage of hate crimes legislation that includes bias-motivated violence based on sexual orientation and gender identity.

The 2012 presidential campaign also saw the first public declaration of support for same-sex marriage by a sitting president of the United States. And, finally, the Supreme Court ruled in June 2013 that the Defense of Marriage Act (DOMA), which sanctioned marriage only between heterosexual couples, was unconstitutional. The ruling, while not so sweeping as to invalidate state laws on same-sex marriage, was nevertheless powerful, as it affirmed the dignity of all people to join in matrimony if they so choose:

> DOMA singles out a class of persons deemed by a State entitled to recognition and protection to enhance their own liberty. It imposes a disability on the class by refusing to acknowledge a status the State finds to be dignified and proper. DOMA instructs all federal officials, and indeed all persons with whom same-sex couples interact, including their own children, that their marriage is less worthy than the marriages of others. The federal statute is invalid, for no legitimate purpose overcomes the purpose and effect to disparage and to injure those whom the State, by its marriage laws, sought to protect in personhood and dignity. (Terkel, 2013)

These 5 years have witnessed what can be a remarkable organizing lesson for all practitioners: By opposing same-sex marriage in California, Prop 8 and its proponents helped unleash a tidal wave of activity for and against same-sex marriage and LGBTQ equality across this country that greatly energized the seemingly defeated LGBTQ anti–Prop 8 forces of 2008. Social work practitioners need to remain aware of this dynamic interplay between the push for social change and the social and political backlash to reassert and even strengthen the status quo, as new issues and challenges—and obvious opportunities— will emerge in the years ahead. Thus, at the same time as technology advances at what seems like ever-faster rates and figures even more prominently in people's lives, the use of these technologies to bring about change underscores even more poignantly the power of human beings themselves—their desires, their suffering, and their enormous ability to connect deeply with one another and the world around them.

Prop 8 and LGBTQ Equality

As the work of JTI makes clear, one can see how in a matter of weeks two women could spawn an online community of thousands that led to street protests of a quarter million people in 320 cities in 2008 and 2009. As happens so often in organizing efforts, JTI is no longer as active as it was during those emotional times, but its impact in California and on the LGBTQ equality movement is still felt 4 years later.

In a similar fashion to JTI, one of the leaders in the fight for these efforts has been Courage Campaign (CC; www.couragecampaign.org), an online organizing network of 750,000 members advocating for LGBTQ equality and other social and economic justice issues in California and across the United States. CC was founded in 2005 by Rick Jacobs—a former businessman and campaign manager for Howard Dean in California— as an online grassroots movement in California fighting for equality for the LGBTQ community. In recent years, CC has been a key player in the fight to defeat Prop 8 and legalize same-sex marriage in California and nationwide. CC's huge online network is spearheaded by Adam Bink, director of Online Programs, and a staff of three. Bink oversees all communication with CC's members through Twitter, Facebook, blogs, and traditional e-mail. CC defines a "member" as any person who has participated in at least one online action with the organization. The issues that CC chooses to advocate for can be divided into what Bink calls the "gay shop" and the "not gay shop"—that is, issues related to LGBTQ equality and those that on the surface are not LGBTQ related (e.g., health care, tax reform, education funding) (A. Bink, personal communication, 2012). Some issues are California specific, while others are specific to other states—such as getting out the vote for same-sex marriage in Washington during the November 2012 elections. Other campaigns have national implications, such as the movement to repeal the federal Defense of Marriage Act, which allows states not to recognize same-sex marriages performed in other states. In short, CC has deepened the use of social media and Internet technologies in the LGBTQ equality movement since the passage of Prop 8 that also will inform other organizing efforts in the fight for social justice.

From Blogs to Videos to Facebook Timelines

The legal process that Prop 8 ignited since 2009 has been complicated and progressing along different tracks that have made their way through the courts simultaneously. (For a detailed description of the timeline of the case along each of these tracks, see www.couragecampaign.org.) *Perry v. Brown,* the trial in California following passage of Prop 8, was filed in 2009 in the U.S. District Court for the Northern District of California, on behalf of two same-sex couples who were denied marriage licenses. A nonjury trial took place and resulted in a ruling striking down Prop 8 as unconstitutional in August 2010. This was followed almost immediately by an appeal to the Ninth Circuit Court of Appeals by the proponents of Prop 8. The appellate court stayed the previous ruling by the lower court, which meant that same-sex marriages would be put on hold. A stay on a ruling is granted if it can be shown that not overturning the ruling would lead to particularized injuries to the parties involved. Due to complicated legal circumstances, the hearing on the appeal was delayed until late in 2011. A ruling on the appeal was issued in early 2012, whereby the appellate court maintained that Prop 8 is unconstitutional. This was followed by a request by proponents of Prop 8 for a larger panel of judges in the appellate court to reconsider the appeal. Due to a complex set of legal circumstances, this request was denied. As a result, the proponents of Prop 8 asked the U.S. Supreme Court to take up the case. Despite opponents of Prop 8 asking the Supreme Court not to take up the case, the high court eventually decided to review it. At issue for the court is whether the Equal Protection Clause of the Fourteenth Amendment prohibits the state of California from defining marriage as the union of a man and a woman. The Equal Protection Clause was the basis for the *Brown v. Board of Education* ruling that led to the end of legalized racial segregation in education.

In 2010, the U.S. Supreme Court overturned a California judge's ruling allowing the *Perry v. Brown* trial to be televised. As a result, the public could have no access to the court proceedings as they unfolded. In response, CC set up the Prop 8 Trial Tracker (now Equality on Trial; equalityontrial.com), which covered the trial live from the courthouse and collected all the latest motions and court rulings on one website. Bink started the Prop 8 Trial Tracker as a blog in the summer of 2010 to provide information about the trial and document and respond to right-wing attacks on the legal process.

As a good organizer developing his campaign, Bink's early intention in blogging was to make the details of the Prop 8 trial accessible to the layperson. At the same time, the Prop 8 Trial Tracker was also used to track and publicize the movements and activities of anti-LGBTQ-equality organizations, such as the National Organization for Marriage. Because of his consistent blogging, if one types "Proposition 8" into the Google search engine today, one of the first hits will be for Equality on Trial (formerly the Prop 8 Trial Tracker). As community practitioners know, information is power—and ready access to information through the Internet is power squared.

The level of real-time detail in Equality on Trial was astounding. For more than a year, Bink and his staff provided almost up-to-the-minute developments as the trial unfolded in the courtroom. The Prop 8 Trial Tracker was also a forum for blogging and commenting about the trial among its members—a powerful community-building tool for informing, engaging, and energizing membership around the nation. Four years after what seemed like the defeat of LGBTQ activists and their allies, prop8trialtracker.com (now equalityontrial.com) had reached more than 5 million views and received 175,000 comments (see www.couragecampaign.org)—hardly the end of a movement, as some commentators had expected 4 years earlier.

Online technology brought the Prop 8 trial to people's living rooms. This highlights the importance of transparency in trials dealing with socially divisive issues and the need to provide real-time accurate information to members of a community concerned with a particular cause (with or without trials). Communication forums such as Equality on Trial provide people who may live hundreds of miles apart the chance to bear witness together and participate collectively in the making of history.

GROUP OR INDIVIDUAL ACTIVITY

Choose a vital organizing issue for your group:

- What type of blog could you create that would post at least weekly updates?
- How would you sign up members?
- What would you have them comment on?
- How often (if at all) would you call for other activities?

Bink explained that in many ways social media "drove" the Prop 8 trial. For example, in early 2011, the Ninth Circuit Court of Appeals in California announced that it would take up the appeal against the ruling that Prop 8 was unconstitutional only later that year. In the meantime, same-sex couples in California would have to continue to wait in limbo and would not be allowed to get married. Upon hearing of this delay in the trial, CC asked its members to send in videos documenting their experiences. For example, two elderly men—one with Alzheimer's—who had been together for decades and could not get married, sent in their story. These videos went viral, and eventually mainstream media outlets such as *The New York Times*, the *Los Angeles Times* and *The Washington Post* covered the effects of this delay on the lives of same-sex couples. Through videos of powerful and moving personal testimonies, information about the trial could be made public and then have an impact on public opinion. Similarly, after the recent decision by the Supreme Court to take up the Prop 8 case, CC launched a campaign to raise funds to "educat[e] the Supreme Court, chang[e] hearts and minds so a larger majority of Americans support marriage equality, and mov[e] stories into the media and public sphere that show how important marriage equality is to same-sex couples" (Courage Campaign, 2012).

Videos continue to be a powerful tool in online activism. During the 2012 presidential campaign, the CC Super PAC, in collaboration with American Bridge 21st Century, created Mittgetsworse.org. Using video testimonies from LGBTQ folks who lived in Massachusetts when Mitt Romney was governor, the site provides an oral history of Mitt Romney's record of stripping rights from LGBTQ Americans. In addition, the site contains a link to a Facebook timeline created by CC staff documenting Romney's statements, positions, and voting record on LGBTQ issues over his political career. Tools such as the Facebook timeline once again show the power of images in conveying a powerful narrative while efficiently and effectively providing detailed information. Using these Internet media, CC helped mobilize the LGBTQ base in the recent presidential election.

Influencing Public Attitudes Toward Gay Marriage: Connecting Campaign Narratives

After the national and state elections of 2012, 13 states and the District of Columbia now have full marriage equality. Six of these passed same-sex marriage in 2010 or later. Seven more states have broad relationship recognition laws; in other words, through civil unions or domestic partnerships, they extend to same-sex couples all or nearly all the state rights and responsibilities extended to married couples (see www.familyequality council.org). At the same time, however, laws in a number of states continue to be or have become more restrictive in the recognition of same-sex relationships. Public support for same-sex marriage has steadily increased. Attitudes toward gay marriage in the United States significantly liberalized from 1988 to 2006, with 71% opposing gay marriage in 1988 and 52% opposing gay marriage in 2006 (Baunach, 2011). Baunach attributes most of this attitudinal shift to intracohort change, which is individuals changing their attitudes over time; the remainder is due to later (and younger) cohorts replacing previous ones. For example, surveys in 2012 show that 66% of people under age 30 support gay marriage, compared with just 29% of those over 65 (Cohen, 2012).

One of the questions addressed in the first edition of this chapter was how online organizing affects the constituencies for various causes and more quickly connects them to one another. According to Bink, since 2009, social media and the Internet have sped up public support for same-sex marriage and equality. People who once were opposed to same-sex marriage, or those who perhaps had not given marriage much thought and had taken this right for granted, are now advocating for same-sex marriage. When asked who these people are, Bink spoke about the "movable middle" (A. Bink, personal communication, 2012). Much was said in the run-up to the 2012 presidential election about "swing voters" and "independents." What moves the "movable middle" when it comes to same-sex marriage and other LGBTQ-related issues?

CONTEXTUALIZING THE PRESENT-DAY STRUGGLE TO LONGER-TERM ORGANIZING EFFORTS

As with any organizing effort, first it is important to locate the present-day actions within the long-term narrative developed by previous generations. For example, any gain in the LGBTQ movement today gains greater authority by using the narrative threads of past LGBTQ issues to frame its demands. The author and activist Baunach (2011) argued that the two dominant and opposing constructs that have been used historically to frame gay marriage are *equality and morality*. Those fighting for gay marriage and other rights for LGBTQ people have often used the language of equality to highlight discrimination and to advocate for more just and equitable laws and policies. Those opposing gay marriage have often done so on the grounds that homosexuality is morally wrong and that sanctioning gay marriage would weaken the moral fabric of American society. Baunach claims that public opinion about gay marriage has moved toward an equality perspective and away from a morality perspective over the past several decades. This example mirrors the civil rights struggle led by African Americans that began in the South more than 60 years ago, where activists moved the discussion toward equality and social justice and away from respect for tradition and fear of violence. And just as public opinion shifted then, leading to the Voting Rights Act of 1965, so, too, do the opinions and attitudes of political leaders shift today. LGBTQ activists and practitioners alike can take hope for the long-term direction of their movement, as recent years show an unprecedented number of elected officials endorsing equality for LGBTQ people.

Using CC's example, how can community activists working on a social issue or program find a common cause when groups have had a history of division and distance? One of the powers of social media is that it provides a forum for linking multiple issues. For example, the *narrative of equality* has allowed activists in the LGBTQ movement to encompass a wide range of social issues, from LGBTQ people serving in the military to LGBTQ youth being bullied to same-sex marriage. Thus, someone who is not in favor of marriage rights for same-sex couples may be moved by a Facebook post about LGBTQ teens being bullied and committing suicide. The post may contain a video sharing the story of the teen's parents or a graphic showing rates of bullying among different groups of teens. Bink explains that the combination of

- ✓ the content of the post,
- ✓ the manner in which information is conveyed, and
- ✓ the fact that it was posted by a "reputable" source (e.g., one's family member, a trusted Facebook friend)

contribute to shifting the attitude of the user about that issue and related issues.

In short, social media allows for long-term organizing narratives to be immediately and powerfully connected to the issues of the day to make connections across issues, populations, and programs. CC has done this—as can all community practitioners.

INDIVIDUAL OR GROUP ACTIVITY

Reexamine the issue you identified above. What common narrative can you create that links your issue to the "movable middle" needed to make your campaign a success?

1. Identify the common narrative value (equality, fairness, choice, voice, etc.) _____

_____

2. Create three concrete examples that reflect that same narrative value.

   a. _____

   b. _____

   c. _____

3. Now connect those three issues/concerns to your primary campaign, using CC's three tactics:

   a. The content of the post (the issue at hand, framed with a long-term narrative or value): _____

   b. The manner of the posts (Facebook campaigns/posts, Twitter, etc.): _____

   c. Reputable sources (family members, members of communities, etc.): _____

   _____

Think Local, Act Global

Internet technologies allow folks to pursue specific goals that are localized and yet still have a multipronged and comprehensive organizing agenda that has global reach that can engage and mobilize far more people than found within a geographic community—from petition campaigns to look at the ingredients in Gatorade, to support for Islamic girls wanting access to education in Afghanistan. Internet technologies give organizers and organizations unprecedented access to get involved in a wider variety of campaigns. For example, one click on the "Actions" link on the CC website shows a dizzying array of initiatives and calls to action on issues such as LGBTQ equality, health care, equity in education, tax reform, youth issues, the War on Drugs, and voting rights—to name just a few. Visitors to the site are invited to participate in a range of activities: put pressure on lawmakers through online petitions, share progressive voter guides, raise funds for television advertisements, participate in door-to-door get-out-the-vote campaigns, submit video and photo testimonials. While "real" organizations tend to do one or two actions at a time, different readers of the webpage can commit to differing levels of activism at the same time: One person may choose armchair activism through donations or testimonials, another to attend a militant demonstration targeting some opposition figure or event, and still another to become deeply involved in local efforts to get out the vote for an upcoming election or ballot initiative. Providing ways to involve multiple layers of membership at the same time is an important innovation of Internet organizing that undoubtedly will be refined over the coming years with even more effectiveness.

Decision Making

When asked how CC makes decisions about what campaigns to pursue, Bink explained that the staff poll members about which campaigns they feel are most important to devote resources to. For example, when faced with limited resources and gay marriage referenda being voted on in three states in the 2012 elections, members voted to devote all their financial and on-the-ground resources to get out the vote in Washington State.

In addition to developing an LGBTQ advocacy agenda that encompasses multiple progressive issues, one of the major shifts in recent years is that mainstream media outlets have begun to cover LGBTQ issues and causes. No longer are LGBTQ issues covered only in the small presses and media outlets on the fringes. Mainstream news and entertainment sources such as *The New York Times*, CNN, and ESPN are making gay rights prominent news items. The Prop 8 Trial Tracker, for example, attracted coverage from *The New Yorker, The New York Times*, the *San Francisco Chronicle*, and many other media outlets and blogs. Social media outlets such as YouTube and Facebook have been catalysts and portals for siphoning information to these mainstream outlets. Comunello and Anzera (2012) explain that social media serve two functions in mobilization. They serve as a means of organizing protest activities and as a vehicle for the spread of information through grassroots journalism. This illustrates what Jenkins (2006) describes as a "convergence culture" (p. 308), where old and new forms of media intersect and information from independent grassroots media and mainstream broadcast media flow back and forth.

The work led first by JTI and carried on by CC in the fight for same-sex marriage suggests that social media can serve several functions for any progressive social movement. They provide a space and forum for connection among those already in support of the issue (in this case, same-sex marriage). They offer vehicles to disseminate information about initiatives, legislation, statements, and positions almost continuously. They provide a means of linking issues and allow people a chance to see connections among issues. For

CC, this is particularly important for shifting attitudes toward same-sex marriage, gay and lesbian rights, and homosexuality, and for "reaching" folks whose attitudes may be "in the middle." Other movements, from Occupy Wall Street to environmental activism to those fighting for the rights of the mentally ill or the rights of immigrants, can do the same. In a related way, social media normalize or "mainstream-ize" issues that may otherwise be deemed fringe or alternative. By disseminating information so rapidly and on such a widespread scale, mainstream media are almost pressured into covering the issues.

Deepening the Political and Ideological Debates

Furthermore, established social media outlets such as CC also reawaken and reenergize long-standing political and ideological debates that are unique to the movement itself. For example, the use of social media to propel "gay" issues into the mainstream raises long-term ideological questions about the "gay movement" that LGBTQ activists have been having off and on for generations. What are the consequences of the mainstreaming of the gay movement? Is the national gay movement losing its potential for radically changing societal institutions (Epstein, 2013)? Some argue that focusing on issues such as the right to marry and serve openly in the military reinforces oppressive social institutions that sanctify patriarchy, aggression, and violence, rather than supplanting these institutions with new ways of thinking about and organizing social relations (Conrad, 2013). In the race for equality through the securing of rights to marriage, certain ideologies may become further sanctified, such as the notion that the only way to lead a good and moral life is by being in a monogamous relationship. To what extent are the needs, wishes, and rights of single LGBTQ people—particularly those who are poor or working class—being represented? Similar debates, altered to fit the content and texture of a particular movement's issues and actions, have long been under way in racially based civil rights movements, the environmental movement, and the recent Occupy Wall Street movement (Freeman, 2013).

Movement Expansion

The work of CC suggests that by using social media to bring together actions on a multitude of social and economic issues, there also is the potential for more of the LGBTQ community to be represented in other social action movements. How do social media play a role in shifting the culture and values of a movement? In the long run, people determine the culture of a community—but that culture is dynamically shifting as people interact and communicate with one another in an increasing number of different ways. Perhaps the speed with which people can connect through social media makes it hard to control the evolution of a movement's culture. All these are questions that beg future research.

THE OBAMA CAMPAIGN'S IMPACT ON INTERNET ORGANIZING

JTI's and CC'S widespread success suggests that there may be a new age of LGBTQ activism inspired and ignited by Barack Obama's initial presidential campaign, subsequent election, and powerful Internet-based reelection. Many younger folks—both LGBTQ identified and others—were inspired by Obama and subsequently campaigned for him and the social, economic, and political issues he championed. As is well-known, Obama is not only this country's first African American president; he is also the first with an extensive background as a community organizer, skills he used brilliantly over the course of his campaign (Moberg, 2007; Nather, 2008). Obama and his campaign strategists were masters of using Internet tools to organize campaign events, disseminate information about policy issues, and raise funds. Through e-mails, text messaging, online videos, and blogs on sites such as Facebook, YouTube, MySpace, Twitter, and Hulu, the Obama campaign ignited discussion, dialogue, collaboration, and tremendous initiative simultaneously on national, state, and local levels.

Of course, for almost as long as there has been an Internet, there has been Internet organizing. Kahn and Kellner (2004) nicely trace the history of present-day Internet activism back to the indigenous EZLN Zapatista movement in Mexico in the early 1990s and protests against neoliberalism and transnational capitalism beginning in the late 1990s. A number of social and political movements have also begun to employ tools of the Internet, particularly social networking, in their organizing and advocacy strategies. These include groups as disparate as labor unions (Pinnock, 2005), Catholics fighting for abortion rights (Bloch, 2007), transnational nongovernmental organizations (Custard, 2007), immigrant rights groups (Lovato, 2008), people living with HIV-AIDS (Gillett, 2003), and electoral/political organizers such as MoveOn.org (Newman, 2009). What distinguished Obama in his presidential race was that he and his staff saw a critical need in a critical mass of people at a critical time—the need to act and become involved both individually and collectively to bring about change in this country.

Realizing that this same mass of people comprised users and creators of the next revolution in Internet technology—social networking—Obama seized the opportunity to meet this need using powerful social-networking platforms. Obama's campaign website, myBarackObama.com (or myBO.com, as it was lovingly called by many of his supporters), provided an online space that encouraged individual initiative while promoting lasting relationships and collaborations among his supporters. The Obama campaign masterfully capitalized on these two forces by creating an online community forum where people could mobilize quickly and effectively for offline activism, a phenomenon called *flash activism* ("Wetpaint-Powered Flash Activism," 2009), all of which was expanded throughout the Arab Spring and Occupy Wall Street later on.

The Obama campaign illustrated the ways technology can give communities the capacity to self-organize on a large scale (Lovato, 2008). Kahn and Kellner (2004) describe how networks of citizens connected through technologies such as laptops, personal digital assistant (PDA) devices, cell phones, and global positioning systems (GPS) on blogs, wikis, and other online communities can be transformed from "'dumb mobs' of totalitarian and polyarchical states into 'smart mobs' of socially active personages" (p. 89). These smart mobs can then become flash mobs (Kahn & Kellner, 2004) that rapidly gather at sites to carry out particular actions. (JTI is such an example.)

In just a few years, Obama grew an online constituency of more than 13 million people and raised $750 million in campaign funds, half of which was in small donations made online (Borins, 2009). Obama's roots as a community organizer in Chicago were evident throughout his campaign. According to Stirland (2008), "the blend of gumshoe canvassing and information processing [was] a hallmark of the Obama campaign" (p. 3). While embracing new online technologies to recruit, mobilize, and inspire people, Obama and his campaign strategists never lost touch with the process of on-the-ground field organizing. Obama used technology as a "partner . . . bringing the efficiencies of the Internet into the real-world problems of organizing people in a distributed, trusted fashion" (p. 3). Underlying the enormous growth in Obama's grassroots support was his understanding of the need for evolving communication strategies at a time when new technologies were continually emerging. Through his persistent experimentation with new communication tools, Obama modeled the innovative spirit and risk taking he espoused as a presidential candidate ("How Obama Used Social Networking Tools to Win," 2009).

What sustained the energy of Obama's supporters over such a long period of time? Stirland (2008) explains that Obama appealed to people's right brains—the affective and emotional drivers of their activism—rather than focusing solely on stimuli associated with the left brain, such as people's need for logical and reasoned arguments around policy issues. An example of this strategy is the use of personal storytelling in the training workshops developed for campaign organizers. Personal storytelling was used as a way to motivate others to action by bringing together the personal and the political, something Obama demonstrated in his many speeches (Stirland, 2008). Senge (1990) similarly speaks about the integration of reason and intuition as essential to "personal mastery" (p. 167). Obama's use of social networking helped his supporters gain a "sense of ownership, a kind of positive entitlement" (Carr, 2008, para. 17). The dynamics of these online communities encouraged two-way conversations between activists and their leaders, which promoted a new kind of transparency in campaigning and governance (Carr, 2008). Obama's use of social-networking platforms during his campaigns has encouraged transparency and citizen dialogue (Borins, 2009).

What lessons can be learned from the Obama campaign? One question that has emerged is whether community organizers and activists for social justice can embrace the power of media and technology and their integral links to governance and power (Lovato, 2008). Sen and Kahn (2003) argue that we are now in an era when community organizers should support new social movements in gaining large-scale progressive change. This signals a shift in tactics. Whereas in the past, community organizers may have chosen smaller-scale issues that were "winnable" in the short term, community organizing groups in recent years have begun to organize the most marginalized people around issues that may be extremely difficult to change in the short term (Sen & Kahn, 2003). It is through a "think local, act global" approach that the difficulties and isolation that some groups experience at the local level may be overcome.

JTI is a wonderful example of a social justice movement that has seized and harnessed the power of Internet technology at a critical moment in this nation's history and in the history of LGBTQ civil rights.

IMPLICATIONS FOR FUTURE COMMUNITY ORGANIZING

Employing and embracing Internet technologies has implications for community organizing regarding four powerful elements that impact strategic development:

- Resources
- Constituencies
- Trust
- Collective identity

The following sections lay out each of these elements and then offer several questions that community organizers and other macro practitioners can explore through future practice and research, not only to use Internet technologies effectively but also to ignite campaigns capable of sustaining social justice movements.

Time as a Resource

Internet technologies can change the nature of time as a resource in community organizing. Social-networking sites such as JTI make it possible for a person to get involved in a flash. The lag time between feeling the urge or need to do something about an issue, finding an opportunity to get involved, and then taking action becomes extremely small—perhaps only a matter of minutes. The days are over when one had to find a phone number for a local community organization, call the organization, leave a message, and then wait for a return call before taking action. When technology provides opportunities for almost immediate action, time ceases to be a barrier to getting involved.

Furthermore, sites such as JTI shift people's use of time. With Internet access, a person can become involved in a campaign at any time of day from virtually anywhere in the world for any amount of time. Thus, the Internet allows people more flexibility with their use of time. One can become involved for as little or as much time as one wishes and do so while attending to the myriad other responsibilities and demands of one's life. The Internet allows people to integrate their organizing and activism into the rest of their lives.

Constituencies and Coalition Building

To understand how the Internet has been helping reshape coalition building in organizing, one needs to go back to the first major event launched by JTI: the massive city hall rallies following the passing of Prop 8 on November 15, 2008. On that day, more than 250,000 people in more than 320 cities in 11 countries simultaneously staged rallies at city halls to protest Prop 8 and celebrate the beginning of what some described as the "civil rights battle of our generation." More than 3,000 people attended the rally at City Hall in New York City. Immediately upon arriving at the rally site, one was struck by the youth of the organizers on stage and of the participants. All but one of the New York City organizers for JTI was of college age. In other cities, the age range was more varied. According to Balliett (personal communication, 2009), people involved with JTI and subsequent organizing since those November rallies include activists who have been fighting for LGBTQ equality since the Stonewall rebellion and before, as well as younger LGBTQ activists who have grown up in the Internet age and are savvy about the many uses of electronic media. As also seen through the Occupy Wall Street movement in 2011 to 2013, it is clear that intergenerational campaigns become feasible through Internet work.

Perhaps following messages from the Obama campaign, one of the predominant cries at many rallies that day was to find new allies who would champion the cause of LGBTQ equality. Speakers called on LGBTQ folks not to make assumptions about a person's stance on LGBTQ rights and equality based on his or her religious affiliation, political leaning, or sexual orientation. Speaker after speaker called for reaching out across identity divisions, to "our Republican allies, our straight allies, our Christian allies." Many reminded the crowds that though someone may not favor same-sex marriage on a moral or emotional level, he or she may fight vehemently for equal rights for LGBTQ people as a matter of principle and upholding democracy. This call for connecting with others proactively rather than defensively is reflected in JTI's mission statement:

> Our movement seeks to encourage the LGBTQ community not to look towards the past and place blame, but instead to look forward at what needs to be done **now** to achieve one goal: Full equality for ALL. We stand for reaching out across all communities. We do not stand for bigotry, for scapegoating, or using anger as our driving force. Our mission is to encourage our community to engage our opposition in a conversation about full equality and to do this with respect, dignity, and an attitude of outreach and education. (JTI, 2008)

The sheer energy, anger, and optimism of the folks revealed something significant happening in the history of movements for LGBTQ equality. While responding to the present crisis and envisioning the future, participants also created an atmosphere of reflection on where we are as LGBTQ communities, where we have come from, and where we must go. Furthermore, the Internet is shifting: The "who" is encompassed within *we*. Today's organizing is operating in a more complex era, where boundaries between individuals, communities, nationalities, nations, and groups have been narrowed in many ways. These boundaries have been blurred and in some instances eliminated through the Internet, which has brought people together who might never have come together during the predigital age. Using electronic media, JTI has helped expand the constituency fighting for LGBTQ equality and justice.

Throughout the campaigns following Prop 8, the tenor of the debate surrounding same-sex marriage and LGBTQ rights often invoked the spirit and language of the civil rights movement. Some have called the mass mobilization that followed the passing of Prop 8 the "second Stonewall." At the November 15 rallies, many people carried signs invoking Martin Luther King, Jr. and his dream for African American people and this country. Spurred on by Obama's now-infamous phrase, "Yes we can," organizers repeated the mantra, "Yes we will," suggesting that same-sex marriage and full equality for LGBTQ people are bound to become reality throughout this country. At the heart of this expansion of constituency, newfound energy, and a shift in the discourse around LGBTQ issues is the practice of new forms of Internet-based communication and dialogue. How have tools and strategies offered by the Internet fostered this communication to catalyze people to come together for a common cause?

Shifting the Discourse

One of the most significant aspects of JTI is that it has provided a forum for people to express their opinions and engage in meaningful dialogue with one another about some of the most emotionally and politically charged issues in contemporary society. For example, a woman from Los Angeles, Jane _____,[1] who became active soon after JTI was launched in November 2008, immediately identified herself as "straight, White, and Christian." Jane grew up in the segregated South. She had worked on the "No on 8" campaigns in California prior to the November elections. When Prop 8 was passed on November 4, she, like many others, was enraged. She began looking for ways to get further connected to the LGBTQ community and become even more involved in fighting for LGBTQ equality and justice. She joined the Human Rights Campaign, one of the nation's largest LGBTQ advocacy organizations. Within a few days, she came across JTI and noticed a section on the website for straight allies. She started participating in a discussion around the question, "How to get more straight allies?"

Importantly, Jane stated that speaking openly with others via discussion boards has been easier than speaking in face-to-face meetings, where she feels more discomfort talking to people she does not know. Jane explained that online conversations do not have the nonverbal communication that can impede face-to-face and even phone communication. Through these online discussions, Jane has become involved with boycotts of products and companies that do not support LGBTQ equality and campaigns to contact elected officials regarding LGBTQ rights. Jane said that through JTI, she has learned so much so quickly. This is important, she says, for people such as her who, until recently, had not thought about marriage from an equality perspective. She admitted that, for most of her life, she had thought that "marriage is between a man and a woman and that's it." It was not until she started realizing that certain folks in this country were denied the right to marry that she began to look at marriage through the lens of equality and justice. She sees Prop 8 as a violation of the principle of separation of church and state and a matter of equal access under the law. Jane's experiences suggest how potent Internet communication can be in stimulating reflection and action, the essential ingredients for cultivating what Freire (2000) calls *critical reflection*. How can Internet chat rooms on other sites like JTI foster this kind of sustained dialogue for people who can become allies?

Such questions are important to answer. Jane, when asked about what it was like for her to be a straight person working for LGBTQ equality, replied that most of her conversations on JTI and in offline organizing groups she volunteers with in Los Angeles are with LGBTQ folks. She explains that at actual meetings, "it is awkward to be the only straight person in the room." She is often met initially with some skepticism about her motivations for being there. She finds that she and her LGBTQ allies "have to go out of their way to break the ice." At the same time, Jane's activism with the LGBTQ community has spurred conversations with her straight friends and family members, often with the intention of informing them of issues they may not have thought about in terms of equality for LGBTQ people. Jane's experiences suggest that Internet technologies might be shifting the nature of trust in relationships among activists and organizers and creating new ways to build this trust. This phenomenon has been described as the *virtual trust* in Internet communities (Alfredson & Themudo, 2007). How does one use the dialogue in chat rooms to extend this trust into our meeting rooms in local communities so that everyone who is supportive feels welcome?

Virtual Trust: Creating a New Collective Identity?

What are the dynamics of trust in virtual communities, such as in discussion boards and online task groups? Traditionally, trust in community organizing groups is built on the reliability of following one's words with concrete actions and the credibility gained by doing what others do not want to do (Kahn, 2010; Staples, 2004). Alfredson and Themudo

(2007) raise the question of how to generate this kind of trust in the absence of face-to-face communication in what they call *dot-causes*. Most of the emerging literature on virtual trust is in the area of consumer–business relationships in online business enterprises, virtual organizational teams in the business sector, and online learning communities (see de Laat, 2005, for examples). De Laat offers evidence that shows that people do, in fact, invest high levels of trust in one another in different types of Internet communities, including trading communities involving the exchange of goods, online task groups, and support groups. The building and sustaining of trust in online organizing and social justice communities such as JTI is an important area for future exploration.

We can learn something about the nature of trust from the ways Obama led his presidential campaign. He not only appealed to people's capacities for reason and logic when considering political issues and social policies (the left-brain approach); he also drew on their need to connect emotionally with the issues, with one another, and with him as a person (the right-brain approach). Obama and his overall campaign struck a deeply personal tone with so many people, which ignited a fervor, commitment, and follow-through not seen in this country for a generation. JTI has ignited and nurtured a similar fervor by making the fight for same-sex marriage and issues of LGBTQ rights and justice deeply personal and about not just changing policies but also changing hearts and minds and developing new kinds of relationships with one another. The conversations that are happening are shifting the discourse from an "us versus them" paradigm to one of "us" as people in this country who deserve equal access and treatment under the law. Jane and people like her voice the concern that measures such as Prop 8 and others that limit or eradicate rights for LGBTQ individuals undermine the very principles and spirit on which this country was built.

By emphasizing and championing the building of genuine alliances, JTI is championing a shift in the mentality of LGBTQ organizing by actively changing the discourse from a victim-oriented discourse to one that heralds LGBTQ people and their allies as agents of change. Of course, this shift did not just happen overnight after the November 4, 2008, election. However, the interpersonal dynamics created through electronic communication are accelerating this change in the tenor of LGBTQ organizing and can do the same in other movements. Consequently, the culture of organizing within LGBTQ communities fighting for same-sex marriage rights is changing. Sen and Kahn (2003) explain that the organizing process can help build a new collective identity and transform the culture within communities. Gorton (2009) similarly describes the Stonewall riots of June 1969 as a time when the "GLBT community coalesced and forged a collective identity . . . mark[ing] the beginning of a decisive shift in consciousness, when gays and lesbians in ever increasing numbers affirmed their sexuality as healthy and natural" (p. 6). Can the interactive support and dialogue offered through websites such as JTI and CC, as well as Occupy.net, create an equivalent affirmation today as activists go about their local work?

NEW DILEMMAS AND MORE QUESTIONS

No change, be it in an individual or in a community, comes without its own tensions. In fact, what Peter Senge (1990) calls "creative tension" (p. 150) signals a gap between our vision and our current reality. The recognition of this gap and the willingness to embrace the tension it evokes is, according to Senge, a vital source of energy. Internet technologies compel us to examine our assumptions about communities, communication, and interpersonal relationships and to envision new possibilities for collective action. At the same time, the use of Internet technologies by social justice campaigns such as JTI raises several dilemmas and questions concerning the sustainability and scope of online community organizing and flash activism. First, how does the trust that develops between participants in virtual organizing communities translate into reliable follow-through with concrete actions? In some respects, people may be more apt to commit to actions in cyberspace and subsequently not follow through because they feel less accountable when they are not meeting face to face. At the same time, participants may feel more free to move forward on their ideas with concrete actions without the barriers that face-to-face meetings create in terms of planning and interpersonal dynamics.

Second, to what extent does the Internet help organizing groups reach out further into all segments of their communities? Are the most marginalized within disenfranchised communities being drawn in or further marginalized through the Internet? Some critics of the same-sex marriage movement within LGBTQ communities emphasize that only certain segments within those communities may be interested and have the resources to fight for same-sex marriage rights (see, e.g., Polikoff, 2008). They argue that queer people of color and transgender people, particularly those who are at lower socioeconomic levels, are likely not to hold marriage as a top priority in their advocacy and organizing efforts. Concerns about economic security and immediate safety are likely to dominate their agendas. Fighting for marriage equality, some say, is too narrow an agenda, and what is needed is a broader effort to legally and economically recognize family and relationship diversity (see, e.g., BeyondMarriage.org, 2006). Such arguments hark back to similar discussions within the welfare rights, homelessness, and battered women's movements of the past (Hopper, 2003; Piven & Cloward, 1993; Schechter, 1999).

To what extent does using the Internet influence activists' capacity to pursue specific goals while maintaining a comprehensive agenda? It is both interesting and promising that JTI and the many organizations fighting for same-sex marriage following Prop 8 have used the same-sex marriage platform to ignite a larger dialogue around full equality and justice for *all* members of LGBTQ communities. An example of this is the emergence of discussion boards and forums on JTI about the struggles and rights of transgender people. To what extent organizations such as JTI can successfully use the Internet to broaden their scope without diluting their efforts remains to be seen.

Finally, to what extent is the opportunity for spontaneous action that the Internet provides also a possible impediment to strategic organizing requiring a long-term perspective on social change? Eight months after the passage of Prop 8 and the creation of JTI, some major financial backers of same-sex marriage in California, fearing another political loss, cautioned gay rights organizations not to move forward too quickly with trying to overturn Prop 8 in 2010 (McKinley, 2009). A coalition of organizations fighting for same-sex marriage, Prepare to Prevail (see preparetoprevail.com), stated that a push to overturn Prop 8 in 2010 would be risky. This put them and large gay and lesbian rights organizations such as the National Gay and Lesbian Task Force at odds with grassroots LGBTQ organizations such as JTI, which had pushed to keep the momentum and continue the fight to overturn Prop 8 in 2010. Grassroots LGBTQ organizations created and fueled through the Internet, such as JTI, have offered opportunities for spontaneity, creativity, and quick action on issues mainstream groups may be unwilling to face. At the same time, large established and well-funded advocacy organizations such as the Human Rights Campaign and the National Gay and Lesbian Task Force have demonstrated stability in human, financial, and political resources and the power to weather crises and defeats. The dynamics between these established organizations and the more activist ones, such as JTI, echo the struggles that occurred between Martin Luther King, Jr.'s Southern Christian Leadership Council and the more militant student-led Student Non-Violent Coordinating Committee (Branch, 2006). They are also reflected in the present-day struggles within Occupy Wall Street and those who would work on specific campaigns, as opposed to those influenced by a focus on "solutions" rather than the singular "demands" of a campaign, such as Occupy Student Debt. How grassroots Internet community activists and traditional advocacy organizations can partner and join forces around their respective strengths to promote a unified social justice agenda is an important question for organizers across movements.

Since early 2009, organizing around defeating Prop 8 has in large part been directed by the progression of the legal case involving Prop 8. As was described earlier, community organizers and organizations such as CC have played critical roles during this long and complicated journey of the Prop 8 case to the U.S. Supreme Court. It is interesting to consider that the dynamics of these organizing efforts have in large part been directed by the progression of a court case. To some extent, the dominance of this court case has focused the efforts of different arms of the same-sex marriage movement, from local grassroots organizers to national mainstream organizations such as the Human Rights Campaign and the National Gay and Lesbian Task Force.

Coming Back to Basics?

Just as Internet activism around Prop 8 needed to be understood in the context of the ways Obama harnessed the Internet for his first and second presidential campaigns, recent developments around LGBTQ equality need to be understood in relation to the Arab Spring and Occupy Wall Street movements. Both of these movements are powerful examples of using social media in massive online and on-the-street actions. The extent to which social media "drove" these revolutions is a subject of debate. One narrative is that smartphones, Facebook, and Twitter led to the Arab Spring. Some critique such a unidirectional causal explanation for complex social movements (Comunello & Anzera, 2012). Commentators have tended to take dichotomous positions on the relationships between social media engagement and civic engagement, with so-called "digital evangelists" emphasizing the revolutionary and transformative role of social media, and "techno-realists" (Jurgenson, 2012) minimizing its impact on offline on-the-street action (Comunello & Anzera, 2012). The Arab Spring and, to a lesser degree, Occupy Wall Street have spawned a wave of empirical research by Internet scholars into the role of social media in political activism. The findings are still tentative on the weight and influence of social media on the events that brought about regime change in countries such as Tunisia and Egypt, and such conclusions can appear only in later editions of this textbook.

The reality, both inside and outside of cyberspace, is that people, not technologies, are the ones who desire and work for change in their lives. And repressive social, economic, and political conditions lead to suffering, discontent, and eventual uprising. The strategic and tireless work of CC members these past few years underscores people's deep need for support and a sense of companionship. As technologies become faster and more integrated, and as people are able to connect with one another and with issues almost simultaneously, their need for heartfelt support and communication will perhaps grow even more. Virtual communities provide these different types of support in an ever-faster and more complex world. In a way, social media provide people with a crucial witness of their own experience. And as a result, what we see both online and offline is the igniting of confidence and belief that one's voice should and can be heard.

Anyone engaged in organizing and social work advocacy must continue to reflect on the main ingredients in building a campaign for major reform. Such ingredients include a critical level of discontent and a critical mass of people willing to own their discontent and, rather than blaming themselves, willing to look to the systems that are creating these conditions. They also include the need and wish to be informed and not to be in the dark anymore. Above all, a core ingredient for social change is the wish no longer to struggle alone. We are never alone in this world, but the traumas from our personal histories and the subjugating forces of dominant individuals, groups, and institutions can make us believe that we are in it alone and that we are supposed to be. The combination of information, connectedness, and awareness that social media offer create an energy and momentum that propel us to begin to question what we may have taken for granted and then act to improve our own lives and the lives of those around us.

CONCLUSION

The work of JTI and other social movements using Internet technologies signals an important juncture for community organizers, an opportunity once again to harness the creative tension that Senge (1990) describes as so vital for personal mastery and growth. The Internet and the communities it can help create, like other technologies, can both remind us of where we are and where we have come from and help us envision who we can become individually and collectively. Therein lies the enormous transformative potential of the Internet to push us to look deeper within ourselves while embracing more of the world around us.

For all macro practitioners, the opportunities seen through the example of JTI suggest that new forms of organizing are possible, whether through local, state, or national efforts. It is clear that sifting through how much can be spontaneously created through social networks and how much can be sustained only through genuine relationship and community connection will continue to be a primary task over the coming years.

ACTIVITY FOR EDUCATIONAL POLICY 2.1.5: ORGANIZING THROUGH A SOCIAL NETWORK

1. Choose a campaign or organizational activity that can benefit from a social network:

   _____

2. Review present social networks (Facebook, LinkedIn, etc.) for possible websites, chat rooms, and blogs that would be supportive of this campaign.

3. Can you join? What are you requesting by joining? What are you committing to do?

   _____

   _____

4. Can you use Wetpaint to create your own webpage?

5. Who can you enlist to help you with these efforts? _____ In your agency? _____ In your community? _____ Other parts of the country? _____

   _____

Keep a notebook on questions and dilemmas as they emerge through this work. And remember to have fun, too!

THE COMMUNITY TOOLBOX

A helpful section of the Community Toolbox related to the Internet can be found at http://ctb.ku.edu/en/tablecontents/sub_section_main_1900.htm, under the heading "Using Internet-Based Tools to Promote Community Health and Development." It details both specific purposes for Internet usage and important links to other sites that can assist organizations and campaigns in developing their Internet capabilities.

REFERENCES

Alfredson, L., & Themudo, N. (2007, February). *Virtual trust: Challenges and strategies in Internet-based mobilization.* Symposium conducted at the 48th Annual Convention of the International Studies Association, Chicago.

Baunach, D. M. (2011). Decomposing trends in attitudes toward gay marriage, 1988–2006. *Social Science Quarterly, 92*(2), 357–374. doi:10.1111/j.1540–6237.2011.00772.x

BeyondMarriage.org. (2006, July 26). *Beyond same-sex marriage: A new strategic vision for all families and relationships.* Retrieved from http://beyondmarriage.org/full_statement.html

Bloch, J. (2007). Cyber wars: Catholics for a free choice and the online abortion debate. *Review of Religious Research, 49*(2), 165–186.

Borins, S. (2009). From online candidate to online president. *International Journal of Public Administration, 32,* 753–758.

Branch, T. (2006). *Parting the waters: America in the King years: 1954–63.* New York: Peter Smith.

Carr, D. (2008, November 10). How Obama tapped into social networks' power. *New York Times.* Retrieved from http://www.nytimes.com/2008/11/10/business/media/10carr.html

Chapman, P. (2008). *Thou shalt not love: What evangelicals really say to gays.* New Rochelle, NY: Haiduk Press.

Cohen, J. (2012, May 15). Voters split on Obama's gay marriage announcement. *Washington Post.* Retrieved from http://www.washingtonpost.com/blogs/behind-the-numbers/post/voters-split-on-obamas-gay-marriage-announcement/2012/05/14/gIQALve4PU_blog.html

Comunello, F., & Anzera, G. (2012). Will the revolution be tweeted? A conceptual framework for understanding the social media and the Arab Spring. *Islam and Christian Muslim Relations, 23*(4), 453–470.

Conrad, C. A. (2013). *Gays against gays in the military.* Retrieved from http://invasionanniversary.blogspot.com/

Courage Campaign, (2012) http://equalityontrial.com

Custard, H. (2007, May 24). *The Internet and global civil society: Communication and representation within transnational advocacy networks.* Symposium conducted at the annual meeting of the International Communication Association, San Francisco.

Davis, T. (1999). *Weary feet, rested souls: A guided history of the civil rights movement.* New York: W. W. Norton.

de Laat, P. B. (2005). Trusting virtual trust. *Ethics and Information Technology, 7,* 167–180.

Epstein, B. J. (2013, June 13). Gays against gay marriage. *Huffington Post.* Retrieved from http://www. huffingtonpost.co.uk/bj-epstein/gays-against-gay-marriage_b_3426051.html?just_reloaded=1

Fisher, R. (1994). *Let the people decide.* New York: Twayne.

Freeman, J. (2013). *A model for analyzing the strategic options of social movement organizations.* Retrieved from www.jofreeman.com/socialmovements/analyzesoc.htm

Freire, P. (2000). *Pedagogy of the oppressed.* New York: Continuum.

Gillett, J. (2003). Media activism and Internet use by people with HIV/AIDS. *Sociology of Health & Illness, 25*(6), 608–624.

Gorton, D. (2009). Why Stonewall matters after forty years. *Gay & Lesbian Review Worldwide, 16*(4), 6.

Hopper, K. (2003). *Reckoning with homelessness.* Ithaca, NY: Cornell University Press.

How Obama used social networking tools to win. (2009, July 10). *INSEAD Knowledge.* Retrieved from http://knowledge.insead.edu/innovation/how-obama-used-social-networking-tools-to-win-1600

Jenkins, H. (2006). *Convergence culture: Where old and new media collide.* New York: New York University Press.

Join the Impact. (2008). *Our mission statement.* Retrieved from http://jointheimpact.com/about-us/mission-statement/

Jurgenson, N. (2012). When atoms meet bits: Social media, the mobile web and augmented revolution. *Future Internet, 4,* 83–91.

Kahn, R., & Kellner, D. (2004). New media and Internet activism: From the "battle of Seattle" to blogging. *New Media Society, 6,* 87–95.

Kahn, S. (2010). *Creative community organizing: A guide for rabble-rousers, activists, and quiet lovers of justice.* Bennington, MA: Berrett-Koehler.

Lovato, R. (2008, November–December). Upload real change. *Color Lines.* Retrieved from http://colorlines.com/archives/2008/11/upload_real_change.html

Mattiane, S. (2003). *To see with two eyes: Peasant activism and Indian autonomy in Chiapas, Mexico.* Albuquerque: University of New Mexico Press.

McKinley, J. (2009, July 26). Backers of gay marriage rethink California push. *New York Times.* Retrieved from http://www.nytimes.com/2009/07/27/us/27gay.html?pagewanted=all

Moberg, D. (2007, Spring). Obama's third way. *Shelterforce.* Retrieved from http://www.shelter-force.org/article/681/obamas_third_way/

Nather, D. (2008, August). A quick rise on a non-traditional career path. *CQ Weekly,* 2180–2193.

Newman, M. (2009, October 22). A public option sprint. *New York Times.* Retrieved from http://query.nytimes.com/gst/fullpage.html?res=9F0DE3D91F30F931A15753C1A96F9C-8B63&ref=moveon.org

Pinnock, S. (2005). Organizing virtual environments: National union deployment of the blog and new cyberstrategies. *WorkingUSA, 8*(4), 457–468.

Piven, F. F., & Cloward, R. (1993). *Regulating the poor: The functions of the welfare system.* New York: Penguin Press.

Polikoff, N. (2008). *Beyond (gay and straight) marriage: Valuing all families under the law (queer ideas).* New York: Beacon.

Schechter, S. (1999). *Women and male violence: The visions and struggles of the battered women's movement.* Boston: South End Press.

Sen, R., & Kahn, F. (2003). *Stir it up: Lessons in community organization and advocacy.* San Francisco: Jossey-Bass.

Senge, P. M. (1990). *The fifth discipline: The art and practice of the learning organization.* New York: Doubleday.

Shepard, B., & Hayduk, R. (2002). *From ACT UP to the WTO: Urban protest and community building in the era of globalization.* New York: Verso.

Spaeth, M. (2009). Presidential politics and public relations in 2008: Marshall McLuhan 2.0. *Journalism Studies, 10*(3), 438–443.

Staples, L. (2004). *Roots to power.* New York: Praeger.

Stirland, S. L. (2008, October 29). Obama's secret weapons: Internet, databases and psychology. *Wired.* Retrieved from http://www.wired.com/threatlevel/2008/10/obamas-secret-w/

Stoecker, R. (2002). Cyberspace vs. face-to-face: Community organizing in the new millennium. *Perspectives on Global Development and Technology, 1*(2), 193–197.

Terkel, A. (2013, June 26). U.S. v. Windsor ruling: The best Justice Kennedy quotes from the court's DOMA decision. *Huffington Post.* Retrieved from http://www.huffingtonpost.com/2013/06/26/windsor-v-us-ruling_n_3454920.html

Vaid, U. (1995). *Virtual equality: The mainstreaming of gay and lesbian liberation.* New York: Doubleday.

Wetpaint. (2012). *Wetpaint: Building massive loyal audiences.* Retrieved from http://www.wetpaint.com/page/about

Wetpaint. (n.d.). *What is a social website?* Retrieved from http://www.wetpaint.com/page/What-Is-A-Wiki

Wetpaint-powered flash activism turns out tens of thousands of Prop 8 protesters. (2009). Retrieved from http://www.prnewswire.com/news-releases/wetpaint-powered-flash-activism-turns-out-tens-of-thousands-of-prop-8-protestors-61987967.html

Williams, J., & Bond, J. (1988). *Eyes on the prize: America's civil rights years, 1954–1965.* New York: Penguin.

NOTE

1. Jane requested that we not use her last name. All quotations are from an interview conducted in September 2009.

CHAPTER 10

Political Advocacy

The Social Work
Practitioner in the Political Arena

BE CAREFUL WHAT YOU WISH FOR!

Kay looked at her friend, her cheeks ashen with worry. Back at their favorite diner, she had switched to tea to calm her nerves.

"Ellis, I so wish you could do this! Representing our NASW chapter with that legislative committee is the last thing I want to do. I hate being in rooms with mahogany all over the place and big leather chairs! I'm intimidated before I walk in!"

Ellis smiled at his friend, sipping his standard cup of decaf. "Careful what you wish for, my friend. You did all that work on the NASW task force on housing debt and increased homelessness, and somebody's actually gonna listen. What's wrong with that?"

"Okay, okay. You taught me to appreciate data and its impact on our work, but there's data and there's power. Remember me back in that school with that CEO? I got tongue-tied as soon as I saw her and her Saks Fifth Avenue suit. Now I'm gonna be in a huge room with all those suits! It's too much!" She took two gulps of tea, wincing at the heat against her tongue. "I wish I were back running a support group in the shelter."

"Hey, you know this is part of social work now. If we don't advocate for us, who will? You think the banks don't have lobbyists telling everyone the crisis is over, the housing debt a thing of the past?"

(Continued)

(Continued)

"I know, I know. The chapter has three task forces, and they all are hoping to get their day inside these chambers. I just don't think I'm cut out for this kind of public speaking."

"First off, when you lobby or speak, you need your bullet points. I use data to center what I have to say—takes the pressure off. I can help you with those bullet points, for sure." He paused, and his face lit up. "Hey, I just thought of something that's sure to work!"

Kay looked at Ellis, doubt on her face. "Yeah? What? You know I don't do drugs." They both laughed.

"No, better than that! Remember Shoshanna, from our organizing class back in the day? She's an aide to Senator Walker, his assistant chief of staff. Why don't you meet with her and find out how best to present your findings. She staffs those kinds of meetings, and she'll know how long to speak, what emphasis to make, what sways people and what doesn't. You know, with her experience she can give you a road map on how best to be a lobbyist."

"Well, I will never be a lobbyist, but that is one great idea! Shoshanna is smart and has got to know those ins and outs. We even did a project together at school. I will definitely give her a call. My nerves are already better." She looked at her half-empty cup of tea. "It's time to switch to coffee!"

They clinked their cups in a toast to their friendship. "That's the Kay I know, caffeinated and opinionated!" Ellis drained his cup as the waitress approached. "You'll just have to get used to being a lobbyist, my friend. In today's world, that's just another social work job!"

Educational Policy 2.1.8—Engage in policy practice to advance social and economic well-being and to deliver effective social work services. In this chapter, readers will learn that "social work practitioners understand that policy affects service delivery, and they actively engage in policy practice. Social workers know the history and current structures of social policies and services; the role of policy in service delivery; and the role of practice in policy development." There will also be examples of social workers who "analyze, formulate, and advocate for policies that advance social well-being; and collaborate with colleagues and clients for effective policy action."

INTRODUCTION

The social work Code of Ethics makes clear that the profession is expected to advocate both with and for the oppressed and politically marginalized. While every social welfare history textbook triumphs the role of social worker Harry Hopkins in Roosevelt's New Deal policies, the powerful influence of Whitney Young in Lyndon Johnson's 1960s War on Poverty, and the growing emergence of more and more social work professionals at every level of government, far more pervasive roles for social workers have been either as behind-the-scenes campaign tacticians, centrally located legislative aides maintaining focus on key legislative items of the current legislative session, or front-of-the-room lobbyists working in coalition with others as they seek support for vital programs. No political candidate wins or rewins an election without strategists able to mobilize voters and issues that lead to victory. Later on, because politicians must respond to multiple constituencies and innumerable issues in each legislative session, their aides are crucial in sifting what fits their bosses' long-term political agenda of reform. Likewise, few politicians can long ignore a well-orchestrated and politically powerful lobbying effort championing the specifics of a particular cause or issue. All these tasks are increasingly undertaken by social workers. As we will see later, local chapters of the National Association of Social Workers (NASW), as well as its national office, are involved in each legislative session to push legislative agendas and elect officials who will be supportive of social welfare policies and programs.

Such political involvement is critical in the 21st century for two overlapping reasons. The first reason is "political"—that is, because the issues central to the field and to the people with whom we work are going to be contested and debated as to how "worthy" they are of support. As such, they reflect a historic debate as old as the profession itself—what populations and issues are "deserving" or "undeserving" of political and programmatic support (Jansson, 2011; Reisch, 2012; Trattner, 1999). For example, what about poor, pregnant mothers receiving good nutritional supplements so their babies will thrive at birth and during those crucial first 3 years of development? That program certainly sounds deserving enough. What about poor elementary school children whose educational performance will suffer if they don't receive free or reduced-cost breakfast and lunch programs at school? That's pretty deserving, too—it's not their fault there may be little nutritional food to eat in their homes. How about their older brothers and sisters who, lacking employment opportunities, are considering joining gangs? Are they "deserving" enough to receive gang-prevention efforts? What about that family member of theirs who landed in prison for 6 years for selling marijuana? How "deserving" is he or she? What if he or she sold heroin? Used a gun? What about people who find themselves homeless and unemployed after getting out of prison?

The above continuum of different but overlapping populations and possible program interventions in support of them underscores that interpretations of who is and isn't "deserving" are almost always determined through a shifting political discourse that can and will change in part on the basis of the larger public perception of whether a population and its concerns are legitimately deserving of support. Such discourse is further politicized by broader ideological arguments over the appropriate mix of individual or societal responsibility to ameliorate or prevent social problems from occurring in the first place. Is the cause of that school child's lack of good, daily nutrition that the parents are lazy and uninformed, or is it poverty and lack of economic opportunity? The greater the agreement on "social" causes that extend beyond individual responsibility, the more societal arrangements will be perceived as rightly and necessarily intervening in and at times even controlling people's behavior. (Think about anti-smoking regulations today compared with just 15 years ago!) Large segments of U.S. society agree that all children should receive an education. Thus, there is little controversy over federal, state, and local governments mandating that from the age of 5 to 16, all children *must* receive schooling. What quality of education they receive, who will provide it and where, and what content must be covered are of course different, "political"—debatable—matters entirely. Who "wins" such a debate is at play all the time and thus requires our serious attention.

The second reason for social workers' political involvement is economic. That is, who pays for that multitude of programs—from pilot projects working with young transgender people so they can confront developmental milestones with a minimum of threat, to federal entitlement programs such as Social Security for the retired elderly? As the current, volatile national debate over the debt ceiling, the size of our deficit, and levels of progressive taxation have underscored since at least 2008, there is no easily arrived at answer to this part of the discourse. The wars between "red" and "blue" have grown more entrenched, reflecting hardened attitudes supported by established constituencies that make budgetary compromise difficult at best (Gelman, 2010). Whether the rich pay far more in taxes so we will have revenues capable of funding all the "deserving" programs found across social welfare or we adopt fiscal policies that greatly lessen the tax burden on the corporate and wealthy sectors while slashing social programs to balance the budget and thus regrow the economy is a stark and volatile debate that is far from over.

It is thus incumbent on social workers throughout the social work profession to enter and engage in this political debate or risk further marginalization that would push our core programs, as well as our central beliefs, onto the margins of society. Luckily, an increasingly large number of social workers have been developing the campaign, legislative, and lobbying skills that will be needed over the coming years. While a number of highly visible social workers are now serving as U.S. Senators, members of Congress, and a variety of state and local officials elected in every state of the nation, the focus of this chapter will not be on how you can get elected to office. It will instead focus on the kinds of jobs social workers can do that may begin as entry-level positions but evolve, because of a mix of strategic smarts, hard work, and professional skill, into roles as genuine political operatives capable of influencing the direction of important social legislation vital to our field.

What follows are three case studies of social workers who have worked in the three central domains of political advocacy: election campaigns, lobbying efforts, and legislative policymaking. All began as interns with relatively little political experience; each has evolved to be seen as a significant political actor in his or her own right, with a skill set and political acumen capable of working in the committee rooms and legislative chambers where policy is shaped. A fourth case study will highlight a seasoned professional strategist whose work with his local social work chapter has modeled the ways state and local chapters of NASW can work effectively as political advocates.

FROM CAMPAIGN "GOFER" TO VALUED POLITICAL LIAISON

As Haynes and Mickelson (2009) make clear, campaigns have two very demanding—and very different—sets of tasks. The first set is the nuts and bolts of campaign management: raising money, registering voters, handing out leaflets, calling and recruiting new volunteers, canvassing, buying lots of coffee and donuts, stuffing envelopes, and getting people to the polls. It's all the little things that go into the daily ins and outs of a campaign. Because these tasks are also time focused—with the exception of presidential elections (which seem to be no less than 2 years for challengers and at least 1 year for incumbents), electoral campaigns may last anywhere from a few weeks to a number of months—the greatest underlying skill here is *time management.* Time, money, and personnel are the primary resources that dictate how a campaign is run. With lots of money and plenty of time, media and mailings can substitute for people on the ground. With the exception of multimillionaire and billionaire candidates, most campaigns must rely on a relatively small number of people willing to work very, very hard to get their candidate elected. The campaign managers who know how to target volunteers to maximize their value throughout a campaign have a greater likelihood of success. Is it leafleting at key commercial centers or work sites with large numbers of workers? Is it calling on likely supporters for donations? Is it running a daily blog or tweeting four times a day? Is it arranging speaking engagements? Knowing how to manage your time and personnel to maximize their impact is a vital skill in electoral politics. While the day-to-day work associated with these demands is simple and straightforward—and, as a campaign wears on, exhausting—its importance cannot be underestimated.

The other key skill set for effective campaign management is the opposite of nuts and bolts: the candidate's *electoral strategy.* This kind of strategic work has three key dimensions: (a) developing and refining the candidate's platform, or what policies and programs he or she is campaigning for; (b) distilling and responding to his or her opponent's campaign platform and evolving political statements; and (c) proactively responding to constituent interests and campaign issues as they shift and change over the life of the campaign (Hamilton & Fauri, 2013). While this can also seem straightforward, in the throes of a campaign, it is not. Initial positions of two opposing candidates may be stark: Your candidate is running on a platform to tax the rich, support public education, and block any cuts to Medicare; the opponent wants to cut all taxes, expand charter schools, and rein in Medicare costs. The strategic demands here seem simple: appeal to targeted constituent groups who wish to support one or all of these issues, show why your opponent is a threat to such interests, and get out the bigger vote.

If only it were that simple. As campaigns evolve, an opponent attempts to strategically undermine your candidate through tactics designed to weaken his or her credibility: The tax proposal will hurt far more people, and an attractive older couple is recorded saying how much they'll be affected by more taxes; smiling children at a charter school speak happily of all they're learning compared with at their former public school. Campaign managers and their staff need to strategically prepare for such attacks; indeed, here one will use the chessboard in advance, forecasting what the attacks will be and having ready responses to vitiate the attack. This kind of tactical back and forth is crucial to the long-term effectiveness of your campaign. Such tactical flexibility that does not lend itself to an attack of inconsistency (a charge Republican candidate Mitt Romney in 2011–2012 was never able to overcome) can occur only if the candidate and lead staff of a campaign underline their strategic principles and positions well in advance of the election cycle. While doing such work can seem initially time-consuming and not so important, it can prove of great value later on in the excitement and urgency of daily campaign demands. Like Obama in 2012, being flexible on levels of tax rates while staying firm on the principle of "the well-to-do must pay more for the sake of equity and fairness" can help strengthen a candidate's reputation, which staff members will want to reinforce and bolster further as the long nights of a campaign slog on.

Jihoon Kim's story of volunteering in electoral work underscores the importance of both time-management skills and strategic smarts. Having been a social work intern in a New York state senator's office, he was hired to serve in constituent services representing the Upper West Side and Washington Heights areas of New York City. As he recalls, it was pretty straightforward work that in classic fashion built from "case to cause" again and again.

> I got to see up close that my boss [state Senator Eric Schneiderman] took the issues of his constituents very seriously, especially when he could see they impacted so many of them. We had many individual tenants with problems, and he worked to bring tenant groups together to fight this one landlord who had a lot of bad buildings. . . . It was good work.

As such, the young staffer's efforts included the basics of entry-level strategy formation covered in Chapter 8: Connect a series of people and their issues to form a manageable campaign with realistic targets for change and improvement. In doing so, the state senator could use his political strength to get state and city regulatory housing agencies to enforce codes requiring the landlord to improve his buildings.

It was solid, impressive work, and Kim might have been satisfied to remain in this kind of position for many years—except, once again, "history moved." Obama's election to the presidency in 2008 also had the effect of propelling Schneiderman and the Democratic Party into state senatorial power, becoming the majority in the State Senate for the first time in years. Kim's boss was now more influential statewide, resulting in a need for them both to be aware of and responsive to statewide issues. Likewise, Schneiderman's political ambition led him to decide to run for statewide office 2 years later, for attorney general. The strategic chessboard had suddenly become much more complex.

Every state's election cycle varies in how it works and what is required to run for office; you will have to know yours when you get involved. (The League of Women Voters website in your state is an excellent place to get such information; see www.lwv .org/.) For New York Democrats, the key election was not the general election (which had favored most Democrats since the 1970s) but, rather, the primary. Adding to the pressure, to get on the ballot, candidates had to receive at least 25% of the votes at the Democratic convention, where party loyalists from across the state would meet to choose potential primary candidates. As such, this "pre-primary" election cycle is challenging first in terms of time management: New York State is relatively big geographically, with Buffalo 400 miles from Manhattan, Binghamton 225 miles from Buffalo, and the Hamptons 100 miles from the Upper West Side of New York City (where Schneiderman lived). Getting around to meet and greet the local leaders, as they expected, would be a daunting task. Furthermore, the state is culturally and politically diverse—New York City urbanites and Westchester County suburbanites need to mingle with North Country farmers and small-city politicians who live far closer to the Canadian border than to Times Square.

Branded a "Manhattan career politician" by his opponents, Kim's boss knew he would have to crisscross the state if he were to have any chance of winning. He also was far more liberal than his opponents, another cause for concern with upstate and suburban politicians. Finally, his strongest opponent was a woman already recognized as a rising star in prosecutorial circles for her hard-hitting trials on Long Island. Schneiderman and his team would have to put in extremely long hours if he were to have a chance of winning. And, given the travel dilemmas in the state, where flying into small airports could take longer than road travel, a lot of those hours would be spent in a car traveling from one campaign spot to another.

It would perhaps be understandable if a professional social worker initially thought that being his boss's driver was a lowly task, but Kim didn't hesitate. "In volunteering, I knew I was going to work incredibly hard, and we did. . . . It was exhausting for all of us." He paused for emphasis. "But there's a lot of strategic work behind the wheel, too. We got to talk a lot about what was next, what the issues were at the next stop. . . . Sometimes there was no one else in the car, and he needed a sounding board for what issues to emphasize."

Kim's social work skills came in handy as well.

Anxiety can be high in a campaign when there's no clear frontrunner. Plus, we're all over-caffeinated . . . people who hadn't smoked in years were back puffing away. . . . I saw that our [social work] relational skills mattered. I talked people off the ledge of over-anxiety and reaction a lot. Also, it became my [strategic] job to filter every call that came into the car so people didn't overload Eric. I had to learn to push back on how time got used, and on what.

Kim could take more and more strategic risks in how he worked on the campaign because his hard work day in and day out, combined with his strategic skills in assessing issues and his relational skills in calming the campaign waters, gave him credibility with his boss and the top campaign managers. While he would be the first to tell you that the campaign was won by Schneiderman's progressive views, campaign smarts, and ability to connect to voters across the state, it is nevertheless compelling that a social worker gained enormous credibility inside a campaign that, by definition—an attorney general's race!—is dominated by lawyers. At present, he has signed on as an upstate Intergovernmental and Community Affairs representative for the attorney general, working on regional and statewide issues impacting voters. The attorney general never forgets to call Kim on his birthday, and he is invited to strategy meetings in New York City and Albany. This social worker remains a political player well after the campaign.

JIHOON KIM'S INTERNAL STRATEGIC VISION WORKING ON A STATEWIDE ELECTION CAMPAIGN

Who: Both the candidate for New York State attorney general and the constituents who would benefit from his election—including tenants, consumers, women of domestic violence

What issue: Election of a Democratic Party candidate with an established history of progressive politics related to tenants, consumers, and unfair corporate influence

How he works: Available on an as-needed basis throughout campaign; uses social work skills to diminish reaction and anxiety among exhausted campaign staffers; helps candidate assess shifting contexts throughout the campaign as new issues arise

Core values consecrated in action: Confidentiality, loyalty, fairness, balance, equality, social justice

A LEGISLATIVE AIDE MOVES A NEWLY EMERGING BABY BOOMER ISSUE "FROM CASE TO CAUSE"

The legislative process can be a long, detailed, and at times seemingly mysterious under-taking that can begin with either a previously unrecognized problem—homelessness in the 1970s, AIDS in the '80s, immigration in the '90s, climate change today—or an issue whose previous laws and regulations had proved inadequate. Public education, child welfare, and mental health are all examples of decades-long efforts seeking reform through legislation. As Haynes and Mickelson (2009) outline, a bill can go through at least six steps before it has any impact: introduction in the legislative body, committee assignment and amend-ment by committee members, reconciliation between a Senate bill and a legislature's bill, voting, executive signing, and implementation by a state, city, or federal agency.

Anyone who expects to influence legislation must know the ins and outs of the munic-ipal and state legislative process. While all states have basic outlines similar to what Haynes and Mickelson (2009) provided, the Texas lieutenant governor's office, for exam-ple, has a great deal of influence in legislation, while in California the same office has little influence. Likewise, the Speakers of the House in New York and Illinois' General Assembly control almost all legislation, while in Montana and Wyoming power is more dispersed (Keefe & Ogul, 2002).

What is often left out of these primers on legislative action is a singular insight that any experienced lobbyist or advocate knows. At each stage of this process are staffers and aides, people like Jihoon Kim, whose combination of policy smarts, loyalty to their bosses, and ability to handle the give-and-take of legislative action make them key bro-kers throughout any legislative session (Jansson, 2006). While at first this may sound undemocratic, how could it be any other way? Politicians do not have time to actually write bills; their aides do. The research they need on an issue is conducted by a staffer. Once all have agreed on what bottom lines will not be crossed (how much revenue to spend, what town or city a new program must be located in, etc.), these same aides meet with their counterparts to negotiate and draft final bills (which are then reviewed by the politicians themselves—one hopes). Such aides are thus critical in legislative development, and advocates and lobbyists will need to build relationships with them as well as with the assembly member or senator.

There also are times when this legislative role can become even more critical to legis-lative development. Like Kim, almost all aides in state and local government engage in constituent services—meeting one-on-one with individual citizen and local groups who have their own concerns and issues. Most of these issues are idiosyncratic and individual-ized—a problem with a landlord, a zoning requirement to be modified. But occasionally, those constituent issues begin to cohere into something that goes beyond one or two peo-ple's concerns and seem to speak to a larger problem that a politician may seek to address.

Here, a legislative aide gets to combine a mix of skills, from clinical social worker to political broker to behind-the-scenes advocate.

An example of such a dynamic role is Alice Fisher, at present the director of community outreach for the New York regional office of Senator Liz Krueger. Fisher came to her present position as a top legislative aide after a career working as an advocate and organizer with the National Conference for Community and Justice, formerly the National Conference on Christians and Jews (NCCJ)—same acronym but a more ecumenical title to match our 21st century religious and cultural mix (see www.nccjstl.org/). While her story has much overlap with Kim's—she, too, was an intern with a senator; she, too, got a job working on constituent services, with a special focus on housing and the elderly, which make up a large segment of Senator Krueger's constituency—what makes part of her story so compelling is this long-term organizer's use of clinical insight and diagnostic skills that have now moved a once-invisible issue understood "case by case" to an emerging "cause" that promises to significantly impact the populations affected and the programs expected to work with them.

Senator Krueger, long recognized as a smart and politically savvy social justice advocate in the State Senate, assigned Fisher to revitalize a senior advisory board that had been moribund for years. As she herself is an astute tactician, Fisher changed the name of the group to "Roundtable for Boomers and Seniors" and the meeting time to 8 a.m. Her ongoing work with people over age 60 left her well aware that "calling people south of 70 years old 'seniors' was a turn off in the way 'boomers' was not." She also had assessed that this group, as well as many active older people, got up early and were open to an 8 a.m. meeting—something her younger colleagues thought was crazy. The result of her innovative outreach efforts? Her first roundtable had 100 attendees—an increase of more than 400% from the previous year!

She also was aware that this educated and engaged group would not stick around for follow-up sessions if there was not real substance that affected their lives. Through her assessment, she saw that caregiving issues were paramount—but not "Health for the Elderly 101." She and her team developed a five-part series on caregiving, with a focus on emerging issues related to longevity: potential chronic illness, the problems of caregiving for boomers and their elderly parents, and how agencies were and were not responding to these issues.

During this time, a little-talked about issue arose out of the many constituent calls that Fisher takes from seniors seeking assistance for a variety of problems. The issue, desperate case by desperate case, began to emerge as having real programmatic and policy implications for many of the social service agencies with whom Krueger's office worked. The issue was hoarding. Seniors threatened with eviction because of their severe cluttering and hoarding habits were calling the senator's office for help to keep their apartments. As Fisher soon learned,

> reality TV has popularized the issue while managing to trivialize it as well. Popular TV makes it seem like it's the problem of sad, eccentric loners living out on their own, in their own homes. As the calls kept increasing in volume, we began

to see that it was so much worse . . . and that there was a huge potential for an urban crisis in senior evictions.

The legislative aide went on to analyze the issue in the context of problems raised by boomers and elders at the roundtables. Fisher contextualized their private troubles in demographic terms.

> Americans are starting to live longer, a lot longer, and that means that more and more people will suffer from dementia and Alzheimer's—perhaps up to half the population 85 and over. What seems like an individual issue in each family is going to grow exponentially as boomers retire and live on.

She went on to clarify a powerful, seemingly "individualized" problem.

> In cities, hoarders don't live alone like you see on TV. They are apartment dwellers who have neighbors next door, above and below them. The problem starts with one person, but the vermin and infestation becomes a health problem for an entire floor of four or five apartments or even a whole building.

Ever the good social worker, she paused for emphasis.

> I was living what got talked about in policy class. . . . That "personal problem" of the "old guy in 3-C" warps into a "public issue" when 10 tenants or building management files a complaint with the Health Department and the NYC Department for the Aging!

With the hoarding issue now clearly far more than a set of individual cases but a problem of safety, health, and well-being for a larger and larger part of the community, Fisher went about investigating what was being done. After all, good legislation needs to be built on firm data both for the need itself and for the present programmatic response to it if the legislation is to have any clout. As was discovered, almost every social work agency Krueger's office worked with had its share of hoarders, and they all were handled the same way.

> It turned out that the only agency with any resources and skills to deal with this as a defined problem was a public agency, Adult Protective Services, a solution of the last resort when adults, including the elderly and disabled, have no support network of family or friends, and are unable to care for themselves.

Private nonprofits and foundations had previously funded the cleaning out of some of these apartments. To their amazement, however, when they went to check on the client as little as 6 months later, the place "looked as if we had never been there!" As a result, private funding was pulled back and is virtually nonexistent today. Agencies that had previously looked at these isolated cases as a housing issue soon came to realize that there was a mental health component that was not being addressed.

Fisher then organized a professional roundtable of city agency leaders, legislative aides confronting this issue within their own districts, and social work directors from a variety of senior service agencies also stymied by the growing problem. More than 40 people— from agency staffers to legislative aides to public agency managers—attended this work group session sponsored by Senator Krueger, with the strategic objective of assessing the depth of the problem, the type of resources available, and possible policy recommendations for future legislative sessions. Those at the meeting identified the need to educate the public about hoarding and the implications of cluttering habits.

Fisher engaged a clinical colleague, Susan Siroto of Search and Care, to help oversee the development of a best practices handbook, *What to Do With All That Stuff: Senator Liz Krueger's Best Practices for Clutter and Hoarding*. This publication can be used by agencies, landlords, co-op boards, hoarders themselves, neighbors, and caregivers (often baby boomers caring for their elderly parents), and in turn will help develop even more documentation needed to push policy reform—and add needed financial resources to a complex and growing problem. The topic and the booklet were introduced at the current roundtable program, Longevity and Its Impact on Society. The session, titled "What to Do With All That Stuff," was viewed as addressing one of the challenges of longevity (i.e., the longer we live, the more we accumulate). A social cause had begun to be created.

While the individual cases have been turned into a cause, Fisher and her colleagues are under no illusion that the needed changes in service delivery will occur overnight. But a legislative aide has used a mix of her political smarts and social work skills to focus attention on a problem previously at the margins of social welfare policy. While still identifying a legislative "fix" to the problem, it is hoped that Senator Krueger will introduce legislation that addresses the problem more systematically. "From case to cause" has moved from a long-ago historical concept to the basis for genuine social change.

ALICE FISHER'S INTERNAL STRATEGIC VISION IN CONSTITUENT SERVICES AND LEGISLATIVE ADVOCACY

Who: Both isolated elderly involved in hoarding and their caregivers, including family members, social work agencies, and city and state bureaucracies charged with oversight of this population

What issue: Hoarding, "from case to cause"

How she works: Acts as liaison to both families and agencies impacted by this problem, data analyst, large- and small-group facilitator, and advocate

Core values consecrated in action: Safety and well-being, human dignity, community, social justice

INDIVIDUAL ACTIVITY

1. Review the "individual" work you have been doing. What issues seem to be emerging as "case by case" that could be reframed as a "cause"?

2. Review what Fisher did. What do you need to make this a cause that a politician or funder might consider supporting?

   a. Type of data

   b. Breadth of issue

   c. What is now being done

   d. New needs

   e. Other

3. Formulate three bullet points that could turn this into a "cause" and that you can use to speak about it with someone in authority.

   a. _____

   b. _____

   c. _____

FROM BEHIND-THE-SCENES LEGISLATIVE AIDE TO UPFRONT POLITICAL LOBBYIST FOR SOCIAL JUSTICE

Of course, most legislative activity doesn't begin through an aide's advocacy. The most common way issues become causes and causes become legislation is through lobbying—that mix of influence and power in formal and informal ways that lead first one and then many politicians to vote an issue into law. In some cases, that influence process can be as long as a century and require the strength of social movements, as was true with the civil rights and suffrage movements needed to win and keep the right to vote for people of color and women. Such challenges continue to this day, as witnessed in the 2013 Supreme Court ruling that voided the National Voting Rights legislation of the 1960s. Other laws come through traditional, more corporatized means, with lobbying firms paid by major industries to protect or enhance their interests. For example, most readers who followed the last two or three presidential elections will have heard of the oil and gas industry lobbying for land rights for drilling or the lumber industry wanting to expand logging rights (Gelman, 2010). But what about the Free Speech Coalition—a "nonprofit" lobbying arm of the multibillion-dollar pornography industry (see www.freespeechcoalition.com)—or the National Potato Council—a lobbying group supported by both Coca Cola and farm groups that successfully advocated for pizza to be labeled a "vegetable" for school lunches (Nixon, 2011)? In 2013, there are more than 13,000 registered lobbyists in Washington, D.C., alone, with each of the 50 state capitals having their own significant share (Keefe & Ogul, 2002). Obviously, lobbying is big business, and lobbyists' hefty fees are paid because of their success in influencing the legislative process—on pizza and porn, oil and timber . . . and social legislation, too.

As Haynes and Mickelson (2009) point out, successful social welfare lobbying cannot use the dollars of major industries to gain influence. Social welfare advocates create access and influence through two primary resources: numbers and facts. While others may be able to afford dinners at expensive restaurants, social workers' successful use of the following tactics can pay off in significant influence over a bill's passage:

- Letter writing
- Social media petitions and videos
- E-mails
- Phone banking
- Giving testimony

These can all be effective strategies in a well-orchestrated lobbying effort. Such efforts may take years, not months, and may overlap with more than one legislative cycle before passage; skilled political activists will take into account the degree of support and level of opposition as they build momentum for the campaign. Done with consistency, these tactics can make all the difference in whether or not a bill moves from committee to a full vote and eventual passage.

Perhaps the least expensive tactic, letter writing nevertheless must be organized carefully to be effective. As Haynes and Mickelson (2009) suggest, letters should be brief, neatly written or typed, and have three paragraphs: (1) your introduction, stating the subject and the specific bill tied to it, as well as why you are concerned about the issue; (2) your perspective on the matter, with a concrete example backing up that perspective; and (3) the specific action you are requesting the politician to take (e.g., vote yes, vote no, add an amendment). These letters need to come from a variety of actors, especially across the politician's district. Oftentimes a social work chapter or union will prepare postcards and standard letters for members to sign and send in. The dilemma here is obvious: Standard postcards and letters increase your numbers but may water down the overall impact; personal letters can have much more emotional impact but may result in far fewer letters being sent.

With the use of *social media and e-mail,* traditional letters are becoming less and less used in favor of popular sites such as Facebook and Change.org, both of which have served as successful platforms for campaigns to stop domestic violence and improve health care regulations for at-risk children.

Groups are increasingly using other forms of social media to counter the power of more financially wealthy lobbying groups. By combining their *Twitter accounts with smartphone dexterity,* their influence can grow exponentially. Indeed, the prevalence of smartphones has led to the creation of apps used specifically for grassroots lobbying efforts. For example, the rock star Bono's antipoverty group ONE uses an iPhone app that figures out who your member of Congress is, brings up his or her phone number, and provides you with a handy script to read off to the receptionist or intern who answers the phone in D.C. (Ali, 2011).

By combining a systematic letter or e-mail campaign with the immediacy of your smartphone or social media petition efforts, your lobbying campaign begins to gain the kind of traction that can capture a politician's attention. Assuming your influence has grown, a bill may then be debated in legislative hearing—an opportunity for you and/or other members of your campaign to give *testimony* before the committee discussing the merits of a bill. Such testimony needs to be both put in writing and orally presented.

This is where your greatest resource is the facts and information your campaign can provide, not just the numbers of people who support it. The written testimony is the completed document for your cause. It should provide history, context, data, powerful stories, and case examples—all resulting in strategic justification for your campaign's success. As such, it can be the backdrop to your oral testimony, which tactically will be briefer, more visual, and provide the powerful highlights of what is written. Both take professional skill to deliver well—the data must be compelling and accessible, the talk forthright and delivered with authority. For a first-timer (or second-timer, for that matter), such presentations require practice, practice, practice, for you will be understandably nervous inside the legislative chambers. Such thorough preparation is another of the resources needed to counter other, better-financed campaigns that may be opposed to your calls for improved child safety, healthier school lunches, or more dollars allocated to homeless shelters.

With testimony completed, petitions counted, and arguments heard, all that's left is the vote. Here is where telephoning can prove tactically important. Done right before the vote, this strategy can provide the final push for a vacillating legislator to move to support your campaign. Of course, with the overuse of telephone banks, often with hundreds if not thousands of automated calls replacing the personal influence of direct calls, such efforts are a matter of strategic choice for any campaign's leaders. Often taking place on the day before the vote at a chapter or union office that can provide trunk lines to minimize the cost of such calls, these calls are the culminating tactic in a long-term lobbying strategy that the social work profession and its allies use more and more to achieve their members' goals and objectives.

Gary Parker had come to appreciate the strategic importance of lobbying while working as a legislative aide. As with Kim and Fisher, he had enjoyed his behind-the-scenes responsibilities for New York's first openly lesbian state legislator, Deborah Glick, using his advocacy and strategic skills to develop seemingly isolated issues into strong advocacy campaigns supported by his progressive boss. For example, various block associations in the Greenwich Village neighborhood were concerned about the expansion of the Port Authority's transit infrastructure in ways that would negatively impact the historic architecture and charm of the old neighborhood. Parker saw up close how connecting seemingly disparate groups was the only way to develop enough social and political capital to influence a huge multibillion-dollar state bureaucracy far more accustomed to setting and acting on its own agenda, unimpeded by outside citizen groups. The young aide realized that without a consistent marshaling of support from groups across the district, there was little way to slow down forces more interested in their own power than in fostering community dialogue (Stolle & Hooghe, 2003).

The political insights Parker gained as he built a determined coalition of neighborhood actors confronting a massive and often hostile opponent stood him in good stead as his own political career as a social justice advocate evolved. During the early years of the George W. Bush Administration, he was increasingly aware of the entrenched "pro-heterosexual family" attitudes and policies across the country that had been growing since the passage of the In Defense of Marriage Act under the Clinton Administration (Jansson, 2011). A committed gay activist himself, Parker knew that his community faced further marginalization if these sentiments hardened into even more conservative social policies.

At the same time, his work in the trenches of legislative reform made him equally aware that the level of cohesion between the various LGBTQ political clubs was minimal at best. Through the long battles around AIDS and due to the distinct cultural and class differences between the smaller, outer-borough clubs such as Staten Island and the racial differences experienced by the Out People of Color Caucus (which cut across the boroughs, called counties in other parts of the state and country), there was not enough unity and alignment for such groups to lobby effectively against the trends of anti-homosexuality emanating from Washington and Albany in the early 2000s. If New York state politicians were to take a progressive stance on these issues, something would have to happen to begin fostering a unified political message from LGBTQ activists around the city and state. Experienced in coalition work by this time, Parker knew that the first step would have to be helping groups put to rest their previous antagonisms so that hidden agendas didn't undermine long-term clout (Mizrahi & Rosenthal, 2001).

His first step was to develop a partnership with one other club leader, Brad Hoylman, who was based in Brooklyn. Their partnership would demonstrate the outline of the kind of cross-city coalition that they were seeking. Rather than start with an overt political meeting, they tactically went a different way. They had a social, inviting people for drinks and appetizers with a low-key call about the Bush Administration's attack on gay rights.

Using the event as a foundation for a more political direction, Parker and Hoylman allayed fears of the smaller and more conservative club on Staten Island and the less financially secure Out People of Color Caucus that the political lobbying campaign would be dominated by wealthier and further-to-the left groups in Manhattan and Brooklyn. They did this in two ways: by making donations voluntary rather than a flat fee that some might not be able to afford and by stating that they were a "nonpartisan" Coalition of Progressive Clubs motivated by a simple mission—"Our community is under attack, and now is the time to do something about it." The willingness to tactically embrace nonpartisanship gave the smaller yet important Staten Island club room to politically maneuver within its more conservative borough; the voluntary dues structure maintained the authority of the Out People of Color Caucus within the coalition itself, an authority that would have been diminished if the fee structure were uniformly high.

The result of Parker's strategic brokering was the creation of a powerful citywide LGBTQ Coalition of Progressive Clubs that developed the clout to wage a unified lobbying campaign for marriage equality in the middle of the conservative Bush years (2000–2008), which resulted in the state legislature taking a firm pro-marriage-equality stance well before most other states. "I knew if we worked to strengthen our social capital we'd get more political capital. In lobbying, having tactical flexibility without losing sight of the underlying cause for our community was the key to our success." The ensuing letter campaigns, political meetings, rallies, and testimonies built in momentum and influence across the state. While it would be a few more years of political deal making and shifts in the governor's office under Andrew Cuomo before gay marriage was adopted in the state, Parker's lobbying efforts were a central building block in the long-term success of this campaign for marriage equality.

GARY PARKER'S INTERNAL STRATEGIC VISION IN LOBBYING EFFORTS ON BEHALF OF MARRIAGE EQUALITY

Who: LGBTQ political activists and all LGBTQ people seeking marriage equality

What issue: Marriage equality for the LGBTQ community

How he works: Acts as liaison to different political clubs, political broker, advocate, and lobbyist

Core values consecrated in action: Equality, fairness, human dignity, community, social justice

THE CARE AND TENDING OF "NATURALLY OCCURRING NETWORKS": A SEASONED SOCIAL WORK PROFESSIONAL BUILDS A LOCAL NASW CHAPTER INTO A STATEWIDE POLITICAL FORCE

Social work's growing effectiveness in the legislative arena and as a successful lobbyist for member and community interests is perhaps best understood by seasoned professionals who have operated in the political trenches of state and local chapters of NASW itself over the past 30 years. One of the most skilled operatives is Robert Schachter. Schachter began his professional social work career in the late 1970s, at a time when the local NASW chapter defined "politics" as "influencing policy through discussion." He noticed that the core of NASW leadership worked on individual membership concerns while mildly advocating particular causes through the development of policy and position papers—such as for the infamous Wilder case in child welfare, where placements were made on the basis of a child's skin color (Bernstein, 2002), and the growing homeless problem (Baxter & Hopper, 1981; Fabricant & Kelly, 1986).

Such a "white glove" approach to advocacy did not sit well with the young organizer, nor did the times warrant it. The "city crisis" of the mid-1970s had already decimated social service roles (David, 2012), and Schachter, working at the Community Council of Greater New York, searched and soon found others who, working outside of the chapter, were forming political alliances advocating more forcefully for change. Connecting to established but less traditional social work leaders such as Ruth Brooks and Barbara Brenner, he saw the value in their work with veteran Democratic Party politicians that most in the profession still avoided. "I could see that legislation that made a difference in our communities and our own work required real organizing, not just policy papers."

This insight was soon put to the test as then-mayor Ed Koch proposed cutting the entire Youth Employment Training Program that affected thousands of inner-city youth. By this time working inside the NASW chapter as head of its political action committee, Schachter put out a call for members to join in a planned march and rally at City Hall to protest the cuts—an unprecedented call to political action by the chapter. This powerful tactic was a significant boost inside a powerful media campaign under way to end these cuts. With support from Democratic politicians as well as many other groups and activists from across the city, revenue was found, the cut funds were soon restored, and the training program continued.

The local NASW chapter and its newly hired director of public affairs—Schachter—changed to meet the far more politicized environment in which the social work profession was becoming an increasingly active player. His political mentor Brooks was recognized for her leadership inside the chapter and was able to invite established, powerful politicians such as state Senator Al Vann and Congress member Major Owens to address the chapter. While not ignoring traditional membership concerns, Schachter, Brooks, and Brenner saw that building and maintaining these political relationships would serve the profession well in later years. As it turned out, this nurturing of political alliances in the 1980s proved crucial to the well-being of the profession 20 years later.

Schachter reflected on how he developed his strategic vision at the very beginning of his career:

> I worked in SROs [single-room-occupancy hotels for the homeless] early on, and I saw how powerful and important "naturally occurring networks" were in helping people live their lives with a little dignity. That term has stayed with me throughout my career.

For Schachter, the importance of *supporting one another* and providing *key, timely information*—primary qualities of such networks—was the hallmark of what the NASW chapter could be. What was different, of course, was that the timely use of information was two-way—from and to political actors across the state. And that support would be internal for members, as well as occurring between members and other, non-social-work allies—who, together, could create alliances that would strengthen each other.

While in retrospect this kind of alliance building can seem straightforward and simple, at the time it was anything but. Because of his work on the city crisis cuts in services and his own members' identified concerns, Schachter knew that the conditions of the workplace—hours, pay, amount of paperwork—would grow in importance for chapter members (Fabricant & Burghardt, 1992; Fabricant & Fisher, 1999). He also knew that his NASW chapter—as anywhere else—was primarily composed of both frontline workers impacted by these changes to workplace conditions and managers and executives who had to undertake these often drastic, cost-cutting measures. In short, tensions between social work managers and workers common to the workplace were found within the chapter as well.

Luckily, by the mid-1990s, the young executive director had a key ally in the chapter president, Brenner. Herself a hospital administrator and aware of the erosion of working conditions for medical social workers, Brenner saw the potential of forming an alliance with one of the strongest unions in the state, 1199 (Hospital and Health Care Workers), led by Dennis Rivera. Toward that end, Schachter and Brenner and other NASW leaders organized more than 1,000 social workers to attend a major indoor rally sponsored by 1199, at which prominent politicians would be speaking. From this platform, they hoped, a more formal alliance with the union could be created to work on key legislative issues. "To me, when it comes to politics, a 'naturally occurring network' takes a lot of work to create and sustain. And that's where we were going."

Not that the chapter leadership wanted to go there. When Schachter proposed the alliance with the union, the majority of the chapter board responded in disbelief at the thought of being coerced into union-like activity. Ever the tactician, Schachter knew an immediate alliance was off the table if the union asked the chapter to do anything. His advice to his union counterpart: "Ask [the chapter] for nothing. If you do, other possibilities will happen over time. Just ask for nothing now."

Working in the legislative halls of the state capital, the union consistently represented social work interests as it pushed for support on Medicaid, Medicare, and other health-related issues. Gratified by such support, a year later the NASW Board overwhelmingly voted to align cuts with 1199 in a statewide alliance focused on health and social service legislation. It had taken work, but the naturally existing network between the profession and a major union had taken shape through Schachter, and strategic insight and hard work had paid off.

The true value of this network became clear a few years later. Across the social work profession, a vast majority of its members desired a licensing bill that would protect them for insurance reimbursement as well as elevate the status of the profession itself. At the same time, many Black and Latino social workers, especially members of the Association of Black Social Workers, were concerned about potential marginalization among members who were far more committed to work within minority communities than to traditional forms of private practice. Wanting to be supportive of both groups, Schachter soon realized that a way through the impasse lay in the legislation being debated at the state level. Union 1199 needed support in stopping the managed-care cuts that would lose hundreds of jobs for its members and reduce services needed in the poorest communities—core issues for Black and Latino social workers everywhere. At the same time, licensing still mattered, and so he approached the political director of 1199 about supporting the issue. The union was the only actor in this fight that could bring along the Black and Latino Legislative Caucus—given veto power that session by the Speaker of the House on licensing—to support the licensing bill. Given the 15 years of their work together, the political director agreed to do so. The licensing bill passed soon after. The naturally existing network of union local and professional chapter had held.

As a transformative strategist (see Chapter 8), Schachter wasn't finished. The concerns raised regarding potential racial bias within the licensure testing were still present. Working now with Mary Pender-Green, a nationally recognized leader in antiracism work, the NASW executive director saw it as his ethical obligation to continue addressing those concerns. Some of his work took the shape of coordinating with the board to have all members take the People's Institute's antiracism workshop to better understand the multiple dimensions of racism in the field and in their own agencies. But more important here, a recent action in 2012 was to host a chapter program to assist people who for any reason had had difficulty with the licensing test. "I am happy to report over 450 people showed up to get support." For the first time, large numbers of Black and Latino professionals, among others, felt that there was hope to pass the exam given the information shared and the support they received. Schachter's vision of a naturally occurring network continued to live on inside the largest NASW local chapter in the nation.

**BOB SCHACHTER'S INTERNAL STRATEGIC
VISION FOR A "NATURALLY OCCURRING NETWORK"
IN THE POLITICAL DEVELOPMENT OF HIS NASW CHAPTER**

Who: NASW chapter members

What issue: Improved Medicaid reimbursement, licensing, member test taking

How he works: As executive director, strategic broker with previously distant organizations, and tactician using building blocks for long-term goals

Core values consecrated in action: Support, fairness, equality, high standards, collaboration

CONCLUSION

What all these stories have in common is the strategic growth and political influence of the social work profession itself over the past 30 years. Today, the NASW webpage can help connect any member to his or her PACE (Political Action for Candidate Election) affiliate, helping mobilize social workers and their allies in election campaigns of local, state, and national importance (NASW, 2009). A brochure is also available to help social workers learn how to run their own campaigns for office (NASW, 2013). A list of legislation in Congress requiring action is updated monthly so state and local chapters can mount their own campaigns to influence future outcomes. In short, 21st century social work places the political and legislative process central to its mission. As the above four stories suggest, it will be an arena increasingly populated by professional social workers skilled in political advocacy and legislative acumen as well.

ACTIVITY FOR EDUCATIONAL POLICY 2.1.8

1. Review your local NASW chapter's list of activities. What are the priorities for the chapter in terms of legislation?

2. Determine at what stage in the legislative process the top priorities are—part of bills, need to be introduced as new legislation, or to be voted on?

3. Speak to other NASW members involved with the activity about possible aides or staffers whom they know. Together, design steps to meet and influence one of these aides.

   a. What is your "ask"? What needs to happen concretely to move the legislation along?

   b. Plan out those steps over the next 2 months with chapter members.

THE COMMUNITY TOOLBOX

The Community Toolbox has more than 151 webpages devoted to different kinds of political advocacy, including specific campaigns for health, pollution, and child safety. Some of the more basic strategic items are as follows:

Advocacy Over and for the Long Term

Systems Advocacy and Community Organizing

General Rules for Organizing for Legislative Advocacy

Overview: Getting an Advocacy Campaign Off the Ground

Developing a Plan for Getting Community Health and Development Issues on the Local Agenda

Lobbying Decision Makers

Changing Policies to Increase Funding for Community Health and Development Initiatives

Conducting a Direct Action Campaign

Changing Policies to Increase Funding for Community Health and Development Initiatives

Online Tools for Advocating for Change

Identifying Opponents

REFERENCES

Ali, A. (2011). iPhone app will help you lobby. *Roll Call*. Retrieved from http://www.rollcall.com/issues/56_132/iPhone-App-Will-Help-You-Lobby-206125–1.html

Baxter, E., & Hopper, K. (1981). *Homeless adults on the streets of New York City*. New York: Community Service Society.

Bernstein, N. (2002). *The lost children of Wilder: The epic struggle to change foster care*. New York: Vintage.

David, G. (2012). *Modern New York: The life and economics of a city*. New York: Palgrave-MacMillan.

Fabricant, M., & Burghardt, S. (1992). *The welfare state crisis and the transformation of social services work*. Armonk, NY: M. E. Sharpe.

Fabricant, M., & Fisher, R. (1999). *Settlement houses under siege*. New York: Columbia University Press.

Fabricant, M., & Kelly, M. (1986). No haven for the homeless in a heartless economy. *Radical America, 20,* 23–34.

Gelman, A. (2010). *Red state, blue state, rich state, poor state: Why Americans vote the way they do.* Princeton, NJ: Princeton University Press.

Hamilton, D., & Fauri, D. (2013). *Social workers political participation: Strengthening the political confidence of social work students.* Bristol, UK: Policy Press.

Haynes, K., & Mickelson, J. (2009). *Affecting change: Social workers in the political arena* (7th ed.). New York: Pearson.

Jansson, B. (2006). *Becoming an effective policy advocate* (6th ed.). New York: Brooks/Cole.

Jansson, B. (2011). *The reluctant welfare state* (7th ed.). New York: Brooks/Cole.

Keefe, W. J., & Ogul, M. S. (2002). *The American legislative process: Congress and the states.* New York: Pearson.

Mizrahi, T., & Rosenthal, B. (2001). Complexities of coalition building: Leaders' successes, strategies, struggles, and solutions. *Social Work, 46*(1), 63–78.

National Association of Social Workers. (2009). *Lobby day tool kit.* Washington, DC: Author. Retrieved from http://www.socialworkers.org/advocacy/grassroots/lobbyday.pdf

National Association of Social Workers. (2013). *NASW advocacy.* Retrieved from http://capwiz.com/socialworkers/home/

Nixon, R. (2011, November 1). School lunch proposals set off a dispute. *New York Times.* Retrieved from http://www.nytimes.com/2011/11/02/us/school-lunch-proposals-set-off-a-dispute.html?pagewanted=all&_r=0

Reisch, M. (2012). *Social policy and social justice: Social work in the new century.* Thousand Oaks, CA: Sage.

Stolle, B., & Hooghe, M. (2003). *Generating social capital: Civil society and institutions in comparative perspective.* New York: Palgrave-Macmillan.

Trattner, W. (1999). *From poor law to welfare state.* New York: Free Press.

CHAPTER 11

The Reemergence of Environmental Activism Within Social Work

Kristin LeBourveau and Meredith Ledlie-Johnson

GOING GREEN

Ellis was on the phone with Kay, talking about a possible collaboration with her program, even though it was across the continent.

"This foundation wants us to see if we can expand our environmental focus into other, more traditional forms of social work. They're open to a pilot in four cities. So I thought of you and the homeless work you do. What do you think?"

"Hey, I'd love to work with you, but adding in an environmental thing seems beyond our scope. We work on healthy meals in the shelters, and our mental health programs stress wellness. But they've got enough to deal with—unemployment, bad housing, lousy schools. The social environment is tough enough—going green sounds like a California thing, not a New York one."

Ellis laughed. "What? Now I'm the crunchy-granola, latté-drinking one? Truth is, working on these ecological issues has really turned me around, Kay. How can kids do well in school if they don't eat well? How can they eat well if their community is a food desert— you know, nothing but bodegas and delis for food? As for mental health, do you know social scientists have found that a patch of green nearby, even a small one, is good for our well-being?"

He went on, clearly animated by the subject. "You know me. I started doing some research on this. It turns out a heroine of yours, Jane Addams, way back in the day was as much into sanitation and healthy living as Dr. Oz!"

"You must be kidding. Jane Addams founded settlement houses, was antiwar to the point that she went to jail, and big into social justice. I never heard a thing about her and the green environment." Kay still sounded skeptical.

"Who do you think created the Fresh Air Fund? Social workers like her! She was the sanitation officer for her ward!"

"No way! You mean we had the natural environment itself in our work back in the day? I'll be...." Her voice trailed off in wonderment for a second. "Okay...I'm open to hear more. What's the pilot entail?"

"Well, of course, food deserts need new markets with fresh foods to come in, so we start with ways to create a green market up there in Harlem." Her old friend was off and running. "Those markets are just a part. They create local jobs for your kids." Pretty soon, he connected the effort to a civil rights struggle in the South more than 30 years ago. Kay sighed happily. *Only my dear friend,* she thought, *could connect green grass and social justice. Thank goodness he's in my life.*

Educational Policy 2.1.7—Apply knowledge of human behavior and the social environment. In this chapter, the reader will see how "social workers are knowledgeable about human behavior across the life course; the range of social systems in which people live; and the ways social systems promote or deter people in maintaining or achieving health and well-being.... Social workers utilize conceptual frameworks to guide the processes of assessment, intervention, and evaluation; and critique and apply knowledge to understand person and environment."

A RETURN TO SOCIAL WORK'S "NATURAL" ORIGINS

At one time in social work's history, Ellis and Kay's argument might never have happened. Settlement houses in the late 19th century were champions for the creation of parks and playgrounds, and social workers were among the first recreation specialists in the country. This chapter analyzes what caused social work to move away from this environmental focus and why practitioners have recently started bringing the profession back to awareness of and engagement with the natural environment as central to our work.

For a long time, professional social workers have approached their work from a person-in-environment perspective—facilitating an intervention that considers a person's intellectual and physical abilities and also outside influences such as the communities in which they live, economic and educational opportunities, and the civil rights they may or may not enjoy; that is to say, a person-in-*social*-environment perspective. This has been the dominant emphasis for generations in social work curriculum. Ironically, the natural environment—our land, our air, and our water—was once seen as central to social work, only to be pushed aside as the profession turned away from influencing societal problems and more toward individualized interventions. Over the past 40 years, with evidence surfacing on the impact of climate change and other manmade toxins on our natural world, we again are increasingly aware of how much a healthy environment supports living healthy lives. That said, despite clues from our professional ancestors, modern social work practice has yet to fully embrace a new concept of environment that is inclusive of the natural world. This chapter is written by practitioners of a new (or very old, depending on your point of view) paradigm for social work practice—one that does not consider macro practice as entirely separate from the individual-level approach or believe that the two are mutually exclusive. This chapter instead supports a practice perspective that includes the natural environment so that the professional again is fully engaged in creating a more cohesive and comprehensive approach to improving the health and well-being of individuals and eradicating those conditions that undermine our society's sustained and equitable use of resources so that well-being can be assured.

The Environmental Roots of Social Work—and of Two Social Workers' Careers

The story of how we got involved in ecological social work begins when we first met, at the start of our graduate school careers at Hunter College (now Silberman) School of Social Work in September of 2007. Sharing a small office inside a (very old) church building at PICO (once known as the Pacific Institute for Community Organizing) affiliate Brooklyn Congregations United, we took comfort in sharing our trepidations as a way of normalizing the uncertainties we faced. As full-time graduate students, we spent a fair amount of time grounded in reflection, aware that each course, paper, and project was shaping our approach to the work we would someday "really" do. Meanwhile, we were full of curiosity and apprehension over what and where we would someday be.

Lucky for us, as we talked, we discovered we had similar reasons for becoming social workers dedicated to community organizing, and we quickly became good friends. As we began negotiating our classes and fieldwork, we spent hours in conversation about what we were struggling with, what skills we felt good about, and what issues we wanted to work on in our careers. At that point, we had only vague ideas of wanting to change the world, but we were not sure how or where to start. Our initial encounter with the concept of including the natural environment as a tool in our work was short and provided just enough promise to persuade us to dig deeper. A lunchtime conversation that started with "Hey, have you ever heard of Red Hook Farms?" became the proverbial seed that started our careers.

Meredith:

I applied to social work school after working with adult vocational ESL (English as a second language) students at the Center for Immigrant Education and Training at LaGuardia Community College. My time there had shown me that while job counseling and support helped individual students reach their goals, policy changes on a larger scale would help a whole group of people at once. I didn't know how change like that happened, but I wanted to learn.

As Kristin and I got deeper into our studies and field placement assignments, we both discussed how anxious we were about not having a cause that we felt connected to. While we enjoyed the challenge of the work we were doing, we were each looking for something we could call our own. So it was with great excitement that I told Kristin about how I had stumbled on Red Hook Farms and similar urban agriculture organizations. I came across them after researching the term "garden therapy" on a hunch after a walk in a city park. As our research opened our eyes to the wide array of organizations working on environmental justice, food sovereignty, and similar issues we both began to realize that we were in the middle of something big. We both felt that there were strong connections between what we were studying and the changes these organizations were seeking. We couldn't wait to get involved.

Kristin:

My career in social work began at the Missouri Children's Division, as a frontline caseworker for families with children placed in alternative care. I knew the work of a frontline caseworker would be exhausting and emotionally difficult at times, but I was keenly aware that I had found my path. My work revealed a complex system of policies and laws that made serving the best interests of both children and their families prohibitive, and I felt the need to approach the issues my clients faced systemically, with the hopes of crafting community policies that promoted preventive services. It was the time I spent in graduate school that introduced me to the idea of combining my personal passion—gardening—with my professional desire to strengthen underserved communities.

Once our attention had been turned toward the growing use of gardens and green space in community-based work, Meredith and I began researching the concept of horticultural therapy. We found that the profession was almost exclusively dedicated to individual therapy and physical rehabilitation, and we knew from what we learned that there was indeed a great deal of room to bring the principles of the work into macro practice.

We were both especially drawn to the history of the campaign to create and protect community gardens in underserved neighborhoods of New York City (details about this campaign are explained later in this chapter). We regularly brought up the campaign and the tactics used in our community organizing classes, where our classmates likely began to think of us as the "garden girls." The more we learned about horticultural therapy, environmental justice campaigns, and the local food revolution, the more excited we became—although we often worried that what we were interested in was not "real social work." Would we be able to find jobs in line with our interests? We were still new to organizing, in addition to the world of horticulture, urban planning, and urban agriculture that we now hoped to connect with our practice. We felt that the issues we were interested in were closely aligned with social work values, but we did not quite know how to unite them. Perhaps if we had known more details about the beginnings of social work and its efforts to combat what was seen as "urban ills," we would have felt more confident in our new direction.

Social Work's Start as the "Answer" to the "Problems of City Life"

That the rise of parks, recreation, and social work are closely intertwined from the late 19th century on makes good sense if thought through fully: The effects of industrialization and urbanization were just beginning to be felt, and all three were designed to combat the effects of crowded living conditions and long factory hours. Jane Addams's Hull House is famous for many types of reform, a number of which affected the environment of the community surrounding the settlement house. For example, Addams was appointed garbage inspector for her ward after hassling the mayor about the lack of municipal attention to the mounds of garbage on the streets (Blum, 2004, p. 202).

The conditions of the streets in poor immigrant neighborhoods, and their effects on the children who played in them, can be pinpointed as one very visible motivation for the work of the reformers of the Progressive Era. Reformers such as Addams, Riis, and Wald were driven to create areas of respite, such as settlement houses, parks, and playgrounds, for the families that relied on these streets for play and socialization (Blum, 2004; Cranz, 1982).

While the history of the creation of settlement houses is well-known to most social work students, the parallel history of the role of social workers in the creation of parks and playgrounds may not be. This history begins with the creation of the first urban parks, designed "not from European urban models but from an anti-urban ideal that dwelt on the traditional relief from the evils of the city—to escape to the country" (Cranz, 1982, p. 5). These first parks, built in the last half of the 1800s, were "pleasure grounds" designed to re-create nature and filled with unstructured activities (p. 5). Parks were seen as a needed antidote to the increasing number of hours workers spent inside. During this time, what was acceptable for inclusion in these new public areas was fought out—"refined" activities such as riding and skating were allowed; "unrefined" activities such as selling goods, gambling, and political rallies were not (pp. 17–19).

By the 1900s, park administrators, influenced by the ideals of the Progressive Era, began to be more interested in the social role of the parks than in their aesthetic design. During this time, social workers began to advocate and provide programming for parks.

> The reform era saw the first professional incursions into the area of public welfare—as opposed to city beautification. Social workers were the first professionals regularly employed by parks departments, and the development of the paid social worker parallels the shift from philanthropy to professionalism in park work as a whole. The profession of social work incubated in settlement houses and park houses and then developed independently of the park system. (Cranz, 1982, p. 169)

Improvements in working conditions (shorter workweeks, higher wages, and child labor laws) had created a new reality: leisure time. This time needed to be filled with healthy activities to counteract the siren call of the saloon and the streets (Cranz, 1982, p. 62). Reformers of this time were especially worried for children and began to advocate for playgrounds as a prominent feature of municipal parks (p. 63). Children's play was supervised in these new playgrounds, and "the care of the playground was entrusted only to play leaders who understood that the significance of [the] play instinct was its relation to the physical and social development of young people" (p. 67). Recreation became a new specialty for social workers. Park life was no longer merely a substitute for the country; parks were smaller and tucked into neighborhoods as a part of the city's social reform tool kit.

These neighborhood parks were programmed year-round. One important aspect of this project was vegetable gardening. Parks and schools often collaborated in teaching gardening to youth, and adults were given plots as well. These plots were an important part of feeding the populace during the World Wars and were seen to encourage self-reliance and hard work (Cranz, 1982, p. 76).

The next explosion of park building occurred in the 1930s—much of it fueled by New Deal Works Progress Association funding, which eventually led to the professional separation of park administration and social work (Cranz, 1982, p. 99). Parks departments became increasingly focused on building their facilities and infrastructure, virtually eliminating the idea of using parks as a tool for reforming society. As time passed, the two professions went on to focus on their own challenges; park administrators had to deal with declining cities and shrinking budgets, and social work (while dealing with the very same challenges on a macro level) turned to focusing on individual mental health and influencing policy on a variety of issues, such as welfare reform, child welfare, and the rights of the mentally ill.

THE EMERGENCE OF "ECOLOGICAL THEORY" — WITHOUT THE NATURAL ENVIRONMENT

Social work was pioneered in an urban environment, so these urban roots led to an unfortunate shortage of examples of social workers realizing the benefits of nature as a whole, beyond urban parks and other human-made settings.

Pioneers such as Richmond and Addams helped establish parameters for social work's focus on the social conditions of the environment through attention to housing, sanitation, and public health. Besthorn (1997, as cited in Coates, 2003, p. 40) states that their emphasis on the social environment laid the groundwork for the field's neglect of the natural environment. They were not entirely to blame. Coates traces the field's shifting attention as it grew beyond its settlement house roots: from the influence of psychoanalysis and its allegiance to individual change and through talk therapy unrelated to such environmental factors. Likewise, in the 1960s, leaders of the field sought a unifying theory to settle the debate between "individual service and environmental action" (Besthorn, 1997, as cited in Coates, 2003, p. 41). This search led to the "goodness of fit" and "ecological" models of Bronfenbenner, Meyer, Gordon, and others, though these models focused on understanding the interactions between only the social environment and the individual (Coates, 2003, pp. 41–42). The ecological model developed the idea that people and their environment had a reciprocal relationship; professionals thus studied factors in the social environment that affected an individual's ability to cope. This ecological model eventually became a leading theory in the field (p. 42). As Besthorn (1997, as cited in Coates, 2003, p. 43) pointed out, however, social work's construct of person-in-environment has a tendency to view the natural environment as a benign and unchanging background for human activity, and removes the idea of nature from person and environment.

It is interesting that this dualistic worldview (the social environment vs. the natural environment) is reflected in the argument at the heart of social work—namely, whether social workers should focus on individual mental health or larger policy and societal change issues. The ecofeminist assessment of this issue concludes that Western thought is full of dichotomies such as humanity versus nature (Hoff, 1994, pp. 19–20). The term *ecofeminism* refers to a school of thought that has combined feminist values with ecological concepts. Ecofeminist theory asserts that the reasons for the current state of our environment lie in Western culture's devaluation of the natural world. It proposes "alternative values and conceptual models of social systems, which would support environmental restoration and sustainability" (p. 19). The view of nature as "the other," as something that can be willfully exploited or ignored altogether, is an assumption that is at the heart of the foundation of much of modern society, including social work. As we begin to realize the full effects of such thought, social work is just beginning to bridge this divide by widening the definition of ecological social work to include the natural world.

From Lost Theory to Emerging Social Work Practice: Some Lonely First Steps

As for the start of our own careers in environmental social work, the road has often been a winding one. Uncovering the connections that bond your personal passion to your work can be both thrilling and precarious. While finding a true home for your skills can bring a sense of incomparable purpose to your work, there can be fear in learning that you may be lonely in your conviction or that your intentions are already marked by defeat. In the hopes of learning more about what had been done, what was being done, and what may be left to do, we pursued information and enlightenment from a broad range of sources and quickly learned that a great variety of disciplines and tactical approaches were being used to join the once-distinct struggles of restoring both healthy environments and healthy communities.

We often felt more acutely aware of what we did *not* know than of what we *did* know. We began by taking advantage of the many opportunities to learn about urban agriculture, community gardening, and horticultural therapy that abound in New York City. We learned that while we were still relatively on our own, we were not the only social workers interested in the benefits of a healthy environment.

At this point, we had finished our first-year field placements with Brooklyn Congregations United. We had each struggled with the faith-based backbone of the organization and had learned an immeasurable amount. Not unlike the social construction of practice issues highlighted in Chapter 5, the skills we had learned included building relationships around sharing our personal values, bringing seemingly disparate groups together around those shared values, and using those values to envision a better future. These were skills we would depend on in our next placements and beyond.

We were both placed to work with teens for our second year of fieldwork. Kristin helped train high school–aged peer educators on issues surrounding reproductive health care, and Meredith worked at an after-school service-learning program in a supportive housing complex. Leadership development not unlike that discussed in Chapter 5 and long-term project planning were the skills we each endeavored to build on during that year. Meanwhile, our coursework had shifted to cover the basics of legislative advocacy. In volunteering with the Domestic Workers United campaign, which successfully fought for an increase in labor protections for domestic workers in the state of New York, we began to connect the dots about how community organizing actually occurs. Big, visual actions such as rallies and protests are few and far between (and surely unsuccessful) without the careful and difficult work of leadership development, goal setting, target identification, and power analysis. We were finally beginning to grasp the day-to-day work of an organizer. Our next steps would be to get out there and practice these skills for the causes that interested us the most. When we did so, we uncovered further historical connections between environmental work and social justice.

THE ENVIRONMENT AS A SOCIAL JUSTICE MOVEMENT

While the environment had not been a principal focus of the theories initially sustaining our professional work, it became clear to us that it had played a conspicuous cause in the fight for social justice, a core social work value. While social workers today do not typically turn to parks or gardens as an outlet for their practice skills, the macro practitioner may find herself examining the natural environment as it relates to the community members with whom she works—issues of open space, environmental justice, and food deserts are not unfamiliar to today's organizer. Not unlike issues such as housing, immigration, and health care, environmental issues have arisen in the context of a market economy and are being addressed as a distinct civil rights issue of our time.

As we discovered, the environment and racism were two common, independent areas of focus for many practitioners until the early 1980s. When the rural, poor, and predominantly Black Warren County in North Carolina was chosen to house a large toxic waste dump, community members protested their way into the national spotlight, permanently underscoring how the two issues were interconnected. They were not the first to challenge such action, however what happened in Warren County propelled local (and often isolated) opposition against toxins and waste facility sites into a multi-issue, multiethnic, and multiregional movement (Bullard & Johnson, 2000).

In the late summer of 1978, more than 30,000 gallons of toxic oil contaminated with PCBs (polychlorinated biphenyls) were illegally jettisoned along 240 miles of roadside shoulders across 14 North Carolina counties (Bullard, 1993). The Environmental Protection Agency recognized the dumping grounds as a threat to public health and designated them as superfund sites (Bullard, 2009). Warren County was chosen by the North Carolina Department of Environment and Natural Resources and the Environmental Protection Agency as a landfill site to dispose of the contaminated soil (Bullard, 2009).

The plan to site the hazardous waste facility in Warren County brought cause for concern to community members. Initially, resistance was raised by (mainly) White landowners who endured 3 years of legal challenges, which were wholly unsuccessful. The group, known as Warren County Citizens Concerned about PCB had no knowledge of or experience in direct action. The decision to shift to disruptive direct-action tactics necessitated the need for coalition support. The group turned to a local Baptist church, with whom they had been in contact previously and whose members lived adjacent to the site. The church leadership embraced the opposition and gained the support of the United Church of Christ Commission for Racial Justice and the Southern Christian Leadership Conference (of which Dr. Martin Luther King Jr. had once been president), which led to local business and political support as well. The caliber of leadership drawn from the African American community helped legitimize and empower the movement (McGurty, 2000).

Bolstered by the addition of experienced leaders, they developed a direct-action campaign evocative of the civil rights movement of the 1960s. Long-distance marches, mass meetings, and the incorporation of prayer in the protests all shared lineage with the protests of 20 years earlier. Symbolic blockades, created by people lying down in front of trucks entering the site, were also used successfully to delay dumping and to increase visibility of the movement (McGurty, 2000). Their actions led to more than 500 arrests—the first ever arrests made over the siting of a landfill—and gained the attention of the national media (United Church of Christ Commission for Racial Justice, 1987). While the battle eventually ended in defeat, the protests in Warren County are widely known as the conceptual beginning of the environmental racism movement (Bullard, 1993; Skelton & Miller, 2006). Leaders from the civil rights movement diagnosed the environmental struggle as an extension of the same economic and education issues they had long been fighting (Skelton & Miller, 2006). It became clear to those involved that the civil rights movement, long rooted in social justice, and the environmental movement, rooted in injustice, had common conceptual links that were emerging in a new paradigm for collective opposition.

The initial opposition to the siting of the landfill was marked by a not-in-my-backyard frame. The shift in tactics toward collective action also created an interesting shift in the framing of the problem, which was insightfully expanded to blame not only the decision makers in the siting of the landfill but also long-standing historical racial discrimination throughout the South (McGurty, 2000). The scope of the problem also underwent a significant shift beyond Warren County—leaders realized there were Warren Counties throughout the South and helped solidify the concept of environmental racism as a distinct form of oppression.

The movement was also marked by an intensified focus on research as a tactic in combating the oppression they faced. The actions in Warren County led to the publication of a 1983 study by the U.S. General Accounting Office examining the location of landfills within communities of color and their disproportionately negative impacts on those communities, as well as a landmark 1987 study commissioned by the United Church of Christ Commission for Racial Justice—titled *Toxic Wastes and Race in the United States*—which directly challenged the relationship between communities of color and the siting of toxic waste dumping (Bullard, 2000). Employing research in this new battle for social justice was a departure for many who had long relied solely on more traditional tactics borrowed from the civil rights movement, including protests, demonstrations, and community forums (Bullard, 2000, p. 43).

The birth of the environmental justice movement culminated in the First National People of Color Environmental Leadership Summit in 1991, which lasted 3 days and produced the Principles of Environmental Justice.* Reminiscent of the Denver Principles, created in the early 1980s in an effort to protect and expand the rights of people with AIDS, the Principles of Environmental Justice aimed to reconnect people of color with their natural world and broadened the scope of the environment to include the places "where we live, work, learn and play" (Turner & Wu, 2003). The consideration of "place" was now more apparent than ever as a complex and layered factor in both the mental and physical health of a community.

UNEARTHING COMMON GROUND: THE ORIGINS OF URBAN ENVIRONMENTAL ORGANIZING

Farther north, the struggle for environmental justice was cropping up in vacant lots across New York City's Lower East Side. The fiscal crisis of the 1970s and the resultant cuts to city services had begun to take its toll on the neighborhood, which was hit especially hard and characterized by large-scale disinvestment and abandonment, a lack of police and fire services, and empty lots that were literally filled with trash.

In the spring of 1973, a small grassroots movement led by artist, experienced activist, and Bowery resident Liz Christy opted to respond to the blight of their neighborhood in a new way. Together, over the course of a few months, they liberated a vacant lot at the corner of Bowery and East Houston streets, hauling out trash, leveling the ground, and bringing in loads of soil (www.ecotippingpoints.org). The group soon gained the attention and support of neighbors who also wanted to help in the effort. By summer, they had collectively transformed the lot into a community garden where community members could grow their own produce and come together in a joining of the natural and social environment, and they had created a sense of unity and purpose in the process. Once an informal social network, The Green Guerillas (as the group became known) emerged from their efforts united and began working to help other communities plan and design their own gardens.

News of the garden spread quickly and was well received—except by city officials who threatened to put a stop to the horticultural trespassing (www.ecotippingpoints.org). The *New York Daily News* had taken interest in the garden and ran a story that led the city not only to back down but to lease the gardeners use of the land for $1 per year. The media attention helped create a shift in public perception of the garden, which underscores the importance of issue framing and the power of a sympathetic city. Soon after the story ran, city-owned vacant lots became popular targets for new community gardens, and in 1978, the city created Operation Green Thumb (today known simply as GreenThumb) to help manage the leasing of these spaces (www.nycgovparks.org).

The leases were a way for the city to provide legal and *temporary* use of the vacant land, and were conditioned such that the gardens could be removed by the city should the opportunity for development arise. Despite these conditions, the gardens became well rooted as community fixtures. The introduction of GreenThumb allowed community members a feeling of protection and security, and they focused their efforts on learning about urban horticulture, no longer fearing imminent destruction of their gardens.

By the late 1990s, New York City was home to 1,906 community gardens (American Community Gardening Association, 1998, as cited in von Hassell, 2002) and an estimated 14,000 community gardeners (Neighborhood Open Space Coalition, 2000, as cited in von Hassell, 2002). Ultimately, the success of community gardens in these neighborhoods became the root of their potential demise. Neighborhoods such as the Lower East Side had once again become desirable, and real estate developers were seeking land on which they could build.

In 1996, New York Mayor Rudolph Giuliani ordered an auction of all "disposable" vacant land over a 5-year time period, and approvals for new gardens ceased. The community gardens that had been granted leases on city-owned lots became income targets for the administration and the city. The move gave community members cause to bridge the pavement that separated them and raise their collective voice. The threat of large-scale elimination of the gardens carried the organizational impetus of the movement beyond the Lower East Side to Brooklyn, the Bronx, and the Upper West Side of Manhattan. Strengthened by an exponential increase in protesters, a coalition formed around the already well-organized Lower East Side gardeners, who took the lead in coordinating a citywide voice. The gardeners offered sympathy to others who were facing the loss of their gardens at auction, as a way of creating a paradigm shift in the community members—by asking how their gardens were started and what they most enjoyed planting, they were able to reframe the situation as injustice and gain support in their efforts (Martinez, 2009).

The framing of the movement proved to be critical to its success. The garden activists understood the risk of being perceived as selfish when compared with the interests of the city as a whole, as the development of low- to moderate-income housing could potentially help offset gentrification of their neighborhoods. Further, they knew that their claims were solely moral—the contracts they signed with the city provided temporary use of the land. By telling their stories—collectively held narratives and histories as gardeners—they sought to move public perceptions of the gardens. By sharing the grief associated with their loss, they contradicted the city's claim of bringing no harm and simultaneously found gardeners to unite around a common purpose (Martinez, 2009).

The gardeners used a variety of tactics to reframe the issue and gain support for their gardens. Early on in the movement, gardeners demanded that each garden be discussed by name. This tactic went beyond symbolism and acted as an objection to the characterization of the gardens as unencumbered lots, forcing community boards to recognize the gardens as "places" (Martinez, 2009). They engaged the media to help increase visibility and public support. Wholly sympathetic, news stories ran often and commonly portrayed the gardeners' plight through a "paradise lost" lens (Martinez, 2009). Elaborate performance pageants were also a common tactic, which served to illustrate resistance and told compelling narratives portraying gardeners as victims. Political allies were also to be found, especially in the city council and, most notably, with Attorney General Eliot Spitzer. Disruptive action and intensive protests, including the release of thousands of crickets at one auction site, increased as the auctions drew closer.

In the weeks and months leading up to the auction, a number of environmental nonprofits had attempted to purchase the gardens as land trusts, and were each refused by Giuliani. The movement had succeeded in articulating a sympathetic frame for the public to embrace, and once joined by the inspired Bette Midler and her considerable resources, two private organizations—the Trust for Public Land and the New York Restoration Project—came together and purchased just over 100 garden sites from the city at the near-market-value cost of $4.2 million (Elder, 2005; Martinez, 2009; Steinhauer, 2002). The gardens they purchased now operate under the private jurisdiction of these organizations, though much of the daily control remains in the hands of the garden members.

INDIVIDUAL OR GROUP ACTIVITY

1. Review a project you are working on and consider in what ways you could tactically include a "natural environmental." issue (consider the following options):

   a. Use of local space ("the commons")

   b. "Greening" options

   c. Health and wellness related to the environment

   d. Environmental justice issues

2. Consider the ways social workers can make a contribution to such efforts:

   a. Micro skills

   b. Group work skills

   c. Macro skills

3. What new allies can be developed here?

This battle for green space, while contextually different from other social movements, relied firmly on theories and tactics from a community development model of organizing. Its strength, as discussed in Chapter 7, was in building true grassroots power from within and gaining the broad support of the media, neighborhood groups, and government officials.

Today's community gardens have symbolized a community's response to increasing land development and decreased power (both actual and perceived) over their environment. Ferguson (2001, as cited in Chitov, 2006) reasoned that the community gardening movement that began in the 1970s marked a much stronger shift away from government provision and control of the gardens, and paralleled the ideological shift that was happening in urban communities. Unlike their counterparts earlier in history (the WWII Victory Gardens), these gardens emerged "not out of government support, but rather its neglect" (Ferguson, 2001, as cited in Chitov, 2006, p. 442). Increased disenfranchisement led to a desire to reclaim neighborhood spaces, an effort that was and continues to be led at the grassroots level (von Hassell, 2002, pp. 42–44).

THE ENVIRONMENTAL PRACTITIONERS' JOURNEY CONTINUES

Our journey during the end of our second year and after graduating took us through parks, gardens, and classrooms—and to different parts of the country. While we didn't know it yet, we were graduating into a recession.

Kristin:

Becoming more familiar with the basic principles of social capital theory, I began incorporating research on community gardens and civic engagement into my existing coursework, tailoring my assignments whenever possible. The ongoing project culminated with a paper dedicated to the use of gardening as a tool in social work practice and officially convinced me (if not others) that I would indeed be doing "real" social work. Having spent the year working with mostly legal professionals, I was comfortable as a social worker in a nontraditional role and continued to research and network, in the hopes that it would prepare me for work with a multidisciplinary organization.

Through this process, I formulated a strategic vision, that with the engagement in the transformative process of community gardening, I hoped to connect people of all ages from working-poor communities and communities with little social capital, with the values of growth, sustainability, and social and economic justice. I crafted my vision with a great deal more ease than I had expected, and have not desired to change a word of it since. The difficulty, I feared, would be in finding (paid) work that allowed me to live up to my ideals.

After graduating, I moved to Denver and continued learning about the work being done, while becoming familiar with local organizations I was interested in working with. I indulged in my rediscovered square footage by planting a large garden. Like any organizer, I practiced patience (though not always well) and continued searching for the right opportunity.

Meredith:

After graduation I felt anxious about my prospects of finding work related to my new interests, as I did not know where to begin looking for a job in ecological social work. On a whim I searched agricultural jobs on Craigslist and applied to be a farmer's market manager for Greenmarket. I was thrilled to be offered a seasonal position and was given 3 weekly markets to manage. One market was in a prosperous neighborhood on the Upper East Side, one straddled a public housing complex on one side and a brand new high-rise condo on the other (also on the Upper East Side), and one was outside of Lincoln Hospital in the South Bronx. Two of these markets accepted SNAP (food stamps) and participated in Health Bucks, a program designed to help low-income families purchase more food from the market by matching the amount of SNAP benefit dollars they spent there.

Greenmarket is a forward-thinking organization, and I was exposed to both challenges and solutions I hadn't considered before; from the little things (I had never observed a family using their SNAP benefits before, or the decisions they made when using them) to the large (balancing the need to serve a "food desert" in a lower-income area with making a certain profit in a higher-income neighborhood). I most enjoyed interacting with customers and hearing directly from them about what had brought them to the market that day. The reasons ranged from simple curiosity to being able to purchase culturally specific foods to concern for the environment as a whole. For me, it reinforced the lesson that a successful program or campaign is one that many types of people can feel engaged in for a variety of reasons. This was something I had witnessed at Brooklyn Congregations United, the domestic workers' rights campaign, and was now seeing the effects of in the fight to get more healthy food to all New Yorkers.

After my seasonal position ended with Greenmarket, I was uncertain I would find similar work but ended up being hired by the park advocacy group New Yorkers for Parks (NY4P). NY4P has a long and storied history, beginning with park and playground creation at the turn of the century and continuing up to present day with a focus on equality of access to and maintenance of public open space in New York City. Throughout the years, NY4P and its predecessor organizations relied on a variety of organizing models, but it has most recently used a civic model of organizing. NY4P's biggest strength is its research, which it uses *to build a history of data on issues related to New York City's parks (maintenance, amount of open space per neighborhood, land use, etc.). These independent reports are made available to community groups so they can use the information to urge the Parks Department and local politicians to move on their community's concerns. Additionally, NY4P hosts an annual event where parks-related organizations and activists can meet directly with their city council member about their local park. My role at NY4P included helping maintain our relationship with the hundreds of park-related groups in New York City and training citizen activists to use our tools to advocate for their local parks. The job opened my eyes to the way caring for shared public space is often the first step in a long journey toward neighborhood improvement (as Kristin's research into community gardens had shown me in graduate school). I fell deeply in love with parks and their ability to be the heart of a community, and gained a deeper understanding of what moves government officials to change. I worked with and learned from many types of experts—environmentalists, lawyers, urban planners, community gardeners, municipal officials, and more. I was often (but not always!) the only social worker at the table, and it was gratifying to marry my skills with theirs in working toward a common cause. **This was the major lesson I learned from my time at NY4P—social workers may not be environmental experts, but they are skilled in the mix of micro and group work skills of helping guide groups toward positive change.***

DIGGING DEEPER: THE POTENTIAL FOR SOCIAL WORK WITH TODAY'S ENVIRONMENTAL ORGANIZING

Today the number of organizations highlighting the importance of the environment seems limitless, and many choose to focus on merging the natural environment with its urban, human-made kin. A keen example of what can be done within the scope of this work is Growing Power. Founded in Milwaukee and later expanded to Chicago, Growing Power operates a number of urban farms as community food centers. Equipped with gardens, greenhouses, farm animals, kitchens, aquaculture, and food distribution centers, the organization endeavors to build equitable, affordable, and sustainable food systems (www .growingpower.org).

Growing Power also seeks to engage low-income youth for nutrition and gardening education programs, as well as entrepreneurial job-training programs. Within these programs, participants connect to food production in a way that highlights the planning, cultivation, harvesting, and marketing of their crops within their own communities. Enabling employment and education preparedness for the youth participants is central to the focus of the programming (www.growingpower.org).

As companion to the youth training programming, Growing Power also actively participates in local food policy and food justice initiatives in an effort to develop responsible policies to improve access to nutritional and affordable food options and increase food security. In addition, they provide technical assistance to other urban farmers and community members through outreach and education (www.growingpower.org).

Similar to the Added Value program at Red Hook Farms, Growing Power brings agriculture into the city, a common strategy for combating today's "urban ills," such as food deserts. The organization encompasses a diverse set of issues aimed at overcoming the singular and complex problem of food justice. (The focus on green-collar job preparedness is also common among many organizations today and creates an economic incentive with the larger goal of strengthening community food systems.) Growing Power acknowledges the link between access to green space and community well-being, and the gardens provide respite from vacant lots and abandoned buildings. Social justice is explicitly addressed through policy initiatives, as well as through community involvement and increasing sustainability measures in underserved areas.

Emerging Professional Attention to the Concept of "Environment"

As exemplified by ongoing environmental justice movements and the basic principles of horticultural therapy, the idea that social work needs to pay attention to the natural environment has been gaining traction. Weick (1981, p. 141) named four areas that social work should assess to place the individual within the broadest possible environment: the internal-social, external-social, internal-physical, and external-physical. This shift allows social work as a field to address the macro versus micro debate, as well as allowing for inclusion of exploration of the physical environment within the individual (addressing the mind/body dichotomy) and without (finally giving social work a platform to address nature and built environments; pp. 141–142). Weick writes, "To view behavior accurately, all four sets of environmental influences must be considered. The result is a broader diagnostic base that acknowledges the significance of not only psychological and social factors but also the physical factors shaping human behavior" (p. 142).

	Internal	External
Psychosocial	Thoughts, feelings, personal goals	Socioeconomic status, political economy
Physical	Genetic traits, organ functioning	Climate, food, noise

Schmitz, Matyók, Sloan, and James (2012) highlight a holistic and interdisciplinary view of the skills social workers will need to engage in practice that takes into account the natural environment. Drawing on peace studies and economics, Schmitz et al. believe that social workers must help bring about the paradigm shift toward compassionate, regulated use of shared natural resources. They state that social workers are historically change agents and leaders, and have the skills to help guide the interdisciplinary work that must take place to bring about the societal changes needed to protect the natural environment. Additionally, Schmitz et al. trace many of the challenges faced by the populations social work seeks to engage, such as the urban poor, low-wage workers, refugees, migrant workers, and the like, and connect them back to Western capitalistic ways of doing business. The authors profoundly assert that an equal way of using and protecting natural resources would help alleviate some of the most entrenched problems social work faces. "The interconnection between poverty, food insecurity, inequality, environmental degradation, sustainability and development is well established" (Soubbotina, 2004; World Commission on Environment and Development, 1987, as quoted in Schmitz et al., 2012).

> Those on the margins of society are little able to advance environmental justice as long as it is separated from the responses to the structural issues of war, violence and poverty. Environmental degradation, poverty and war are inextricably linked, and the human and social dimensions of this crisis are tied to issues of human rights and social justice. (Mearns & Norton, 2010, as quoted in Schmitz et al., 2012, p. 281)

Finally, the best example that the field of social work is beginning to expand its focus on the social environment is that both the National Association of Social Workers (NASW) and the Council on Social Work Education have proclaimed protecting the environment to be an important role for social workers, as it affects so much of their clients' and communities' lives.

THE HEALTH CONNECTION: MICRO MEETS MACRO

Why are the field's leading professional organizations urging social workers to join the cause for the environment? In large part, because research and anecdotal evidence are pointing to the negative health effects on both individual and community levels from the current state of our deteriorating natural environment. Focusing on improving our natural environment will add an array of new interventions to the arsenal of both micro and macro social workers as they push to better the health of their clients and communities.

Much has been written in the past few decades on the environmental determinants of health and health disparities. Research to date has focused on whether there is a causal relationship between green space and overall health, and thus far, the evidence is anecdotal at best—finding that *perceptions* of health are higher when people live in "greener" areas (Maas, Verheij, Groenewegen, de Vries, & Spreeuwenberg, 2006). Other research has found that contact with, or even a view of, the natural environment corresponds with shorter recovery times from illness, improved cognitive functioning, healthy childhood maturation and development, and enhanced coping and adaptive behavior (Kellert, Heerwagen, & Mador, 2008). The relationship between green space and mental health is stronger, in part due to the fact that green space tends to lead people outdoors and thus increase levels of social cohesion (deVries et al., 2003; Sugiyama et al., 2007).

In addition to the many benefits examined through one's direct contact with the natural environment, the relationship between community health and the natural environment can also be viewed as positive and productive. Accumulating evidence in research shows that shared social environments—in this case, shared common space such as parks and gardens—have a significant effect on a person's health above and beyond individual effects (van der Linden, Drukker, Gunther, Feron, & van Os, 2003). Findings suggest specifically that family and neighborhood social capital are important predictors of children's health and well-being (Almedom, 2005, p. 954; Day & Wen, 2007). In short, access to open space may improve overall health, both at an individual and at a community level, but the key factor implicated in improved health is *the engagement in and use of the space*. Neighborhoods that demonstrate high levels of social capital (characterized by high levels of informal social control and feelings of trust and reciprocity) are healthier (Almedom, 2005, p. 954; Day & Wen, 2007; Sugiyama et al., 2007; van der Linden et al., 2003). While research continues to evolve, we posit that in addition to the benefits enjoyed from breathing clean air and drinking clean water, the act of joining your neighbors in the garden or at the park may also ease your stress and make you feel a bit better. From this, we gather that the binary approach to social work practice (treating the individual or treating the community) is shortsighted—as is the neglect in incorporating the natural environment in our work. Compartmentalizing our efforts will not wholly limit our results, though a more comprehensive and layered approach can begin guiding us to more robust results.

INDIVIDUAL OR GROUP EXERCISE ON CONNECTING MICRO AND MACRO

- Examine a "social" (macro) or "individual/interpersonal" (micro) issue to determine its natural environmental elements.
- How might those factors be impacting your intervention?
- Add one "environmental" focus to your work that can be addressed concretely over the next 2 months of work with your individual or group.

The Environmental Activists' Internal Strategic Visions Take Shape

Aware once again that we might be lonely in this, we set out to continue our work with a full consideration of social work practice—inclusive of individuals, communities, and both natural and social environments.

Kristin:

I joined the Chicago Park District, one of the largest municipal park districts in the country and a leading provider of programming and recreation opportunities, where I am excited to have a home for my skills and expertise. Tasked with supporting both the community gardens and the youth-focused Harvest Garden program, I find myself engaged in work that is both physically and intellectually satisfying. While there is a great deal of gratification in the labor of preparing the children's gardens for planting in the spring and seeing the first sprouts emerge from the soil, my work is validated by the interactions between the gardeners. As they come together on a Saturday morning to tend to common areas in the garden, the sense of stewardship they have over this small plot of land within a city park is apparent. As they work and chat, I hear them offer recommendations to one another for successful planting, and I can see a community forming.

Chicago is widely diverse with respect to both cultural and socioeconomic identities, and while statistics show a decline, the city is also the most segregated city in the United States (Glaeser & Vigdor, 2012). Armed with the knowledge that many of Chicago's neighborhoods are considered food deserts, Harvest Garden is a three-season gardening program designed to introduce Chicago's youth to healthy organically and locally grown food. The program operates through a social justice lens, with the goal of teaching children how to grow and prepare fresh produce in neighborhoods where access may otherwise be unlikely.

Throughout the Chicago Park District, I am surrounded by a diverse group of professionals who are striving to provide the best in nature, recreation, arts and culture programming, and special events. With an intensified focus on Chicago's youth, the Chicago Park District released a strategic plan in 2012 underscoring a commitment to provide opportunities for children and their families. The main focus of the organization is to provide programming that will engage kids for a lifetime. Adherent to the belief that parks are the unsung heroes of our communities, I share in the values of the organization and believe that the work we do can act as a gateway for Chicago youth to lead healthy, active lives.

KRISTIN LEBOURVEAU'S INTERNAL STRATEGIC VISION AS AN ENVIRONMENTAL SOCIAL WORK PRACTITIONER

Who: Working-class and poor people in underserved communities

What issue: Environmental, economic, and social justice

Her role: Facilitator, educator, and advocate

How she worked: Calling attention to the connection between community members' producing locally and the principles of social and environmental justice that it supports

Core values consecrated in action: Growth, sustainability, equality, diversity, respect, social justice

Meredith:

In 2012, I moved to Virginia and was hired by the Family Nutrition Program of Virginia Tech, where I run a project designed to increase the food security of the families in our statewide SNAP-Ed (nutrition education) program through a variety of ways: by helping them access and use their SNAP (food stamp) benefits at the local farmer's market, counteracting food deserts by helping farmer's markets open mobile and pop-up locations, and teaching the basics of vegetable gardening to the youth in our programs. I am seeking to engage both our participants and the many players in the local food system (farmers, market managers, and local officials), and to help them learn more about each other and how both communities and families can benefit from a strong local food system. I don't think deep change is possible if you seek to engage just one side of an issue. Both sides are experts in their personal challenges and solutions; sometimes the best course is to help them connect and learn from each other. The work I am beginning now is a mix of the women-centered model of organizing and the civic model of organizing, in that the focus is on building reciprocal partnerships with other institutions and government agencies to support the nutritional health of low-income families.

The core values in my career are respect for each individual's experience, curiosity, reciprocity, and hope. The food-security project is quite new, but my plan is that our participants will teach us what would help them make healthy choices for their families and that the markets we work with will continue to evolve to better serve low-income families' needs while also helping grow their local economies. I have been able to put my personal values into action in my career through recognizing that what interested me the most was helping make sure low-income communities had equal access to the things that could have a positive effect on their mental and physical health—be it safe, clean, and well-programmed parks or healthy local food—and that has been an honor.

MEREDITH LEDLIE-JOHNSON'S INTERNAL STRATEGIC VISION AS AN ENVIRONMENTAL SOCIAL WORK PRACTITIONER

Who: Limited-resource families

What issue: Food security and access; social justice

Her role: Project manager, coalition member, and advocate

How she worked: Directly with SNAP clients, state-agency representatives, and farmer's market managers to understand all challenges and opportunities, and identify areas of mutual benefit for all three

Core values consecrated in action: Respect for each individual's experience, curiosity, reciprocity, hope, social justice

---

A SUMMARY EXAMPLE: FINDING COMMON GROUND ACROSS SOCIAL WORK METHODS THROUGH COMMUNITY GARDENS

As both the long, once-neglected history of the physical environment and social work and our own journeys into environmental activism make clear, there are many ecological arenas in which individual need and community purpose can find common cause. Perhaps nothing demonstrates this more cogently and concretely than community gardens. In all these examples, the gardens do not exist simply to beautify an area; they "represent places within which life occurs" (von Hassell, 2002 p. 32). In other words, the gardens serve to underscore the connection between individual and community well-being. A central tenet of community organizing theory asserts that individuals acting alone do not reap the same benefits as those who are a part of a larger group effort—this concept is mirrored by social capital theory. Whether organized by a city, a nonprofit organization, a park department, or a block association, gardens are an outlet of control and ownership by the gardeners. For some, it is the only "investment" they have in their community. For a macro-practice social worker, it can be a platform from which greater community growth can be facilitated. Community gardens, parks, and other forms of public open space provide a nice framework in which to merge the underlying goal of a strong, healthy community with the surplus benefit of strong, healthy individuals.

Community gardens require members to participate in a process involving shared chores, shared space, and shared responsibility. As mentioned, individuals who participate in this process are believed to benefit from the interactions with other members of their community. These benefits stem from a number of variables associated with the activities encompassed by community gardening, including an environment that supports the process of socialization; the facilitation of cooperation, decision making, and in some instances leadership skills; and the emerging presence of social norms such as trust and reciprocity. Whether a member shares watering duties with a neighboring plot or participates in yearly elections, the exchange facilitates a process of cooperation and encourages trust.

By promoting community-level decision-making abilities, Jamison (1985) and Linn (1999) contend that community gardeners have the capacity to feel an increased sense of ownership or stewardship in their communities, which may empower them to take on more active roles in other neighborhood development activities (as cited in Glover, 2004, p. 69). The complementary processes of empowerment and leadership development, embodied by the efforts of organizations such as Growing Power, reflect the attributes needed in a community-building effort. These qualities might be demonstrated in one's ability to mobilize resources, coordinate partnerships or collaborative efforts, and recruit others to assist in the physical efforts a garden inevitably requires. As a result, community gardens begin to serve as potential sites for community building (Glover, 2004).

Much of the current research on community gardens, leadership development, and empowerment intuitively overlooks the engrained dichotomy of individual versus macro practice historically found in social work curriculum. As discussed in Chapter 5, this divide limits us as practitioners. Much of environmental justice work operates just the same—recognizing that healthy individuals and healthy communities go hand in hand. As social workers, we are now charged with creating a new practice framework that acknowledges this duality as limiting and allows us to act on our dynamic world without boundaries.

TACTICAL IMPLICATIONS FOR
THE ENVIRONMENTAL PRACTITIONER

Bullard (2000) identifies eight prevalent tactics in the environmental justice movement: government legal action, government administrative action, private legal action, demonstrations, petitions and referenda, lobbying, press campaigns, and violence (see www.thechangeagency. org). Conspicuously absent from his list is research, which is common and increasing in environmental justice campaigns (Minkler, Breckwich Vasquez, Tajik, & Petersen, 2006). Community-driven research, specifically, is well suited to environmental justice campaigns (and all social justice campaigns), as the tasks involved also serve to increase the capacity of community members. Aimed at educating legislators, policymakers, and the media, methods may include secondary data analyses, geographic information systems mapping, survey research, and scientific and anecdotal data collection (Minkler et al., 2006).

Partnerships with hospitals, universities, and other larger organizations also complement the research process, as well as the overall strategy of the campaign: Not only can they add skills such as research, media relations, and fundraising, but they can enable groups to enter the policy arena from a more influential position, increase their ability to mobilize their base, and provide additional human resources (Minkler et al., 2006). As seen in Warren County, informal partnerships, collaborations, and alliances also add to the value of many campaigns through shared resources, information, and collective identity.

In large part, the work that has emerged from the environmental justice movement is rooted in the context of the civil rights movement—and appropriately so, as the foundation for the injustice is kindred. Chapter 8 discusses why having an understanding of the historical antecedents of community organizing can position an organizer to contextualize present-day issues in a way that allows learning from past mistakes and the ability to make the necessary modifications to capitalize on effective campaigns. The early environmental justice movement demonstrates this point well, with prominent civil rights leaders who joined the old brand to new conflicts.

CONCLUSION: IMPLICATIONS FOR THE NEW ENVIRONMENTAL PRACTITIONER

While times of struggle are susceptible to an increase in collaborative work in a quest for social justice, times of peace also reflect active participation (Chitov, 2006). The ability to identify and expose the self-interest of community members (e.g., garden members) is a key factor in maintaining participation. Chitov reinforces this point, adding that incentives for engagement are a critical element to the sustainability of a community garden. There must be a feeling that it is in an individual's best interest to support the greater group or community. Marcus and Green (2012) note that much of what we choose to do is a reflection of our anticipation of an expected return, though this return can include the understanding that there is value in the action itself. In addition, the belief that investment now will result in a reward later is also important to building and maintaining social capital. The key concepts of obligation, expectation, and trustworthiness rely on a reciprocal relationship (Laser & Leibowitz, 2009). This process contributes to the overall levels of sustainability that can contribute to the longevity of the community while maintaining active participation.

Midgley and Livermore (2009), supported by the research of Robert Putnam, suggest that community-based social workers and community organizers have the ability to mobilize social capital and build not only social and political power but also economic power. Social workers, and especially community organizers, possess the skills required to mobilize social capital. Skills such as "defining the target need or population, analyzing community resources and problems, creating local community agencies, facilitating setting goals and objectives, selecting effective strategies for community action, implementing programs and projects and evaluation outcomes" (Midgley & Livermore, 2009) are often found in the repertoire of a macro practitioner and paralleled by individual-level professionals. Further, many community organizers facilitate the development of individual leadership as they explicitly forge connections between community stakeholders, local leaders and politicians, civic groups, clergy and churches, schools, and local businesses— therefore increasing civic engagement and collaboration, and empowering individuals within the community. Literature reinforces the consequence of such work, touting that an increased democratic effect is embodied by those who take a more active role in further developing the community (Glover, Parry, & Shinew, 2005). This is not unlike the activities commonly played out in community gardens, or in the creation of green spaces in urban communities.

Efforts within the environmental justice movement can be influential on the community level by reclaiming public space through the transformation of vacant lots or neglected common space; increasing security by creating safe, open, green spaces that increase foot traffic and community gatherings; and allowing members to participate in creative nonviolent resistance to the market economy and political processes that so often shape their lives and communities. In underserved or marginalized communities, the ability to reduce dependence on high food prices and limited selection of healthy choices, and to provide people with the opportunity to grow their own food, encourages both economic and environmental justice.

As the field of social work moves forward, the concept of "person-in-environment" is sure to continue to evolve into something more complete and all encompassing. Social workers are well placed to see the effects that polluted, unhealthy environments have on their clients and communities. The reasons for the harm caused to the environment are just as thorny as those for the social injustices social work already challenges: Racism, classism, and valuing profits over the health and viability of communities are just a few of the interlocking forces driving the current misuse of the environment.

As the effects of global warming and the fight for ever-dwindling natural resources begin to grow clearer to the general population, social workers with skills in community organizing, visioning, leadership development, and facilitation will be needed to help organizations of all kinds meet the challenges of this new reality. Collaboration with other professionals—ecologists, city planners, health care workers, researchers, parks professionals, and others—will be one important way social workers can contribute their skills and ensure that underrepresented populations get a seat at the planning table. The social work profession has been informed and supported throughout its history by a variety of disciplines and practice methods. Professional social workers encompass the ability to utilize a broad and diverse range of skills, while calling on a wide range of disciplines for support. Through these partnerships, we are better prepared to serve our diverse and dynamic community members.

ACTIVITY FOR EDUCATIONAL POLICY 2.1.7

1. Reimagine how the "social environment" impacting an issue or campaign can include the "natural environment." Examine how the two are intertwined. How does this change the focus of your work, if at all?

2. What new actors can you invite into this work?

3. How can your social work skills sets be used in this environmental activism?

THE COMMUNITY TOOLBOX

Ecological Sanitation Closes the Loop Between Health, Sanitation, and Food Security

Neighborhood Design and Zoning for Community Buildings

Improving Parks and Other Community Facilities

Improving the Quality of Housing

Neighborhood Design and Zoning for Community Buildings

Protecting Environmental Quality

Example(s) of Strategic and Action Plans (Related to Clean Drinking Water)

Take Charge Challenge: Self-Determined Physical Activity Program

Determining Service Utilization (related to recreation)

Improving Services (for physical activity)

REFERENCES

Almedom, A. (2005). Social capital and mental health: An interdisciplinary review of primary evidence. *Social Science and Medicine, 61,* 943–964.

Blum, E. D. (2004). Settlement House Movement. In R. Stapleton (Ed.), *Pollution A to Z* (pp. 202–203). New York: Macmillan Reference.

Bullard, R. D. (1993). Environmental justice for all. *National Humanities Center: TeacherServe.* Retrieved from http://nationalhumanitiescenter.org/tserve/nattrans/ntuseland/essays/envjust.htm

Bullard, R. D. (2000). *Dumping in Dixie: Race, class and environmental quality* (3rd ed.). Boulder, CO: Westview Press.

Bullard, R. D. (2009). *VOICES: Investigate EPA's treatment of black communities in the south.* Retrieved from http://www.southernstudies.org/2009/09/voices-investigate-epas-treatment-of-black-communities-in-the-south.html

Bullard, R. D., & Johnson, G. (2000). Environmental justice: Grassroots activism and its impact on public policy decision making. *Journal of Social Issues, 56*(3), 555–578.

Chitov, D. (2006). Cultivating social capital on urban plots: Community gardens in New York City. *Humanity and Society, 30*(4), 437–462.

Coates, J. (2003). *Ecology and social work: Toward a new paradigm.* Black Point, Nova Scotia: Fernwood.

Cranz, G. (1982). *The politics of park design: A history of urban parks in America.* Cambridge: MIT Press.

Day, J., & Wen, M. (2007). *Social capital and adolescent mental well-being: The role of family, school and neighborhood.* Presented at the annual meeting of the American Sociological Association.

De Vries, S., Verheij, R.A., Groenewegen, P.P., Spreeuwenberg, P. (2003) Natural environments - healthy environments? An exploratory analysis of the relationship between greenspace and health. *Environment & Planning, 2*(10).

Elder, R. (2005). Protecting New York City's community gardens. *NYU Environmental Law Journal, 13,* 769–800.

Glaeser, E., & Vigdor, J. (2012, January). *The end of the segregated century: Racial separation in America's neighborhoods, 1890–2010* (Manhattan Institute for Policy Research, Civic Report N. 66). Retrieved from https://www.manhattan-institute.org/html/cr_66.htm

Glover, T. (2004). The 'community' center and the social construction of citizenship. *Leisure Sciences, 26*(1), 63–83.

Glover, T., Parry, D., & Shinew, K. K. (2005). *Mobilizing social capital in community garden contexts.* Retrieved from http://lin.ca/Uploads/cclr11/CCLR11–46.pdf

Hoff, M. D. (1994). Environmental foundations of social welfare: Theoretical resources. In M. D. Hoff & J. G. McNutt (Eds.), *The global environmental crisis: Implications for social welfare and social work* (pp. 12–35). Aldershot, UK: Ashgate/Avebury.

Kellert, S., Heerwagen, J., & Mador, M. (2008). *Biophilic design: Theory, science and practice.* New York: John Wiley.

Laser, J. A., & Leibowitz, G. S. (2009). Promoting positive outcomes for healthy youth development: Utilizing social capital theory. *Journal of Sociology & Social Welfare, 36,* 87–102.

Maas, J., Verheij, R. A., Groenewegen, P. P., de Vries, S., & Spreeuwenberg, P. (2006). Green space, urbanity, and health: How strong is the relation? *Journal of Epidemiological Community Health, 60,* 587–592.

Marcus, D., & Green, D. (2012). *Feasibility assessment of 3 potential community garden sites in Burlington, VT.* Retrieved from http://www.uvm.edu/rsenr/experientiallearning/community basedlearning/PDFs/NR206_f12_GreenandMarcus_GardenSiteAssessments.pdf

Martinez, M. (2009). Attack of the butterfly spirits: The impact of movement framing by community garden preservation activists. *Social Movement Studies, 8*(4), 323–339.

McGurty, E. (2000). Warren County, NC and the emergence of the environmental justice movement: Unlikely coalitions and shared meanings in local collective action. *Society & Natural Resources, 13*, 373–387.

Midgley, J., & Livermore, M. (Eds.). (2009). *Handbook of social policy.* Thousand Oaks, CA: Sage.

Minkler, M., Breckwich Vasquez, V., Tajik, M., & Petersen, D. (2006). Promoting environmental justice through community based participatory research: The role of community and partnership capacity. *Health Education & Behavior, 35*(1), 119–137.

Schmitz, C. L., Matyók, T., Sloan, L. M., & James, C. (2012). The relationship between social work and environmental sustainability: Implications for interdisciplinary practice. *International Journal of Social Welfare, 21*, 278–286.

Skelton, R., & Miller, V. (2006). The environmental justice movement. *Natural Resources Defense Council.* Retrieved from http://www.nrdc.org/ej/history/hej.asp

Soubbotina, T. P. (2004). *Beyond economic growth: An introduction to sustainable development* (2nd ed.). Washington, DC: World Bank.

Steinhauer, J. (2002, September 19). Ending a long battle, New York lets housing and gardens grow. *New York Times.* Retrieved from http://www.nytimes.com/2002/09/19/nyregion/ending-a-long-battle-new-york-lets-housing-and-gardens-grow.html

Sugiyama, T., Leslie, E., Giles-Corti, B., Owen, N. (2008) Associations of neighbourhood greenness with physical and mental health: do walking, social coherence and local social interaction explain the relationships? *Journal of Epidemiology & Community Health 62* (5).

Turner, R. L., & Wu, D. P. (2003). *Environmental justice and environmental racism: An annotated bibliography and general overview, focusing on U.S. literature, 1996–2002.* Retrieved from academic.research.microsoft.com/Paper/3040083

United Church of Christ Commission for Racial Justice. (1987). *Toxic wastes and race in the United States.* New York: Author.

van der Linden, J., Drukker, M., Gunther, N., Feron, F., & van Os, J. (2003). Children's mental health service use, neighborhood socioeconomic deprivation, and social capital. *Social Psychiatry and Psychiatric Epidemiology, 38*(9), 507–514.

von Hassell, M. (2002). *The struggle for Eden: Community gardens in New York City.* Westport, CT: Bergin & Garvey.

Weick, A. (1981). Reframing the person-in-environment perspective. *Social Work, 26*(2), 140–143.

NOTES

*Delegates to the First National People of Color Environmental Leadership Summit, held October 24 to 27, 1991, in Washington, D.C., drafted and adopted these 17 principles of environmental justice. Since then, the principles have served as a defining document for the growing grassroots movement for environmental justice.

1. Environmental Justice affirms the sacredness of Mother Earth, ecological unity and the interdependence of all species, and the right to be free from ecological destruction.

2. Environmental Justice demands that public policy be based on mutual respect and justice for all peoples, free from any form of discrimination or bias.

3. Environmental Justice mandates the right to ethical, balanced and responsible uses of land and renewable resources in the interest of a sustainable planet for humans and other living things.

4. Environmental Justice calls for universal protection from nuclear testing, extraction, production and disposal of toxic/hazardous wastes and poisons and nuclear testing that threaten the fundamental right to clean air, land, water, and food.

5. Environmental Justice affirms the fundamental right to political, economic, cultural and environmental self-determination of all peoples.

6. Environmental Justice demands the cessation of the production of all toxins, hazardous wastes, and radioactive materials, and that all past and current producers be held strictly accountable to the people for detoxification and the containment at the point of production.

7. Environmental Justice demands the right to participate as equal partners at every level of decision-making, including needs assessment, planning, implementation, enforcement and evaluation.

8. Environmental Justice affirms the right of all workers to a safe and healthy work environment without being forced to choose between an unsafe livelihood and unemployment. It also affirms the right of those who work at home to be free from environmental hazards.

9. Environmental Justice protects the right of victims of environmental injustice to receive full compensation and reparations for damages as well as quality health care.

10. Environmental Justice considers governmental acts of environmental injustice a violation of international law, the Universal Declaration on Human Rights, and the United Nations Convention on Genocide.

11. Environmental Justice must recognize a special legal and natural relationship of Native Peoples to the U.S. government through treaties, agreements, compacts, and covenants affirming sovereignty and self-determination.

12. Environmental Justice affirms the need for urban and rural ecological policies to clean up and rebuild our cities and rural areas in balance with nature, honoring the cultural integrity of all our communities, and provided fair access for all to the full range of resources.

13. Environmental Justice calls for the strict enforcement of principles of informed consent, and a halt to the testing of experimental reproductive and medical procedures and vaccinations on people of color.

14. Environmental Justice opposes the destructive operations of multi-national corporations.

15. Environmental Justice opposes military occupation, repression and exploitation of lands, peoples and cultures, and other life forms.

16. Environmental Justice calls for the education of present and future generations which emphasizes social and environmental issues, based on our experience and an appreciation of our diverse cultural perspectives.

17. Environmental Justice requires that we, as individuals, make personal and consumer choices to consume as little of Mother Earth's resources and to produce as little waste as possible; and make the conscious decision to challenge and reprioritize our lifestyles to ensure the health of the natural world for present and future generations.

More info on environmental justice and environmental racism can be found online at www.ejnet .org/ej/.

Section V
Transitions and Evaluation

No service or practice intervention can be maintained for long if it cannot provide evidence that it is making a difference in some way: larger numbers reached, services expanded, policies changed. This emphasis on evaluation becomes more pronounced as one develops in one's professional career. After all, the greater authority one gets in agency life, the more accountable one becomes for the results the agency or program must deliver.

Chapters 12 and 13 explore the importance of ongoing evaluation from a unique perspective—through the transitions, both programmatic and professional, that practitioners undertake as they develop their careers and expand their programmatic focus over time. Chapter 12 emphasizes one of the greatest and most difficult transitions in a practitioner's life—from frontline activist to program supervisor. It shows the ways *a practitioner must sift the various evaluative criteria of his or her own career objectives* in deciding whether to transition to greater supervisory responsibility of others (with ensuing agency constraints) or remain solely as a frontline fighter for social justice.

Chapter 13 focuses on professionals with major executive responsibilities. Through four case studies of social work leaders who have maintained principled commitments throughout their professional lives, it shows how their increasing skills with analyzing hard data and evidence need not compromise their underlying beliefs in social justice, equality of access, and fairness. Through their underlying use of internal strategic visions as part of how they evaluated the programs and populations they were responsible for, each transition undertaken serves as an example of how transformational practice is possible at all levels of the profession.

CHAPTER 12

Crossing the Great Divide

A Grassroots Organizer Evaluates
How to Be a Socially Committed
Supervisor and Beyond

STEPPING UP OR SELLING OUT?

Ellis listened patiently as Kay spoke. They were back at their favorite diner, but her coffee had grown cold. The coffee, he knew, was fresh and tasted just fine; he was on his second cup. Kay, however, was so agitated by the dilemma she confronted that she'd forgotten to take a sip.

"I love doing grassroots work, Ellis, love it! I've been able to work with women coming out of terrible DV situations in ways I've always wanted to. Just this last year we got more shelter beds for domestic violence victims passed through city council. To see that more women can be safe and get on to safely building their lives is everything my vision is all about." She paused, looking down at the cold, murky brown liquid in her cup. "But now our director has left her job to move to Minnesota, and they want me to take her position! I don't think I can do that!"

"Wait a second, my friend! Back in the day when we were in social work school, you always said you wanted to run your own agency. You can't just do that working in the trenches. I made my choice, and the trenches is where I'm gonna stay. That's what suits me. I still wanna change the world, not run an agency. You do." He drained his coffee cup again. "What's so bad about that? You're not gonna turn into an oppressor overnight, are you?" He smiled warmly as he motioned for a third cup.

"Well, no, I guess not, but as I've been working in an agency as a professional and not just a student I see all the demands on supervisors and directors. Funders want outcomes; government contracts expect numbers. I see the people who run this place dealing with all that paper and it makes me grind my teeth to think about doing the same. I *love* working with the women, not paper!"

"Yeah, and you always told me that your boss was a great person. 'Patty goes the extra mile for us,' you'd tell me. She didn't sell out, did she?"

Realizing she hadn't had a drop of the cold liquid in front of her, Kay gave a gratified smile as Florence, their favorite waitress for years, wordlessly replaced her cup with a new, hot one as she poked her in the arm and signaled her to drink up. Kay did just that, reflecting on Ellis's insight. "Well, yeah, she's been great, but she's older than me and has been supervising for years. I'm gonna have to supervise people I've been peers with for 2 years. That sucks! I mean, now I'm responsible for whether they do their job and time sheets, and quarterly reports, and . . ." her voice trailed off. The coffee was growing cold again.

Ellis looked at her for what seemed like an hour, a sly grin spreading across his face. "Oh, I get it! You and I are more alike than we like to admit, Kay. You love to challenge authority down at City Hall, but *having* authority freaks you out." He picked up a huge fried onion ring from the pile on his plate and started to chew. Swallowing quickly, he went on. "And isn't one of your peers you'd be supervising a woman who takes 2-hour lunch breaks and couldn't care less what happens to the group she runs . . . you know, the group on safety that everyone keeps dropping out of because they feel humiliated by her? What'd you call her last year? Cruella DeVille?"

Kay put her head in her hands. "Uggh! Exactly! I'm pretty sure Patty was working on writing her up to remove her, because no matter what was tried, Marsha never changed, never came through. I know she sees the job as just a paycheck. *And,* Ellis, she's also a single mom and 10 years older than me!" She drank her coffee, not even noticing how tepid it was now. "How am I gonna handle all of that?"

"Well, back in school, our macro teacher used to say it was not whether you had authority or not, but it was how you used it. 'Authority doesn't give you *carte blanche,*' she said. 'Done well, it gives you a chance to grow.'" Ellis reached over and gave his friend's arm a warm squeeze. "Those women need you in that job, Kay." He squeezed again. "Now I guess you get to grow."

They stood up to leave. Kay leaned over and whispered in his ear as she took the check. "You know, I've decided I hate you." Then she kissed him on the cheek.

Educational Policy 2.1.2—Apply social work ethical principles to guide professional practice. In this chapter, readers will see how "social workers have an obligation to conduct themselves ethically and to engage in ethical decision-making . . . [and to] recognize and manage personal values in a way that allows professional values to guide practice; make ethical decisions by applying standards of the National Association of Social Workers Code of Ethics . . .; tolerate ambiguity in resolving ethical conflicts; and apply strategies of ethical reasoning to arrive at principled decisions."

Educational Policy 2.1.3—Apply critical thinking to inform and communicate professional judgments. This chapter also underscores how "social workers are knowledgeable about the principles of logic, scientific inquiry, and reasoned discernment. They use critical thinking augmented by creativity and curiosity. Critical thinking also requires the synthesis and communication of relevant information."

RESOLVING PROFESSIONAL DILEMMAS OF POWER AND AUTHORITY ON THE SIDE OF SOCIAL JUSTICE

The dilemma Kay confronts occurs for any macro practitioner as he or she decides to move into positions of agency authority. As a grassroots organizer, the dilemma was perhaps the opposite: While lacking much formal organizational authority, one could stay closer to the people with whom one worked. A potentially deeper connection and relationship with people in the community could compensate for being less involved in and lacking much power inside an agency. For Kay—and anyone about to become a supervisor or director responsible for running an agency program—this shift in the dilemma one wrestles with can be emotionally draining and, at times, cause unforeseen problems on the job with former peers, fellow supervisors, and community members.

This chapter sorts through the powerful dilemmas confronting the new supervisor and provides a direction one can take to minimize the tensions wrought by having a new position of expanded authority. We'll begin with a brief review of the kinds of human services organizations that macro practitioners find themselves working in and address the primary tensions that emerge for the progressive macro practitioner in each type as he or she moves into greater and greater organizational responsibility and authority.

THE THREE TYPES OF HUMAN SERVICES ORGANIZATIONS: VARYING CONSTRAINTS AND OPPORTUNITIES

Macro practitioners in the United States work in three primary types of organizations designed to serve the needs and interests of communities and their members: (1) social justice organizations, which may or may not have nonprofit status; (2) traditional nonprofit agencies; and (3) public-sector departments or agencies. Each places different kinds of constraints on the macro practitioner; each provides special opportunities as well. Each type has a different *auspice,* or organizational mandate, under which it operates that impacts the choices a practitioner will make. Knowing the distinctions about each can help a macro practitioner decide which set of dilemmas he or she wishes to struggle with.

1. *Social justice organizations* are organizations purposefully developed with mission statements and activities primarily focused on social justice, oppression, and clear-cut inequalities in our society. From People Improving Communities Through Organizing (PICO) to Greenpeace to Urban Justice Center to Sisters-UNITE!, these organizations have a distinct clarity to their goals and objectives and equally clear targets for change that emphasize their own autonomy, unimpeded by the programmatic constraints demanded by governmental and most foundation funding.

For example, PICO's value statement reads:

PICO believes in the **potential for transformation**—of people, institutions, and of our larger culture—and the power of people of faith to lead this transformation.

PICO believes that **people should have a say in the decisions that shape their lives.** We trust democracy—the original principle of the American Revolution that organized and vigilant citizens are the best defense against special interests.

PICO believes that **ordinary people know best what their families and communities need** and that their voices need to be at the center of political life. One of our basic principles is "never do for others what they can do for themselves." Ordinary people, given the proper training, motivation and support, can take extraordinary steps to improve the quality of life for their communities.

PICO believes that **when people have power they can protect the things that are important to their families and their communities,** and that one way to have power is to build strong, broad-based, democratic organizations.

PICO believes that **strong democratic organizations are rooted in the needs and resources of local communities.**

PICO believes that **government can play a vital role in improving society, but that civic leaders and organizations need to have the power to shape policy and hold public officials accountable.** (PICO National Network, n.d.)

PICO was founded in 1972 under the leadership of Father John Baumann, a Jesuit priest who had learned community organizing in Chicago. PICO began as a regional training institute to help support neighborhood organizations in California. With guidance from Dr. Jose Carrasco, a veteran organizer and teacher, and Scott Reed, PICO developed a new congregation–community model. In this model, congregations of all denominations and faiths serve as the institutional base for community organizations. Rather than bringing people together simply based on common issues such as housing or education, the faith-based or broad-based organizing model makes values and relationships the glue that holds organizations together. These innovations have resulted in the development of a national network of powerful, long-lasting community organizations (PICO National Network, n.d.).

PICO's strategic focus was to use the power of faith regardless of denomination as the basis to begin organizing. Likewise, its ecumenical emphasis on churches, synagogues, and mosques (as well as some schools and community centers) was born from the simple fact that such places of worship were some of the few sustained organizations inside poor rural and urban communities, and this could serve as a natural locus for organizing for social change. Its focus on the average citizen was important, for its projects—whether housing or school improvement—emanated from a belief in the capacity of nonprofessionals to be the leadership basis for community-wide reform.

This approach, with its social justice emphasis on people indigenous to the community as crucial stakeholders in any community change effort, has been highly successful in maintaining a grassroots approach to organizing efforts. Macro practitioners whose primary identity is first as an organizer and then as a social worker are often drawn into their ranks, working either through the national PICO office or hired from the local faith-based group's offices. At present, PICO's success has led to more than 53 federations in more than 150 communities in 17 states, fighting for housing, educational justice, immigration reform, and other social justice efforts (PICO National Network, n.d.). As PICO's webpage makes clear,

> PICO seeks to guarantee that their affiliated organizations have a degree of independence from traditional funding sources of the public sector by challenging the faith-based groups to develop their own funding streams. The most common way in which a PICO organization is started is that a group of people, often but not always clergy, invite PICO staff to meet with them to help build a new community effort. People involved in the effort may participate in PICO National Training sessions to learn more about congregation-based organizing. Based on an assessment by experienced organizers, local leaders raise funds and recruit institutions to participate on what PICO refers to as a Sponsoring Committee. This committee sponsors the development of a new organization effort during its first few years of existence. (PICO National Network, n.d.)

Such a demand for financial independence allows PICO affiliates to more easily chart their own course without fear of fiscal retaliation from politicians or public-sector funding sources that may have become the target of their efforts. For example, some 2010 campaigns focused on the rights of immigrants in Colorado, the demand for stronger bank regulation and the stopping of foreclosures in California, and health care reform with a public option nationwide. Such strong positions, emanating from their communities' concerns for equitable treatment of the poor and disenfranchised that is a hallmark of social justice campaigns, are easier to maintain because of the PICO federations' financial independence, unfettered by grants from the public targets they may be denouncing.

With its clear focus on the rights and responsibilities of poor and working families to take control of their lives in such direct economically related issues as health care and housing, and by backing up its commitment through a willingness to confront those whom they perceive as either blocking reform or maintaining inequality, PICO stands as one of the largest national social justice organizations of its kind. As such, many macro practitioners at the early stage of their careers are drawn to work with PICO or similar kinds of groups as the best of what social justice work has to offer (Fisher, 2009).

There are, of course, sharp dilemmas in working for PICO, as well as for most social justice organizations (including all three types discussed here). As full-time activists within Occupy Wall Street know, perhaps the sharpest dilemma is what a frontline social justice organizer is paid. Because most social justice organizations have limited funding due to their desire for independence from funding requirements (INCITE!, 2007), the yearly salary in 2009 for most staff was between $18,000 and $25,000 a year, which, given the long hours they work, is perhaps little more than minimum wage (Fisher, 2009). While these organizers will tell you they do not feel exploited, a macro practitioner's ability to live on such an income will also require other lifestyle commitments that are part of many social justice activists' worldview: shared housing arrangements in intentional communities (Christian, 2007) and communal approaches to food, energy, and other ecologically shared resources (Shepard & Hayduk, 2002). Clearly, these are harbingers of new trends in how our less resource-rich world will survive late in the 21st century (Senge, Scharmer, Jaworski, & Flowers, 2005; Shepard & Hayduk, 2002). Such commitments to work and life carry with them enormous personal demands on the practitioner that many will admire but not wish to pursue for more than a few years.

Other social justice activists take an even more pointed position on working within nonprofit human services organizations. Led by such groups as INCITE! Women of Color Against Violence, a national radical feminist organization, these activists purposely eschew nonprofit status so that their analysis and actions will not be compromised by either the government or foundations (INCITE!, 2007). Their work asks pointed questions such as these:

- How did politics shape the birth of the nonprofit model?
- How does 501(c)(3) status allow the state to co-opt political movements?
- Activists or careerists?
- How do we fund the movement outside of this complex?

Their work goes on to provide a powerful social justice–based critique to work inside the nonprofit world:

A $1.3 trillion industry, the US nonprofit sector is the world's seventh largest economy. From art museums and university hospitals to think tanks and church charities, over 1.5 million organizations of staggering diversity share the tax-exempt 501(c)(3) designation, if little else. Many social justice organizations have joined this world, often blunting political goals to satisfy government and foundation mandates. But even as funding shrinks and government surveillance rises, many activists often find it difficult to imagine movement-building outside the nonprofit model. (INCITE!, 2007, p. 138)

Their work, *The Revolution Will Not Be Funded* (INCITE!, 2007), draws on essays from around the world that critique the "nonprofit industrial complex" and offer arguments for building membership-based (dues-paying) organizations whose financial independence strengthens their ability to critique and organize against the government and economic actors who otherwise might be co-opting their militant activism through funding arrangements and service-based contracts that move people away from activist organizing.

Such arguments have the power to ignite thought and reflection in every macro practitioner as he or she seeks strategic effectiveness in combating society's ills. What is the balance between trenchantly critiquing the economic and political causes of major social problems (such as homelessness, domestic violence, low-wage labor, the exploitation of undocumented workers, educational inequality, continuing racism, and homophobia) and either standing outside the messiness of reform or entering the fray with what some may perceive as only Band-Aids to offer? A call for social justice without a commitment to actively help those in need is simple elitism masquerading as sophisticated political commentary. Likewise, working fervently to help those most afflicted by inequities in our economic and social system without some attention to that system is purposeful naiveté cloaked most often in self-righteousness and exhaustion. Social justice organizers who do manage to maintain their critique while working in the trenches of reform force all macro practitioners—like Kay and Ellis—to think through the strategic mix of reform and radical change to which they are committed (Fisher & Schragge, 2001; Reisch, 2005).

REFLECTIONS ON THE SOCIAL JUSTICE DILEMMA

Working for social justice has its rewards and its challenges.

Reflecting on your own work in social justice, cite two concrete examples of those rewards.

_____

_____

Now cite two challenges you live with in this work.

_____

_____

How do you keep a balance between the rewards and challenges so that you remain committed and effective in this work?

_____

2. _Traditional nonprofit agencies_ are those human service organizations whose auspices are chartered with tax-exempt 501(c)(3) status. Often called nongovernmental organizations (NGOs) in other parts of the world, within their ranks can be found nonprofits as large as the Bill and Melinda Gates Foundation ($60 billion) and in-name-only groups of a few people using their nonprofit status for doing business as consultants, daycare providers, or other small mom-and-pop operations. What they all have in common to achieve their nonprofit 501(c)(3) status is a board of directors that reviews operations and a commitment not to make profits for shareholders or providers of the operation but, instead, to use all funds for services and programs. They maintain their nonprofit auspice by also agreeing not to engage in political/electoral activity (Patti, 2008).

For most macro practitioners, their interests are with neither something as large as a $60 billion foundation nor a mom-and-pop shop but, rather, with the vast array of settlement houses, community centers, shelters, drop-in centers, advocacy groups, improvement associations, housing redevelopment corporations, and after-school programs in which the majority of us can be found working. However, before we turn to the professional dilemmas confronting organizers-turned-supervisors like Kay, there is one other contextual issue that needs to be addressed: What caused the explosion in nonprofits since the late 1970s in the first place?

As Robert Fisher and Howard Karger (1996) cogently argued in the mid-1990s, the vast expansion of nonprofit organizations is in great part a reflection of the social and personal contradictions wrought by a world increasingly privatized and individuated in the ways human needs were to be met. Confronting a global economy that further dispersed its workforce around the world and further fragmented community supports, nonprofit organizations began to emerge as a response to needs that could no longer be met through the traditional means of extended family, religious affiliation, or neighborly intervention (Fisher & Karger, 1996). Furthermore, with the post-1980 Reaganite push for antigovernment and antistate activities and the ascendancy of the free market as the privatized choice for individual improvement and reform, more and more community members left out of that market had to turn to voluntary associations, church groups, and others who supported their needs through nongovernment-based assistance. More recently, Fabricant and Fisher (2003) have written on the cost-containment strategies implicit in the state's contracting out its services to nonprofits as ways to meet those increasing service needs while diminishing overall state costs.

These works have clarified the primary dilemma of most nonprofit activity: Fulfilling important service needs and creating imaginative forms of advocacy often buckle against the constraints of fiscally insecure and often underfunded programs. On the one hand, nonprofit, community-based organizations provide a wealth of needed services that hark back to the days of settlement houses and friendly visitors. A brief review of the National Association of Social Workers' (2013) webpage on social workers in the news finds the following services and programs offered by established nonprofits from around the country:

- Hospice care for the elderly
- Addiction prevention programs for formerly incarcerated prisoners
- Suicide-prevention work with young Latinas
- Gang-prevention youth leadership programs in small Midwestern cities
- Advocacy for improvements in mental health diagnoses
- Expanding social skills and job training for the developmentally disabled
- Support and services for gay veterans

Such nonprofit work reflects the combination of 19th century traditions (work with the elderly and the mentally ill), continued attention to issues and populations that surfaced in the 20th century (domestic violence and gay issues), and global dynamics new to the 21st century (work with young Latina immigrants, the spread of gangs into smaller cities). It supports Fabricant and Fisher's (2003) argument that macro practitioners can and will be challenged to continue to respond to increasing needs that can be met only through the kinds of consistent, organizational efforts that these nonprofits provide.

While they are fewer in number nationwide, almost every city can also boast of nonprofits engaged in advocacy, empowerment, and development programs. Here, the incubation of and support for new ideas and opportunities for challenging some of the inequities of 21st century life can be found. A quick look at the Association of Community Organization and Social Administration's (ACOSA) website (www.acosa.org), the collaborative of macro academics and practitioners, captures the flavor of this widespread macro activity:

- A Pittsburgh–Youngstown–Cleveland MIS collaborative training session on Cleveland's Northeast Ohio Community and Data for Organizing, where participants learned the latest Internet data-mining techniques for organizing in their communities (Teixeira, 2008)

- A presentation by Neighborhood Progress, Inc., Cleveland community development partners working on housing creation and service development with their human service counterparts (Teixeira, 2008)
- Attention to community-based approaches to conflict mediation in the Middle East
- Alignment with the International Association Schools of Social Work (IASSW) and the United Nations Declaration of Human Rights (as a vehicle to fight torture, genocide, and female genital mutilation across the globe)
- Notation of collaborative efforts under way with the following populations and issues:

  o LGBTQ youth
  o Intergenerational work with youth and elders
  o Expanded advocacy regarding homelessness
  o Social justice issues for the formerly incarcerated
  o The struggles of documented and undocumented immigrants
  o Joining environmentalism and human service work
  o Sustainable local economies and community development projects

What the preceding listing makes clear is how many of those involved in the nonprofit world are also at the cutting edge of social trends, issues, and emerging populations that the rest of the field may be just learning about. Whether joining in efforts to provide services and training through sustainable, local agricultural projects (Netting, 1993); working with transgender youth and other members of the LGBTQ community in the worldwide fight against HIV-AIDS (Shepard & Hayduk, 2002); or expanding their organizing effectiveness through Internet projects and Internet software (Kiesler, 1997), nonprofit macro practitioners are right to be excited by the efforts under way across the United States, North America, and beyond.

That meaningful work, both in terms of service and advocacy, is a hallmark of the human services nonprofit world seems evident. The fiscal constraints under which these organizations operate are unfortunately also evident; charitable giving in 2009 experienced its largest drop in 50 years (Strom, 2009). Likewise, with all but two states (Wyoming and North Dakota) running deficits and seeking to rein in costs through cutbacks in the social-service sector, nonprofit leadership has had to again scramble for what Fisher (2005) identified as "the search for contract availability and requests for proposals (RFPs) rather than internal goal-driven" (p. 50) approaches to their agencies' work (Brilliant, 1992). This "going for the gusto," as macro practitioner John Weed years ago described it (J. Weed, personal communication, 1982), entails the danger of chasing dollars for survival rather than staying true to the core mission that inspires its staff and community members to take on this work every day.

REFLECTIONS ON THE NONPROFIT DILEMMA

Working in a traditional nonprofit has its rewards and its challenges.

Reflecting on your own work in a nonprofit agency, cite two concrete examples of those rewards.

_____

_____

Now cite two challenges you live with in this work.

_____

_____

How do you keep a balance between the rewards and challenges so that you remain committed and effective in this work?

_____

_____

Fighting to hold on to the meaning of one's work while trying to survive and live well is a primary dilemma for all nonprofit macro practitioners. We will return to how one can do so later in this chapter. But first let's look at the final arena in which macro practitioners can be found—the public sector.

3. While not always widely analyzed in macro practice, the *public sector* is nevertheless a pivotal arena in which macro practitioners are employed. Their auspice stems from federal and state-level legislation, often granting them funding status to solicit RFPs to nonprofits whose programs support the populations whom practitioners are charged to service. Equally important, a large percentage of funds for nonprofit agencies comes through public sources, whether through grants, RFPs, or as part of private–public partnership collaborations in supportive housing, economic development, child welfare, education, mental health, youth development, and aging programs. A brief review of the case studies in Weil's (2005) extraordinarily wide-ranging *Handbook of Community Practice* found that almost all had examples of public sector–based collaboratives or initiatives in which community-based work was under way—from Community Economic and Social Development projects (Rubin & Sherraden, 2005) to community-building initiatives in support of family-centered service collaboration (Mulroy, Nelson, & Gour, 2005) to community-based children's mental health projects among Native Americans (Cross & Friesen, 2005).

Because there is also a noted shift under way from the antistate, free-market approach to government services and programs of the past 25 years (see Chapter 2), it is perhaps an extraordinary moment in which macro practitioners working within the public sector can play an increasingly important role in the new forms of community practice that emerge over the next decade. While such work has its own unique dilemmas, which are discussed below, the size and scope of the resources the public sector offers can provide macro practitioners—whether frontline community partners in neighborhood collaboratives or middle-level managers running million-dollar programs—extraordinary access to influence community services and programs.

To get an idea of how far ranging the public sector's influence is in community-based nonprofits, the list of programs that the U.S. Department of Health and Human Services (HHS) publishes can help. Its breadth of more than 300 programs, consolidated below, touches on almost every sector of community life, whether large urban city, rural community, or Native American reservation:

- Health and social science research
- Preventing disease, including immunization services
- Ensuring food and drug safety
- Medicare (health insurance for elderly and disabled Americans) and Medicaid (health insurance for those with low income)
- Health information technology
- Financial assistance and services for low-income families
- Improving maternal and infant health
- Head Start (preschool education and services)
- Faith-based and community initiatives
- Preventing child abuse and domestic violence
- Substance-abuse treatment and prevention
- Services for older Americans, including home-delivered meals
- Comprehensive health services for Native Americans
- Medical preparedness for emergencies, including potential terrorism (HHS, 2009)

All these programs accounted for more than $967 billion in 2013 (HHS, 2013), a sum equal to almost a quarter of all federal government outlays, with obvious heavy funding for Social Security, Medicare, and Medicaid. While often indirectly related to community programs, this funding is critical for social service initiatives: Supportive housing for the mentally ill requires Social Security payments; innovative child welfare programs and community partnerships are indirectly supported through Title IV payments that provide foster care; the activist elderly would be less so without their Medicare and Social Security payments. Macro practitioners who oversee such programs and how they are allocated in their locales are indispensable allies in the progressive work others undertake.

Similarly influential positions are occupied by macro practitioners who work for individual state and municipal agencies, whether they are local Head Start program officers helping advance health-and-wellness prevention programs or local county officials helping support alternative sustainable agricultural programs in rural areas (Carlton-LaNey, Murty, & Morris, 2005).

Furthermore, HHS macro practitioners, through their state and municipal offices, administer more grant dollars than all other federal agencies combined. HHS's Medicare program is the nation's largest health insurer, handling more than 1 billion claims per year. Medicare and Medicaid together provide health care insurance for 1 in 4 Americans.

The magnitude of public-sector expenditure also makes clear the primary dilemma for most of its practitioners. Their work, while powerfully impacting the scope and direction of much progressive nonprofit activity, occurs away from the front lines or the grassroots. Responsible for regulating and monitoring the contracts and activities of the nonprofit sector, public-sector practitioners are less likely to get the satisfaction from community member participation and grassroots involvement that their nonprofit colleagues do. As we will see in the next chapter, this does not mean that one becomes a faceless bureaucrat. It does mean that one's satisfaction and meaning will come in other, less direct, yet still important ways of supporting and guiding efforts occurring outside of agencies and in the communities themselves.

REFLECTIONS ON THE PUBLIC-SECTOR DILEMMA

Working for the public sector has its rewards and its challenges.

Reflecting on your own work in the public sector, cite two concrete examples of those rewards.

_____

_____

Now cite two challenges you live with in this work.

_____

_____

How do you keep a balance between the rewards and challenges so that you remain committed and effective in this work?

_____

_____

FROM GRASSROOTS ORGANIZER TO AGENCY SUPERVISOR: ROLES, RESPONSIBILITIES, AND TENSIONS

Regardless of the agency type in which one works, the transition from frontline activist to agency supervisor is initially difficult for many reasons. For example, as Kadushin (1976) noted in his classical synthesis of the social work supervisor, a supervisor will be called on to work on three important tasks: *administrative, educational, and supportive* (p. 21). Equally important, these tasks are no longer undertaken simply for one's own development: A supervisor now has the additional *responsibility* to undertake them with supervisees. Finally, and perhaps most important for the macro practitioner, a supervisor is expected to have the *authority* to help evaluate, guide, and, if necessary, direct staff so that the tasks at hand are accomplished in a timely and successful way.

Distinguishing Frontline Practitioner and Supervisory Tasks, Responsibilities, and Authority

As Cousins (2004) argues, the work of the frontline practitioner and that of a supervisor are distinct, because the demands and expectations of the former are primarily shaped by how he or she is performing with community members and less immediately by agency demands. While agency expectations may focus the direction of a practitioner's work, he or she is internally struggling with and learning how to motivate, plan with, and learn from the people of the community group or coalition to which he or she is assigned. The ensuing mind-set of the practitioner is primarily focused on how he or she influences, guides, and responds to others through the best mix of individual and professional skills and personal temperament to get the job done. Developing tactical self-awareness (see Chapter 2) challenges the singular macro practitioner to examine external situational demands and his or her own capacity for meeting them in a tactically flexible, dynamic manner, not only for the agency but also for the community—and for oneself.

It is thus no accident that a successful macro practitioner, upon being promoted to oversee a program, will initially be as flummoxed as Kay is in our opening scenario. She has not had to think of her tasks primarily through the prism of agency need but, rather, has approached them more from her own skill sets and those of the people with whom she is organizing. When you combine this individual focus with the telling finding that the overwhelming majority of human-service supervisors and managers receive next to no formal training in their new positions (Burghardt & Tolliver, 2009), it becomes clear why so many macro practitioners initially shy away from their new tasks and responsibilities.

Looked at closely, the three tasks Kadushin (1976) outlines are in and of themselves not especially challenging for a skilled macro practitioner. The *administrative tasks* relate to the paperwork of a human-service worker's life: reports on measurable results or out-comes, staff time sheets, work logs, weekly schedules, and so forth. *Support* functions are tied to staff development, whereby a supervisor meets with workers and listens to and communicates with them on the frustrations, challenges, and opportunities of the job. As Shulman (2006) points out, through this support function, supervisors must develop "their communications and relationship skills. . . . The very qualities which initially attracted the supervisor to work with people can be rediscovered in the ongoing relationships with staff" (p. 118). I would argue that a good frontline macro practitioner, through tactical self-awareness and his or her immersion in the community and the demands, fears, expectations, and developing leadership capacities of its members, will have already developed some of these skills. The same is also true for the *educational* function: What organizer hasn't been involved in educating others, providing information, and promoting new ideas as part of frontline assignments?

New Responsibilities

What will be new—and thus a heavy lift—will be that you, as a new supervisor, are now weaving into your role the *responsibility to guarantee that results occur each week from others in your program and not just from yourself.* It can be a real identity shift from supporting community members as they take on the responsibility to run their own meetings to overseeing that your program staff responsibly show up each and every day for the work leading up to those meetings. As Kay said at the beginning of the chapter, taking responsibility for time sheets and quarterly reports feels a lot different than taking responsibility for whether community members do what they've agreed to do.

As will be discussed later in this chapter, the distinction between overseeing time sheets and developing membership capacity has less to do with a person's degree of responsibility—both are fairly high—*and more to do with developing one's own internal strategic vision and seeing how the way one handles these tasks remains at least a partial reflection of that vision in one's new role.* That it's easier to visualize meaning with membership development than well-done, reliably accurate time sheets doesn't mean that time sheets are lacking in actual value for a program's success. Growing personally comfortable with both tasks is what causes so much initial consternation for new supervisors as they try to ease into their new positions.

Educational tasks are fundamental to any community practitioner's role as well, whether on the front lines or as a supervisor. Whether informing community members about the latest changes in rent guidelines in a large city or about what qualifies for sustainable, local agricultural subsidies in a small rural town, a macro practitioner is constantly involved in providing educational opportunities through his or her work. The same is true for an agency supervisor, only the content may extend from the strategically substantive (such as providing workshops on tenants' rights or small farmers' access to subsidies) to agency-based mandates caused by new contract guidelines or shifts in focus from foundations. This, too, becomes a responsibility of the frontline supervisor. For example, much work on homelessness has shifted from a focus on a provision for shelter to the need for subsidized housing (McCormack & MacIntosh, 2001), with a corresponding shift in what community-based agencies are expected to provide in the way of services and programs. Supervisors are expected either to educate their staff on such changes or to provide workshop opportunities for them to learn how a community program's work and focus may be changing.

Issues of Power and Authority

Of course, the cause of most underlying tensions for macro practitioners becoming supervisors relates to power and authority. As Shulman (2006), Kadushin (1976), Hill (2003), and others (Cousins, 2004; Patti, 2008) relate, the greatest tension for new supervisors is how they use their power and authority over their staff, many of whom may have been former peers and even friends. As Hill documented in her classic study on new managers, the most "profound psychological adjustment a new manager or supervisor must make is a transformation of professional identity" related to the responsibility and authority that person now carries in the new position (p. 121). Just as Kay's greatest fear was over how she would use her power with her new staff, almost all new supervisors fear how they will handle the demands of performance evaluation, worker accountability, and what to do when work performance is not satisfactory (Cousins, 2004). Because most new supervisors in human services begin their jobs having had, at best, a mixed experience with previous supervision (Cousins, 2004), the concerns over how power will be handled is understandable.

That said, as Cousins (2004) stressed, "We are kidding ourselves if we pretend that power differences either do not matter or have been overcome" (p. 177). All this is heightened for community practitioners whose commitment to social justice and against oppression is a pervasive, widespread part of their identities as change agents (Homan, 2004; Rubin & Rubin, 2005; Staples, 2004). It cannot be sidestepped; as Cousins states, "While we may work to create a supportive environment, the reality is that it is also the job of the supervisor to raise performance issues" (p. 177). A new supervisor must use authority to make demands on others that some staff may not like at all. While in the role of a fellow community worker one might have been bothered by a peer's underperformance, one had neither the responsibility nor authority to handle these problems (unless, of course, it impacted one's own work).

Becoming comfortable with using the authority of one's supervisory position can and will be daunting at first, but it cannot be avoided for long. For as Hill's (2003) research documented, a new supervisor will eventually be held responsible for a worker's failure to perform well. As one of her subjects wrote, "It's humbling that someone who works for me could get me fired" (p. 51). To become a supervisor is to take responsibility for a program and the team who works there. Over time, a program's underperformance, while it may be caused by only one or two workers, will be your responsibility. Realizing this may cause initial consternation and fear, and it needs to be addressed quickly.

The structural reality of a supervisor's position is that you are in the middle: responsible for developing and sustaining the people below you while held to standards and program performance from the people above (Oshry, 2007). Instead of finding yourself freed to act, you learn that actions must be balanced between what your staff will respond to and what your bosses above are demanding. As one of Hill's (2003) new managers stated, "I never knew a promotion could be so painful" (p. 51).

Hill (2003) found that many new managers, confronted with this dilemma of feeling trapped between above and below, resolve their role tension,

> mistakenly believing their power is based on the formal authority that comes with their . . . new position. . . . This operating assumption leads many to adopt a hands-on, autocratic approach, not because they are eager to use their new power over people but because they believe it is the most effective way to produce results. (p. 52)

It is not hard to understand why the use of this autocratic approach occurs in human services, even among community-based macro practitioners. Confronted with the dilemmas of their position and offered no formal training or mentoring on how to resolve the tensions of being "the monkey in the middle," a new supervisor is trapped in the cognitive-dissonance–creating ambiguity of too much responsibility and too little power. Cognitive dissonance occurs when a person is confronted with and must decide between two seemingly irresolvable choices: "horizontal" social justice versus "vertical" supervisory control (Festinger, 1957), feeling uncertain about which organizational pole to adapt to (*Respond to the staff I am with every day? React to my bosses' new demands?*). Hill (2003) suggests that most initially resolve this tension by using only their formal authority to dictate solutions.

This tendency to resolve the ambiguity in one's supervisory role by adopting an overly rigid response to power has created one of the more troubling ironies in human-services work. Oftentimes, supervision in the nonprofit and public sectors is far more inflexible and unsupportive than that found in the corporate sector (Fabricant & Fisher, 2003). In some ways, this seems reflective of the lack of formal management training and mentoring within human services that a United Way study suggests is one of the primary causes of staff turnover in agencies (Burghardt & Tolliver, 2009). It also corresponds to one of the key findings of Hill's (2003) landmark work: that new managers and supervisors learn primarily from experience as they work with those above and below them. However, if that experience continues to be built on others' rigidity and failure to mentor, the ensuing learning will be cast in equally rigid lessons. In short, it would seem as though a silent yet troubling cycle of frontline practitioner promotion, initial supervisory role ambiguity in authority and responsibility, and the less-than-satisfactory yet jarring experience of being left adrift creates a permanently rigid reliance on one's formal authority among many supervisors and managers. It is cause for genuine concern if this occurs among supervisors and managers in the human services, where the profession's ethical commitments to empowerment, strengths-based practice, and respect are some of its central tenets. If such ethical practices are not also applied among staff, can they truly be sustained with clients and community members (Burghardt & Tolliver, 2009; Cousins, 2004)?

APPLYING TACTICAL SELF-AWARENESS TO THE SUPERVISORY ROLE

Facing this quandary, what is a macro practitioner with commitments to social justice to do? What is available to help mitigate the pressures toward unintentional rigidity and accidental misuse of authority that can otherwise occur? Hill's (2003) findings on learning from experience are powerfully important here, for they suggest that *the resolution to one's dilemmas as a new supervisor may lie as much with how one has practiced in the past as it does with present demands as a new supervisor.*

We again turn to Paulo Freire (2000) for guidance. He writes as follows of how critically reflective practitioners respond to interpreting and acting on the conditions they confront in their lives, whether as a new grassroots organizer, as a community member elected head of a tenants' council, or as a newly promoted supervisor or educator:

> Humans . . . because they are aware of themselves and thus of the world—because they are *conscious beings*—exist in a dialectical relationship between the determination of their own limits and their own freedom. [*Through reflection-in-action*] as they separate themselves from the world, which they objectify, as they separate themselves from their own activity, as they locate the seat of their decisions in themselves and in their relations with the world and with others, people overcome the situations which limit them: the "limit-situations." . . . Once perceived as . . . obstacles to liberation, these situations [including being in a new supervisory role!] stand out in relief from the background, revealing their true nature as concrete historical dimensions of a given reality. Men and women respond to the challenge with . . . "limit acts": those directed at negating and overcoming, rather than passively accepting the "given." . . . *Thus it is not the limit-situations . . . which create a climate of hopelessness, but rather how they are interpreted by women and men at a given historical moment.* (p. 89; italics added)

Freire's challenge to people committed to progressive, liberating practice is the development of this dynamic interplay between structural conditions impacting a person's life (whether the demands are those of a new supervisor or the constraints on local agricultural development, funding levels for youth projects, etc.) *and* what one perceives, responds to, and acts on regarding those conditions. Staying with our examples here, for Freire a new supervisor's "limit-situation" bound up in new authority and responsibility is just that: *challenges, not chains.*

The deeper challenge is not the new supervisory role; it's whether the macro practitioner has developed the capacity to see the role in its historical dimensions of a given reality: A new role with more authority can be interpreted so that one inflicts arbitrary, abusive power over others, or it can be struggled with in ways that make the educational, supportive, and administrative tasks of the job with one's staff an opportunity for further transformation.

It is here where Hill's (2003) findings on experience as the key to learning and Freire's (2000) framing of how to perceive and act on the limit-situations for a new supervisor converge. *What will impact the degree of rigidity and overutilization in a new formal supervisory role will be determined not by the role itself but by how a macro practitioner has previously dealt with the former limit-situations he or she had encountered as an organizer.* If one's organizing experience created rigid boundaries between the organized and the organizer, then the boundaries between supervisee and supervisor will begin with that same overly formal separation. Likewise, if the frontline macro practitioner has relied on only external markers of achievement in measuring his or her own professional growth, then only the external measures of supervisory responsibility will be factored into that person's success as a supervisor.

As Freire is suggesting, however, a more dynamic process of growth and development is possible for a new supervisor if one has taken on the internal challenges of reflection in action while a community organizer. Continuing to use tactical self-awareness can allow a macro practitioner to do just that as he or she begins a new supervisory role. As we saw in Chapters 2 and 3, tactical self-awareness is a tool to help a professional reflect on his or her own strengths and limitations in relationship to the external demands of practice. As such, its ongoing utilization helps one become comfortable with the dynamic interplay among one's own personal fit with task and process, new and old assignments, and the other demands that fill up an organizer's work life. Used as an instrument to deepen one's reflection for improved action, over time tactical self-awareness will have helped the frontline community practitioner create his or her own powerful limit-acts on the limit-situations before him or her.

Thus, for example, when a community-wide meeting is being held, a young macro practitioner assesses how he or she can be most tactically effective at that meeting and where others will be tactically better. Using skills developed over time in countless organizing situations, he or she is doing more than practicing tactical self-awareness and good strategic decision making for the group in the moment. He or she is also deepening personal leadership capacity and flexibility so that he or she will approach future positions, whether as supervisor or director or executive, with the same internal awareness to remain open to new limit-situations in the new authority and responsibility. These new responsibilities, while obviously still challenges, emerge quickly as opportunities to grow from rather than as dreaded designers of a climate of hopelessness that can be met only with rigidity and fatalism.

Rather than rigidity, a new supervisor can review Kadushin's (1976) three main supervisory domains in the same tactically self-aware manner as he or she reviewed organizing assignments (see Table 12.1).

Kadushin's (1976) three primary supervisory functions easily lend themselves to the same task and process dimensions outlined in Chapter 2. *A practitioner would utilize the table to identify those areas where he or she was more or less tactically flexible so that he*

Table 12.1   Tactical Self-Awareness and Primary Supervisory Functions

Administration		Support		Education	
Task	**Process**	**Task**	**Process**	**Task**	**Process**
Collect data; prepare reports; fulfill funding requirements	Explain policies and procedures	Schedule time for coaching/ mentoring	Support staff challenges	Conduct systematic performance appraisals	Review staff skill development
Monitor staff performance	Elicit feedback on projects		Listen to staff feedback on limits and opportunities	Provide workshops, trainings, practice	Provide teachable moments on dilemmas
			Provide teachable moments through your tactical self-awareness		
(. . . ongoing professional and strategic development . . .)					

or she did not ignore assignments that were more taxing or become overly rigid in handling them. Unlike the community organizer, who can work with peers and community members on assignments, the supervisor has less discretion in assigning such tasks to somebody else. (Of course, having utilized tactical self-awareness through one's organizing practice can help make the transition easier in handling the above tasks than it otherwise might be.)

It is important to note that all the above tasks do not happen each and every day—after all, there are only 24 hours in a day! They should, however, occur within a month's time, and some (such as administrative tasks) will occur with greater frequency than others. Kadushin (1976) identified these three areas because they also provide balance for a supervisor in the mix of responsibilities to meet agency needs, ongoing staff development, and programmatic achievements. Only through ongoing practice—Hill's experience—will knowing how to achieve that balance occur.

EXERCISE ON TACTICAL SELF-AWARENESS FOR THE NEW SUPERVISOR

Using tactical self-awareness, reflect on the task and process demands of a supervisor within each of the three functions. Where are you strong? Where will you need support and training? How will you go about getting that support? In what way could you offer support to others?

Administration	*A Strength*	*A Challenge*	*Support From*	*Support To*
Tasks				
1.				
2.				
Process				
1.				
2.				
3.				
Support	*A Strength*	*A Challenge*	*Support From*	*Support To*
Tasks				
1.				
2.				

Process

1.

2.

3.

Education   *A Strength*   *A Challenge*   *Support From*   *Support To*

Tasks

1.

2.

Process

1.

2.

3.

Administration

The administrative functions of a supervisor are the most apparent and are directed toward clear agency needs related to funding requirements, project outcomes, and concrete data. It's the paperwork that almost every human-services practitioner loathes, but if it is avoided, it will mean the agency goes out of business. Impossible to avoid and at times likely to be overlooked by some new supervisors concerned with their support and educational responsibilities, it requires internal vigilance related to a macro practitioner respecting agency needs and not just the staff's.

The process parts of the administrative function relate primarily to a supervisor learning how to explain the various policies and procedures to staff so that everyone in your program understands how programs work, what new guidelines or mandates have come from either private funders (which may relate to new criteria for program completion or meeting program milestones on attendance, membership involvement, etc.) or changes in public regulations (which can range from directives on smoking to employee protections on the job to new Social Security regulations regarding reimbursements). For some new supervisors, these tasks will be the foundation on which they develop their primary role definition; for others, they may appear as irritants to avoid. You use tactical self-awareness here to make administrative functions neither supervisory armor held over those beneath you nor bureaucratic chains that bind you to staff in opposition to the executives above. Administrative work is both exacting detail that keeps people employed and a tool that provides at least partial clarity about what matters in often-ambiguous strategic situations. Developing the internal capacity to hold these differing external tensions is the purpose of tactical self-awareness for the supervisor.[1]

Support

The support functions relate to what Shulman (2006) identified as the ways supervisors build trust with their staff and provide a safe environment in which professional development can occur, especially in those areas most troubling for a staff member. As Cousins (2004) also suggests, a supervisor establishes this kind of supportive atmosphere by permitting mistakes, encouraging open expression of concerns, and letting workers share their thoughts and feelings on authority. A supervisor's task functions here are straightforward: to schedule time for this supportive activity to occur. Remembering to schedule and keeping the commitment to this area of professional development when other programmatic demands can seem to take a higher priority are the essence of what management writer Steven Covey (2003) identified as scheduling Quadrant II behaviors—that is, those items that are important but not urgent inside a program[2] (Covey, 2003, 2004).

By paying attention to this supportive task, a supervisor is using time for the process activities Cousins (2004) and Shulman (2006) identified: listening, hearing concerns, and so forth. This empathic capacity can be strengthened by a supervisor using teachable moments based on his or her own tactical self-awareness. Teachable moments (Parker-Pope, 2008) are examples of what supervisors provide their team members through experiential learning. Working from the concerns and challenges a staff member has raised, a supervisor uses a teachable moment based on an equivalent experience of how he or she handled such an issue, raising questions along the way so that the staff member can reflect on his or her own way of handling the issue in the future. Based on tactical self-awareness, what has been added to this experiential learning has been the supervisor providing both an equivalent example and his or her own strengths and limitations in handling that or an equivalent problem. For just as the organizer provides a new form of democratic leadership development by sharing skills and acknowledging areas of need and difficulty in mastering tasks with community members (see Chapter 4), a *supervisor creates a powerful learning experience for staff members when he or she provides glimpses into his or her own struggle to develop professionally rather than only simple answers on how to do it right.* Support and encouragement to share difficulties in the work is far easier when a supervisor has spoken not only of how to get things done but also of how difficult it was to learn to achieve such mastery for the supervisor.

Of course, it takes personal comfort in one's approach to work to be able to provide teachable moments based not only on the right way but also on how demanding doing the right thing can be. Tactical self-awareness operates from the search for excellence, not perfection—whether one is a new grassroots organizer or a recently promoted supervisor. By using your own limits and strengths applied to practice as vital tools for learning, you expand the opportunities for sharing lessons, professional skill development, and personal mastery. Use the support function of supervision to provide an arena in which this struggle to grow personally and professionally is one of the genuine rewards provided by a supervisor—for your staff and for yourself.

PERSONAL ACTIVITY

Reflect on your own tactical self-awareness on where you have had a struggle to improve and what you have done. What are you doing to improve and to develop a teachable moment that models the kind of effort to change that you would like a staff member to make (or a fellow team member who is struggling)?

Your tactical self-awareness challenge: _____

The effort to improve required/s me to . . .

_____

Teachable moment: "I have had a struggle to improve as follows":

_____

"AND, I'd like you to reflect on [ISSUE AT HAND] and how you might apply my example to what we've just talked about related to your work":

_____

Education

Buttressing the support functions that build internal professional and personal capacity are the education functions that focus on skills and knowledge needed to run a project or program well. The empathy required to help others grow has to be matched by the challenge to get the job done professionally for either to be of long-term value.

Here the task functions are tied to specific performance appraisal work on how well a staff member is accomplishing his or her job. As countless human resources manuals have detailed, performance appraisals are meant to be learning tools with no surprises for staff members at the time of yearly performance evaluations; an equal number of books document how often unhappy surprises occur (Grote, 2002). There is no simple way to overcome this impasse other than to see the appraisal as a necessary task in supervision that a supervisor must guarantee occurs. An appraisal is built on a previous yearly evaluation where strengths have been noted, deficits or areas of improvement spelled out, and a clear direction provided for how those improvements can occur and how strengths can be built on. Raising those areas inside supervision on a monthly or quarterly basis provides the supervisor with information on the work that he or she might not have and guarantees that the staff member gets no surprises later in the year that cause unnecessary tension within a program.

Another task for the supervisor is to help locate and provide support for workshops and trainings that a staff member may need for improvement. While such tasks will most likely be undertaken in consultation with upper-level managers or executives and need to be fit within budgetary considerations, a supervisor has the responsibility to communicate what would be most beneficial for a staff member's performance improvement. By demonstrating attempts to help others develop, a supervisor builds goodwill through such efforts after the sting of informing someone of needed improvement fades.

The process functions within education relate mostly to knowledge and skill development as macro practitioners. Here, it is the substance of skill development and the knowledge needed to be strategically effective in your housing group, LGBTQ elders' program, or sustainable agriculture project. Engaging in substantive talks, peer-to-peer workshops, and late-day (or night) strategy sessions builds the kind of substantive expertise and strategic flexibility your staff and programs need to remain vital and effective in the larger community.

As part of this work, a supervisor wants to include time spent with the practice dilemmas embedded in any strategic solution or tactical direction taken by a program. When you chose a set of allies, whom did you leave out? By emphasizing a piece of legislation for family-run farms, what corporate lobbyists' arguments will you have to counter? Just as tactical self-awareness poses personal dilemmas in assessing one's strengths and limitations in any given situation, this kind of strategic assessment examines a community program's campaigns and projects.

Taken together, the administrative, support, and education functions of a supervisor are less distinct domains than they are a weave of task and process activities that ground a supervisor in a rich and rewarding approach to the work he or she has undertaken. To create such a weave and avoid an overly formal approach to the role, a new supervisor will have been practicing tactical self-awareness as a community organizer so that the flexibility born from reflecting in action in the past continues into the present demands of the new job. Rather than being the imposed limits of agency hierarchy, these demands become the limit-situations capable of inspiring new ways to think, act, and join with others—your own limit-acts—that transform fear to hope and constraints into new arenas for growth inside your agency.

PERSONAL ACTIVITY ON PERFORMANCE APPRAISAL

1. Reflect on your staff's overall performance issues. Where are they strong? Where are there challenges? Are there any serious breaches in performance standards that need to be addressed?

2. Using your own tactical self-awareness, plan on a systematic conversation on these issues with each staff member.

3. If there are serious issues, speak with your own supervisor or human resources director on how best to proceed.

"EMBODY THE CHANGE YOU SEEK": USING YOUR INTERNAL STRATEGIC VISION IN MASTERING ROLES, RESPONSIBILITIES, AND POWER IN A NEW SUPERVISORY POSITION

Of course, no amount of tactical self-awareness can fully prepare someone for the demands of a new position such as program supervisor or project director. There will still be former peer relationships to rework, new levels of authority and power to adjust to, and the dawning (and often frightening) awareness that you are responsible for developing your team and not just yourself.

Equally important, tactical self-awareness tends to be applied in terms of your own development as you reflect on and assess your strengths and limitations in a campaign or program operation. There also are other, more external markers of strategic impact to which a macro practitioner must pay attention. A community-based practitioner is confronted daily with a variety of opinions, ideas, and beliefs about what is and is not important, who is of value, and what matters to the long-term direction and dreams one cast as a young organizer—ideas that, on a day-to-day basis, can sometimes seem far, far away. How do you avoid falling into the trap of constructing convenient beliefs that may unintentionally and yet everlastingly alter your commitment to and faith in the capacities of others, especially from the community, when you have less and less contact with the community in your new supervisory role?

Carolyn Strudwick confronted these challenges while working as an extraordinarily effective outreach worker with Safe Horizon/Harlem Streetwork, now located in Harlem. A strong, insightful, and courageous community practitioner born in Jamaica and raised in a West Indian middle-class home where *Black* and *powerful* meant the same thing, she came to the United States at the age of 18 to further her education. Landing at a local community college in New York State, she was initially thrown off by others' responses to her forceful and unintimidated manner as she dove into her class-work and outside activities. Because she was used to a dynamic give-and-take of ideas inside her home and at West Indian schools, it took her a while to understand that some Whites, including professors, were hostile to her presence, while some native-born African Americans suggested that she slow down so as not to make it harder for all of them at the college. Only after an older African American activist, Abdul Wahid Cush, had helped her understand some of the dynamics at play in America did she begin to understand the mix of historical and structural oppression that many of her White class-mates and professors wished to ignore and that some people of color hoped she would stop raising.

Strudwick slowly began to make peace within herself and with those around her regarding what she clearly identified as social and racial injustice:[3]

> Coming from the islands, where these issues didn't play out in the same way, it took me a while to understand that some American-born people of color had to have different responses to racism than I did. I could also see that just telling White Americans about their "internalized superiority" wasn't going to keep the conversation going, either.

Strudwick continued to reflect on her lifetime commitment to racial and social justice and her desire to be strategically effective. "If I was going to have an impact on helping kids of color in my little corner of the world overcome racial barriers, I was going to have to learn to handle things differently."

Her passion for social justice led her to Safe Horizon's Streetwork project, a program providing preventive services to homeless and at-risk youth. She became a member of an outreach team working with these troubled and often isolated young people. As a frontline community practitioner, she had to develop an easy and immediate rapport with wary, frightened, and often abused teenagers who made their living and found their shelter on the streets of New York City. Raised by a father who was a born organizer and a mother who kept the home open to everyone, Strudwick had little difficulty in adjusting herself to the testing and wariness of the young people she was trying to recruit off the streets and help toward a healthier, longer life. She described her approach this way:

> Those kids mean everything to me. I could work on their needs and help them see that the causes to their problems wasn't just them. But I wasn't afraid to challenge them, either. Hustling on the streets of New York City too long is a death sentence, too.

As a frontline community practitioner working with young people on the streets of New York City, it was relatively straightforward for her to put into practice the strategic vision that she carried inside.

CAROLYN STRUDWICK'S INTERNAL STRATEGIC VISION AS A COMMUNITY PRACTITIONER

Who: Young people, especially of color

What issue: Preventing homelessness and risk of HIV-AIDS infection; social justice

Her role: Outreach worker, street counselor, and advocate

How she worked: On the streets, building trust through respect and confidentiality, demonstrating openness to discussing issues with teens, and being both nonjudgmental and at the same time challenging

Core values consecrated in action: Respect, safety, trust, fairness, equality, reciprocity, social justice

---

What animated Strudwick in her work was her ability to see her values related to social justice concretely applied through the way she worked with young people on the street. When people—whether a 15-year-old street hustler or a human-services executive from downtown—meet her, they encounter a down-to-earth, humorous, and open woman with a lilting West Indian accent who speaks to them directly no matter the subject, as demonstrated here:

> Kids need to know you are not afraid of them and that you respect them. I have to show that respect from the beginning by being able to handle whatever they bring to me without judgment. How are they ever going to listen to me if I don't

listen to them first? . . . That pretty much works with everybody, I think, whether up the chain of command or down.

Her team members and program director appreciated her forthright discussions on underlying social justice issues that were impacting these kids' lives: jobs, employment, housing, and the racially disproportionate disadvantages that impacted their lives and those of their families (Derman-Sparks & Phillips, 1997). Given her leadership skill set and her newly minted master's degree in social work, she was soon elevated from frontline activist on the streets of New York City to senior director for the Streetwork Harlem site, where she became a supervisor of a four-member supervisory staff. She describes the role transition this way:

It was an adjustment, but I knew I could do this. It wasn't about changing my vision to fit the new job. I had to see if I could make the job fit the vision, too. It just had to look different. I just had to see it was still about helping those at-risk kids of color and the larger issues of social justice that are there, too.

Strudwick went about approaching her new role with the same direct, matter-of-fact, and powerful leadership she'd used on the streets. As she detailed how she went about working with the staff as well as the teens, the shape of the vision took place. As you will see, what changed was not the vision but how it manifested in her new supervisory responsibilities.

CAROLYN STRUDWICK'S INTERNAL STRATEGIC VISION AS A FRONTLINE SUPERVISOR

Who: Young people, especially of color

What issue: Preventing homelessness and risk of HIV-AIDS infection; social justice

Her role: Supervisor, coach, advocate, and mentor

How she works: More in the agency, building trust through respect and confidentiality with her staff and expecting them to do the same with young people, demonstrating openness to discussing issues with staff and teens, being both nonjudgmental and at the same time challenging to both, and creating a safe atmosphere in the office for staff and youth

Core values consecrated in action: Respect, safety, trust, fairness, equality, reciprocity, social justice

---

Here's how Strudwick describes applying her vision to her new role:

I have the same vision I always had. For me, it just meant I had to work with staff in the same ways I work with kids. For example, I have a young Youth Advocate who's White and comes from a pretty privileged background. He struggles with that as he works here in Harlem. I let him know I love him for that, that he works with who he is and doesn't forget it when working with the kids. He also doesn't let that stop him, and I respect that, too. Social justice isn't about race; it's about many things. So the fact that he works hard at the same things I care about means a lot more than what his background is. I make sure he knows I believe that. . . . I learned from my mentor Abdul back in local Community College that I can't just be angry about oppression. It's gotta be something we deal with while we do our job, but we still have to meet and recruit those kids to our program, too. I also feel it's an asset to work in diverse settings and important we make the effort to get along with each other and find common ground in the face of diversity. So in meetings I raise these issues so they stay front and center in our minds, but we also have the rest of our job to do. My vision gets to show up here and there, and that makes a difference to me and how I feel about this work. . . . My vision and commitment to the work is also strengthened from a self-preservation perspective, as an investment in each young person and promoting social justice is also helping to secure the environment I share with others. We all gain from that. A good vision can make you healthy, too!

For Strudwick, her new supervisory role had been a challenge met by finding concrete actions that make her vision real, not a set of fetters that limit her commitments:

Some weeks are easier than others, and it can be hard dealing with so many issues. I won't deny that either. But at the end of the day, I still love what I do. It's still all about the kids.

REFLECTIVE EXERCISE

As a supervisor, critically reflect on and respond to the following issues related to your position:

A. What are your primary tasks?

_____

_____

_____

_____

(Continued)

(Continued)

B. What amount of responsibility do you have to complete team/unit tasks?

_____

_____

_____

C. What level of authority do you have to ensure that unit tasks are completed?

_____

_____

_____

- How do you respond to tensions between B and C?

– Role rigidity and overuse of authority

_____

– Ignoring role responsibilities and underusing authority

_____

– Flip-flopping between the above two

_____

– Balancing authority and responsibility

_____

- What steps can you take to achieve better balance in your role?

– External steps

  ○ Approach director for support
  ○ Reestablish team norms and standards
  ○ Delegate more effectively (if overly rigid)
  ○ Set professional boundaries (if overly loose)

– Internal effort

  ○ Reflect on internal strategic vision and values consecrated in action, and reapply
  ○ Consider long-term legacy and commitments
  ○ Balance "career" and "courage" mix

A CAREER OF COMMITMENT: SOCIAL JUSTICE ADVOCATE AS ENTRY-LEVEL EXECUTIVE

Over the past few years, of course, Strudwick's bosses recognized her mix of genuine commitments and top-flight skills and promoted her again—this time to an entry-level executive position overseeing other programs beyond Streetwork. Perhaps even more challenging, this promotion meant going downtown to executive-level meetings, where the team comprised mostly White professionals, many with Ivy League degrees. Once again, Strudwick was confronted with issues of power and privilege—some of which, she admitted, required some personal work.

> I had to look at whether I could use my own voice all over again . . . did my voice really matter? . . . What power did I really have? . . . I had to work on ways to speak up and be diplomatic, too. . . . Being too loud, I could see, was just my own intimidation, and intimidation is "just a story" I had to get past.

Strudwick's brilliant insight here spoke to the "dance of oppression" that can occur when a person from an oppressed population (in this case, a woman of color) begins working in a new, more challenging environment. Her mindful insight (see Chapter 7) was to note that (a) the room was indeed filled with mostly White, highly educated professionals (who may or may not have been aware of their power and privilege), and (b) her own internalized identity had to break free from "the story" that she was inevitably excluded from the group, made to be intimidated, and had to react with either anger or upset to be heard. As she went on, acting from a place of perceived intimidation and ensuing anger would have danced her right out the door!

This doesn't mean that she didn't recognize a responsibility to keep the voices of her staff and clients at the executive table. Her internal strategic vision didn't disappear just because she was in a new room; it now had to be applied, tactically, in new ways to fit the contours of that room. She recognized a dilemma: On the one hand, Harlem Streetwork was a poster child for much of what her parent agency, Safe Horizon, was all about—serving the most vulnerable, marginalized populations in all of social services. The agency was proud of the program and often brought funders to the sites to see its work. On the other hand, not everyone can work with young, homeless, street-smart youth who have been traumatized repeatedly as young children, thrown out of their homes (often because of their sexuality), and forced to steal, sell their bodies, and commit to a daily hustle just to survive. Such extraordinary staff are often themselves either from the streets or have experienced the kinds of long-term trauma wrought by social oppression due to a mix of sexuality, race, gender, and class. They are, in short, a feisty bunch little interested in diplomacy and far less impressed by position than are most other professionals. People meeting with them who are not comfortable with street-smart confrontation have a very long day ahead. The ensuing dilemma is obvious: People may love the program from afar but not up close. In today's fiscal climate, both may be required.

Strudwick therefore saw her responsibility as twofold. First, she trained herself to better use hard data as evidence to justify her program's continuation. Arguing with others without evidence to back up her claims as they evaluated program options would never work over the years ahead. At the same time, her internal strategic vision's values consecrated in action went beyond data-driven commitments. They included social justice, respect (for those with less of a voice, in this case her staff), and fairness. While she developed her abilities to present data-driven results, she also advocated for her new group of executive peers to attend the People's Institute's antiracism workshops as a way for them to develop a deeper understanding of both structural racism and the dynamics of privilege and power. Rather than defensively lecturing people inside a boardroom, she found a way to help others from that boardroom understand the issues through others' lessons, not hers.

This tactical mix of evidence and advocacy in support of her values is on full display every year at the holiday party Streetwork hosts for senior staff, funders, and themselves. Clients formerly on the street who have used Streetwork's services present some of their stories, including both the painful past and the more optimistic present. One of the most moving encounters retold happened almost by accident. A staff member was on vacation in Florida when a young African American man approached her while she was shopping at a mall. Confirming who she was, he went on to say, "Hey, you guys made all the difference! Look where I am now, working and living well!" (He had been living on the streets of New York and hustling to survive.) He described the ARC program Strudwick and others had emphasized. "That stuff you guys did made a difference . . . you know, yoga, acupuncture . . . having a place to talk."

ARC stands for "attachment, resilience, and competency" (Blaustein & Kinniburgh, 2010). The Streetwork staff understood that long-term oppression requires respect, trusting relationships, and long-term healing from the prolonged trauma of marginalization, hurt, physical violence, and oppression that these young people have experienced for years and years. Strudwick's ability to combine data with the young people's voices at this event demonstrated the mix of hard and soft evidence that allows her to keep effectively fighting for this program's survival. The dynamics of power and privilege that continue to exist in any agency have hardly disappeared, nor is the funding for marginalized, poor youth guaranteed in times of greater and greater fiscal austerity. But a once-gutsy grassroots organizer for social justice is now, 15 years later, a spirited entry-level executive still committed to social justice. Only the arenas for struggle have changed.

CAROLYN STRUDWICK'S INTERNAL STRATEGIC VISION AS AN ENTRY-LEVEL EXECUTIVE

Who: Program staff, mostly new professionals with their own lived experience of marginality

What issue: Maintaining programs for young people to prevent homelessness and increased risk of HIV-AIDS infection; social justice

Her role: Executive peer, program head, and advocate

How she works: Both in her programs and in executive offices, building respect and interest for her programs for her staff and clients, and finding her voice in new arenas so that she presents evidence of program effectiveness as well as issues of power and privilege that may be at play across the agency

Core values consecrated in action: Respect, voice, fairness, equality, reciprocity, social justice

CONCLUSION: DEVELOPING NEW PROFESSIONAL ROLES FROM PERSONAL MASTERY

Strudwick has used her two promotions to deepen and expand the ways she expresses her vision, supporting and educating staff as well as young people. The flexibility she demonstrates in her work as she interprets new assignments flows from measuring what is and reflecting in action on how to fold her consecrated values into her new work. In doing so, she is demonstrating what Senge (1990; Senge et al., 2005) and his colleagues at MIT have identified as a key measure of sustained leadership, which we saw at play in Chapter 8 with organizer Eric Zachary—*personal mastery* (Schön, 1995). As we saw with Zachary, personal mastery relates to one's ongoing capacity to correctly distinguish "what is" from what one perceives, and in so doing effortlessly adjust to the demands of one's environment. Strudwick's adjustment to becoming a supervisor and, years later, an executive came about through the internal work she had done on maintaining her vision *before she was ever promoted*—and promoted again. As with Senge's (1990) master potter, her ongoing reflection, interpretation, and action while an organizer allowed the same committed leader to emerge in her new positions (Argyris, 1993).

For the community practitioner moving into supervision, the tools of tactical self-awareness and internal strategic vision explicated in this chapter are designed so that any macro practitioner may someday throw his or her own artful pots—using the limit-situations of his or her work, whether as supervisor or street activist, executive or grassroots organizer—as the clay from which progressive macro practice is formed continues to powerfully take shape.

INDIVIDUAL ACTIVITY FOR EDUCATIONAL POLICIES 2.1.2 AND 2.1.3

- How did Strudwick handle the dilemma of her new position as an executive?
- Explore the ethical dilemma between "holding the voice of her staff" and "being responsible for an agency's financial well-being"?
- What did she use to deepen the critically reflective skills needed in her more complex work environment?
- Reflect on your own choices for where you will work (social justice, nonprofit, public-sector organization). How will you maintain the balance between your commitments and what the agency's auspice requires?

THE COMMUNITY TOOLBOX

The Community Toolbox has a number of chapters on leadership, management, and supervision, including the following, at http://ctb.ku.edu/en/tablecontents/chapter_1015.htm.

Becoming an Effective Manager

Section 1. Developing a Management Plan

Section 2. Providing Supervision for Staff and Volunteers

Section 3. Providing Support for Staff and Volunteers

Section 4. Promoting Internal Communication

Section 5. Day-to-Day Maintenance of an Organization

REFERENCES

Argyris, C. (1993). *On organizational learning.* Cambridge, MA: Blackwell.

Blaustein, M., & Kinniburgh, K. (2010). *Treating traumatic stress in children and adolescents: How to foster resilience through attachment, self-regulation, and competency.* New York: Guilford Press.

Brilliant, E. (1992). *The United Way.* New York: Columbia University Press.

Burghardt, S., & Tolliver, W. (2009). *Stories of transformative leadership in the human services: Why the glass is always full.* Thousand Oaks, CA: Sage.

Carlton-LaNey, I., Murty, S., & Morris, L. C. (2005). Rural community practice: Organizing, planning, and development. In M. Weil (Ed.), *The handbook of community practice* (pp. 402–417). Thousand Oaks, CA: Sage.

Christian, L. (2007). *Finding community: How to join an eco-village or intentional community.* New York: New Society.

Cousins, C. (2004). Becoming a social work supervisor: A significant role transition. *Australian Social Work, 57*(2), 175–185.

Covey, S. (2003). *The 7 habits of highly effective people.* New York: FranklinCovey.

Covey, S. (2004). *The 8th habit: From effectiveness to greatness.* New York: FranklinCovey.

Cross, T., & Friesen, B. (2005). Community practice in children's mental health: Developing cultural competence and family-centered services in systems of care models. In M. Weil (Ed.), *The handbook of community practice* (pp. 442–459). Thousand Oaks, CA: Sage.

Derman-Sparks, L., & Phillips, C. B. (1997). *Teaching/learning anti-racism: A developmental approach.* New York: Teachers College Press.

Fabricant, M., & Fisher, R. (2003). *Settlement houses under siege: The struggle to sustain community organizations in New York City.* New York: Columbia University Press.

Festinger, L. (1957). *A theory of cognitive dissonance.* Palo Alto, CA: Stanford University Press.

Fisher, R. (2005). History, context, and emerging issues for community practice. In M. Weil (Ed.), *The handbook of community practice* (pp. 34–58). Thousand Oaks, CA: Sage.

Fisher, R. (2009). *The people shall rule: ACORN, community organizing, and the struggle for economic justice.* Nashville, TN: Vanderbilt University Press.

Fisher, R., & Karger, H. (1996). *Social work and community in a private world: Getting out in public.* New York: Addison-Wesley.

Fisher, R., & Schragge, E. (2001). Challenging community organizing: Facing the 21st century. *Journal of Community Practice, 8*(3), 67–83.

Freire, P. (2000). *Pedagogy of the oppressed.* New York: Continuum.

Grote, D. (2002). *The performance appraisal question and answer book: A survival guide for managers.* New York: AMACOM.

Hill, L. (2003). *Becoming a manager: How new managers master the challenges of leadership.* Cambridge, MA: Harvard University Press.

Homan, M. (2004). *Promoting community change: Making it happen in the real world.* Florence, KY: Cengage Learning.

INCITE! Women of Color Against Violence (Ed.). (2007). *The revolution will not be funded: Beyond the non-profit industrial complex.* Cambridge, MA: South End Press.

Kadushin, A. (1976). *Supervision in social work.* New York: Columbia University Press.

Kiesler, S. (Ed.). (1997). *Culture of the Internet.* Mahwah, NJ: Lawrence Erlbaum.

McCormack, D., & MacIntosh, J. (2001). Research with homeless people uncovers a model of health. *Western Journal of Nursing Research, 23*(7), 679–697.

Mulroy, E., Nelson, K., & Gour, D. (2005). Community building and family-centered service collaborative. In M. Weil (Ed.), *The handbook of community practice* (pp. 460–474). Thousand Oaks, CA: Sage.

National Association of Social Workers. (2013). *Media room.* Retrieved from http://www.social-workers.org/pressroom/default.asp

Netting, R. (1993). *Smallholders, householders: Farm families and the ecology of intensive, sustainable agriculture.* Palo Alto, CA: Stanford University Press.

Oshry, B. (2007). *Seeing systems: Unlocking the mysteries of organizational life.* San Francisco: Berrett-Koehler.

Parker-Pope, T. (2008, September 15). It's not discipline, it's a teachable moment. *New York Times,* p. H5.

Patti, R. (Ed.). (2008). *The handbook of human services management.* Thousand Oaks, CA: Sage.

PICO National Network. (n.d.). Retrieved from http://www.piconetwork.org

Reisch, M. (2005). Radical community organizing. In M. Weil (Ed.), *Handbook of community practice* (pp. 181–194). Thousand Oaks, CA: Sage.

Rubin, H., & Rubin, I. (2005). *Qualitative interviewing: The art of hearing data.* Thousand Oaks, CA: Sage.

Rubin, H., & Sherraden, M. (2005). Community economic and social development. In M. Weil (Ed.), *The handbook of community practice* (pp. 475–493). Thousand Oaks, CA: Sage.

Schön, D. (1995). *The reflective practitioner.* Surrey, UK: Ashgate.

Senge, P. (1990). *The fifth discipline: The art and practice of the learning organization.* Cambridge: MIT Press.

Senge, P., Scharmer, O., Jaworski, J., & Flowers, B. (2005). *Presence: Exploring profound change in people, organizations and society.* London: Nicholas Brealey.

Shepard, B., & Hayduk, R. (2002). *From ACT UP to the WTO: Urban protest and community building in the era of globalization.* New York: Verso.

Shulman, L. (2006). *The skills of helping individuals, families, groups, and communities* (5th ed.). Florence, KY: Thomson.

Staples, L. (2004). *Roots to power: A manual for grassroots organizing.* Santa Barbara, CA: Praeger.

Strom, S. (2009, June 9). Charitable giving drops, a report finds. *New York Times,* p. A16.

Teixeira, S. (2008). Regional collaboration opens doors for community information systems and more. *ACOSA Update, 21*(4), 2–3. Retrieved from http://www.acosa.org/updt_sum2008.pdf

U.S. Department of Health and Human Services. (2009). About HHS. Retrieved from http://www.hhs.gov/about/index.html

U.S. Department of Health and Human Services. (2013). *FY2014 budget: HHS budget in brief.* Retrieved from http://www.hhs.gov/budget/fy2014/fy-2014-budget-in-brief.pdf

Weil, M. (Ed.). (2005). *The handbook of community practice.* Thousand Oaks, CA: Sage.

NOTES

1. Fabricant and Fisher (2003) document that in some agencies, paperwork and executive demand for quantitative outcomes may become so onerous and time-consuming that it makes support and educational functions all but impossible to carry out. If, after prolonged assessment, you find this to be the case in an agency and there is no opportunity for redress, you must find work elsewhere if you are to continue doing the kind of work that brought you into the field. See Fabricant and Fisher's (2003) *Settlement Houses Under Siege.*

2. Covey (2003) identified four quadrants that account for how managers and others make decisions about how to use their time: Quadrant I (urgent and important), where genuine crises, quarterly reports, and the like are found; Quadrant II (important but not urgent), where relationship building, self-care, and long-term planning occur; Quadrant III (urgent but not important), where unattended-to problems and crises caused by miscommunication, turf wars, poor planning, and so forth require immediate attention; and Quadrant IV (neither important nor urgent), where passive, burned-out activities such as net surfing and reading junk mail happen. Covey argues that spending time in Quadrant II is critical to lessening time spent first in Quadrant III (stress-inducing tasks that never should have happened) and then in Quadrant IV, where burned-out, stressed staff go when they have spent too much time in Quadrant III. See Chapter 2 in Steven Covey's (2003) *The 7 Habits of Highly Effective People.*

3. All quotations are from a personal interview with Strudwick in August 2009.

CHAPTER 13

So Much Information, So Little Time

Human-Services Executives' Strategic, Evidence-Based Search for Social Justice

---

GETTING TO THE TABLE

It was 7 years from that first cup of coffee. Same diner, same booth, same two friends. Only the conversations were different. Or were they?

Kay was talking. "Yeah, well, now it's my turn to be crazed again. I know that there's a big part of me that wants to take this new job for the city. They have access to all the dollars, and I want to make some of them available to the folks who deserve it. I know I could make a difference as an assistant commissioner. But, damn, the crap you have to do at the top—"

Ellis interrupted Kay so that she'd finally eat the increasingly cold turkey burger in front of her. "Sure, there's crap at the top. There's crap at the bottom, too. You think it's fun spending twice as much time to get a flyer out than it ought to? And people show up late for meetings so much that we call them a half-hour earlier than we expect to start. Why do you think it's gonna be so different from when you were program director of that shelter?"

"I see some of the city and state people at meetings, and they scare me. Most of them have such dark circles under their eyes, I don't think they sleep. They carry briefcases bigger than

(Continued)

(Continued)

yours and mine combined! And all those policies they deal with—from the mayor, the city council, the state regulators, blah, blah. I mean, they deal with so much *stuff!*"

"Kay, slow down a little, okay? I mean, if it's all such a big bureaucracy, why would you bother? Besides, everybody works hard in human services." He paused for a second as he finished his own burger, this one made from beef. "You wouldn't do this just to make a better salary." Ellis and Kay had often spoken about the fact that most public-sector jobs paid better, with better benefits than found in their nonprofit work. "Not that that's a bad thing." They both laughed.

"I know everybody who does this works hard. Domestic violence work can take you anywhere, day or night. And our planning meetings can stretch into the 5-hour zone." She reflected on what she was trying to say. "I guess it's more the kind of work, the pushes and pulls that execs have on them." She paused again to eat some more. "I've spent my whole career so far where at least some part of my day is with the women I care about. I'm not sure as a honcho or honcha I get to do that."

"So you're worried about becoming a faceless bureaucrat, huh?"

"Well, something like that. I like being with people, and I don't need to be in the front of the room. But not in the room at all? I think that's what worries me. With this title and access to decisions on where the dollars go, I'll get all sorts of attention now. But I've been around long enough to know that it's not attention I'm after." She took a sip of her coffee and grimaced at the cold, stale taste it left in her mouth. "I guess I'm going to find out if I can be an executive and keep my commitments to those women I've been working with all these years when they're no longer in the room."

Her friend reached over and gave her arm the same squeeze she'd once given his. "They'll still be inside you, right?" Kay nodded slowly in the affirmative. Ellis's fingers tapped against his chest. "If they're there—and I know they are—you'll find a way, Kay. You just gotta look for it."

Educational Policy 2.1.6—Engage in research-informed practice and practice-informed research. In this chapter, readers will learn through case studies how "social workers use practice experience to inform research, employ evidence-based interventions, evaluate their own practice, and use research findings to improve practice, policy, and social service delivery."

Educational Policy 2.1.8—Engage in policy practice to advance social and economic well-being and to deliver effective social work services. In this chapter, students will learn that social work agency leaders "understand that policy affects service delivery, and they actively engage in policy practice.... [They] know the history and current structures of social policies and services; the role of policy in service delivery; and the role of practice in policy development" *so that they can "analyze, formulate, and advocate for policies that advance social well-being; and collaborate with colleagues and clients for effective policy action."*

INTRODUCTION: FACELESS BUREAUCRAT OR FIERCE ADVOCATE?

Kay's fears spring from a mix of impressions that many younger or less experienced macro practitioners begin to have as they advance in their careers. To a grassroots organizer involved directly with people in daily struggles for survival in the community, human-services executives can seem distant, withholding, and all-powerful. Seeming to make decisions with little or no community input, these executives, from the street level, appear to embody everything that some say is wrong with the field of social work: uncaring, unmotivated, disconnected.

As practitioners move forward in their careers, however, they begin to rub up against those faceless bureaucrats in coalitions, task forces, and alliances related to legislation, policy formation, and basic advocacy. While some still manage to reflect that indifference, up close, many of these human-services executives can be recognized as the fierce and committed advocates they always have been (Burghardt & Tolliver, 2009). They work as many if not more hours, and, lacking direct contact with people in the community, often receive fewer direct rewards for the work they undertake (Drucker, 2006, 2007). This chapter explores the conditions under which human-services executives work, how those who continue to act on their core values manage to overcome some of the daunting constraints they face, and how some are able to maintain a powerful social justice agenda no matter their distance from the daily community struggles that first got them involved in macro practice.

THE CONSTRAINTS AT THE TOP

A Personal Vignette

Because I am a teacher of community organizing with far more years of experience in the community than in large-scale organizations, my own exposure to the greatest constraint confronting executives unfolded in the mid-1990s as a group of us worked with executives from New York City's child welfare agency, the Administration for Children's Services—the largest municipal agency of its kind in the nation. Having already been impressed by the caring and hardworking commitment of executives such as Nicholas Scoppetta, William Bell, and Linda Gibbs, we were certain that the recommended systems improvements in response rates for children at risk would occur, given the investment in a multimillion-dollar e-mail system for all staff—from frontline workers in the community responding to reports of possible abuse to the top floor of the newly renovated building housing the executives and other child-welfare staff. Surely the desired collaboration and information sharing so critical to team building and problem solving would occur soon after. *How great,* I thought, *community building inside a giant child-welfare agency!*

A few weeks later, I raised my hopeful observation with a small group of child-welfare executives who had been intimately involved in this improved communications system. Giving me a slightly bemused look, Zeinab Chahine, one of the key leaders who oversaw the borough offices directly involved in child protection, gently asked me how many work-related e-mails I thought she got a day. Reflecting on my own and doubling the number, because I knew how hard she worked, I said 40. The answer was *75 . . . a day . . . that in some form or fashion had to be responded to!* I was stunned, only to learn that she was not an exception at the table: John Benanti, head of all administrative operations, had the same number, while Diane Connolly, in charge of quality improvement, had about 70. Obviously, community building inside a child-welfare agency through e-mail was going to be a lot harder than I had ever imagined . . . and that was in the mid-1990s!

Constraints Caused by Information Overload

This vignette captures what any human-services executive learns quickly: The greatest constraint on an executive is created by the amount of information he or she is bombarded with every day from myriad sources, all of which impact the time available for thoughtful decision making and critical reflection. Such information is both constant—those daily e-mails pile up pretty rapidly when executives take even a 2-day vacation—and about actions or events that the executive must in some way respond to. As Drucker (2007) wrote in his classic work on executives, "One responds to events that impact you before and after an operation . . . what events are relevant and important and not merely distractions the events do not indicate" (pp. 10–11). In other words, the information an executive is receiving is not only coming in at a high volume; it also must be sifted for its legitimacy, immediacy, and value to how the organization operates. So much information necessarily requires an executive to filter out what for others may be of enormous import.

Being able to *distinguish what is urgent from what is important* (Covey, 1990, 1992, 1996) is further complicated for an executive because he or she is responding to so many sources of information and events: Board members, union representatives, politicians, other executive staff, community folks, and funders are all vying for access, with information to share or receive. Ironically, "an executive's time tends to belong to everybody else . . . from a 'best customer' to a high official in the city administration" (Drucker, 2007, pp. 10–11). Being able to handle so much information from so many sources with too little time to respond to it all is a fundamental directive in an executive's life that is not so much resolved as handled, much the same way a juggler handles multiple balls in the air. At any one moment, some balls are briefly touched while others are up there, heading skyward and out of reach . . . only to be quickly handled and just as swiftly released. If the juggler pays too much attention to any one ball, disaster soon ensues. Of course, that a juggler doesn't look directly at his or her audience for very long is forgiven, for the balls being tossed are visible to everyone. For the executive managing as many items, such visibility does not exist.

Constraints Caused by Answering to Multiple Stakeholders

As Oshry (1994) makes clear in his compelling *In the Middle*, people at the top, while having vast authority, can keep their authority only by being responsible to all the stakeholders in their agencies: board members who want outcomes at the lowest possible cost, employees who want respect and good salaries, local officials who expect immediate attention to their constituent needs regardless of resource limitations. As this brief list suggests, some of each stakeholder's interests may compete and conflict with others: Fiscal accountability might be incompatible with good salaries; immediate responsiveness to constituent needs must be balanced against long-term interests for staff to be trained and skilled at what they do. The competing requests can be neither completely ignored nor totally granted, resulting in the need for even more information sharing as multiple sources are consulted to give balance within, across, and outside the agency.

Constraints Caused by the Impossibility of Personal Intervention

An executive "is effective only if and when other people make use of what he contributes, and many of whom over which he has no [direct] control" (Drucker, 2006, p. 27). The higher up in an agency one travels, the less one is engaged in *doing* the work of the organization and its stated mission, whether providing shelter, mental health services, child care, or foster care. Instead, the work is necessarily turned over to people who oversee other people who do such work. This being the case, an executive may wish something to happen and can even mandate it, but there is still a large gap between stated desires for policy or program development and actual implementation, which may occur three floors down or 5 miles away from the executive office. Because he or she is involved in the overload of competing information discussed above, it could not be otherwise. What an agency is known for doing and what the executive is doing, day in and day out, can seem to be very different things—a policy and program dilemma that cannot be resolved simply by an agency's leadership individually taking up more work.

FROM CONSTRAINTS TO COMPLIANCE: INEFFECTIVE LEADERSHIP IN A TIME OF INCREASING COMPLEXITY

Confronted with so many constraints in what others assume is a position of unbridled authority and power, executives must quickly learn to resolve the tensions in what all these competing and often overlapping information sources are telling them. This alone is a dilemma, further deepened by the insight provided by the well-known organizational development theorist and practitioner Meg Wheatley (2001). As she writes, most of us suffer not only from information overload; because of our training, there is also a problem in the way we look at and interpret information:

> Information theory has treated information as something that is tangible . . . as a quantity, bits and bytes to be counted, transmitted, received, and stored. . . . This strong focus on the "thingness" of information has kept us from contemplating its other dimensions: the content, character, and behavior of information. (p. 94)

If the executive confronts his or her constraints only from the simple overload of it all, it is inevitable that eventually the reaction will be to try and control the seeming chaos overload creates through a command-and-control approach to organization. That, in turn, results in emphasizing short-term reportable results and selecting a career workforce whose sole focus is compliance and the replication of compliance-based systems that streamline information so that it appears in repetitively similar ways (Public Sector Consortium, n.d.). This is what happens when units of service and timeliness of reporting become the *only* measures of an agency's effectiveness (Fabricant & Burghardt, 1993; Fabricant & Fisher, 2003).

Of course, no service-based agency could survive without some focus on compliance—for example, reliable data to measure outcomes or clear reporting that systematizes practice so that workers are held accountable in the delivery of fair and equitable services for every community member who walks through the agency's doors. Furthermore, nationally known executives such as John Mattingly and William Bell in children's services and Steve Coe in mental health have demonstrated that in the training of staff in the handling of data sets, they are improving the overall leadership effectiveness of middle managers in preparation for their future work with the multiple stakeholders referred to above (Brody, 2004).

That said, Wheatley (2007) has also made the startling point that, on their own, "outcomes are fear-based" (p. 28). By this, she means that, stripped of the possibility that feedback in organizations may also include "content, character and behavior" (p. 67), outcomes come to substitute for knowing or understanding what is happening, how it occurs, and what it may actually mean to the mission of the agency and the people it serves. *Having a need to be in relationship with others is replaced by hoarding information needed to justify one's position.* That a frontline worker has met with six clients in a day does not necessarily mean good practice has happened, let alone best practice. If such data are void of other meaning or are not balanced with other narratives sharing other forms of knowledge about agency policy and practice, then it is information of justification through quantification, not understanding. Neither the qualities of justness—what fully fits the needs of the community—nor those of justice—what the community equitably requires—fit within these narrow "outcome" parameters.

Such narrow human services agencies exist, as do executives who replicate the very worst of compliance-driven culture. As Fabricant and Fisher (2003) carefully document, even some settlement houses known for their democratic and egalitarian character at the turn of the 20th century are now compliance-based shells of their once-noble past as we move fully into the 21st century. However, that some social service agencies are now run by executives who give meaning to the fears Kay anguished over at the start of this chapter does not mean that executiveship is inevitably synonymous with social indifference. As the rest of this chapter makes clear, there are those whose sense of mission and accomplishment is as focused at the top of their careers as when they first began.

We will address three ways different executives have responded to some of the constraints addressed above:

- Handling opposing points of view among agency stakeholders, including board members and key staff, without sacrificing the core mission of the agency
- Responding to systemic racial inequities in the profession that were also found within the agency, without antagonizing other influential actors
- Developing a community organizing strategy to shift away from the compliance-based focus common to child welfare without dropping the focus on outcomes

We will then trace their work since the first edition of this book to see how they have continued to bring their vision alive in new ways.

As you will see, the ability to handle these constraints derives less from special individual qualities of the people involved and more from the underlying leadership methodology by which they approach the demands of their roles as executives.

AN EXECUTIVE'S STRATEGIC BALANCE BETWEEN CONTENDING STAKEHOLDERS

Gladys Carrion, born and raised by her working-class Puerto Rican parents in the South Bronx, had gone to law school for only one reason: to advocate on behalf of the children and families who were similar to those with whom she'd grown up—the poor Black and Brown children of New York City. She explains her motivation this way:[1]

> Growing up in the South Bronx, I had never even met a lawyer, other than Perry Mason on TV. But I knew that's what I wanted to be. For some reason, I always knew it was the kids I saw on the streets who mattered to me most. . . . I could make a good living, maybe not rich, but rich in other ways, by doing this work.

"This work," at the time, was as executive director of Inwood House, the oldest agency in the United States serving pregnant and parenting young women. (She is at present New York State commissioner for the Office of Children and Family Services.) Its special mission, begun in the 1830s with young Irish and German immigrants, was not only services but also advocacy on the behalf of young women who had confronted sexual and physical violence, poverty, and drug abuse within their families before they arrived at Inwood House's doors—some of these women as young as 13 and none yet 20 years of age.

Many of those who worked in the agency were also fierce advocates and had developed their social work careers as feminists and fighters for the rights of women. As such, their antagonism toward President George W. Bush's abstinence-only sex education program was absolute. From their firsthand experience, they knew that a focus on abstinence alone, given the realities of these young women's lives, was a little like trying to block a waterfall with a thimble. Without a full range of options that included safe-sex practices and fully understanding sexuality, staff were convinced, these women would be at greater, not lesser, risk. They clearly communicated to their executive director their opposition to the legislation and were adamant that their agency never receive such funding.

Inwood House's board of directors was composed of very different kinds of people from the staff. Because the agency had such a distinguished lineage, its board was made up of business leaders from Fortune 500 companies, lawyers from Wall Street firms, and society folks who also served on boards of major museums and other charities. Yearly fundraisers were emceed by the likes of NBC's Tom Brokaw and CBS's Katie Couric. As with all boards, members saw their primary responsibility as fiduciary rather than programmatic, so when the large amounts of money funneled through abstinence-only programs became available, some board members wondered about the possibilities such funding offered the agency. After all, as a contract agency rooted in the community and reliant on government and foundation funding for the majority of its programs, wouldn't the agency welcome such a major windfall?

Staff would be up in arms over such funding; some board members saw the funding providing a variety of other valuable services. What to do? For Carrion, the answer lay not with this dilemma but with the strategy she had employed when she first signed on to the agency as an already-known progressive advocate. Like a master organizer in Chapter 7, Carrion was using her entire chessboard from the moment she arrived at Inwood House:

> You can't expect to influence the Board when you need to if you haven't paid attention to who's on it from the beginning. People knew I was an advocate when I arrived here. I knew if I was going to keep to my progressive agenda I'd have to have a Board that agreed with me.

From the outset, Carrion sought to bring on new board members who both supported the agency mission and would be amenable to her progressive stance on policies impacting the young women in her agency. "When openings occurred, I sought out ways to make the Board more socially diverse, people who knew the communities we served and had a similar agenda." Such a strategic focus from the beginning made it possible for her to easily argue against the funding and its failure to directly help the young women at the agency. By the time she confronted this funding dilemma, the chess pieces had been moved on the board to guarantee that the members approved of her direction.

Part of her credibility came from being fiscally responsible and not simply from being an advocate. At the time, abstinence dollars were plentiful enough that they could be applied with many different age levels. Working with seasoned social work practitioners who knew the importance of sex education for various age levels, she had learned that early sex education with a focus on abstinence was both uniquely effective and appropriate for one particular group—fifth-grade boys. Because research had pinpointed this as the age at which sex education needed to begin if it were to be effective (Alford, Cheetham, & Hauser, 2007), and because fifth graders were still young enough not to be sexually active, Carrion had little difficulty in working with staff to obtain these funds:

> At first, a few staff were upset, but not for long. It wasn't about ideology or saying no just to be anti-Bush; it was about being sensible and principled at the same time. It made sense to support abstinence for the fifth-grade boys, because it worked and helped them. It was principled for other groups because abstinence didn't work, and we weren't going to take dollars to run the agency and then have a program that hurt the girls' chances to go back to school or stay employed.

Carrion found it easier to maintain her principled stance because such principles informed her strategic approach to working with the board from the moment she walked through Inwood House's door. When confronted with policy and practice dilemmas—as all executives are, often each day—such principled commitments moored her approach to resolving tensions in policy and practice that otherwise can seem overwhelming. Her values in action serve as sifting agents for conflicting information, helping her balance one set of directives against another. Having used the chessboard from the moment of her arrival as the agency's executive, she remained fiscally responsible and principled at the same time.

GLADYS CARRION'S INTERNAL STRATEGIC VISION AS INWOOD HOUSE'S EXECUTIVE DIRECTOR

Who: Working-class and poor communities, especially young people of color and their families

What issue: Pregnant and parenting young mothers and fathers and their children

Her role: Executive director, advocate, and leader

How she worked: Used the chessboard to recruit a diverse board of directors for future decision making; with staff, interpreted policies for practice with principle and practical application

Core values consecrated in action: Safety, fairness, equality of access, access to complete information, transparency, integrity

PERSONAL REFLECTION

Reflect on people who have recently joined your agency or campaign. As you sought them out and interviewed them, did you assess how their skills, talents, and values might impact the later work of the group? How can you tell when there is value alignment? Did you hear a story or concrete example that brought those values to life? How do such values in action fit with other work under way inside your group or agency?

"IT'S ALL ABOUT MY KIDS": AN EXECUTIVE MINES THE EVIDENCE IN SUPPORT OF SYSTEMIC TRANSFORMATION

Carrion had demonstrated strategic savvy in balancing competing interests between her agency board and her committed staff. In her new position as Commissioner of New York State's Office of Children and Family Services, she would need strategic brilliance, because the number of constituencies now confronting her vision were more organized, more political, and less influenced by her position, as powerful as it was. For she was "all about the kids," and the evidence, she soon learned, showed that those kids were not being well cared for at all.

Her responsibilities as a statewide commissioner included both child welfare and juvenile justice, where more than 1,400 young people could be found in residential facilities—small prisons—across the state. At the same time, being new to juvenile justice, she recognized that her first responsibility was to review the evidence on conditions in those facilities and among those children before she could form a direction for her vision.

> I knew I had to read—there was A Human Rights Watch report, an Inspector General's report, a review of a death of a child at the facility in Fort Tryon. . . . That data was the backbone to any advocacy I wanted to undertake, so it started there. . . .
>
> I became data driven. I learned the demographics. I studied the type of offenses, and saw over 50% were nonviolent. I read the case histories of the kids as well, where they came from and what their lives had been like. . . . Over 90% were Black and Brown kids, almost all from New York City even though they were being kept upstate, sometimes 8 hours from their homes and families.

She paused only for a second before she went on. "I went and visited the facilities upstate to see what conditions were like, and talk with the kids. They looked like my own son. . . . They were from my own community."

The no-nonsense, data-driven executive went on. "After each visit, I'd go back into my car. Then I'd cry." For Carrion, her vision had always been about the kids. To make a difference in their lives, she'd have to get them back closer to home, where their families, schools, and communities were. That would mean closing down facilities in upstate communities that depended on these jobs and had politicians in the state legislature ready to do battle to protect them. As emotionally committed as she was to this systemic change, she knew a simple form of advocacy was doomed to failure. What she developed would require patience and persistence—key traits of anyone who *lives his or her strategic vision* and thus can consistently work at the building blocks of reform over a long period of time. Her work would also have to encompass a *transformational strategy*, one capable of supporting contending approaches within the same overarching plan—just as Eric Zachary did in Chapter 8 in fighting for educational reform.

"I knew I was in for years of work. So I sought out the best-thought leaders on juvenile justice, on child development." In her approach to advocacy, she didn't stop there. "I needed external partners from universities, other social service programs that worked with these children and their families [such as education, mental health, developmental disabilities, and criminal justice advocates]." She was also armed with powerful evidence on the failure of the system. "You would have an upstate facility with 32 staff and 4 or 6 kids, and some of the workers didn't know their names!" The data, she went on, showed that incarceration beyond 6 months did little good, and yet most children were staying for a year and beyond. Finally, there was the financial wallop to further buttress her advocacy agenda. "It cost $240,000 a year to house a child upstate. That, I would argue was the high cost of failure." In tough fiscal times, it all made for a compelling argument.

At the same time, however, Carrion also kept a service agenda alive—one designed to support staff as well as the kids who would remain in care. She convinced the Governor's Office to increase her budget so she could hire 156 new staff, primarily mental health and education positions that supported the deescalation model of residential care that she espoused, a model that deemphasized restraint and punishment. "I brought in people from the best program in the country, out in Missouri, to speak with staff and train us on how best to work with young people in these facilities." This gave her credibility with upstate actors suspicious that she was simply an advocate.

In short, her push toward systemic advocacy was complemented by her pull toward programmatic reform. While her longer-term goals sought diversion so that young people ended up either out of the residential facilities or at least back closer to their communities, she did not ignore the shorter-term needs to improve the way children were treated in the facilities in the here and now. That such programmatic reform would later be applied to the systemic changes in New York City was a building block of change Carrion had in play from the start.

After a year and a half, this work alone would have created a solid legacy for her administration. She had needed patience as she sifted the data and put in place the fundamentals of her mix of systemic advocacy and programmatic reform. But persistence isn't the same as patience—it means continuing to work toward that inner strategic vision, no matter how seemingly small or large the building blocks might be. She courted advocates. She spoke with union leaders and politicians from New York City as well as rural areas of the state. She hired a press secretary who could target her message to different media outlets. And all the while, she kept searching for the dollars to make the diversion from residential care possible.

"My 'aha!' moment came when I realized that diversion [rather than sending kids away upstate] could never happen without new resources, and there was only one place for those financial resources to be found: the empty beds." Of course, to close facilities, even those filled with empty beds, meant to incur the wrath of both unions whose members needed those jobs and politicians whose communities had few other streams of revenue.

There was a sudden increase in kids going AWOL from facilities; for the first time, a van at one facility was left open so kids could escape. I knew what was at play here: They wanted me to back down. My response was simple: push to close them down even more quickly, while continuing to support better mental health treatment, the Sanctuary Model of clinical intervention (Bloom, 1997) . . . and all the while remaining transparent with the press and the public about what was going on.

Instead of being intimidated, she took her argument further, creating a blue-ribbon commission comprising legal, academic, law enforcement, district attorney, and advocacy panelists whose charge was to review the conditions at play inside these facilities.

> If it's about the kids, it's not about me. I wanted others to share the stage. People like Judge Lippman and Kevin Whelan of the governor's office deserved credit and to be seen in the leadership roles they played . . . not me. I went to the foundations to get funding, and they all did. I got over $500,000 for a systematic year-long review with all the stakeholders of juvenile justice playing a part.

The commissioner was confident that the panel could reinforce her arguments for systemic reform while doing so with a kind of impartiality that would begin to limit some of the political foes now lined up against her. A master strategist is primarily motivated by her vision, not by ambition; being committed to "my kids" and their chance to live decent lives trumped the withering accusations hurled at her by antagonists who tried to refute data with lurid, untrue tales of residents attacking staff and holding "sex parties" in the facilities. Confident in the mix of factual clarity and the underlying values of her vision, Carrion never blinked at what many state commissioners in the past might have run from.

And then the U.S. Department of Justice showed up for a system-wide investigation of her juvenile justice facilities, bringing a lawsuit drawn up around three primary complaints: (a) lack of mental health services; (b) punitive conditions of confinement; and (c) sexual abuse. Rather than resist, she instructed her staff to be fully cooperative. The Department of Justice carted away 1,000 boxes of data for review. Never speaking to her throughout the entire process, they 6 months later issued a "letter of findings," documenting in 33 concise pages the very reasons for reform that she had been pushing since her visit to a residential facility 2 1/2 years earlier. The report was a stinging indictment of the state system—except for its opening paragraph, which noted that Commissioner Carrion had already started the work of addressing the exact issues that informed the report.

With the clout of the federal report, the findings of the blue-ribbon panel, her own impassioned efforts both to divert kids from residential facilities and to provide nonpunitive forms of training for staff, Carrion had created the strategic leverage that at last made transformational change of an unchanging system possible. Three years of patience and countless hours of persistence led the staffs of Governor David Patterson to begin closing down underutilized facilities and using the $60 million dollars of freed-up resources to create a powerful diversion program that would be housed where the children lived, in New York City. While she would be the first to tell you that much work remains to be done, Carrion's kids were coming home.

GLADYS CARRION'S INTERNAL STRATEGIC VISION AS NEW YORK STATE COMMISSIONER OF THE OFFICE OF CHILDREN AND FAMILY SERVICES

Who: Primarily young people of color incarcerated in residential facilities far from their own communities

What issue: Ending punitive residential programs and closing down vastly underutilized residential facilities

Her role: Commissioner, advocate, and leader

How she worked: Used the chessboard to develop a multipronged plan of reform and systemic change, enlisting stakeholders from across the state through patience, persistence, and the use of hard data to support her cause

Core values consecrated in action: Safety, fairness, community integration, access to information, transparency, integrity

INDIVIDUAL ACTIVITY

1. Distinguish the two complementary prongs of Carrion's transformational strategy.

2. How did these prongs—major tactics—change as her campaign for reform went on? How did improved training for staff come to benefit the children who would gain from diversion?

3. What strategic purpose did the blue-ribbon commission serve?

4. Why did she embrace a federal investigation, when state officials normally resist outside reviews?

5. In what ways did her internal strategic vision sustain her in this work?

SEEKING SOCIAL JUSTICE WHILE RESPONDING TO PUBLIC OVERSIGHT AND THE NEVER-ENDING NEED FOR COMPLIANCE: FIGHTING RACIAL DISPROPORTIONALITY

Perhaps no other human-services system requires the amount of information and compliance-based outcomes that child welfare does. Given the enormous responsibility to assess the safety and well-being of children and the unique legal mandate to remove a child from his or her home if that assessment finds reason to do so, child-welfare professionals at the federal, state, and local levels have created an unprecedented set of protocols, procedures, and assurances so that at-risk children are protected in safe and permanent homes (Lindsay, 2003). From the moment calls of possible abuse or neglect arrive at any state's central registry, the amount of oversight on the promptness and reliability of the professional intervention will run into the hundreds of pages before a case is closed.

And that's just for one case. In a large city, a worker involved in child protection may have up to 12 such cases; his or her supervisor oversees five to seven such workers; that supervisor is overseen by a frontline manager who oversees 7 to 10 supervisors. Keeping the multiplication going, the executive may have upward of 10 to 20 managers; in New York City, it can increase to more than 200. Now pause and reflect: How much information can that executive possibly keep track of? Of course, he or she must be focused on little else—not only his or her job but also the lives of children depend on it. Imagine: In other kinds of organizations, poor or inadequate information may mean a product isn't sold or a service is underutilized. In child welfare, it may mean that an innocent child either dies or is grievously harmed. When such a tragedy occurs, a review begins immediately on the quality of information and who was responsible for it—and this review is carried out by the press and politicians, not only by professionals. Because of this pressurized environment, many human services professionals decide they would rather not work in child welfare.

Given such pressures, there is little wonder that the primary focus of most child-welfare executives is on the quality of compliance, period. And yet, when New York City's Administration for Children's Services was struck with the tragic death of Nixmary Brown in 2006 (Pérez-Peña & Newman, 2006), two executives managed to include social and racial justice as part of the agency's long-term reform efforts. How did they manage not to be overwhelmed by the accountability demands for better information coming from legal and political sources? How were they able instead to connect the focus on better oversight wrought by this crisis to projects for a more racially balanced leadership and an attack on racial disproportionality? How did they, in the words of Wheatley (2009), realize at this time of great anguish inside their agency "that the journey to newness is filled with the black potholes of chaos . . . that it is [through] these dark moments . . . [that one finds] the only route to new ways of being" (pp. 190–191)?

At a quick glance, Liz Roberts and Anne Williams-Isom, two deputy commissioners inside New York City's child welfare agency, the Administration for Children's Services, couldn't seem more different. Roberts, a White woman who grew up in a family headed by her banker father and housewife mother, had lived around the world until settling into a well-to-do suburban town in Connecticut as a teenager. Williams-Isom, the product of a West Indian family headed by a strong and forceful mother, grew up in New York City, attending its parochial schools in Queens, learning to handle the typical demands from its streets as she rode the city's public buses to school with her brothers. One's history shows a lifelong and deeply held commitment to feminism; she was involved as an organizer for the rights of abused women before attending social work school. The other paid little attention to social issues in college and had little plan for what she was going to do, "being guided more by spirit,"[2] as Williams-Isom put it, that led her inexorably from law school to neighborhood services for kids of color.

And yet they became close collaborators and strategic partners fighting for social justice at a time of great crisis inside the compliance-driven world of children's services. While wrestling with all those e-mails, compliance demands from the state, and the ever-present, looming mandates to speak at City Council hearings to justify the work of their staffs, *they nevertheless experienced the Nixmary Brown crisis in ways that elevated rather than diminished their commitment to social justice.* The lacerating pain of remorse and reflection over what had been missed felt across the agency also included for them the awareness that another child of color had been needlessly lost. The route out of their own pain included new attention to the unsettling national trends of racial disproportionality that were also reflected within their own agency. Roberts, with Williams-Isom clearly in support, began working with others to understand and address the reason why so many more African American children were within the New York City child welfare system than were within the general population.[3] Furthermore, Williams-Isom took the lead, and found support from Roberts, to alter the equally unsettling reality of having so few people of color among top executive staff. How did these two women, whose work calendars and e-mail inboxes suffered from the same overload as any other executive's, manage to create a social justice agenda focused on policy innovation in a bureaucracy traditionally unsuited for social change?

As they would be quick to tell you, their ability to work on this agenda took place within an environment where their boss was supportive of their efforts. Both Roberts and Williams-Isom held their executive positions under Commissioner John Mattingly, a national child-welfare leader who for years had expressed interest in and cared about these issues. Because his position at the very top precluded much direct involvement as he dealt with the multiple political and legal actors involved in this case and the rest of his enormous reform effort under way, it was still up to Williams-Isom and Roberts to carry out this work. Furthermore, their colleagues within the agency's senior team were not opposed to their efforts. Working among other bright, capable, and hardworking deputy and assistant commissioners, they thus were able to undertake their work within an environment where the competing agendas were time, money, and resources, not active hostility or hidden agendas seeking to undermine their goals.

That didn't mean that the issues they sought to work on were easy. Given the demands of the day in any human-services agency, raising social issues that are complicated and not easily resolved puts you at risk, professionally, of potential marginalization from your peers. After all, executives are promoted to get large amounts of work done, not to make more work for everybody. The pressures on people to stay the course on what is already an overly full agency plate are enormous. This is where Roberts's background as an organizer and her lifelong commitments to social justice were key factors in her decision making about racial disproportionality. "I began work while in Cambridge at HarborMe, a domestic violence shelter. The shelter had a real mix of women of color and White working-class women. You had to pay attention to race and gender issues." She saw then that "issues of race and culture had to be dealt with by the staff if we were to be effective advocates and genuine allies of these women." *Learning that this social awareness of race, gender, and culture helped make her effective as a young organizer prepared Roberts for how she approached her job as an executive.* The question wasn't whether such issues should be addressed; it was how to be most effective in a demanding work environment where the resources of time and focus were at a premium. The crisis caused by a lovely little Latina girl's death brought into sharp relief how important those commitments formed at the start of her career still were.

It helped mightily that she knew she had an ally and fierce fighter for justice in her colleague Williams-Isom. For more than 10 years at the agency, Williams-Isom had been the one member of the senior team who consistently raised issues of race as they impacted the children and families the agency served. Equally important, she saw the importance of having a leadership team that was reflective of the larger community. That those singled out for public condemnation by the press on this tragic case had all been people of color intensified her resolve to change conditions inside the agency. However, Williams-Isom's own growth as an executive carried with it the awareness that it was not enough to promote people of color into positions of authority if they did not have the preparation to match their potential. Effectively handling all that information—whether quantitative data, political hearings, or staff conflicts between two programs—requires a mix of managerial skill and internal confidence. She knew all too well that creating access to the executive boardroom was one thing; staying there as a player was another.

Thus, while Roberts and others began to move on the development of a Racial Equity and Cultural Competence Task Force, Williams-Isom was simultaneously embarking on the creation of a Leadership Academy for all 270 frontline managers in the Division of Child Protection, child welfare's largest and most publically identified division. These managers—85% of them people of color—worked in borough offices across the city where they were expected to oversee 40 to 70 staff investigating cases of possible lack of safety and neglect. More than capable of handling emergencies, staffing demands of the day, and the complexities of daily practice, they were seasoned veterans who demonstrated courage, tenacity, and commitment every day of the week. At the same time, most also grew either tongue-tied or temperamental when given the opportunity to meet with the more senior team over at the central office.

Reflecting on her own experience, Williams-Isom said, "I had been given an opportunity to develop my voice and my confidence to disagree and still do the work together." Certain that others needed the same opportunity, as an African American woman, she also understood that a leadership program that emphasized skills without also addressing the dynamics of race, oppression, power, and privilege as key dimensions would be insufficient to her vision of a genuinely inclusive, multiracial world. She therefore sought support for and was able to fund curriculum designers whose experience included weaving into the skills-based content these social issues that demonstrated respect for the academy participants and the external barriers they had lived with as people of color, while also challenging them to deal with any internalized oppression that blocked advancement. "My own boss [John Mattingly] let me fly and be free to develop. . . . The frontline managers needed the same opportunity."

What is striking about these two executives is that *their approach to social justice and racial equity was consistently present in their work at a time of crisis without drawing constant attention to it.* Consistency of effort around social issues in organizations that have little time for anything beyond the demands of the day comes from their underlying personal comfort with such issues as being simply a part of their lives and, by extension, inevitably filtered into their work. As Wheatley (2009) wrote:

> Self reference is the key to facilitating orderly change in the midst of turbulent environments. . . . A clear sense of identity—the lens of values, traditions, history, dreams, experiences, competencies, culture—is the only route to achieving independence from the environment. When the environment seems to demand a response, there is a means to interpret that environment. (p. 86)

The agency's crisis, while as painful for these executives as for everyone else, thus served as a prod to bring them back to core values in action that required new dedication, not just more and better (and overwhelming) information. It was the solidity and steadfastness of their previous commitments to social justice—Wheatley's (2009) lens of *values, traditions, history, dreams*—throughout their lives that made the new commitments possible.

Liz, herself a parent of a child of color, went on to serve as co-chair of this task force for more than 2 years. While she is keenly aware that much remains to be done, she and the other members of the task force recognize that there is a new and healthy environment in which people can discuss race. "It used to be 'cultural competency' and 'inequities.' . . . Now it's more real, more textured as we discuss a child, the family, the worker." Such an environment, where racial issues are woven into ongoing conversations and problem solving, has been identified as central to diminishing agency-based causes of racial disproportionality (Hill, 2004).

Furthermore, "people used to be uncomfortable when the issues came up. . . . Now you don't have to fear for your job" as these discussions take place. Such openness is central to the kind of problem solving that must take place as professionals and families assess what works and what doesn't in the lives of children who may be at risk. Equally important, Roberts, a former social anthropology major, is happy to see that race and culture are being looked at by people more and more from "a multiple lens" that speaks to the richness and diversity we have in communities.

Williams-Isom, besides serving as "the godmother to the task force," saw the Leadership Academy advance from an aspiration to a realized part of her legacy. The leadership curriculum for frontline managers emphasized a mix of leadership skills, reflective activities, and increased capacity to handle data in all its forms, all the while weaving in issues of race, oppression, power, and privilege in a way that neither dwells on nor denies their impact on participants' lives. Evaluated by outside researchers, the academy's program was lauded as an exemplary model of exacting professional standards that in no way detracts from the important social issues at play in the program.

The results have perhaps been most evident at the biweekly ChildStat meetings created by Commissioner Mattingly, where selected protection cases are reviewed by the commissioner and his most senior team in front of a room of other executives. The meetings are modeled after the famous CompStat police review programs begun under the administration of Mayor Rudolph Giuliani and his police commissioner, William Bratton (Bratton & Knobler, 2003), and now used nationwide. Frontline managers are brought before the panel to examine how a case was handled, the decision making involved, and lessons learned for future practice. At its inception, ChildStat was a forum of such anxiety and personal tension that once-articulate people became so tongue-tied they couldn't speak and so nervous they threw up before the sessions began. Months after the Leadership Academy had completed its first three cohorts, some of the same people who once had been so nervous were now poised and thoughtful in the give-and-take between the commissioner and themselves over how best to have proceeded with a case. Not unlike the grand rounds in a hospital setting, ChildStat has become a learning environment for both executives and frontline managers. Indeed, as more than one executive noted, what had once been a miserable professional experience was becoming an audition for future promotion! Williams-Isom's vision of a training ground for future executives has become an active part of the legacy she expects to leave behind.

LIZ ROBERTS'S INTERNAL STRATEGIC VISION AS A DEPUTY COMMISSIONER OF CHILD WELFARE: ERADICATING RACIAL DISPROPORTIONALITY

Who: Children at risk, especially young people of color and their families

What issue: The safety and well-being of children

Her role: Deputy commissioner, advocate, and organizer

How she worked: During an agency crisis, worked with others to refocus attention on racial disproportionality and disparity in child welfare as part of overall reform efforts

Core values consecrated in action: Fairness, equality, equity, responsibility to end power and privilege created through gender and racial advantage

ANNE WILLIAMS-ISOM'S INTERNAL STRATEGIC VISION AS A DEPUTY COMMISSIONER: LEADERSHIP ACADEMY

Who: Middle-level, frontline managers, mostly people of color

What issue: Development of executive talent among frontline staff to lead the agency in the future

Her role: Deputy commissioner, leader, and facilitator of dialogue

How she worked: During an agency crisis, used previous discussions on race and equal opportunity to advocate for a high-level, demanding Leadership Academy for middle managers

Core values consecrated in action: Fairness, equality of opportunity, high standards for education and training, support and challenge on overcoming internalized oppression

REFLECTIVE ACTIVITY

Reflect on a recent crisis inside your agency or campaign.

List the negatives of what happened:

_____

Now think about some opportunities that emerged from the crisis: policy innovation, personnel, improved systems, better communication and attention to underlying social dynamics related to power and privilege.

_____

Examine your internal vision. In what ways could your values in action related to *who, what issue*, and *how* have been utilized to make a positive impact?

_____

Could your values in action have been consecrated in a small yet meaningful way as policy and/or practice was reviewed and improved?

TWO NEW EXECUTIVE OPPORTUNITIES . . . AND
ONGOING INTEGRITY TO ONE'S INTERNAL STRATEGIC ·

New opportunities have emerged for both these women over the past few years. .
Roberts, it was to become chief program officer for Safe Horizon, the nation's largest
agency serving clients and communities victimized by crime, trauma, abuse, and neglect
(see www.safehorizon.org). While hardly a switch in terms of size and scope from her
previous position as deputy commissioner of prevention in New York City's public
child-welfare agency, the new position would be focused much more on the ongoing,
immediate service needs of a more diverse set of programs: domestic violence, youth at
risk, elder abuse, and victims of crime. While in a position of genuine power within the
agency, the mix of diversity of programs and the unending need for fiscal accountability
in tough economic times meant moving carefully and systematically to assess the programs, their staffs, and what she could provide as their new leader.

Long accustomed to reviewing data and the search for hard, outcome-based evidence
on the value of programs, Roberts nevertheless joined her systematic review of programs
with her underlying values and commitments to people with less power and privilege than
she. To meet Roberts is to know someone who carries her privilege well—that is, not at
all. She is a great role model for young practitioners who struggle with whether they
"belong" in the fight for social justice given their own more socially comfortable backgrounds. Having been in the trenches for 25 years, her modest personal manner is fused
with a steely commitment that whatever she does will at some point benefit those less
fortunate than she. She doesn't announce such commitments or carry them on her shoulder; *she lives them.*

As chief program officer of a major nonprofit agency, most of her days are spent with
budget items, programmatic developments, and personnel issues. At the same time, she
knew that frontline staff—the vast majority of them young professionals of color—would
have the opportunity to advance only if they, like her, were given high-level skill sets to
meet the bar of excellence that promotion would require. She thus developed alongside a
skills-based parents' program an equally powerful quality supervision program for her
staff. "I knew Safe Horizon would invest in not only client enrichment but staff excellence,
and my goal was to do both."

Roberts set about developing a quality supervision training program as *policy for
the agency,* an important distinction. A training program may be terrific in its client-
centeredness and emphasis on excellence, but if it is not backed up with the power of
being agency policy, it can be an attractive add-on, not a norm. Roberts used her powerful position to help develop such a policy so that all staff would be expected to be
trained in how to provide good documentation, trained in client-centeredness, and given

support through coaching to improve over time. These program elements alone would be worthy of mention here as social justice exemplars of "excellence for all and not just the few." But Roberts and her staff went further by implementing an in-depth, weekly set of case reviews within each program, where teams met and supportively yet thoroughly reviewed a different team member's case in terms of the handling of data, the degree of knowledge and awareness associated with the client's history, and, when possible, how the case directly or indirectly related to funding of the program.

In short, Roberts developed a policy and program for lower-level staff that emphasized the mixed skill set of handling data (a systems skill), client awareness (client-centeredness, a clinical skill), and funding (a fiscal skill) that in combination were the kinds of skills anyone seeking promotion must have—and that many people, lacking access to acquire this kind of skill development, would otherwise never have. Such lack of access guarantees further marginality in the workplace. What better measure of social justice through access to excellence could an executive provide?

LIZ ROBERTS'S INTERNAL STRATEGIC VISION AS CHIEF PROGRAM OFFICER TO FRONTLINE SUPERVISORS

Who: Frontline staff, mostly young professionals of color

What issue: Staff development through quality supervision policy and program

Her role: Chief program officer, advocate, and educator/trainer

How she worked: As she reviewed her roles and responsibilities across the agency, identified ways for frontline staff to gain executive-level skill sets and experience through training and case reviews

Core values consecrated in action: Fairness, equality, equity, responsibility to end power and privilege created primarily through social advantage

---

Williams-Isom's career path led her to a position as chief operating officer of an agency whose entire purpose was equality of access and opportunity through excellence—The Harlem Children's Zone (HCZ), Geoffrey Canada's renowned agency committed to providing complete access and opportunity to children of color denied such access because of their race and class.

I get to live my vision every day, with people who share the same vision. We're committed not just to individual transformation but community transformation.

You can't change a person or even individuals if the community itself isn't changed. Our work is to get kids to want to come back here so that transformation continues. True equity and social justice is about proving that those who come from an economically disadvantaged background can and will perform as well as anyone else . . . and that their community will benefit from that.

Like Roberts, Williams-Isom also works from data and not just conviction. "Without data, both that helps us inform programs and prove we're justifying investment, we wouldn't survive." An interesting example of how data have infused programs is HCZ's Baby College.

We have a Baby College . . . it's as much for parents as it is the children. The latest science says brain development before 3 years is crucial. Parents and kids learn together on how to create an enriching home environment. People come here and are encouraged, not shamed, to learn how to do that.

She went on to detail some of its core elements.

Parents learn the difference between discipline and punishment so they stay out of the child welfare system. Good health care is provided so that chronic health problems are prevented. . . . There's a pipeline from programs to the families that over time build the same kind of social capital as found elsewhere.

The executive was clear that having this kind of commitment to children and families didn't mean the work got easier. "For us at HCZ, love and commitment to these families in Harlem can mean having to make some hard calls along the way, calls based on that love but also the well-being of the child and the entire family." She paused for emphasis. "We had a young child in our Baby College where I got to know the mom pretty well. We really connected. I'm a mother of three, just like she was, with two littler ones soon to come here, too."

But we began to notice that the child wasn't doing too well in school, and a quick check at home showed the other kids weren't looking well either—nothing dangerous, but not well dressed, not as clean as they need to be. I spoke with the mom, and it was clear she was having some mental health problems with all the demands on her as a single mom. She knew I cared about her, and she also knew we expected her to get help so her kids could thrive. Loving someone doesn't mean you let other things slip.

As much as she wanted to change, she couldn't, at least not with the stressors in her life. . . . We did what we had to do for her and her children. . . . We called in her case and had the children temporarily removed so she could commit to working on herself in ways that would eventually make her be the mother she wanted to be.

Williams-Isom was well aware of the seeming incongruity of an agency deeply committed to the children and families of Harlem having children temporarily removed from their parent.

> Remember what I said . . . love and commitment is hard. If you really love those kids and are committed to their future, sometimes the work gets hard. Of course the mother was angry with us. But when she met with me, I had to hold up what we're about. She knew I cared, that Geoff cared. . . . Sometimes the work requires some struggle to get where she and her family needed and wanted to go.

The result? Three months later, the mother was doing much better. She was soon reconciled with her children, and the child in Baby College and her younger sister were dressing better and had their energy back. Through HCZ respecting—and loving—them all enough to challenge the mother to take steps to improve, what in other communities could end up fracturing a family had strengthened this one.

Williams-Isom went on to make clear that staff—many of them drawn from the Harlem community and a significant number of them already having benefited from HCZ programs—express their love and commitment by creating a spirit of camaraderie inside and outside the agency and school. For example, prizes for perfect school attendance are given at various social events, and staff knock on doors in the neighborhood to see how people are doing, not as a "checking up" but a "checking in."

Williams-Isom also has significant fiscal issues to deal with each day, in addition to the variety of systems' problems any large agency experiences. "But I'm okay with that. I signed up for that, too." For a moment, her eyes filled with tears.

> But every day, there are stories of love in this place. I get to see love in action—there's some 15 year old who gets a hug while working on some family issues . . . a 5 year old who smiles a smile as big as the moon as he shows his drawing to me.

She smiled again, her eyes now reflecting steely determination. "There's an urgency here, too. We know how hard it is for kids . . . and the community . . . to get to the next level. But it's all worth it."

ANNE WILLIAMS-ISOM'S INTERNAL STRATEGIC VISION AS CHIEF OPERATING OFFICER AT HARLEM CHILDREN'S ZONE (HCZ)

Who: Children and parents who participate in HCZ schools and programs

What issue: Development of young people in the skills and leadership commitments to return to Harlem so that the community maintains its vital position in New York City

Her role: Chief operating officer, leader, and broker of social capital

How she worked: Daily engagement in leadership development, social capital formation in neighborhood, and one-on-one attention to HCZ community members with respect and challenge

Core values consecrated in action: Love and commitment, fairness, equality of opportunity, high standards for education and training, support and challenge in overcoming internalized oppression and providing enriching learning environments

A MOTHER'S WORDS AND DEEDS INSPIRE A CEO'S STRATEGIC VISION FOR A MULTIBILLION-DOLLAR FOUNDATION

Dr. William Bell is president of the Seattle-based Casey Family Programs (CFP), a multibillion-dollar foundation started by Jim Casey, the original owner of United Parcel Services (UPS) who established a number of foundations in honor of his wife and in support of children across the United States. Arriving at CFP in 2005, Bell found a deeply committed staff located in six Western states whose primary mission the provision of services to children whom public-sector programs were underserving due to a lack of financial resources to ensure their safety and well-being.

While Bell was impressed with the genuine effort of each state's frontline staff and aware of how hardworking the Seattle central office team was in providing the training and information their staffs needed, his vision was to utilize CFP's resources for all 50 states, not just six. At the same time, it would never be possible to set up shop in all 50 states as had been done with the half-dozen. For all its endowment, CFP would have to be strategic in where it leveraged its dollars and its professional staff, figuring out a way to maximize results without heedlessly spending money everywhere in equal fashion. Likewise, the CFP staff would have to be won to a new vision, for they were happy and successful where they worked, even if it was in but a few states. At the same time, as a national expert in child welfare, Bell was called on by other groups—from federal oversight panels to state legislatures to other national advocacy organizations. Dealing with others' multiple agendas and the magnitude of information that went with them, Bell's time to devote to CFP's evolving approach was limited. Reflecting on the chessboard in front of him, he knew he had to do some serious and focused work before embarking on his next set of moves. With that in mind, he turned to what had successfully guided him throughout his career: the lessons and wisdom of his Mississippi mother, Mrs. Alberta Bell.

Like that of the other macro practitioners found throughout this text, Bell's resilience in remaining both principled and strategic in his approach to practice at the front lines, whatever his own position, relied on core values that were expressed in concrete ways both large and small. For him, those values were consecrated first through the words and deeds of his mother. Raised in the 400-person rural town of Pace, Mississippi, Bell saw his mother "work in the fields picking cotton the way a man would do"[4] and then come home and help with the small harvest her own family raised on its small patch of land. "We worked in the garden," he remembered, pickling and preserving everything they could to eat later in the year. While their shelves might have been full, they were rarely overstocked. As a young boy, he saw that an even poorer and older neighbor, Mrs. Williams, would come and pick from the garden whenever she chose. When he asked his mother why they allowed this, since they had little to offer, his mother, a deeply religious woman, smiled and quoted scripture: "Cast your bread on the water and know it shall be returned." Young William saw servant leadership in his own household long before it was written about elsewhere (Greenleaf, Beazley, Beggs, & Spears, 2002).

Distilling such scripture in his own life as he moved to New York, the young social worker framed his practice through two important principles. First, "just keep giving and you will always have." For Bell, "giving to others, not getting all we can, was the essence of success." Tied to this was another critical value: that hard work, humbly rendered—as his mother had demonstrated—would allow him to "be a mirror for people" who could then on their own decide what was best for themselves. Alberta Bell, with no more than an eighth-grade education, first worked in the fields and then became a domestic for the landowners of those fields, a step up followed by another cooking in the local school cafeteria. While she remained in that position for years to provide for her children, she later went back to college, graduated, and became a Head Start teacher. Hard work, applied in service to others so that they, too, may be in a position to better themselves, was Alberta Bell's creed and commitment—and one her son took into his social work practice.

His own practice principles grew from that foundation, first in information and referral work and later as a group and family worker, where he worked long enough and hard enough to see that holding up a mirror for others while they struggle over their life choices was more important than giving advice or providing a handout. He grew comfortable with letting people grapple with their commitments rather than rushing in too quickly to solve their problems or just to relieve the tension in the room. Over time, as he was plucked from the front lines and moved into management positions, his life purpose became much like his mother's. "My purpose [through my work] . . . was to see others less blessed grow out of their situation and their challenges to be more than they thought they could be." This purpose—holding up a mirror as a sign of both challenge and respect for those with whom he worked—was the essence of what Freire (2000) identified as the true task of the humanist:

> It is not our role to speak to people about our own view of the world, nor to attempt to impose that view on them, but rather to dialogue with the people about their view and ours. We must realize that their view of the world, manifested variously in their action, reflects their *situation* in the world. [A practice] which is not critically aware of this situation runs the risk either of "banking" or of preaching in the desert. (p. 96)

Moving to shift CFP's direction and focus, this major child-welfare executive would draw on many resources to develop his work: words of wisdom from mentors such as Willie Dean Smith, his principal at a segregated high school, and Dr. J. White Treiss, the first African American school superintendent in his Mississippi county. Strategic lessons drawn from Bell's community organizing classes in social work school and readings on servant leadership and systems thinking were beneficial as well (Greenleaf, 2002; Senge, 1990, 1999). But he would be the first to tell you that at the core of CFP's new direction were his mother's values and deeds. CFP's Strategy 2020 may flow from the strategic vision of William Bell, but its foundation was built by Mrs. Alberta Bell in her family garden 40 years ago.

Strategy 2020 is a bold national strategy designed to reduce by half the number of children in foster care by the year 2020. Creating four regions of between 12 and 14 states run by seasoned child-welfare professionals, the substance of the work includes attention to racial disproportionality, a focus on family-to-family interventions, attention to youth aging out of foster care, and other child-welfare programs and policies. At its heart, though, are the following strategic principles that allowed the foundation to marshal its resources without losing sight of its goal for the young people of America:

• CFP professionals work with states on their priorities and practice models as long as they are consistent with CFP's. Respecting where the people are, plus one, as the basis of the work is as fundamental an organizing principle as there is, even when the people are the professionals running a child-welfare system.

• A focus on outcomes has both short-term and long-term objectives and is determined not in uniform lockstep back in Seattle but by the regional leadership and the state personnel with whom they work. When such data were used to guide decisions about which states could receive the most attention, this variability allowed a region to experience "combined and uneven development" among its dozen states. Recognizing such variability breaks down some of the fear Wheatley referred to, as noted earlier. By analyzing results across a region and allowing each state's particular needs and strengths to be evaluated differentially, the information CFP strategists collect has some of the textured content and character that is at the heart of reflective, strategic thinking rather than reaction.

- Bell and his top executives held up the mirror to the Seattle staff as they were challenged to use their resources for quality, support, and best practice development that could benefit the variety of states requesting their aid. Shifting from a central role within the old model of programmatic services for six states to a support function for 50 was not without its strains. But Bell's mother's words rang true here as well: "The struggle for humility is only with one person . . . yourself." Rather than simply fight resistance, Bell modeled the way forward through his own actions—not with perfection but by admitting to the turmoil and struggle that change creates. "I knew out of the turmoil good would come, just as my mother did. She did not have an easy life, and there was turmoil for her, too. But she never gave up on her beliefs. Why would I?" For Bell, to hold up a mirror for his staff was to hold one up for himself as well. He has attempted to "embody the change he seeks."

Well into the middle of this long-term campaign, enormous success in a variety of states has already happened since this major strategic shift. Working with CFP staff, state agencies with the largest child-welfare populations, such as Georgia, Indiana, California, and New Jersey, have made identifiable strides in expanding models of practice that hold up mirrors to families in ways that respect and challenge them so that rates of recidivism, length of time in care, and numbers of adoptions are already improving. Texas child-welfare officials, originally supported through CFP funding, have made significant progress in reducing racial disproportionality in the state, successfully convincing the state legislature to pass legislation mandating and funding the People's Institute's powerful antiracism workshop for all child-welfare workers. This remarkable effort has since been transferred to other states with whom CFP staff are working so that, as of 2012, the number of children in care had dropped from more than 500,000 to 375,000 nationwide—a remarkable 25% drop in less than 6 years (CFP, 2013).

As with other executives in this chapter, Bell would be the first to tell you that there is still enormous work to be done and that much of it depends on the continuing hard work of his staff, not just him. There is nothing smooth and easy at the very top: It can be lonely and isolating, too, as more and more information pours in each day from across the country, all of it necessitating time to reflect and respond strategically. For Bell, it's not easy, but he never thought it would be. His mother modeled the inner grace that comes with effortless giving, not with an easy life. To be successful, he simply plans to follow her lead all the way to 2020 and beyond.

> **WILLIAM BELL'S INTERNAL STRATEGIC VISION AS PRESIDENT OF CFP: STRATEGY 2020**
>
> *Who:* Children at risk, especially young people of color and their families
>
> *What issue:* Reducing by 50% the number of children in care across the nation by 2020
>
> *His role:* Foundation president, leader, and strategist
>
> *How he worked:* Shifting the foundation's focus from regional programs to technical assistance and support across the nation, enrolled board and staff through ongoing engagement in a flexible strategy emphasizing long-term efforts for permanent outcomes that would change the face of child welfare; "held a mirror" for people to reflect and make choices for new programmatic focus
>
> *Core values consecrated in action:* Support, equality, work ethic, respect, perseverance, belief in others' capacity to grow, social justice

SOMETIMES IT TAKES MORE THAN A VILLAGE: LEADERSHIP RISK IN SUPPORT OF ONE'S INTERNAL STRATEGIC VISION

If Bell were the kind of organizational leader satisfied only by child-welfare outcome measures, the results in the reduction of care would be enough for him to feel satisfied. But he is a man motivated by his vision, not his laurels. His commitments to children at risk, especially those aging out of care who all too often ended up in some other system, especially criminal justice and mental health systems, left him to ponder what underlay such stark results.

> The evidence was telling. No matter how hard people work—and they do—the results of where young people ended up was not good on any measure.... [Therefore,] I had to look at the entire child-welfare paradigm. The traditional child-welfare model had [in a city or state] 700 case workers with 25 cases working diligently to return kids to permanency [either in their own families or adoptive families].... However, unless we change the conditions in families, and the conditions in which those families live, what kind of permanency have we created?

The former community organizing student now running a major philanthropy began to see that young people could be safe and well only if their communities and families were healthy, too. The result has been a systemic attempt to unite the "micro" work of traditional child welfare services with the "macro" integration of key community actors in new ways that foster social capital needed for young people not to survive but to thrive.

Called "Building Communities of Hope 2020," the CFP pilot initiative sought two key systemic changes. The first was to invite other institutions in the community that are impacting the life of the child, such as education, mental health, and criminal justice, to work together rather than separately so that true social capital—the web of connections that stabilize families and individuals so they can live productive and safe lives—could be created.

The old paradigm of separate bureaucracies working with individual children and their families has the kind of limits that cannot on their own impact the larger conditions of communities and families. Bringing these actors together for the greater good has got to be part of how we configure services going forward.

Doing so in new ways, however, required a key dimension of leadership not always discussed in the literature: *risk*. As is discussed in Chapter 5, "risk" is implicitly associated with danger—it suggests upsetting traditional ways of doing things, calling into question standard ways of operating, and reassessing one's role and authority as one challenges other key stakeholders' basic assumptions.

The traditional path of philanthropy and all funding agencies is to develop a concept of intervention, put out an RFP, have agencies bid on it, award some, and then evaluate its success or not over the next couple of years.

He paused for emphasis. "A grant cycle does not fit the life cycle of a child. We all have to figure out a way to break from that if that child's life is paramount."

One such focus was to reconnect a village's institutional actors in new and more effective ways. The other innovation was to expand who was part of the child-welfare village. Here, CFP's leader explicitly focused on nontraditional child-welfare actors while implicitly continuing to honor his mother, Alberta Bell, and her legacy. Bell and his staff developed a faith-based pilot initiative that called on local churches in Richmond and Atlanta to deepen their own local missions. For example, in Richmond, church leaders expanded their Family Life Centers to tend not only to their members but also to the older youth population aging out of foster care, as well as their families. Tutoring, mentoring, and after-school programs were inspired to work with new children and families with some (but not large) financial resources and with the inspiration of the Golden Rule to guide their work.

Such inspiration to serve others did not come about simply through exhortation but through example and the building of strong relationships that demonstrated respect for the religious institutions as well. Bell, an ordained minister, united this "micro" skill of relationship building with these religious leaders while maintaining a focus on the "macro" call for strong social capital formation as central to these young people's long-term chances for success. His mother would have been proud.

> ## WILLIAM BELL'S INTERNAL STRATEGIC VISION APPLIED AS PRESIDENT OF CASEY FAMILY PROGRAMS: STRATEGY OF HOPE 2020
>
> *Who:* Children at risk, especially young people aging out of foster care and their families
>
> *What issue:* Building more connected community and neighborhood institutions so that the conditions of a community could support families and young people aging out of care
>
> *His role:* Foundation president, leader, strategist, and advocate
>
> *How he worked:* Deepening the foundation's community-based as well as individually based strategies, emphasizing social capital formation and faith-based initiatives so community conditions were strengthened
>
> *Core values consecrated in action:* Support, equality, respect, perseverance, belief in others' capacity to grow, social justice, faith, the Golden Rule

CONCLUSION: IT'S HOW YOU LIVE, NOT JUST WORK

First, executives who practice a progressive agenda through their work at the top have held on to and utilized core values in action throughout their lives. Whether the executive saw them modeled by his or her mother, learned them as lessons from school mentors, or discovered them as a young feminist, *these values were shaped and refined over time regardless of levels of formal power so that they were usable by either a young activist in the grassroots with few resources and fewer organizational constraints or a top executive with far more resources who yet was constrained by the competing agendas of organizational life.* As the stories of the executives in this second edition exemplify, the core values consecrated in action do not change—simply their focus, so that they remain tactically effective and powerful. That's why their internal vision is *strategic,* not simply a nice-sounding abstraction.

Second, for all these executives, such values were tied to a core belief expressed through their work that everyday folks, whether poor Puerto Ricans or White working-class battered women or African American kids and their families, were just as capable of excellence as anyone else, including themselves. As Freire (2000) noted, the "true humanist can be seen by one act of generosity rather than countless words." These leaders embody this through everyday actions that culminate in large-scale differences inside and outside of their agencies.

It takes persistence and patience to continue to act on those values and beliefs, because information roadblocks from other stakeholders will be competing for attention. None of the programs described here was completed in a year, and in most cases they have been many years in the making. Furthermore, those people wounded by a lifetime of being either ignored or marginalized understandably do not immediately act on such positive beliefs simply because an executive has espoused them. Oppressed people, too, will need to see actions connected to that belief in themselves well before risking the transformation such beliefs and values in action require: mutual respect *and* genuine challenge.

As with all successful leaders, these four executives are shaped less by the immediate demands of the environment than by the inner principles that guided them for so long. When either a crisis occurred or an agency culture had to change, their strategic vision, honed by years of practice, was diamond-like as it carved itself carefully into new and often pressing agendas within their agencies.

Embody the Change You Seek . . . Early in Your Career

Finally, their work started humbly and modestly, as it does for almost all social work practitioners: One was an entry-level information specialist, one an advocate and case manager in a homeless shelter, and two worked on legal briefs for individual clients. When you meet executives like them, they all have stories somewhere in their pasts that sound a lot like what recently happened to Yolanda Johnson-Peterkin, newly appointed as an assistant executive director for programs for the Brooklyn-based Women's Prison Association (WPA). Having moved up rapidly from case counselor and team supervisor to entry-level executive, 6 months into the job she found herself overwhelmed by the financial details of the position and frustrated by the lack of connection to the women she had so recently served.

Seeking an outlet for her frustrations, she signed up to bring a WPA team into the maximum-security prison, the Bedford Hills Correctional facility, to lead the female prisoners in an HIV-AIDS walk inside the prison. Each woman had donated 75 cents to support women with HIV-AIDS on the outside, which amounted to more than 2 hours of work inside the prison. At the last moment, Johnson-Peterkin decided to bring along her boom box and a mix tape with "Electric Slide" beats to spark the group. "I thought, they're donating 2 hours of their pay and will be walking in the same prison yard they walk in every day. They deserved something better." Cranking the music up loud, Johnson-Peterkin soon had a line of 100 women prisoners and 10 volunteers dancing to the side, then the left, then the right, and snapping their fingers to the music. Cheers for the walk soon rang out, and, looking up, she saw the fully armed guards in the towers moving to the music as well.

When it was over, the group cheered mightily, the work for the day done. One woman, slightly older, with a touch of gray in her dreads, shyly approached Johnson-Peterkin. She took her hand, tears in her eyes, and said, "Thank you so much. Thank you! I've been in this prison for 16 years, and today is the first day I feel like a human being." Tears rolled down both women's cheeks as they embraced.

That next Monday, Johnson-Peterkin went into her executive director's office to talk. As she related, "I just got back from Bedford Hills and reconnected to what matters to me. I can't do this job if I am not connected to the lives of these women." They talked for a while before Johnson-Peterkin made her request: training on budgets so that she could handle all the new data coming across her desk and perform as an executive needs to *and* an added assignment to work directly on advocacy for those women in Bedford so she could live her strategic vision with passion and commitment.

The WPA executive director quickly agreed. A macro practitioner and fighter for social justice to her core, Johnson-Peterkin plans to be an executive director someday, too. She had learned that living her vision and rising to the top could go hand in hand. Five years later, as director of program operations for Reentry Services, her rise—and her vision—continue.

GROUP AND INDIVIDUAL ACTIVITY FOR EDUCATIONAL POLICIES 2.1.6 AND 2.1.8

Reflect on an agency program or policy initiative that impacts the community in which you work. Now, using William Bell's or Liz Roberts's approach, rethink the policy or program with a community organizer's strategic focus. Include in it process goals that increase community voice, as well as task-related outcomes.

With others, plot out a yearlong goal(s), with 3-month objectives that are concrete and relate to both process and task completion, as Carrion did. Finally, what values have you consecrated in action that show up concretely, as seen from all four leaders' examples? Can you develop your own phrase, such as "hold up a mirror," that helps ground you in the strategic meaning and direction of your work?

THE COMMUNITY TOOLBOX

One of the underlying themes of each executive's development—both personal development and development of the people with whom they worked—was training, staff development, and work with outside consultants as they took on the challenges inside their agencies. The Community Toolbox offers a number of skill sets and suggestions regarding this important work at http://ctb.ku.edu/en/tablecontents/chapter_1012.htm.

Providing Training and Technical Assistance

Section 1. Identifying Core Competencies for the Work

Section 2. Designing a Training Session

Section 3. Delivering a Training Session

Section 4. Conducting a Workshop

Section 5. Organizing a Conference

Section 6. Organizing a Teleconference

Section 7. Organizing a Retreat

Section 8. Choosing a Consultant

Section 9. Serving as a Consultant

REFERENCES

Alford, S., Cheetham, N., & Hauser, D. (2007). *Holistic programs that work to prevent teen pregnancy, HIV and sexually transmitted infections.* Washington, DC: Advocates for Youth.

Bloom, S. L. (1997). *Creating sanctuary: Toward the evolution of sane societies.* New York: Routledge.

Bratton, W., & Knobler, P. (2003). *The turnaround: How America's top cop reversed the crime epidemic.* New York: Random House.

Brody, R. (2004). *Effectively managing human services organizations* (3rd ed.). Thousand Oaks, CA: Sage.

Burghardt, S., & Tolliver, W. (2009). *Stories of transformative leadership in the human services: Why the glass is always full.* Thousand Oaks, CA: Sage.

Casey Family Programs. (2013). *Other Caseys.* Retrieved from http://www.casey.org/AboutUs/OtherCaseys/

Covey, S. (1990). *The 7 habits of highly effective people.* New York: Simon & Schuster.

Covey, S. (1992). *Principle-centered leadership.* New York: The Free Press.

Covey, S. (1996). *First things first.* New York: The Free Press.

Drucker, P. (2006). *The practice of management.* Burlington, MA: Butterworth-Heinemann.

Drucker, P. (2007). *The effective executive.* Burlington, MA: Butterworth-Heinemann.

Everett, J. E., Chipungu, S. P., & Leashore, B. R. (2004). *Child welfare revisited.* New Brunswick, NJ: Rutgers University Press.

Fabricant, M., & Burghardt, S. (1993). *The welfare state crisis and the transformation of social services.* Armonk, NY: M. E. Sharpe.

Fabricant, M., & Fisher, R. (2003). *Settlement houses under siege.* New York: Columbia University Press.

Freire, P. (2000). *Pedagogy of the oppressed.* New York: Continuum Books.

Greenleaf, H. (2002). *Servant leadership: A journey into the nature of legitimate power and greatness* (25th anniversary ed.). New York: Paulist Press.

Greenleaf, R., Beazley, H., Beggs, J., & Spears, L. (2002). *The servant-leader within: A transformative path.* Mahwah, NJ: Paulist Press.

Hill, R. B. (2004). Institutional racism in child welfare. In J. Everett, S. Chipungu, & B. Leashore (Eds.), *Child welfare revisited* (pp. 57–76). New Brunswick, NJ: Rutgers University Press.

Hill, R. B. (2006). *Synthesis of research on disproportionality in child welfare: An update.* Baltimore, MD: Annie E. Casey Foundation.

Lindsay, D. (2003). *The welfare of children.* New York: Oxford University Press.

Oshry, B. (1994). *In the middle.* New York: Power & Systems.

Pérez-Peña, R., & Newman, A. (2006, January 18). A child's death commands lasting attention and outrage. *New York Times.* Retrieved from http://www.nytimes.com/2006/01/18/nyregion/18deaths .html?pagewanted=all&_r=0

Public Sector Consortium. (n.d.). *Learning programs.* Retrieved from http://www.public-sector.org/ learning_programs.html

Senge, P. (1990). *The fifth discipline.* New York: Broadway Books.

Senge, P. (1999). *The dance of change.* New York: Doubleday.

Wheatley, M. (2001). *Leadership and the new science: Discovering order in a chaotic world* (Rev. ed.). Burlington, MA: Butterworth-Heinemann.

Wheatley, M. (2007). *Finding our way: Leadership for an uncertain time.* Burlington, MA: Butterworth-Heinemann.

Wheatley, M. (2009). *Turning to one another: Simple conversations to restore hope to the future.* Burlington, MA: Butterworth-Heinemann.

NOTES

1. All quotes come from a personal interview with Gladys Carrion in October 2009.

2. All comments from Liz Roberts and Anne Williams-Isom are from interviews held in October 2009.

3. In the United States, data suggest that a disproportionate number of minority children, particularly African American and Native American children, enter the foster care system. National data in the United States provide evidence that disproportionality also may vary throughout the course of a child's involvement with the child-welfare system. Differing rates of disproportionality are seen at key decision points, including the reporting of abuse, substantiation of abuse, and placement into foster care. Additionally, once minority children enter foster care, research suggests that they are likely to remain in care longer. Other research has shown that there is no difference in the rate of abuse and neglect among minority populations when compared with Caucasian children that would account for the disparity. See Hill (2004, 2006) and Everett, Chipungu, and Leashore (2004).

4. All quotations from William Bell are from interviews conducted in October 2009 and 2012.

Conclusion

CHAPTER 14

Summing Up, Moving Forward

Key Lessons and New Directions for 21st Century Practice

Kay Francis and Ellis Frazier, the two macro practitioners who opened every chapter, were fictional, but their stories are not. The questions they raised throughout their professional development as they struggled to remain true to the values and commitments they held as young organizers are the same questions that the remarkable group of real men and women have asked in my community organizing classes over the past 35 years. Being honored to witness the integrity and honesty that animated such questions as these students moved from the classroom into the rough-and-tumble of day-in and day-out community work—the quest that so many undertook as they became lead organizers, program directors, and agency executives—has served as the primary framework for this book.[1] The results, of course, have been less about answers arrived at than lessons received that frame how they handle the new dilemmas of practice that inevitably emerge with whatever path they have taken: lifetime organizer committed first and foremost to social justice, program director overseeing a mix of youth development and elder programs, or executive of a multimillion-dollar agency.

LESSONS BUILT ON FROM THE PAST

Some of the lessons are distilled from *The Other Side of Organizing*, made richer from the inspiring lessons people provided over the years as they tried out core skill sets and leadership stances within their own macro practice frameworks.

1. *Tactical self-awareness (TSA) has immediate effectiveness in helping ground a new practitioner in his or her approach to the various demands of the day; its longer-term value is as a tool for the development of personal humility as one goes about the courageous act of trying to change the world.* TSA helps right away in the self-acceptance of being good at some things (and thus tactically effective in some situations) and not so good at others (thus requiring more planning, delegation, and sharing of tasks along the way as one begins the longer process of one's own professional improvement). As I learned over the years, the added benefit of TSA is that its emphasis on accepting your own strengths and limitations develops an internal perspective on performance that is self-accepting of what you do well while also remaining fully aware that such excellence will inevitably be replaced by ongoing efforts to master other tasks . . . again and again. If you practice TSA over many years, there is both greater flexibility in approaching your work and a personal perspective of modesty that reflects neither the grandiosity of always being right nor shame when things go wrong. Furthermore, such modesty maintains the internal capacity to more easily respect the struggles of others, year after year, as they show up in your work: the timid community member seeking her voice; the boastful new practitioner whose grandiosity masks fears of performance; the agency colleague who is too hard on himself. TSA provides an experienced practitioner a lifetime of teachable moments from stories told not about what someone should do but about your own struggle to master, again and again, how getting it right never lasts . . . and doing it wrong won't, either.

2. *In many ways, TSA also serves as the foundation to new models of coleadership that share power and decision making within community groups and in agency projects.* That almost every macro practitioner is keenly aware of the abuse of power when it occurs does not mean one can easily alter such dynamics once one has formal authority over others. As is made clear early in Chapter 12, some progressive people become tyrants once they achieve authority because of their discomfort in the role's power and their own awkward handling of it. TSA, in its practice of strengths and limits, builds up an internal resilience and flexibility in the approach to power as well: If internal control over one's performance is less of an issue, then the need to dominate the external world lessens as well. Through your own internal sharing of strengths and weaknesses, you also can more easily share the tasks at hand and the decisions that need to be made.[2] Through such a model of leadership, decision-making power, rather than being the prerogative of the few, becomes the domain of the many: Community members and frontline staff have gained power, while the practitioner, whether organizer or manager, has lost none.

3. *Fostering models of individual professional development and coleadership that allow for limitation and share power are reflective of a "win–win" paradigm that constructs your democratic practice by breaking down method dichotomies rather than reinforcing*

them. Community organizing can heal while it provides hope in the midst of a difficult struggle for social justice. Likewise, a micro practice that restores others to the dignity they deserve can foster commitment to a socially just world as much as an organizing campaign can. As the case studies and examples from this book make clear, good macro practice is built in part on effective individualized interventions; good individual work can do the same for social justice (Lundy, 2004). Over a lifetime, any macro practitioner will do such individual work (including on himself or herself); so will the micro practitioner engage in larger issues as he or she seeks to better the conditions of the people he or she sees each week (and, it must be said, for the conditions of his or her own life).

4. *As developed here, coleadership models that are genuinely democratic and social constructions of practice that are transformative both develop from a deeply held belief that the capacities of others, given the opportunity to flourish, are equal to one's own.* The richness of Paulo Freire's work stems from this belief as he applied it to literacy training among peasants. Its importance rests on his tacit knowledge, gained over years of effort, that such a belief can be made manifest only through the consecrated, daily implementation of a methodology that allows that belief to emerge—slowly, painfully, and yet, step by step, fully—in active relationship first between the teacher and the taught, finally to bloom as colearners together. *Problem-posing is less a set of questions than a method of inquiry that seeks to learn with others, including the oppressed, in ways that will transform everyone involved.* As such, Freire's dialogue is a lot more than a meaningful conversation. "Naming the word to transform the world" requires a belief in others' humanity and your own openness about what that struggle to be fully human requires of us all: "The midwifery of liberation" is both painful and a source of joy. Applied to macro practice here, the patience and persistence such a methodology requires can be maintained only if the belief in others' capacity to colead, teach, and transform the organizer as well as the organized is genuine. That this belief in others stems in part from a capacity to foster an equivalent belief about oneself is one of the sweet, liberating ironies of what it means to do great practice.

5. *The attention to the not-so-hidden realities of race, gender, sexuality, and other social factors in one's practice continues to be as pressing an issue today as it was 30 years ago.* While Barack Obama's ascendency to the presidency of the United States as the nation's first African American president is of historic meaning, his success by no means vitiates the need for further vigilance on social matters. The often virulent antipathy to his holding this office, as witnessed by the response to his health care initiative at town hall meetings held in 2009 and the growth of the Tea Party in 2010, makes clear that social issues such as race remain front-burner issues of great concern for macro practitioners across the nation (Krugman, 2009). Likewise, the 2013 Supreme Court ruling that undercut significant sections of the 1965 Voting Rights Act, allowing states to change their voting laws without prior federal review, attests to the continuing antipathy to full racial equality

in the United States (Silver, 2013). Within social work, the encouraging response to the work of the People's Institute in combating racial disproportionality in child welfare is one that people can model throughout the profession. As the People's Institute's work makes clear, there is an untapped desire to learn ways to effectively handle the microaggressions that occur within our programs and agencies so that social work becomes a model of engaged antioppressive practice. As this book suggests, learning to weave discussions of oppression into our work that neither dwell on nor deny the "-isms" at play in the profession is a central part of one's transformative practice—for ourselves and for those with whom we work (Burghardt & Tolliver, 2009; Chisom & Washington, 1997; Lundy, 2004).

NEW LESSONS LEARNED

There are also important new lessons learned over the years. These are the most important:

1. Seeking to transform the world without transforming yourself is impossible. Whether working to develop a new paradigm for coleadership or finding yourself on the front lines of debate on issues such as race and sexuality, this is not just hard external work. As demanding as those kinds of campaigns are, they make for hard internal work, too. The personal mastery required to remain open to interpreting the world as it is with its multiple truths of, say, greater advances for lesbians and gays *and* greater threats of homophobic violence requires any dedicated practitioner to spend perhaps unforeseen time on the well-being of one additional person: himself or herself. As leadership develops more from an internal process than an external one (Bennis & Nanus, 2003), part of the demand placed on a practitioner committed to social justice is to remain internally balanced enough to handle what can appear to be the competing interpretations of what is happening in your world: more opportunity and greater violence; racial advancement and further racial marginality; more attention to the elderly and greater elder isolation. Doing this requires an attention to self-care that values your own internal well-being as equally fundamental to your work as developing an effective campaign strategy for immigrants' rights is. As my friend and colleague Willie Tolliver and I wrote elsewhere, *"If the work is sacred, then so are you"* (Burghardt & Tolliver, 2009). Developing awareness that one's physical, emotional, and spiritual well-being need tending to is hard work: There's always another meeting to attend, a rally to plan for, a conference call to make that momentarily justifies why one eats muffins on the run or forgoes that brisk walk to or from work. Without the inner balance created through attention to your self-care, the external balance in your strategic decision making, sharing of power, and accepting of personal strengths and limitations grows more and more limited. As Freire suggests and this work builds on, changing the world for others must include a heartfelt commitment

that such change is needed for yourself, too. *To that end, the practice of the Second Golden Rule—do unto yourself as you seek to do unto others—makes both personal and strategic sense for a lifetime of meaningful and balanced work.*

2. *Your internal strategic vision is developed and refined as an internal tool for both short-term effectiveness and lasting meaning, regardless of the position you hold.* Your internal strategic vision initially reads like a job description: what issues you work on, with whom, the roles you play. What distinguishes it is its emphasis on the *values consecrated in action* regarding how you do such work. As such, your vision more often becomes embodied by the little things you do each day than by the large commitments you work away at with others. Everyone in social work is committed in one way or another to social justice; unfortunately, fewer treat the community members who enter their agencies as they would treat their own families. The same is true when applied to sharing the limelight at forums, running meetings democratically, or including mention of everyone's names on reports and grants. The macro practitioners referred to throughout this text are often in positions of genuine authority and influence, but one of the other distinguishing qualities most of them share is a personal modesty that can at first almost seem odd given their official stature: Eric Zachary prefers to bartend at events rather than work the room; Gladys Carrion spends Halloween making zippy little lollipop ghosts to share with staff; Anne Williams-Isom is known as much for her booming laugh at her own foibles as for her passionate social commitments. *Because they live their visions each and every day, they are able to take the work, but not themselves, seriously.* By refining their vision as something with daily application in little things, they have less need to force distinctions between work and life in ways that make them different people in one arena or the other. The resultant comfort in themselves flows in part from the certainty that what they are about matters over a lifetime of consecrated acts, not occasional big events.

3. *You begin to develop your tenacity to hold your vision for social justice when you have little power, not when you gain it.* Professional development, where you learn both skills for doing things and a framework for doing them justly and well, is a lifetime process, not a task completed while you are in social work school. It may begin when you are a student, when, as Laura Lindstrom (personal communication, 2009) noted perceptively in one of her final graduate classes, "wisps of wordless thought" begin reconfiguring an inexperienced social worker's construction of herself and what she seeks to master. As Lindstrom began to experience, it was not just the tasks at hand but also a way of sharing them that has allowed her to learn, while others get to grow, too. Applying new ways of being in the world that comfortably share power when you have none can be harder than you think . . . those wisps of wordless thought can feel scary at first! What if through the sharing, other people get undeserved credit? How do I get recognition without denying others theirs? Am I getting more attention through the power and privilege

of my race and gender? Less? How do I really know? It is through the commitment to these kinds of questions that you develop emotional sinew and moral tenacity when confronted not only with broad-scale injustice but also with small-group unfairness and personal competition that all too often mar academic and agency life. The willingness to consistently ask these questions, again and again, deepens that resilience, even when what animates those concerns may be no more than the wisps of fear from old (but exceedingly familiar) constructions of identity based on individual competition and win–lose paradigms for success. The courage to keep at those questions in the early stage of your professional development creates over time personal and strategic flexibility throughout your career . . . and your life.

4. *The communities in which social work practitioners work and live will become more and more virtual in ways that create more opportunity for connection and relationship . . . as long as social workers become part of the cyber community and not ancillary to it.* As my friend and colleague Mohan Krishna Vinjamuri wrote in Chapter 9, the ability to mobilize far greater numbers for campaigns is possible today in ways that expand definitions of community and connection. As he made clear, the Obama presidential campaigns encapsulated the incremental gains from other Internet activities and brought them to a new level of development. From household-to-household fundraising to organizing neighborhood "get-out-the-vote" drives on the day of the election, the Obama campaigns showed how powerful an organizing tool Internet technology can be. When that technology is applied to social services, agencies' capacities to assess and categorize needs, share and identify resources, and fundraise are all possible in new ways that can transform agency and community life (Lohmann & McNutt, 2005). Whether such activity builds from virtual trust to agency engagement and community empowerment, as Vinjamuri makes clear, remains to be seen. Does virtual trust sustain relationship as well as direct, albeit limited, worker-to-member contact? Can people identify as strongly with their wired community as they do with their geographic neighborhood? The answers to these and other Internet-based issues will be answered by those who commit to utilizing these tools now and helping create the answers together with others. Remaining aware of the social and economic disadvantages for those who remain without Internet services—some of social work's primary constituents: the poor, immigrants, the isolated elderly—is all the more reason for social work practitioners to become genuine actors in the changes under way through the Internet and its tools of connection.

5. *Meaningful social work practice is determined not by the position you hold but by what you do with the position.* This text makes clear that great practice is not simply the strategic choices you make; it's also how you handle the dilemmas created by those choices. Confrontation risks alienating key targets; consensus may rob your campaign of clarity among your stakeholders. Likewise, there are dilemmas in whatever position you

take inside an agency or in running a campaign: The higher the position of responsibility, the greater the number of stakeholders you must consider; lower down, you have more leverage to keep focused on the campaign's primary goal and less power to move toward it. Living within such dilemmas and still being able to act based on your consecrated values is the lynchpin by which you create transformative practice—for your community and its members, for your agency and its workers . . . and for yourself.

EXPANDING THE DISCOURSE: SOME OF THE CHALLENGES AND OPPORTUNITIES OF THE 21ST CENTURY

As a group, effective macro practitioners are people who engage in issues others either shy away from or have yet to identify in ways that move them from problems to programmatic issues. Whether leading the fight for social security in the 1930s (Fisher, 1994; Reisch & Andrews, 2001), equal employment and educational opportunity in the 1960s (Jansson, 2004; Piven & Cloward, 1991), a woman's right to protection from male violence in the 1970s (Abramovitz, 1999; Schechter, 1982), an end to the medical and social marginalization of gays and lesbians in the 1980s (Vaid, 1996), or undocumented workers in the 1990s (Ness, 2005), organizers and social work professionals inside agencies have been vital partners in developing discourse on previously invisible issues and problems that cried out for reform. While they were often met initially with incredulity at best and active indifference at worst, over time their courage in raising to the fore what others could not or would not recognize has been a hallmark of what macro practice committed to social justice is all about (Burghardt & Tolliver, 2009; Fabricant & Fisher, 2003; Reisch & Andrews, 2001; Wagner, 1989). Some of the issues that seem to inform our discourse over the coming years will include the following:

1. *The flux in societal authority . . . and the altered societal place of social work.* As noted in Chapter 2, the 21st century's Great Recession in 2008 to 2009 not only undid financial markets; it also momentarily upset the 30-year balance of power held by conservative and economic actors, putting in play new possibilities in the relationship between the state, the economy, and the national community in ways not seen since the 1960s. In late 2009, for example, a federal court vitiated the bonuses for Merrill Lynch from Bank of America due to the bank's failure to alert stockholders of the bonuses as it took over the failing financial firm. In language "invoking justice and morality" (Kouwe, 2009, p. A-1), the court went on to excoriate the Securities and Exchange Commission for its lax regulatory authority in reviewing the bank's takeover. Such a response from the judiciary on banking practices and executive pay has not been seen since the 1930s. On the other hand, the visceral and freewheeling responses to the Obama Administration's health care policies at town hall meetings across the nation in 2009, and continuing as it moves toward

enactment in 2014, also are reflections of how some forces are responding quite distinctly to this shift, clearly desirous of a return to laissez-faire, free-market, antistate practices that until now have dominated political discourse since the Reagan era. While their proposed solutions are wildly different, Tea Party activists are reflective of this anger at traditionally dominant actors and at the underlying economic and social dislocation so many of their ranks are now experiencing for the first time in their lives. Better off than most Americans, they are fighting to hold on to what the last 30 years gave them!

Whether progressive actors seize this opportunity to reignite a genuinely more progressive response to social and economic programs remains to be seen. For example, while the Obama Administration has invigorated the state response to economic problems, as seen by the financial intervention inside the banking system and the bailout of industrial behemoths such as General Motors and Chrysler, there has been little to no discussion of a redistributive tax policy at the federal or state level that could easily resolve the present-day deficits and seemingly unending crises of state and local governments. For example, Nobel Prize–winning economist Joseph Stiglitz (2006) and others (Krugman, 2009) have pointed out that a modest increase in the tax rate for the top 20% of households (returning to tax rates of the 1950s) would alleviate the Social Security crisis, handle potential increases in health care costs, and pare down the national debt over the next 10 years. The same would be possible in individual states as well, ranging from the once near-bankrupt California to the deficit-ridden states of New Jersey, Michigan, Illinois, and 12 others, most of them with the largest populations in need of a larger, not smaller, social services sector.

That at present such tax redistribution is a near impossibility reflects the continued belief of Americans that it is more unfair for the well-off to pay proportionately more in taxes than it is for everyone, regardless of income, to bear the equal costs of user taxes such as sales taxes, luxury taxes on items such as hotel rooms, and sin taxes on soda and tobacco. Equally telling, the popular perception remains that such taxes would be wasted on public inefficiency rather than well spent, even as the needs for elder care, child care, education, and mental health services continue to rise as the population grows both younger and older, more urban and more isolated, with smaller households and yet greater individual needs.

How social work and social workers respond within the growing contradictions between expanding social needs and politically determined fiscal constraints will be a powerful harbinger of whether social work returns to a central position within the debate on social reform or remains a sideline player. The immediate crises wrought by the Great Recession and the ensuing losses of public tax revenues, private foundation endowments, and charitable giving understandably cause each and every agency within the field to scramble to survive: Keeping staff, responding to expanding need, and juggling diminished revenues are daunting tasks. Nevertheless, to perform only from a reactive stance in the midst of this political and economic crisis is to limit social work's actors to a minor role at best. Many of the field's leaders in the past have used crisis not for retreat but for structural reform: New York's child welfare commissioner, John Mattingly, used the crisis of the tragic death of a child to deepen reform, not to stop reform in how services are delivered to children at risk. His deputy commissioners Liz Roberts and Anne Williams-Isom did the same regarding issues of racial equality and disproportionality. Van Jones and others in Oakland, California, responded to the deepening crisis of unemployment for young people of color by advancing a new and creative agenda for green jobs as a vehicle to end poverty and fight racism.

As seen in Chapter 12, how one responds to crisis has less to do with the urgency of the problem at hand and more to do with the internal resilience and vision of some who move from reaction to opportunity. At present, the public and political focus on the fundamental issues of the field—poverty, children, families, mental health, community cohesion—has perhaps never been dimmer, save for in the 1920s (Fisher, 1994; Reisch & Andrews, 2001; Sullivan, 2013). The challenge such disengagement creates for social work is a matter no longer for the few but for the many. This historic moment of the early 21st century, both crisis driven and wrought with unimagined opportunity a few years ago, will require historic action, too.

2. *The United States of America is now fully integrated into the global community, not a nation apart from it.* This nation's culture of exceptionalism, whereby the class, social, and economic dilemmas and fissures common to other countries seemingly evaded us by dint of America's unique economic power and social integration, while objectively never true (Chomsky, 2009; Zinn, 1991), maintained its extraordinary power over the American imagination until September 11, 2001, when four planes commandeered by 21 men from a Middle-Eastern terrorist organization changed all of that. The Al Qaeda terrorist attack, coupled with the spread of viruses, flus, and airborne illnesses arriving from across the globe and showing up in our food chain, our waters, and our local take-out joints, has reconfigured America's sense of itself as secure from what goes on outside its borders. Americans are finally aware that we are no more or less safe from outside influences than any other nation. The ensuing expansion of the security arm of the state into domestic affairs has been one of the great growth industries of the past 10 years and will continue to be so for the foreseeable future (Cooper & Block, 2008). Much of this is outside the purview of this book's focus on social work macro practice, save one essential dimension: the response to the people from around the world who arrive as immigrants—some documented, some not—to work and live in communities as diverse as De Moines, Iowa; St. Paul, Minnesota; and Los Angeles, California (Holtzman, 2007).

Perhaps not since the turn of the 20th century and the huge influx of Eastern European immigrants to the United States has the popular debate on immigration been as virulent, fearful, and yet equally hopeful and ever changing in the face of ongoing shifts in American demographics (Ngai & Gerstle, 2005; Werner, 2013). The animosity could be captured as the first edition to this textbook was being published; elected officials across the country called for electronic border fences, "English-language–only" laws, and heightened use of Homeland Security for domestic raids on factories and farms (Fernandes, 2007). Such anger took a more virulent form as well. In part fueled by the increasing economic marginality of the average White male worker (see Point 3 below), violence against immigrants, especially immigrants of color, in 2008 was at its greatest since records have been kept (Potok, 2009). Such violence understandably kept immigrant communities isolated and fearful, making both service interventions and community mobilization more difficult for practitioners (Farrell & Johnson, 2005).

Those were difficult times, and yet, as so often happens with organizing efforts, the demand and expectation for a better life can inspire people to transform fearful times into hopeful ones. Led primarily by young Latino and Asian immigrants, members of Congress from their home districts kept introducing the Dream Act, legislation designed to provide a road to citizenship for young immigrants who came to this country with their parents as very young children. Emboldened by the Dreamers' consistent lobbying, President Obama signed an executive order in 2013 requiring Homeland Security no longer to relocate them to their parents' country of origin and instead opening up avenues toward their eventual citizenship. Building on both this action and awareness of the stark results in immigrant voting patterns from the 2012 elections, Republicans for the first time in years joined a bipartisan bill leading to the passage of an immigration bill that created a path to citizenship for 11 million undocumented immigrants now living in the United States (Werner, 2013). While the bill faces significant hurdles in the House and requires an expanded border fence that will cost billions of dollars, there is little doubt that the language and tenor of the immigrant debate has shifted rapidly over the past 5 years.

Such rapid political shifts speak to how much the social fabric of America is changing. Such social transformation will lead to ongoing changes in social identity as well, with ensuing effects on how people approach and use social services within their communities. For social workers, being able to navigate the cultural labyrinth of the 21st century American community so that all its people are offered a foundation of services and support is an enormous challenge equal to that faced by Jane Addams and Florence Hollis more than a hundred years ago (Jansson, 2004). As the newly mobilized Dreamers are inspiring everyone to consider, only through such engagement can the implied economic and social reciprocity embedded in full citizenship emerge in ways that benefit both new and established community members alike (*Dream Activist*, 2013). *Such issues once again underscore social work practitioners' comfort with their own cultural identity and their capacity to work within an increasingly rich cultural mosaic where Whiteness and its cultural artifacts are but one rather than the preeminent measure of national and social identity.*

3. *We are witnessing the reemergence of social class divisions and the intensification of racial tension in our communities.* The present economic crisis is not just about numbers, as striking as those can be; it is about the structural realignment of the American economy as it is reconfigured within the global, information-based, and highly competitive system that world capitalism has become (Krugman, 2009; Stiglitz, 2006). In 2013, the numbers remain frightening. Using official federal statistics—which count only those looking for work and do not include those who are underemployed or who have given up looking—15 million Americans were unemployed, nearly 10% of the workforce. Thirteen percent of Latinos were unemployed; so were nearly 15% of African Americans (Bureau of Labor Statistics, 2013). Other data sets argue for nearly double for all those percentages if one factors in underemployment and those no longer eligible for unemployment benefits because they have dropped out of the labor force due to an inability to find work.

Little has changed to alter the findings first reported by *New York Times* columnist Bob Herbert in 2009, from the work of Rutgers University economists Carl Van Horn and Cliff Zukin. They detailed the great social shifts that lay behind the stark numbers. More than half the respondents in their national survey said it was the first time they had lost their jobs, and 80% felt that they would not get their jobs back. Reflecting how profoundly different those unemployed are from the unemployed in previous recessions, one of four of those unemployed for the first time had been earning more than $75,000 a year. Such numbers are shocking; so is the 40% unemployment rate of African Americans identified in other surveys that monitored those working part-time or less for more than 6 months (Herbert, 2009; Lind, 2004).

These numbers, as serious as they are, reflect a more profound issue at hand: The U.S. economy is shedding numerous jobs, many of them solidly middle income, that will not return as the economy begins to grow again. Simply to return to the job level of 2007 would require the creation of 9.4 million new jobs, which would mean creating about 850,000 jobs a month over an entire year (Krugman, 2009, 2013). Likewise, while federal economists in late 2009 speak of a "jobless recovery" (Parker, 2009), by 2013 there is little evidence that the recovery itself can be sustained without a level of job creation that no one is predicting (Shierholz, 2013).

Every previous recession ended because of a growth in spending by American consumers (Crutsinger, 2008). However, we now understand that such spending levels were maintained not by an expansion of American workers' wealth but by too-easy credit, including home refinancing, easy access to credit cards, and usurious money lending that put cash in people's pockets for purchasing. The ensuing multitrillion-dollar debt in American households, where the ratio of household debt is four times greater than its savings, has now reined in spending with a vengeance as average Americans learn to live on less to pay off the loans, mortgages, and credit card balances that now are part of their weekly ledgers. If American buying power has ended other recessions, how can Americans, who will work at new jobs for lower wages and are paying off more debt at higher intere s, be expected to buy much at all?

The ensuing recovery, as it occurs in terms of a return to business growth ar fit- ability, can be expected to happen without all boats rising with it. As Americans to experience a downward shift in their standard of living that cannot be maintained t gh access to easy credit, and as they work at jobs paying less than what their parent e, we can expect that issues of social class not seen since the Great Depression will ree e as the differences between the haves and the have-nots become more readily apparel of June 2013, for example, 8.2 million workers are classified as "involuntarily employed that is, working part-time while seeking full-time work (Shierholz, 2013). These increas social class differences became intensified as Wall Street bonuses from bailed-out financi firms rose into the billions at the end of 2009 and returned to pre-2008 levels in 2013. A present, there is little evidence that people are responding as their grandparents did, when the trade union movement grew in the 1930s and '40s in ways that benefited all wage earners with improving hourly pay scales, health benefits, and pension plans (Jansson, 2004; Moody, 2004). Indeed, political attacks are often raised against such benefit pack- ages as being part of the problem in the economy, resulting in a labor movement shrinkage to 11.3 of the labor force, down from 11.8 in 2012.

There has been some movement on progressive taxation, with Obama able to raise tax rates on those whose family incomes are above $400,000—the first time such a progres- sive tax has been passed in more than 30 years. However, at the state level, conservative Republican majorities across the Midwest and South in 2013 are in control of both the state legislatures and the governor's office, resulting in red-state–led efforts to further reduce all forms of progressive taxes while slashing social service and education budgets (Werner, 2013).

Given these rollbacks, that more and more formerly middle-class people are coming to rely on social service programs (including child care, elder care, and other services) for their own family members is one part of the discourse that social work practitioners must undertake if newly marginalized, once-middle-income people ever are to see a robust welfare state as a benefit to their lives and not a burden. Seeking collective answers to problems they once imagined as simply an individual's responsibility, whether those answers be trade unionism, national health care, expanded social secu- rity, alternative economic development, or access to inexpensive higher education—all pie-in-the-sky possibilities as of this writing—is also part of the discourse that macro practitioners need to foster. Indeed, the passage of the dramatic "sequestration" of social service cuts now taking place in 2013 and over the next 10 years, if not altered through Congressional action, will result in a significant reduction in the size of the welfare state itself. In short, the social work profession and the populations it serves will be in peril (Matthews, 2013).

…e of that discourse will also be about race. A quick read of American history …s that as economic insecurity grows, socially regressive answers multiply along the …can fault line of race (Jansson, 2004; Nauert, 2007; Robinson, 2006). Commentators …ried as economist Paul Krugman and former president Jimmy Carter suggest that …se of the antagonism toward President Obama is fueled by racial hatred by those …ite seeking a return to what they perceive as the rightful place of White Americans …thin the political and economic mainstream (Krugman, 2009). Such antagonism is …red not only at the Obamas but also toward the Black, Latino, Asian, and Southeast Asian middle classes, whose entry into the job market at executive and managerial levels, …e still well below that of Whites, now serves as a further marker of once-middle- and …rking-income Whites' relative decline in economic and social access.

Such antagonism, of course, belies the actual data on the successful entry and security of African Americans and Latinos in the economic mainstream. Recent reports by Ehrenreich and Muhammed (2009) and by the Brandeis Institute on Social Assets reveal that Hispanic and African American financial instability as measured by family assets (homeownership, savings, and levels of education) dropped by 60% and 33%, respectively, between 2000 and 2006—well before the Great Recession of 2008 to 2009 (Shapiro, 2006). Indeed, the Pew Charitable Trusts in 2006 reported that "nearly half of African Americans born to middle income parents in the 1960s plunged into poverty or near poverty as adults" (Fletcher, 2007, p. A-1). Reports in 2013 suggest little shift in these data (Shierholz, 2013).

Forty-five percent of Black children whose parents were solidly middle class in 1968—a stratum with a median income of $55,600 in inflation-adjusted dollars—grew up to be among the lowest fifth of the nation's earners, with a median family income of $23,100. Only 16% of Whites experienced similar downward mobility. At the same time, 48% of Black children whose parents were in an economic bracket with a median family income of $41,700 sank into the lowest income group (Isaacs, 2008). Five years later, there is no upward shift yet occurring.

As it has been well documented that the current recession has hit people of color hardest through the housing loan scandals of the home finance industry (Ehrenreich & Muhammed, 2009; Stiglitz, 2012), the overall financial security and economic stability of people of color looms as a continuing crisis that so far has received scant attention from either the popular press or politicians, who instead prefer to focus on the overall financial crisis faced by more and more Americans. Whether a color-blind approach can be successful in addressing the overlapping yet distinct concerns of racial groups as the nation seeks solutions to present economic trends remains to be seen. Social work practitioners need to remain in the forefront, responding to such issues so that America's racial fault line will not be drawn more deeply with once-again tragic results.

In human services, the issues of race are intensified by what is today identified as the *crisis of disproportionality* affecting child welfare, incarceration, homeless rates, and school dropout rates. Blacks are 6 times and Latinos 2 times as likely to be imprisoned compared with their White counterparts ("Racial Disparity," n.d.); 25.4% of all Native Americans drop out by the ninth grade, the highest dropout rate in the nation; 56% of African American and 54% of Latino students graduate overall, compared with 78% of Whites (Greene, 2001).[3] As for child welfare, Whites and Asian Americans continue to be underrepresented relative to their size in the general population; Latinos, while overrepresented in terms of reporting, are equally represented in child welfare in proportion to their general percentage of the population, while both African Americans and Native Americans are significantly overrepresented inside the child welfare system, with far lower rates of reunification and far longer rates of stay within the system.

What distinguishes this discourse on racial disproportionality from earlier discussions on race is not the identification of structural and historic conditions of racial oppression stemming from slavery, Jim Crow laws, or employment and housing discrimination that still exist today (Powell, 2009). While hardly denying these structural factors, the focus has shifted to the roles that human-services, medical, and educational professionals play as gatekeepers and diagnosticians of people of color, whereby their practices intensify the likelihood of those groups either entering and remaining in systems where far fewer Whites will be found (as in child welfare and prison) or leaving systems deemed necessary for economic and social stability (education). Examining the interplay between perceptions of pathology (whether related to family cohesion or the potential for violence) that reinforce structural oppression rather than lessening it is now an active discourse inside the human-services professions in ways that hold promise for how macro practitioners and other human-services professionals work with community members in combating racism wherever it is found.

4. *Working effectively with 21st century families will require further macro and micro practice, not less.* The historic origins of social work included significant emphasis on interpreting and meeting the needs of family units scarred by the excesses of the Industrial Revolution of the 19th century (Jansson, 2004; Trattner, 1998). One hundred and fifty years later, with less than 25% of all American households comprising nuclear families (Schmitt, 2001), the focus on what makes up a family unit has significant cultural, political, and social dynamics at play that Jane Addams could hardly imagine. The fights for and against gay marriage, as more and more states adopt the rights of all couples to marry and as lesbians and gays lead state-by-state battles for marriage with significant religious groups in powerful opposition, are only the most visible reflection of how much households and family structures have changed . . . and where they have not. Thus, while the 2013 Supreme Court ruling against the solely heterosexual marriage provisions in the Defense of Marriage Act, while groundbreaking, did not vitiate state laws that disallow gay marriage. Other data reflect how much the family unit has changed from popular images of heterosexual, male-headed households with 2+ children: The majority of Black

households are headed by single women; 75% of all children are growing up in households that are without two parents; the creation of new, extended household units with family-like responsibilities for adults ranging from traditional assisted-living facilities to alternative cohousing arrangements is on the rise (ScottHanson & ScottHanson, 2005). Such dramatic shifts carry with them the potential for misdiagnosis as to their value as well as a willingness to romanticize alternative units for their potential rather than their actual purpose. As Alice Fisher's groundbreaking "case-to-cause" example of hoarding suggests, being part of this examination and cocreation by all social work practitioners, regardless of method, can only serve social work well.

5. *Clarifying the myths and realities of the nonprofit industrial complex.* A popular and growing debate inside social work practice classes and symposia has been the critique of human services through an analysis labeled the "fight against the non-profit industrial complex" (INCITE!, 2007). Examining the demands by public-sector funders and foundations for outcome-based results that focus on individual units of service over longer-term campaigns for social justice, their critique has created a resonant chord of interest among young practitioners. Many community activists are uneasy about the emphasis on empirical practice measures at the expense of more ideological stances that stand up against the excesses of capitalist exploitation of our poorest workers. Likewise, they express active disinterest in social work practice frameworks that would marginalize community members rather than professionals at the forefront of social change (Kivel, 2007). Citing the debate on racial disproportionality as an example of the self-perpetuating interests of social work professionals to keep their clients in care longer than they need to be there, they champion a model of membership-based funding that gives them the independence to politically act with the community in ways they argue the mainstream profession is unprepared to do. The removal of Van Jones from the Obama Administration because of his leftist history as a Black activist and the attacks on ACORN that extended beyond the organization's obvious mistakes, are further evidence to them of the limits the larger society places on practitioners committed to wide-scale social change.

The underlying dilemma in their critique, of course, is that the size of their organizations and the level of funding they can expect will limit their direct influence on large-scale debate and minimize the number of staff who can afford to live on the modest salaries their stance requires. Likewise, it is clear that their work will not be about service to populations in need as much as about advocacy and change for those populations. Organizations with fewer than five full-time paid staff can do very effective advocacy; whether they can positively and directly impact the lives of those with whom they work is another matter. Becoming clear on such distinctions is important as this debate continues, for widespread need requires levels of service that will inevitably lead to public and foundation funding. Likewise, living at wage levels far lower than found elsewhere in the profession requires a commitment to a lifestyle of communal-like living and economic sufficiency that, as mentioned in Chapter 8, may be a harbinger of future directions in community life that demand personal sacrifice that some may not yet be willing to make. How one combines genuine advocacy for social justice within agencies and the community has been a paramount theme of this book. At the same time, some of the constraints the nonprofit industrial complex analysts speak to are experienced by all social work practitioners and thus must be addressed as new opportunities for economic redistribution and further social equity appear over the coming years . . . or recede as conservative alignments reassert their dominance.

6. *Local economic development and going green are new possibilities for the field of human services.* The focus of social work at its creation was woven from a series of responses to and reactions against 19th century industrial capitalism, the rising urban industrial working class and its families, and the communities in which they lived. Today's social work confronts a global economy, a workforce bound neither by workplace location nor community custom, and a new set of stressful conditions wrought by an increasingly depleted environment that bodes poorly for future generations unless those conditions change. As the inspiring examples of LeBourveau and Ledlie-Johnson suggest, macro practitioners are often in the forefront of our field's new directions. Their activism, increasingly uniting micro and macro work, can be seen in their efforts as well as the efforts of others in supporting sustainable agricultural projects and local farmer's and craft markets, and improving health through food movements. Such work is an exciting portent for the profession's new and revitalized approach to the social conditions our communities confront. Whether emanating from the slow food movement as a critique of mass food production and an opportunity for better, healthier eating (Petrini, 2007) or student-led campaigns for better food in school cafeterias (Waters, 2009), with its potential to aid local farmers and train the next generation of leadership, the focuses on the green economy and the environmental crisis are pathways for social work that macro practitioners have already begun to walk (Olopade, 2009). Others have used the focus on local market campaigns for small businesses and family farms as a way to rebuild community cohesion and develop outreach across class and other ethnic divisions that remain from earlier periods of our nation's history. Being open to organizing trends that initially fall outside of the mainstream of the field is a way the profession can attract and keep young organizers and macro practitioners drawn to forms of activism distinct from yet clearly as vital as those undertaken by the rank-and-file movement of the 1930s or the welfare rights movement of the 1960s (Fisher, 1994; Reisch & Andrews, 2001).

7. *Developing a "learning organization" culture inside our agencies also can build learning circles and communities of practice that extend agency life across the community and into the larger society in ways that potentially generate widespread support for*

a progressive human-services agenda in our nation. As this work has attempted to delineate, flexible leadership capable of sharing power and remaining open to others' ability to inform one another is developed over a lifetime of practiced TSA and personal struggle to grow and change. Such leadership is pivotal to what Senge (1990) defined as an agency's *learning organization,* whereby both individuals and the systems they operated remained open to and capable of transforming themselves as societal needs and demands shifted over time (Senge, 1990; Senge, Laur, Schley, Smith, & Kruscwitz, 2008). Given the social networking found on the Internet, many professionals have begun experimenting with communities of practice and learning circles that expand the networks of like-minded, engaged individuals in issues, ideas, and activities that once could be done only through monthly meetings or late-night caucuses. Set up on a particular issue or topic and held over a series of weeks or months, these new forms of learning and cocreation have the potential to widen the circle of who can be involved and the level of learning and information sharing that takes place. For them to flourish, agency leaders need to trust both themselves and their staff that the ongoing learning is of great value that transcends the immediate demands of daily agency life (Burghardt & Tolliver, 2009). As Liz Roberts's approach to training inside her agency suggests, exploring how to make this happen can serve as another tool in the remaking of democratic culture in our society (Fisher, 2005; Weil, 2005).

8. *Social media will both enrich social work practice and challenge the profession as never before.* As Vinjamuri's Chapter 9 makes clear, social networking is transforming how we all act on the world. From Google maps to provide data for community assessments, smartphones to stay in contact with clients, Facebook petition pages to accelerate social causes, chat rooms for every kind of mutual support, websites to raise philanthropic dollars, and Skype to help practitioners conduct transcontinental therapy, the scope and depth of change under way in how we work with, help, and serve one another has only begun to be imagined. The agency that does not take advantage of such rapid changes and the practitioner satisfied with only face-to-face interactions (whether community or individual or group) do so at their professional peril.

9. *Transformative leadership in social welfare today is being led by those willing to take risks that the old practice paradigms in which they work—and, indeed, have led—need to be completely reimagined and redone.* Eric Zachary's work with the American Federation for Teachers implicitly seeks to shift the old, uneasy paradigm of unions and community collaboration to one of genuine partnership and mutual support, willingly confronting years of resistance and mistrust to forge a new direction in at least some educational reform circles. Gladys Carrion, as commissioner of a state child welfare and juvenile justice system, saw the need to basically end the model of residential care under her watch, even though it created a firestorm of resistance from politicians and unions

from across the state. Dr. William Bell, as the CEO of Casey Family Programs Foundation, broke through the traditional funding cycle in child welfare to focus on a collective impact strategy that would eradicate the silos of bureaucratic response to generational child welfare problems. Working with major stakeholders from across the nation, he strategically helped shift conventional thinking so that the Obama Administration's Child Welfare Improvement Act would include 4-E spending waivers for those states willing and able to (a) commit to both the safety and well-being of their children *and* (b) use preventive funds focused on upfront community- and after-care services. As of this writing, 17 states have done so.

At earlier stages in their own careers, LeBourveau and Ledlie-Johnson were doing the same thing, creating connections between social work and environmentalism—even in the face of initial indifference from their peers and apprehension from their employers. Such risk taking must continue if social work is to return to its place at the table where social reform is debated and social welfare decisions are made.

10. *A transformative model of macro practice can lead to a lifetime of meaningful, strategic practice . . . and a life of meaning.* Because the early 21st century promises to be a time of enormous change that further reconfigures community and agency life, social work practitioners capable of ongoing learning, cocreation of strategic direction, and the sharing of power and resources will be needed more than ever. Such practitioners, found as organizers, supervisors, and managers across the United States, are modeling a leadership stance of reflection in action that perhaps looks like this:

This model emphasizes your own ongoing transformation through a humble commitment to the short-term reflective demands of daily TSA and the long-term effort to consecrate your internal strategic vision through your ongoing work. This internal effort serves as the foundation to your critical reflection in action. Using this internal effort to guide you, you move with increasing personal mastery between the individual/small-group work of problem-posing and dialogue and the strategic activities of the agency and community. In this dynamic, interrelated work, naming the word, with its emphasis on coleadership *and* strategic results, transforms the world for you and the people with whom you work. Because your values are consecrated through actions large and small—social justice campaigns won, meetings successfully facilitated by young community members—the separation between the process of dialogue and the task of strategic outcomes is replaced by the ongoing, transformational possibilities that link both. If you carry this practice forward over a lifetime, agency and community, as well as practitioner and community member, transform together. While there can be no guarantee of widespread social and political transformation, courageously and fully living and working together with others as subjects of history creates a meaningful way to live and act on the world.

Please use the following model (Figure 14.1) to examine your own on-going transformation, as well as the activity below it to reflect on ways to bring that transformation into your daily life and work:

Figure 14.1   A Transformative Model of Macro Practice

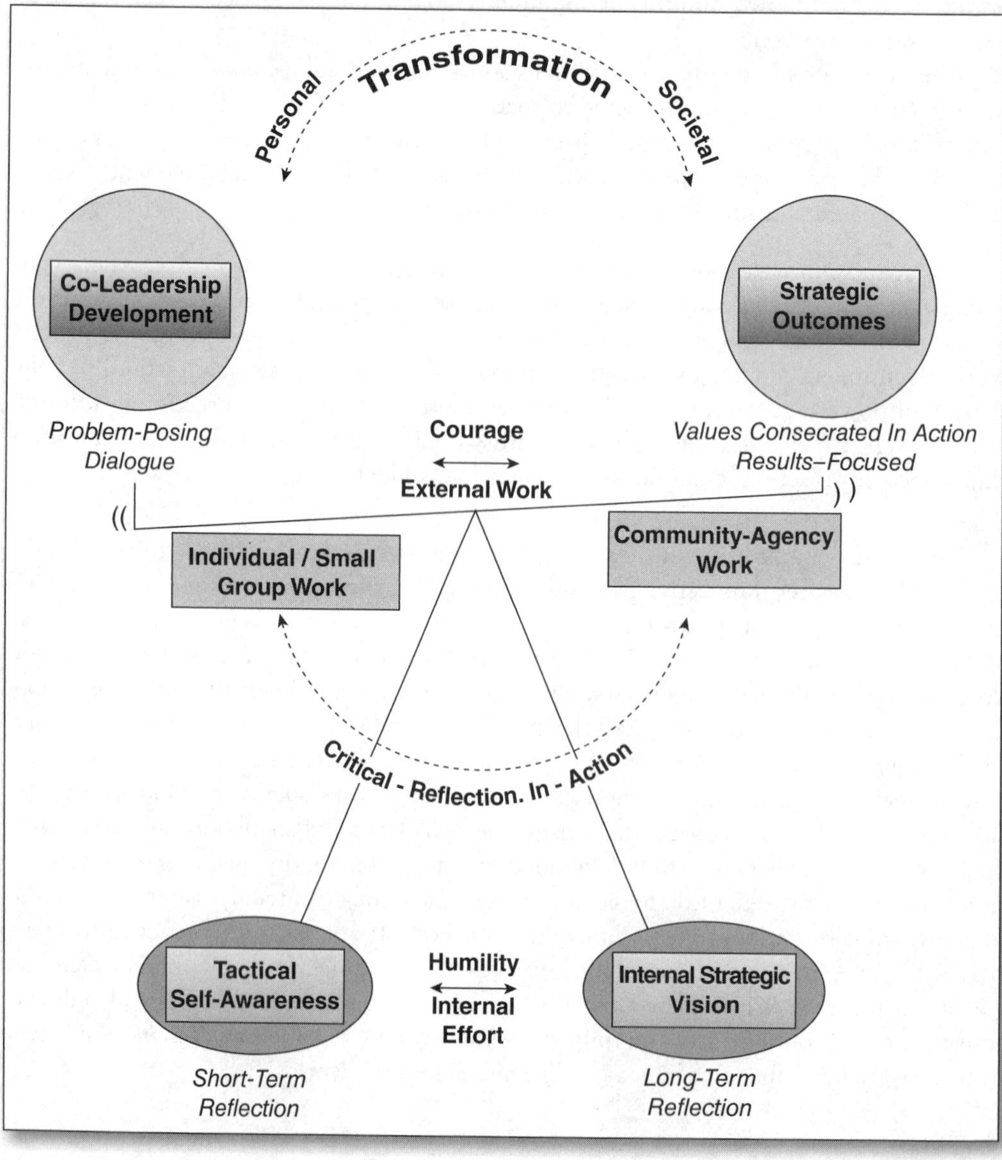

**Individual Exercise Building Your
Transformative Model of Macro Practice**

(External Work)

Co – Leadership
Development

Strategic Outcomes

1. Problem – posing questions:

_____

_____

_____

1. New Leaders-in-Action:

_____

_____

_____

2. Teachable moments from your TSA:

_____

_____

_____

2. 3-month measurable objectives
to attain:

_____

_____

_____

Concrete Actions
With Individuals & Groups

1.

2.

3.

4.

Concrete Actions
in a Campaign or Agency Project

1.

2.

3.

4.

(Internal Effect)

What are your TSA
Strengths & Limitations?

_____

_____

_____

_____

What are the key
Values Consecrated-in-Action
within your internal strategic vision?

_____

_____

_____

_____

CONCLUDING COMMENT

There are, of course, many other issues at play in the 21st century—from the importance of spirituality in communities and agencies to the growth of intergenerational projects that reunite old and young to gain from the energy of the latter and the wisdom of the former . . . or is it the reverse? Happily, there are projects under way and attempts at social change unfolding that have yet to be discovered, but they will be soon. There are transformative macro and micro practitioners and community members out there making sure we all learn about what else is needed to engage and change our nation for the better.

And so this text concludes in ways not dissimilar from the one crafted more than 30 years ago, as *The Other Side of Organizing: Macro Practice in Social Work for the 21st Century: Bridging the Macro-Micro Divide* has had as its primary theme the idea that widespread societal change without personal transformation makes such change impossible. As Paulo Freire might have said, taking the risk to change the world by having the courage also to transform oneself won't be easy, but the task of liberation never has been. How nice that it might just make for a wonderful career as a transformative social work practitioner.

REFERENCES

Abramovitz, M. (1999). *Regulating the lives of women: Social welfare policy from colonial times to the present.* Boston: South End Press.

Bennis, W., & Nanus, J. (2003). *Strategies for taking charge.* New York: HarperCollins.

Bureau of Labor Statistics. (2013, January). Table A-2. Employment status of the civilian population by race, sex, and age. Retrieved from http://www.bls.gov/news.release/empsit.t02.htm

Burghardt, S., & Tolliver, W. (2009). *Stories of transformational leadership: Why the glass is always full.* Thousand Oaks, CA: Sage.

Chisom, R., & Washington, L. (1997). *Undoing racism: A philosophy of international social change.* New Orleans, LA: People's Institute.

Chomsky, N. (2009). *Hegemony or survival: America's quest for global dominance.* New York: Metropolitan Books.

Cooper, C., & Block, R. (2008). *Disaster: Hurricane Katrina and the failure of Homeland Security.* New York: Henry Holt.

Crutsinger, M. (2008, January 5). Consumer spending, a key bulwark against recession, weakens. *Denver Post,* p. 1.

Dream Activist. (2013). Retrieved from http://www.dreamactivist.org

Ehrenreich, B., & Muhammad, J. (2009, September 12). The recession's racial divide. *New York Times.* Retrieved from http://www.nytimes.com/2009/09/13/opinion/13ehrenreich.html?pagewanted=all&_r=0

Fabricant, M., & Fisher, R. (2003). *Settlement houses under siege.* New York: Columbia University Press.

Farrell, W., & Johnson, J. (2005). Investing in socially and economically distressed communities. In M. Weil (Ed.), *The handbook of community practice* (pp. 387–396). Thousand Oaks, CA: Sage.

Fernandes, D. (2007). *Targeted: Homeland Security and the business of immigration*. Boston: Consortium Books.

Fisher, R. (1994). *Let the people decide*. New York: Twayne.

Fisher, R. (2005). History, context, and emerging issues for community practice. In M. Weil (Ed.), *The handbook of community practice* (pp. 34–59). Thousand Oaks, CA: Sage.

Fletcher, M. (2007, November 13). Study: Black families struggle to stay middle class. *Washington Post*, p. A-1.

Greene, H. (2001). *High school graduation rates in the United States*. Retrieved from http://www .manhattan-institute.org/html/cr_baeo.htm

Herbert, B. (2009, June 23). The changing face of the American worker. *New York Times*, p. A-28.

Holtzman, J. (2007). *Nuer journeys, nuer lives: Sudanese refugees in Minnesota*. Boston: Allyn & Bacon.

INCITE! Women of Color Against Violence. (2007). *The revolution will not be funded: Beyond the non-profit industrial complex*. Boston: South End Press.

Isaacs, K. (2008, February 20). *Economic mobility in the United States*. Retrieved from http://www .economicmobility.org/

Jansson, B. (2004). *The reluctant welfare state: American social policies—past, present and future*. Berkeley, CA: Cengage.

Kivel, P. (2007). Social services or social change? In INCITE! Women of Color Against Violence (Ed.), *The revolution will not be funded* (pp. 44–61). Boston: South End Press.

Kouwe, Z. (2009, August 14). The bottomless headache. *New York Times*, pp. A-1, A-26.

Krugman, P. (2009, August 7). The town hall mob. *New York Times*, p. A-32.

Krugman, P. (2013, July 8). Defining prosperity down. *New York Times*. Retrieved from http://www .nytimes.com/2013/07/08/opinion/krugman-defining-prosperity-down.html?_r=0

Lind, M. (2004, January 20). Are we still a middle class nation? *The Atlantic*, pp. 37–46.

Lohmann, R., & McNutt, J. (2005). Practice in the electronic community. In M. Weil (Ed.), *The handbook of community practice* (pp. 301–317). Thousand Oaks, CA: Sage.

Lundy, C. (2004). *Social work and social justice: A structural approach to social justice*. Toronto, Ontario, Canada: UTP Higher Education.

Matthews, D. (2013, March 1). The Sequester: Absolutely everything you could possibly need to know, in one FAQ. *Washington Post*. Retrieved from http://www.washingtonpost.com/blogs/ wonkblog/wp/2013/02/20/the-sequester-absolutely-everything-you-could-possibly-need-to- know-in-one-faq/

Moody, K. (2004). *Time out! The case for a shorter work week*. Detroit, MI: Labor Notes Press.

Nauert, R. (2007, March 16). How fear is learned. *PsychCentral*. Retrieved from http://psychcentral .com/news/2007/03/16/how-fear-is-learned

Ness, I. (2005). *Immigrants, unions, and the new U.S. labor market*. Philadelphia: Temple University Press.

Ngai, M., & Gerstle, G. (2005). *Impossible subjects: Illegal aliens and the making of modern America*. Princeton, NJ: Princeton University Press.

Olopade, D. (2009, September 21). Green shoots in New Orleans. *The Nation*, pp. 17–19.

Parker, J. (2009, July 1). Krugman: U.S. headed for "jobless" recovery. *ABC News*. Retrieved from http://abcnews.go.com/ThisWeek/Politics/story?id=7966402&page=1

Petrini, C. (2007). *Slow food nation: Why our food should be good, clean, and fair*. Rome, Italy: Rizzoli Ex Libris.

Piven, F. F., & Cloward, R. (1991). *Regulating the poor: The functions of the public welfare*. New York: Vintage Books.

Potok, M. (2009). *Climate of fear: Latino immigrants in Suffolk County, N.Y.* Retrieved from http://www.splcenter.org/get-informed/publications/climate-of-fear-latino-immigrants-in-suffolk-county-ny

Powell, M. (2009, June 6). Bank accused of pushing mortgage deals on Blacks. *New York Times*, p. A-16.

Racial disparity. (n.d.). *The Sentencing Project*. Retrieved from http://www.sentencingproject.org/template/page.cfm?id=122

Reisch, M., & Andrews, J. (2001). *The road not taken: A history of radical social work in the United States*. Philadelphia: Brunner-Routledge.

Robinson, E. (2006, January 27). Using our fear. *Washington Post*, p. A-26.

Schechter, S. (1982). *Women and male violence: The visions and struggles of the battered women's movement*. Boston: South End Press.

Schmitt, E. (2001, May 15). For first time, nuclear families drop below 25% of households. New *York Times*, p. A-1.

ScottHanson, C., & ScottHanson, K. (2005). *The cohousing handbook: Building a place for community* (2nd ed.). Gabriola Island, British Columbia, Canada: New Society.

Senge, P. (1990). *The fifth discipline: The art and practice of the learning organization*. New York: Doubleday.

Senge, P., Laur, J., Schley, S., Smith, B., & Kruscwitz, N. (2008). *The necessary revolution: How individuals and organizations are working together to create a sustainable world*. New York: Broadway Books.

Shapiro, T. (2006). *Black wealth/White wealth: A new perspective on racial inequality*. New York: Routledge.

Shierholz, H. (2013, July 5). Four years into the recovery and we're just a fifth of the way out of the hole left by the great recession. *Economic Policy Institute*. Retrieved from http://www.epi.org/publication/years-recovery-hole-left-great-recession/

Silver, N. (2013, June 25). Geography, not the voting rights act, accounts for most majority-minority districts. *New York Times*. Retrieved from http://fivethirtyeight.blogs.nytimes.com/2013/06/25/majority-minority-districts-are-products-of-geography-not-voting-rights-act/

Stiglitz, J. (2006). *Making globalization work*. New York: Penguin Books.

Stiglitz, J. (2012). *The price of inequality*. New York: W. W. Norton.

Sullivan, M. (2013, June 5). Following up on poverty coverage in the times. *New York Times*. Retrieved from http://publiceditor.blogs.nytimes.com/2013/06/08/following-up-on-poverty-coverage-in-the-times/

Trattner, W. (1998). *From poor law to welfare state* (6th ed.). New York: Free Press.

Vaid, U. (1996). *Virtual equality: The mainstreaming of gay and lesbian liberation*. New York: Knopf Doubleday.

Wagner, D. (1989). Radical movements in the social services: A theoretical review. *Social Service Review, 63*(2), 171–188.

Waters, A. (2009, September 2). A healthy constitution. *The Nation,* pp. 22–25.

Weil, M. (Ed.). (2005). *The handbook for community practice.* Thousand Oaks, CA: Sage.

Werner, E. (2013, July 8). Senate immigration bill would remake economy. *TIME.* Retrieved from http://swampland.time.com/2013/07/08/senate-immigration-bill-would-remake-economy/

Zinn, H. (1991). *Declarations of independence: Cross-examining American ideology.* New York: New Press.

NOTES

1. And, needless to say, greatly influenced me and the direction of my own life and work. I could not facilitate discussions on social justice for the long haul if I had not run up against my own dilemmas and the ensuing struggles I had to resolve along the way with the support of these remarkable people inside the classrooms, agencies, and community campaigns over all these years.

2. Those with more formal authority and accountability, whether in an agency or a campaign, of course have final responsibility for decisions, as they may have information that cannot or should not be shared with others on fiscal matters or political dynamics that need to remain confidential. That said, there are numerous meetings, project decisions, and campaign issues that can embody collaborative, democratic leadership that fosters others' development as well.

3. The overall graduation rate is 71%, ranking the United States 12th among industrialized nations—hardly a comfort for any American, regardless of social background.

Index

About the Author

Steve Burghardt, PhD, is professor of social work at the Silberman School of Social Work at Hunter College, City University of New York, and partner of the Leadership Transformation Group. He is a recognized expert in community organizing, democratic leadership, and popular education. He has taught, trained, consulted, and organized with both grassroots community groups and large-scale public agencies on new models of practice throughout his career. The author of seven other books and numerous articles, he has won numerous awards for his teaching on community organizing through popular education, political economy of social welfare, and theories of social change.

⑤SAGE research**methods**

The essential online tool for researchers from the world's leading methods publisher

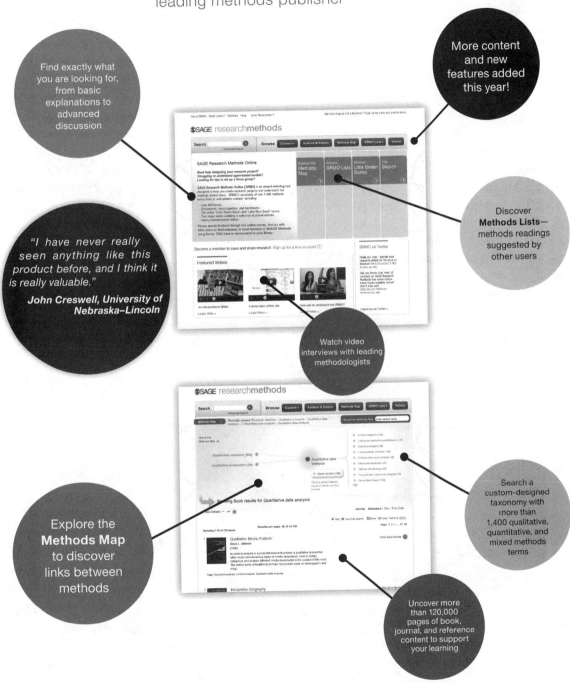

Find exactly what you are looking for, from basic explanations to advanced discussion

More content and new features added this year!

"I have never really seen anything like this product before, and I think it is really valuable."

John Creswell, University of Nebraska–Lincoln

Discover **Methods Lists**— methods readings suggested by other users

Watch video interviews with leading methodologists

Explore the **Methods Map** to discover links between methods

Search a custom-designed taxonomy with more than 1,400 qualitative, quantitative, and mixed methods terms

Uncover more than 120,000 pages of book, journal, and reference content to support your learning

Find out more at
www.sageresearchmethods.com